REBEL CROSSINGS

*New Women, Free Lovers, and
Radicals in Britain and America*

SHEILA ROWBOTHAM

VERSO
London • New York

In memory of two redoubtable rebel women and dear friends, Rosalyn Fraad Baxandall (1939–2015) and Swasti Mitter (1939–2016), with profound thanks for their inspiration and encouragement on life, politics and radical history.

First published by Verso 2016
© Sheila Rowbotham 2016

1 3 5 7 9 10 8 6 4 2

Verso
UK: 6 Meard Street, London W1F 0EG
US: 20 Jay Street, Suite 1010, Brooklyn, NY 11201
versobooks.com

Verso is the imprint of New Left Books

ISBN-13: 978-1-78478-588-8
ISBN-13: 978-1-78478-591-8 (US EBK)
ISBN-13: 978-1-78478-590-1 (UK EBK)

British Library Cataloguing in Publication Data
A catalogue record for this book is available from the British Library

Library of Congress Cataloging-in-Publication Data
A catalog record for this book is available from the Library of Congress

Typeset in Garamond Pro by MJ & N Gavan, Truro, Cornwall
Printed in the UK by CPI Mackays

Contents

List of Illustrations   vii

Introduction   1

PART I: HOPES

1. Radical Endeavour: Helena Born   11
2. Subversive Intimations: Miriam Daniell   27
3. Awakenings: Robert Allan Nicol   39
4. Exaltation: Autumn 1889   52
5. Seekers: 1890   73
6. New Bearings: America 1890–1894   94
7. 'Knotty Points': William Bailie   116
8. Wanderers: 1892–1894   132

PART II: QUESTS

9. Revolutionary Lineages: Helen Tufts   153
10. Whitmanites and New Women: 1894–1897   168
11. Fabianism and Free Love: Gertrude Dix   187
12. Cosmic Vibrations: 1894–1897   207
13. Love, Pure Food and the Market: 1897–1899   225
14. Family Ructions and Political Exploration: 1900   252
15. 'Separation': 1901–1902   266

PART III: ECHOES

16. 'Clues and Meanings': 1898–1902   281
17. A New Beginning: 1901–1902   300
18. Romancing the West: 1902–1908   314
19. Bundles of Contradictions: 1903–1907   327
20. Political Reorientation and a New Arrival: 1907–1914   344
21. Elusive Realities: 1908–1914   363
22. Loose Endings   377

Acknowledgements   396
Notes   401
Bibliography   474
Index   487

List of Illustrations

Fig. 1   Helena Born (Bristol Reference Library), p. 22

Fig. 2   Walt Whitman (Labadie, Special Collections Library, University of Michigan), p. 25

Fig. 3   Miriam Daniell (Bristol Reference Library), p. 36

Fig. 4   Patrick Geddes, p. 42

Fig. 5   Cover of Beauty for Ashes, p. 47

Fig. 6   Robert Allan Nicol (Courtesy of Georges Rey, Private Collection), p. 50

Fig. 7   Great Western Cotton Factory, Barton Hill, by Samuel Loxton (Bristol Reference Library), p. 62

Fig. 8   Bristol Socialist Society's Songbook, p. 79

Fig. 9   Dan Irving (Bristol Reference Library), p. 90

Fig. 10   Enid Stacy (Bristol Reference Library), p. 98

Fig. 11   Benjamin R. Tucker, c. 1887. Studio portrait by Falk, New York (Labadie, Special Collections Library, University of Michigan), p. 102

Fig. 12   Archibald H. Simpson, c. 1889 (Labadie, Special Collections Library, University of Michigan), p. 127

Fig. 13   William Bailie, c. 1902. (Helen Tufts Bailie Papers, Sophia Smith Collection, Smith College), p. 131

Fig. 14   Helena Born and Helen Tufts Bailie under umbrella on beach, 1896 (Helena Born Photograph Collection, Tamiment Library and Robert F. Wagner Labor Archives, New York University), p. 167

Fig. 15   Sarah Elizabeth Holmes (Labadie, Special Collections Library, University of Michigan), p. 181

Fig. 16   Katharine St John Conway (Bristol Reference Library), p. 194

Fig. 17   Cover for *The Girl from the Farm*, p. 202

Fig. 18   Robert Allan Nicol with Sunrise at White-nights ranch in Weimar (Courtesy of Georges Rey, Private Collection), p. 209

Fig. 19   Edward Carpenter in sandals at Millthorpe, near Sheffield, by Alf Mattison (Carpenter Collection, Sheffield Archives), p. 219

Fig. 20   Helen Tufts Bailie and Helena Born, 1897 (Helen Tufts Bailie Papers, Sophia Smith Collection, Smith College), p. 226

Fig. 21   J. William Lloyd (Labadie, Special Collections Library, University of Michigan), p. 227

Fig. 22   Helen Tufts Bailie on the stone wall at Epsom, New Hampshire, 1898 (Helen Tufts Bailie Papers, Sophia Smith Collection, Smith College), p. 231

Fig. 23   Helen Tufts Bailie with a group of family and friends, Epsom, New Hampshire, 1898 (Helen Tufts Bailie Papers, Sophia Smith Collection, Smith College), p. 242

Fig. 24   Cover for *The Image Breakers*, p. 283

Fig. 25   Robert G. Tovey (Bristol Reference Library), p. 290

Fig. 26   James F. Morton (Labadie, Special Collections Library, University of Michigan), p. 302

Fig. 27   Robert Allan Nicol (Courtesy of Georges Rey, Private Collection), p. 316

Fig. 28   Gertrude Dix, c. early 1900s (Courtesy of Georges Rey, Private Collection), p. 318

Fig. 29   Robert Weare, September 1905 (Bristol Reference Library), p. 342

Fig. 30   Boston-1915 Movement, *Sunday Herald*, 4 April 1909 (Wikipedia Commons), p. 352

Fig. 31   Sunrise with Margot and Amaryllis (Courtesy of Georges Rey, Private Collection), p. 364

Fig. 32   Hilda and Juliet Wartnaby Dix (Courtesy of Georges Rey, Private Collection), p. 369

Fig. 33   Margot by Edward Weston (Courtesy of Georges Rey, Private Collection), p. 379

Fig. 34   Amaryllis by Edward Weston (Courtesy of Georges Rey, Private Collection), p. 380

Introduction

In the mid 1970s, I found a little book in the British Library, *Whitman's Ideal Democracy and Other Writings by Helena Born, With a Biography by The Editor, Helen Tufts*. The essays, written after Helena Born emigrated from Bristol to the United States in 1890, reveal a new woman with radical, unconventional views. Helen Tufts' 'Biographical Introduction' relates how, in Bristol during the late 1880s, Helena established a close friendship with another middle-class rebel, Miriam Daniell, became a socialist, supported strikers and left home to settle in the slums. In America Helena lived on a ranch in California, became a staunch member of the Boston Walt Whitman Fellowship, and was influenced by anarchism. Her inspirations were the American writers, Walt Whitman and Henry David Thoreau, along with the English libertarian socialist, Edward Carpenter.[1]

I was already interested in Carpenter, the mild-mannered iconoclast who, from the 1880s, challenged the subordination of women, the suppression of same-sex desire, class inequality and environmental pollution. Rejecting Victorian acquisitiveness and antimacassars, he proclaimed the virtues of 'simplification', stone floors, bare stained boards, sandals and a vegetarian diet. Like many of his contemporaries, Carpenter's socialism was about changing personal life as well as society.[2]

Helena was expecting a visit from him at 12 noon on 25 January 1890, when she wrote from 9 Louisa Street in St Philip's, one of Bristol's poorest neighbourhoods, to her cousin in Devon, 'I have made the floor of my room shine with extra brightness this morning, in anticipation, with aid

of a little beeswax, "turps" and "elbow-grease".'[3] Maybe it was the beeswax
sinking into wood, or perhaps Helena's anticipation, so resonant of the
hopeful days of early socialism, which made this apparently inconsequential morning of rubbing and polishing wing vividly across the decades.
The curiosity it evoked continued to hover.

Writing *Edward Carpenter: A Life of Liberty and Love* (2008) returned
me to Helena in St Philip's pursuing the aesthetic of simplification, while
endeavouring with her friend Miriam Daniell to organise the unorganised. Again time concertinaed and I was left wondering what lay beyond
those bare bees-waxed boards of a house that no longer existed.

I began in 2009 with a perplexing jigsaw of missing pieces and empty
spaces, for Helen Tufts fails to mention that Miriam's lover, a young Scot
from Dunfermline, Robert Allan Nicol, was also living with the two
women in St Philip's. Moreover, she excises the anarchist basket-maker,
William Bailie, with whom Helena later formed a free union in Boston.
Many other questions followed. Why did a Google search for William
Bailie direct me to the papers of a Helen Tufts *Bailie*? How was it that
the forthright exponent of sexual emancipation, the new woman novelist,
Gertrude Dix, who met Robert in the Bristol Socialist Society in 1889,
ended up joining him in California in 1902?

Being a nosy person, committed to digging about in bits of the past
buried in layers of obscurity, on I went. As the gaps filled, interweaving
images emerged of a group of six searchers who tried to change society
and themselves. *Rebel Crossings* traces the five migrants from Britain to the
United States: Helena Born (1860–1901), Miriam Daniell (1861–94),
Robert Allan Nicol (1868–1956), William Bailie (1866–1957), Gertrude
Dix (1867–1950) and American-born Helen Tufts (1874–1962).

Gradually I began to see how they interacted with one another; Helen
Tufts testifies in the journal she kept throughout her life: 'I fell in with
Helena Born, and with her a new world opened to me, – her world of
Walt Whitman, Thoreau, radicalism.'[4]

I found that I, too, 'fell in' with the lives of all six. None are particularly well known, being the kind of figures who surface as names and
then slip tantalisingly back into the shadows. Helena, Miriam, Robert
and William are mentioned in passing by historians writing on socialism
and anarchism.[5] Gertrude's two novels *The Girl From the Farm* (1896)
and *The Image Breakers* (1900) have earned her a literary niche as a 'new
woman' writer, while historians studying women and the American right
have recorded a brave stand by Helen in 1928.[6] By then she had shed

many of her anarchist ideals, but clung to a firm belief in individual liberty. Helen (now Helen Tufts Bailie), proud of her ancestors who had fought the British, and a member of the Daughters of the American Revolution (D.A.R.), exposed how a blacklist operated within it to exclude liberal and leftist speakers. She was expelled from the D.A.R. in a glare of publicity.[7]

This kind of visibility was the exception. Instead, the six cluster in dissident networks mainly outside both the mainstream news and national metropolitan centres. Their geographical migrations spanned Bristol, Dunfermline, Edinburgh, Belfast, Manchester, London, Massachusetts and California, so *Rebel Crossings* follows them and the transmission of radical ideas back and forth across the Atlantic from diverse sites.

It was far more difficult than I initially imagined. Discovering what my six rebels had done involved innumerable labyrinthine trails. Working out what they thought and felt was necessarily a tentative process, for quite often the evidence simply was not there. In some instances I could establish juxtapositions without being able to prove an explicit intellectual provenance. As for feelings, attempting to explore the motivations of the famous who declare themselves is difficult enough; pursuing the relatively unknown is far more testing. For, even when their deeds are on record, their subjectivity often is not. Nonetheless, starting from apparently obscure vantage points opens new perspectives, modifying how wider interconnections and movements can be regarded.

Helen and Helena left collections of papers, and the other four created a paper trail through their writings and activism, which could be supplemented by family documents and memories.[8] So I was able to trace opinions shifting and relocating as new concepts were grafted upon old, and gradually the six ceased to be simply names and acquired personal and social biographies. Looking at an interacting group revealed their consciousness emerging dynamically through their *relationships* with one another.

Helen's extensive manuscript journal was invaluable. She began keeping it in 1886. Hence, from the age of twelve she lived self-consciously; documenting, collating, editing and eventually typing it up in the 1950s. Compelled by a desire to ascribe meaning to what was happening to her, periodically she would express doubts about *why* she was recording so obsessively in a journal most probably no one would ever read. While Helen did not literally migrate, the journal chronicles her metamorphosis from a Massachusetts Unitarian girlhood into a Boston new woman and anarchist. It takes us back into the America she inherited and on towards the ideal democracy of the woman she regarded with such loving devotion – Helena Born.

The values she encountered through Helena and then William mingle with her own internalisation of her family's historical rebellion against British rule, along with the standards and prejudices characteristic of her upbringing in a down-at-heel wing of the WASP elite. While Helen never knew Miriam or Robert, nonetheless, through Helena, their lives indirectly impinged upon hers.

By the time Helen met Helena in 1895 in Boston, the older woman had experienced several geographical uprootings, broken dramatically with the conventions of middle-class womanhood, and experienced social turmoil and hardship. Before joining Bristol's socialist and labour movement in 1889, Helena's early influences were the Unitarian Church and the Bristol Women's Liberal Association, which had links to American freethinkers and women's suffrage radicals. When she settled in Boston, she found followers of Walt Whitman, including a bevy of advanced women, who enabled her to express her aspiration for a fuller unconventional individuality. Eschewing boundaries, she sought a left politics in which social change flowed from individual expression.

Miriam acted as a catalyst in Helena's life, bringing her into the socialist and labour movement in Bristol in 1889. In her own life Miriam transgressed not simply the political convictions of her background but its accepted codes of sexual behaviour. In America during the early 1890s, Miriam moved towards the Individualist Anarchism propounded in Benjamin Tucker's journal *Liberty*, which carried her articles, poems and allegorical stories. Her political rebellion fused with a mysticism, which defied the boundaries of perception, along with the constraints of gender. It foreshadows the interest in the esoteric which is evident in the late 1890s and early 1900s.

Miriam also exerted a powerful effect upon Robert, the Dunfermline shop-keeper's son, who became secretary of the militant new union, the Gas Workers and General Labourers' Union, in Bristol in 1890. In Boston he gravitated towards anarchism, encountered Max Stirner's anti-authoritarian ideas of Egoism, and sought alternative forms of spirituality in California. His letters to Edward Carpenter, written between 1894 and 1896, proffer a glimpse of an incipient bohemia in the foothills of the Sierras. They signal that pantheistic desire to transform inner being, which has taken myriad forms on the West Coast.

In contrast, William sought ceaselessly to understand why injustice and inequality prevailed. He went from an apprenticeship in a Belfast basket workshop, via the Unitarians to Salford and Manchester, where he discovered secularism, socialism and anarchism and learned of American labour struggles through working-class migrant networks. Consumed by the hope of revolution, he propagandised at meetings and in the streets, organised workers and took direct action in what became a protracted battle for free speech in Manchester. In Boston from 1891, like Miriam and Robert, he was linked to the Individualist Anarchist circle around *Liberty*. Tucker became his mentor and, from the late 1890s, Helena and Helen also affected his life and his thinking as he did theirs.

Gertrude was the last of the group to migrate. As a young woman she travelled from her devout High Anglican family in Bristol towards a London literary bohemia that encompassed reformist socialists in the Independent Labour Party and the Fabian Society, revolutionary émigrés and anarchists. Advocating free love, interested in sex psychology and the symbolists, she was self-consciously avant-garde, and her two novels secured her a modest reputation in the United States, as well as in Britain. Her mysterious departure for California and Robert altered the course of her life.

I was drawn to the life-stories, social worlds and aspirations of the six puzzled idealists in this book because in differing ways, all six sought to combine their quest for the personal development of individuals with the creation of a society based on co-operative association, rather than competition and profit. They were going against the grain, for they came to left politics in the late nineteenth century, amid the bitter schism between anarchism and socialism. Henceforth anarchists were to carry the flag of liberty and socialists that of collectivity. As the abyss widened during the twentieth century, criss-crossing between these two wings of radicalism became harder.

Familiar with the emergence of movements for social equality through collectivism and solidarity in the late nineteenth and early twentieth centuries, researching the trajectories of my six rebels I realised how intense, resilient and diverse the strands of individualism had also been.

Rebel Crossings traces the contexts in which their hopes were nurtured. All six rebels participated in fluid political, cultural and spiritual networks; consequently their affiliations reach into feminism, secularism, socialism, anarchism, mysticism, mycology, free love, health foods, sex psychology and rational dress. Their lives lead us into their circles and through their eyes we observe more familiar figures such as Edward Carpenter, Havelock Ellis, John Ruskin, Patrick Geddes, Eleanor Marx, Peter Kropotkin, Benjamin Tucker, Emma Goldman and Charlotte Perkins Gilman.

Helena, Miriam, Robert, William, Helen and Gertrude followed exhaustive trails in the belief that another world was possible, and the women in *Rebel Crossings* made brave bids for love and independence. Their ideas take shape in a tangled, unsystematic manner through their reading, their correspondence, their meetings and their friendships. But the quests they embark upon highlight, from unexpected angles, key cultural preoccupations of the late nineteenth century and early twentieth century.

In this period the questioning of Christian belief, encouraged by evolutionary theories and historical studies of the Bible, led to secularism and to searches for alternative bases for ethics through altruism and humanitarianism. The social and economic problems of capitalism, fostered both socialism and social reform. This commitment to changing society in material terms often existed alongside an inner assertion of self-expression and self-determination. The desire for personal freedom carried especially explosive meanings for women curtailed by male control and a hypocritical sexual double standard. Proliferating forms of heterodox spirituality and new fields of thought like sex psychology wrestled with dilemmas of body and spirit.

By shaking the kaleidoscope, newly nuanced patterns come into view. All six characters in *Rebel Crossings* carried altruistic hopes of free association, imagined communities and visions of a new society. They were also inspired by concepts of individual rights and self-ownership bequeathed by the Enlightenment, along with Romanticism's enthusiasm for the expansion of human possibility. They struggled in various ways to balance altruistic service and egoism, union and personal desire.

Like utopian aspirers in other eras, they found that their lived experience jostled against their hopes and quests. A future without dreams of what might be did not come easily to any of them. The four who survived into the twentieth century necessarily adapted to new circumstances. Still, though the sweeping hopes and schemes were set aside, echoes of their former ideals persisted. Some passed on through the generations.

As I wrote, I came to recognise how I was being driven by a quest that resembled theirs. My socialism was formed at a time when the new left in many countries was seeking an alternative to the repressive aspects of Communism under Stalin. In the early 1960s I took part in the Campaign for Nuclear Disarmament. It included many anarchists and involved non-violent direct action – the imprint of learning through doing stayed with me. Then came the women's liberation movement with its emphasis on the connections between personal experience and social change. In the 1970s, this led me to begin looking at women's struggles for emancipation not simply through feminism, but in socialism and anarchism historically. A continuing preoccupation has been how to comprehend the elusive interaction of inner feelings and the external expression of resistance.

I first discovered the little group of rebels in this book when I, myself, was young and convinced the world was about to change for the better. Then, thwack, capitalism changed gear, appropriating free-expression, raiding collective spaces, shredding non-marketable aspirations, social solidarity and fellow feeling. Now that I am in my seventies and hence incontestably old, it is evident that a good society, along with a new radical and emancipatory social consciousness, will take longer to realise than I had imagined. Like many in my generation, I accept this reality rationally, but emotionally find it ineffably baffling.

It was often painful, charting my puzzled idealists tussling with dilemmas I, too, had come to know all too well. Neither they, nor I, offer neat resolutions. Nevertheless, I believe the *combination* of liberty, love and solidarity they stumbled towards is even more needful in our twenty-first century.

I declare my bias; in writing about six people long ago whose hopes were high, whose awareness did not fit decisively into any received categories, whose ideas were collected from here and there, expressed in small meetings and circulated through barely remembered networks, my aim is subversion sustained by humour and enjoyment.

PART I

HOPES

ONE

Radical Endeavour: Helena Born

Helena's origins were in the Devon countryside. Her grandfather Richard Born farmed 120 acres at Coham, near the small village of Black Torrington, and Helena was born there on 11 May 1860. By the time the 1871 Census was taken, forty-one-year-old Richard Born, his wife Elizabeth, aged forty-nine, and their young daughter, Mary Helena, were living a few miles away with relatives, the Southcombes, at Moorhead Farm.[1] Perched high up on the edge of Hatherleigh Moor, the farm looked out upon a breath-taking vista of yellow heath, backed by greener fields and grey blue hills just visible in the far distance. They were only about a mile from the bustle of the market town of Hatherleigh, but the short walk would have seemed a long way to a small child and Helena's world in her early years revolved around the farmhouse.

The 1871 Census records Richard Born's 'Work, Profession or Occupation' as being 'Out of Business – Interest of Money'. He had somehow acquired capital and no longer worked on the land. Helena's father is classified as a lodger, while John Southcombe and his sister, Susannah, 'Milliner and Dress Maker', were joint heads of the household. The connection between the two families was close, and, after Elizabeth Southcombe was born in 1873, Helena adopted a protective and affectionate relationship towards her younger 'cousin' who was always known as 'Minnie'.[2]

Hatherleigh had developed as a centre for the woollen trade, and its poor inhabitants, known as 'potboilers', retained a medieval right to graze their sheep on the Moor. Decline set in during the eighteenth century, leaving it a tiny market town by the 1860s. Nevertheless, its trading ethos, marked by a Stock Market and several inns, distinguished it from the surrounding villages. The Anglican church, St John the Baptist's, loomed over the cottages in the narrow streets below.[3] According to Helen's 'Biographical Introduction' to *Whitman's Ideal Democracy*, Helena went to a day school in the village, possibly the Anglican National School, still attended by most local children. However, the Borns may have been Nonconformists, for, in an 1885 essay, 'A Chat about Bazaars', Helena recalls assisting at a bazaar to raise money for a 'Dissenting body' in a small town so 'bigoted' that few graced the event, compelling the sellers to duplicate as buyers.[4] Her training for life with a minority outlook began early.

Shortly after the 1871 Census, the Born family moved to Stoke St Mary near Taunton, a town with strong Dissenting traditions, and Helen records that Richard Born sent his daughter to 'an academy' in Taunton. The school was clearly advanced in its approach to girls' education, for she states that the young countrywoman 'excelled in her studies, evinced a taste for mathematics, and looked longingly toward a college training'.[5] But this was not to be.

On 16 February 1876, when Helena was fifteen, the *Exeter Flying Post* announced the sale of the Born's 'FURNITURE', 'Pianoforte', 'Hack Horse, Dog Cart and Harness'.[6] An abrupt change was afoot: Richard Born had become sufficiently wealthy to move the family to Bristol, which had prospered from trading in slaves, sugar and tobacco. By the mid 1870s, its ancient port was being overtaken by competitors, but the city had developed a varied range of industries and a strong financial sector.[7]

The Borns' new rented home was 65 Whiteladies Road, in the elegant suburb of Clifton. Helena's father appears to have invested in land and property, for the 1881 Census states that he derived his income 'from House'.[8] In the early part of the nineteenth century Clifton had attracted impoverished aristocrats, along with up and coming manufacturers, retired army officers and professionals. From the 1860s, as more and more of the aspiring middle class settled high above the city's slums, Clifton turned into a distinctive suburb of Bristol. With its magnificent Downs, its origins as a watering place, its links to the powerful Society of Merchant Venturers and its grand Regency houses, Clifton was no ordinary suburb. In 1862, a new public school for boys, Clifton College, was established there with spacious grounds and playing fields. During the 1860s and '70s many churches and chapels were built, their charities extending the ethos of high-minded endeavour through the city.

By the late nineteenth century Clifton had acquired an unusually large number of women paying rates and heading their own households. These independent middle-class women became a force, not only in the suburb's religious and charitable projects, but in its politics and culture. They established organisations for women's rights, agitating for suffrage and higher education, along with the anti-vivisection cause. They also played a crucial part in the controversial movement for the repeal of the 1860s Contagious Diseases Acts, which had introduced the seizure, forced inspection and confinement of women (but not men) suspected of having venereal disease. The long campaign that resulted in the Acts' repeal in 1886 raised not just individual rights, but the demand for women's control over their own bodies and persons, in a startling assertion of autonomous self-ownership that crossed boundaries of class and gender.[9]

With its Debating Society, Antiquarian Club, Shakespeare and Browning Societies, Clifton pulsated with meetings, not to mention art exhibitions and concerts. It even evolved its own styles – with just a hint of daring. Some aesthetic Clifton women were to be seen in clinging Pre-Raphaelite garments, others favoured voluminous velvet dresses signalling a distinguished intellectual and aesthetic recoil from conformity. The genteel and cultured suburb on the hill thus allowed for choice and diversity among its female inhabitants – albeit those who belonged to its variegated elites. Though Helena was never able to study at university, her surroundings educated and changed her nonetheless.

In 1879 Helena started to keep a scrapbook, and it reveals how her preoccupations alter. Initially devout and patriotic, she carefully cut out reports of addresses by famous preachers along with verses about the Royal Family. Within a year, however, the scrapbooks' contents become more radical. The stimulus most likely derived from the Unitarian church she attended on Oakfield Road near her home. Built in 1862 with local red stone in Gothic style, the church's architecture epitomised rational, harmonious aspiration. Its first incumbent had been the enlightened J. Estlin Carpenter, a probing scholar of comparative religion who supported women's rights. When Helena went to Oakfield church the broad religious tolerance and radicalism he personified still persisted. The current preacher, Revd William Hargrave, shared Helena's scientific interests; he had an MA in Botany and was a keen member of the British

Naturalists' Society. Politically he was a Radical Liberal, part of a growing current in the Liberal Party opposed to the old Whig aristocracy, and Helena came to share many of his views.

Radical Liberals like Hargrave wanted to remove all impediments restricting individual freedom and development. He and his wife, Jane, participated in the agitation against the Contagious Diseases Acts and defended women's rights to suffrage and legal independence. Hargrave's commitment to individual freedom extended to a critique of class prejudices and he was prepared to defend trade unions and land nationalisation. Moreover, he was a supporter of the radical secularist MP, Charles Bradlaugh, expelled from the House of Commons in 1880 after refusing to take the religious oath of allegiance. From that year, cutting after cutting on the protracted Bradlaugh case appear in Helena's scrapbook.[10]

Living without God was being debated in the newspapers and journals Helena perused so assiduously. The erosion of religious faith removed the reassurance of immortality, opening a space for alternative kinds of spirituality and secular ethical values. It also reinforced aspirations for individual fulfilment on earth rather than in heaven. Yet a revulsion against a mechanical materialism was widespread. Like many Victorian young women, Helena's passions, spiritual and sensuous, were aroused by the Romantic poets, especially Percy Bysshe Shelley and John Keats. Algernon Swinburne and Robert Browning appealed too, perhaps because they explored parameters of doubt while intimating realms of personal free expression. Browning, like the novels by William Thackeray and George Eliot that Helena read, also probed the generation of individual personality – a pursuit Helena would make her life quest.

A favourite of Helena's was the less known Bristol poet, John Gregory, a self-educated shoemaker employed at Clifton College to mend the boys' shoes. His poems appeared in local papers, such as the *Bristol Mercury*, mixing sentiment with protest against social injustice. In 1880 Helena cut out his 'Beauty's Choice', with its rejection of worldly esteem, and his 'Reward of Labour', exhorting the reader to 'look onward, upward'.[11] Despite their differing circumstances, Helena could identify with Gregory's call to resist the thwarting of spiritual and creative aspiration. Over the next few years many more verses by this remarkable man were to be pasted into the scrapbook.

Born in 1831, Gregory's radicalism reached back to the Chartist movement, for he had read the *Northern Star* as an apprentice in Wales. In Bristol, Gregory became active in the Boot and Shoe Union and the

Bristol and District Labour League, an organisation formed to promote working-class candidates. He denounced the upper classes graphically as 'fat calves of Fortune [who] lay at ease as Caterpilars [*sic*] basking in the sunshine on leafs [*sic*] of Cabbages', and was a supporter of the Bristol Socialist Society which Helena later joined.[12]

The Bristol Socialist Society began as a discussion group started by two brothers who were supporters of Bradlaugh, John Sharland, an engineer, and Robert Sharland, a wire-puller, along with a Republican carter called William Baster. Then another Sharland brother, Will, enrolled, bringing along his neighbour, a Christian Socialist factory worker, Robert Weare. They had become friends through talking over the garden wall about socialism and the ideas of the American land nationaliser, Henry George. In 1884, this little band of working-class dissidents turned themselves into the Bristol branch of the recently formed Marxist Social Democratic Federation (S.D.F.) before becoming autonomous early in 1886.[13]

Committed to ending the 'private ownership of land and the means of production, distribution, and exchange', the Bristol Socialist Society also aspired to 'the attainment of the higher ideals of life' regardless of class or sex.[14] They met in local coffee houses, wrangling over politics and economics or enjoying readings from their favourite poets – Gregory, Whitman, Shelley, William Morris – and the musical Sharland brothers singing rousing glees.

Edward Carpenter was one of their most popular speakers. In August 1885, his message of love, liberty and equality at the Castle Street Coffee House gained a new recruit for the Bristol Socialists, the Labour League member, Robert Gilliard. Gilliard, a solicitor's clerk, wanted more than working-class men in Parliament or even public ownership. A profoundly spiritual man, he was concerned about creating alternative values of loving association, alongside external social and economic changes.[15] So from the early days of Bristol socialism various kinds of Christian Socialists rubbed shoulders with secularists.

Before long Gilliard was addressing the group on one of his heroes, John Ruskin, whose ethical and aesthetic revolt against capitalism attracted many on the left regardless of his Tory views. The future Labour Prime Minister, Ramsay MacDonald, recalled hearing the talk in 1885, after winding his way up a 'long wooden staircase' to a 'dimly-lit small upper room' and sitting with the Bristol socialists on their 'hard penitential forms' amid 'the odour of sawdust and steaming coffee' in the 'coffee-shop' below.[16]

Within a few years Gilliard, the Sharlands, Baster and Weare all became close friends of Helena's.

The shocks to the seemingly unstoppable progress of the British economy began to provoke questioning among the well-to-do. In Bristol, as elsewhere, social unease was fed by religious doubt. From the early 1880s Helena's interest in the Bradlaugh case gradually broadened and her scrapbook entries suggest a questioning of the status quo. In January 1883 she cut out a newspaper report of a lecture in London by Louise Michel, headed 'The Female Apostle of Anarchy'. Imprisoned under harsh conditions after the defeat of the Paris Commune in 1871, Michel had been released under an amnesty in 1881. She was in London to raise funds for imprisoned anarchists and to support soup kitchens for striking workers. The report confirmed that she thought 'property was robbery' and 'had no religion': 'A religion implied a belief in God, and she could not believe that a just and beneficial Being would have permitted such misery as the poor suffered to exist.'[17] Helena also diligently pasted in news items on insanitary housing; an Exhibition of Women's Industries; the Bristol Quaker, Thomas Pease, calling for equal moral standards for men and women at a Social Purity meeting; and items on rational dress, vegetarianism and anti-vaccination.[18] Like vivisection, vaccination aroused the ire of some Victorians, not only because of the danger for human beings, but because it utilised calf lymph.

Helena's conservative parents surely disapproved. However, their serious, socially awkward daughter had acquired an obstinacy that would endure. A compulsion towards enquiry and duty propelled her towards unconventional ideas and dangerous causes. This propensity was accentuated after Elizabeth Born's death early in 1884. Mother and daughter had been close, almost sisterly companions. Her loss left Helena emotionally alone, for Richard Born appears to have been a remote father. Despite his wealth, he employed only one maid at the house in Whiteladies Road and, after her mother's death, household duties devolved heavily on Helena. With a countryman's expectations of a plain daughter, her father assumed she would take over as his cook and housekeeper.[19]

The Unitarian church in Oakfield Road provided Helena with an irrefutably legitimate escape route. She loved playing the piano and singing, and just after the death of her mother made an important friendship with a fellow choir-member, Beatrice Taylor. Taylor remembered, how, after choir practice, Helena used to accompany her home. Taylor's father, who liked talking about social and political affairs, urged Helena to express her ideas, and she would make her points 'in a rapid, nervous manner', engaging in 'vigorous argument' with him, before falling silent. Despite remaining unconvinced, Helena would end the conversation 'with a laugh'.[20]

Encouraged at last to articulate her own opinions, Helena began to practise speaking in public at Oakfield's Debating Society. On each occasion she had to force herself to rise and was only able to utter a few words. Taylor was well aware what agonies even these had cost her friend who was afflicted by 'extreme diffidence'.[21] Helena struggled hard to combat her reserve, but the shy self-consciousness was never entirely overcome.

With her new friend, however, Helena could be completely at ease. The two young women accompanied one another to dances and discovered a mutual delight in walking long distances. One expedition took them miles out into the countryside where they ate their lunch sitting together like vagabonds 'upon a haymow'.[22] It was the first of several intense, joyous companionships with women.

Helena's interest in science led her towards the evolutionary and social theories of Charles Darwin and Thomas Huxley, along with the startling freethinking German naturalist, Ernst Haeckel. In her November 1884 essay on 'Bias', preserved in a notebook, Helena referred with approval to Alfred Russel Wallace, who had independently arrived at the idea of natural selection and was, moreover, a supporter of land nationalisation. 'Take nothing for granted that has not been demonstrated', noted a sceptical, scientific Helena.[23]

While the Unitarian church offered stimulating and sustaining fellowship, Helena's reading was unravelling her Christian faith. Not simply her study of evolution, but Bradlaugh's secularism, the revolutionary politics of Tom Paine, the American freethinker Colonel Robert Ingersoll, and the agnostic Leslie Stephen left the received religious views of her childhood increasingly threadbare.[24] By the mid 1880s she was ready for new outlets.

Helena's friends the Hargraves were associated with a grouping that proved even more significant to her than the Oakfield church – the Bristol Women's Liberal Association (B.W.L.A). Jane Hargrave was a valued member and William Hargrave had lectured for the Association. In 1885, the year the Hargraves left Bristol, Helena started donating 1s as a member. She would soon be on the committee, her election noted by the *Bristol Mercury and Daily Post* in March 1886.[25] Richard Born's daughter was starting to become a minor local public figure, though the journalists evinced much difficulty in grasping the spelling of her name.

The creation of the B.W.L.A. in 1881 initiated a national movement as Liberal Party women in other parts of the country started establishing branches, creating a national rival to the Conservatives' 'Primrose League'. The official aim of the Bristol Association was 'to promote Liberal principles and to diffuse knowledge on political questions of general and local interest among the women of Bristol'.[26] However, the politic phrasing belied an exasperated impatience over women's suffrage among doughty campaigners like the B.W.L.A President, Anna Maria Priestman, who voiced their steely refusal to 'work for any Parliamentary candidate who was not in favour of equal laws for men and women'.[27]

Through the B.W.L.A Helena landed in the midst of an extraordinary network of exemplars linked to wide-ranging radical and feminist campaigns, nationally and internationally. Anna Maria Priestman saw women's suffrage as part of a broad extension of democratic citizenship. She was prepared to support radical workers' causes and advocated women's trade unionism.[28] In 1870 Anna Maria and her sister Mary had refused to pay their taxes as a protest against women's exclusion from the franchise. Mary Priestman, the B.W.L.A Treasurer, took part in the campaign against the Contagious Diseases Acts. Another sister, Margaret (Mrs Arthur Tanner), also opposed the Contagious Diseases Acts and was a Vice-President of the B.W.L.A.[29] All three women had participated in the anti-slavery movement and had signed the first women's suffrage petition in 1866.[30]

Their niece, Helen Priestman Bright Clark, married to the Quaker owner of Clark's shoes in the nearby town of Street, was yet another Vice-President. The daughter of the leading Radical Liberal, Joseph Bright, in 1883 she had won round the majority of delegates to women's suffrage at a large Liberal conference in Leeds.[31] The American radical suffrage campaigner, Elizabeth Cady Stanton marvelled, 'For a daughter to speak thus … in opposition to her loved and honored father … was an act of heroism and fidelity to her own honest conviction.'[32]

Yet another Quaker, Emily Sturge, co-founder with Anna Maria Priestman of the B.W.L.A., was also honorary secretary of the Bristol and West of England Society for Women's Suffrage. Especially interested in education, she was elected to Bristol's School Board in 1880 and became the first woman on the Council of Redland High School for Girls' in 1883.

In 1885 Emily was just one of seven Sturge women in the Association, closely followed by five Tanners. Bristol's radical families swelled the rolls of the B.W.L.A.[33]

Participation in multifarious causes linked these B.W.L.A. members to national and international social movements. The Unitarian, Mary Estlin, was not on the committee when Helena became a member, but was one of the larger donors paying a subscription of 5s. She had led the renowned Bristol and Clifton Ladies' Anti-Slavery Society in the 1850s, later supporting women's suffrage and opposing the Contagious Diseases Acts. Moreover, she had been friendly with the militant anti-slavery leader, William Lloyd Garrison, until his death in 1879, and was in contact with the radical wing of the American women's rights movement, which included Stanton.[34] These interconnections still operated when Helena joined the B.W.L.A. In 1885 they invited the freethinking American friend of Stanton's, Moncure Conway, to speak on 'Women and Evolution'.[35]

In December 1886 a 'Miss Barne' appears in the *Bristol Mercury and Daily Post* supporting a Bill for the extension of the franchise to women, along with the Misses Priestman, the Sturges, Helen Priestman Bright Clark and Bristol's pioneering woman doctor, Eliza Dunbar.[36] Helena's involvement occurred during a disheartening period; the Liberal Party was ignoring women's suffrage and the movement was divided. While one wing deplored any break with conventions and believed in seeking votes only for *unmarried* women and widows in an effort to placate husbands, the Bright-Priestman group opposed such cautious pragmatism and saw women's rights as rooted in radical individualism.[37]

In 1887 they were studying a pamphlet, *For Liberty* by the Individualist Auberon Herbert, who opposed state compulsion of any kind, whether for taxation or vaccination. The former MP and eccentric aristocrat was living with his family in a cluster of cottages in the New Forest, and Helena had a personal connection to this elegant, individualistic bohemia because Beatrice Taylor went to work there as a governess to Herbert's daughter 'Nan'.[38]

Yet Helena was painfully aware of the consequences for women like herself of breaking with convention. In January 1887, in notes for a talk entitled 'Pro Bono Publico', she reflected that 'for women (with few exceptions) public service does not lead to glory and emolument, but is attended with odium and ostracism'.[39] Even so, she was being shaped by a political milieu which asserted not simply the individual's duty to defy

unjust laws and oppressive customs, but *women's* personal responsibility
to witness. Both Quakerism and the campaign against the Contagious
Diseases Acts fostered these connections. 'The Personal Element in
English Politics', discussed at a B.W.L.A. meeting in 1887, was a topic
particularly close to the Quaker women's hearts.[40]

The Bristol middle-class women's assertion of individual rights and
personal service combined with a social altruism that sought to gain working-class support for women's suffrage, encourage women's trade unions
and improve conditions at work.[41] Helena was attracted to this ideal of
service and clearly admired B.W.L.A member, Maria Colby, who, after
knocking on door after door in working-class St Philip's and St Jacob's,
became so weary of objections to women's suffrage, 'based on the idea
that the primary duty of women is to darn stockings', that she submitted
her own ironic request for a holey-socked husband to the local paper. An
amused Helena preserved it in her scrapbook in 1886.

> Wanted –
> A postman to marry, who walks with might,
> Or policeman on duty by day and night,
> Or telegraph racer with heels of horn,
> Who'll bring me daily some stockings to darn.[42]

In December 1887, Emily Sturge, who, like Anna Maria Priestman,
supported trade unions for women workers, stressed the significance
of the cross-class connection. In her talk, 'Am I My Sister's Keeper?',
she argued that B.W.L.A. members should help to form unions and co-
operatives among working-class women and use their buying power as
middle-class women to improve working conditions.[43]

Upon coming across a long, detailed article on women's labour in a
Bristol paper-bag factory, Helena carefully placed it in her scrapbook. It
was by an American woman journalist, 'J.M.B.', and covered not just the
work itself, but the women's survival tactics. J.M.B saw how the workers
broke up the 'dull routine' by joking, and supported one another in misfortune – saving fragments of cake for a workmate's sick child. No need
for them to be *told* about solidarity, she said; they came down 'like a meat
fly' on anyone who gave offence.[44] Helena must have been intrigued by
this insight into an unfamiliar world for she pasted in page after page of
graphic reportage.

The mix of individualism and altruism that inspired Bristol's radical women is evident in a revealing letter they sent to the first meeting of the International Council of Women organised in 1888 in America by Stanton and her colleague, Susan B. Anthony:

Dear Sisters, – We have heard of your intended gathering with deep interest. We are not able to send one of our number to represent us; but we write to tell you that your zealous labours in America strengthen and encourage our work here, to bid you God-speed, and to assure you that we are one with you in the conviction that women must stand by women – the most educated by the most ignorant – the most sheltered by the most unprotected – until every barrier raised by law and custom in the way of women's full development and freedom shall be broken down.[45]

Signed, 'In the Fellowship of Womanhood', it included Helena's name nestling second after Anna Maria Priestman's. Other signatories included Margaret Tanner, Helen Priestman Bright Clark, Emily Sturge, Mary A. Estlin, along with John Stuart Mill's sister, Mary Colman, suffrage campaigner Maria Colby, and Louisa Swann, a Quaker activist.[46] The letter was read out to the forty-nine radical delegates who, after vigorous singing of 'Equal Rights for Ever' to the tune of 'John Brown's Body', set to work on their programme which embraced not only suffrage but prison reform, social purity, trade unions and co-operatives.[47]

Helena's chance to speak for the Bristol Women's Liberal Association came in May 1888 on the somewhat prosaic topic of 'The Budget'. B.W.L.A. members, having become increasingly involved in municipal politics, were confronted with a Conservative Bill for local government reform and joined the working-class Liberal Operatives Association to talk through its funding implications. Both radical groupings faced a dilemma of how to square their distrust of the state with much needed local social provision. This conundrum was by no means peculiar to Bristol. In London, studies of poverty, stimulated by social settlements like Toynbee Hall, were convincing some Liberals of the need for more generous state support, and the social reformer, Francis Gilmore Barnett, whose clergyman brother Samuel had founded Toynbee Hall, was present at the Bristol meeting. However, the complexities of local government finance resulted in the crucial question of the 'budget' being 'unavoidably postponed'. 'Miss Born' was billed as one of the speakers expected to elucidate at a follow-up meeting on May 14th. Emily Sturge took the chair, and Helena, with her head for figures, stepped into the breach. Her views

Helena Born
(Bristol Reference Library)

went unreported; but she was clearly proud of this opportunity to take the platform, as she kept the notice all her life.[48]

Helena's time in the B.W.L.A. introduced her to the practicalities of organising and brought her into contact with the respectable working class. Her reliability and thoroughness were recognised by older members. In 1887, she was recruited by the philanthropic Dr Eliza Dunbar onto the committee of the Marlborough Workmen's Flower Show and Home Industry Society. The aim of the society was to encourage gardening, housewifery and handicrafts. By 1888 Helena had been made secretary, enabling Dr Dunbar to take a backseat.[49]

Through the B.W.L.A. Helena entered the wider world of Liberal politics. Her membership coincided with a serious rift over Home Rule for Ireland, which was supported by the Radical wing of the Liberal Party and opposed by 'Unionists'. In March 1886 she had served on the Election Committee for the unsuccessful Liberal Home Rule candidate James Judd, only to see Gladstone's Home Rule Bill defeated and the Unionists defect to the Conservatives.[50] Over the course of 1887, the Conservative and Unionist government responded harshly to the Irish tenants' rent rebellion. The Priestman, Clark, Tanner wing of the B.W.L.A. joined other Radical Liberals in protesting. In February 1888 Anna Maria Priestman icily condemned Coercion in Ireland at the B.W.L.A. soiree in the Victoria Rooms.[51]

Predicting 'a stimulus' to Liberalism in Bristol 'with the help of the ladies', Mr H.T.M.C. Gwynn, chairman of the Clifton Ward Bristol Liberal Federation, welcomed Helena and Maria Colby onto the committee on February 27th with the words 'the Liberals of Bristol were determined to leave no stone unturned in order to do justice to Ireland'.[52] During February and March 1888 Helena was present at anti-Coercion meetings in the Bristol suburbs of Bedminster and Montpelier.[53] On March 13th at a B.W.L.A. meeting in Montpelier where 'Coercion in Ireland' was unanimously condemned, 'Women in Politics' was also discussed; Helena's voice was to be heard as it closed, urging 'the advantage of organisation' and the establishment of a new B.W.L.A. branch in Bristol North.[54] She preserved a cutting that summer reporting a meeting of the Wells Women's Liberal Association attended by Anna Maria Priestman and Louisa Swann condemning the death in prison of the Irish tenants' leader, John Mandeville, and the imprisonment of the Nationalist MP, John Dillon.[55]

Throughout Britain resistance to Coercion in Ireland was creating the basis for political alliances between Radical Liberals and other groupings. Bristol was no exception. In August 1888 the Bristol Operatives' Liberal Association mounted a demonstration with the Trades Council, Irish Nationalists and socialists opposing Dillon's arrest. Robert Tovey, from the Clothiers' Cutters Association and a prominent figure within both the Trades Council and the Labour League's agitation for working men candidates, declared he was 'representing the labour party', and 'held out the right hand of sympathy with his Irish brethren'.[56] Tovey was soon supporting Helena in organising women workers.

A key figure in bringing the Liberal Operatives together with other groups against Coercion was their imposing President, Dan Irving. His life history personified liberal self-help ideals. Despite leaving school at thirteen to go to sea, Irving had risen to become a foreman shunter on the railway until an accident resulted in the loss of his leg and a humiliating downgrading in position and pay. This harsh treatment shook his Baptist faith and began to alter his political thinking.[57] Like many other working-class Radical Liberals, Irving soon moved towards socialism, becoming one of Helena's firm friends.

The resolution denouncing Coercion was put by a young socialist solicitor H.H. Gore. Hugh Holmes Gore was the secretary of the Clifton and Bristol Christian Socialists and a leading figure in the Christian Socialist movement nationally. Influenced first by John Ruskin's social economics, and then from the mid 1880s by the socialism of William Morris, Gore was hostile to the Radical Individualism of the Liberal Party left, which he saw as perpetuating class inequality through free market economics. He distinguished between a self-centred 'individualism' and the expansion of individuality he saw arising from socialist relations of 'mutual love, forbearance and help'.[58] Gore, who was friendly with Edward Carpenter, became an important link between the Christian Socialists up in Clifton and the working-class socialists in the Bristol Socialist Society.

Helena's political radicalism developed alongside an inner rebellion against the crushing of individuality she experienced as a middle-class woman. In her 1887 notes headed 'Pro Bono Publico', Helena pronounces: 'once the unfettered soul has grasped the full meaning of life', all the petty, material details of daily life would fall into insignificance. In that chiliastic moment, 'the fashionable observances of custom's slaves and conventionality's handmaidens' would be 'unmasked'.[59]

In her April 1888 essay, 'Insincerity', she deplores the 'reticence' that allowed 'worn out customs and creeds' to prevail. Observing how the 'timid' were 'deterred from following the dictates of their reason', she describes how they were stunted by a 'vain endeavour to regulate their thoughts and actions in accordance with that which society appears to approve'. Helena considered such insincerity to be particularly prevalent in relations between the sexes. It constituted a 'source of much mischief, undermining the mutual helpfulness which might be derived from frank interchange of thought'. Consequently, men and women were 'far from understanding each other, and hence do each other unintentional mischief'.[60]

Helena was drawn to the scientific approach to ethics expounded by Herbert Spencer. In his 1851 book, *Social Statics*, Spencer had linked the evolutionary ideas of J.B. Lamarck to humanity's progress, promulgating personal evolution through exercising control and circumspection, an approach to conduct Helena made her own. In his early work an optimistic Spencer maintained that as individuals became more aware of their individuality they would take pleasure in the freedom of others. Following 'the law of perfect freedom' meant doing as one desired as long as it did not prevent others doing likewise.[61] Spencer popularised the term 'altruism', as used by the French Positivist, Auguste Comte, envisaging an inevitable process of individuation leading towards an ideal of perfect competition that seamlessly folded into mutualism.[62]

In *The Man Versus the State* (1884), however, an older, more irascible, Spencer protested against arguments for collectivism as endangering the desired equilibrium of the free market. He singled out as false prophets the art critic turned social economist, John Ruskin, the land nationaliser, Henry George, along with William Morris and Henry Hyndman, the founder of the Marxist Social Democratic Federation.[63]

Ostensibly in 1888 Helena still dwelt amid a world of decorous propriety, contributing as a member of the Flower and Needlework Guild to the 'chaste decorations' commended by the *Western Daily Press* at the October wedding of the Liberal employer, Sir Joseph Weston.[64] However, over the course of 1888 and 1889, Helena came round to many of the ideas of Spencer's bugbears, while always endeavouring to *connect* individual freedom and personal expression with her vision of social transformation.

Two convulsive forces exercised a catalytic impact upon Helena. The first was Walt Whitman. Nothing Helena had read prepared her for either the form or content of his poems in *Leaves of Grass*. Whitman's voice pierced through the restraining reticence cloaking polite behaviour, in an unfamiliar, startlingly direct style. Moreover, he wrote about topics beyond Helena's wildest imaginings. Here was a poet celebrating body and self while merging with everyone and everything; a poet who revelled in 'I' and transcended 'I'. The frank energy of Whitman seized hold of Helena, shaking down her carefully cultivated persona. From Whitman, glorying in his own explosive being across the Atlantic, came an intimation of the extraordinary, expansive individuality for which she yearned; henceforth Helena carried Whitman within her.[65]

The second force came from closer to home – from the new, Bristol North branch of the B.W.L.A., to be precise. Miriam Daniell's name first appears in the 1888 Report, as a member donating 3s.[66] Miriam (née Wheeler) was married to a successful Liberal solicitor, Edward Tuckett

Walt Whitman (Labadie, Special
Collections Library, University of Michigan)

Daniell. The couple had moved in 1888 from Westbury-upon-Trym, then just outside Bristol, to a large, rather gloomy house at 28 Hampton Park, Redland, only a short walk from the Borns.

The two young women gravitated to one another. While they shared a potent idealism, Miriam was everything Helena was not. Whereas Helena laboured at making herself indispensable by being level-headed and reliable, the charismatic Miriam effortlessly attracted people to her. She was impetuous and bursting with conviction and passion. This is how Helen later depicted Miriam and Helena's early friendship:

> Miriam was an artist, a poet, and a socialist. Her studies in economics, her intimate knowledge of the lives of the working people, and her deep sympathy with them in their efforts to improve their lot led naturally to her embracing the socialist gospel, then spreading amongst the advanced guard of the labor movement. In the course of frequent walks into the country in all weathers Miriam imparted to Helena her own enthusiasm. They were kindred souls, both richly endowed with the artistic temperament, and sought the natural beauties of field and flower, rain and sunshine, and in them found joy and inspiration.[67]

Helen relates how their passionate reciprocity resulted in a great mass of 'unsocial customs' being thrown irreparably to the winds.[68] In meeting Miriam, Helena experienced a transformative release, emotionally and politically. And Helena, who was reading Edward Carpenter's Whitmanite prose poem *Towards Democracy*, Henrik Ibsen's plays, William Blake's poetry and the aesthetics of Walter Pater, surely shared her excitement with Miriam.[69] Carpenter's combination of spirituality and left politics, Ibsen's assertion of individual freedom, Blake's exultation of energy and enthusiasm and Pater's mix of sensuousness and asceticism were to mark Miriam for the rest of her life.

TWO

Subversive Intimations: Miriam Daniell

Robert Rogers Wheeler and his wife, Catharine, could never have imagined their baby girl, Elizabeth Miriam, born on 29 October 1861, would transmogrify into an intransigent rebel.[1] There was nothing extreme about the Wheelers; they appeared as solid as solid could be.

Miriam's father had started work as a sales assistant in a grocer's in Moulton, Northamptonshire, marrying Catharine Freeman, the daughter of a substantial Norfolk grocer. He then set up a grocery shop and became a tea importer in Bristol. The shop at Portland House, Clifton, prospered by catering for the elaborate culinary tastes of the suburb's aspirational inhabitants, and the Wheelers gradually accrued wealth by selling them fine teas and new-fangled products, such as Nelson's Opaque Gelatine.[2]

Robert Rogers Wheeler was also a significant figure in Pembroke Congregational Chapel, which happened to be at the other end of Oakfield Road from Helena's Unitarian church. The successful trader acted as the chapel's treasurer and, during the 1870s, was responsible for a large rebuilding project that replaced the original iron structure.[3] The new building, an ample stone chapel, exuded affluent self-assurance.

His grandson, the well-known archaeologist, Sir Mortimer Wheeler, remembered Robert Rogers simply as a 'bluff old boy', yet he clearly had social and cultural ambitions for his six children, two boys and four girls, employing a governess from Zurich to educate them. Miriam's mother, Catharine, is described by Sir Mortimer Wheeler as 'a little gentle, good-looking old lady with a streak of cynical piety in her composition'.[4]

Miriam's Victorian upbringing appears to have been comfortable, pragmatic and conventionally religious; however, in the sixteenth century, when faith had been a matter of life and death, one ancestor of the Wheelers *had* made an extreme and principled choice. John Rogers had been converted to Protestantism by William Tyndale in Antwerp. After Tyndale's violent death in 1536, Rogers helped to prepare a revised translation of the Bible and was burned at Smithfield in 1555 for his Protestant views. The memory of John 'the Martyr' Rogers lived on in the Wheeler family. It was perpetuated in Miriam's father's second Christian name and, in the 1890s, Miriam's elder brother, Robert Mortimer, proudly told his young son, Mortimer, 'Your ancestor Rogers the Martyr was burned at Smithfield for saying what he thought.'[5]

While the first Wheeler boy, Herbert, stayed securely within the orbit of Bristol Congregationalism, Robert Mortimer proved more restless; he went up to Edinburgh University to study classics under John Stuart Blackie. A supporter of Home Rule for Ireland *and* for Scotland, Blackie was an ardent advocate of Scottish culture and also supported the efforts of campaigner Sophia Jex-Blake to open the University to women medical students. Another guiding figure was the Professor of Literature, David Masson, who transmitted his love of Emerson and Whitman. He and his wife Emily Rosaline, a suffrage activist, were also keen campaigners for women's higher education and Masson lobbied for many years within the University for women's entry into the Medical Faculty.[6]

Through Edinburgh University, Miriam's brother entered circles utterly different from his Bristol Congregational upbringing, becoming, in his son's words, 'an advanced free thinker of the militant type of the early 'eighties', whose friends included the secularist writer and friend of Bradlaugh, John Mackinnon Robertson. Robert Mortimer came home with an MA, infused not simply with free thought, but with radicalism and Romanticism. After lecturing in Bristol, he returned to Scotland in the late 1880s and taught in the Glasgow University Extension Movement.[7] Dreamy, democratic Robert Mortimer undoubtedly communicated these startling enthusiasms to his younger sister, Miriam.

However, all was still calm, on a bright, frosty November day in 1880, when the *Bristol Mercury* sent a reporter to cover the Congregationalists' Bazaar in the Victoria Rooms. The Bazaar aimed to clear the debt from Pembroke's new chapel building, and the Wheeler family had been mobilised in support. The 'Misses Wheeler' caught the reporter's attention, seated behind a stall draped in pink cloth covered with white lace. Miriam had just turned nineteen; sister Catharine was twenty-two, while a precociously artistic Mary was fifteen and already winning prizes at Bristol School of Art. The youngest sister, Ellen, being only nine, was presumably too young to have contributed to the handicrafts on display. These were described in the *Bristol Mercury* as including 'fearfully and wonderfully made combinations of textile fabrics' along with 'that modern vagary of fashion, the Tam o'Shanter hat'.[8] Women had started to favour the Scottish men's round flat hat in velvet or crocheted, topped by a bobble, and the 'Misses Wheeler' were au fait with the latest styles.

Miriam had inherited her mother's good looks, and must have made a striking saleswoman. She had already acquired an approved suitor, Edward Tuckett Daniell, whose elder brother, James Livett Daniell, had handled the legal side of Pembroke Chapel's building programme.[9] It is tempting to imagine treasurer Robert and solicitor James mooting the match over legal papers, tempting too to wonder whether Edward dallied by the Misses Wheelers' stall, ostensibly admiring those Tam o'Shanters.

Miriam married Edward at Pembroke Chapel in July 1881; she was nineteen and he was twenty-seven. Robert Rogers Wheeler had contrived his daughter's move into the professional classes, for Miriam's husband was not only a fellow Congregationalist, he was a partner in the solicitor's firm, Daniell, Strickland and Daniell, with chambers on St Nicholas Street.[10]

Edward Tuckett Daniell was both personally and professionally dependent upon his elder brother. The Daniells' childhood had been fraught with Dickensian misfortune. After their father, 'a General Merchant', died, their mother, Martha Tuckett, was reduced to penury and forced to work as a housekeeper. A solicitor, James Livett, had looked after young James and assisted his career in law. James in turn took brother Edward under his wing, and, after marrying Sophie Day Baynes in 1870, brought him into their home in Clifton, as well as into the firm as a clerk, and later a partner.[11]

James Livett Daniell appears to have been the driving force, navigating the business through the complex web of piety, power and liberalism that constituted Bristol nonconformity. He nursed political as well as social ambitions, as an active Radical Liberal who opposed the Contagious Diseases Acts and endorsed women's suffrage, Social Purity and the anti-vivisection movement. His wife, Sophie, loyally supported her husband by backing suitable charities such as the Bristol and Clifton Association for Home Teaching of the Blind and Industrial Employment of Blind Women, patronised by the philanthropic son of Bristol's Quaker chocolate manufacturing family, Sir Lewis Fry MP. In 1884 Sophie Daniell became a member of the British Women's Liberal Association and later participated in the Clifton branch of the National Association for the Abolition of Government Regulation of Vice led by the Quaker reformer, Margaret Tanner.[12] Despite being in contact with radical reformers, she always, unlike Miriam, adopted the conventional custom of signing herself as 'Mrs J.L. Daniell'.

In 1882 Edward Tuckett Daniell and his young wife settled down at Churchfield Villa, a new house near Holy Trinity Church in West-bury-upon-Trym. Miriam's interest in art was shared by her husband, and they both submitted paintings to the Bristol Academy Fine Arts Exhibition in 1884. Whereas the *Bristol Mercury* enthused about 'Mrs E.M. Daniell's "Nasturtiums"' as 'rich and glowing with colour', the paper dismissed 'Mr E.T. Daniell's evening scene "New Arthog, North Wales"' as 'a pretty view very much over painted'.[13] It must have been somewhat galling for Edward Tuckett Daniell, already overshadowed by his older brother, to be outpaced by his talented and beautiful wife. Moreover, she was acclaimed under *her* initials not his, still an indicator of social dissent in a provincial city. While fashionable refinement appears to have characterised the work reviewed, Miriam was heading towards the 'circle' of 'gifted men and women, artists, musicians, those who cherished ideals', mentioned so reverentially by Helen in her 'Biographical Introduction' to *Whitman's Ideal Democracy*.[14]

A key figure in Bristol art circles was Henry Stacy, who had made great efforts to revive the Bristol Society of Arts. A former principal of Weston-super-Mare's art school until it foundered, by the early 1880s Stacy had been reduced to earning a meagre living for his family by offering private lessons to Bristol's young ladies, but he occupied a respected niche among local artists. Stacy was a convivial High Church man, with socialist sympathies, and the indigent but vibrant Stacy household attracted the Clifton young, who clustered there to talk and dance. The fun mingled with principles and politics. Stacy's son Paul helped to organise the Clifton and Bristol Christian Socialists with Hugh Holmes Gore. Daughter Enid joined the Bristol Women's Liberal Association in 1884, soon moving leftwards.[15]

Henry Stacy knew the controversial William Morris, whose lecture on 'Art and Labour' in March 1885 at the Bristol Museum and Library provoked turmoil in the local art world. Miriam may well have been among the great crowd who heard the fearless, shaggy-headed figure in his blue serge jacket announcing 'the human pleasure of life is what I mean by art'. Even if she was not present, she would have heard how he had called on the educated leisured classes to join the camp 'of the people'.[16]

Morris met workers from the Bristol Socialist Society that March, for he was intent on recruiting for his Socialist League, which had recently broken away from Hyndman's Social Democratic Federation. His visit left Bristol buzzing with debates on socialism versus individualism, emboldened Hugh Holmes Gore to publicly declare his socialism, and led Enid Stacy to start reading the American socialist, Laurence Grönlund, whose 'luminous common sense' convinced her that capitalism would evolve into socialism.[17]

Miriam's political opinions remain veiled in the mid 1880s, and her father Robert Rogers was probably still congratulating himself on his perspicuity in steering his highly strung daughter towards the cool, level-headed Edward. That July a letter penned by Miriam appeared in the *Western Daily Press*, pleading for extra troughs on the Downs so that the 'poor panting sheep' suffering from the heat would not have to drink from a depleted 'pestiferous puddle'.[18] Such empathy might have slightly raised fashionable eyebrows, but it was the signature 'E. Miriam Daniell' which would have alerted guardians of propriety. It indicated that Miriam was intent on becoming her own woman. 'E.T.D.' stepped in quickly with a letter the following day corroborating 'Mrs Daniell's complaint' about the plight of the sheep.[19]

Externally the Daniells might still have seemed a well-matched couple and their contrasting personalities construed as complementary rather than conflictual. However, the first recorded indication that something was deeply amiss occurred the following year. In 1886 Miriam became ill and had to undergo an operation, after which 'by medical advice cohabitation ceased'. This information surfaces in the *Bristol Mercury*'s account of the Daniells' divorce in 1894, along with the statement that she subsequently visited Edinburgh 'from time to time' and the bland observation, 'They lived more or less happily until 1889.'[20] In contrast, Helen, whose negative perspective was shaped by Helena, termed it 'An unhappy marriage of many years'.[21]

Reynolds's Newspaper indicates that Miriam went north 'for the benefit of her health', but several other newspapers note that the operation in 1886 was conducted in Edinburgh.[22] The reason for the operation is not specified in the divorce reports; their discretion suggests she went in search of treatment for a 'women's complaint'. Miriam's brother, Robert Mortimer, would have been aware that the campaigner for women's medical education, Sophia Jex-Blake was practising privately and teaching midwifery at the Edinburgh School of Medicine for women that she had just founded.

Over the next two years Miriam's interests, which had been mainly aesthetic, extended towards politics. She joined the Bristol Women's Liberal Association in 1888, the year she met Helena. By then she was no longer out in Westbury-upon-Trym, but ensconced in 28 Hampton Park with its four storeys and grand bay windows, conveniently close to Helena's home in Whiteladies Road. Edward Tuckett Daniell was no doubt gratified by a report in the *Englishwoman's Review* that on 19 February 1889 a drawing room meeting had been held there by 'Mrs M. Daniell' with Mrs Margaret Tanner occupying 'the chair'. The topic was Ireland.[23]

If Sophie Daniell was put out by her sister-in-law's rise to prominence in the B.W.L.A., she need not have worried; Miriam was far too engrossed in her fulfilling friendship with Helena to be competing over drawing room meetings. Though Miriam assumed the role of trailblazer, inwardly she needed Helena who could comprehend her enthusiasm while channelling the ricocheting fancies that exhausted her. Miriam's wild energy was complemented and sustained by a warm, trustworthy and non-judgemental Helena. Two very different women at odds with conformity, questioning convention, and contemptuous of hypocritical compromise, had found one another. Their interaction proved so intense it was as if they had merged.

Helen records that a rebellious Miriam had already embraced 'the socialist gospel' when they met.[24] Exactly how Miriam became interested in socialism is unclear, though one obvious influence would have been Morris' lecture in 1885, while another may have been Henry Stacy. By the late 1880s other possible sources had multiplied nationally. The Christian Socialists, the Social Democratic Federation, the Socialist League, the Fellowship of the New Life and its breakaway the Fabian Society, not to mention several autonomous bodies comparable to the Bristol Socialist Society, were all energetically propagating their versions of socialism.[25]

But the group Miriam would have been most likely to encounter locally was the Clifton and Bristol Christian Socialists founded by the solicitor, Hugh Holmes Gore.[26]

One direct personal link with the Daniells is on record, for Gore was associated with Miriam's husband in a campaign to preserve public footpaths. In December 1888 the two men both signed a memorial to the Docks Committee urging the repair of a neglected path.[27] Edward Tuckett Daniell had been drawn into the Footpaths' Preservation Society through a new addition to the firm, Richard Clapton Tuckett (later to become Henry Stacy's son-in-law). Other preservers included the social reformer, Francis Gilmore Barnett, Bristol University's bicycling zoologist, Professor Conwy Lloyd Morgan, and Francis J. Fry, from the prominent Quaker chocolate family. Their Ruskinian commitment to keeping the public pathways resulted in clashes not only with private landowners, but with Bristol's powerful Merchant Venturers.[28]

John Ruskin's moral and aesthetic challenge to market values had inspired Gore's Christian Socialist group. In 1887, when the London Christian Socialist, Emily Guest, addressed the Clifton and Bristol Christian Socialists on 'The Religious Basis of Socialism', she had invoked Ruskin's critique of capitalism's destructive impact on the environment. Guest emphasised the interconnectedness of daily life and argued that the Christian commitment to loving one's neighbour required social transformation. In the chair was the young High Church woman, Gertrude Dix, then aged twenty and already assuming a public political role.[29]

Helen tells us that in 1888 Helena too was assiduously reading 'the social and economic writings of John Ruskin, besides most of the current works on socialism and kindred subjects', while Miriam's socialism had led her to read on economics and acquire 'an intimate knowledge of the lives of the working people'.[30] Together the two young women came to the conclusion that not simply the *conditions* of capitalist production, but its nature and purposes, were profoundly flawed. Exploited labour resulted in the making of useless and ugly things. Helen summarises their thinking:

> In ministering to artificial tastes, silly fashions, and unsocial customs, the labour of a considerable proportion of the producing classes was utterly wasted; hence the producers themselves were exhausting their energies to supply the multitudinous demands of the idle rich, while unable to secure for themselves a sufficiency of wholesome sustenance.[31]

Edward Carpenter digging his market garden at Millthorpe, near Shef-field, was propagating an alternative to bourgeois acquisitiveness; Miriam and Helena too decided 'that social regeneration would only come through the simplification of life'.[32] From Carpenter, and their reading of Thoreau's *Walden* (1854), came the ethical and aesthetic imperative to reduce wants. 'Simplicity in dress, in house-furnishings, in tastes and habits' became a 'cardinal tenet'.[33] They both became vegetarians – still a startling act of dissidence in the late 1880s. As Miriam and Helena's friendship brought them closer, they started to question the fashion-able materialistic preoccupations of Clifton, despising luxury and those who 'seek only comfort and pleasure'. The drawing room meetings, the clothes, the gossip now seemed 'as dross'.[34]

Miriam and Helena greatly admired Carpenter's long prose poem, *Towards Democracy* (1883). Inspired by Walt Whitman, it is infused with longing for more direct, democratic forms of personal relating. To Miriam and Helena, along with many other late-nineteenth-century rebels, *Towards Democracy* expressed desires for other ways of being in the world.[35] Over the course of 1888 and 1889 their opposition to cap-italist society merged with a resolve to make personal changes in how they lived.

This assumption of personal moral agency was not uncommon on the left. In 1883 the Fellowship of the New Life had been formed with the intention of changing perceptions, culture and life-style, alongside exter-nal social reforms. Carpenter was associated with the group and one of its initiators, Edward Pease, was the son of the prominent Bristol Quakers Thomas and Susan Pease. Pease soon moved on to become secretary of the breakaway Fabian Society, but another member, Cecil Reddie, a school-master at Clifton College between 1887 and 1888, remained a 'new lifer' in the Fellowship as well as a Ruskin enthusiast.[36]

The working-class members of the Bristol Socialist Society also sought a new life of mutual self-development, alongside transforming society.[37] However, by the late 1880s, the close-knit band of comrades were being pulled away from their sawdust-floored coffee house by severe unemploy-ment in working-class Bristol and by the agitation around Home Rule and Coercion in Ireland; in June 1887 they took a bold stand against the royalist razzmatazz surrounding Queen Victoria's Golden Jubilee.[38] Robert Weare was able to announce cheerily in *Commonweal*, the organ of William Morris' Socialist League, that 'Socialism is making good progress in Bristol.'[39] Indeed Robert Gilliard was later to observe how even before Miriam and Helena joined the Bristol Socialist Society, 'we had already begun to make things hum a bit'.[40]

The humming occurring on the streets was fostered and sustained through discussion groups and loyal friendship networks. During the grim winter of 1887, when the Bristol Socialist Society had unsuccessfully demanded public works for the relief of the unemployed, Robert Gilliard drew on his clerical skills by starting a small class to teach shorthand, useful for minute-taking. It included Robert Weare and met on Sunday mornings in the sitting room above the shop of Henry Stacy's friend, the Labour League member, James W.D. Marshall. They wandered from shorthand to discussing writers like Carlyle, Emerson and Mazzini, and their numbers swelled until, in September 1888, they formed themselves into the Bristol Sunday Society, 'for mutual improvement in Science and Literature'.[41]

Similar Sunday Societies were starting elsewhere at this time and Weare and Gilliard's project quickly attracted distinguished supporters, including the socialist artist, Walter Crane, and Darwin's pugnacious populariser, Thomas Huxley. Several Bristol social reformers, concerned about the gulf between classes, became involved. Among these were the ubiquitous Francis Gilmore Barnett, along with the Principal of Clifton College, Revd James Wilson, and his Christian Socialist brother-in-law, Revd Thomas William Harvey, who worked in the College's Mission, running adult education classes for workers and opening his church, St Agnes, to the unemployed.[42]

On 11 February 1889, the Sunday Society was formally inaugurated at a conference to organise lectures on 'Science, History, Literature and Art' held at the Castle Street Coffee House. Miriam was the only woman elected onto the committee. This is the first public mention of Miriam's name in association with the Bristol socialists; her election indicates that somehow she was already in contact and had won their confidence. Other members included Gore, his solicitor friend, E.J. Watson, and the Bristol Socialist Society men, Gilliard, Weare and Baster. The Radical Liberal, Dan Irving, was also elected to the Sunday Society Committee. Gilliard and Weare's homes were close to his and they won him over to socialism on their walks home from meetings.[43]

The Bristol Sunday Lectures proved a great success, attracting large audiences to mainly scientific topics. Weare, however, wanted a group that reflected the personal fellowship and 'social' character of the original band of socialist mutual improvers, and created yet another Society. Initially this was to be 'The Bristol Sunday Rambling Society', for he was a keen geologist, and, like Miriam and Helena, a great walker. In deference perhaps to the less athletic, they became 'The Bristol Sunday Research and Recreation Society'.[44] Both Miriam and Helena's names were to appear on the list of people offering lecture topics to Weare's alternative series of lectures under the auspices of the Socialist Society.[45]

During 1889 Helena continued to attend B.W.L.A. meetings and, in February 1889, was present at a discussion on Home Rule. Her scrapbook shows she was following the reports emerging from Lord Dunraven's Select Committee on 'The Sweating System', which exposed the harsh conditions of low-paid workers. Early in 1889 she cut out an article about the 'girls' who blew the bellows in the small chain-making workshops at Cradley Heath near Dudley in the Midlands.[46] Perhaps Helena's probing intelligence was already leading her to wonder whether the personal changes she and Miriam were attempting were sufficient in the face of class inequality.

Within a few days, contemplation became impossible, for the two women were thrust face to face with desperate Bristol working-class families whose precarious lives had been devastated by floods. On March 8th, the low-lying areas of the city were engulfed when heavy rainfall and a snowstorm caused the River Frome to swell and burst its banks. The *Bristol Observer* reported that 'a raging torrent' of water had overcome

Miriam Daniell
(Bristol Reference Library)

working-class Eastville, and started to spread towards Merchant Street and Broadmead. The streets turned into fast-flowing rivers, filling basements and reaching up to the height of bedrooms. The water stopped tramcars and swept furniture away. A horse was spotted desperately swimming amid the debris.[47]

Bristol had long been subject to flooding, but by the 1880s commercial development had increased the danger by covering over the natural basin of meadows between Mina Road and Stapleton. Only a few years before, in 1882, floods had led to calls for new drainage precautions, but these would have been costly and were ignored by the council. The 1889 floods were more severe; the police and sanitary authorities could barely manage to deliver bread and water to stranded victims.[48]

Voluntary efforts were vital. One of the earliest to respond was Revd Harvey, who telegrammed Revd James Wilson from St Agnes, 'District flooded; come at once'.[49] Wilson hurriedly left a Clifton musical party and descended by cab to find the area inundated and the occupants of the small four-roomed houses, which typically contained two families, trapped by the rapidly rising water. Their belongings were claimed by the flood.[50]

Miriam and Helena both threw themselves into the relief work, but it was Miriam who quickly emerged as a crucial figure alongside Revd Harvey, collecting and distributing dry clothes and boots. On March 14th the *Western Daily Press* printed an appeal from 'Miriam Daniell' for donations, announcing that supplies were being 'judiciously distributed' from Harvey's St Agnes Mission House, Newfoundland Road, and her own address, 'Torryburn, 28 Hampton Park, Redland'.[51] Edward Tuckett Daniell's feelings about living in a relief station go unrecorded. By this time he must have known his wife did nothing by halves.

The floods aroused outrage. Harvey chaired 'An Indignation Meeting' at St Agnes, where tradesmen threatened to withhold payment of their rates, Robert Tovey, from the Trades Council, demanded improved flood protection, and calls were heard for the whole of Bristol's municipal council to resign.[52] The impact of the floods upon Miriam and Helena was traumatic. Helen insists in her 'Biographical Introduction' that their efforts to relieve suffering were, 'Not in the guise of charity, but as co-workers, anxious to be of service.'[53] Nonetheless, close contact with Bristol's poor must have been a sobering reminder of the privilege of their own class position.

Miriam and her husband moved shortly after the floods to an even grander house on Seymour Road, in what then was Stapleton (now Ashley

Down). They took the name of their former Redland home, 'Torryburn', with them as if it carried some special meaning. 'Torryburn', a beauty spot near Dunfermline in Fyfe, uncannily anticipated the upheaval ahead.

Helena resumed the round of her former political activities. That April she attended a B.W.L.A. meeting at the Misses Priestman's elegant house at 9, Durdham Park, up near the Downs, to reflect on 'The Personal in Politics'. In the discussion, Dr Eliza Dunbar expressed warm approval of the idea that 'Political interests dealt with individuals', while the radical Quaker, Louisa Swann, remarked on the importance of personal fellowship within the Women's Liberal Association itself. A staunch Home Ruler, she regretted how this had broken down tragically in the split with the Unionists over Ireland. Helena and Miriam, too, had been pondering over the personal and the political, but Helena, who must have been bursting with suppressed thoughts of her own, just modestly thanked the Misses Priestman for their hospitality.[54] The following month she was dutifully serving as a B.W.L.A delegate, along with Emily Sturge, at the Liberal National Reform Union.[55] In limbo, Helena reverted to her customary reticence and restraint.

Helena and Miriam's walks and the talks ceased that summer. Miriam had abandoned the new house, departing once again for Edinburgh. It is not clear what took her north – but this visit was to change everything.

THREE

Awakenings: Robert Allan Nicol

If Edward Tuckett Daniell had paid close attention to the books his wife and her odd friend were reading during 1888 to 1889, he might have been forewarned of trouble ahead. His suspicions would most likely have fastened on works by socialists like Edward Carpenter, or perhaps the plays of Ibsen, notorious for encouraging wives to slam doors on unhappy marriages, rather than the mystical poetry of Blake or the aesthetic criticism of Pater. Yet imperceptibly it was Blake, kissing 'the Joy as it flies' and celebrating the 'lineaments of gratified desire', who slithered under the careful frontage of his marriage, along with Pater's disturbing contention that only 'exquisite passion' could set the spirit free.[1]

Through those visits to Edinburgh, Miriam had met a handsome Scottish student, Robert Allan Nicol, who proved to be Edward Tuckett Daniell's nemesis. Born on 1 June 1868, Robert was eighteen when Miriam first went to the city; three years later, in 1889, he left Scotland with her for Bristol.

Robert's family were from Dunfermline where they had been running a hatters' and hosiers' shop at various sites on and around the High Street since 1847. Dunfermline, Scotland's ancient capital, had prospered in the eighteenth century from its damask linen produced by hand-loom weavers. Around the time that Robert's grandfather (Robert Nicol senior) was opening his first shop, the tall belching chimneys that accompanied the power loom began to appear on the skyline. They were soon to dominate, and while young Robert was growing up linen and coal mining provided the main sources of Dunfermline's wealth. Demand for hats and clothing enabled the Nicols to thrive; Grandfather Robert took his son into partnership until 1877, when Robert Nicol Junior started out on his own.[2]

Both Nicols served on the Town Council and were known locally for being radical and ornery. Grandfather Nicol had earned the sobriquet 'The Peoples' Hatter' for his politics, along with a reputation for not being 'easy dissuaded from his purpose'.[3] Turning adversity to advantage after his shop burned down in December 1878, he took to announcing himself as 'Burnt-out Nicol'.[4] Nevertheless, the long cycle of depressed trade, combined with a second fire at the rebuilt shop in November 1882, meant that his business never recovered. Fires were common in the town at the time, but the attic flat above the shop happened to be occupied by a policeman and his wife who lost all their possessions, and the police bestirred themselves. A report appeared in the local papers that 'an elderly man of average height, stout build, and wearing a shooting jacket and white muffler' had been seen 'loitering about the premises in a highly suspicious manner'. Nicol Senior was arrested. He was found not guilty, but went bankrupt all the same.[5]

Henceforth the family fortunes rested with the next generation, Robert and Margaret Nicol. Their first son had died in infancy in 1865 and Robert Nicol Junior had consequently assumed that the next son would follow in his footsteps into the hatters' shop. So, in 1868 the new baby born on June 1st was duly named Robert Allan Nicol.[6] By the early 1880s the Nicols and their six children, including young Robert Allan, were living at Railside Cottage on Pilmuir Street, a solid three-storey stone house fronted by two bay windows which backed onto a linen mill. A tall chimney towered behind Railside Cottage, which, because it was near to the Coal Depot, was surrounded by mills. So many workers came in from neighbouring small towns that, when the six o'clock hooter sounded in the evening, it was said to be impossible to 'walk up Pilmuir Street against the tide of women in clogs coming down to catch the train home'.[7] The Nicol family had industry literally on their doorstep.

Trade continued to be depressed, Dunfermline workers were restive, and the radical People's League, which opposed the House of Lords and inclined to Republicanism, was active in the town. In 1886, when the Dunfermline People's League encountered resistance from the Committee of the Carnegie Free Library over the introduction of the radical *Reynolds's Newspaper*, Robert's father defended the radicals. When the dispute came before the Town Council, the Library Committee maintained they were excluding *Reynolds's Newspaper* because it was 'immoral', whereupon 'Mr Nicol', a stalwart of St Andrew's Parish Church, led the attack. Arousing laughter and support by asserting that he read it himself, he opined it was 'not in accordance with the spirit of the age to keep the people from having a peep at a Radical newspaper if they desire it'.[8] The clash was ironic, for Andrew Carnegie, the Dunfermline boy turned American industrialist, who had given the town its library, had himself spoken out against the House of Lords, royalty and hereditary privilege.

'R. Nicol Junior', as Robert's father was known, was an ingenious salesman. By 1887 he was the owner of a shop not only at number 2 on the High Street, but at 2 Bruce Street as well, and had branched out into women's as well as men's apparel. His stock ranged from luxury goods, like astrakhan gloves for both sexes, to waterproof coats and work wear. Adapting Robert Nicol Senior's trademark by calling himself 'Hatter to the People', he issued novel advertisements in the local paper scorning 'self-crowned Philosophers, who know nothing about business, attempting to preach to the people about the rights and wrongs of Trade'. The Forth Bridge, then being built between Dunfermline and Edinburgh, provided him with a trading opportunity, and Nicol offered 'BLUE SHIRTS and BLUE SEMMETS. Splendid Lines for Workers on the Bridge.' That December the venturesome shopkeeper was off to Manchester and Glasgow to stock up on 'Christmas novelties'. His imagination roved further afield, leading him to speculate on the potential global demand for hats, shirts and semmets, not just in 'busy Europe', but in the snowy north of Russia and Scandinavia and in a 'young democratic America'.[9] Ingenuity, an eye for the main chance and far-flung perspectives appear to have been part of the Nicol heritage.

Robert Nicol's energetic promotion of his shops was necessary, for, by 1887, he had a costly son at Edinburgh University. Bright young Robert Allan had studied at Dunfermline High School for seven years, doing so well that he then went on to the august Royal High School, an imposing Greek-Doric building on Edinburgh's Calton Hill, dating from the eighteenth century. As one of the old grammar schools, it could boast ancient origins going back to the twelfth century. When Robert became a pupil, the 1872 Education Act had brought it under the auspices of the School Board and the erudite John Marshall was Rector. Though he specialised in the Classics, Marshall also encouraged the arts and athletics, and in old age Robert would express pride in the 'fine all-round education' he received.[10]

In 1884, an earnest, scholarly Robert, aged sixteen, was preoccupied with writing for the school magazine and considering his future. As Robert's education progressed, his father had come to recognise that he was not going to be a shopkeeper. The next son in line, William, was being primed for the hatters, and it was agreed that Robert would study medicine at Edinburgh University. His mother, Margaret, encouraged this move and Robert later claimed she was related to a well-known Scottish medical family.[11]

Robert had found an intellectual mentor, Patrick Geddes, a member of a 'Secular Positivist' debating group called the Environmental Society, which envisaged social harmony through research and planning. Geddes worked as a senior demonstrator in botany and zoology at the University's Medical Faculty. The position was neither well paid, nor particularly academically distinguished, but the irrepressible Geddes with his lively eyes and bushy eyebrows was a magnetic figure who attracted adherents and retained their loyalty. Among them was Cecil Reddie, who had studied at Edinburgh before teaching at Clifton College in Bristol. Reddie was a lifelong friend of Geddes' outstanding student, John Arthur Thomson, who Robert came to like very much. Thomson had arrived at the University planning to study theology, but had been lured by Geddes into zoology and botany. Later to collaborate with Geddes, Thomson described the older man as 'the most educative person I have known'.[12]

Patrick Geddes

Geddes' own education had been unconventional. Despite his father's plan for him to be a banker, he had eventually studied under Thomas Huxley at the same time as fellow zoologist, Conwy Lloyd Morgan, Bristol's professorial footpath preserver. Geddes had then worked on a marine station in Brittany, examining how minute protozoa morphed into metazoans, a fascination that would inspire his approach to the structures of human society. While in France, he was impressed by the evolutionary social theories of Auguste Comte and Frederic Le Play which offered an ethical alternative to conventional religion. Back in Edinburgh, in 1884, these thinkers would lead him to the Secular Positivists, and thence to the Environmental Society.[13]

How sixteen-year-old Robert met Geddes is not known, though he was evidently dazzled by the prospect of studying under the 'educative', sophisticated thinker. But the 'Hatter to the People' put his foot down, and, writing from Lorne House, Dunfermline in September 1884, his son had to explain that his father wanted him to start his medical degree straightaway: 'He is not a man of independent means, and is anxious that I should get my degree, in order to have it to fall back upon if anything happened to him. After I get my degree, I am at liberty to go on with science or <u>otherwise</u>.'[14] He must have made an impression on the older man, for Geddes responded with an offer to coach him for a science scholarship.

An inveterate connector of disciplines, ideas and people, Geddes imparted his enthusiasm for knowledge without boundaries to all and sundry. His interests embraced not simply botany and zoology, but housing reform, urban planning and the social and economic benefits of art. When Robert made contact with Geddes, the older man had decided Ruskin's economic and social model of the household dispensing welfare and well-being presented a means of undermining the laissez-faire faith in unrestricted market forces. Against claims that social reform would disrupt an imagined equilibrium, Geddes' 1885 lecture on 'The Conditions of Progress of the Capitalist and the Labourer' rejected competition as the driving force in evolution, stressing instead a co-operative organic development modelled on idealised impressions of the ancient Greeks and medieval cities.[15] Moreover Geddes argued for widening the scope of economics to include the everyday activities associated with the biological and social reproduction of life. Under his aegis the Environmental Society would quickly transmute into the Edinburgh Social Union, committed to improving and beautifying the living conditions of the poor.

Geddes was a supporter of the University Extension Movement's efforts to offset the exclusive character of higher education by offering lectures to students outside the universities. In 1885 he started a summer school for elementary school teachers at Granton Marine Station on the coast near Edinburgh, along similar lines to the Extension courses. One of his students describes how he spoke so fast it was impossible to take notes, wandered far from his original subject, neglected to prepare them for exams and disregarded any need for food. Nevertheless, she recounts how they found Geddes' boyish enthusiasm and humour, combined with his penetrating intellect, irresistible. His greatest gift was teaching them to 'ask the "how?" and "why?" of Nature'.[16] It is not hard to see why Robert was drawn to Geddes. Father Robert Nicol's suspicions were clearly well founded; here indeed was a man likely to entice a youngster away from a sensible vocational education.

Nonetheless, seventeen-year-old Robert's name duly appeared in Edinburgh University's 'First Matriculation' records for 1885 to 1886 under 'Medicine', and in March 1886 Robert informed Geddes he was gaining first-class marks in practical chemistry, so perhaps he *had* received that extra coaching after all. The impact of his mercurial mentor is ominously evident in Robert's letter; regardless of the pressure of Preliminary Examinations bearing down upon him, Robert had been running a seminar for Geddes on Greek mythology. The uptake was disappointing; Robert itemised gloomily how numbers were down to three and even he had been forced to miss the final class because of his examinations. Aware of Geddes' critiques of exam-oriented learning, the harassed student was only too ready to agree that '"Reformation in a flood"' was required in the university system.[17]

Robert's dedication to Geddes extended to ploughing through Thomas Carlyle's chaotic satire on academia and the church, *Sartor Resartus*, written in instalments over 1833–4. He also tells Geddes how he had been enjoying a *History of Our Own Time*, a lengthy work of several volumes, written by Justin McCarthy, a member of the Irish Land League. Like Geddes, Robert's interest in the past combined with excitement about the modernity of the International Exhibition on Industry and Science which was being mounted on the meadows opposite his lodgings in 1886, at 9 Marchmont Crescent.[18]

Robert appears to have established a personal friendship with his teacher, later describing himself as having been 'a close companion of Sir Patrick Geddes who lived at the time on Princes Street'.[19] Geddes' upper storey flat, which looked over at the Old Town, was a popular gathering place for students, and Robert mentions visiting it when Geddes was away in March 1886. It seems he conferred with Geddes' housekeeper, for he wrote, 'The Good Wife tells me that she has only had a bad cold since you left and is defeating your idea that she ill-uses herself when you are away. She bade me say that no letters of seeming consequence have arrived for you.'[20]

The following month Geddes married Anna Morton, who shared his interest in social reform. The daughter of a wealthy Liverpool merchant, she had worked with Josephine Butler in the campaign against the Contagious Diseases Acts, as well as with the Ruskinian housing reformer and footpath preserver, Octavia Hill. The newlywed couple defied convention by setting up home in a tenement flat, 6 James Court, off Lawnmarket, in Edinburgh's Old Town. They stained and polished the uneven floors, filled it with good second-hand old furniture, installed a piano, and started improving the sanitation of the dingy overcrowded Court below.[21] Investigations of conditions in the area abounded, but upper-middle-class settlers were an intriguing new phenomenon. Edinburgh progressives soon adopted 6 James Court as their rendezvous, mounting three flights up the dark stairs to the Geddes' flat with its resplendent view of Princes Gardens and the Firth of Forth.[22]

News of the Geddes' reclamation spread far and wide. The Russian anarchist exile, Peter Kropotkin, who had renounced his own princely heritage for revolutionary politics, wrote in excitement to a former Communard, the geographer Elisée Reclus, 'It is a complete reawakening.'[23] The Socialist League member, James Mavor, later to teach in University Extension with Miriam's brother Robert Mortimer Wheeler, was inclined to be somewhat more sceptical, but even he compared Patrick and Anna Geddes to the Russian Narodniks who went to live among the peasants.[24] People began to refer to this 'circle of university and town folk whose interest ran to social and economic questions' as the 'Geddes group'.[25] Robert was an enthusiastic acolyte.

In later life Robert reminisced about 'working at the University with Sir Arthur Thomson, one of the most charming men & so kind always to me'.[26] John Arthur Thomson was only seven years older than Robert, but had already studied abroad, first with the iconoclastic naturalist, Ernst Haeckel, in Jena, and then, in 1885, at the Zoological Institute in Berlin.[27] Unlike Robert, Thomson was consumed by his scientific studies, engaging closely with Geddes on theories of evolution and natural selection, struggling to assess the relative significance of hereditary and environmental factors. While a student, Robert lodged with the Thomson family at 10 Kilmaurs Road, conveniently close to the University, and remembered his friend's, 'dear old Mother & sisters – all very clever & good cooks' with fond affection.[28]

The 'dear old mother', Isabella Thomson, widowed after the death of her clergyman husband and in her late fifties when Robert was living with them, was, indeed 'clever'. From a family of naturalists, she had encouraged her son's interest in botany and zoology.[29]

Helped by Geddes, Robert presumably became a junior demonstrator, because he mentions meeting 'young men from all over the world & they loved to be taught by me'. Edinburgh Medical School's reputation was international and he was particularly impressed by '2 rajahs from India' who were 'keen after knowledge'. Robert also claimed to have 'loved being a help to suffering men'.[30] Medical students were sent to practise on the poor when they were too ill to go to the dispensary, so he may well have entered tenement homes in the Old Town, around James Court.

As an old man in 1955, Robert looked back on his medical studies through rose-coloured spectacles simply 'as happy days'.[31] However around 1886 or 1887 he made a decision he would subsequently regret; he gave up medicine. In the University records on Matriculation covering 1884–8, 'Medicine' is crossed out and replaced by 'Arts'.[32] Robert was not unusual in dropping his medical studies, for a high proportion of students stopped before completion. Fees were high and the bursaries available did not cover the extra costs; medical students were obliged to buy not just books but equipment, including an expensive microscope. Those who failed a course could sit it again, but the extra expense favoured those from richer families.[33]

Robert appears to have excelled in tests, so the move from medicine was presumably because the interests awakened by Geddes and his circle distracted him. Not only was Robert to shift away from science, he also moved to the left. In March 1886, he had commented in passing to Geddes, 'There has been a riot lately in London headed by the Socialists', yet by 1889 he was ready to throw himself into socialist agitation.[34]

A young man with a radical background and an enquiring mind would have come across several rebellious movements in 1880s Edinburgh. The biblical fundamentalism of some sections of the Free Church of Scotland was under attack from freethinkers and sceptics, while the case for land nationalisation had a special pertinence in a country where the historical memory of forced evictions was raw and bitter. Resistance over rents and Home Rule in Ireland resounded in Scotland, stimulating both political nationalism and interest in Celtic culture. Trade unions were stirring and Edinburgh's women were campaigning for suffrage, higher education, housing reform, even birth control.[35] Robert would also have encountered fiercely contested strands of socialist and anarchist ideas. Visiting speakers to Edinburgh included Kropotkin as well as Morris, and the city provided refuge to the Communard, Léo Melliet, who taught French at the University and was a critic of both the 'authoritarian' Marx and the S.D.F. leader Hyndman.[36]

By the mid 1880s Edinburgh had branches of the Social Democratic Federation and the Socialist League, which was affiliated to the Scottish Land and Labour League, while Melliet had helped set up the Edinburgh University Socialist Society. Its first 'Appeal', 'Beauty for Ashes' (1884), announced 'Utopia now: we can bring it about' and was evidently significant both for Robert and for Miriam, because a copy bears his initials, 'R.A.N.', followed by her signature, 'Miriam Daniell'.[37] We have no means of knowing when they put their names on it, but Robert must have been in contact with the University Society during 1886 because he also signed his copy of its Report for 1885 to 1886.

Though Edward Carpenter, the Positivist Professor Edward Spencer Beesly, and the American evolutionary socialist, Laurence Grönlund,

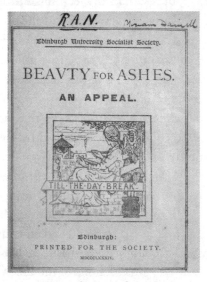

Cover of Beauty for Ashes

were among its early speakers, 'utopia' failed to attract many students; so, deciding 'Socialist' was not 'a happy label', over the course of 1885 and 1886 the Society's members replaced it with 'Social Reform'. The Edinburgh University Social Reform Society's Report for 1885–6 in Robert's possession urges 'reintegration' and 'regeneration' as opposed to the 'disintegration' of violent revolutions, noting the 'interesting discussion, mainly on the Religious Aspect of Socialism', which followed Grönlund's lecture. Commenting approvingly on initiatives for housing reform, the simple life and outdoor recreation, the Society promoted a forthcoming lecture series on 'The Claims of Labour' which was being organised by Geddes' friend James Oliphant with the Trades Council, the Co-operators and the Socialist League. The Report for 1885–6 concludes with the statement, 'I am the Divine Idea, the Soul, the Will, of the universe. My spirit, the Spirit of Love, is that which *creates*, and recreates or *redeems*. I am God. For God is love, and Love is God.'[38] A transcendent spirituality evidently features along with a commitment to social change in Robert's early political influences.

Before long socialism and sexual emancipation were being added to the mix. After being in difficulty in the mid 1880s, by March 1887 the Edinburgh Socialist League had acquired sufficient revolutionary élan to critique Geddes' lecture, 'The Theory and Practice of Social Reform'. The Socialist League's *Commonweal* observed scathingly, 'Some of the Socialists present seemed to think that "reform" might be brought about with somewhat more rapidity than the lecturer indicated.'[39] In 1888, an undeterred Geddes, enthusiastic about a blossoming of Scottish culture and identity, maintained an individualistic materialistic society was being replaced by a more 'socialistic' one. Lecturing on 'Co-operation versus Socialism', he postulated an ideal of 'public splendour and refined private simplicity' capable of combining collectivity with a creative individuality.[40] James Court was the protozoa which he envisaged extending into urban reform, creating the City Beautiful and ensuring social transformation without class conflict.

In the late 1880s Geddes and Thomson were briskly producing articles on 'Environment', 'Evolution', 'Reproduction' and 'Sex' for the popular encyclopaedias, so central to Scottish intellectual life. These were still regarded as risky topics for popular science, and, when their contents were bundled together into book form in 1889 as *The Evolution of Sex*, the two authors acquired fame and a certain notoriety. Geddes and

Thomson link evolution to a combination of individual freedom and altruistic mutuality. One diagram in the book depicts protoplasmic identity forking into two strands, 'Hunger self-regarding egotistic', takes one direction, while 'Love, other-regarding, altruistic', goes in another.[41] The aim was harmonious blending.

Geddes regarded men and women as different but equal and complementary, arguing that women as reproducers and nurturers shaped economic and social circumstances, a viewpoint which resonated with some contemporary campaigners for women's rights. He proposed that women carried a unique potential for a higher form of civilisation, in which self-interest would be curbed by 'other-regarding' concerns for reproduction and the survival of humanity. Geddes was careful not to reduce women to biology, but his new women found fulfilment in love and maternity rather than work or politics, and his allocation of an idealised cultural role to women could confine as well as release actual women's potential.[42]

Nevertheless, in the context of 1889, *The Evolution of Sex* provided scientific ballast for an ethical endorsement of desire – empowering for a generation who may have abandoned Christianity, but still experienced guilt: 'Sexual attraction ceases to be wholly selfish; hunger may be overcome by love; love of mates is enhanced by love for offspring; love for offspring broadens out into love of kind.'[43] Most controversially, the book included a defence of contraception as a means of relieving women from frequent childbirth, though Geddes, a high-minded, Romantic moralist rather than an advocate of free love, hastened to explain that this should be after marriage, rather than before.[44] Geddes not only stirred Robert; his idealised female archetypes figure in mystical form in Miriam's later writings, while Helena was profoundly affected by his approach to knowledge.

Robert was twenty-one in the summer of 1889 when Miriam returned to Edinburgh. To him, intellectually adrift, picking up ideas jackdaw-like and open to change, she must have seemed an all-knowing fireball of energy, enthusiasm and conviction. Miriam, beautiful, angry and sexually unhappy, responded. Perhaps the grim misery of the Bristol flood had stimulated a desire to escape into some pleasurable diversion. There may have been a hint of scandal surrounding Robert, for according to family memory he had been implicated in an affair with the wife of one of his professors. Fantastical rumours of a duel in which Robert murdered his rival elaborate this story. More likely the languid opinionated young man possessed a capacity to charm, and perhaps there was gossip. If Miriam *was* warned off, she would surely have defied any admonitions.

How, when and where they were initially introduced remains unknown, but both were reaching out towards political, personal and social emancipation, while the circles in which they moved were inter-woven. By switching to 'Arts' Robert would have encountered the radical David Masson, as did Miriam's brother Robert Mortimer Wheeler. Geddes, Thomson and Wheeler worked in University Extension and had acquaintances in common, such as the socialist, James Mavor. Conwy Lloyd Morgan and Cecil Reddie, who had returned to Edinburgh and taught a University Extension course in autumn 1888, were friendly with Geddes and had links to Bristol. The Women's Liberal Association's net-works also spanned both cities, while Dr Eliza Dunbar was in touch with Edinburgh campaigners for women in medicine.[45]

When the time came for Miriam to return south, presumably they could not bear to be parted for she took the unusual step of bringing Robert back to stay at Torryburn. Edward Tuckett Daniell, who had only recently got rid of all those charitable boots and clothes, now found his new home unpleasantly cluttered by an arrogant and beautiful boy. Worse, the intruder sprawled around declaiming socialism with his wife. Miriam was not slamming any doors; instead she was stripping off the accumulated layers of that careful front of respectability Edward had worked so hard to establish. Miriam's behaviour had always been somewhat bizarre, but in returning with Robert she was courting serious

Robert Allan Nicol (Courtesy
of Georges Rey, Private Collection)

danger to her reputation. Her contained, punctilious husband must have regarded her indifference to scandal with incredulity.

If Helena grounded and restrained Miriam, Robert animated and escalated her wilful energy. Together they generated a wild courage. Miriam, politically righteous, driven by Blake's enthusiasm and trembling with Pater's 'exquisite passion', had freed her spirit from convention. Through her meeting with Robert she embarked on the course Pater indicated, the inward, elusive 'success in life' that despised the formation of habits. Henceforth the aesthete's aspiration, 'To burn always with this hard, gem-like flame, to maintain this ecstasy', defined Miriam's path.[46]

FOUR

Exaltation: Autumn 1889

When Edward Tuckett Daniell sought a divorce from Miriam in May 1894, the court was told that during the summer of 1889 in Edinburgh, 'A great intimacy sprang up' between Miriam and Robert.[1] Quite when this intimacy became sexual goes unrecorded. Not only is a divorce court a lubberly source for the inner matters of the heart, the legal documents give only a brief outline, so the story of Miriam and Robert's early love comes down to us filtered through a mesh of newspaper reports, for the case was reported widely.

Alluding to Miriam's medical complaint, the *Cheshire Observer* cites Edward Tuckett Daniell as saying in court that he had thought 'any improper intimacy' was 'unlikely' because 'he was told it could prove fatal'.[2] He maintained, according to the *Daily News*, that he had 'believed in her purity of motive but knew what sentimental friendship would lead to'.[3] Allowing for his awareness as a solicitor of the need to explain his delay in seeking a divorce, it is conceivable that an idealistic Miriam *did* bring her ardent young Scottish companion to Bristol on a political mission, before they actually became lovers.

Whatever the actual nature of their relationship, Robert's presence surely accentuated the discordance between Miriam and her husband. When he was asked in court, 'Did your wife hold views about Socialism?', the reply was, 'Very strong views. She used to take a leading part in demonstrations. Mr Nicol used to share these views.'[4] The newspaper accounts contain small but confusing variations. One version of the divorce trial has Miriam urging her husband to leave his home and live in the slums; another records her as proposing that *she* should live with the poor.[5] The class gulf must have been highlighted by the list of goods auctioned from their former home at 28 Hampton Park that September. The superfluous accoutrements of Miriam's life with her husband, mahogany and walnut suites, marble-top dressing tables, carpets, engravings, 'time pieces' and a piano 'by Able and Smart' were all going under the hammer around the time she was becoming active in the Bristol Socialist Society.[6]

That September, encouraged by members of the Bristol Socialist Society, Miriam and Robert began to investigate complaints from workers at Fry's chocolate factories; some of the men resented the unequal allocation of a pay award, while women workers wanted shorter hours.[7] These rumblings of discontent among the workers at Fry's were one sign of a wider rebellion.

After long years of uncertainty, depression and insecurity, unemployment was down and a new militancy was emerging. In 1888 there had been a series of strikes involving women, from female cigar makers in Nottingham to cotton and jute workers in Dundee, while the well-publicised strike of London match women at Bryant and May's factory demonstrated how supposedly 'unskilled' women could organise. They inspired others. Early in 1889, the newly formed Gas Workers and General Labourers' Union (G.W. & G.L.U.) secured the eight-hour day in an historic victory inaugurating a 'new unionism' that mobilised unskilled and semi-skilled workers, women as well as men. London dockers, casualised and unorganised, took action that August. They, in turn, aroused a veritable 'strike fever' in East London and, under pressure, their employers settled in early September.[8]

Ben Tillett, the London dockers' leader, was Bristol born, and during August 1889 Gore and Tovey urged the Trades Council to collect for the strike fund. These links to new unionism proved important. During mid September, while Miriam and Robert were investigating Fry's, fifty-four men at John Lysaght's galvanising iron works in Bristol, led by Frank Rawle, became involved in a dispute. After they joined the Gas Workers and General Labourers' Union, followed by many of their workmates, John Lysaght swiftly agreed to a pay rise. The powerful contagion of hope had reached Bristol.[9] A new labour movement was in the making.

Miriam and Robert's entry into labour organising occurred when it seemed as if the old social order was cracking open. New unionism had such an impact partly because it demonstrated that workers outside the skilled craft unions could mobilise effectively; this combined with a vision of a broad and inclusive working-class solidarity emblazoned in its motto, 'Love, Union and Fidelity'.[10]

Breaking with the traditions of the craft unions, which had excluded women, new unionists encouraged them to join. At the Lysaght victory rally, James Vickery from the Bristol G.W. & G.L.U. demanded, 'was there no Annie Besant in Bristol to fight the battle of the poor oppressed female workers of the city'.[11] Annie Besant's support for the match women and other strikers meant she was well known to the Bristol left. By autumn 1889 she had moved away from socialism and was immersed in Theosophy, a spiritual movement that introduced Eastern religious ideas to westerners. However, Eleanor Marx, who was a member of the Socialist League, continued to support the organisation of the unskilled and semi-skilled through new unionism. On 10 October 1889, she formed a Women's Union at Silvertown, in London, as a branch of the G.W. & G.L.U., enabling her to become a member.[12]

Miriam and Helena had already become heavily involved in a strike at Redcliffe Crown Galvanising Iron Works. Miriam spoke at their first meeting with Albert Vincent, from the Trades Council, Frank Rawle, from Lysaght's, and Robert Sharland from the Bristol Socialist Society. When a strike fund was set up, Miriam became treasurer and Helena its secretary.[13] New unionism's openness to recruiting women and support from socialists like Sharland partially explains how they so quickly took a central role.

One of Edward Tuckett Daniell's grievances in the divorce case was his wife's connection 'with some Union in Bristol'.[14] No doubt he winced to read how, at the demonstration in support of the strikers on October 5th, the socialist banner 'EDUCATE, AGITATE, ORGANISE' was carried high by his wife's friends. Even worse, there was Miriam distributing strike pay: 6s 3d for married men with 6d extra per child, single men 5s, boys and women – assumed to be dependent on a male wage – 3s 4d. The Redcliffe Crown owner settled speedily, and on October 8th 'Mrs Daniels' [sic] is reported in the Western Daily Press as saying 'She was very glad to know a settlement had been arranged and that the women were also going in again with an increase in wages. Their victory showed them how necessary it was to organise in such matters and not fight separately.'[15]

Bristol's gas workers came out on October 9th, whereupon the Gas Company tried to bring in 120 scabs from Exeter. This was a mistake: the

Socialist League's *Commonweal* records them being met 'by an immense populace, armed with bricks and stones'.[16] After some wisely decided to return to Exeter, those who remained were taken in vans towards the Avon Street Gas Works. They never arrived; the vans were blocked by a barricade of overturned carts at the bridge in St Philip's Marsh, where they were assailed with missiles and the demonstrators happily consumed the provisions intended for the scabs! The following day the shaken directors, aware that Bristol would soon be without power, settled with the strikers.

When ten thousand people turned up to celebrate, the new unionist, James Vickery, voiced the surge in confidence: 'With the combination of the workers, capital must give way.' Translating Marx into direct speech, he claimed that 'Anything and everything they saw around them was produced by the workers, and if they produced all they ought to have a share in all.' Standing on the platform with Vickery was Robert Weare from the Bristol Socialist Society. Suddenly finding himself with a mass audience, he spoke from the heart against the dehumanising alienation imposed by capital and the class system: 'They did not fight merely for an increase in wages, but to prove that they were men and not merely beasts or "hands".'

Miriam and Robert's pamphlet, *The Truth about the Chocolate Factories or Modern White Slavery its Cause and Cure*, begins on a similarly lofty note:

> The Workers, for long the sport and victims of Private Enterprise, are awakening to the truth that they are *men* – that they have the rights to live, breathe and act like men – that until they get their rights, at least a little more than the bare necessaries of life, they will be prevented from fulfilling their duties to God and Humanity.[17]

Lysaght's, Redcliffe Crown and the Bristol Gas Workers' strikes are mentioned, so the pamphlet was probably finished around the second week in October. By then Edward Tuckett Daniell had for some time been enduring the handsome young Scot, perched like a cuckoo in his home, while his wife was running wild with people he would surely class as rioters. The pamphlet proved the proverbial last straw, for now Miriam's politics were encroaching directly into his business affairs. The Daniell brothers were lesser lights in the Liberal commercial and political circles in which the Fry family played a leading role. Worse, civic-minded

Francis James Fry, a supporter of the Footpaths Preservation cause, held a substantial share in the family's chocolate business and signed documents as co-proprietor. Though not personally close to his cousin, Joseph Storrs Fry, who actually ran the firm, their interests were closely linked.[18]

Even the title was a provocation. It echoed Annie Besant's widely known article about the match women, 'White Slavery in London', published in her magazine *The Link* in 1888, and implied that adherents of the Social Purity cause publicised the sale of 'white slaves' into prostitution, while ignoring economic slavery. It so happened that Joseph Storrs Fry's sister Susan and his brother-in-law Thomas Pease (parents of the Fabian secretary, Edward Pease), were prominent in the Social Purity movement, as were James Livett Daniell and his wife Sophie.

The contents of the pamphlet went on to challenge both the firm's image as a benevolent employer and Joseph Storrs Fry's paternalistic management. Miriam and Robert's summary of the 'Facts' gathered from the workers is sobering. The hours of work were from 6 in the morning to 6 in the evening, though shorter for women in the summer. Yards' men carried sacks weighing one to two hundredweights, stacking them seven feet high. Chocolate grinders and pressers laboured amid ceaseless dust; operators of the pans and rollers toiled in extreme heat. Women and girls producing the mint cream for Fry's famed chocolate bars or 'tablets' had to swing constantly from side to side, lifting tablets weighing up to thirty pounds.[19] Miriam and Robert ask bluntly, 'Would the rich Cliftonians, some of whom live on the labour of these girls, allow their daughters to run such risks?'[20]

The workers complained they were fined for resting, for putting their head out to breathe through a window or for being one minute late. Wage differentials served to control the labour force, loyalty being rewarded with extra pay.[21] The pamphlet crystallises the employees' discontents into demands for an increase in pay, an eight-hour day and a fair standard of wages for all, rather than the 'favouritism' bestowed by Joseph Storrs Fry.[22]

The workers did not want the information broadcasted, but Miriam and Robert concluded publication was 'a duty that we owe to the Public at large'.[23] The Fry's workers no doubt wavered out of fear of victimisation, but also because they were aware that far worse forms of employment existed. Joseph Storrs Fry was not the stereotypical 'sweated' employer, on the contrary, he prided himself on being a benign industrialist and marketed his products on this basis. His concern for his workers' welfare was well known. If workers were sick he helped to secure treatment; bibles and copies of Mrs Beeton's cookery book were issued when women left to be married. However, Fry's adherence to a strict Quaker moral code was double-edged, leading him to supervise the workforce outside as well as within the factories. In the context of the late 1880s, being forced to make grovelling apologies for drunkenness while being paid less than 'virtuous' colleagues rankled.[24]

An underlying problem was Fry's preference for the familiar traditions established by his father. He had resisted moving the works to a new site, so, as mint chocolate bar sales went up, production expanded and more buildings were crammed into Union Street and the Pithay. As a result, workers' conditions had become increasingly cramped and unpleasant.[25]

Not content with piecemeal demands, Miriam and Robert drew on the American socialist, Laurence Grönlund's popular book, *The Co-operative Commonwealth* (1884), to question the profit system as a whole. Miriam and Robert reveal an interesting ambivalence on the alternative form of production that would replace capitalism. Socialists in the late 1880s were divided on whether industry should be directed by the state or through workers' associations, and *The Truth about the Chocolate Factories* calls for producer co-operatives and price controls through a 'National Trades' Council' *or* by 'the States' [*sic*], which, like Grönlund, they define as '"organised society"'.[26]

In contrast though to Grönlund's down-to-earth style, Miriam and Robert issue a chiliastic warning to 'philanthropists': 'To avert the physical revolution which at any time now, may with white and red flames of hate and bloodshed cremate the pestiferous corpses of once living and useful institutions, it is necessary that they should be transformed with new and different life.'[27] This suggests Miriam's pen – she had a penchant for the word 'pestiferous'.

The pamphlet ends with a call for 'A Spiritual evolution', and poses a stark dichotomy of living 'with love' or dying 'with hate'. It declares for 'Freedom, not fetters: Democracy, not aristocracy: Brotherhood not isolation: Co-operation not capitalism: Humanity not inhumanity.'[28] It was not uncommon for political and spiritual heterodoxies to travel in tandem: the Bristol Socialist Society included Christian Socialists, Theists and Spiritualists as well as Secularists, while Robert Gilliard was interested in the mystical Emmanuel Swedenborg whose followers in the Church of the New Jerusalem had influenced William Blake. However, *The Truth about the Chocolate Factories* adopted a prophetic millenarian style, extreme even by the standards of contemporary spiritually minded socialism.

With a passionate cry to dwellers in 'homes' that 'are luxurious and lethargic' to tear 'the bandages of selfishness, custom and opinion' from their 'eyes', Miriam and Robert admonish their readers to:

Hail the great *Sun*; the source of energy which brings joy to the hearts of countless of your despairing brothers and sisters. No, as you are noble men, gentle women, true maidens and youths, you will come out from the West where the day died, and turn to the East to welcome the splendid Light of Love and Liberty which are not two, but one and Indivisible. For God is Love and Unity. And there is no Spirituality unborn of His Breath.[29]

This is a curious exhortation to appear in a pamphlet on work, published in a series called 'Facts for the Times'. It derived from an esoteric figure, Thomas Lake Harris. Believing that God was neither Male nor Female, but combined the two sexes in One, Harris saw the Divine Breath as a means of acquiring a state of mind in which spiritual unions with counterparts could be achieved and set up various communities, including Fountain Grove near Santa Rosa in California. He was ambivalent towards physical love but composed highly sensuous poems celebrating 'Woman' as an ideal.[30]

Despite loathing socialists who endorsed class conflict, Harris was attracted by Laurence Grönlund's perspective of altruistic reform and outlined a Theo-socialist order in which the mystical 'Divine Breath' could sustain 'creative and redemptive evolution'.[31] Gilliard may have introduced Miriam and Robert to Harris' writings, but he also had followers in Scotland.[32]

According to reports from the divorce case, Edward Tuckett Daniell 'greatly objected', not to the 'Co-operative Commonwealth' or the mysticism, but to 'misstatements' in *The Truth about the Chocolate Factories* about Fry's relations with their employees, and declared to Miriam that he would take 'steps to stop it'.[33] In response to her husband's agitated threats, an infuriated Miriam told him 'she would leave his house'. According to the *Morning Post*, 'She went to live with some Socialistic friends in Bristol against his wish and consent.'[34]

*   *   *

Miriam was not only defying her husband, she was disgracing her family and cutting herself off from the cultured middle-class circles in which she moved. Her departure with Robert constituted an extraordinary break with convention, especially shocking in a religious, provincial city like Bristol. She could not have survived the calumny such a move entailed without being sustained by the Bristol Socialist Society's strong fellow-ship. This was expressed not just in their activism but in their poetry readings, glee singing and 'Tea Meetings' where they whirled around their 'Palace', the Coffee House in Castle Street, dancing 'in time and out of time' to the piano.[35] Gilliard later reflected to Helen: 'Whitman sings beautifully of loving comrades, but his verses do not begin to touch upon the real delight of the actual bliss of comradeship in practice.'[36] After the gloom of her unhappy marriage, Miriam was enveloped by their kindness and conviviality.

The respectable members of the Bristol Socialist Society, who were far from being free lovers, accepted and respected Miriam regardless of her disregard for the gender codes of Victorian womanhood. In his letter to Helen, Gilliard 'could hardly explain why – and no amount of kicking over the conventional tracks seemed to affect our regard for her, except to increase it'. He struggled to 'convey' the impact of Miriam's charismatic courage upon them: 'She was such an exceptional woman that I and my friends have never seen any other to begin to approach her. The regard which she excited in those who came in close contact with her bordered closely upon reverence.'[37]

Miriam had little time to ponder the consequences of her actions.

On 19 October 1889 the Fry's workers assembled at the British Workman Coffee House in New Street; Miriam spoke to the women downstairs while Albert Vincent from the Trades Council met with the men upstairs. Miriam sought to encourage the women by saying that the strike fund committee set up to support the Redcliffe Crown workers was available to help them if their claim was 'just'.[38] The men pledged to form a branch of the Gas Workers and General Labourers' Union and a group began working with the Trades Council.

Fry's responded with alacrity and sophistication, dividing the workers and isolating the most disgruntled by calling a meeting at the factory on October 22nd, to which Joseph Storrs Fry sent a pained message assur-ing his employees that they were free to join a union if they 'so wished' but hoped 'the unity of spirit … would not be severed by outsiders'. A spokesman from the company announced an increase of 1s a week for *male* workers, but while the men had won a raise, the others had not. The rebellious mood dissipated, as long-term employees affirmed their loyalty and gratitude and a vote of confidence in the 'heads of the firm' was passed 'amid loud cheering'.[39]

When a second edition of *The Truth about the Chocolate Factories* was produced on October 24th, Miriam and Robert noted the advance of 1s, the one and a half hours allowed for meal times out of the 12, the bonus of 2s for a month's punctuality, the provision of 'a duck jacket' to protect clothing, along with tea and coffee.[40] Fry's had made some ameliorations, thus reinforcing the loyalty of the more privileged workers and breaking the attempt to unionise.

In contrast, other Bristol employers were making substantial concessions. On October 24th, C.P. Thomas, a soap maker in St Philip's, who was a supporter of Helena's Oakfield Unitarian church, swiftly averted a strike by offering increased pay. Several other employers did likewise.[41] The militancy of new unionism and the support it was attracting took them by surprise.

The momentum of resistance continued. Towards the end of October, two major industrial conflicts erupted in Bristol: on October 21st, 2,300 dockers came out, closely followed three days later by over 1,700 cotton workers, the majority of whom were women. With James Vickery from the Gas Workers and General Labourers' Union, Miriam, now an accepted strike organiser, headed parades of cotton workers from the gates of the Great Western Cotton Works at Barton Hill into Bristol. Four thousand people demonstrated in support of the cotton workers on October 25th.[42]

The following day, a Saturday, the dockers were celebrating victory in euphoric style. The new unionist leaders, Ben Tillett, Tom Mann and Will Thorne, all of whom were socialists, were greeted at Temple Meads station by John Gregory and Robert Tovey from the Trades Council, the reformer, Gilmore Barnett, and Bristol Socialist Society members, Irving, Weare and Robert Sharland. Tillett, Mann and Thorne then marched triumphantly through Bristol at the head of a large procession of around fifteen thousand people, with the venerably bearded Gregory in a carriage and Miriam and Helena in a four-horse open brake. Over a thousand women cotton marchers linked arms and tripped along, keeping deftly in step to the music of the Lysaght's brass band. Up and up they went towards Clifton, their numbers increasing as they climbed. When they reached the fresh air of Durdham Downs, Gregory proudly introduced 'the noble trio' of new unionist leaders.[43]

The crowd listened respectfully, but it was the frail-looking, emotional Tillett with his Bristol origins who was their favourite. At thirty he was carrying a weight of responsibility on his shoulders; acutely aware that new unionism operated on a knife-edge of legality, he urged the crowd 'not to lose their heads for nothing'.[44] Platforms around the Downs carried other speakers, including Weare and the veteran Republican, Baster, from the Socialist Society. Bristol's labour movement had materialised.

After the demonstration, the new unionist leaders stayed over until the Sunday to advise on strategy and to sort out an inter-union dispute over whether the dockers should join Tillett's union or the Gas Workers. When a Strike Committee to assist unorganised 'workers of both sexes' was elected, Robert, Miriam and Helena, along with other members of the Bristol Socialist Society, were propelled into positions of leadership. Robert's name headed the list, a testament to his capacity to impress. His assertive keenness and unbounded energy, along with his per-suasive powers, had evidently compensated for his lack of experience. Miriam's name followed Robert's, and the new committee also included Helena, along with Gregory, Gore, Gilliard, Weare, John and Robert Sharland.[45]

On the Monday, Robert was appointed secretary for the Strike Com-mittee, on a salary of 30s a week, with Robert Gilliard as assistant-secretary. The ad hoc Committee took on the truly daunting responsibility for the city-wide revolt of labour. Helen relates how Miriam and Helena 'seemed to be needed everywhere at once'.[46] All three newcomers found them-selves at the epicentre of an inchoate eruption of militancy.

One key player, the managing director of the Great Western Cotton Works, George Spafford, remained implacable in opposing new unionism. The company had been reinvigorated in 1885 as a result of investment and reorganisation, but Bristol's cotton industry struggled in relation to Lancashire. The costs of restructuring combined with depressed condi-tions of trade had led the Great Western directors to introduce a wage cut of 10 per cent. Now, with the upturn of trade during the late 1880s, the workers, who had a long history of sporadic rebellion, wanted their wages to be restored.[47]

Though not unionised, the cotton workers, 1,350 women and 200 men, were far from submissive. Aware that their wages were significantly lower than those of the Lancashire workers, they were adamant about their right to that 10 per cent increase. They knew that they were still paying out of their wages for the new machinery installed in 1885. Then there were the fines, the obligation to pay for the cotton bobbins, and the money for doctors taken from their wages and partially pocketed by the company. They complained too about inadequate ventilation, the subterfuges adopted if factory inspectors came, and the ways in which their dinner hour was encroached upon.[48]

Spafford accepted a deputation on October 24th, saying pointedly to Miriam that 'he could not allow her to interfere between the management and the work people'.[49] By October 28th, faced with the prospect of finding strike pay for over a thousand cotton workers, some members of the Strike Committee began to balk, suggesting lowering the demand to 5 per cent. A fast-thinking Miriam, for whom retreat was anathema, intervened: 'They would be taking a great responsibility on themselves by advising the women to accept 5 per cent if the company could afford 10.'[50] She suggested they should seek information.

This gained a little time, and she and an uneasy Gore, who was well aware of the company's financial predicament, were deputed to go and meet Spafford. The chairman of the Board of Directors was Sir Joseph Weston, whose wedding Helena had helped to decorate. A former Liberal

Great Western Cotton Factory, Barton Hill,
by Samuel Loxton (Bristol Reference Library)

MP with Home Rule sympathies, Weston was active in municipal politics and had a philanthropic track record. A placatory Gilmore Barnett
wondered 'whether it would be wise' if he were to sound Weston out,
as he was 'personally acquainted' with him.[51] Neither approach yielded
anything.

An impasse had been reached. Spafford was threatening to close the
vast mill, even to burn it, rather than concede. So, on October 29th,
a sub-committee to collect funds was set up, composed of Miriam as
treasurer, Helena as assistant treasurer and secretary, along with Gilmore
Barnett, Robert Weare, Dan Irving and the Lysaght's worker, Frank
Rawle.[52] They faced a well-nigh impossible task.

The minutes of the October 30th Strike Committee meeting note the
need to help 'Mrs Nicol'; the mistake was scribbled out and replaced by
'Daniell', the minute taker had presumably assumed the inseparable pair
to be man and wife. Unusually the minutes bear witness to some personal crisis. The Committee instructed Robert and Miriam to go home,
requesting them 'to do nothing in the Strike business ... until 10 o'clock
tomorrow morning'.[53] Presumably an overwrought Robert and Miriam
were being given an enforced holiday.

It is not clear exactly where their 'home' was at this point. However, on
November 4th, the Strike Committee decided that 'Nicol's' remunera-
tion was inadequate for the 'many hours' he was 'devoting to the duties'.[54]
Robert's salary was accordingly increased from 30s to £2 a week and the
office closed at 8 p.m. instead of 9 p.m. This may have been the point at
which he and Miriam acted upon her conviction about the need to live
in a poor area. In *The Truth about the Chocolate Factories* they had called
St Philip's a 'filthy and wretched slum'.[55] Yet they set up house at 9 Louisa
Street, a narrow cobbled road, just around the corner from C.P. Thomas'
soap factory and relatively close to Lysaght's and the Barton Hill cotton
workers.

A contemporary commentator describes 1880s Bristol as a 'city of
extremes', with the 'cankering sores' of 'vermin-ridden warrens' merely 'a
stone's throw' from 'the stately factories' vaunting the prestige of the 'merchant princes' who owned them.[56] In another mood Miriam, too, might
well have denounced St Philip's as 'pestiferous'. Instead, with Helena
providing a threadbare cover of respectability, 9 Louisa Street became a
mini-settlement in action. Helen has left an account of the transformation effected by the idealistic settlers who created:

An example of practical simplicity in household matters, showing aesthetic possibilities in color and ingenious and artistic adaptation which
were a revelation to their neighbours. With their own hands they tinted
the walls of their rooms and waxed the uncarpeted floors, while from
the most commonplace materials they improvised many articles of
furniture and decoration, combining both beauty and utility.[57]

According to Helen, they sought to gain 'the confidence and respect'
of their neighbours,[58] but in fusing Carpenter and Thoreau's ideas of simplification with Patrick and Anna Geddes' reclamation of the Old Town
in Edinburgh, the aesthetic improvers neglected a significant distinction.
The bare boards, imposed upon rather than chosen by the nineteenth-
century poor, were likely to betoken scrubbing and discomfort rather
than any 'new life'.

Edward Tuckett Daniell appears to have accepted the situation at face
value, perhaps hoping Helena's presence might mitigate scandal. He
maintained contact with Miriam, later claiming that members of her
family also visited her. One certainly would have been Miriam's sister
Mary, who joined the Strike Committee on November 2nd. In 1894,
Daniell testified in court that he had offered Miriam an allowance of £1
a week at Louisa Street, 'and more if she left that style of life'.[59] He could,
of course, have been lying, for a husband was expected to give financial
support when a couple became estranged. However, he was a fair man, if
undemonstrative, and such an offer would have appeared reasonable to
his legally trained brain. Miriam of course viewed it as a cynical payment
to enforce outward conformity, and scorned his money. Mutual incomprehension marked their relationship. Gilliard described Daniell as 'a
long-icicle kind of a man (very tall & very cold)', adding 'when the little
pure fiery-hearted soul of a wife of his used to touch him one expected
something to happen like a fizzing sound; and could only attribute the
fact that it did not happen, to her kindness to him'.[60]

Gilliard was hardly neutral, being utterly bowled over by Miriam. He
was not alone. The force of Miriam's personality evoked Helena's adoration, swept Robert away from Edinburgh, charmed the socialists and
encouraged the strikers. Somehow, she had evaded the internalised fear
keeping most women of her generation rule-bound. Miriam did not
bother to break the rules; she simply behaved as if they were irrelevant.
This, along with the sheer power of her convictions and her capacity
to impose her view of events upon others, gave her the advantage. The

surprising mix of fragility and iron will contributed to her charisma, personally and politically.

If Miriam aroused devotion, she also provoked antipathy. According to Robert, Cecil Reddie disliked her; a disgruntled Richard Born, who had lost his house-keeper, blamed her for leading Helena astray; and, not surprisingly, Bristol's business community abhorred the woman they branded as an agitator. On October 31st an angry letter appeared in the *Western Daily Press* from Charles Helton Tuckett. He had been present at the meeting with Spafford and accused Miriam of declaring, 'I will take them out to the last woman', adding ominously, 'The men as might have been suspected followed in support of this woman.' Cast as an incendiary seductress, Miriam 'utterly' denied the accusation, responding, 'I said to Mr Spafford that probably the girls would come out if their demands were not granted.'[61] Indeed, Miriam could not have *conjured* such extreme resistance among workers; all she could offer them was hope and support.

While Miriam was the visible figure, Helena stayed in the background, working behind the scenes. A puzzled Gilliard reflected: 'She was always the same quiet thoughtful person never displaying much *outward* enthusiasm about the work she was about, but never idle.'[62] Helena immersed herself in internal committee work, but on October 31st, overcoming her shyness, she had gone with trade unionist Frank Rawle to speak to low-paid women pipe makers employed by Messrs Hawley and Co. whose wages averaged around 7s 6d for a sixty-hour week.[63]

Through the autumn of 1889 Helena also continued to participate in the Bristol Women's Liberal Association, signing a memorial for women's suffrage to John Morley MP presented by Emily Sturge at the Conference of the West of England W.L.A. The signatories included Helena's other former associates, Anna Maria Priestman, Margaret Tanner, Maria Colby and Louisa Swann.[64] However, the demands of the Strike Committee were increasingly pulling her away from her former political engagement with Bristol Liberalism, while the intensification of militancy exacerbated political divisions between the Liberals and the socialists.

On November 2nd, the Socialist League's *Commonweal* hailed the 'Great Revolt of Labour at Bristol' and the Strike Committee was deluged with calls for assistance from all manner of workers encouraged by the victories. Out came sawyers, carters, coal carriers, warehouse men, cigar, brush, box, pipe and black lead makers, along with scavengers, quarrymen, French polishers, hatters, colliers and charcoal workers.[65] On November 9th *Commonweal* reported how Bristol bargemen had taken direct action by blocking the Feeder canal that led into the Floating Harbour. They chained their barges together under a bridge and sympathetic crowds refused to allow the blockade to be moved, dropping paving stones on one steam launch that tried to break through.[66]

Miriam was everywhere, meeting the pipe makers with Helena on November 10th, then answering a call from colliers in the Forest of Dean.[67] Along with Helena and the rest of the Strike Committee, she also faced the formidable problem of how to find funds for the cotton workers. On November 12th the cotton company reaffirmed their refusal to negotiate and, yet again, the cotton workers voted by a large majority to stay out. Miriam and Helena issued appeals to papers like *Commonweal*, the *Factory Times* and the *Women's Union Journal*, the organ of the Women's Trades Union and Provident League, as well as to individuals. The spirit of solidarity among workers was high; when the carters' dispute was settled some of the men sent money.[68] Overall the trade unions proved the most reliable source of financial aid.

The Strike Committee appealed in vain to Bristol's Nonconformist and Anglican clergy. Only the Christian Socialists, Revd J.R. Graham at St Jude's and Revd T.W. Harvey at St Agnes, responded with personal donations and collections from their congregations. In an effort to gain sympathy from church-goers, the Strike Committee adopted a shaming tactic used by the Chartists and revived during the 1888 London match-women's strike. Early in November several hundred cotton workers, mainly women, dressed in their white aprons with shawls over their heads began to arrive at churches on Sunday. When three hundred appeared at Tyndale Baptist Chapel, Revd R. Glover, who had initially shown support, responded by lecturing them on how working-class conditions had improved.[69]

At All Saints on Pembroke Road, the High Church vicar tried to ignore them. It was raining outside and the drenched and emaciated women strikers marched down the aisle, standing in silent reproach between the congregation and the altar rail at the critical moment of the High Celebration, when the choirboys were hailing the Presence. Inside the church the fragrance of flowers mingled with the incense, but one worshipper, Katharine St John Conway, a graduate of Newnham College, Cambridge, who was teaching at Redland High School, was conscious only of the protestors. Overwhelmed by guilt, the following day Conway went to offer her services to the Bristol Socialist Society. Initially greeted with scepticism, 'tall, gentle' Robert Weare rescued her saying, 'Give her Carpenter's *England's Ideal*. That's what she needs.'[70]

It was a wise choice and she found the book revelatory: 'It was as if in that smoke-laden room a great window had been flung open and the vision of a new world had been shown me.'[71] Two more middle-class High Church recruits soon followed. Enid Stacy, also teaching at Redland High School and a worshipper at All Saints, was already interested in socialism. The arrival of the cotton workers, 'wet and desperate after many weeks of sullen holding out for even a right to combine', made her feel compelled to join the strike movement.[72] Yet another High Church middle-class woman, Gertrude Dix, from the Christian Socialists, joined the Strike Committee that November. On November 19th the Howes hatters had come out in support of the reinstatement of a woman worker who subsequently withdrew from the strike. The employers proceeded to sack those they perceived as leaders. In response to a desperate appeal made by Robert on November 25th, Gertrude, who had just joined the Strike Committee, was elected to a sub-committee raising funds and struggling to stop the victimisation.[73]

Early in November Robert Sharland had knocked up a hundred wooden collection boxes so the cotton workers could raise money for the strike themselves.[74] Their lively zeal provoked one irate correspondent in the *Western Daily Press* on November 7th to complain that when 'accosted' by a woman striker, he had enquired what they would do that winter if they did not return to work. Expecting a deferential supplicant, he was horrified to receive the lippy reply, 'Oh! ... we are going to live on the rich' – she had taken the socialists' propaganda literally.[75] But the temptation of ready cash proved too strong for one of the cotton workers, Mrs Cooper, who confessed to having got drunk on the donations she had taken. Helena, the merciful, urged that it 'should not be dealt with harshly'.[76] The money was declared 'lost'.

Helena's mix of diplomacy and attention to detail proved invaluable. When a vital promised donation from Tom Mann went to the Trades Council by mistake, she tracked it down and restored it to the Strike Committee. It was Helena who persuaded people to provide premises and Helena who organised benefits. And it was Helena who liaised with Anna Maria Priestman on the running of a much-needed soup kitchen at Barton Hill.[77]

It was a shock therefore to the Strike Committee when the self-effacing secretary of their fund-raising committee read out an 'insulting' letter she had received from Revd James M. Wilson, the headmaster of Clifton College.[78] Its contents were not recorded by the minute taker, and Wilson would later claim he had sent the wrong version. But the gist can be inferred from his open letter to the cotton workers, printed in the local press on November 22nd. Wilson urged the cotton workers to trust their directors rather than 'any one else who is busying himself or herself' in 'the strike'. The directors could not 'defraud the share-holders of their just claims for interest'. He went on to maintain that the workers had been 'MISLED … Not wilfully but in ignorance' by 'foolish people with WARM HEARTS and WEAK HEADS'.[79] Wilson's letter established a narrative through which Bristol's clergy and Liberal social reformers, briefly upstaged by the Socialist Society, could regain the moral high ground. On Sunday, November 24th, the vicar of Emmanuel Church and the minister of Trinity Wesleyan Chapel picked up the cue, and, when the strikers appeared, reiterated the refrain that the workers had been misled.[80] Robert Weare's reply from the Strike Committee in the *Western Daily Press* on November 25th reminded Wilson that it had been the strikers who had voted not to return to work. Contesting the assumption that dividends of at least 5.5 per cent had to be an 'inexorable and divine law', Weare dismissed this as 'a transitory precept to which we no longer submit'.[81]

The shareholders of Bristol were no doubt still spluttering over the transitory status decreed for their profits when Helena sought help for '1,300 cotton operatives on strike in Bristol' from the Positivist dis-ciple of Comte, Professor E.S. Beesly, well known for his sympathies towards trade unions and labour representation. In a long letter metic-ulously outlining the cotton workers' conditions and demands, Helena stated: 'they have all joined a Union and we have so far educated them, that they begin to grasp the great and grave problems of Capital and Labour'.[82]

Exhausted and angry by what had occurred that November, Helena does not display her customary equanimity. Scorning the directors and shareholders' philanthropic pretensions, she wrote:

They support 'Hospitals' and head subscription lists for the (Happy) Heathen. Meantime their workers toil and cry, diseased with unhealthy joyless work and ill-drained hovels for homes.

Must these things not be brought to light and these women encouraged to stand against a system which drives them to supplement their wages by Prostitution, and which wrecks the bodies which hold the future health of England.[83]

Helena stressed the 'girls' were 'firmly resolved ... to fight on to the end', even if it would result in the closure of 'such a shameful specimen of the results of interest, of money and competition'.[84]

Bristol's first woman Poor Law Guardian, Mary Clifford, had a quite different take on the strikers' consciousness. She had been 'meeting some of the men and women privately' along with some of her friends and her view was that while the men were 'very full of reasoning of the socialist kind', in contrast, the women were 'very open to being led' by people such as herself.[85] Clifford was indeed a popular figure in the Barton Hill community. Dressed in startling art nouveau garments, she often took local children on outings up to the Downs or to the windy beach at Weston-super-Mare. Believing that personal contact could overcome class hostility, Clifford urged social reformers to display understanding and enlarge their outlook in order to bring 'countless needs into sight'.[86] She baulked, however, at demands.

On November 26th, the Strike Committee finally secured a formal response from the Great Western directors to the written demands of the cotton workers. Management agreed to abolish the hated fines for accidental damage and the payment for bobbins. They accepted stops for meals at 8.30 a.m., 1 p.m. and 5.30 p.m., better ventilation, inspection by workers of their money paid to company doctors, and no victimisation. But they rejected any wage increase. The meeting between the Strike Committee and the strikers to discuss the offer proved painful and difficult. Only after a debate that lasted an hour and a half did the cotton workers miserably accept the Committee's recommendation that they should return to work. Far from wavering, they had been starved into submission. Clifford's assessment had been mistaken.[87]

Clifford was relieved by the 'helpful' presence of Clementina Black, who had come from London to mediate.[88] As a young woman Black had been friendly with Eleanor Marx, and then, through her sister, Constance Garnett, moved in Fabian circles. Troubled, like Helena, by sweated work, from 1887 to May 1889 Black was the secretary of the Women's Trade Union Provident League, which encouraged the formation of women's unions.[89] However, by the time she came to Bristol, Black was active in the newly formed Women's Trades Association. Conceived in the wake of the London dock strike and formally launched at a conference on October 8th, the new organisation included social reformers from the churches and social settlements along with new unionists, Mann, Tillett and John Burns. It argued for 'self-supporting and self-governed unions', aiming not simply at better wages but 'sanitary conditions' and 'proper treatment'.[90] Its remit of 'strong Trade Unions' discussing peacefully with employers was acceptable to the Bristol Socialist Society, as well as to Mary Clifford, but did not extend to Eleanor Marx from the Socialist League. Barred from its founding conference, she formed the Women's Branch in the Gas Workers and General Labourers' Union just two days afterwards.[91]

Helena scribbled rough notes around the margins of one of the Women's Trades Association leaflets for her contribution to Weare's lecture series. Helena's topic was all too familiar, 'Why Women Should Organise', but now she could draw on the bitter experience of the cotton workers' strike. She reflects that wages are only 'Kept above starvation level by continual war with the Employer & workman'. Detecting a 'sense of compunction' among 'the better hearted among the comfortable classes' over wage levels at just about starvation, Helena observed the rich 'beginning to be a little ashamed of their comfort in the face of this misery of those they call their fellow creatures'. Paying tribute to 'A. Besant', she added acerbically: 'They begin to talk in Drawing Rooms. Are they prepared to make any sacrifices.' Socialism would make philanthropy unnecessary; people would simply 'prefer to be charitable'.[92]

The premise behind Weare's lecture series was that while 'combination' was vital for 'both sexes', trade unions were 'not in themselves sufficient for workers' emancipation'.[93] Helena, like Edward Carpenter, describes them as 'Bridges', a means of reaching a better state of affairs, not an end in themselves. Like many other socialists caught up in new unionism, Helena was trying to think through its implications. Her notes include a heading 'the Labor Candidates'.[94]

While 'the labour movement' had appeared as a new term, the revolutionary left tended to be dismissive of trade unions. Hyndman, the leader of the S.D.F., grumbled because the new unions did not declare themselves as socialists, while some members of the Socialist League favoured the creation of revolutionary unions. Theorising tended to limp along behind activism, for in practice, in Bristol, and indeed all over Britain, socialists threw themselves into new unionist organising. Friedrich Engels' clarity was unusual. He staunchly encouraged Eleanor Marx's work with the Gas Workers and General Labourers' Union, perceiving how the workers' militancy not only secured tangible gains but dislocated the powerful ideological assumption 'of an identity of interest between capital and labour'.[95]

Emily Sturge approached unions from the opposing vantage point of a shared interest. In her address on December 16th for the B.W.L.A at Redland Park Hall, on 'Women and the Labour Movement', she maintained that if a women's union had existed at the cotton works, 'the employers might have been met, and a fair arrangement come to which could have prevented such a strike'.[96] By implication she was accusing Helena and Miriam of rabble rousing and causing unnecessary suffering. Wrongly assuming, like Clifford, that the women workers would have been amenable to compromise, she was equally over-optimistic about the directors' inclination to offer concessions.

In contrast Miriam and Helena, having witnessed in practice the power of solidarity between men and women, emerged as advocates of militant new unionism. A gulf had opened between two conflicting perspectives on how best to organise women workers. This intensified Helena's alienation from her former Liberal political associates. Helen's 'Biographical Introduction' to *Whitman's Ideal Democracy* records that supporting 'the labouring folk brought forth much criticism and remonstrance' for Helena, who felt 'this disapproval' from 'old and respected friends ... sorely'.[97]

Estranged by her new political allegiances and closeted at 9 Louisa Street in an awkward threesome, Helena's closeness to Miriam must have been affected by her friend's passionate love for Robert. Submersion in work, checking records and adding accounts, long after the Strike Committee office closed, would have been her salve. Meanwhile she was still trudging up to Whiteladies Road to placate an irate Richard Born by cooking his weekly pies.

As for Robert, after the *Chocolate Factories* and his appointment as secretary to the Strike Committee, over the last two months of 1889 he had been involved with a wide range of workers on strike, from hatters to miners as well as the cotton workers. He proved himself capable of handling the routines of organising and his personable sociability had also been spotted by John Sharland and James Vickery as a potential asset for the G.W. & G.L.U. They started taking him out on union business to meetings with workers, which drew them, rather agreeably, towards pubs like the Old Fox on Redcliff Street.[98] Robert was being groomed for a new job.

Even after the cotton workers returned to work, the pressure on the Strike Committee did not let up. After an unofficial strike of shoemakers, the employers locked them out and John Gregory was faced with 8,000 boot and shoe workers to maintain, many of whom were women and children, working at home, and without any means of livelihood.[99] They needed funds beyond the capacity of the unionised craft workers. Such hardship meant that a Christmas gift of 'a fine hamper of vegetables' from one of the blacklisted workers to Helena, Miriam and Robert constituted an act of moving generosity. They allowed themselves three days' holiday over Christmas, tramping off on 'long country walks' through 'the ever-present mud'.[100] But it proved only the briefest of respites.

FIVE

Seekers: 1890

The mud hardly had time to dry on their boots before the meetings began again. That January the ad hoc Strike Committee reconstituted itself in a more structured manner as the Workers' Organising Committee (W.O.C.).[1] Like the Strike Committee, the Organising Committee was based at the British Workman Coffee House in New Street and the same names occur in the minutes. Along with the trade unionist Tovey are the socialists Robert, Miriam, Weare, Irving, Gilliard, Gore and Watson. Gertrude Dix too was formally 'nominated and unanimously elected' on 4 January 1890.[2] The political influence of the socialists is evident in the Committee's aims to unionise the unorganised and encourage 'a federation of labour' to overcome the divisions between trades, and to 'promote lectures and addresses on the Social question so far as it affects Capital and Labour'.[3]

The topics offered for Weare's lecture series indicate that the Bristol socialists gave 'the Social question' a wide remit. Weare covered 'Industrial War', 'Social Peace', 'Work, Wages and Wealth' and 'Principles of Socialism'; the railway worker, Irving, proposed 'Land Nationalisation', 'Communism, the True Basis of Society'; Gilliard, 'The Social Hive', as well as 'Christian Socialism' and 'Is Socialism Inevitable?' Along with 'Why Women Should Organise', Helena's heading was 'The Aristocracy of Sex', the scornful phrase Susan B. Anthony had used in 1869, when American reformers opted for 'manhood' rather than universal suffrage. Miriam's enthusiasms extended to 'Cosmopolitanism and Patriotism', 'Evolution of Women', 'Socialism and Art' and 'Nihilism'.[4]

The Workers' Organising Committee retained the Socialist Society's ideals of personal comradeship and these were bolstered by humorous fellowship. One sub-committee, composed of Robert Nicol, Robert Sharland, Robert Weare, Robert Gilliard and their ally from the Trades Council, Robert Tovey, was named 'the Five-Bob Committee' with the ironic trailer, they 'couldn't raise one between them'.[5] Robert Nicol might have lacked 'bobs' (shillings), but he did have a new position. Now the District Secretary of the Gas Workers and General Labourers' Union, he begins to emerge from Miriam's shadow over the following months as a union organiser.[6]

Yet it was she who evoked love and reverence. On the evening of January 12th, a torch-lit procession of shoe workers cheered her as, small and defiant, she called for an eight-hour day, declaring that 'Capitalists must be content with less profit.'[7] Gregory had turned around what had seemed a desperate situation and effected solidarity between craft trade union men and the non-unionised women outworkers. Four days later, when the dispute was settled by a Board of Arbitration, the united shoe workers were able to influence the terms. It seemed as if a viable model had been found which could be adapted for other low-paid women outworkers.[8]

Just before the shoe makers' strike was resolved, Miriam, Helena and Robert Tovey, with his Clothier Cutters' Association cap on, produced a leaflet, 'REASONS WHY TAILORESSES SHOULD JOIN A UNION: Addressed to "FELLOW-WORKERS"'. It stated:

> During the great strikes in Bristol repeated appeals have come to us for aid and advice in the Formation of a Union for the Tailoresses of the city. Press of work entailed by the great rush of all sorts of workers to join Unions has prevented any response being given on the part of the Union or Strike leaders, but, now the labour world is quieter for the moment, representatives from your comrades of the Amalgamated Society of Tailors; the Clothier Cutters' Association; the Bristol District of the G.W. & G.L. Union and the Workers' Organizing Committee have met together and are taking immediate steps to get every *Tailoress* in Bristol into a Trade's Union.[9]

By paying a sixpenny entrance fee, and then one or two pennies a week, the promise was that the new union would secure fair wages and the abolition of fines, 'in an amicable spirit if possible'. Organising could bring down the daily hours of labour to eight a day and reduce the time wasted by 'outdoor hands' while waiting for their work to be checked and new material delivered. The tailoresses were told how unionisation could prevent undercutting, along with the antagonism this provoked between men and women in the trade. Moreover, the union meant 'women shall get a wage equal to that of the men for doing the same work'.[10] Though expressed in moderate tones, the implications of these proposals were radical indeed. However, trouble lay ahead.

Thirty-nine women enrolled in the new tailoresses' union at a meeting on January 13th, a modest start that met with protests, not only from several decidedly unamicable employers, but also from Mary Talbot and the Bristol Association of Working Women.[11] The Bristol Association's origins went back to the mid 1870s. Because women were excluded from male craft unions, separate local bodies for women workers had been set up with the Women's Protective and Provident League (from 1888 the Women's Trades Union Provident League) acting as an umbrella.[12] While the Bristol Association's membership numbered in total only around seventy in 1890, Talbot possessed influential allies, including Mary Clifford, suffrage women and some of the craft trade unionists.[13] Nevertheless, supported by Tovey, Vincent and Gregory on the Trades Council and backed by the Workers' Organising Committee, the tailoresses became a branch of the G.W. & G.L.U.[14]

In part, Talbot, who had conflicted with Tovey in the past over women's unionisation, was fighting a turf war over recruitment. But, as in the cotton workers' strike, differing concepts of the role of trade unions were in collision. For Talbot and her allies, the purpose of a union was primarily defensive. Joining a union constituted a collective form of self-help, which could develop women's confidence and provide welfare, such as sick pay, in times of need. In contrast, militant new unionism focused on winning better pay and conditions and carried an implicit critique of the profit system itself. Reaching out to all workers, not just a craft elite, solidarity was its lifeblood. Both wings of the Bristol women's labour movement envisaged unionisation as enhancing character and consciousness; Talbot defined this process in terms of self-respect and morality, while Miriam and Helena conceived a 'loving comradeship' for the tailoresses.[15] They were in accord with the G.W. & G.L.U. motto, 'Love, Union and Fidelity', and Tillett's Dock, Wharf, Riverside and General Labourer's Union Journal, the *Monthly Record*, which quoted Shelley's 'The Revolt of Islam' on its masthead: 'A NATION MADE FREE BY

LOVE. A MIGHTY BROTHERHOOD LINKED BY A JEALOUS INTERCHANGE OF GOOD.'[16]

The reality was less glorious. As January came to a close, Helena described in her letter to Minnie Southcombe the difficulties of organising seamstresses in the outlying villages. Leaving Tovey to deal with ideological skirmishes in the newspapers, Helena was tramping out into the surrounding countryside, trekking sometimes for thirty miles some days, to meet women working in their homes.[17] The recruitment efforts staggered on for several months; at the end of April, Helena, Miriam, Tovey and Irving all went out to the village of Frampton Cottrell in a horse-drawn wagonette to induce women to join the union.[18] But the bitter truth was that few women seamstresses joined either the G.W. & G.L.U *or* Mary Talbot's association.

Helena took the tailoresses' cause to heart, keeping the little union rulebook all her life. Even though they had failed to bring home workers into the union, Helena, Miriam and Tovey's leaflet had put forward the startling demand for equal pay. This had been raised by Clementina Black at the 1888 Trades Union Congress; the attempt to unionise the tailoresses introduced it into Bristol's new unionism.

Helen relates how Helena, excised from her old 'Musical, artistic and literary circles' was abandoned by many 'whilom' friends. One who did remain loyal was an artistic governess, Alice Willway, who visited Louisa Street early in 1890. Sipping tea and talking with a friend had become a rare treat.[19] Helena, whose diligence and reliability generated ever more tasks, was barely at home. As well as serving on several committees and attending meetings, the Minutes of the Workers' Organising Committee record Helena helping to find a name for a sympathetic brass band, contacting women workers, and dealing with the expenses incurred in organising the tailoresses.[20]

Her January letter to Minnie Southcombe reveals an unsalutary aspect of home-life in Louisa Street: 'Our only domestic pet at present is a brown rat which has emigrated from the drains and located itself in our coal house adjoining our dining room. It does not mind us in the least and runs about regardless of our presence.'[21] Helena took a stoical approach to rats, though even she panicked one night when she imagined the over-friendly creature in her bedroom. She was missing Minnie, confiding 'My heart often longs for you', while despatching austere advice: 'Happiness only comes to us, dear, when we want nothing for ourselves, and when our lives are in accord with the Great Spirit of Love which animates the universe.'[22]

As she wrote, Helena, wielding her beeswax and 'turps', was excitedly awaiting that visit from Edward Carpenter, whose writing she so admired, telling her cousin, 'For the next few hours I shall be discreetly inhospitable, in view of the muddy pavements outside!'[23] Carpenter, who could never have imagined the preparation and expectation under way at 9 Louisa Street, was already friendly with the Sharlands, Gore, Weare and Gilliard but this was his first encounter with Helena, Miriam and Robert. He later recollected meeting Helena 'once or twice', retaining a perception of 'absolute trueness & a sort of reliance in her'.[24] No comment on Miriam survives; it was Robert who caught his attention and Robert who would be invited to his home at Millthorpe.

Carpenter's visit coincided with a second dispute at Lysaght's galvanising iron works. After Christmas the firm had started laying off their more experienced workers who had participated in the previous strike. At an angry meeting they resolved to strike, despite the mutterings of a punctilious Robert who knew they had an agreement to give a week's notice. He was overridden by the trade unionist, Frank Rawle. John Lysaght then locked the men out. Once again Miriam and Helena, along with Tovey, were raising money and another battle for moral support ensued. Two hundred and fifty Lysaghts' workers attended a service on Sunday January 26th at Bristol Cathedral before going to Shaftesbury Hall, in St Philips, to hear Carpenter address them.[25]

The following day he was lecturing to a packed meeting at the Castle Street Coffee Palace on 'The Breakdown of the Industrial System'. With Dan Irving chairing, Carpenter portrayed capitalism as 'a tissue of fraud and adulteration'. Questioning the immutability of the present form of production, he posed the possibility of alternatives. Like many contemporary socialists he considered the capacity of trade unionism to change consciousness by creating the 'Solidarity of Workers' as more important than winning immediate pay increases, or even the eight-hour day.[26]

Within a few weeks it became clear Lysaght's were not prepared to negotiate. Instead they were about to pull the carpet from under the feet of the militants. The firm was using the lock out to reorganise production, modernising the plant, so the skills of the experienced workers would be less vital. Many strikers returned to work, leaving around a hundred still out and without jobs. Amid the bitterness of defeat, on February 21st Rawle accused Miriam of maladministration of the strike fund.[27] The audited accounts were published in the press and his charge proved unfounded, but for Miriam, who lived for ideals and thrived on heroic moments, the accusation would have been devastating. She had no talent for messy politicking.

Next came the prosecution of pickets for alleged intimidation in a dispute at the Bristol Flour and Bread Company owned by Isaac Wilmot. Picketing had been made legal in 1875, but intimidation remained an offence. This could encompass 'watching or besetting', for which three of the Howes hatters had been gaoled. An impatient Miriam was dismissive of legal niceties: 'if picketing was not legal it ought to be made so'. However, on March 28th the decision of a sympathetic Justice Cave that the pickets had *intended* to abide by the 1875 Act did prove crucial for the bakers. The case against them was dropped.[28]

Miriam inclined to absolutes rather than nuances. A photograph of her from this period (see p. 36) shows her hair drawn back severely, haloing her head. Her face looks tense and weary but her gaze is unflinching and resolute. Miriam identified with the Russian revolutionaries known as 'Nihilists', women as well as men, who had pitted their lives against the Tsar's autocratic powers. She was not alone; their eloquent exponent Stepniak (Sergey Mikhaylovich Stepnyak-Kravchinsky), author of *Career of a Nihilist* (1889), was being lionised in radical British and American circles, for his 'grand presence and fine conversational powers'.[29] Miriam's entry into activism had occurred in such extreme circumstances, the compromises of the everyday tended to appear like distasteful betrayals.

Robert, too, was happiest in heroic mode and had composed a song for the Bristol Socialist Society's *Labour Song Book* declaiming, 'An offering to the shrine of power/Our hands shall never bring', and honouring 'those/Who bade the world go free'.[30] It was given pride of place on the first page, with instructions that it should be sung to the tune of 'Ellacombe' or 'The Hardy Norseman'. Yet, by March 1890, Robert's day-to-day union work meant he was all too aware of the odds against new unionism. He would, moreover, have picked up the critical theoretical rumblings against new unionism emanating from both Hyndman's Marxist Social Democratic Federation and from the anarchist-influenced Socialist League. Along with other socialist new unionist supporters, he was seeking ways of complementing industrial power.

Among the topics Robert had proposed for Weare's lecture programme were 'The New Trade Unionism – a Means to an End' and 'The New

Religion'.[31] Both themes merged in a pamphlet he and Miriam were preparing that March, *The New Trade Unionism: Its Relation to the Old; and
the Conditions of Its Success*. Again Robert and Miriam adopt a chiliastic
tone. The unconcerned rich living 'upon interest of money ... wrung
from the wretched poor' are warned they are inviting violent conflagration.[32] However, this second pamphlet also reveals them trying to assess
and comprehend the implications of the intensive activism of the last
few months. Conscious the employers have mounted an offensive, by
'organising speedily into phalanxes', starving workers into submission or
utilising the police and military, they single out for praise the scrupulous judgement of Justice Cave as evidence of a degree of independence
within the judiciary.[33]

Combining factual material on recent disputes with references to
the history of trade unionism, Miriam and Robert take the long view,
locating new unionism 'as merely a big incident in the labour war' and
criticising the leadership as too preoccupied with 'shallow success' and
'material gains'.[34] This was in accord with some Marxists and anarchists'
suspicions that by achieving 'palliatives', new unionism would dampen
revolutionary ardour. But Miriam and Robert deplore the folly of calls
for 'a physical revolution' coming from some anarchists who were gaining
strength in the Socialist League.[35]

Bristol Socialist Society's Songbook

Struggling to come to terms with their disappointment as the momentum of the strike wave began to falter, their faith in the pure 'social instincts' of the people is now tempered by an uneasy recognition of the need for education.[36] By this they do not simply mean formal learning. They argue that an inward spiritual transformation must accompany efforts to better workers' conditions. And, although Miriam and Robert want change to come from workers' own efforts, they conclude that some external group is required to bring the alternative spiritual principles into their lives, 'to bind them into loving and, therefore, living unity'.[37] The pamphlet thus expresses a tension between the perceptions of the subordinated and the knowledge of the faithful, a node of attrition in both socialism and anarchism that continued to trouble them both.

The New Trade Unionism also engages with the problem that had caused the Fabians to split from the Fellowship of the New Life: how to balance political and personal transformation. The pamphlet begins with a quote from Thomas Lake Harris, the mystical community builder and Grönlund enthusiast: 'Reformers fail because they change the letter,/And not the Spirit of the World's design.'[38] The necessity of linking an inner change with external social transformation was a familiar theme in a left still cast within the Christian search for redemption. Miriam and Robert present a human-centred mission:

> The greatest Union of all – the union of the Souls of Mankind in a perfect Love, out of which will emanate perfect and eternal Peace, which will express itself, not in religious trances or in lethargy, but in active, beautiful, and simple service, sacrifice and life.[39]

A workers' movement based on love and Miriam and Robert's stress on the 'value of the unity and equality of the sexes' could be encompassed within the broad church of ethical socialism.[40] But ethical eyebrows would have started to go up when they pronounce, 'the male and female principles will be symbols of God on earth'.[41] The gas workers, tailoresses and bakers who signed up for new union membership could hardly have bargained for the predicted inrush of love:

> All days shall be Sundays, love days as Christ decreed, and, God will walk on earth with and in man. The advent of Christ will have been consummated. The People is the Church, and with the ideal of love filling their lives, the Unity, divine woman and divine man, will reign in it supreme as Lord of creation.[42]

The New Trade Unionism does not simply seek a transcendent alternative to capitalist society through inner as well as outer change, it spills over into an antinomian rejection of all boundaries. The 'spirit of love' is not to be found in any Church, for love 'is smitten with deadly pain, and flees from us when we attempt to limit it'.[43] Christianity's divorce between 'body and soul' must be refuted.[44]

Robert and Miriam's pamphlet floats inexorably towards the search for arcane sources of revelatory enlightenment, which exercised a powerful attraction in the late nineteenth century. Dilemmas of power, sex, guilt and asceticism tended to be expressed in a quasi-religious idiom. Some, like Annie Besant, turned to the East, through the Theosophists; others such as Anna Kingsford, an animal rights activist popular in socialist and feminist circles, revived Neo-Platonist mysticism and reinterpreted heretical strands of Christian thinking.[45] Ideas of divinity dwelling within every human being, a rebalancing of male and female as symbolic principles of reason and intuitive love, along with a heterodox form of redemption through the exaltation of 'Woman', flit through Thomas Lake Harris' writings. Similar ideas can also be found in fragmented notes left by the metaphysical thinker James Hinton, whose ideas on the interrelatedness of good and evil influenced both Carpenter and his friend, the sex psychologist Havelock Ellis.[46]

However, the most obvious source of Miriam and Robert's subversive spirituality lurked closer at hand. They quote the Swedenborg-influenced, Bristol Socialist Society member, Robert Gilliard at some length at the beginning of their pamphlet:

> If Humanity has lost its Edenic state of innocence and love, by the beguilement of the serpent, the allurement of the senses, the only antidote against the deadly poison of the sensualism with which men are bitten in to-day's wilderness is the looking toward the elevation of this very sensual principle itself in the recognition that in its proper relation to the inner spiritual life, IT also is Christ-like, Human and Divine.[47]

Gilliard's fascination with the transformatory union of spirit and sensuous desire, of seeming good and apparent evil, resonated powerfully. Miriam's sister, Mary Wheeler, who designed the frontispiece, visually reinforces Gilliard's words. She depicts men and women holding aloft a staff around which a serpent is coiled, reaching upwards and biting the sun. The image, which figures in Christian iconography of healing, is also redolent of the awakening of yogic energy symbolised by the serpent mounting the spine.

The 1890 pamphlet on new trade unionism sets out recurring tropes around spirit and matter, which Miriam and Robert pursued in varying ways through their lives. In Gilliard's view their quest lacked 'proper balance'.[48] He considered: 'They were as true as steel to the cause but had a tendency to drift off into new bold and untried projects in it.' He was right, they were attracted towards extremes; however, during that summer of 1890 at least, the two iconoclasts did make valiant efforts to face a new reality.

The New Trade Unionism was published when the certainties of autumn 1889 were being seriously buffeted. From March 1890, regular reports on Bristol strikes appear in 'A Weekly Paper Devoted to the Interests of the People', called *The People's Press.* Edited by Robert E. Dell, a young journalist on the Fabian Society's Executive Committee and an enthusiastic advocate of new unionism, it included Eleanor Marx as a contributor.[49] The March 22nd issue carried a rather belated 'Report of Bristol Strike Committee' by 'Miriam Daniell, Treasurer and Helena Born, Secretary'. Noting 'the organisation of unskilled labour of all kinds into Trades Unions', they warn that 'liberty is never gained for ever, but is constantly liable to attacks if not jealously guarded'.[50] The author of 'Bristol Labour Notes', probably Robert, announces: 'Employers have now recovered from their surprise', and were endeavouring to trick workers with 'bonuses and profit-sharing schemes'.[51]

That March Miriam was greeted by several hundred cheering cotton workers in the G.W. & G.L.U.[52] But it is apparent that Miriam and Robert were struggling to adjust to new circumstances. Robert, no doubt remembering the Lysaght's fiasco, was warning Bath gas workers that the victimisation of their leaders campaigning for the eight-hour day could well be the directors seeking to force a strike at a time of year 'most favourable to themselves'. Miriam and Helena, too, urged that if they could 'stand firm to one another', striking might be unnecessary.[53]

Bristol socialists change tack and start to explore complementary strategies in order to reinforce an increasingly beleaguered industrial militancy. Gore, now a Fabian, began working closely with the Bristol Miners' Association leader, William Whitefield, mooted as the Labour candidate who could take the demand for the eight-hour day to Parliament. The Labour League's idea of a 'Labour Party' begins to assume capital letters early in

1890.[54] Similar local initiatives around the country were eventually to cohere as the Independent Labour Party in 1893.

Socialist education and small prefigurative projects were favoured by Carpenter's friend, Raymond Unwin, who spoke that spring with Miriam on the 'Labour Question' and addressed the Clifton and Bristol Christian Socialists on 'Democracy'. In the Socialist League paper, *Commonweal*, Unwin reported that the great wave of labour unrest in Bristol was showing signs of being 'spent'; nevertheless, the serious mood of the Clifton and Bristol Christian Socialists impressed him: 'The younger people especially – high school mistresses, and youths just starting in life – appear anxious to find out the right and to work for it.'[55]

Unwin's serious young seekers sound like Katharine St John Conway, Enid Stacy and her younger brother Paul. Among them no doubt was also Gertrude Dix, who, like Robert, became a friend of Unwin's. Twenty-two-year-old Gertrude was moving away from both her devout High Church background and even from the relatively respectable orbit of Clifton Christian Socialism. After working with the ad hoc Strike Committee, on January 4th she had been unanimously elected onto the Workers' Organising Committee. In 1890 Gertrude attended the cotton workers' G.W & G.L.U. branch meetings with Robert and Miriam and later recalled walking with Robert out to meet the miners.[56] She was also on a sub-committee consisting of Robert, Miriam, Helena, Gore, Watson and Irving, which hoped to further socialist education by setting up a 'Labour Newspaper' for Bristol and the West of England.[57] Gertrude, having joined the Bristol Socialist Society, followed, in her own distinctive manner, paths beaten out by Miriam and Helena. Neither she nor Robert could have imagined how significant their encounters in 1889 and 1890 were to be.

Early in April, an expansive Robert, addressing the Masons' Labourers, who had recently joined the G.W. & G.L.U., argued for a federation of all unions into 'a large labour army' on the model of the Miners' Federation.[58] He was expressing an idea circulating among the wing of the socialist movement looking to the formation of a 'Labour Party'. Then, on April 16th, he proposed to the Workers' Organising Committee a Bristol May Day march. Such a visual show of labour solidarity no doubt appealed more than the meetings of the Bristol Committee for Promoting the Better Housing of the Poor that Robert was currently attending as the representative of the Gas Workers' Housing Committee. Along with

Helena, Gore and Irving, Robert was pursuing a policy of appeasement with reformers such as Mary Clifford and Mary Talbot. Theoretically he was extending new unionism beyond production, but in actuality a leaflet on Bristol's 'insanitary evils' no doubt seemed somewhat paltry.[59]

As District Secretary of the G.W. & G.L.U. Robert was moving into the wider world of left politics. The decision to celebrate May Day had been made by the socialist movement internationally the previous summer and, by April 1890, two opposing proposals had emerged for the march in London. The anarchist-influenced Socialist League opted for May 1st itself, which was a week day, but most of the large new unions, the London Trades Council and the S.D.F. backed a Sunday march in support of legislation for the eight-hour day. The anarchists, however, would have no truck with Parliament.[60]

Undeterred by the split in London, Bristol's Workers' Organising Committee, helped by friendly members on the Trades Council, Tovey and Vincent, sought a broad consensus by inviting trade unionists, social reformers, radicals and Liberals as well as socialists to take part. Mary Talbot accepted, but Bristol's Liberal MPs all declined. By moving the date to Saturday May 3rd, Bristol secured the flamboyant Radical MP Cunninghame Graham and Eleanor Marx, who, being impoverished, had to request her travel expenses. They sent her 30s, and, deciding this was excessive, she dutifully returned 10s.[61]

On May 3rd around 2,000 May Day demonstrators assembled with their banners at the Ropewalk; gas workers, cotton workers, box, soap and pipe makers, boot and shoe workers, bricklayers, masons, labourers, oil and colour men, potters and tanners, all affected by the unrest of the preceding months. As they marched through the city, onlookers along Old Market Street, Castle Street and Wine Street joined in. Collecting a strong reinforcement of firemen, dockers and seamen at the Drawbridge Hotel, the march wound its way up to Whiteladies Road in Clifton. Mary Talbot and the banner of the Association of Working Women bobbed along in the crowd, and the Bristol Socialist Society, bearing a big red banner designed by Miriam, brought up the rear. Henry Stacy, looking out from his friend James Marshall's upstairs window, compared the procession to 'a serpent', adding cannily, 'but the sting is in its tail'.[62]

On reaching the vast green expanse of Durdham Downs, the demonstrators spread out to listen to Eleanor Marx and Cunninghame Graham make the case for the eight-hour day and call for the election of independent labour candidates. The resolution for a forty-eight-hour week by 'every legitimate means in their power' was carefully worded to include both the parliamentary and the anti-parliamentary left.[63] Tovey, Gore and Gilmore Barnett, all municipal councillors, chaired the platforms. Local speakers included Robert from the G.W. & G.L.U., proud to be on the same platform as Eleanor Marx and impressed by her 'splendid voice and flashing eyes'.[64]

Bristol's first May Day reaffirmed the institutional presence of a labour movement in the city, but it was smaller than the organisers had hoped, forcing Tovey to appeal for funds. Also the miners' agent, William Whitefield, abruptly withdrew, meaning there was no labour candidate to put forward. Whereupon, the pushy but slippery leader of the National Amalgamated Sailors and Firemen's Union, Joseph Havelock Wilson, offered to stand.[65] On May 6th when the Election Committee met to interview Havelock Wilson at 9 Louisa Street, a suspicious 'Miss Born' enquired if he would 'abide by the decision of this Committee?' She took the view that a parliamentary candidate should be a paid labour delegate, rather than an unpaid freewheeling 'representative'.[66] In the event, Wilson, who evaded the question, suffered a humiliating defeat from the Liberal Great Western Cotton Mill magnate, Sir Joseph Weston. Worse, Havelock Wilson's supporters were bombarded with turf and stones thrown by miners and shoemakers.[67] Running labour political candidates, and raising proletarian consciousness, proved more volatile and tricky in practice than in theory.

Robert was blessed with a buoyancy of character, which inclined him to press on to the next eventuality rather than dwelling on past set-backs. Between May 19th and 21st, he was in south London at the Workman's Club in Gye Street, Vauxhall, with James Vickery, representing Bristol, at the first delegate conference of the G.W. & G.L.U. Young 'Bro. Nicol' played a surprisingly vocal and assertive part. On May 19th the Conference Report records him moving that the union should commit itself to obtaining 'the same wage for women as for men, when doing the same work'. It was seconded by Mrs Burgess from the Norwich Women's Branch of the G.W. & G.L.U. and passed onto the rule book with a rider stating that whenever the words 'man', 'him' or 'his' occur, they should be taken to mean 'man or woman'. 'Our Union is of men and women and our Rules apply to both.'[68] It was a significant precedent.

The following day Robert spoke out forcefully against union funds being invested in private companies:

We do not believe in interest, we all have to suffer from this damnable interest-mongering. We object to sweating, and can therefore not profit by the sweating of the sweating companies. At the present time I know we must make a compromise and must invest somewhere. I propose we invest only in Government and Municipal Securities – not that we are ignorant of the fact that the Government to-day is also a sweater, but because we hope one day to control the state, and on that ground can invest in Government stock where we cannot rightly invest in interest-paying Companies.[69]

This proposal seemed fanciful to Robert's trade union mentor Vickery, who asserted that as 'practical Trades Unionists', they had to get the highest possible rate of interest for 'working men'.[70] Nonetheless, Robert's resolution was passed.

He scored another victory when he declared workers should do their utmost to obtain direct representation on all governing bodies, parliamentary and local, and 'heartily support' the 'labour party' in its efforts to obtain such representation.[71] Robert was evidently in accord with Eleanor Marx's efforts to link new unionism with a broad labour political project. The Conference Minutes reveal her displaying an impressive knowledge of the union rule book, as well as skill in cutting through potential log-jams. When Robert wanted the number of members required to form a branch reduced from one hundred to twenty-five, she quickly intervened, saying that branches could make their own by-laws. Robert, along with the other delegates, clearly held her in high esteem. On one issue though his Scot's upbringing and the Celtic nationalist influences he had encountered in Edinburgh resulted in a clash. He spoke in favour of autonomy for the Scots, Irish and Welsh regions and was overruled.[72]

Robert's persuasive qualities stood him in good stead at the conference and he made his mark. However, when the delegates were selected to go to the Trades Union Congress, it was the more experienced and pragmatic Vickery who was chosen to represent the Gas Workers and General Labourers' Union.[73]

Robert's address in the Conference Report is given as 6 Shaftesbury Street, Heath Street.[74] He, Miriam and Helena had moved to a cottage backing on to the Gilliards' home in Lower Eastville. It was comradely and congenial; the Gilliards and their young neighbours used to talk over the garden wall, visit each other and take meals together. They became close friends and though Gilliard continued to admire Miriam, he was aware how she and Robert provoked one another's proclivity for exalted excess:

> They feared nothing! and being heart-strong and head-strong in pursuit of anything they considered to be good, they were unable to constrain themselves to act within the limits of prudence which is necessary of course in all causes, much less could they be repressed by anyone who opposed them.[75]

He watched a 'self-abnegating' Helena exert a 'modulating influence', contriving to check her friend through her 'quiet unobtrusive counsel, silent and loving rebukes diffidently conveyed (as if they were of little consequence & only meant in fun)'. Irving and Baster, who lived in the neighbourhood, frequently dropped by and joined in the discussions. To Gilliard's bemusement, Edward Tuckett Daniell also came to the cottage 'as a kind of friendly visitor'.[76] His grand residence, 'Torryburn', was not too far away.

The move enabled Robert to be closer to the large Stapleton Gas Works just across the river. It also rescued the trio from one of the 'insanitary evils' of 9 Louisa Street. Over time, befriending rats may well have proved an altruistic step too far, even for Helena. However, a new imperative undoubtedly propelled their migration. By May 1890, Miriam was two months pregnant. She had defied propriety on many fronts, but giving birth to a child out of wedlock in Bristol in 1890 was a terrifying prospect. Robert Gilliard later confided to Helen that it would have been 'out of the question' for 'our Socialist women to overturn the conventional tables as Miriam did', yet he felt deeply protective, and so too did his wife Mary. 'My wife, who was one of the purest women who ever lived, often used to speak of her as a person she should like to "hug".'[77] Mary Gilliard may have been pure as snow, but having borne ten children she would have detected the signs of pregnancy. However, love, union and fidelity held strong; Miriam's secret was staunchly guarded.

Still, over the summer, Miriam would have been counting the months, knowing that soon even a modicum of subterfuge would be impossible. Signs of the strain she must have experienced erupt in a letter to her husband written three years later in 1893. Responding to his claim she had 'left the burden of shame' to be 'borne' by others, including himself, Miriam acknowledged she had displayed a 'reserve' over her relationship with Robert, but angrily denied any suggestion of 'shame' on her part.

Accusing her husband of 'an exaggerated self pity', Miriam dismissed external conventions. Had she not 'lived with Robert Nicol for nearly a year in my own city, meeting my fellow-citizens daily in my public work'.[78] Her vindication was the purity of her inner motivation, yet the vehement rage indicates how vulnerable, a proud, pregnant Miriam actually must have been in 1890.

Gilliard regarded Miriam and Robert as 'high strung souls' who could 'brook no restraint'. In combination they blazed as 'fiery enthusiasts (in the best sense) whose vital forces could not be suppressed',[79] however, by the summer of 1890, it must have felt as if the options of the previous autumn were, one by one, closing down.

Like Gilliard, Helena was accustomed to political engagement in less dramatic times, and she simply reverted back to the routines of local activism. She attended a cotton workers' branch meeting with Robert on June 11th and supported the joint work of the Bristol Socialist Society and Christian Socialists by speaking that June in Eastville with Robert Gilliard and Paul Stacy.[80] In the same month, at Trinity Church in Stapleton, she, Watson and Robert Sharland attracted a crowd of two or three hundred people. Helena managed a few remarks on the 'position of women under the present system'. She was forcing herself to become a public speaker.[81]

Accustomed to life not going her way, she had acquired iron self-control and strategic wisdom. Gilliard discerned she was 'no less determined' than Miriam and Robert, but did not drive at difficulties head on as they did. Instead she displayed a considered 'knowledge of the consequences of every act & word of hers'.[82] This mix is evident in Helena's response to a friend in the Women's Liberal Association, who had criticised her for recruiting women into the G.W. & G.L.U. It seems to have been written shortly after Robert's equal pay resolution passed into the union's policy:

> Our union is one of the few unions initiated by men which accords women full representation on its councils, and has included among its objects the obtaining, wherever possible, the same wages for women doing the same work as men. You know I am in favor of men and women working hand in hand wherever practicable, instead of in separate organizations, which tend to favor an unnatural antagonism.[83]

Helena argued that 'Equality and freedom for women is one phase only of an ideal of universal freedom and equality.' Her social vision was organic, the suffering of one part 'injures every individual', and her socialism was based on the premise of a shared responsibility, 'we cannot isolate ourselves from the mass'. She told her B.W.L.A. friend she regarded socialist principles as 'economically incontrovertible' and believed they contained 'spiritual ideals of unity and brotherhood which alone can transmute the materialism of our time'. Stoutly defending her Bristol Socialist Society comrades, Helena insisted that 'Their antagonism is not directed towards individuals of the capitalist or any other class.'[84] She assured her friend, 'I have not taken up a new position without carefully thinking it out. If at any time I see beyond, I shall be prepared to abandon it.' Affirming 'that the only effectual way to convince others of the truth of one's principles, and to bring about the new time, is by living them', and heeding the 'spirit of love', Helena quoted Whitman on the joy of '"being tossed in the brave turmoil of these times"'.[85]

The strike wave had released a new found power in Helena. Her friend Helen would describe this phase in Helena's life as 'one of self-denial and arduous labor', accompanied by 'self-realization and much happiness'.[86]

Gilliard contends that Miriam and Robert had no 'power in themselves to adopt with any continuity, quiet and plodding grooves'.[87] This catches the temperamental difference between them and Helena, but is too sweeping. They did keep trying that summer in Bristol. After the G.W. & G.L.U. conference, Robert, who the Workers' Organising Committee reports as dealing with the minutiae of meetings and accounts, continued to cast around for a political vehicle to promote the aims of new unionism. On June 2nd the *Bristol Mercury* reports him moving a resolution for 'a labour party' at a large meeting chaired by Tovey in the 'Castle Coffee Palace', which led to the formation of the Bristol Labour Emancipation League with a programme of parliamentary representation and municipal reform acceptable to radicals as well as socialists.[88] Moreover, on June 11th Robert was to be heard exhorting the cotton workers 'to have the magic of patience and proceed in a quiet way and not rush into battle at inopportune moments'.[89]

Even more galling, he, Miriam and Helena, found themselves entangled with Bristol's Chamber of Commerce in establishing a Board of Conciliation and Arbitration for the city. On June 12th, Robert, representing the G.W. & G.L.U., along with Miriam and Helena, from the

Dan Irving (Bristol Reference Library)

cottonworkers' and tailoresses' branches, assembled at the Chamber of
Commerce. Several male trade unionists from the previous months' disputes were present, along with Dan Irving (Railway Workers), Gilmore
Barnett (Dockers), Mary Talbot (Bristol Association of Working Women)
and Gertrude Dix (Clifton and Bristol Christian Socialists). After a long
argument, the meeting managed to agree that the Board would be composed of an equal number of workers' and employers' representatives.[90]

In January, arbitration had seemed a good way of preventing disputes from dragging on; by June the initiative had shifted towards the
employers. Moreover, the workers' representatives were split. Some of
Bristol's craft trade unionists were hostile to new unionism. At a follow
up meeting to discuss the proposed Board, attended by Robert, Miriam,
Helena, Gertrude and Dan Irving, their lack of power was revealed.
Efforts by Robert and Irving to ensure that the Board could elect its
chair, as the shoemakers had done in January, were blocked by an alliance
of employers and craft trade unionists; the chairman of the Chamber of
Commerce, W. Dove Wilcox was duly elected.[91]

The constitution of the Bristol Board of Conciliation and Arbitration
met with approval from members of the Chamber of Commerce, from
craft unionists and from the Association of Working Women. Robert,
Miriam, Helena and Gertrude did not add their signatures, but Irving
did. On August 2nd, *The People's Press* duly labelled the Board 'the brat',
and scorned the signatories for 'Licking the Boots of the Capitalists'.
Irving was singled out. 'It seems a pity that such a good fighting union
as the General Railway Workers should connect itself with the brat.'[92]

Irving no doubt would have argued it was necessary to concede to a temporary defeat and continue to resist from within – he was after all an experienced trade unionist. But he was also a proud man and the barb would have struck home. To Robert and Miriam, acceptance of 'the brat' surely appeared as treachery on the part of the Social Democrat from whom they had learned so much. Helena, being both forbearing and pragmatic, remained his friend.

At some point over the course of that summer of 1890 Robert paid a visit to Carpenter's home at Millthorpe. He must have gone North in tumult and Carpenter's wry, sage-like manner, combined with the beauty of the Cordwell Valley, would have been a welcome diversion. Unlike Eleanor Marx, the charismatic Carpenter was sympathetic to the anarchists and, though supportive of new unionism, not particularly interested in the nitty-gritty of labour representation. Already familiar with Neo-Platonic writings on matter and spirit, Carpenter was becoming absorbed in Eastern religious thinking. The visit had a significant impact upon Robert, politically and personally. Carpenter possessed a gift for reassuring comradeship, and Robert quickly established an easy intimacy. Four years later he retained a sensuous memory of 'Fox Lane and the road to Chesterfield for did not Edward C. come home in the dusk with me from Chesterfield one summer evening his arm in mine. And it was sweet!'[93]

It is probable that as a result of this visit Robert met Alexander Ellis and his sister Kate, soon to marry a Whitmanite and Carpenterian enthusiast, Henry Binns. Alexander and Kate were dissident off-shoots from a wealthy Quaker family with business interests in collieries and railways, living at The Gynsills near Leicester. The encounter with Alexander Ellis was to prove of great significance for Robert's future. The repercussions were myriad, both immediately and long term.

After attending Bootham, the Quaker boarding school at York, Alexander Ellis had worked in the collieries as a clerk and later became an auditor. Leicester, though a secularist and Socialist League stronghold, also harboured Swedenborgians, along with several American unorthodox religious transplants including Spiritualists. Instead of following the Radical Liberal trajectory of his father, at twenty-three Alexander inclined towards utopias and heterodox religion. In 1890 he was about to venture off to Australia and then America where he planned to earn a living from journalism.[94] Robert thus made direct contact with someone close to his own age ready to go across the globe.

Miriam, facing personal ignominy and, like Robert, politically dismayed by the obstacles blocking their aspirations, was ready to shake off the dust of the old world. She is recorded as saying 'there was a wider sphere of usefulness in America'.[95] Miriam and Helena 'had dreamed of a pilgrimage to the land of Emerson, Thoreau and Whitman', but Helena had less cause to break her ties with Bristol.[96] She agreed to go because Miriam asked her to, even though leaving her Bristol Socialist Society friends resulted in 'mingled feelings of uncertainty, regret, and hope', and she went with the expectation that at some point she would return.[97] Carpenter may have encouraged their migration, for the American Whitmanite writer, William Sloane Kennedy, maintained that he gave Helena a letter of introduction to Whitman. A meeting with the poet would have been a dazzling prospect, but an ailing Whitman seems never to have replied.[98]

Towards the end of August, when the trio set off from Bristol's Temple Meads station, a mystified Gilliard spotted Miriam's husband among the people bidding them farewell. Gilliard felt the occasion ought to have been tragic. But that was not as it seemed. He was confounded by the tall, cold man and by Miriam's composure: 'I cannot begin to describe her manner, the sadly-sweet, mirthful-melancholy smile.' She was neither bold nor self-assertive towards her husband. Through the haze of his devotion, Gilliard saw Miriam for the last time, infused with 'determination and unalterable ideas', with 'her halo of love and beauty overshadowing it all'.[99]

The train was taking them to the *Majestic* liner in Liverpool docks. On August 20th Miriam was entered on the passenger list as 'Mrs Daniel [*sic*], Marital Status Single.' With nearly two years knocked off her age, she appears as twenty-seven with the occupation of 'Housekeeper'. Robert stated that he was a 'Mechanic' – the first in a long line of fluctuating job descriptions. On arrival in New York, he was demoted to 'labourer', while Miss Bone/Born, described as aged twenty-five instead of thirty, left as a 'spinster' and arrived as a 'servant'.[100] Helena carried with her an unabridged edition of John Bunyan's *Pilgrim's Progress From This World to That Which is to Come: Delivered Under the Similitude of a Dream.* Inscribing her name and the date '1890' on the top right hand of the title page, she kept the book throughout her life.[101]

Their departure evoked tributes from *The People's Press*. Robert was commended for 'the able manner' he had displayed as secretary of the G.W. & G.L.U. For Miriam and Helena there was a heartfelt warmth in the thanks for 'yeoman service in organising the tailoresses and pipe makers'; and for their contribution in the cotton strike, when 'No one toiled harder.'[102] Their legacy would be the space opened for the next tranche of 'new women' who opted for socialism in Bristol: Miriam's sister Mary Wheeler, Katharine St John Conway, Enid Stacy and, of course, Gertrude Dix.

The 'exalted enthusiasm' and 'brave turmoil' of their experiences in Bristol during 1889 and 1890 were so extreme and exceptional that they defied assimilation and analysis. Psychologically, Miriam and Robert were inclined to move on, but Helen notes that even the reflective Helena was never able 'to keep a record of events, and could never in later years recall the details of her life at this period, so as to furnish a consecutive story'.[103]

SIX

New Bearings: America 1890–1892

T he voyage from Liverpool to New York on the SS *Majestic* took just six days. Launched the previous year, the *Majestic*'s maiden voyage had been in April 1890; state of the art wrought iron and steel, she could steam along at the impressive speed of 20 knots carrying Helena, Robert and Miriam, six months pregnant, to the new world.[1] Released from their cramped lurching cabin and dazed by the glaring shock of the city's August heat and cosmopolitan bustle, they wandered into a market, where they came across a huge cannon ball of a fruit. Assuming that such an exotic object must be a rarity, they pounced upon it, lugging it all the way to Cambridge, Massachusetts in their already bulky hand baggage, only to discover that America was a country full of watermelons![2]

Their next revelation crystallised more slowly. They had selected Cambridge as the hub of Transcendentalist enlightenment and, along with other cultural tourists, did indeed trek out from their lodgings to gaze at Concord and Walden Pond, where Helen pictures them delighting in the vivid beauty 'of the autumn foliage and lingering over landmarks grown familiar to them through Thoreau', before plunging sublimely into the 'placid waters' of the Pond.[3] But gradually it became apparent, even to the idealistic trio, that the Cambridge of their imagination did not match reality.

Since Thoreau's day the population of Cambridge had grown from around 8,500 to about 70,000. In 1890, though its core retained an ethos of shaded scholarship and elegant culture, to the east, furniture makers, glass blowers and book binders combined with noxious meat packing plants. To the north, clay pits and brickyards provided employment for Irish immigrants fleeing poverty.[4] Along with the immigrants from the British Isles, the Boston area attracted Italians, Spanish, Portuguese, Armenians, Germans, Russians, Poles. Lost in this great crowd, confused by their abrupt change in circumstance, Miriam, Robert and Helena passed un-regarded, with only one another to rely upon. With no accepted place, or any clear sense of purpose, they had to realign themselves to the strangeness of their surroundings.

The transition was especially sharp for Miriam. On November 3rd she gave birth to a baby girl, named 'Miriam Sunrise', because, in Miriam's words, they were 'hoping her arrival would prove the advent of brighter days'.[5] She was registered under the surname 'Nicol', Robert is there as Robert A. and Miriam becomes Miriam D. turning 'Daniell' into a Christian name.[6]

Miriam, who seems to have previously displayed little inclination towards motherhood, underwent a transformation. Cut off from the meetings, the marches, the speeches, she turned her considerable emotional energy towards Sunrise. Holding the small, helpless bundle of utopia evoked obsessive anxieties and wild conjectures. Helen records: 'With Miriam's intense mother-love went a tendency to conjure up imaginary dangers. Her mind was in constant terror lest some calamity should befall the child.'[7] Infant mortality remained high and some degree of nervousness could be expected from a first-time mother, but Miriam's fears for her baby's health were compulsive, and accompanied by a fixation about cleanliness and contamination. Miriam insisted that the uncarpeted floors of their rooms 'must be scrubbed on hands and knees' every morning.[8] A sacrificial Helena complied.

Helena threw herself into work. Disapproving of parasitical dependence on unearned wealth, she was determined not to ask her father for help. Having resolved that their survival rested upon her, she decided to acquire a practical skill and spent three months without pay in a Waltham printing office in order to learn typesetting. She then worked on a Waltham newspaper, before finding a position in a Boston office. It is unlikely that any of them had given much thought to labour market prospects in migrating to the land of Emerson, Thoreau and Whitman, but Boston and Cambridge with their multiplicity of newspapers, learned journals, books, publishers and printers *did* offer modest opportunities for women. Helena was able to earn around 7 or 8 dollars a week, and, as an educated woman, she could aspire to proof-reading, averaging around 9 dollars and 50 cents, still less than a skilled cloak maker on an aristocratic 11 dollars a week.[9]

Helena told Minnie Southcombe, 'I start from home at 7 a.m. daily, and arrive home at the same time in the evening.' She added, 'My cooking, sewing, scrubbing, correspondence, etc., I get in when I can at odd times.'[10] After scrubbing the floor, walking to work in all weathers, doing a twelve-hour day, reassuring Miriam about Sunrise's well-being, and presumably acting as the main bread-winner, Miriam and Robert expected Helena 'to prepare her own meals after she returned in the evening'.[11] It was an ironic twist of circumstances for a campaigner for an eight-hour day.

Typically, Helena found compensatory joys in her arduous routine. 'I have a three and one-half mile walk each way, passing over the beautiful Charles River, and across the Common, by the lake.'[12] Three evenings a week, she joined fellow commuters on one of Boston's pioneering 'electric cars'. Rapidly replacing the horse-drawn trolleys, these rattled along at speed, leaving no dung in their wake. Helena only indulged so she could study 'book keeping and advanced French' at the High School in Cambridge.[13]

Helena dispensed more sobering advice to young Cousin Minnie: 'If one is really to accomplish anything in one's life-work the first lesson to be learnt is to give up *some* pleasures and concentrate one's energies.' Stressing that work 'done with a view to helping others' would always be 'blessed', she announced, 'We are well and comfortable in our quiet, restful home.'[14] Helen, following the gloss given by Helena, provides a grand rendering: 'After the turmoil, strife, and publicity they had passed through in England they were singularly retiring now and held aloof from all but a few whom kindred interests and warm appreciation of Miriam's intellectual brilliancy had brought within their circle.'[15] By responding to Miriam's plea to journey to America, Helena had become even more isolated than when they had been in St Philip's.

In the notebook she began to keep in 1891 Helena copied out Emerson's poem 'Give all to love; ... obey thy heart; /Nothing refuse'.[16] Regardless of her loving altruism, the circumstances of the trio did accentuate tensions, hinted at in Miriam's testimony, 'To H. Born', written 'with love' in July 1891:

Lena, of all who called me friend in name.
And all who said they loved me more than life,
Who did compete for favour with sweet strife,
And watched me close through long years without blame,
How few at last could judge me by my aim
Or trust me when I cut with spirit knife
Those false ties which but gave me <u>name</u> of wife,
Yet which were making me exist a lie
But you dear sister woman saw beyond
Mere form and custom, and were unafraid,
Hearing the pathos of the human cry,
To stake your reputation as a maid,
And find society in sea and sky
Denied by those you sought, like Christ to aid[17]

Miriam acknowledges her need for Helena, by graciously granting her friend divinity. Helena could dispense with divinity, but she did need to be needed. That tiny edge to the idyll, the 'sister woman' competing for favour, 'with sweet strife', surely refers to Helena's relationship with Robert. But Helena was too principled and too self-controlled to admit her jealousy, and Robert, if inclined to spar, appears to have breezed away grudges.

Robert, as ever, has left few traces. It is not clear whether he actually worked as a mechanic, a labourer, a teacher or a clerk. But in 1894, reminiscing in a letter to Edward Carpenter, Robert says he had 'cared for Walden Pond and Boston Town and dear old red-brick Harvard' because Miriam, 'happy, beautiful and free', was with him.[18] Helen's memoir of Helena, too, mentions 'pilgrimages to Walden afoot, and numerous tramps into the woods of Arlington', referring to 'attendance at lectures open to the public at Harvard'.[19] These lectures may have been the source for Robert's boast in old age that when he 'visited Harvard' during his stay in Cambridge, 'They offered me a professorship. I met Louis Agassiz but he was leaving for South America. I liked him very much. He was kind to me. I met a number of professors. Nice chaps.'[20] Robert may have met Harvard professors, but they were hardly likely to make him one of their number, moreover the Swiss-born naturalist Agassiz had died in 1873. Robert had become so accustomed to inventing his own life that over time he probably came to believe his own fantasising.

One acquaintance though was real enough: the artist, J.W.A. Scott. In 1896, Robert would ask Carpenter to send the popular landscape painter copies of *Towards Democracy* and the four 'sex pamphlets', *Woman*, *Sex-Love*, *Marriage* and *Homogenic Love*. Scott lived at the corner of Pleasant and Cottage Street, quite close to the Green Street apartment Robert, Miriam and Helena were renting in 1891. Robert also mentions to Carpenter a young, aspiring artist called Harris Osborn, with whom he made friends while in Cambridge.[21]

These artistic contacts tally with Helen's account of Miriam's frequent visits to Boston Art Museum, then in Copley Square, and her vain attempts to earn money through 'decorative painting' without any notion of how to market her work. Other spare moments from her all-consuming anxiety about Sunrise were spent writing 'poems, sketches, short stories, essays'. According to Helen, these were mostly far too 'radical' to make 'acceptable copy for the average editor', so Miriam simply stored them away.[22]

A letter from Miriam to Enid Stacy, written in October 1891 and suffused with esoteric mysticism, indicates why Miriam might have faced problems selling her wares. Since Miriam and Robert had emigrated, Stacy had become a member of the Socialist Society and the Clifton and Bristol Fabian Society, which had emerged from the Christian Socialists. As well as being active on the Workers' Organising Committee, she had taken over as honorary secretary of the Association for the Promotion of Trade Unionism among Women and was becoming an effective

Enid Stacy
(Bristol Reference Library)

speaker at outdoor and indoor meetings.[23] Evidently feeling that she was following in Miriam's political footsteps, she had sent Miriam a paper she had written. This could have been her lecture on 'The Russian Nihilist Movement', delivered to the Bristol Socialist Society in February 1891 describing how an underground of terror had arisen as a result of persecution, or a new one she was preparing on 'Women, Work and Wages'.[24] Both would have been topics likely to engage Miriam a year before, but now she responded only with a cursory 'We like to keep in touch with home matters' and a conventional aside about love to 'comrades'.[25]

She proceeds to adopt the voice of a transmigratory prophetess: 'I wish you to know I stand often by you – am near you – (waiting till you see me!).' In an oblique, uneasy reference to the scandal that still shuddered on in Bristol, Miriam pronounced: 'We are not unconscious of each other by any means though for the present silence rules our tongues.'[26] Disillusioned with the democratic hopes of her socialist past, she has acquired a mysterious calling as a member of a female elect, destined to free women despite themselves, and she addresses Stacy as an acolyte:

> I have a deep faith that some day we may work together for the emancipation of woman; not from mere wage slavery or from economic disability but from real fetters. Her dethronement from her high birth right is but a symbol of the general materialism of today – of the descent of the soul of man – the earth bound spirit into matter. We, who are women, have to set our faces sternly to the task of unheeding the poisoned arrows bent skilfully towards us from those we seek to aid. And with no temporary windy impulse, but with everlasting vital enthusiasm we must free ourselves to render her free.[27]

Miriam's aspirations for women's fulfilment in a new moral world are expressed in spiritual terms. The mystical orientation already incipient while she was in Bristol has moved into the ascendant. Miriam's inchoate letter becomes intelligible as an expression of an overwhelming heart-hunger for an alternative to a mechanistic materialism; it also resonates with a specifically gendered need. Creative self-hood and active individual agency were psychologically as well as practically difficult for late nineteenth-century women, reared to subordinate their own desires through service to others. Reworking esoteric knowing by asserting femininity as love and 'Woman' as the means of redemption could offer a powerful source of legitimation.[28]

It is not clear whether Miriam was calling upon Stacy to join a particular religious group, or simply drawing eclectically upon a range of the heterodoxies flourishing in Cambridge and Boston during the early 1890s. Among the fissiparous contenders for truth were Theosophists, Spiritualists, Esoteric Christians, plus followers of Thomas Lake Harris and of an aspiring community leader who had engrossed several of Harris' tenets, Hiram E. Butler. Butler and his Boston adherents formed the Boston Esoteric Publishing Company and a journal called *The Esoteric*, before departing in the summer of 1891, with a handful of the faithful, for Applegate, in Placer County, California, amid recriminations from the Theosophists.[29]

Miriam urges Stacy: 'Dear Comrade let us if we think we see higher heights and purer lights than another not shun that climbing Soul on its low level but bend to point the way we take, in loving reason.' Intimating that Stacy might demur, she adds, 'No petty superficial difference must delay us from uniting on our underlying agreement.' Miriam proffers the unbounded natural beauty she had found in America, 'our lakes pure deep broad, and … our woods, wild odourous [*sic*] vast', as an entry into another dimension of perception. Infused by the splendour of a Massachusetts fall, Miriam relates how amid 'peerless sunlight', the 'blazing woods undulating in orange waves to a blue horizon' were imprinted with decay. Yet Miriam sees 'Autumn' as 'the apotheosis of the year' revealing the 'real beauty of Death'. She insists that death is not 'a spectre, a skeleton, a grinning and icy terror, a black phantom of the night in which we grope'. Instead it is 'the Friend of the triumphant discerner of the meaning of Life', able to lead 'to new light and love'. A fascination with the 'fugitive elusive luminous tints of Death', as a means of 'shattering the false curtain of sense', recurs in Miriam's later poetry and short stories.[30]

In this strange, revelatory communication to Stacy, Miriam asks: 'Will you not take part in our plans for England? We could move the world if we write.' She ends her letter with:

> Once long ago one took me by the hand and for ever removed the power of pain to hurt me – Life too, so full as it seemed of jarring notes – became a harmony: I can also give you the secret if you will let me. Only in handing it to others does it yield its best to us.
>
> Yours in deed
> Miriam[31]

Miriam's preoccupation with achieving harmony through occult divination held no attraction for Stacy, for whom individual development was integrally connected to creating a socialist co-operative commonwealth. Nevertheless, Miriam lingered as a sufficiently significant figure for the younger woman to keep this letter.

In Boston, over the course of 1891, Miriam and Robert encountered a strand of political and social radicalism which prioritised the personal autonomy of the individual – the Individualist or Philosophical Anarchism of the group around Benjamin Tucker and his paper *Liberty*. From January 1892, Miriam's writings start to be published in *Liberty*, while Robert's name and address appears on an undated list of the Boston Anarchist Club, which Tucker had helped to found in 1887.[32] It is not clear whether Robert joined the Club or was associated more loosely as a contact, but Tucker and the Liberty circle were to be very important to Miriam.

Born in 1854, Benjamin Tucker was in his late thirties when they met, and the key figure in a milieu that would have intrigued Miriam. Brought up in a prosperous Quaker family and exposed to American reform ideas from his youth, he had imbibed the arguments of the radical abolitionist, Garrison, and the Transcendentalist, Emerson. He studied Mill, Darwin, Huxley and the anti-statist Spencer at New Bedford's Friends Academy before going on to the Massachusetts Institute of Technology in Cambridge. Becoming convinced of the need for self-ownership and individual sovereignty, he was drawn towards Spencer's assertion that liberty had to be compatible with respect for the freedom of others.[33]

In the early 1870s, Tucker came across campaigners for economic equality in the New England Labor Reform League in Boston and there he met the free-thinker and fearless sexual radical Ezra Heywood, who edited *The Word*. Through Heywood and the Labor Reform League Tucker encountered the veteran abolitionist William B. Greene, a follower of the French pioneer of anarchism, Pierre-Joseph Proudhon; and Josiah Warren, who had created the libertarian community 'Modern Times' near New York in 1851. Greene and Warren persuaded Tucker that root and branch financial reform and the equitable exchange of labour were vital aspects of individual freedom. Though Tucker concurred with the English Individualist, Auberon Herbert, in distrusting the state, he differed from Herbert and the small band of Individualists in Britain in believing that the cost of making goods should decide their price.[34]

Benjamin R. Tucker, ca. 1887. Studio portrait by Falk, New York (Labadie, Special Collections Library, University of Michigan)

Tucker thrived on controversy, upsetting some of his own supporters by dismissing natural rights and inclining instead towards Max Stirner, the German author of *The Ego and His Own: The Case of the Individual Against Authority* (1844). A fellow anarchist, William Walstein Gordak, described the editor of *Liberty* as 'that glittering icicle of logic'.[35] But Tucker was open to dissent. He published the Fabian statist, George Bernard Shaw as well as Kropotkin, despite regarding his approach to anarchism as too communistic. He set up an exchange between *Liberty* and *Commonweal*, joining all the other irritated correspondents who complained about the Socialist League's inefficient mailings. Welcoming visiting British radicals, he took a special pleasure in convincing socialists and Kropotkinite anarchist communists of the superiority of the Individualists' approach. Disputatious in print and a nervous speaker in public, he could be warm and affable in small gatherings.[36]

Like Miriam, Tucker opposed violence, while admiring the bravery of the Nihilists' struggle against Czarism, publishing Stepniak, along with the influential novel *What's to be Done?* (1863) by N.G. Chernyshevsky, which upheld the application of reason to domestic and sexual life in the revolutionary movement. Tucker's intransigence, which earned him the sobriquet of 'plumb-liner', would have appealed to Miriam. In 1881 he had defied the ban on Walt Whitman's unexpurgated *Leaves of Grass*. On sex, Tucker was more circumspect, unlike the outspoken American proponents of free love, Ezra and Angela Heywood or Moses Harman,

who were prepared to face prison on charges of obscenity. Tucker's radicalism nevertheless encompassed the civil and personal liberties that were
so vital to Miriam.[37]

The breadth of Tucker's views on women's emancipation would have
been equally inviting. In 1892 *Liberty* advertised *The Story of an African
Farm* – the novel by the 'new woman' writer, Olive Schreiner, a friend
of Carpenter and former love of Havelock Ellis – as 'A work of remarkable power, beauty and originality'. Tucker published the utopian story
of woman-power, *A Strike of a Sex* by George Noyes Miller (1891), as
well as the perceptive *The Rights of Women and the Sexual Relations: An
Address to an Unknown Lady Reader* (1892), by the German émigré revolutionary Karl Heinzen. Culturally exploratory, he initiated translations
of Tolstoy, Zola, the German Stirnerite poet, John Henry Mackay, and a
'Tendency Novel', *The Rag-picker of Paris*, by the sharp-eyed observer of
French bohemianism and class inequality, Félix Pyat.[38]

But Tucker's trump card was undoubtedly *Liberty* itself; the journal
offered Miriam an outlet for all that pent-up creativity.

Miriam and Robert's new association with Tucker coincided with
Helena's decision in 1892 to pay a visit to Britain. Most probably she
missed her Bristol socialist friends; perhaps too she wanted to break
away from jockeying with Robert for Miriam's favour. Even so, her loyalties remained painfully divided, for America now held not only her
beloved Miriam, but Sunrise, who was just learning to walk, stump-
ing resolutely along. That February, aware how deeply Helena loved the
little girl, Miriam scribbled a note on a scrap of paper in large emphatic
handwriting:

> Dear Helena
> Stumpy & me
> Wants you to be
> Quick back
> from England
> Yours
> Miriam[39]

Helena's Bristol homecoming was unlikely to have been particularly
comfortable. Already estranged from her father, she now had a new step-
mother to meet, for after his daughter departed he had married again.

The house Helena knew was no more, for her father and his new wife, Maria Jane Born, were now living at 1 Keswick Buildings, in Clifton.[40] Moreover she would have found the Bristol socialists struggling against hostility, not only from employers and the police but from some of the cultured elite. Enid Stacy was soon to endanger her own teaching position by supporting the 'sweet girls' at Sanders factory.[41] Helena pasted a sardonic rhyme by the socialist solicitor, Edward J. Watson, a friend from new unionist days, into her scrapbook, along with a sentimental verse by Katharine St John Conway. If Helena listened to gossip, she would have heard that Conway was lodging, somewhat uneasily, with Dan Irving and his ailing wife, Clara, while Miriam's two younger sisters had moved into 'Torryburn' with Edward Tuckett Daniell.[42]

Helena was reading Carpenter's *Towards Democracy*, Part III, published in spring 1892. She carefully copied out long sections into her notebook, fastening upon 'To Thine Own Self Be True', in which Carpenter admonishes 'patience … till the season of liberation', promising, 'when the love comes which is for you it will turn the lock easily and loose your chains'.[43] Her attention was caught too by his poem 'The Secret of Time and Satan', which subverts conventional boundaries of good and evil through an inner knowledge of self. Carpenter's Satan lands 'Feet first', standing magnificent, 'erect, dark-skinned, with nostrils dilated with passion – / (In the burning intolerable sunlight …)'.[44] He annihilates dichotomies:

> The ascetics and the self-indulgent divide things into good and evil – as it were to throw away the evil;
> But things cannot be divided into good and evil, but all are good so soon as they are brought into subjection.[45]

Despite the wrench of leaving Miriam and Sunrise, Helena's trip to Britain renewed her confidence in herself. It also confirmed her love of ideas and learning. In July she made her way up to Edinburgh to attend Patrick Geddes' 'Summer School of Art and Science', which had grown out of the vacation courses for pupil teachers.[46] The University Extension Movement's scheme of peripatetic lecturers was labelled the 'University on Wheels', but Geddes' version took place on foot.[47] The students tramped not only through the streets of Edinburgh, but over to Dunfermline and up the Pentland Hills, enabling Geddes to apply his approach of 'working from the concrete to the abstract', freshening students minds through 'observation' and 'impressions' with the aim of encouraging independent thought.[48]

That 1892 Summer Meeting ran from late July through August. Helena was in her element, studying sociology alongside biology with Geddes and taking Thomson's zoology course. Helen describes Helena's 'copious notes', but it was Geddes' 'keen insight and human sympathy' for 'social and economic problems' that truly inspired her.[49] Geddes, who was still warning students against being drawn into 'any one narrow groove of thought and research', offered a sociology syllabus that began with 'Actual Life Around Us (What is going on?)'. Next came 'Analysis of Activities. (How does Social Life go on?)'. This was followed by 'Social Statics. (Institutions as they are)'; 'Social Evolution (Whence are we? And wither tending?)'. Geddes concluded with 'Practical Economics and Ethics', to which he added Chernyshevsky's question, 'What is to be Done?'[50]

She met a fellow spirit in an American, Virginia E. Graeff, who was similarly animated by Geddes' vision of the learning process. Writing in the American University Extension Society's journal, Graeff praised Geddes' combination of 'accuracy' on 'details' with his 'breadth', saying he was able to bring the 'scientific knowledge of the specialist, in harmony with the general knowledge of the citizen of the world'. She was especially impressed by the Summer School's 'translation of thought into action'. Its motto was 'Vivendo Discimus' – 'We Learn by Living' – which she liked, but proposed adding the dictum of the German child-centred kindergarten pioneer, Friedrich Froebel, 'We Learn Through Doing'.[51]

Helena undoubtedly accompanied Graeff and the other students to socials at the Geddes' home in James Court. But, as usual, she stayed on the side-lines. In response to a later enquiry from Helen, one of the organisers, Kate Crooke, retained only a dim memory of 'a woman of great social enthusiasm' and wondered if Anna Geddes could recall more, 'I did not get to know her intimately as I believe Miss Graeff did.'[52]

Helena formed another new friendship in Edinburgh that summer with the Secularist, John Mackinnon Robertson, who Miriam's brother, Robert Mortimer Wheeler, admired. But if Carpenter's name came up they surely clashed. In April 1892, the plain-speaking Robertson reviewed *Towards Democracy*, Part III, and was *not* impressed. Sniffing religiosity in a new guise, he wanted to know why 'Mr Carpenter' chose to address his readers 'like a fakeer [sic], rather than a cultured Englishman'. Robertson dismissed the Whitmanite style caustically as the 'chopping up of ragged lumps of language by way of separate paragraphs'.[53]

Nonetheless Carpenter continued to be Helena's lodestar. She copied his words into her notebook, 'If to gain another's love you are untrue to yourself then you are untrue to the person whose love you would gain.' While Miriam and Robert moved into Tucker's Individualist orbit, Helena was sufficiently impressed by the anarchist communism of Kropotkin to cut out a review of *La Conquête du Pain* (1892), marking a passage on the need for revolutions to extend beyond changing 'Governments' through 'associations for free labour' that would transform production and daily life.[54] Relishing this rare period of space and time for reading and thinking, Helena lingered on in Britain.

Meanwhile Miriam, Robert and Sunrise left Cambridge for the wider vistas of New York. Tucker had taken a job with the *Engineering Magazine* and moved *Liberty* with him. Miriam, who had concluded that she, too, needed to acquire a trade, planned to learn typesetting. She and Robert were to help produce *Liberty*.[55] The ideas Miriam encountered in the Liberty circle made explicit her critique of marriage and provided her with an ideological justification for the self-ownership she sought. Proximity to the journal provided a glorious opportunity for Miriam to release the store of stories and poems swirling through her mind as she looked after Sunrise. She blossomed.

Her first story, 'A Daughter of the Gods', was a moral allegory about the corrupting effect of money and repressive sexual hypocrisy upon a farming family. First they cast out a servant who becomes pregnant, leading Miriam to ask how a man could 'leave a woman to bear the brunt of shame alone' and how 'sister women can combine to be like iron arrowheads to pierce the one who differs from them?' Rejecting the rich suitor selected for her, the daughter Cora, a true Romantic heroine, 'tall and straight and supple' with white skin and 'soft blue-black hair in waving clouds drawn back from her chiselled forehead', acts decisively. Taking 'a long black cloak' she plunges into the Charles River. A sole, understanding voice delivers Miriam's message on sexual relations: 'Many who pass judgement on her are yielding their bodies not from love, or honest sexual passion, a healthy rampant animalism, but from money under the cloak of marriage, which screens many a real adultery and lust.'[56]

Sardonic humour makes her second allegory, 'The Un-Henly Hen', less mechanically didactic. The hens in the coop turn against 'the impudent baggage', a 'blue stocking' hen who stands 'staring at the sky instead of scratching the ground like an honest hen'. The gossips concur that she does it to attract attention, that she aspires to crow like cocks. Only a little bantam speaks up for her. Why worry about her becoming a bad wife 'for she is not such a fool as to get married under present conditions'.[57] Miriam knew women who broke with convention were not simply condemned by men, but by other women.

Allegory enabled Miriam to stretch beyond simply protesting against present circumstances; dreams could turn into revelations. In the nightmarish 'The Black-Caps', published by *Liberty* in May 1892, her brain feels like a kicked skull; she is taken to an icy hill where she fancies her blood congeals. Losing consciousness, she awakens in 'The Old Theatre', where the sufferings of humanity appear before her. She sees Christ on the cross, for subverting the 'social order by teaching the divinity and equality of men'; the Nihilist, 'Sophia Petrovskaia', condemned as a 'Terrorist' and sentenced to execution; while the blood of the Chicago anarchists' accused of the Haymarket Bombing splashes upon 'those around them with crimson stains'. Miriam, steeped in the history of Protestant martyrs' blood as the seed of faith, foresees the growth of 'Anarchy'.[58]

Miriam's vision of anarchy challenges the sexual as well as the political order. When a syphilitic young prostitute is dragged into 'The Old Theatre', she writes, 'As long as Love is denied or fettered, Lust will obtain entrance into the Soul.' Her allegory contests any clear-cut ethical divide between 'good' and 'evil'. Evil lies in disharmony and 'disproportion'. In the words of the 'sinewy', satanic 'guide', 'God' is 'Love and Intelligence, or Heat and Light, or Female and Male, a dual principle forever working rhythmically in the Universe'. Miriam's quill becomes the trumpet calling the 'People' to the day of 'Love and Light and Liberty'. Refusing the convention of 'those tiresome dream stories' in which the narrator awakes, Miriam, the seer, challenges the world as it is from another dimension, writing from a 'tear jar ... of things as seen from the air circle'.[59] Like many utopians, she adopted allegorical fantasy in order to expand the possibilities of expression. Yet the form reveals her sense of helplessness in relation to reality; the wrongs Miriam depicts are so cosmic that any specific efforts appear negligible.

Over the spring and early summer of 1892, Miriam's poems in *Liberty* examine a dilemma closer to home: how to *combine* love and liberty. In 'Form and Spirit' she writes, 'Love is a beam of light' not to be caught or seized. Nor can it be consciously comprehended:

> Love is like a filbert nut
> Which, if you eat the kernel out,
> Keeps its life a secret shut.[60]

The June 25th issue of *Liberty* contained two poignant poems. In 'Epigram', on the first page, Miriam states:

> I live to love, I love to live,
> But love than life is stronger.
> And now my love is dead, I'd give
> My life to live no longer.[61]

The last page of the same issue carried 'The Price of Love':

> I loved him; he had made more sweet
> The wine of Life for me;
> I loved him, but the price of Love
> Was loss of Liberty.
>
> He liked me not for what I was,
> Or what I hoped to be;
> He had an ideal self, and gave
> It me as livery.
>
> I wore it, was his lackey, dumb
> For his dear sake one year;
> And then the dread of losing him
> Was lost in larger fear.
>
> 'You love me not; I am the peg
> On which you would suspend
> Yourself; a glass to mirror you
> An adjunct, not an end.
>
> You have a gilded cage, with seed
> And water set for me;
> I droop and pine; how can I sing,
> With birthright to be free?

You worship your own image; I
Am needed but for shrine;
See for your sake, I starve my soul,
Equal with yours, divine.'

He smiled, remote, amused, as one
Upon Olympus set,
And answered: 'Why think silly thoughts?
Kiss me, and then forget.'

To him one day I said: 'Anew
Let's fashion marriage.' He
Regarded me as mad. The price
Of Love was Liberty.

He loves me not, not ever did,
Methinks; nor can I cry.
Since I belong no more to him,
But have my Liberty.

And yet I can conceive a Love
That seeks not to possess.
That is itself, and lets you be
Yourself, not more nor less.[62]

These two poems resonate with Miriam's own experiences, the emotions springing directly off the page. She is, moreover, asking a startlingly modern question: can desire be emancipated? Ahead of the early twentieth-century feminist avant-garde, she strains to envisage how advanced women influenced by free love might embrace passion without losing a fragile new autonomy. In both poems Miriam tethers feelings and thoughts tightly together and the contained tension enables her to find a form that works. However, in 'Toleration', the following month, an abstract poem in which she tries to subvert fixed horizons of knowledge, the link is missing and the style awkward.[63]

Miriam experimented with differing forms of writing according to her subject matter. Like other 'Gilded Age' writers she adopted a colloquial manner and a jogging rhythm in her verses protesting, albeit pessimistically, against inequality and wage labour. In July 1892, several men died when Carnegie's steel plant at Homestead saw a pitched battle between Pinkerton detectives and locked out workers defending their right to unionise. He might be Dunfermline's benefactor, but his firm was out to break the union, which had secured an increase in wages. In Miriam's poem he is depicted as 'The Bandit' on 'his prancing steed', bequeathing death and misery. In 'Awake' and 'The Coach and Four', the people are duped by the 'tinsel' of grandeur. In 'Modern Trade' the hounds are 'Necessity', and the hares can think of nothing except escape. 'Any Worker to Any Strikers' is similarly pessimistic about revolt. Striking brings 'no lasting cure', and 'The strike is lost as strikes must be'.[64]

In contrast, when depicting a utopia beyond present imagining in the poem 'In Robes of Anarchy', Miriam reverts to the imagery of her mystical writings. 'Truth' is first symbolised as the 'Sun', manifesting herself, 'With hair of dazzling gold and eyes that burn!' Then, no longer 'trim-clad', it shape-shifts, and, Miriam writes, 'I see/You in wind-driven robes of Anarchy'.[65]

Scattered among these overtly propagandist poems are evocative protestations against personal constraint. In 'Pastures', reminiscent of those Durdham Down sheep, Miriam muses:

> Life tethered me upon a globe to graze,
> Sweet herbs, green grass to nibble all around,
> But still, I tugged my cord, and strained my gaze
> To see beyond horizon of my ground.[66]

Another poem, 'Chains', describes struggling against the bonds of religion, state power, materialism and conventional love. Miriam exposes the hurt of contempt.

'Men loathed me as a reptile thing/Who strove towards a bird's wing'. Casting off the bonds of love proved the hardest:

> so slight
> A chain, so sweet a pain, the Night
> Shook bats about me when I brake
> Love's bonds for freedom's sake.

Exhausted, the poet is left with a final, unassailable restraint, 'Necessity'.[67]

Isolated for so long as a poet, Miriam restlessly sought differing forms, aware that she needed advice on how to develop her craft. A breakthrough occurred that July after her review of 'The Gothic Minster', by Harry Lyman Koopman, brought her into contact with the author. At thirty-two, Koopman was already a published poet. He had translated some of John Mackay's poems from German for Tucker, and his own work appeared frequently in *Liberty*. In 1892, after working in libraries, he was studying for an MA at Harvard. Miriam praised Koopman's stylistic skills and approved his intimation of new life immanent in the everyday. However, she censured a cameo of a worker happily wandering by the Minster with his children; 'The fruit of energy', Miriam informed the poet, should be 'conserved for work and not expended in sexuality, or exhausted by the toil of procreating and rearing a family'. She also sternly decrees that Gothic relics 'emit odours of dissolution' and hence were not to be regarded simply as aesthetic. Referring the American poet to Carpenter's 'York Minster' in *Towards Democracy*, Miriam notes the contrast between the magnificence of the building and the 'pinched faces' of the people in the surrounding streets, 'The Church has failed to meet the growing needs of Humanity.'[68] Koopman took her criticism on the chin, sending her a copy of a collection of his poems.

Miriam continued to spin off fragments of allegorical prose. 'Not in Hell' features a 'coarse, voluptuous' Mrs Flesh, the embodiment of materiality, and a truth-telling Satan who confesses that the Chicago Anarchists 'did not belong' with him in Hell.[69] In 'You Positively Must' and 'You Must Not', Miriam ridicules coercive custom, beef is forced on the vegetarian, and the artist warned not to wear a 'red necktie' in case he might be suspected of anarchism.[70] The tone of 'Conjugal Bliss' on September 24th is more pointed. When Tom complains about Jessie's 'chum', Ellen, visiting, he implies that the house is not theirs but his. When his wife retorts, he urges her '"Be reasonable, you are always extreme"'. Jessie's response sounds suspiciously like Miriam: '"I might earn as good a living as I desire if I spent my time and strength in printing or teaching, instead of in bringing forth and rearing our children and doing the housework etc."'[71]

Instead of engaging in a debate on how to put a value on domestic labour and child-care, Tom, who appears to be Scottish, tries flattery: '"Your chap loves his wee wife"'. Jessie is unyielding; realising what she had '"thought was gold is only brass"', she tells Tom:

'I am a slave. I, who am your acknowledged equal in learning and accomplishments, failing the muscle, have to knuckle under, deceive you, or go. Which of the three ways, the first two so well-worn, the third so lonesome, thorny, and untried, I take, remains to be proved but – '.

Exit Tom, banging the door and whistling 'Yankee Doodle'.

Miriam, oscillating between pinnacles of hope and abysses of despair, boundless and life-affirming one moment, censorious and stringent the next, was, indeed, always 'extreme'. Moreover, she was the mother of a toddler and desperate to write. This was not the kind of woman Robert's upbringing had prepared him for. In the abstract he might favour women's emancipation, but it is unlikely that responsibility for domestic work and child-care figured significantly in such a schema.

Helena's absence would have exposed the impractical couple to material pressures, for there is no evidence of Robert being in regular employment. He had abandoned medicine for literature; abandoned literature for Miriam, abandoned his job in Bristol for America and now he was stuck without any particular place for himself. Miriam, meanwhile, was once again acquiring celebrity. It is not inconceivable that Robert would respond to incipient signs of Ibsen's Nora in Miriam by whistling 'Yankee Doodle'.[72]

Even though Miriam had found recognition and affinity through Tucker and *Liberty*, it was not too long before they clashed. Both parties being 'plumb-liners', it was short and sharp. Their dispute was provoked by another protégé of Tucker's, William Bailie, who had arrived in Boston during 1891. The new immigrant, a basket maker born in Belfast in 1866, was already a veteran left activist. While living in Manchester he had been drawn to Secularism, and then to the Marxist Social Democratic Federation, before moving towards the anti-authoritarianism of the Socialist League. Inspired by Morris' anti-statist socialism and then Kropotkin's anarchist communism, he knew both Carpenter and Unwin. Although he, too, had been involved in new unionism, Miriam and Robert did not meet him until they were in Boston.[73]

Miriam may have felt a twinge of irritation over Tucker's interest in William Bailie, who was allowed a great deal of space in the paper, but on 25 June 1892, an article by him in *Liberty*, 'Bursting a Bubble', really vexed her. Pricking at the 'hubris' of the type of reformer who 'believes he has a mission, and that self-sacrifice is its primary condition', he warned how the 'fire and enthusiasm' of idealists could turn to ash, 'as the cold truth forces itself upon them, … that the people thank them not'. Miriam's revered sacrificial Nihilists failed to impress him: 'We must be willing to discard enthusiasm, vain hopes, false theories.' Ireland and the Manchester Socialist League had dented William Bailie's faith in 'rapid transformations, and a quick-coming millennium'. He had witnessed the consequences of burn out. 'Not to die, but to live, not to suppress, but to realise and expand, should be our endeavour.'[74]

The antithetical views of the Irish Mancunian unsettled the core of Miriam's certainties. She responded with 'Enthusiasm', an angry poem in defence of 'The creative instinct Ardor', in which she sneers at 'Puritans' and 'sober Quakers' who 'Crushed life's forces' as well as those content with 'coarse sense pleasures' who 'smoke and breed and feed their clay'. Miriam contrasts both with an image of creative energy, the 'virile youth' who 'still has desire' and thus a chance to find 'life's well-spring'. 'Art', asserts Miriam, is 'enthusiasm's child'.[75] This was her coup de grace and she may well have expected Tucker, the experimental publisher, to concur. By invoking enthusiasm, she was tapping rich Romantic currents within nineteenth-century writing while touching on older forms of religious fervour.[76]

Tucker the man of culture, however, differed from Tucker the political thinker. 'I fully share Miriam Daniell's enthusiasm for enthusiasm', he declared in an editorial headed 'Picket Duty', but warned, 'The most horrible acts of tyranny that stain the world's history were the work of … enthusiasts.' Against dramatic stances, he advocated 'quiet, patient, steadfast, unshakeable determination', even if this meant it 'lost its froth and foam and bubble (and mayhap, alas! its sparkle also)'.[77]

Miriam did not, of course, take kindly to being told to calm down and could never abide anyone lecturing her. She now took on Tucker as well as young William Bailie. This really was upping the stakes. *Liberty*, it was true, was packed with debates; but Tucker held the ring. Moreover, while the journal was committed to women's individual freedom, only Sarah Elizabeth Holmes writing as 'Zelm' in 1888 had contested male contributors' attitudes to women, and even she had not confronted Tucker himself.[78]

Miriam assumed a tone of breezy defiance. Even though Tucker pretended to be just whispering 'in her ear', she knew this was no whisper, but the word of male authority. His allusion to 'froth … foam and bubble', and the gallant reference to 'sparkle', must have irked her. On 10 September 1892, Miriam sparkled sharply back, informing 'Mr Mentor' that his 'whisper was unnecessary'; she was perfectly aware how enthusiasm could 'be a strong devil as well as a smart angel'. He was, moreover, apprised that his 'flat beverage' did not interest her one iota. She preferred to stick with the 'foam and bubble' variety; an intense healthy life, in her view, could afford to be 'exuberant'.[79] Miriam had no compunction about challenging masculine hubris from the moral high ground of the Victorian angel of the hearth, while aiming below the belt. In a sideways swipe at her rival, she declared that if enthusiasm was to be discarded, 'there is but one means to that end, asceticism, – which I can scarcely think Mr Bailie would advocate'.[80] William, who had married young, was the father of a growing family.

Aware that in challenging Benjamin Tucker she was in combat with 'a giant', Miriam reached for aesthetic cover.[81] A woman embracing 'enthusiasm' signified a display of femininity out of control, which could be easily marginalised. Miriam needed to assert female *power* amid passion, and she selects not Blake but 'Michael Field', stating that in praise of enthusiasm, 'he has written a long classic drama thereon entitled Callirrhoë'.[82] Miriam's choice of this 1884 reworking of a Greek myth is intriguing on several counts.

The plot weaves together sensuous longing, love, resistance, sacrifice, sublime excess and the strength of female self-determination against the odds. The result is an obliquely subversive allegory about gender. Callirrhoë desires both the Dionysian priest Coresus and the Maenad, Nephele, yet she rejects their new religion of excess and transgression and thus is condemned. Yet, at the moment when she is to be sacrificed, Coresus, true to *his* love for *her*, turns the knife on himself. Whereupon, in obverse renunciation, she chooses to give herself to Dionysius as a passionate Maenad, then takes the sacrificial knife and entering a wood, stabs herself.[83]

'Michael Field's' verse drama, published in London and Clifton, was well received by critics, until Robert Browning revealed that two *women* were the actual authors. It was not unusual for women writers to adopt male pseudonyms, but it was somewhat surprising to have an aunt and her niece collaborating on erotic works of literature. Moreover, when their secret was exposed, Katharine Bradley and her niece Edith Cooper were living in an ardent union in Bristol, where both supported women's suffrage and Bradley was the honorary secretary of Clifton's Anti-Vivisection Society, to which James Livett Daniell also belonged. By 1890, 'Michael Field' was being called 'she' by reviewers.[84] Was Miriam being loyal to their assumed identity in using 'he', or simply ignorant of *Callirrhoë's* true authorship?

Miriam's parting shot also drew on her wide reading of English literature, by quoting from Samuel Butler's seventeenth-century satire *Hudibras*. Comparing herself to a yeoman who wore a resplendent purple velvet patch on his fustian clothing to mark the sacred spot where he had been kicked by a 'live lord', Miriam announced that she, too, knew what it was to be 'kicked until they can feel whether a shoe be Spanish or neat's leather'. She added, 'Some like myself … will appreciate the delicacy of your mental kicking; and besides, are we not always too happy when we of the common herd come in contact with a lordly foot.'[85]

Her opponent parried with a scathing psychological metaphor of Niagara, 'a very shallow stream, capable by itself of nothing but ruin (and beauty)'. The image begins to pull Tucker into Miriam's metaphorical mind-set and he quickly steadied himself with a reference to Proudhon. Insisting that 'Anger from the feeling of oppression' was not sufficient, Tucker advocated a 'controlled intensity' deriving 'peace from the knowledge of the truth'. The search must be for 'that tranquillity of soul which arises from the clear perception of evil and its cause, and which is much more powerful than passion and enthusiasm'.[86]

Back she came on 17 September 1892, with a letter headed, 'Enthusiasm and Tranquillity'. Far be it from her to suggest that 'passion should not be controlled'. Nevertheless, she remained adamant that enthusiasm was not be 'crushed or discarded'. It was 'a biological fact; … the Love force from which our advancement as well as our degradation may proceed, the raw material for good or evil'. Again Miriam quotes 'Michael Field' in her defence of Romantic enthusiasm, 'the sap of the Tree of Life, the spring and origin of all good fruit'.[87]

Accustomed to adoration, as well as hostility, the conflict with Tucker, who could diminish as decisively as he could empower, left Miriam bereft of a literary mentor. She found her poetic knight in Harry Lyman Koopman. Evidently amused and delighted by her clash with Tucker, Koopman penned 'To Miriam Daniell', comparing her to her clever, combative namesake in the Bible.[88]

SEVEN

'Knotty Points': William Bailie

T he young Irish Mancunian William Bailie, whose mistrust of enthusiasm had provoked Miriam's wrath and who was later to be so important in Helena and Helen's lives, would have found Tucker's respect for his abilities inestimably precious. William's life had been short on praise. The Bailies were a Northern Irish Presbyterian farming family with Scottish roots; William was born on 25 November 1866, in Belfast. Helen records that his father, James, worked as a carpenter for the Ulster Railroad and William retained happy memories of riding on the engines and being allowed to pull the whistle when he was a small child. But fortune did not proffer William a good hand. An inflammation of the eyes resulted in a permanent loss of sight in one eye after a criminally inept doctor 'spurted acid' into his eyes.[1] A bout of scarlet fever followed. Then, when he was nine, his father died of consumption, leaving five children. Hannah (Maxwell) Bailie was unable to care for them as she had to go work in the linen mills.

William quickly learned survival techniques, acquiring a much sought after paper-round by avoiding the tough boys jostling at the door, and creeping inside through a distribution window. Small for his age, but bright and studious, he attended the National School and read his way through the Presbyterian Church Sunday School library, though when he selected Edward Gibbon's *The Life of Mahomet*, the minister replaced it with a copy of *Pilgrim's Progress*, from which a youthful William learned of Christian's unrelenting struggle with his burdens.

At eleven, his mother apprenticed him to a wicker workshop. They were too poor to wait until he was fourteen, when he would have been eligible for the better-paid trades involving machinery. So William was bound to serve his term until the age of eighteen, which at eleven must have seemed an eternity. He had entered an ancient craft ruled by custom. The workshop consisted of eight men under a foreman and, as the new boy, he was at the bottom of the pecking order. He ran errands, not only for the foreman, but also for the men, who sent him off to buy beer.

Hastening through the streets of Belfast, William happily anticipated the tips he could spend on the *Boy's Own Paper* and the *Union Jack*. If *Pilgrim's Progress* instilled earnest endeavour, the tales of W.H.D. Kingston and G.A. Henty took him into a virtual world of English boys' public school pranks and naval battles. Along with many of his contemporaries, William absorbed an ideal of the Victorian manly man, plucky, honest, modest and loyal to the British Empire.

Disaster struck again. Traditions of a more unruly manliness prevailed in the workshop, and the twelve-year-old 'was thrown – in joke – from a ladder'. The consequences were 'a compound fracture in his left leg' and a return to the hospital where the same 'quack' doctor who had ruined his eye proposed to amputate his leg. Luckily for William, the doctor in charge of the ward overruled him, and with 'skill and patience' enabled the boy to walk again. In later life though the old wound would continue to cause pain.

When the slight, studious boy returned to the workshop he found acceptance as a scholar; the old custom of selecting someone to read out loud during work still survived in the Belfast basket workshop and William slipped into this role. The Catholic sweeper had begun to study for the priesthood and helped him with grammar and arithmetic; the shillings William earned each week enabled him to buy second-hand books and cheap tickets to the theatre. Like other apprentices, in learning his trade William also absorbed the broader cultural milieu of his fellow workers. Religion and politics were hotly debated by the older wicker workers, who were both Protestant and Catholic. Though William had been brought up in the Presbyterian faith, his father had resigned from the Orangemen's Lodge because he disliked sectarian hatred. An enquiring William listened to his workmates, and went to hear the evangelical revivalists, Moody and Sankey, *and* the Catholic Bishop, to find out what they said. He inclined to neither.

But the all-pervasive talk of Home Rule *did* interest him. In the late

1870s Protestants and Catholics had found a convincing leader in the aristocratic Charles Stewart Parnell, who was able to combine the politics of Home Rule and the economics of the land question. William used to wind his way through the Catholic part of town to hear speakers on the downs.

His weekends were spent with friends rowing on the river, sitting in the harbour, or climbing up Cave Hill. But William wanted something beyond working-class Belfast. By the time he reached fourteen he had imposed a harsh code of self-discipline, starting three-hour night classes at the Working Men's Institute in mathematics, science and agriculture. Five days a week he would wait at the workshop gate until it opened and then run a mile to the classes, arriving just after they started at 7 p.m. Four years later he obtained a hard-won certificate from the Belfast School of Science and Technology, which he kept all his life.

In May 1882, while William was attending the Presbyterian Sunday School, classes were interrupted by the superintendent. A secret Republican society called 'The Invincibles' had assassinated the Chief Secretary, Lord Frederick Cavendish, and his deputy, T.H. Burke. Inevitably, reprisals for the murders extended beyond 'The Invincibles' and, as the number of prisoners mounted, William found himself helping to make willow chairs for them. His workshop had been given the government order for the jail. It may have been this assassination and its consequences that contributed to William's life-long horror of violence.

His interest in radical ideas was stimulated when Henry George, the American author of *Progress and Poverty* (1879), toured Ireland in 1881, arguing for a single tax on land, and William went to hear him speak in Belfast. William then found a congenial Unitarian church in the market area of Belfast. Its minister, Revd James Christopher Street, was an Englishman with radical sympathies who tried to help the poor and campaigned against the appalling conditions of women in the linen industry. He encouraged debates on Tolstoy and Buddha in his non-denominational Rosemary Street Mutual Improvement Association, and ran a bookstore in the church where William picked up a pamphlet by William Morris, *Art and Socialism*, just before he left Belfast by boat for Scotland.[2]

Aged eighteen and having served his apprenticeship, he sought better prospects, first in Glasgow, then in Edinburgh, without success. In Newcastle his money ran out and he persuaded a guard to let him sleep in the baggage car of a freight train bound for Leeds. From there he hitched and walked across the Pennines, following the routes over which the Chartists had marched only a few decades before.

William had calculated that if ever there was a place in need of his baskets, it would be Manchester. No provincial city could rival the great industrial centre which had expanded beyond its original manufacturing base in cotton, devouring outlying villages. Neighbouring Salford, where William settled, survived as a distinct borough, though it, too, became part of the same vast conurbation. The newcomer had to find his way through unfamiliar streets, scouring for orders for 'the heavy rattan crates', called 'skips', used in industry.[3] All the wily skills he had learned in Belfast were needed, not just to obtain orders but in negotiating a tough city, where gangs of 'scuttlers', with their white mufflers, pointed clogs and caps cockily positioned on the back of their heads, fought over turf as hard as any Mancunian capitalist.[4]

At eighteen, the street-wise young William, alone with his baskets in a basement, was ignorant of the perils of love and desire. Helen recounts how an Irish match-maker pursued him in order to arrange a marriage with her husband's sister, twenty-one-year-old Ellen Donnan. The hardworking, aspiring basket maker was regarded by the Donnan family in Belfast as 'steady', and Helen observes acerbically that Ellen Donnan 'caught him'.[5] Their marriage was registered in Salford, in the summer of 1885. Their first child, Annie, was born in 1887, Ellen two years later and William (Willie) in 1890.[6]

Ellen Bailie may soon have come to wonder whether the unusual man she had married really was 'a catch' after all. When he was not working, he was invariably either reading or at meetings. True, he always maintained her and the children, but he was utterly absorbed in politics and ideas. Whether they were happy in the first years of marriage is impossible to say, but they had nothing whatsoever in common, apart from the children.

Before long William began attending meetings of the National Secular Society, which had strong roots in Manchester. He heard both Charles Bradlaugh and Annie Besant, respected by freethinkers not only for their oratory but because they had braved abuse and physical attacks for their views. Soon he was also reading the Social Democratic Federation paper, *Justice*, and attending meetings of the Salford S.D.F. at a 'hall over a tavern'.[7] On 1 May 1886, *Justice* mentions a 'William Bailie' participating in a discussion at the 'Crescent Inn' led by an unemployed decorator,

George Smart, who had been the S.D.F.'s candidate for the School Board the previous year. The topic was Gladstone's 'Irish measures'.[8] William thrived in this egalitarian Marxist mutual education class, so vital within radical working-class culture, and soon became one of the S.D.F.'s speakers. By September 1886 a 'Bailey' was addressing an outdoor meeting at Trafford Bridge.[9] Many more were to follow.

William always remembered the S.D.F. propagandist and organiser, J. Hunter Watts with particular affection. Watts acted as his mentor just as Street had done, moreover he provided a line through to William Morris who became William's hero. Watts had remained in the S.D.F. when Morris split to form the Socialist League in 1884. Nevertheless, he maintained his friendship with Morris, with whom he shared an enthusiasm for education.[10]

Manchester offered a veritable treasure trove of lectures and classes for searchers like William. Among these were the Sunday lectures organised by the Ancoats Brotherhood in the New Islington Hall, on similar lines to the Sunday Society in Bristol. Founded by Charles Rowley, a picture framer with a Morris-style vision of linking craft knowing with high culture, Ancoats was significant enough for William to keep a Brotherhood Christmas card depicting cherubic figures bearing peace and good will.[11] Each year Ancoats welcomed William Morris. The audience in 1888 was larger than usual and afterwards Morris accompanied 'Comrade Hunter Watts', with whom he was staying, to a meeting of the Manchester S.D.F., where he found 'comrades' who were 'as eager and earnest as could be desired'.[12]

Shortly after Morris' visit, William left the S.D.F. for the Manchester Socialist League, which had been recently revived after the collapse of the initial branch started by Raymond Unwin. Helen says the reason for his shift in allegiance was the 'authoritarian character' of the S.D.F., but Morris' genial charisma no doubt contributed.[13] William's name appears in *Commonweal* in April 1889, speaking in Stevenson Square with two other former S.D.F. members: John Marshall, who had established close contact with Manchester's Jewish immigrants by agitating against low-paid 'sweated' labour, and John Ritson who had gone as an economic migrant to the United States, where, in 1887 he had experienced the horror of the Chicago anarchists' executions at first hand.[14]

Outrage over these executions fostered sympathy towards the revolutionary anarchist tendency gaining influence in the Socialist League. The Manchester branch attracted two keen anarchist adherents who often spoke with William at open-air meetings, Alf Barton and Herbert Stockton. Barton, the son of a Bedfordshire foundry worker, was a clerk who had joined the Ancoats Brotherhood when he came to Manchester, and later became a librarian at the John Rylands Library. Stockton got by with a series of odd jobs, eventually becoming an insurance agent.[15]

Helen wrongly presumes that William was the sole intellectual in the branch; in fact others, including Stockton and Barton, shared his scholarly inclinations.[16] Moreover, the Manchester Socialist League was far more diverse than Helen imagined. 'J.B.S.', the author of 'A Revolutionary Reminiscence', describes how 'Lawyers, Schoolmasters, University men mixed and fraternised with clerks, tradesmen and labourers' while the class mélange was enriched by refugees from European revolutionary movements, including 'Russian Jews' escaping 'persecution'.[17] According to J.B.S., all the Manchester Socialist Leaguers shared a tendency to take themselves 'very seriously'; dismissive of the 'trivialities of life', they dreamed of revolution. He recalls a particular coterie as being 'wont to wade through Adam Smith, John Stuart Mill and Karl Marx'.[18] Bailie, Stockton and Barton were certainly part of this little band.

Zealously they combated false prophets in the guise of the liberal University men who lectured at the Ancoats Brotherhood. William and friends attended a lecture on 'Capital and Labour' in autumn 1889, delivered as part of a series on 'Present Day Social Problems' by Professor J.E.C. Munro. Their brisk report in *Commonweal* related how Munro, the President of the Manchester Statistical Society, was 'given a rather hot night of it by our speakers, who lost no opportunity of driving home their principles'.[19] With Mill's iron law of wages discredited, liberal economists were searching for alternative theoretical frameworks and policies, to combat radical and socialist calls for redistribution. Munro's proposition of a sliding scale of wages, by which pay rates would be determined by prices, was regarded with suspicion by the revolutionaries. Another speaker, the Ruskinian University Extension lecturer who supported the Co-operative Movement, Michael E. Sadler, lecturing on 'The Beginnings of Modern Socialism', also failed to please. In January 1890, the awkward squad intervened at Ancoats to put him right on 'the principles of revolutionary Socialism' and overturn his 'economic fallacies'.[20]

J.B.S. recalls how 'The joy of life and the joy of the struggle pulsated through our veins', describing their utter immersion in 'open air meetings, printing leaflets, writing to newspapers'.[21] Indeed, William is mentioned in *Commonweal* week after week, speaking outdoors, rain or shine. His name also appears on an undated list of Socialist League 'functionaries' and 'correspondents', for, from the summer of 1889, he was taking on the internal organisation of the branch, sending in reports, paying for *Commonweals*, sorting out problems and inviting speakers.[22] Only the powerful comradeship of the Manchester Socialist League members made this level of commitment possible. 'Every fibre of our being was devoted to the "cause"', writes J.B.S. They might have been seen by others as 'harmless lunatics', or even 'incendiaries, murderers and assassins', but they regarded themselves as 'comrades in life and death'.[23]

Amid the heat and pressure of intransigent opposition they came to feel a certain detachment from the mass of workers who did not share their viewpoint. Sometimes their isolation and the daunting odds against them took a heavy psychological toll. Moreover, the group's high ideals of comradeship could be strained by the arrival of destructive intruders, such as a wandering alcoholic speaker called 'McCormack' who was scrounging and stirring up trouble that summer. He eventually moved on to other open-hearted anarchist communist sympathisers in Norwich and was revealed as a police informer in 1892.[24]

The creation of the Socialist League Club aimed to foster fellowship. Early in November 1889, they welcomed Kropotkin to the Club and Helen records that it was his 'humanitarian communist-anarchism' that 'set' William towards anarchism.[25] But William was equally delighted by William Morris' hasty postcard, dated 6 November 1889, agreeing to lecture on 'The Class Struggle', which became one of his most treasured possessions.[26] William booked the Secular Hall for Morris, who, in contrast to state socialists like the British Fabians or the Americans, Bellamy and Grönlund, argued that socialism would arise out of resistance and conflict. Morris saw strikes, boycotts, bold propaganda, a readiness to risk fines and imprisonment, as sources of revolutionary consciousness. Characteristically, he selected an historical topic with a message of non-violent direct action – the 1539 'Revolt of Ghent', when citizens refused to pay an oppressive tax – for his lecture at Ancoats in the New Islington Hall.[27]

William shared Morris' love of history. However, along with other comrades in the Socialist League, he felt there was so little time. J.B.S recalled how, braced and invigorated by their convictions, their main fear was that the revolution would arrive before they had time to prepare the people for it.[28] In chiliastic mode, Raymond Unwin came over from Chesterfield to address the Socialist Club in November on 'The Wane of Civilisation', and did an outdoor meeting with William.[29]

Like Miriam, Robert and Helena in Bristol, during 1889 William and his fellow Socialist League members found themselves *living* the class struggle. That autumn they were defending striking tram workers and Jewish tailors, organising carters and lorrymen working on the railways and encouraging militancy among the gas workers. Early in November *Commonweal* reported that men at Berry's Blacking Works had won an 'easy victory' and that 'Bailie and Barton' were urging them all to join the Gas Workers and General Labourers' Union. The gas workers themselves went on strike in December, only to be soundly defeated by scab labour, from which the dismayed Socialist Leaguers learned the bitter lesson that class struggle did not automatically raise consciousness.[30] The set-back did not prevent a great host of other workers taking strike action during 1890; they included cabinet makers, boot makers, waterproof makers as well as tailors, many of whom were Jewish immigrants.[31] In July the *Workman's Times* even reported stirrings among basket makers.[32]

The Socialist Leaguers envisaged their Club as becoming the nerve-centre for 'Socialist propaganda' in Lancashire; Unwin supported it with a donation of 5s and Carpenter gave the large sum of £2.[33] However, conflict at the centre of the Socialist League was making 'Socialist propaganda' increasingly contentious. In January 1890, John Marshall had distinguished Socialist Leaguers as anti-parliamentarians who 'aimed at the realization of Communism and the abolition of authority in its entirety' from S.D.F. members who desired 'to preserve a system called Collectivism'.[34] But bitter disputes were also occurring *within* the Socialist League as the anarchists gained ascendency.[35] When Edward Carpenter spoke at the Club on 31 March 1890, he proffered compromise. His lecture 'The Present and Future Society', proposed that a Collectivist Socialism was a necessary transitional phase, en route to an Anarchist-Communist Society, though quite how such a transmutation would occur was not specified.[36]

Some anarchist communists in the League were adopting an overtly violent, confrontational tone. The polarisation was driven not just by theoretical disagreements, but by despair over the slow pace of change. This tended to feed internal acrimony. On June 28th an exasperated William, having been criticised in a letter to *Commonweal* for inaction, responded: 'It is more easy to draw up a system and explain how it may be carried out than to take one's coat off and settle to the work of putting it into practice.'[37]

Agitation was particularly difficult that summer because the Social-ist Leaguers defied the patriotic enthusiasm surrounding the visit of the imperial hero, H.M. Stanley, to the city, denouncing 'Christianity and Commercialism, whose civilising agents have been fire and murder, the elephant, rifle and the gallows'.[38] His youthful attachment to the *Boy's Own Paper* long discarded, William was staunchly anti-imperialist, and soon found himself in a confrontational free-speech conflict when the police started breaking up Socialist League open-air meetings. Helen records that William was determined 'to put their interference to the test, and volunteered to risk arrest'.[39] He was duly charged with 'obstruct-ing the carriage-way in Higher Chatham Street, Chorlton-on-Medlock', a poor area in the city. On August 4th, William conducted his own defence, stating that until the police had arrived, 'followed by a number of roughs', no trouble had occurred. He also pointed out that the Salva-tion Army and the City Mission, speaking on the same spot, had been left unmolested. He was fined 5s and costs.[40] Helen maintains that 'The judge stopped further interference by the police'; but *Freedom* reported the arrest of 'Comrade Barton' that August.[41] Manchester's free-speech agitation, initiated by the little group of anarchist communists, was to be a long one and would land Herbert Stockton in jail. Eventually taken up by the Independent Labour Party, it would involve Emmeline Pankhurst and gain support from the *Manchester Guardian*.

From August 1890 several insurrectionary anarchist communist speak-ers began touring the provinces; Charles Mowbray, who promised 'to stir up Manchester and Salford', was followed by George Cores.[42] Amusingly, however, Cores the fiery shoemaker was thrown off course in Manchester, admitting, 'I felt very bashful in the presence of so many charming and enthusiastic girls.'[43] The Socialist League Club had helped to open space for young working-class women; the anarchist communists rejected 'the tacit doctrine of some Socialists' of 'no marriages till after the "Rev"', and romance flourished.[44] Herbert Stockton's sister Eleanor married Alf Barton, later playing a leading role in the Women's Co-operative Guild, while her friend, Emily Bradney, became Stockton's wife.[45]

William spoke with Barton that November, denouncing the murder of the Chicago Martyrs.[46] But despite his anger against injustice, William did not dismiss the 'theoretic', preferring to convince by facts and reason. Helen describes him as always the 'rationalist rather than the zealot'.[47] William was a conscientious activist and an organiser, but his real love was a ceaseless quest for knowledge and ideas. *Commonweal* reported him lecturing to the Socialist League Club on 'The Place of Modern Athens in Industrial Evolution' on November 30th.[48] Then on December 5th a probing William opened a discussion on the 'Difficulties of Communism'.[49] As Helen puts it, 'William was never orthodox.'[50]

Nor did his strong convictions make him personally sectarian. During 1890 he befriended a young minister from the Unitarian church in Upper Brook Street, called John Trevor. Trevor was agonising over Christianity's lack of relevance to workers. When he came across the Socialist League Club, William impressed him as 'a remarkable man. Anarchist, Communist, Revolutionist, Atheist, and of course very poor'. Recognising William's 'ability' and scholarly bent, Trevor was amazed by his new friend's dedication, reading long into the night to prepare himself 'to speak to the people' and then mounting 'a broken chair' to address them in the Mancunian rain, while they, sublimely unconcerned, 'flowed past'.[51]

In the spring of 1891 when John Trevor worked out a scheme to take Christianity out of ecclesiastical institutions and into the 'Labour Movement', he was surprised when William 'jumped at it'. William sought to combine revolutionary principles with an outward looking politics and saw Trevor's plan as 'a kind of Socialist Salvation Army' capable of rousing people. He told Trevor it should be called not 'the Working-Man's Church, but the Labour Church, because he was sure I did not want to stand so much for a class as a principle'.[52] Over the next decade the Labour Church provided a vital non-sectarian space for the British left.

However, by October 1891, when the Labour Church was launched in Manchester, William, Ellen and the three children were no longer living in Harpurhey. They had migrated to the United States.[53]

How did William come to make this momentous decision? It seems theoretical doubts were not the only factor; the catalyst was a conflict with the basket makers' trade union. It looks as if William wanted to expand beyond the rattan baskets into making willow furniture, which was becoming popular. When he tried to bring in furniture makers from Leicester, Helen states, 'The union prevented them from working in William's shop.'[54] This was presumably because they belonged to a different craft union from the rattan skip makers. William, as a smaller master seeking to diversify, was caught up in one of the contradictions he was habitually analysing as a revolutionary, an irony that no doubt would have been a source of mirth among his craft unionist opponents on the Manchester and Salford Trades Council.

*   *   *

When William arrived in Boston he settled his family at 166 William Street, Chelsea. Across the harbour, to the north of Boston, Chelsea was conveniently linked to the city by the railway, and William set about building up his business making 'baskets for the factory trade'.[55] He could find few signs of the labour movement activism he had known in Manchester and missed the constant public debate about the relations between workers and capital.[56] However, notices about *Liberty* had appeared in *Commonweal* and he sought out Benjamin Tucker, joining the Boston Anarchist Club.[57] Started by Tucker and a small group of supporters in 1887, it was very different from the Manchester Socialist Club. An account from 1888 evokes an atmosphere of refined subversion. The seventy-eight attendees are described as polite and mainly male, apart from a 'bright intelligent lady engaged in selling various anarchistic pamphlets and papers' while another quietly collected donations 'for the benefit of the widows and orphans of the Chicago "martyrs"'.[58]

The Boston Anarchist Club and the conversations with Tucker and other Individualist Anarchists provided William, the willing pupil, with a keen team of personal tutors and enabled him to develop his thoughts at length in *Liberty*. William's first article for the journal, an allegory about capitalism, 'The Story of a School', appeared in December 1891 and was followed by the partly autobiographical, 'The Martyrdom of the Soul', early in February 1892. In this William wrote with feeling about the crushing of dreams and aspirations through the pressure to make money and gain a standing in the world, as well as the long hours of toil experienced by workers in factories and shops, at furnaces or on the street-cars. Acknowledging that women's lot was harder still, making them 'the slaves of routine, custom, and conventionality', he protested against 'The curb at every turn of Dame Grundy and her progeny, public opinion, custom, respectability'.[59]

Tucker was not only working for the *Boston Globe* and producing *Liberty*, he was also about to launch *The Weekly Bulletin of Newspaper and Periodical Literature*. The idea was to offer a 'catalogue' for 'specialists, students, professional men, *litterateurs*, artists and scientists' of reviewed articles, listed under twenty-eight subject headings.[60] In 1891 William was 'engaged' to scan American and European periodicals and newspapers, 'clipping and classifying' them in Tucker's office near to the *Globe*. 'William was in his natural element', writes Helen, adding that 'George Schumm read proof and translated articles from the German, A.H. Simpson ... set type.'[61] Thrilled to be paid to do what he loved – reading – William abandoned his basket workshop.

Archibald H. Simpson, c. 1889 (Labadie, Special
Collections Library, University of Michigan)

Through the *Weekly Bulletin* William formed two close friendships,
with Schumm and Simpson. Schumm's knowledge of German thought
and literature, and Simpson's familiarity with the American revolutionary left, had a lasting impact upon him. Moreover, through them, and
through Tucker, William was introduced to the ideas of the anarchist, Josiah Warren, whose belief in individual sovereignty had led him
to abolish rules at the community Modern Times, in Long Island, in
1851.[62] Amid this stimulating micro world of radical iconoclasts, William
came across Miriam and Robert, but not Helena, who was presumably
baby-sitting Sunrise.[63]

William's glimpse of fulfilling work was all too brief. The *Weekly Bulletin* was losing Tucker several hundred dollars a week and he was forced
to close it down. When, early in 1892, Tucker went to New York taking
Liberty with him, William was not able to move and must have watched
Miriam and Robert's departure with envy. Left 'high and dry', he resumed
his basket making. Nevertheless, all was not lost. The intellectual affirm-
ation he received from Tucker was galvanising. Helen observes, 'William
wrote and wrote, and Tucker accepted every article he wrote for *Liberty*.'[64]

In February 1892, in 'The Martyrdom of the Soul', William bemoaned
how 'placing', 'settling' and 'worrying' about a growing family absorbed
a man's 'thoughts' and 'time'. His bleak delineation of 'Domestic Com-
forts', as merely 'a sleeping place, where the partner lives who prepares the
food and supplies maternity to the children', indicates the relationship
between William and Ellen had not improved by crossing the Atlantic.
He acknowledges that women's individuality was even more 'suppressed'

than men's, but thought men suffered more because they could glimpse the alternatives barred to them.[65]

Writing at length for publication was new to William and he struggled to find the means of expressing his ideas. He ends in biblical style with a credo he followed all his life:

> Never despise the inner promptings. Know that thou dost possess something worth cultivating; seek for it, and thou shalt in some direction find it. Fear not to think and to express thy thought. Act upon thine own judgement when thou canst brave the calumny and ostracism of the multitude. If thou wouldst possess a soul of thine own, make not gain thy chief business, but be ever ready to sacrifice something for thy soul's sake.[66]

On May 28th, when Tucker allowed William to fill a whole issue of *Liberty* with 'A Mighty Consultation and a Multitude of Diagnoses', he adopted a thinly veiled allegorical idiom to trash a gaggle of 'quacks': Christian Socialists, Secularists, Marxists, along with 'Professor Co-operator English' and 'soul-wandering Besantavatsky'. Towards Kropotkin, 'Prince Pierre' on 'The French Revolution', William assumed a gentler tone, but it was 'Proudhon Redivivus' whom he graced with the last word.[67] William had been listening carefully in those illuminating 'interviews' with 'Mr Tucker'.

The June 25th article that so annoyed Miriam, 'Bursting a Bubble', expressed William's scepticism towards a politics of emotional, heroic self-sacrifice. Though grimly aware of the consequences of casting oneself body and soul against the power of the capitalist state, William was enraged by the eighteenth-month sentence imposed on the British anarchist communist editor of *Commonweal*, David Nicoll, on a charge of incitement, expressing indignation about 'police-hatched plots' that had snared both anarchists and Irish Americans.[68] William's distrust of the state extended to attempts to curb capital through legislation. Writing 'Notes from the United States' for John Trevor's *Labour Prophet* he pointed out that these could rebound on workers.[69] Pragmatically, however, he did not oppose all forms of state intervention, supporting compulsory education in a letter to *Liberty* in September 1892.[70]

By September 1892 William had decided that 'Mutual Banking', one of Tucker's great interests, was relevant for Ireland's economic and political freedom, a view likely to have earned approval from his editor.[71]

Moreover, a keen 'Wm Bailie Chelsea Mass' put his name down for *three* copies of Tucker's collection of essays, *Instead of a Book*.[72] In January 1893 a jubilant Tucker announced that after many 'interviews' with himself 'and other comrades over "knotty points"', 'Comrade Bailie' had finally 'thrown his Communism overboard and is today as good an Anarchist as one would care to see'.[73] Adroitly hegemonic, Tucker reserved 'anarchism' for his own brand, dismissing Kropotkinite anarchists as 'Communists'.

Debating 'knotty points' was William's idea of bliss, and in a rush of energy and confidence he proposed a series of articles offering 'a connected and scientific presentation' of anarchist 'economic conceptions'. Aware of his 'temerity', he hoped to fill a gap and resolve 'confusion'.[74] Tucker rejected 'this too modest announcement of Mr Bailie's purpose', urging 'attentive consideration of what he has to offer'.[75] Such an endorsement would have been the equivalent for William of seeing his name in lights.

The project was indeed ambitious. In the first two articles in his series on 'Problems of Anarchism', which was to run on into August, William takes his readers back to the 'dawn of history', tramping them from primitive society to feudalism.[76] His scope extends beyond anarchism, engaging with a conundrum also troubling liberal and socialist thinkers – how to balance individualism and collectivism. An optimistic William set out to channel Egoism while vindicating altruism: 'The individual freely pursuing his own welfare is led to act for the good of others, to conduct which is altruistic.'[77]

Still angry against class injustice, William argues that modern industry and the state consolidate and secure the unequal division of wealth and fiercely defends the right to private property as well as the 'fruits' of one's labour.[78] Just a hint of his S.D.F. and Socialist League days remains in his swipe at attempts to reform capitalism as 'temporary palliatives'.[79]

On April 22nd his indulgent editor called a pause owing to problems of space.[80] It sounds as if readers had complained that William's articles were too preoccupied with denouncing fallacies, rather than elucidating anarchist economics, for, upon William's return, he called for patience: 'Our investigation will necessarily be occupied as much in sifting out the chaff and rejecting the untrustworthy conceptions among established teaching as in the discovery of reliable and useful principles.'[81]

William's chaff-sifting might have been slightly easier had he confined himself to the history of economic and political ideas. However, his investigative mind tended to stray towards topics that defied clear-cut answers. Already, in 1893, he was wondering about the implications he could observe in America of imperceptible gradations between classes.[82] His own investigative inclinations tended to confuse the political clarity he sought.

'Problems of Anarchism' reveals other tensions within William's approach. Drawn intellectually to objective overviews and total explanations, the William who cleaved to reason and social science was impelled by a William passionately committed to individual agency. Moreover, his subjective perspective forked in contrary directions. Keen to prevent the readers of *Liberty* from pursuing 'will-o'-the-wisps', he criticised the liberal economist Francis A. Walker, who maintained that wage increases had to be linked to greater productivity, as an apologist for 'plunderers'. He pointed out that Walker failed to critique the causes producing and maintaining 'the present arrangement'.[83] This was perfectly true, yet within that same 'present arrangement' William himself was a capitalist, albeit a small one. Regarding himself as crucial for the survival of his basket workshop, he could not accept either Marx *or* Josiah Warren's views on labour as the source of value 'under all circumstances'.[84] Tucker had published William's articles 'regardless of any deviations from *Liberty's* chosen path', but the dismissal of Warren earned a sharp rebuke. William was warned, 'he must not misstate Warren's economics unless he desires to be called to account'.[85]

William's thought may have meandered and his style been somewhat leaden, but his enquiring, original intelligence eschewed doctrinal certainties. He stumbled up against problems that neither he, nor many others after him, resolved. The crux of William's perplexity was how to fulfil needs in conditions of equality and freedom:

> Every Utopian and Communistic scheme formulated that attempts to do without the economic competitive forces replaces them by a reactionary and insufferable hierarchy, or else, like the Communist Anarchists, ignores the necessity for any machinery to adjust economic activities to their ends.[86]

Ironically, his logic left him saddled with competition, even though he knew from his own experience the destruction it wrought. William never did develop his positive anarchist economic theory. Nonetheless, wrestling with all these 'knotty points' was to equip him in the future to synthesise his ideas on anarchism, and to study Warren's life and thought in depth.

William Bailie, c. 1902 (Helen Tufts Bailie Papers,
Sophia Smith Collection, Smith College)

The 'Problems of Anarchism' series was running out of steam and came to a halt in August 1893. For several years, William's contributions to *Liberty* became less frequent, though he continued to speak at meetings. Perhaps he recoiled from being 'called to account' in print. Or he may simply have been exhausted by study, writing and arguing, while running his workshop. Helen later remarked, 'William's hopes of a literary life soon faded, and he had to bend his strength to building up his business ...'[87]

EIGHT

Wanderers: 1892–1894

No overt break with Tucker had occurred after the sharp spats in *Liberty* between him and Miriam. Indeed, on October 1st, Miriam, Robert, Helena and even Miriam Sunrise Nicol are all listed, along with William, as donors to Tucker's compilation of *Liberty* articles, *Instead of a Book*.[1] Moreover, several of Miriam's poems appear in *Liberty* that month. Among them are two loving tributes to Sunrise, 'To Any Natural Child', 'A name is but a sound to mark a thing', and 'Lullaby', which imagines a child at peace amid nature, 'Where the Pacific rollers pour/Their saffron shells on a coral reef'.[2]

Miriam, however, had crossed an invisible boundary; Tucker certainly believed in free debate and female equality, but as editor he maintained control in a predominantly male grouping. Miriam, who quivered with acute antennae of excessive sensibility, would have responded by magnifying the slightest indication of coldness. She needed more than a formal, outward editorial relationship, she wanted the inner recognition from Tucker that had released her creativity.

During the autumn of 1892, Miriam's mood darkened. Several poems from this period ruminate gloomily over the essential loneliness of the human condition. Early in October 'To Each His World' was published:

> In me my world was born,
> With me my world will die,
> And what I see at eve or morn
> Lies folded in my eye.[3]

'Self-centred' the poet stands alone. Keeping one's counsel and 'Forget-ting joy and woe' now become Miriam's poetic endeavour.[4] On October 22nd, in Miriam's 'The Bottom of the Sea', the poet is the diver 'allured' by the 'dreamy light' of the ocean's depths. 'I saw the skeletons in ghastly strife/For gold; their empty skulls grinned: "This is life"'.[5]

Ferociously independent and yet fearfully demanding, Miriam was a woman of extreme and complex contradictions. Solitary in her ima-gination, she required unstinting belief. When this was withdrawn, she erupted, and then crumbled into ashes of despair. In her daily existence she was desperately in want of others. Helena not only provided her with practical support, she sustained Miriam psychologically by assenting to her friend's powers.

Feeling isolated in New York, Miriam summonsed Helena in distress:

> Lena, the equinoxial gales are near,
> The fickle sea has lost its summer mood,
> Its face is angry and its voice is rude,
> That dominates my faith with foolish fear,
> Lest I should lose within its depths my dear.[6]

Panicking that Helena would perish on the voyage back from Glasgow, she longs fervently for Lena's ship to anchor: 'Our faithful friend! So from our hearth and heart/Never again adventure till death part'.[7]

Once again Helena put her life on hold for Miriam. She boarded a ship in Glasgow, arriving in New York on October 18th to find her friend in a state of agitation.[8] From the late summer of 1892, New Yorkers had been regarding the arrival of boats from Europe with dread, for the last great European cholera pandemic had killed many thousands. The New York Health Authorities managed to contain the disease, but Miriam, in terror of contamination, was refusing to handle any of Tucker's mail from Hamburg, one of the ports badly affected by cholera.[9] Helena had no sooner disembarked, when Miriam insisted they should all return to Cambridge. Helena complied because of 'the forceful and magnetic personality of Miriam', and love of Sunrise.[10]

Miriam had another reason for wanting to be back in their old apartment: it would make them neighbours of the Koopmans. Aware she needed to go beyond spontaneous inspiration to attain control over how she crafted her thoughts and emotions in rhyme, she had determined Koopman was to be her poetic mentor. Aware of her own limitations, she felt clumsy even in thanking him for the volume of his poems: 'I know so little. My own singing is an inborn tendency blindly followed rather than a conscious art.' Assuring him she did not write for 'Fame', so inseparable from 'Hate and Envy', Miriam the poetic novice confesses: 'I sing, out of tune often enough like a cage born bird, because I must utter or I should die.'[11]

Along with technical guidance, she intimated that he would also be able to empathise with her Romantic individualism: 'The creative instinct is an imperative one and satisfies itself in expression.' Miriam wanted to break from overtly propagandist verse. 'In a fever of reform I once rhymed because it helped the worker to remember certain things which I then thought it important for him to bear in mind in a species of didactic doggerel which had no literary value and was of small ethical importance.' But it was futile to 'induce the wings of Freedom to grow upon the shoulders of fledgling men and women by rubbing upon them the ointment of our own experience'.[12]

Miriam had moved from socialism to the sun, and thence to the 'wind-driven robes' of 'Anarchy'; now she presented herself to Harry Koopman as lost and wounded.[13] Suffering from an 'inflammation of the larynx & lung' that she claimed was the legacy of the remorseless agitation in Bristol, Miriam, the anxious mother, tells him Sunrise also is ill from 'croup, coughing and struggling for breath'.[14] Saying she believes only 'Thoreau's pines' will secure their recovery, she enthuses at the thought of meeting 'Mrs Koopman & the blue eyed babes'.[15]

They had only been back in Cambridge a few days when Miriam arrived with Robert unannounced at the Koopman's home. Koopman himself was out, and his wife Helen answered the door. As Miriam enquired formally for 'Harry Lyman Koopman', Helen Koopman gazed in wonderment at 'this little woman, so plainly dressed, with the golden diadem over her black hair – oh, she was so beautiful. Her head was like a flower.'[16] As the Gilliards had, the Koopmans took Miriam, Robert and Helena under their protective wing. 'They were so poor, so unfitted to meet the world', reflected Helen Koopman.[17]

Miriam might turn to Harry Koopman for poetic insights, but it was Helen, the mother of a young family, who could advise on Sunrise. Helen Koopman dispensed wisdom on child rearing happily, but became exasperated because Miriam disregarded it. Years later she was still grumbling about the neurotic preoccupation with cleanliness which led Miriam to wash Sunrise's Jaeger woollen clothes each day. Dr Jaeger maintained that wool, being a natural fibre, prevented noxious exhalations, but Miriam, dubious of authoritative voices, kept washing, just in case. Helen Koopman observed practically, 'wool does not need it, and all that washing would get it out of shape'.[18] She told Helen Tufts that Miriam panicked unnecessarily about Sunrise's health:

> She took everything so hard. Sunrise was sick once; they had been feeding her a vegetable diet that did not agree with the baby's stomach and she had a fever. Miriam came to us about it. She 'knew the child would not live over the next night'. Yet it was what I had brought my children through many a time. Next day, Miriam sent for the doctor. Nothing could happen but that somebody must be blamed for it. Miriam could never be got to admit that <u>she</u> was in the wrong.[19]

Helen Koopman appears to have been one of the few people who could extend friendship without regarding Miriam in heroic terms. Yet she came to appreciate Helena, so rarely noticed in the presence of Miriam, as more 'practical' and the 'best balanced' of the trio. She considered too, that Miriam behaved unfairly towards Helena: 'If Sunrise had a cold, it was Helena brought it to her. Helena once went to a funeral "and brought back germs". Helena had a good deal of blame in those days.'[20]

Helen Koopman recalled antagonism from Robert towards Helena: 'He was jealous of Helena too, jealous of Miriam's attachment to Helena; he made life hard for Helena.'[21] It seems Helena's prolonged absence had not resolved the grating irritation she aroused in him. Only Miriam and Sunrise kept the two yoked, and the connection chafed both of them. Helena might have been Miriam's patient Griselda, but she had no more reason to be constantly with Robert than he with her. In later life, Robert's family would describe him as cool and withdrawn, with a capacity for dry, biting comments, and perhaps this was already evident. Helena was a strong woman, who had deferred her own personal fulfilment because of Miriam and Sunrise. She was carrying a great weight of contained anger; in subtle ways she no doubt retaliated.

The emotional and sexual dynamics between Miriam and Robert had shifted too. Living in a confined space at their new address, 230 Pearl Street, allowed them little private intimacy. A troubled Helena confided to Helen Koopman 'that Miriam and Robert had terrible rows at night. Miriam would not let Robert come to her; she believed in that only when they could plan for a child. But they slept in the same room, and Robert was very unhappy.'[22]

Such an assertion of sexual autonomy on Miriam's part was in accord with the commitment to individual control and voluntary motherhood prevalent in the free love circles she encountered in America. Free lovers sought to perfect intimate human relationships but disagreed about the relative virtues of continence and physical sexual intercourse. Some free lovers risked imprisonment to distribute information about methods of contraception. Others rejected it as unnatural, advocating male control over ejaculation or abstinence.[23]

Ambivalence towards the physical was prevalent too in some alternative spiritual movements. There was a tendency to favour celibacy, though some of the less orthodox followers of Swedenborg affirmed the body. The esoteric sects that mushroomed in the second half of the nineteenth century were suspected by the press of orgiastic indulgence, but officially at least, they expressed a reticent wariness about sex. Thomas Lake Harris, whose writing is infused with physical arousal, wanted his followers to sublimate desire in spirit unions, while Hiram E. Butler posited that sex should only be for procreation, specifying with precision that it should occur once every eighteen months.[24]

Guilt about sexual pleasure was culturally pervasive and while Miriam was a proponent of freedom and desire in love, she could well have been affected by the residual puritanism of a Nonconformist upbringing. In practice free love carried differing implications for men and women because of social attitudes and unequal power relations. As a 'new woman', Miriam not only expresses a fine-drawn tension in balancing passion and independence – she lived it.

But practical, rather than spiritual or psychological, reasons could have led Miriam to resist Robert's advances. In 1886 that mysterious illness had caused her to sleep apart from her husband and her ill-health persisted. Rearing one child amid poverty and insecurity would have made her terrified that she would go under with a second. She must have been aware the unsteady Robert was hardly a reliable breadwinner.

Dissension in the bedroom did not curb Miriam's protective loyalty towards Robert. In December 1892, she despatched a contorted letter reproaching Harry Koopman, addressed as 'Dear Comrade', for supposedly stealing one of Robert's ideas in a poem. Amid many crossings out, she asserted that Robert 'consciously knew' an antithetical link between Christ and Shylock 'to be <u>his</u> thought & intended to use it himself in a literary article on Judaism at some future period'. Despite her desire for the Koopmans' friendship, Miriam was prepared to risk losing it for the intellectually insecure Robert. She added a special note to 'Dear Helen' at the end trying to explain her distress that an insight of Robert's she had revealed to them had gone into a poem, 'But I think you will understand I am as jealous as a Mother over all Robert's ideas. And I should not be worthy of your love if I did not prefer truth to it.' She signed it,

> Yours dear and kind comrades
> as ever
> Miriam Daniell.[25]

She was fortunate; the Koopmans remained 'dear and kind comrades', though it is probable that on Helen Koopman's part, good will towards Miriam, so beautiful, so unbounded, and a poet, may have been edged by traces of envy. Miriam, Robert and Helena's wanderings troubled her. 'Their coming to America was a reckless thing', she reflected, 'They burned their bridges behind them; unused to poverty and hardship, they passed through the extremest kind of each. They always seemed to me like birds, flitting from one place to another.'[26]

Helen Koopman presents a picture of Miriam especially as adrift and restless, going on long tramps to Concord or carrying Sunrise in her arms around Boston Art Gallery. Having experienced metropolitan life, she was now apt to sneer at Cambridge. After attending a lecture by the Rus-kinian Professor of the History of Art, Charles Eliot Norton, at Harvard, Miriam remarked on the futility of lecturing people in Cambridge who were so materialistic, 'so dull and dead to beauty'.[27] Helen Koopman interpreted this apparent unsociability as a result of the scarring Miriam had received.

Nevertheless, over the course of 1892 and 1893, Miriam and Robert did establish a strong friendship, not only with the Koopmans but with William Bailie's friend, the anarchist George Schumm, and his wife, Emma Heller Schumm. At the home of the cultured, impecuni-ous Schumms, Miriam could express her enthusiasms without fear of disapproval. The exuberant George Schumm was a great talker, while diffident Emma Heller Schumm, the more subtle thinker, listened with quiet empathy.[28] Though Helena also visited their household, Emma did not really get to know her until later: 'She was somewhat overshadowed by the more attractive, more positive and brilliant Miriam.'[29]

The Schumms proved a wonderful source of ideas and intellectual contacts. They had grown up in Sauk City, Wisconsin, a settlement of free-thinking German immigrants. Their parents were members of a humanistic association called 'Freie Gemeinde', which rejected religion and monarchy while supporting the emancipation of women, black people and workers. George Schumm remembered his father, first a farmer, then a shopkeeper and inn-keeper, possessing a fine library and hanging portraits of Lessing, Goethe and Schiller on the walls.[30]

After graduating from Cornell, George Schumm had worked with the revolutionary émigré and doughty opponent of Karl Marx, Karl Heinzen, on his paper *Der Pionier*. Ibsen and Shaw were important influences upon him. The Schumms' links with Tucker went back to the late 1880s, when they edited a German edition of *Liberty*, called *Libertas*. After it collapsed they continued to translate work that Tucker published. Emma Heller Schumm, whose father was an exile from the German Revolution of 1848, had been the first woman from Sauk City to attend the University of Wisconsin. She translated Heinzen's enlightened *The Rights of Women and the Sexual Relations*, published by Tucker in 1891. The couple helped Tucker to disseminate the ideas of thinkers such as Stirner and Nietzsche.[31]

Miriam and Robert came into contact with these theorists of 'owness' (or self-ownership) and self-becoming through their friendship with the Schumms.[32] In autumn 1893, Miriam was intrigued by a meeting at their home with John Mackay, the German anarchist poet who wrote on Stirner, while Robert took philosophical self-affirmation literally. An amused George Schumm later recalled meeting 'the young Scot in the Harvard Yard' declaring: 'Mr Schumm, if my will were only strong enough, with this fist I could ram through these stones.'[33] Needless to say Harvard remained intact.

Emma Heller Schumm remembered encountering the three migrants from Britain in the early 1890s:

> They had all turned their backs upon conventional society and conventional living. They were serving their apprenticeship in the new life of their choice. There was much enthusiasm for ideas, much storm and stress, much material hardship, but it was all very beautiful. How I longed to shelter them from the world's rough handling.[34]

Though more idealistic than Helen Koopman, Emma was similarly aware of just how harsh American capitalism could be for the insecure and unprotected.

*   *   *

The year 1893 afforded ample cause for anxiety. From February the booming American economy experienced a series of financial shocks. A collapse in funding combined with over-expansion of the railways led to the bankruptcy of railway companies and banks; this in turn contributed to a panic, which exacerbated into crisis. Unemployment figures leapt upwards over the course of the year.

Miriam was so preoccupied with inner consciousness she seems hardly to have registered the external mood of economic pessimism. But two personal threats to her peace of mind did impinge. On 9 May 1893 Edward Tuckett Daniell wrote the first fateful letter broaching the question of their divorce. After receiving two emotional accusatory and discursive replies from Miriam, and Robert's admission that he was Sunrise's father, the cautious solicitor eventually sent Ettie (or Hettie) Hughes, a nurse who had been a mutual acquaintance, to contact them in America. She visited 230 Pearl Street and would later testify in court that she had known the Daniells since their marriage and that she had seen 'Mrs Daniell and Mr Robert Nicol … living together'.[35] She mentioned a child was with them.

Miriam appears to have regarded Ettie Hughes' visit as simply a friendly call. Though she told the Koopmans that her husband's intention of seeking a divorce was causing Robert and herself 'some anxiety', she was airily dismissive, declaring that 'Edward D's' moves were merely for form's sake, attempts to 'condense the vapour of public opinion'.[36] She did not consider the possibility that he might simply have wished to be free to marry again.

Ettie Hughes' arrival enabled Miriam to discuss a medical problem that had been troubling her. Alerted by the nurse, she consulted the doctor who had delivered Sunrise. He told her he thought it was 'something he neglected' at the birth, but assured her it was something that 'may be put right'. She was unable to be specific about what this might be, even to the Koopmans, but at least she now had an explanation for having felt 'often unwell'.[37]

Harry Koopman graduated from Harvard with his MA that summer and was offered a prestigious and secure post as librarian at Brown University. Miriam, distraught, bereft and fearful, arrived at the Koopmans' home unexpectedly on the day they were departing for Providence. Helen Koopman remembered that she looked worn out, with 'black rings under her eyes'. Miriam 'threw herself into a chair' and announced she had found out 'what was the matter with her'. Starvation was staring them in the face, all they had to eat was a can of corn; she began talking wildly of writing a 'blood and thunder story' for money, and revealed they were thinking 'of going to California on foot'. This proposition greatly alarmed Harry Koopman who warned her they would be arrested as tramps.[38]

Shortly afterwards a much calmer Miriam wrote thanking the thoughtful Koopmans for the 'useful gifts' of their coal and oil supplies for the winter. She added 'if we remain', these would ensure them an 'Algerian climate!'[39] The 'if' was significant. Miriam was still entertaining the idea of venturing west and Robert, too, had become excited by California.

Their restlessness had acquired a cynosure in the shape of Alexander Ellis, Carpenter's friend from Leicester, with whom they had stayed in contact. After trying his luck as a journalist in San Francisco, Ellis had bought a ranch in the foot-hills of the Sierras, called 'White-nights', near Weimar, Placer County, only a few miles away from Hiram E. Butler's Applegate Community. When Ellis visited them in Cambridge, he painted a 'glowing picture of life in the Sierras'.[40] The mentality of the 1840s gold rush had persisted and California continued to attract optimistic seekers.

Land, regarded as a speculative investment, was being bought and sold in the hope that minerals might be discovered. Not only was Placer County rich in minerals, during the early 1890s it was being promoted as the place to make money from fruit-farming. Ellis had opted for fruit-farming, but he may well have toyed with mining, which was familiar from his background in Leicester, enthusing Robert with prospects of wealth and adventure.

Miriam, according to Helen, nursed a 'long-treasured' project of 'an Arcadian socialist colony'. This 'enchanting' dream of escaping from 'the squalor and materialism of commercial civilization' was revived by Ellis' 'invitation to hasten across the continent and on the ranch begin the projected social experiment'.[41] In Miriam's imagination his ranch, 'White-nights', was to form the nucleus of the future utopia. She was not the first or the last individualistic spirit to conceive that new ways of relating and alternative values were to be found through a rural communal life. In a letter to the Koopmans that July, Miriam casts Ellis as a mythic prophet of 'Woman', the archetype of enthusiasm and love:

> Alexander works alone in the west, clearing & preparing. Symbolically he works on almost virgin soil there, as by his life he works for Woman – Remote, he is but by the Post Office there flows to him a turbulent stream of bitterness & of denunciation from those he loves, the

Quakers of the old school because he has withdrawn from their Body & has endorsed our position.[42]

It is not clear whether she is referring to one of the esoteric groupings so fervently hunting for threads of secret wisdom from ancient times, or simply her and Robert's mix of spirituality and self-expression. But personal growth and inner development are paramount. In the same letter that July, she mentions revealing 'all' to Harris Osborn, the young artist from Cambridge she and Robert had befriended, and adds: 'Gradually Whitman, Mill, Ibsen etc had prepared him to be with us in this & other matters – in telling him we pulled down [she crosses out 'lost'] the house of our friendship, & builded a roomier palace on a foundation of gold.'[43]

During July, Miriam, Robert and Helena had moved from Pearl Street to an apartment on a hill near the edge of Cambridge. Miriam regarded it as 'a marked improvement', informing the Koopmans that from one side they looked down upon Cambridge's 'roofs and towers' and could see 'its trees & green wrapped life'. In front they had fields, blue hills and fresh air. Nevertheless, the pressures of daily life continued: Along with the expenses of moving, she described Sunrise's 'dysentery', which Miriam sought to cure by abandoning 'house keeping' and taking the small child out 'to the woods', morosely happy that her daughter could now indicate where she felt pain. Miriam wrote in the conviction that the Koopmans could understand 'the miracle of the parent's life in the childs [*sic*], & its joys and pains'. She had 'little time for reflective & tranquil persistent thought – which is why I just now produce sonnets and lyrics instead of prose'. Nevertheless, she assured Harry Koopman he was right to subordinate his writing to 'love', for 'the living is more important than the utterance of principles, or the melody of your brain'.[44]

Inspired by meeting the Stirnerite poet, Mackay, at the Schumms in September 1893, Miriam did manage to write one long poem herself and sent it to Brown for Harry Koopman's criticism that autumn. She told the couple that a recent photo of Harry's 'friendly tolerant face' sustained them. Miriam, who looked out through a veil upon the external world where others dwelt, regarded poetry rather than the library as his 'real work'. 'R earns better & Lena is proof reader', she notes in a cursory material aside.[45]

She elaborates at greater length on how a reconciliation had been effected with her parents. It was clearly important to Miriam that the Wheelers had accepted Sunrise as their grandchild, though she joked,

'Mother takes much comfort from Jehovahs [*sic*] tolerance in the Old Testament to his wicked creations. I am glad she can reason so well on unreasonable ground, and that they did not "defunct" on the blow to their respectability.'[46] The Wheelers had moved out to the rural seclusion of Frampton Cottrell, and were safely ensconced from any malicious gossip, amid the poppies, raspberry canes and 'towering hollyhocks' of a country garden.[47]

Despite being aware that she was unwell, Miriam was still planning to travel to Placer County: 'We are here for the winter if all goes well and shall hope to greet you at our home or yours before flying west next spring when the snows are melted.' Wearied by the city crowds 'of human rags, torn and distraught with nothing to give of the sweetness of a hidden life', she imagined Ellis' ranch as a haven of peace, happiness and contemplation.[48] In Helen's words, the 'western pilgrimage' had been decided; they were simply waiting for the 'means and opportunity'.[49]

Miriam's frangible equilibrium was shattered later that autumn after a visit from the Deputy Sheriff with writs for the divorce and warnings to leave Boston. News came that Robert's parents were planning to send out a messenger to ascertain his sanity.[50] After consulting a lawyer, a panic-stricken Miriam insisted they should set off immediately to join Ellis at his ranch. She later told the Koopmans he had warned them they could be arrested. While the Koopmans were urging marriage, Ellis was in 'sympathy' with 'our protest against the necessity of a vow'.[51]

According to Helen Tufts, Helena's 'inclination and judgement were against this precipitate flight'.[52] Helena had just obtained the job of her dreams. She had not simply become a 'proof-reader', she had been given responsibility and control over 'the work and proof-reading on the Harvard Magazines and job printing, and found the experience congenial & engrossing'.[53] Moreover, possessing the common sense Miriam and Robert lacked, Helena would have been conscious that the proposed journey would take them into wild countryside at a time when winter was approaching in the Sierras and roads could become impassable. She was also likely to have had a better grasp of the economic uncertainty hanging over America.

But Miriam, of course, implored her to go and Helen Tufts describes how Helena yielded to 'the urgent appeal of her harassed friend' out of 'comradeship and devotion'.[54] Helena later quipped, 'And what could I do? ... It isn't easy to live with a genius.'[55] Helen Koopman, being less complaisant towards poetic geniuses, opined: 'Miriam was so impetuous, it was her way, and she carried all before her.'[56]

The Koopmans first heard of the departure from Cambridge from young Harris Osborn. Helen Koopman expostulated in dismay to Miriam, 'Oh, if only you had come instead to Providence. You only needed to go a little way out of the State.'[57] The couple's worst fears about the folly of the migration west were confirmed by a bleak letter from Miriam, written in Sacramento on November 8th. The trio had reached the end of their long train journey and were stranded; Weimar was still about forty miles away and they were down to their last few dollars. Robert and Helena could find no work; they were eking out their money by spending a mere 25 cents each per week on food. Their lodgings were primitive. Forced to leave their household goods behind, all they had there was a stove, saucepan and frying pan, 'We sleep on the floors and the wind blows cold through chinks wide enough to admit light.'[58]

They sat looking at the photos of the Koopman family they had pinned on their bare and draughty wall, searing mementos of past happiness. They were all ill and again, Sunrise was suffering from 'croup', coughing hoarsely. Amid all this privation and despair, Miriam was endeavouring to write 'a kind of literary mush, a demi semi philosophical historical scientific paper for a magazine in faint hope of a dollar'.[59] She was so desperate she told the Koopmans that if the desert had not been between them and the east she would have started to walk back to Boston. Instead she had resorted to writing home for money. Even allowing for Miriam's penchant for melodrama their circumstances were undeniably bad. 'Arcadia' was forgotten now and she decided their flight had been 'forced by puritanism'. Miriam was collapsing; 'I cannot go on with the fight much longer. We must marry & go under, though I hate to haul down the flag.'[60] She appears to have forgotten the awkward fact that she was already married.

The dream of California as a pure natural space soured in Sacramento. By 1893 vast wealth had concentrated in the city. One of the key hubs of the railroad network that had spread westwards as a result of the gold rush, it had grown into a flourishing financial and manufacturing centre. Farmers, carpenters, grocers and lawyers had moved in, along with poor Mexicans, and the most despised and persecuted group, the Chinese. Banned by the 1881 Exclusion Act, the Chinese who remained lived a segregated existence. Like Miriam, Robert and Helena, Sacramento's immigrants had dreamed of America as the land where anything might be possible. But Miriam loathed the place, with 'its flat baked plain and its heated dry odourless air', and recoiled from the people she saw around her, 'the passionate fierce animalism & the repressed Catholic types & the men who have <u>done something</u> & are furtive'. She shuddered with fear and horror when she saw Chinese workers, their faces seemed 'debased' to her.[61] Her racism was, it is true, common at the time. But it is ironic how the acutely sensitive Miriam could be utterly incapable of empathy.

In Sacramento Miriam was no longer able to wrap herself in what she had described to the Koopmans only a few weeks before as 'the sweetness of a hidden life'. There was no superior insight, no esoteric enlightenment, no Arcadia. She was utterly exposed. It had finally dawned on her that all that lay ahead was 'a dirty log cabin' – Ellis' ranch; 'I do not think we can cope with such virgin soil as the pine clad slopes of the precipitous Sierras. I wish I could give you some breath of beauty or of life but I am too sad.' She related to her appalled friends, 'RAN [Robert] is crushed and poor Lena feels up a blind alley.'[62]

Somehow they found the money for the fare from Sacramento. By November 23rd Miriam was writing to the Koopmans from Ellis' ranch near Weimar, Placer County, thanking them for the $10 they had sent and scrupulously returning $5. Rejecting her friends' advice to marry, she was adamant that she and Robert would have no more children. Resolutely Miriam asserted the importance of freedom and her belief that they had found 'the best solution for one phase of the Sex Question … I love Robert. I believe we shall find it is a love till death.'[63] Though Miriam informed the Koopmans loftily that Sunrise was to be raised in solitude close to nature, their living conditions were daunting, and Miriam, who had suffered from lung and larynx problems, was now troubled by a persistent cough. Yet, on November 28th, when Miriam was able to return the final $5 of their debt from furniture they had sold and money from her father, she insisted she was able to adjust to 'rugged simplicity without danger to health'.[64] Miriam and Helena transformed their cabin with paintings and books and the Koopmans sent a present of a 'pretty book' – a missive from the East.[65] Moreover, the scenery and climate of White-nights compensated for their gruelling experiences. Helena told the Koopmans on December 20th, 'Each height we climb reveals new wonders. In one direction you may look on the distant coast range, in the other the horizon is bounded by the snow-capped peaks that lie between us and the great desert.'[66]

Ellis' ranch was in a sheltered valley surrounded by tall pines. The weather that December was miraculously warm and sunny, interspersed with heavy rainfall that swelled the little streams flowing into the north fork of the great American River nearby. After Christmas, in a letter to the Koopmans, Miriam wrote, 'You don't know how I long to send you our weather. In Dec we had strawberries and roses and violets and even now yellow escolchia [*sic, escholia*] and pale sweet manzanita blossoms bring the bees buzzing about.'[67] Fascinated by a canyon down the river and relishing the 'pungent, perfumed evergreen' trees of the Sierras, Miriam would lie down in the red earth with pine needles prickling her back and look up at the 'giant trunks', charred and blackened by forest fires.[68]

Meanwhile, clambering up and down the precipitous passes, discovering watercress and mint, Helena collected 'baskets-full of the pinkest mushrooms – a vegetarian luxury' that sold in Cambridge for a dollar a pound.[69] She was applying Geddes and Graeff's advice to learn through living and doing; and the fungi on the hillsides of the Sierras would lead her to study mycology. She busied herself cropping wood for the stove, clearing and burning fallen branches, and, as usual, taking responsibility for the housekeeping.[70] Helena, who had begun to carve out a cultivated career in Cambridge, characteristically acclimatised to a pioneer life. Stoically, she reflected to the Koopmans, 'Just now it seems to me a sane ideal to live simply, in contact with Mother Earth, to have few needs and to supply them as far as possible oneself on a co-operative basis.'[71]

Ellis' ranch was certainly in the wilds, though not the lawless 'Wild West' of legend. True, up in the north, Colfax remained a rough settlement, and highwaymen could still raid the trains and coaches in Placer County, but Auburn, the county seat in the south, took an increasing pride in its blossoming cultural assets. Weimar itself had originated in a small settlement called New England Mills. Some of the miners had stayed after the 1840s gold rush, to be joined by farmers, struggling to grow fruit in the mountainous terrain. When residents applied for a post office in 1885, they substituted 'Weimar', derived, it seems, from the name of an old Indian chief, 'Weimah' and retaining the pronunciation.[72]

Scattered among these resilient mountain people around Weimar and Applegate, clusters of experimental lifers, seers, healers, mystics and bohemian misfits were to be found, attracted by the prospect of freedom, as well as the invigorating air and natural beauty of the area. On a walk shortly after they arrived, Miriam encountered one of these eccentric settlers, 'Miss Osborne', living in a hut near one of the river's bends. She instantly recognised a soul mate. Miss Osborne had become a hermit because 'she loved nature and wanted to get away from society, with its foolish requirements and insincerity'. Kissing the hermit's worn hand, Miriam pronounced, 'I had no need to ask who the empty huts were for. I knew that they were built and waiting for women of magnetic spirit who had weighed modern life and found it wanting.'[73]

Miss Osborne was a favoured exception; shortly afterwards, Helena relayed to the Koopmans that they had not 'yet responded to the advances of the neighbors to become acquainted'.[74] She also mentioned that Miriam was unwell. Helena, Robert and Sunrise, despite breaking her arm, were flourishing at White-nights, but Miriam's health had deteriorated rapidly and she was bedridden. On Christmas Day, decorating the rafters of the ranch house with white and green mistletoe and red berries, they had to draw the table to her bedside.[75]

Yet still Miriam did not stop writing. Thanks to Helen Tufts, her poem 'Bohemia' later found its way into the anarchist paper, *Free Society*:

> In the land where all law is a shadow
> On seas where each port is a bier
> I have found me a new El Dorado,
> A life that is unhaunted by fear.
>
> I have found me a chamber to dwell in,
> And have carven a seat and a shelf;
> Wrought in a chest that were meet for Greek Helen;
> My walls I have pictured myself...
>
> I have found me few friendships but steady;
> Outspoken, gruff, resolute folk,
> Who have weathered life's storms and sea's eddy
> And tamed the fierce fates to a yoke.[76]

Miriam spent little time in the balmy valley amid the roses, escholia and manzanita. By late December, aware she was 'exceedingly ill', she reported to the Koopmans that she was 'being nursed up enough to go to a hospital for a serious operation'.[77] Miriam, apt to panic before imaginary dangers, faced the threat to her life with a steady inward strength. It was as if all those intimations of death in her poetry had served as rehearsals. Now, her opening night before her, she knew exactly what to do. Sending her love in a shaky hand to the Koopmans, equably she began to make plans for Sunrise's education. She kept on writing, proudly telling the Koopmans that her poems and prose were 'still finding a channel'. Indeed, she had discovered a new outlet, 'The Religio Philosophic Mag', which had published an essay by her on 'the ultimate aggregation'.[78] The *Religio-Philosophical Journal* was edited by Benjamin Franklin Underwood, a thoughtful freethinker and social reformer, married to an outspoken advocate of women's rights and spiritualism.[79] But Miriam had passed beyond the time for new mentors.

Helena remained at the ranch while Miriam went to San Francisco with Robert and Sunrise for treatment. While Miriam lay there sick and in pain on a hospital bed, disaster struck. In a letter from San Francisco she wrote, 'the ranch has vanished. Smoke was seen and a few tongues of flame hungrily licking the outside of the roof ... In a second the place was a whirlpool of flame....' She related how 'In fifteen minutes everything had gone, only smouldering, the lazy smoke blew down the cañon and wreathed about the hilltops quietly. It was over.'[80]

Helena had watched helplessly as the cabin, containing all their beloved aesthetic objects, everything that had belonged to their lives together, burned to the ground. She would subsequently reflect philosophically, 'One needs such an experience, if only once in a lifetime, to teach self-dependence and the futility of relying on material things for happiness.'[81]

Yet to Miriam facing death, it seemed like the annihilation of an identity she had so assiduously cultivated. She observed, 'Truly it is well we do not anchor to things', yet symbolically the objects had accrued profound value:

> I lost all my books many of them authors' presentations and picked editions not to be measured by money standards in their worth to me, vases and pottery which had belonged to my grandmother, and years of work in oil- paintings which I may not hope to do again for my child.[82]

Helen Koopman related that Miriam turned upon Helena in bitterness:

> When the cabin in California was burned, it was Helena who had the blame of that, too – she had built up a big fire to make bread, and had gone off for a little while, – it is just what I would have done. It did not mean carelessness on Helena's part, but a defect in the stove. Miriam

wrote to me about it, and I said then to Mr Koopman, as soon as I read it, 'That is one of Miriam's ways.'[83]

Perhaps the fire signified to Miriam the destruction of a relationship in which Helena had already begun to resist her silently. In 'Bohemia', Miriam is blessed with a light-giving 'angel', but her poem 'The Cross-roads' begins, 'Friends go from me. They say,/"Your way is not our way"'.[84] The cruel paradox was that Helena's busy, productive endeavours to make the best of circumstances not of her own choosing had severed her from the woman she had loved before all others. Whatever happened during Miriam's last days, their paths parted; Helena buried the pain.

In February, Miriam wrote to the Koopmans from San Francisco, 'I am completely invalided and next month have to undergo a more serious operation than we thought.'[85] A 'clever' and 'kind' Jewish specialist who was a Professor at the Medical College 'will perform it probably in his private Hospital'. She had also consulted a second doctor but he 'thinks poorly of my chance of life'.[86] Miriam hoped the Koopmans would 'Keep in touch with my two dear ones if I die & befriend them. Not with money, but with human loving kindness. I hope they will not want now the material bread of existence.'[87] It was Robert and Sunrise not Helena that Miriam regarded as needful of protection and support.

I am suffering much
Dear friends Goodbye, Goodbye
I am full of quiet peace & courage, content to go or stay. There is no chance of my ever being a strong woman again anyhow which makes one more ready to be resigned.
I am glad to have known you
May you be happy and healthy –
Harry write for the people & for Liberty.
Helen here's a kiss to you
Bless the bairns for me.
   Touch their little heads for me in love.
You would like this place with its mountains bolt upright round the bay – and the sun setting through the Golden Gate.
With our love
   Yours now (& <u>after</u>)
   Miriam[88]

At the end Miriam had found her Arcadia, in a city, rather than in nature. But she was never to become a San Franciscan.

On April 15th, awaiting her operation, she told the Koopmans tersely that since the fire Helena 'has left us to go east'. Robert and Sunrise visited her each day. Close to death, she retained some interest in external events; her 'eye' was upon the desperate 'Industrial army' of the unemployed who had left San Francisco late that March to struggle across America. She regretted her inability to 'voice their needs'. Miriam died on 19 April 1894.[89]

By a grim twist of fate Edward Tuckett Daniell was granted his divorce on April 30th; Robert Allan Nicol was named as the co-respondent and ordered to pay costs within six months.[90] But the valley near Weimar was far away, and Robert remained in California.

Back in Cambridge, Helena was left alone with her memories. Helen Tufts, who loved Helena dearly, struggled in her assessment of Miriam. From Helena's descriptions, Helen imagined a tragic, romantic figure: 'Living out her life in defiance of custom and her own upbringing, she ruptured all ties that were less than those of perfect sympathy, and exulted in the hardships to which her course fated her.' Helen presents Miriam as a 'dreamer', 'beautiful', 'spirited', 'sensitive', who 'wandered with her head in the clouds', yet somehow saw the underlying causes of human suffering. Nevertheless, ambivalent towards the woman who had turned against Helena, she also portrays Miriam as 'imperious' and dominating, moving 'in isolation of spirit'.[91]

It was Helen, however, who ensured that Miriam's writings reached early twentieth-century readers, not only through the anarchist *Free Society*, but in the Whitmanite journal *The Conservator*, edited by the poet's devoted amanuensis, Horace Traubel. Helen informed Traubel on 18 December 1901 that the poems she was sending him by Miriam Daniell were among her last works, and 'so far as I can find' had not been published before.[92] In one poem, 'I AM', Miriam echoes Whitman and Carpenter's defiance of self-abnegation. The woman, Miriam, transcends gender boundaries and hierarchies. Her 'I' affirms the democratic voice of the 'vulgar and incurious', excluded by 'Spiritual Monopolists', the complacent, sure, 'Self-patented Nobles'. 'I' inhabits earth, sea, wind, fire and breath:

I am in all things, all life, all people, all that Is.

I am Woman and Femaleness equally with Man and Maleness.

I am the passive and conservative, the active and the radical
principles.

Do you deny the Soul? Do you suffer shame on account of the body
and its tendencies?

Hearken!

There is no part of Me better or worse than another.

I justify Myself in that I am.[93]

Still Miriam longs to fuse body and spirit; still she is the iconoclast convinced that temples, gaols, palaces, colleges of learning, factories, filthy cities, must all turn to dust. But now she recognises only 'the fluid Universe'. And, 'Occult behind your occultation', she defies the exclusive male guardians of the 'mysteries': 'I penetrate the walls which you erect./I leap the boundaries which you set to enclose Me'.[94]

Thus, at the end, Miriam the extreme antinomian rebel against enclosure rejected any single theory of enlightenment and transformation. In another poem, 'REFORM', she writes: 'The eye sees only at one time the thing/Whereon it looks, all else is blurred and faint'.[95] In 'To the Earth', she returns to matter, re-entering the 'Mother' to forget.[96] In 'So Long', a boundless Miriam bids her final farewell:

One last time I girdle earth with these arms; I taste her sweet and sour, I see her million sights – her teeming life, her myriad lights and shadows … Death beckons me, I do not fear him … And yet I linger turn my head, prolong farewell. Not to wipe April tears from lovers' eyes, or shake my shoe dust at my enemies…[97]

Moving beyond torment, Miriam, at thirty-one, had found a 'Love' so powerful it could contain hate within itself. 'Love I taste, hear, see, feel, everywhere … So long! so long! I may not tarry. You in your turn shall see it without aid of mine. Death your hand; here's mine to you.'[98]

PART 2

QUESTS

NINE

Revolutionary Lineages: Helen Tufts

elen was born on 9 January 1874, at the advent of America's
'Gilded Age'.[1] Despite periodic depressions and violent class
and race conflicts, the country she grew up in was moving
towards a position of unprecedented wealth and power. Yet Helen inherited a cultural idyll of an America that was fast becoming obsolete.
Through her parents and grandparents she was imbued with a respect for
learning, a sense of individual possibility and a conviction that life should
be led according to principles. The typewritten manuscript entitled 'The
Journals of Helen Matilda Tufts Bailie, from 1886' documents both how
her consciousness changed and how she remained perplexed by a sense of
mismatch. Somehow lived existence never quite shaped up to her expectations; she was left reaching towards an elusive, imagined America.

As she grew older, Helen became more and more intrigued by forebears and lineages, researching her family's history as if probing for an
explanation of how she, herself, had come about. A summary inserted at
the beginning of the journal goes back to early settlers, some of whom
had arrived in Massachusetts with the Puritan John Winthrop in 1630.
On her father's side were Tuftses and Adamses while her mother's family
heritage included French Huguenots who had fled after Louis XIV denied
Protestants religious freedom in 1685.[2]

Helen was especially proud of her revolutionary great-great-grand-
parents, Peter Tufts and Anne Adams, cousin of President John Adams.
A family story, passed down from generation to generation, told of
Paul Revere, the legendary coppersmith turned courier, waking her

grandparents at Medford in 1775 with his call 'Get up Tufts, the British are coming.' He had evaded an ambush to take news of the British army's movements to American Patriots. Instead of fleeing to safety, the Tufts remained in their home, receiving and caring for the wounded from the battle of Bunker Hill. Helen records how George Washington himself later thanked great-great-grandmother Anne personally.[3]

Family memories bestowed upon Helen an insider's sense of commitment and duty, combined with the conviction that true esteem was earned through service. They instilled spiritual principles too; great-grandfather Joseph Tufts had seceded from the Orthodox Congregationalists in Charlestown to establish the first Unitarian parish in Massachusetts.[4] The Unitarians' questioning of the supernatural, their commitment to reason grounded in education, was inscribed upon Helen's life.

Her grandfather, also called Joseph, was born in 1783 and graduated from Harvard in 1807. He became a lawyer in Charlestown, endowed the town with a library and, in 1827, married Helen Whittemore, also of heroic revolutionary antecedents.[5] The couple had three children; the youngest, William Whittemore Tufts, born in 1831, was to be become young Helen's father and it was he who communicated to her most intensely that sense of a country gone askew.

Joseph Tufts had only just provided his wife and family with a new house, when he died of diabetes in 1835. During her mid-twenties Helen Whittemore Tufts' comfortable and predictable life in Charlestown was shattered. Returning to West Cambridge (now Arlington) where she had been raised, her granddaughter records that the young widow 'identified with the cultured group of the Unitarian parish'.[6] Unitarianism was being riven by a series of traumatic controversies. Ralph Waldo Emerson's emphasis upon the spiritual self-determination of every human being strained even the tolerant ecumenism of the Unitarian faith. Emerson broke with the Unitarian Church, but his Transcendentalist call to be self-reliant, to build one's own world and value personal feeling and friendship, exerted a profound influence upon the Unitarian circles in which Helen's grandmother moved.

In the early 1850s her Transcendentalist connections enabled the attractive and intelligent young widow to obtain a clerical post for bookish William Whittemore Tufts at the publishers, Little, Brown and Co.[7] He soon became restless and, in 1853, struck out on his own with 'Tufts' American and Foreign Literary Agency', selling books by mail and commending himself to the Presbyterian Theological School as a purveyor of 'Truth'.[8] The venture failed and he was obliged to take a clerical post in the New York Commissary, which was a great deal duller than publishing. He found relief from the tedium by becoming a regular frequenter of Shakespeare's plays at Wallack's Theatre and gravitating to Henry Ward Beecher's Congregationalist Plymouth Church in Brooklyn, where he found drama of a different kind. The charismatic preacher was at the height of his powers and huge crowds flocked to hear him fulminate against slavery. Beecher's social commitment and his rejection of a punitive God moved Helen's father so profoundly that he decided he was called to the ministry.[9]

In 1855 the young man wrote a desperate letter to John MacLean Jr, the recently appointed President of Princeton University, telling him 'I love to preach, preach'. Impatient, yet filled with guilt at abandoning his post at the Commissary, he admitted, 'I fear that I am discontented with the situation in this life which God sees fit to place me.' The unsettled pattern that was becoming evident caused concern. His mother, sister, relatives and friends regarded 'the great change as a dampner to all further success in the affairs of the world'. With an ominous prescience, young Tufts announced, 'I shall never be a rich man.'[10] Periodic bouts of righteousness and a chafing conscience indeed destined him to an erratic career course.

The 'great change' was effected and Tufts entered Presbyterian Princeton in 1857, finding a benefactor in Revd Henry J. Van Dyke of Brooklyn, who paid off his debts and helped find him work in the belief that the young enthusiast would defend 'Good Old School Presbyterians'. Managing his finances was never to be William Tufts' strong point; in March 1862 an indigent Tufts nervously enquired whether Van Dyke might happen to have an old carpet 'lying up unused' that he could put down in his college room.[11] Otherwise, though, he flourished at Princeton, contributing to the University's *Nassau Magazine*, which he eventually edited.[12] He had stumbled towards his true metier – the life of a permanent impecunious student.

In 1862, when America was being torn apart by the Civil War, William Tufts was preoccupied with what President Maclean regarded as 'peculiar' theological ideas. As faith had to be 'spontaneous', it followed that 'the unregenerate' should not be 'exhorted to believe in Christ'.[13] Maclean concluded such opinions were not compatible with the Presbyterian ministry, so instead William Tufts became a sub-master at Newark Academy, one of New Jersey's oldest day schools. Once again Tufts had acquired modest prospects, yet before long humanity and conscience got in the way and the new recruit was at variance with the school Principal, a man whom Helen describes as 'a whipper'.[14] After William Tufts challenged the treatment of the boys, the Principal resigned, whereupon the excessively ethical whistle-blower felt honour-bound to give in his notice too.

Newark offered more congenial outlets to a man nursing literary ambitions and Tufts acquired a column in the local paper. But after he wrote a critical series of articles on Newark's ministers it was mysteriously cut. He then fixed on another career move, the study of homeopathic medicine. Like many of his contemporaries, he was attracted to its holistic approach to diagnosis and treatment as opposed to allopathy's reliance on drugs.[15]

When thirty-nine-year-old Tufts qualified from the New York Homeopathic Medical College in 1870, the question of prospects loomed with some urgency, for he had fallen in love. The most fortunate aspect of his sojourn in Newark proved to be lodging with the Terrill family where he met his bride to be, Isabel Terrill. Born in 1848, she was seventeen years his junior when they married in 1870. Like the Tufts, the Terrills had been staunch supporters of the American Revolution. They were also creative and artistic; Isabel's father, Daniel, was a skilled craft engraver and watch-case maker.[16]

The Terrills clearly valued religious toleration, for despite being Presbyterian, they accepted their new son-in-law who now followed the Universalists. The group, which was inspired by Emerson, was close to Unitarianism, but emphasised compassion and universal salvation rather than a rationalistic, critical Deism. Like the Unitarians, Universalists participated prominently in movements for reform, supporting the abolition of slavery and the campaign for women's suffrage. So it was appropriate that William Tufts would present his young bride with a subscription to *The Atlantic*; founded in 1857 by Emerson and Harriet Beecher Stowe, the magazine combined culture with reform.[17] This was to be the ethos in which Helen was raised.

When Helen came to type up her journal she added a graphic account of her early childhood. She was especially cherished, for her parents had lost a child before she was born in Newark, New Jersey. However, the family's economic fortunes were always uncertain; William Tufts never did provide economic security.

When Helen was two, her father spun around once again. Feeling the call, this time to the Unitarian ministry, he brought his family first to West Medford, and then to Cambridge. Between 1876 and 1878 he studied at Harvard Divinity School when it was opening up to the Transcendental Universalism Emerson had inspired. This was the intellectual and spiritual heritage his daughter absorbed as she grew older. In later life she oscillated between reverence and exasperation towards her father, but from him she acquired a sense of life as a quest.

The birth of a second child, Helen's brother Russell, in 1878, added to the pressure on the family's budget. Accordingly, when William Tufts was offered a pastorate in the small town of Warwick, it must have seemed providential. Unfortunately, they made the journey in a Massachusetts winter with deep snow on the ground. Helen was only four, but that first encounter with Warwick remained imprinted on her mind.

> A sleigh took us over from Wendell thro the woods, and along a lovely road. My Mother's horror showed in her face. She must have thot [*sic*] we were moving into a howling wilderness. As we passed into the village and went by the cottage we were to occupy, buried in snow to the second story window, Mama moaned.[18]

For the first few days they lodged with the Joneses who owned their cottage. The civic-minded Nahum Jones was the wealthiest man in the small settlement. He had come from Boston and established a factory turning out thousands of boots and shoes a year. Otherwise farming and logging were the main sources of livelihood. Warwick had been incorporated as a town back in 1763 and some of the original families could still be found there in the 1870s. But the town's growth had been hampered by its inaccessibility and when the Tufts arrived the population was still only a few hundred.[19]

By 17 June 1878, the day of William Tufts' ordination, the snow had long melted and Isabel Tufts had taken down the quilts shielding the windows. Somehow she had found the time to compose a hymn that was sung in celebration at the ordination, an august Unitarian event, attended by many local ministers. In 1937 Helen found a clipping in an old book from the Unitarian *Christian Register* which reported the ceremony with the comment, 'It was fitting that so many of the sons of Warwick should have taken part.'[20]

By the 1870s the Unitarians, with their tall white Meeting House, were the largest religious grouping in Warwick, dominating the governance of the small town. Helen remembered the church, standing opposite her School House on a 'long hill leading down through the village past Albee's store'.[21] A photograph of Abner Albee, who was also Warwick's postmaster, conserved by the Warwick Historical Society, reveals a proud bearded man, hair neatly flattened, elegant in bow-tie and starched white collar. The Tufts' cottage was just at the back of his shop, and in the summer Helen used to push her baby brother Russell in her doll carriage up and down a small incline nearby. In the winter when it became slippery with ice and snow, Helen, wrapped in 'an old pair of Papa's pants', could slither down it.[22]

Warwick offered a delightful freedom to a small girl, but for Isabel Tufts, still in her early thirties and accustomed to cultured Cambridge, it must have felt constricting. She adapted as best she could, becoming a keen member of the Ladies' Archery Club that gathered during the summer at the home of Helen's playmate, Mavorite Reed. The Reeds, one of Warwick's old families, lived in one of the larger eighteenth-century houses, set back from the Athol Road. They held lively gatherings on their long front lawn in summer and delicious maple sugarings in the winter – in old age Helen could still recall the wonderful hot syrup cooling in the snow.

When her mother took the children by stagecoach to stay with their Terrill grandparents at a farm in East Orange, they were pleasurably indulged. Helen recalled licking the sugar off buns there without earning a rebuke. She developed an early love of animals on these visits; too tender-hearted to eat a hen consigned to become chicken soup, she was mightily honoured when a cow was named after her.[23]

She was learning from her surroundings, perceiving Divinity in awe-inspiring nature, long before she read Emerson. It was all around her, cloaked in folklore. From the cottage window in Warwick, she could see Bennett's Hill, named after a 'Mr Bennett' who boasted he had shot a deer bounding over it across a ravine half a mile wide. Even more imposing were the peaks dubbed 'Mount Grace' and 'Little Grace' in memory of a mother and baby captured by Indians in the 1670s; both Graces were green and verdant in spring and summer, but loomed a foreboding purple in the winter twilight. Helen formed a close attachment to her father and accompanied him on long walks in which he used to teach her about the past from the landscape, identifying rocks and boulders or pointing out old cellar holes made by the Indians, as well as abandoned quarries where the early British settlers had mined for ore. The violence with which the land had been taken remained sealed from memory; Helen simply notes, 'Warwick had an Indian history.'[24]

Helen's formal education was dispensed in the local School House. A Warwick Historical Society photograph from the 1870s shows a simple building with a large iron bell and shuttered windows. About twenty children, ranging in age from toddlers to nine or ten year olds, straddle the front entrance in a line. There, in the one-roomed school, Helen learned how to spell 'CAT' and 'RAT', but William and Isabel Tufts wanted more for their intelligent daughter than the 'three Rs'. Her artistic Terrill grandparents possessed a collection of beautifully illustrated children's books and her mother brought her some designed by Walter Crane, the socialist friend of William Morris. The enlightened Tufts parents believed in stimulating the imagination of children rather than simply instilling facts or moral lessons. Helen delighted in the fanciful Ting-a-Ling stories by Frank Stockton, in the *Riverside Magazine for Young People*, and enjoyed the *St. Nicholas Magazine*, which set out to encourage creativity and resourcefulness and included Louisa May Alcott, Mark Twain and Rudyard Kipling among its contributors.[25]

Helen remembered the care her father took in patiently answering her childish questions. But what made the deepest impression upon her was his compassionate example. Local people would come to the kindly minister when they were in trouble, and, because there was no doctor in Warwick, William Tufts began treating people as a homeopath. Helen used to accompany him on visits, recalling how startled he was by one woman patient, a medium who invoked visions of his brother and sister. It was not, however, the spirits, but William's dramatic enthusiasms that led to his downfall. His Shakespeare club at the Joneses, his reading groups devoted to Wordsworth and Browning, might be culturally acceptable.[26] But when the Tufts family started distributing flyers for his production of 'Mother Goose', tongues began to wag. While 'Mother Goose' was successfully performed in the hall above Stimson's store where magic-lantern shows were held, and raised enough money for a new set of hymn books, controversy persisted.[27] A clique of 'back biters' in the church started 'adverse mutterings' against William and a new minister was chosen. 'Papa was never one to fight for himself', remarked a rueful Helen.[28]

Wounded by the back biters, William 'accepted a call to Tyngsboro' (also Tyngsborough). And so after three and a half years, when Helen was eight, the family moved once again, this time to an even tinier settlement situated on the Merrimack River. In the winter, when the river froze, Helen learned to skate. The Unitarian church there was by a rickety red iron bridge and, each spring, when logs floated down from the northern woods they would pile up against it, causing anxiety about its safety.[29] Helen was growing into a serious child, 'devoted' to the Children's Page in the Unitarian *Christian Register*. But moral improvement continued to be leavened by the Transcendentalist imagination; Isabel Tufts introduced Greek myths to Helen and her brother Russell, by reading them Nathaniel Hawthorne's *Tanglewood Tales*.[30]

Isabel became active in Tyngsboro's recently formed 'Unitarian Women's Auxiliary Alliance'. Though they focused on education and raising money for the church, advanced ideas undoubtedly penetrated, for Unitarian women had played a prominent role in early suffrage organising. While Helen's mother was busy organising church fairs and socials, including a 'Little Folks Concert' for the Children's Mission, William Tufts was once again embroiled in controversies with members of the church and the local school. In 1884 the nomination of James Gillespie Blaine as Presidential candidate divided Republicans. Suspecting him of corruption, Helen's father supported a group of high-minded, dissident Republicans who backed the Democrat, Grover Cleveland.[31] Labelled 'Mugwumps', they saw themselves as rising above party, but their opponents regarded their defection as treachery, especially when the Democrats won the election. The local postmaster, Mr Littlehale, was, according to Helen, 'a loud Republican', who branded William Tufts as a political outcast. Feelings ran high, and 'Mugwumpery' led Helen and her desk mate, Cora Littlehale, to quarrel 'bitterly behind our geographies'.[32]

Troubled about the standard of schooling, challenged by a rival candidate for the post of minister and isolated politically and culturally, in March 1884, an anxious and weary William Tufts wrote to the Secretary of the American Unitarian Association, Grindall Reynolds. Mentioning opposition from some of his parishioners, he raised the question of securing a more permanent post.[33]

This was not to be; in 1885 William Tufts abruptly abandoned the ministry and decided to return to medicine. His daughter concluded that, after seven years of banishment, her father 'longed for old friends and old haunts'.[34] They headed back to Arlington, tragically without their horse Chilperic, who had to be sold. Helen's only consolation was a beloved black-and-white English shepherd dog called Pan. Though the move would be beneficial for Helen, she later looked back nostalgically to those happy childhood years in Warwick and Tyngsboro, when she had been particularly close to her father. Even so, she acknowledged that his inclination to dwell upon abstractions rather than earning a living was partly responsible for some of the tribulations to come.

He had fatally failed to register that Arlington did not lack doctors, allopathic *or* homeopathic. Appearances mattered in Arlington, so they moved from their little house in Court Street to Arlington Avenue, in the hope that it would be better for the practice. Instead their costs increased.[35] By summer 1888, whenever a new doctor arrived Helen wished him up in 'the moon'.[36] She bemoaned her father's reluctance to press patients who 'pleaded hard times', sighing that if only he could collect what was owed, 'we would then be easy'.[37]

They were not easy at all and consequently the burden of responsibility came early for Helen. From the age of twelve she was helping her mother in the house, watching the bread, so her parents could take a walk together, and doing the washing and the ironing.[38] Her childhood instilled a genteel frugality of mend and make do; in 1887 Helen made a spool-bag for her mother's thirty-ninth birthday.[39] 'How poor we were in Arlington' she later exclaimed.[40]

Young Helen identified implicitly with her father's values, revering Henry Ward Beecher, and gazing reverentially at the portrait of her principled great-grandfather, Joseph Tufts, while visiting a relative, Cora Brown, at Concord. Though steeped in *Uncle Tom's Cabin* and raised to admire the opponents of slavery, Helen also assimilated the unthinking prejudices that surrounded her. On a visit to her mother's family in New York in November 1886, the children 'blacked up', copying the popular minstrel shows, and Helen fixed red flannel around her head to look like a 'darkey' (*sic*). A year later she was shivering in dread when two of the Chicago anarchists, accused of a bomb plot in the Haymarket, were spared from execution.[41]

The move to Arlington ensured a good education. Helen attended Russell Grammar School, a large, new brick building where she thrived as a pupil until June 1888, when she proudly received her graduation diploma tied 'with a blue ribbon'.[42] She went on to Cotting High School, recording in her journal that she was reading Caesar and Virgil and studying Greek grammar.[43] At home she read avidly, sharing Grandmother Tufts' love of Dickens and acquiring her father's enthusiasm for the theatre.

*   *   *

In June 1892 childhood ended abruptly when Helen, aged eighteen, graduated. Ruefully, she recorded how her parents had decided she must forego a graduation ring.[44] But the most painful denial was not continuing her education. Helen's friends, young women as well as men, were joining the expanding rolls of college students: 'Mary Hadley is going to Boston University; Mary Leavens to Wellesley; Ernest Moore to MIT, also Fred Damon; Arlie White to Harvard.' Her only consolation was the discovery, 'There are grey-haired students at College nowadays.'[45]

Full of youthful aspiration and intellectual vigour, Helen was forced to buckle down and think about earning a living. Encouraged by her father to practise writing in her journal, and feeling special in her bookishness, she nursed higher hopes than 'typing and book-keeping', noting disdainfully how 'The stupidest girls' from school had become 'stenographers'.[46] Hence, like many other young women seeking genteel employment in Boston, the 'Lady of Labor' entered the literary world at its lowly end, packing envelopes for the mass-circulation magazine, *The Youth's Companion*. From October 1892, Helen sat at a long table with a group of other young women sorting and folding circulars which they placed in envelopes. The work was completely unskilled, even the addresses were added downstairs. She toiled from 8 until 6, earning $6 a week – a relatively high salary at the time – but too low for independent respectable survival. Moreover, to her distress, the fares into Boston took $1 each week from her pay.[47]

She was caught in the transit problem currently agitating the city's entrepreneurs and planners. Boston was spreading outwards as more and more middle-class residents fled to the edges of the city to escape the new waves of immigrant poor. By day the commuters returned to an increasingly congested commercial centre. Horse-drawn vehicles were giving way to electric cable cars but, for the time being, both competed for space, slowing down journeys.[48]

In 1893, with help from her father, Helen moved to Cambridge's Riverside Press, a printing works that was part of the publishers Houghton Mifflin. Its founder, Henry O. Houghton, had been a close associate of Little, Brown and Co., before building up his successful business of well-produced books. Helen's mother, who held advanced views on women's employment, favoured typesetting, but Helen found her fingers were all thumbs and soon realised she was not welcome as a woman in the printing trade.[49] The 'vicious' behaviour of the man who ran the press distressed the sheltered new recruit: 'He uses bad language, and talks with the other typesetter in such a way as to shock me on purpose.'[50] To her great relief, a 'crushed' Helen was moved to the proofreading department. There the atmosphere and company were more congenial. However, the close work quickly affected her eyes, glasses had to be bought and a trip to the Eye and Ear hospital followed.[51]

These expenses were incurred when Helen and the whole Tufts family were under severe pressure. Grandmother Helen Tufts was ailing, and money so scarce even younger brother Russell was mowing lawns in an effort to contribute. It all felt unjust:

> Papa should have made a success here. But a doctor must make a show, keep a home and have an oily tongue. Papa will not praise himself, and Mama and Russell and I am proud of him for it. How many poor families he has seen through long and dangerous illness and how few have paid him a cent. Mama, with all her noble and ennobling ambitions, is a slave to the kitchen, eking something out of nothing day after day.[52]

Helen felt her responsibility as the wage earner keenly. To reduce the fare cost she started walking four miles to and from work each day in all weathers – an experience that led her to favour 'sensible bloomers' and wish she possessed the courage to wear them.[53]

Helen's first glimpse of a radical critique of wider social injustice came through the Unitarian church early in 1893. The Unitarians were looking outwards to other faiths, and that March invited the unorthodox German-American Rabbi, Solomon Schindler, to speak on 'Socialism vs. Individualism'. Schindler's enquiring mind had brought him close to the Unitarians and then led him towards the socialism expounded in Edward Bellamy's influential utopian novel *Looking Backward* (1888). Reading Bellamy convinced Schindler of the need to nationalise basic utilities, converting him to the 'Nationalist 'movement, inspired by the novel. When Helen heard Schindler speak, he was working on a sequel to Bellamy's book, called *Young West*, packed with proposals for reforming all forms of inequality through collectivist state intervention.[54] Helen was puzzled and shocked to hear Schindler blaming 'individualists for selfishness and inequality' and was dubious about his interpretation of socialism as 'Evolution, not Revolution'.[55]

Helen adopted the views of her parents for whom violent socialists and anarchists melded into a malign mélange with rowdy Irish men and illiterate immigrants. 'Discontented and ignorant Poles and Italians, Russians and Germans come over and work for less than Americans will, and then, influenced by Herr Most and his followers, turn and rend anyone they can hit.'[56] By the 1890s the foreign-born from many other lands had dramatically augmented Boston's population. Among them was the Bavarian revolutionary, Johann Most. In 1887, outraged by the execution of the Chicago anarchists, Most had delivered an incendiary speech and been put in jail. But Helen exaggerated his influence among Boston's immigrants, many of whom were Catholics, loyal to the Church hierarchy.[57]

Individual rights, however, met with the Tufts' approval and Helen shared her mother's commitment to women's suffrage. In February 1894 she notes that the Massachusetts Woman Suffrage Association (M.W.S.A.) had succeeded in bringing a bill for partial suffrage in municipal elections before the Massachusetts Lower House. They had formed an alliance with the Woman's Christian Temperance Union, which stressed social purity, as well as with the Loyal Women of America, a right-wing, anti-Catholic organization. Nevertheless, the bill was defeated in the State Senate and morale in the Massachusetts suffrage movement slumped.[58]

Helen made a long-standing friend at Riverside, Ella Davis, who she describes as having suffrage and social purity 'much at heart'.[59] The suffrage movement was shifting away from Stanton and Anthony's assertion of women's political and social rights and presenting women as a source of ethical power. This had conservative implications, as it was often assumed that moral standards were not simply inherently female, but embodied by a worthy female elite. However, it contained a transformatory aspect too; the radical edge to social purity was a commitment to equal standards for men and women in personal behaviour.

In May 1894, twenty-year-old Helen, striking out towards emancipation in everyday living, garnered Ella Davis along with Isabel Tufts as allies in the cause of rational dress:

> Bloomers are gradually coming to be accepted as sensible and unalarming. Mama and I like them very much, Papa detests them, and Russell would be dreadfully self conscious if I were seen with him in such a garment. They will have to progress.[60]

Cycling simplified Helen's trek to work, and enabled her to experience the delights of a new self-propelled mobility, but, like many other women, she found her long skirts annoyingly restrictive on a bicycle. The bicycle clubs springing up around the country were recruiting 'wheelwomen' as well as men; conservatives proffered advice to them about how to mount while standing on the pedal, but radicals took to bloomers, which rapidly diversified into new fashion items. French women cyclists favoured bloomers with a long-skirted coat reaching to the knees, New York wheel-women adopted voluminous bloomers extending down to their shoe tops, while the most daring wore knickerbockers only to their knees.[61]

Massachusetts was more demure. In April 1894, when the Massachusetts Bicycle Club came puffing along the route of Paul Revere's Ride and stopped for sandwiches and lemonade at Thoreau's House near Walden Pond in Concord, Helen detected only 'one of the ladies' looking very 'sensible' in her 'bloomers'.[62] William Tufts might have disapproved of his daughter wearing bloomers; nevertheless, the strange 'wheeled horses' on the Revere Ride found their way into the novel he was writing, *A Market for an Impulse* (1895): 'Thousands upon thousands of them ridden by youths of both sexes, trouped by in societies and in small parties.'[63] Helen's generation were abandoning customary proprieties.

Unable to attend college, Helen pursued the extra-mural improvement on offer. In April 1894 she and Ella Davis heard the economist, Francis A. Walker, speak at Prospect Street Church, Cambridge, in favour of 'Bimetallism'. American bimetallists like Walker argued that accepting silver as well as gold as the standard would relieve financial pressure on poor farmers and wage earners. London's Bank of England, being predominant in the international financial markets, was able to exercise global leverage through its management of the gold standard, and Walker lambasted the 'selfish, shallow mono-metallism of London bankers'.[64]

In May 1894 Helen was back at Prospect Street Church to hear Josiah Royce speaking on 'Psychology'. A friend of William James, Royce pioneered a progressive educational psychology which impressed Helen. Though she continued to regard the poor en masse as menacing, she was able to empathise with his focus on the children of a crippled fruit vendor confined in a dark yard.[65] Royce's altruism was far more inviting to her than the pessimism of Schopenhauer which was currently in vogue. Helen, who was copyediting an essay on Schopenhauer, wondered how the philosopher did not recognise the yearning 'to be of use, to do good in the world'.[66]

Helen was not alone in being troubled by the distress and anger pervading America. The financial crisis of 1893 had triggered an economic crisis. Factories and mines were closing, steel and railroad companies going bankrupt. Depression exacerbated the decline in farmers' incomes and resulted in bankruptcies and homelessness. The unemployed took to the streets, their protests encouraged by Populist critics of extreme inequality such as Jacob S. Coxey and the temperance campaigner, Mary Elizabeth Lease, who declaimed, 'Wall Street owns the country.'[67] Revolutionary and reformist socialist ideas were gaining adherents too. American Marxists clustered in the Socialist Labor Party, while Schindler and other followers of Edward Bellamy were known as Nationalists, because, like the gradualist Fabians, they advocated state ownership.[68]

That April, miners in Illinois, Ohio and Pennsylvania went on strike in their thousands. Then, in solidarity with the Pullman workers' resistance to wage cuts and sackings, railway workers, led by Eugene Debs, started a boycott of trains pulling Pullman cars. In the American labour movement militants were talking of a 'new' trade unionism which resembled the upsurge in Britain. But American workers were treated more harshly than their British counterparts. Not only did the employers use overt anti-union violence, Richard C. Olney, the Attorney General in President Grover Cleveland's administration, was closely linked to the rail owners. Though Debs, along with many other strikers and unemployed marchers, was sentenced to jail, he emerged undeterred, talking of a 'Co-operative Commonwealth'.[69]

Helen's incipient social awareness was tempered by her unease about both state collectivism and democracy. Hearing Harvard professor, Charles Eliot Norton, speak about his friend Thomas Carlyle's distrust of the majority, confirmed her doubts.[70] Nevertheless, as 1894 came to a close, she was searching for direction, 'The months fly past. Everyday I think of what I want to do in the world. Day after day it is all only hope. I look through the years to come and see no change from the daily life I lead now. Once I could write. Now it is difficult to put my thoughts on paper.'[71]

The following year Helen was transferred from Riverside to work on Houghton Mifflin's catalogue, earning $9 a week. But a more fundamental change was imminent.[72] Early in April 1895 a troubled Helen noted an unemployed demonstration at the State House in Boston, led by Morrison I. Swift. The maverick activist, who had worked in social settlements in New York and Philadelphia, agreed with the Populist, Jacob S. Coxey, that the federal government should provide those without work with useful public employment, such as improving the roads. Helen dismissed Swift as 'morbid on Socialism', but, when the rousing Mary Elizabeth Lease joined him on the platform in Boston Common, the whole Tufts family turned out to listen.[73]

Along with other Populist women, Lease advocated social equality and believed in women's redeeming mission to bring co-operation and moral regeneration. She combined decidedly intemperate attacks on the demon drink with denunciations of capitalist 'bloodhounds of money'.[74] Mulling over these startling notions in her journal, Helen admitted drink did not account for the destitution of the majority of the demonstrators, but could not accept the proposition that the whole structure of society was at fault. Instead, at a time when hostility to immigration was at a peak in Boston, Helen concluded, 'The present immigrations [*sic*] laws are very much to blame.'[75]

During the spring of 1895, she sought refuge from bimetallists and 'bloodhounds of money' alike by studying 'Medieval History' at classes organised by the philanthropic Social Union.[76] It was there that she met the immigrant from England who offered her the intellectual and political guidance she was seeking, the socialist Helena Born. At twenty-one, Helen could have no conception of the effect this empathetic older woman would have upon her life.

L. to R.: Helena Born and Helen Tufts Bailie under umbrella on beach, 1896 (Helena Born Photograph Collection, Tamiment Library and Robert F. Wagner Labor Archives, New York University)

TEN

Whitmanites and New Women: 1894–1897

Miriam's death left Helena utterly alone. The catalyst of hope and despair, the wielder of intense emotion and of psychological control, had gone and Helena, who had indeed given all for love, had lost her closest, most intimate friend. Yet the grief of separation and bereavement was scarred by their ultimate estrangement. Moreover, Sunrise, who Helena had helped to nurture, was thousands of miles away in the West, across mountains, plains and desert; so young a child could be expected soon to forget. Helena, her stoicism under siege, was forced back upon her own resources in an effort to re-establish inward strength and calm.[1]

Meanwhile turmoil raged in the world outside. In September 1894, thousands of Boston garment workers, many from immigrant backgrounds, mounted a massive strike, helped by members of the social settlement, Denison House. Part of a desperate labour rebellion, this upsurge so reminiscent of the Bristol cotton workers resulted in large wage increases and a reduction in the hours of labour from twelve to nine. Class conflict accentuated the polarisation in American society; socialists and anarchists alike were being branded as purveyors of chaos and subversion.[2]

Helena remained committed to the 'social and economic emancipation' of both men and women, but in those first few months back in Cambridge she was cocooned, focusing on recreating her life and making herself anew.[3] She found work, and a perch in a tiny room on a hill, 'high up among the tree tops', in Beach Street, Somerville.[4] There

Helena meticulously arranged the few possessions that had survived the trip to California; her scrapbook and notebooks, notices from her labour organising in Bristol, some autographed proofs and business letters from famous writers such as Oliver Wendell Holmes, collected during her glory days working on the Harvard magazines. Most precious were the poems Miriam had written for her, along with the Stumpy note and a green cloth folder, embroidered in red with Robert's initials 'RAN'.[5]

Laboriously she was constructing an autonomous self in an aesthetic enclave that fused Carpenter's strictures on simplicity with Morris' respect for craft. Absorbed in wood-carving, Helena designed everyday objects, trays and butter-boxes. She bound her own books, embroidering covers for them. Carving, staining, sewing, possibly helped to salve painful memories of the woman who had awakened her to colour, texture and tone. Going to and from work, she spotted mushrooms, hunting for them further afield on her holidays.[6] Perhaps by sorting small external objects Helena was able to pattern and assume control over her own feelings. In Helen's words, 'From this time on her life moved in paths of her own hewing.'[7]

Helena's search for self-directed personhood returned her to Whitman, whose work had so deeply affected her when she first met Miriam in the late 1880s. In 1892, she had copied a passage from his 1855 Preface to *Leaves of Grass*, into her notebook:

> This is what you shall do: Love the earth, and the sun and the animals, despise riches, give alms to everyone that asks, stand up for the stupid and crazy, devote your income and labour to others, hate tyrants … re-examine all you have been told in school or church or in any book, dismiss whatever insults your own soul.[8]

The 'Good Grey Poet' enhanced Helena's awareness of her own individuality and enabled her to discover others seeking similar unconventional paths.

On the evening of 8 November 1895, Helena braved a snowstorm to attend a meeting of the newly formed Boston branch of the Walt Whitman Fellowship at the home of the writer, Edward P. Jackson, in Dorchester. There, amid the intrepid little band that had made it through the snow, she heard Jackson contrast Tolstoy's asceticism with the body-affirming poetry of Whitman she had discovered in the early days of her friendship with Miriam.[9] Joining the Walt Whitman Fellowship that snowy night marked a vital step for Helena.

The Fellowship had been founded by Horace Traubel. Profoundly affected by his youthful contact with Whitman, from 1888 Traubel dedicated himself to recording the poet's every utterance, whether profound, irreverent or mundane. Following Whitman's death in 1892, friends and admirers started to assemble on May 31st, the poet's birthday. In 1894, Traubel convinced them that a more structured organisation was needed; the Walt Whitman Fellowship International was accordingly established with a branch in Philadelphia and another in New York.

Traubel conceived the Fellowship in grand terms, operating on a global scale, and studded with notables. He successfully persuaded the distinguished professor from the University of Pennsylvania, Daniel Brinton, to be its President. Traubel's sweeping vision, combined with his sense of himself as specially ordained to interpret Whitman, alternately inspired and irritated fellow Whitmanites, but his charm and assiduity meant that Traubel remained the driving force in the Walt Whitman Fellowship, maintaining a broad organisational control through his informal networks of correspondents. He had acquired his experience of organising, along with many useful contacts, from Philadelphia's Ethical Culture Society. Personally bohemian and freedom-loving, Traubel was open to a wide range of radical cultural and political causes; an advocate of women's emancipation and anti-racist, he was sympathetic to anarchists and socialists alike. He created a platform not only for remembering Whitman, but for those seeking to connect inner growth with social change. His magazine, *The Conservator*, became the outgoing organ of the Fellowship, which also published a series of papers.[10]

The Boston branch that Helena joined on 8 November 1894 in Dorchester was well stocked with speakers and writers. The journalist, William Sloane Kennedy, who remembered her having been given a letter of introduction to Whitman by Carpenter, was elected to the branch's first formally constituted committee. Its Secretary Treasurer was Laurens Maynard, who acted as Traubel's eyes and ears. He had initiated the branch in Boston with two literary scholars, Charlotte Porter and Helen Archibald Clarke, who edited their own journal, *Poet-Lore*.[11] Exuding a personal and intellectual confidence Helena must have envied, they asserted 'advanced' feminist views and were politically radical.

Formerly part of Traubel's Philadelphia Ethical Society network, Porter and Clarke had moved to 3 Joy Street in Boston's old elite neighbourhood

of Beacon Hill where they lived happily together in a loving relationship marked by the ceremonial exchange of rings. Their appreciative but
critical guide, *A Short Reading Course in Whitman*, was published as a
Fellowship paper in 1894. Taking seriously the poet's advice to 'dismiss
anything that insults your soul', the acute pair proffered the observation,
'It is a curious fact that might possibly strike only the woman reader,
that in all his singing of comradeship and friendship he makes no direct
reference to comradeship between women.'[12] The two feminist scholars
insisted 'that the manly love of comrades, must include the womanly love
of comrades', and, moreover, that this woman to woman love had 'superiority over the love of a husband'.[13] In October 1894, Charlotte Porter's
'Some of the Pros and Cons of Socialism' appeared in *The Conservator*.
Opposed to the unrestricted rule of 'plutocracts', Porter argued against
competition and profit. But recognising the danger of a socialist society
turning into another type of tyranny, she concluded that the best counter
to any incipient tendency towards a collectivist authoritarianism lay with
the 'individualist philosophy'.[14]

The two editors of *Poet-Lore* attracted other thoughtful, independent-
minded women. The day after the Boston branch gathered at Jackson's
home, a chuffed Laurens Maynard announced to Traubel that Helen
Abbott Michael had joined, explaining how she was married to the
Tufts' College professor, Arthur Michael, and was a 'friend of Charlotte
Porter's'.[15] The well-connected Helen Abbott Michael happened also to
be a scientist, specialising in the chemical composition of plants, as well
as a reformer concerned about poverty.[16] Along with Porter and Clarke,
she was alert to cultural bias and ruffled the male Whitmanites with incisive observations on the poet's gendered ellipses. Writing in *Poet-Lore*, she
noted that despite Whitman's tributes to women, when his writing rose
to 'heights and out-reaching vistas', he invariably ascended 'alone'.[17]

Maynard announced another valued recruit, young Sarah Macdonald,
who lived at 3 Joy Street with Porter and Clarke. Wonder of wonders,
she was a stenographer! Full reports of meetings for Traubel could
now be ensured, and Macdonald was button-holed as minute taker.
It took Maynard rather longer to register the retiring English woman,
'Miss Born'.[18]

In contrast, when a Fellowship member, Mary Stevens, visited Beach
Street she was captivated by the 'commonest things' such as 'a string of
melon seeds … festooned against the wall' serving as 'artistic adornment', and 'the sweet look' in Helena's 'eyes' as she read so earnestly 'from

Carpenter and others'. Stevens came away empowered, 'feeling … rich in the glimpse I had then of new horizons, of new worlds of thought and aspiration and enjoyment'. She reflected, 'It was the first time I had met a woman of this type and I was deeply impressed.'[19]

This was the quietly compelling Helena who chanced across Helen at that Social Union class on 'Medieval History' in Spring 1895. While Helen found a transformatory mentor, Helena gained an affirming protégé. 'Miss Born', with her broad learning and intense life experiences, presented a 'striking figure' to Helen. The younger woman was fascinated by her new friend's 'large bright, dark eyes, her alert movements'; even Helena's tendency to burn bright red in the Massachusetts sun was glossed as an 'expressive face glowing with the high color she brought from England'. Similarly, Helena's dress, 'always so different from that decreed by fashion', appeared most admirable to Helen who appreciated the 'rich coloring of her simple garments'.[20] Helena confirmed Helen's desire to make an independent, striving path through life, enabling the younger woman to brave the uncertainties of new womanhood.

Eager to connect the wonderful new friend from 'Medieval History' with her beloved family, Helen sought some common ground for them to meet. Popular books had encouraged a mushroom-hunting craze, and William and Isabel Tufts duly accompanied Helena and their daughter on a trip organised by the recently founded Boston Mycological Club.[21] Next, Helen and Isabel took Helena to the festival at Longfellow House, doubly significant as the home of the poet *and* the site where George Washington had been visited by John and Abigail Adams while he was planning the siege of Boston in 1775.[22] Helena was being Americanised.

Nevertheless, Helen was aware how Helena 'arrested attention' and that her unusual charisma did not appeal to everyone. While some were attracted by Helena's 'loving enthusiasm and sincerity', others were strongly repelled 'by her unconventionality'.[23] The young American was forced to concede that the efforts at assimilation were not *entirely* successful: 'My prize was not very welcome at home. Helena was too much of an oddity. Mama was kind, Papa suspicious, Russell frankly derisive.'[24] Neither Russell, just starting his first job at a photographer's, or Papa William Tufts, were predisposed to odd women.

Nevertheless, through her friendship with Helena, Helen painfully began to deconstruct the assumptions of her upbringing.

*   *   *

Helena's rejection of customary female behaviour was sustained by the Walt Whitman Fellowship. She had landed amid a coterie of rebellious intellectual women, which included her Edinburgh Summer School friend, 'Miss V.E. Graeff', who was proposed by Clarke as a Fellowship member to Traubel in April 1895.[25] Clarke acted as a self-appointed shop-steward, grumbling in her letters to Traubel, on behalf of members of slender means, about expensive dinners and the $3 subscription fee to the Walt Whitman Fellowship International.[26] 'All but the capitalists are getting poorer and poorer all the time and capitalists somehow do not take to Whitman', she expostulated.[27]

Traubel encouraged women members, partly because he followed Whitman in supporting an emancipated ideal, but also because he would have recognised that their presence allayed an undertow of suspicion about effusive male bonding. Nevertheless, over the course of 1895, some of the distinguished male Whitmanites began to evince unease. In May 1895, Professor Daniel Brinton refused to put himself forward to be President again. He appears to have been disturbed by questions of whether Whitman was attracted to men and confided to the Vice-President, Isaac Platt, that 'women of doubtful character' had been admitted into the Fellowship.[28] William Sloane Kennedy dismissed the murmurings about Whitman's sexuality as an indication of how the warped minds of decadent Europeans misinterpreted American innocence and sincere good fellowship.[29] But he, too, spoke 'slightingly' about the Boston branch to the Canadian Whitmanite, Dr Richard Maurice Bucke, currently working on a sweeping spiritual tome on 'Cosmic Consciousness'. Sure enough, news of this malicious male gossiping reached Clarke, who mounted a swift counter-attack. In a letter to Traubel on 29 May 1895, she upbraided Kennedy, 'so unjust as well as un-Whitmanic'.[30] On May 31st conflict marred the Memorial Meeting on the poet's birthday; a disgruntled Maynard reported to Traubel, 'Kennedy and Miss Clarke had a tiff'.[31] To his surprise Mrs Kennedy thoroughly enjoyed herself, and was intending to come to meetings that fall.

The 1895–6 committee of the Boston branch was well-womanned with Charlotte Porter as President, Helen Abbott Michael as Secretary-Treasurer, and a committee that included not only Helen A. Clarke, but the lecturer and teacher, Mary Dana Hicks.[32] The artistic Hicks headed the Prang Educational Company, which aimed to promote art in schools

Thriving amid this bracing company an expansive, assertive Helena emerges during autumn 1895. The September issue of *The Conservator* carried her article, 'Whitman's Altruism', in which she argued that while the poet's celebration of 'personality' could be seen as Egoism, this was tempered by his practical altruism in tending the wounded during the Civil War.[33] Moreover, she maintained he reconciled the opposing polarities cosmically, and, like Hegel, saw 'self-realization' being effected through 'self-renunciation'.[34] Helena herself had struggled against the denial of self demanded by religious asceticism. She comprehended the ferocious longing for individual expression experienced by new women, yet she sought to balance this with co-operative union, invoking the anarchist communist, Kropotkin and Geddes' collaborator, John Arthur Thomson, in support of her claim that mutual aid was an evolutionary necessity.[35] In 'Whitman's Altruism', Helena first articulated the dialectical relationship between self and others which constituted the core of her own politics.[36]

In autumn 1895 news reached her of the case of Elsa Lanchester, a young middle-class member of the London Social Democratic Federation, who had been forcibly confined in an asylum by her father and brothers because she had decided to live with an artisan, James Sullivan, in a free union. Released only after a campaign by anarchists and socialists, Lanchester's treatment revealed the powerful prejudices of gender and class that Helena detested. In her essay, 'Marriage Safeguards', she challenged the 'cast-iron codes' restricting women's freedom, proposing instead that democratic 'marriage forms' based on comradeship would foster individual development. Helena adopted the approach outlined by Carpenter in his 1894 pamphlet *Marriage in Free Society*, rather than the complete rejection of marriage which some free lovers advocated.[37]

In 'Marriage Safeguards', Helena's take on Grant Allen's novel *The Woman Who Did* is discerning. The book was regarded as scandalous in 1895 because a character in it, Herminia Barton, opposes marriage and bears a child out of wedlock. However, her punishment was harsh – the death of her lover and the opprobrium of her daughter. Helena critiqued the novelist's blank pessimism, arguing that such a choice should not be considered simply in individual terms but as part of a 'momentous social revolution'.[38] For Helena, 'the effort to live one's ideals, even in the face of social ostracism', was a form of 'self-realization' rather than sacrifice.[39]

A newly combative Helena took an arch stand against Traubel's attempts to edit her circumlocutory prose that December. 'It may surprise you that I should prefer my own angularities to the graceful alternatives offered me.' She backed her complaint up with an endorsement of the authenticity of the 'ear' to the ground, gleaned from Geddes' Summer School, informing her editor that 'the manner of delivery 'expresses the individual, therefore I am inclined to reject any veil which may improve the style while obscuring personality'.[40]

In fact, Helena's turns of phrase *were* often cumbersome and some-times unclear. Her tenderness about being edited arose because becoming a writer had been a long painful gestation and her intellectual armoury attained largely through self-endeavour. No doubt, too, she was inclined to bristle at any hint of male patronage, though she did, rather begrudg-ingly, offer thanks to her editor for pointing out a misquotation of Spencer. Traubel, who was far more open than many male intellectuals to women contributors, backed down.

They certainly kept him on his toes. Helena was no doubt gratified to see her name listed in the December *Conservator* with Bucke, Kennedy, Brinton, Porter and Clarke, not to mention the doyen of arts and crafts, Oscar Lovell Triggs, and the literary historian, Hamlin Garland.[41] Nevertheless, a lynx-eyed Clarke noted a subtle gender boundary; while comradely male Whitmanites dropped the customary 'Mr', women's names were still prefaced by 'Miss' or 'Mrs'. The editor of *The Conser-vator* was sharply notified that if he desired to be addressed still as '"Dear Horace Traubel"', equalisation in nomenclature must be introduced.[42]

In February 1896, Helena made her debut as a speaker for the Fellowship. Her topic was 'Poets of Revolt'; she was billed as lecturing on Shelley and Whitman, though Carpenter would be included in the published version of the paper in *The Conservator*.[43] The meeting was held at the apartment of Gustave Percival Wiksell, a radically minded dentist, who became a good friend of Helena's and an intimate comrade of Traubel's.[44] He lived in the Hotel Pelham, on the corner of Tremont and Boylston Streets, an accessible venue for the Whitmanites to gather. One of Boston's earliest apartment blocks, built in the mid nineteenth century, by the 1890s the six-storey building had acquired an air of antique elegance. Helena thus had a rather grand setting for what must have been a momentous event for her.

Helena praised the 'Poets of Revolt' as reformers and seers who embod-ied comradeship and a life close to nature, while supporting democracy and the emancipation of women. By sheltering behind the poets, she was able to explore her own preoccupations with reconciling polarities of inward and external transformation, individual expression and comradely association, body and spirit, 'enthusiasm' and reason. Noting Shelley's political radicalism, and quoting 'A nation,/Made free by love', as well as his famous call, 'Rise, like lions after slumber', she detected in the poet's face 'an enthusiast who has retained much of the spirituality and charm of youth in manhood's early years, when most men have succumbed to the materializing and conventionalizing tendencies of environing influences'.[45] Unlike Shelley, who defied all external institutions, Whitman, Helena observed, was 'neither for nor against them'.[46] He put his faith in balancing body and spirit and the creation of a democratic culture of comradeship, rather than in political solutions.[47]

Whitman had been Carpenter's great inspiration when he began writing his prose poem, *Towards Democracy*, in the early 1880s, and Helena was at one with Carpenter's effort to connect Whitman's preoccupation with body and being to the socialist movement. His utopia was hers, 'a time when men and women all over the earth shall ascend and enter into relation with their bodies', attaining 'freedom and joy'.[48] The voices of her Bristol comrades singing of the 'heroes, patriots, and lovers' in Carpenter's popular labour hymn, 'England Arise',[49] still resonated:

> From mass meetings across the ocean I seem to hear the reverberations from a thousand throats, thundered with the rugged fervor of men whose daily bread was at stake, and whose unselfish aims and persistent sacrifice are a menace to exploiters and a glorification of high endeavor.[50]

Traubel constituted a link with British socialist Whitmanites. In spring 1896, he sent Helena a copy of the *Labour Prophet*, the organ of the non-sectarian Labour Church.[51] Its founder, John Trevor, had taken William's advice and the Labour Church combined social justice with a broad spirituality that drew on Whitman, Emerson and Carpenter. Helena, familiar with Gilliard's democratising of divinity and Robert Sharland's prized first edition of Whitman's *Leaves of Grass*, identified with this ideal of transcendent communion. Traubel corresponded with Edward Carpenter and on April 28th Helena told him she had ordered Carpenter's new book, *Love's Coming of Age*.[52] Published in 1896, it brought together pamphlets he had been writing on sexuality, with the significant exception of one, printed for private circulation, 'Homogenic Love'. Helena refers in her letter to 'the Calamus token from which Walt Whitman springs anew'.[53] The strong Calamus grass symbolised Whitmanite love of comrades, but it is not clear how Helena regarded

Whitman's sexuality or whether she was aware of Carpenter's physical attraction to men. Like many readers of his works she probably saw him simply as advocating a more democratic approach to relations between the sexes and a critique of the subordination of women, which eschewed the extremes of 'free love'. It is doubtful that she could have known how Traubel himself was deeply ambivalent about his own sexual feelings and feared any exposure of Whitmanite comradeship's erotic undercurrents.[54]

On May 27th Helena gratefully acknowledged a recent translation of Paul Desjardins' *Le Devoir Présent* (1892) that Traubel had sent her. Like Geddes, Desjardins had been influenced by Le Play, and sought to transcend the clash between labour and capital through a new social morality arising from an inner spirit rather than an external code. He was due to speak on 'La Grandeur du Moment Présent' at Geddes' Summer School and Helena enclosed the notice in her letter. Helena tells Traubel she planned to lend the translation 'to a comrade in the Sierras for whom it is opportune'.[55] This had to be Robert.

During spring 1896, Helena was busily preparing for Whitman's birthday celebration. The Walt Whitman Fellowship assembled at the recently founded Twentieth Century Club, a centre for radical humanitarian thinking, with a mild bohemian and 'socialistic' tinge. Former friends of the poet, like the white-bearded, cosmic, Dr Richard Maurice Bucke, shared their reminiscences, but the main theme of the day focused on Whitman as an advocate of personal liberty. Helena's contribution was a paper on 'Inequality in Divorce', in which she bravely stated:

> No more immoral lesson could, from my point of view, be promulgated than the suggestion it is righteous to retain by legal bonds the person of an another whose spirit has become alien. To the developed woman it would be an intolerable spiritual degradation for material ends.[56]

Placing herself in double jeopardy, she criticised the eminent freethinker and Whitmanite, Robert G. Ingersoll, for saying that the divorce law should favour women by protecting against their husbands' attempts to divorce them. Helena was insistent on the principles of equality and self-ownership, dismissing special treatment as 'paternalism'.[57]

Neither Helena's egalitarian defence of divorce nor her idealistic assertion that the experience of suffering would enable the soul to emerge, 'not embittered, but seeking for the expression of the love-force higher channels', are likely to have calmed the anxieties of Helen's parents, in the audience at 'Miss Born's invitation'.[58] Helena's call for a break with the 'past' and her condemnation of those who sought to regulate the lives of others 'in accordance with approved models', surely perturbed William Tufts, whose tolerance towards individualism tended to curdle in relation to his beloved daughter.[59]

Nevertheless, Helen persisted in her efforts to bring her family and her new friend together. In June they made a joint expedition to Concord, a tactful choice as they could all concur in homage to the Transcendentalists. Mushrooms took them all to the grounds of Wellesley College in July.[60] Then Helen, keen to communicate her pride in the American Revolution to Helena, 'studied up' so she could act as guide on the excursion of the 'Prospect and Social Unions' to Paul Revere House in Boston.[61] Helen's greatest triumph, however, was the inclusion of Helena in the Tufts' family holiday to Squibnocket on Martha's Vineyard. While there William Tufts happened to trip over a chair and was confined to bed with a leg rigidly in splints, leaving Helen and Helena free to roam in search of mushrooms and blueberries. When they were not walking, they went to the beach where their enthusiasm to acquire a tan left them painfully burnt – a peril of athletic new womanhood (see p. 167).[62]

Back from vacation, Helen records teaching both her mother and Helena to handle 'a wheel'. Along with the cycling craze, gymnastic exuberance was sweeping through Boston; accordingly, she and Helena kept up their exercise at the 'YW gym'.[63] Their friendship enabled Helena to discover a youthful leisure she had never experienced, while gradually Helen started to assimilate Helena's views and interests. That September she began to consider becoming a vegetarian.[64] She also accompanied Helena to a meeting addressed by the eloquent and controversial William Jennings Bryan.[65] Thousands gathered on Boston Common to hear the radical Democratic candidate, hoarse-voiced from his campaign trail, put the case for bimetallism as the cure for the economic pressures on farmers and workers. Emotions ran high on combining silver with the gold standard. The financial lobby, whose fortunes were linked to the London Stock Exchange, were backing the Republican, William McKinley, and smearing the Bryanites.[66] Helena was rather impressed by Bryan's arguments for a mix of silver and gold; Helen just went 'for the fun of it'.[67]

Helen was, however, attracted to the cultural stimulation of the Whitmanite milieu, attending a lecture by Oscar Lovell Triggs on 'Democratic

Art' at the Twentieth Century Club and listening to two very different Whitmanite women, the perspicacious Helen Abbott Michael on 'Woman and Freedom' and the effusive Elizabeth Porter Gould on Whitman's English friend, Anne Gilchrist.[68] Gould had made Whitman acceptable in polite American circles with her expurgated edition of his poems, *Gems from Walt Whitman* (1889). Part of a growing cohort of popular women speakers, she attracted a large female following, with what the *Boston Herald* described as her 'full flow of language'.[69] She bombarded Traubel with letters, verses and press cuttings on her triumphs and dazzled Laurens Maynard, when they met at the Twentieth Century Club.[70]

Helena started to expose Helen not simply to Whitmanite ideals but to her socialism. In November she began to reveal to the mystified young American what Helen described as 'her Bristol work'.[71] And, in December she took Helen to a strike meeting in Faneuil Hall.[72] Memories of Bristol brought out the steel buried beneath Helena's conciliatory demeanour. Early in 1897, her ire was aroused by an attack on unions by the President of Harvard, Charles William Eliot. Outraged by his praise for scabs, Helena compared them to burglars, 'victims of a social system based upon inequality of opportunity, avarice, and self-seeking'.[73] She was in no doubt that the risks and insecurities of the wage earner were far greater than those of capital. It was Helena's lot to abhor conflict, but to side with labour.

At the end of 1896, Helena was elected onto the committee of the Boston Walt Whitman Fellowship. Once again, she had slid into a position of responsibility, this time acting as a buffer between the two militant and assertive 'Poet-Lores', Clarke and Porter, and the noticeably twitchy male Whitmanites. A delighted Maynard, writing to Traubel, pronounced the new Executive 'splendid'; along with 'Miss Born', it consisted of 'Miss Davenport – the pretty girl you met at the dinner', along with 'Mrs Hicks' and three men, Jackson, Wiksell and Harry Young. Smarting from the sharp feminist criticism of the *Poet-Lore* women, Maynard confided, 'There is still a little pull in the opposite direction by a few of the women but they're being squelched every time they show their heads & are good natured in their opposition.'[74]

Predictably, Maynard's delight about the squelching proved premature; his opponents, despite being 'good natured', were apt to take a tough line on masculine presumption. Clarke, for instance, mustered the formidable 'Maiden of the Rainbow' of Norse myth on side. The Maiden had dismissed a would-be suitor with scorn:

> Maidens living with their mothers
> Are like ripe and ruddy berries.
> But the most of married women
> Are like dogs enchained in kennel.[75]

Within a few months Clarke was calling for Traubel to explain why no women had been invited to speak at the annual Fellowship gathering at the end of May, and why she and Porter were expected to share a ballot in elections. She saw these instances of discrimination as systemic. While women were prepared to give men a 'fair representation', when men were 'in charge they overlook women if they possibly can'.[76] A mighty clash followed in which Maynard 'called her down', though they parted, he believed, as 'good friends'.[77] Clarke made her peace with Traubel that August with a somewhat barbed concession. His failings, she believed were not intentional, but 'the result of a carelessness men sometimes manifest through an unconscious inherited bias'.[78]

Helena's own odd-woman tendencies were cloaked in English restraint. But she knew how to operate in political groupings and quietly started to encourage links between the Walt Whitman Fellowship and the other clusters of dissidents she knew in Boston. She had renewed contact with the Schumms, and one Sunday afternoon when she and Emma Heller Schumm happened to find themselves alone, a profound sense of mutual recognition passed between the two women. Emma recounted:

> We caught a glimpse of each other's souls and became friends … I looked into the face of a strong, self-poised woman, not a mere visionary and enthusiast. She had known great sorrow since I had seen her last, and it had made her strong – as she spoke her sincerity, her earnestness and her high aspirations made her plain face beautiful to me. A great joy came over me, and I knew then that I must cling to her, that I must not let her slip away from me again.[79]

The Schumms began to attend meetings of the Walt Whitman Fellowship, and then joined. Quietly, Helena was effecting connections that would become stronger, while she, herself, was developing close friendships among members of the Boston Individualist Anarchist circle, which included advocates of free love and advanced new women.

George Schumm worked for a textbook publisher, Ginn & Company. Its owner, Edwin Ginn, held liberal and humanitarian convictions and was prepared to employ leftists. When Helena, too, was taken on there, she met Schumm's workmate Archibald H. Simpson. Simpson, always known in public as 'A.H. Simpson', was a fellow British immigrant. Initially a Marxist in the Socialist Labor Party, he had been friendly with the 'Chicago Martyrs', and helped to defend them when they were accused of the Haymarket bombing in 1886. A man of ardent principles and an inveterate joiner of causes, he had become convinced by the arguments of the free lovers around Ezra and Angela Heywood, and had written for their journal, *The Word*, not simply on sexual freedom in the abstract, but about the pleasures of masturbation and orgasm.[80]

Falling in love with Angela Heywood's sister, Flora Tilton, brought Simpson into the extraordinary Tilton family. Their radical mother, Lucy Tilton, raised her three daughters Angela, Flora and Josephine to accept sex as natural; not only did Angela write graphically on sexuality, Flora and Josephine defied the law by selling pamphlets on birth control.[81] Upon her arrest in 1877, Josephine is reported as declaring, "'I look upon marriage as a curse, a prostitution of our noblest passions. I believe in free love, Spiritualism and affinity.'"[82] Simpson shifted away from his deterministic interpretation of Marx, helped to form the Boston Anarchist Club, and worked for Tucker, who won him over to Individualist Anarchism. All his life Simpson remained an extreme supporter of extreme causes, yet his somewhat bombastic front concealed a kindly man, utterly devoted to his love, Flora Tilton.[83] He became one of Helena's most loyal friends.

She found a fellow spirit too in the Schumm's unusual lodger, Sarah

Sarah Elizabeth Holmes (Labadie, Special
Collections Library, University of Michigan)

Elizabeth Holmes, who had been associated with the Individualist Anarchist circle for several years. Born in 1847, and related to the Boston literary celebrity, Oliver Wendell Holmes, the well-educated, idealistic young woman developed emancipated views on marriage and gave birth to a daughter in a free union. When the relationship turned sour, her partner took the child.[84] In the late 1880s Holmes and Tucker became 'sweethearts' and she clashed with his friend Victor Yarros and other male Individualists in *Liberty* over women's emancipation.[85] Her own experience encouraged her to point out that abstract principles did not address the complexities of unequal material circumstances and social power, or take into account the nuances of emotional connection and actual dependence when it came to women and children. It aroused a storm of controversy and she retired from the fray. Like many thoughtful women of her era, Holmes belonged to the wrong sex and lived at the wrong time for intellectual and sexual fulfilment.

In her youth a beauty with a 'great mass of black hair', a stroke in her early forties had left Holmes partially blind, turning her hair, now cropped short, prematurely grey.[86] The anarchist poet, J. William Lloyd, who wrote for *Liberty*, recalled a complex, intellectual woman, 'very dignified, cultured ultra-refined and sensitive', but inclined to morbid moods of introspection and dull despair'. Yet in her happy moods, he adds, 'she could be delightfully witty, with a most quaint and unexpected humour'.[87] Wit and cultured conversation did not, however, endear Holmes to the Schumm children, when she found sanctuary with their family. The daughter, Beatrice Fetz, regarded Holmes as parasitical, recalling how Emma Heller Schumm toiled, looking after the children on a low income, while their lodger was 'gung-ho for women's rights and didn't do any housework'. Fetz conceded, 'She did the dishes sometimes as a help to my mother. She'd dust a leg of the piano, go out and read some Browning, then dust the other.'[88] Tucker's sister-in-law, Bertha F. Johnson, confirmed Holmes' lack of interest in domesticity, remembering the 'soft' voice and 'aristocratic demeanour'.[89]

When Helena introduced Holmes to Helen at the 'YW gym' in March 1897, the younger woman noted, with evident respect, that this new acquaintance was in the 'advanced class'.[90] Struggling to situate yet another remarkable person she needed to remember, Helen catalogued this brief encounter in her journal: 'a friend of the Schumms (Individual Anarchists). Have met Mrs Schumm at Whitman meetings.'[91]

Two years of knowing Helena acquainted Helen with far more startling characters and concepts than any university course would have done. At the January meeting of the Walt Whitman Fellowship in 1897, she heard the Boston journalist, Franklin Benjamin Sanborn, reminiscing about Whitman. Sanborn himself was a legendary figure – not only had he known Whitman, Thoreau and Emerson, he had supported John Brown's abortive attempt to start an armed uprising of slaves at the Federal arsenal at Harper's Ferry, Virginia.[92]

Helen met her first Marxist at that meeting, Martha Moore Avery, a wealthy widow who had followed 'Eastern Cosmic Law' under the influence of the fashionable Boston astrologer, Dr Charles D. Sherman, before joining the Bellamy-inspired Nationalists. Avery, attracted by the certainties of the doctrinaire and schismatic leader of the Socialist Labor Party, Daniel De Leon, had then gravitated to the S.L.P. and was notorious for expounding Marx's theories as if they were an esoteric form of higher knowledge.[93]

Helen found all these unfamiliar doctrines confusing. After a visit with Helena to the home of 'the Schumms' and 'Miss Holmes' at Forest Hills, she carefully wrote down, 'They do not believe in the necessity of an intermediate stage of Socialism.'[94] The emotional nuances, too, were hard to fathom, and much still flew over her head, like Laurens Maynard's readings, at the Hotel Pelham in 'Mr Wiksell's office', of Dr Bucke's edition of Whitman's loving letters to the horse-car conductor, Peter Doyle.[95] Drawn to Helena's fascinating friends, Helen was frequently disturbed by what they said and did. Entranced by 'Miss Clarke and Miss Porter' and their aesthetic room at 3 Joy Street, when they broke off their proof-reading of *Poet-Lore* to defend William Jennings Bryan's views on free silver, she 'felt upside down afterward', for, after his defeat by the Republican, McKinley, Bryan and his supporters were being presented as akin to anarchists and criminals.[96] Even the Schumm children startled Helen by playing a game called 'blowing up the Czar … with toothpicks and a match'.[97] A visit with the Schumms and Helena to see Daniel Chester French's bronze, 'Death Slaying the hand of the Sculptor', in Forest Hills Cemetery did not entirely reassure her.

Helen struggled to reconcile what she heard and saw with the American patriotism in which she had been reared, proudly taking Helena to Patriot's Day in Concord that April. Instituted in 1894, it commemorated both the beginning of armed resistance to the British *and* the Civil War. There, by French's statue of the revolutionary soldier, the

'Minute Man', they heard Julia Ward Howe recite her famous 'Battle Hymn of the Republic', with its stirring call, 'let us die to make men free'. Howe, the opponent of slavery, friend of the Transcendentalists and advocate of women's suffrage, personified Helen's pride in America. This, in turn, was closely bound up with her loyalty to her family. It seemed so right and proper that it should be 'Papa' Tufts who helped Howe to her seat on the train.[98] But this kind of American patriotism, along with Helen's ideas and her relationships with her parents, were transmogrifying.

Helen and her young friends, all working for a living, were bursting with zest, and Ella Davis, in particular, took to Helena, joining a rebel cell with Helena and Helen over a vegetarian lunch at Beach Street in February 1897. Calling themselves 'The Sensible Skirt Vindicators', all three resolved to wear their spring outfits a daring six inches from the ground.[99] Helena appeared at Ginn & Company with her 'new woman' hemline, Helen shortened her 'black brigatine', but Ella Davis trumped them both by arriving in bloomers at Riverside, where her male superiors responded with outrage.[100] Helena's friend, Beatrice Taylor, from Oakfield Unitarian days, raised the stakes of adventurous new womanhood by visiting with a rucksack containing 'clothes to last her three months'.[101]

Isabel Tufts tried hard to relate to her daughter's modern outlook and odd circles, joining the gym, crocheting a silk purse for Helena's birthday and presenting her with an 'aesthetic' Japanese tray. Women's personal emancipation constituted common ground and 'Mama' Tufts resolutely puffed away at the 'wheels'.[102] She also accompanied her daughter on an outing to Devil's Den Woods in Arlington, along with Helena, Beatrice Taylor, Sarah Holmes, the Schumms, Ella Davis and Harriet Law. Happily, Helen recorded:

> We talked and talked and talked, – an harmonious mingling of individualists and socialists, monists, astrologists (Harriet). To me the most interesting subject was Absolute Evil, the proposition denying its existence. I took the affirmative side and found I couldn't convince them; though by the time we started home we all thought mosquitoes an absolute evil.[103]

Helen was coming across arcane forms of spiritual heterodoxy through her friend, Harriet Law, who enthused about the astonishing mental powers and teachings on Eastern spirituality of the astrologer Dr

Sherman. Though Helen inclined to scepticism, the esoteric thinking that had intrigued Miriam and Robert earlier in the decade had developed quite a following, its promise of inner power exerting a particular appeal for women. Exploratory Bostonians could attend lectures on 'The Esoteric Signification of the Science of Astrology' or 'Mental Telepathy', or take courses on yoga; the city even boasted a 'Daughter of the Druids'.[104] Helen was more impressed by Harriet's contact with an orange-robed Anagarika Dharmapala, whose version of Buddhism reminded her of Unitarianism, reflecting that while 'Harriet's tendency is very much in, – Helena's is both in and out.'[105]

Helen, attracted to Helena and the possibilities she opened, observed uneasily how her friend was viewed with mistrust by some of the older generation. One day in March 1897, when they joined a group of young women at Ella Davis' home, she noticed that 'Mrs Davis' was markedly unfriendly towards Helena.[106] Ella Davis' mother no doubt spotted the quiet authority and influence Helena wielded amid the excited, chattering young women.

Helen's journal documents how her friendship with Helena formed her radicalism, but it also reveals how she was caught between conflicting worlds. Helen oscillates between her new-found radicalism and bigoted preconceptions, casually remarking how Ella Davis and her young women friends introduced Helena to 'darkey [*sic*] songs' accompanied by a banjo.[107] Acceptable as quaint curiosities, when Helen met African-Americans at close quarters she recoiled. When Harriet Tubman, the heroic abolitionist and former slave who had risked torture and death smuggling slaves to freedom from the south, visited Houghton Mifflin's, Helen dismissed her as 'very plain and unnoticeable and quite black', wondering at the 'reception' given to Tubman by cultured Boston.[108] It was not simply that Helen was racist and ignorant; she clung tenaciously to an ingrained sense of exclusivity. Her lineage may have been revolutionary and the values of her family tolerant, but she was conscious that she belonged to an elite – albeit a much besieged one.

While aspects of Helena's advanced opinions could be absorbed as self-improvement, towards others Helen displayed a prim rigidity. When a storm broke out over Frederick William MacMonnies' statue, 'Bacchante and Infant Faun', donated to the resplendent new Public Library in Boston, Helena was with her aesthetic devotees, while Helen stood with her puritanical opponents. In the short term, the opposition to nudity and intemperance prevailed; Bacchante, grapes and infant Faun were taken down from their 'green wooden pedestal'.[109] Ironically, Mac-Monnies' work later became so famous, many copies were made and one would eventually return to Boston.

Yet Helen *did* harbour longings to venture beyond the confines of her family. One day, in late February 1897, when Helena joined Helen for lunch at Houghton Mifflin, she happened to notice a copy of the socialist Walter Crane's *Claims of Decorative Art* (1892) in the office. For Helen, Crane evoked childhood visits to her maternal grandparents, but the book triggered very different memories for Helena, who began speaking animatedly about Miriam and Robert. Before long the conversation led to California. An excited Helena and Helen began imagining how they would travel West together; it was agreed that Helena would contact Robert.[110] On March 16th Helen wrote in anticipation, 'I feel as if I had started already. I do so want to see this big country of ours.'[111] Floating over this call to explore the wild was the shadowy figure of Robert Allan Nicol, at the remote ranch in Weimar, Placer Country. An enigmatic Helena depicted him as a 'Shelley type'.[112]

ELEVEN

Fabianism and Free Love: Gertrude Dix

The memory of Miriam and Helena continued to reverberate in Bristol socialist circles after their departure. In differing ways, the young 'new women' recruits who followed them into the Socialist Society – Gertrude Dix, Enid Stacy and Katharine St John Conway – took up their complex quest for personal independence and social commitment. Of these three 'sister women', it was Gertrude who pursued self-expression most fearlessly by adopting a psychological idiom rather than Miriam's mysticism.

Gertrude's Christian Socialism had grown out of her family's devout High Church Anglicanism. Such a trajectory was not unique. From the 1880s a radical minority of High Church Christians assailed both capitalism and Victorian hypocrisy. A leading figure was Hugh Holmes Gore, and it had been the close association he fostered between the Christian Socialists and the Bristol Socialist Society that had enabled Gertrude to become active in the strike wave of 1889 and then work in the Organising Committee with Robert, Miriam and Helena before they left in August 1890.[1] In 1891, when the Christian Socialist group became the Clifton and Bristol Fabian Society, the informal links with the revolutionaries in the Bristol Socialist Society persisted and their membership overlapped.

On 9 January 1891 Gertrude was asked by the Bristol Socialist Society to speak to them on Plato, whom she admired. The following week, when both Enid Stacy and Mary Wheeler became members, Gertrude argued that credit was due to Plato for his views on women – whatever his failings on 'Slaves or Helots'.[2] The minutes were taken by Robert Gilliard, who reported a 'splendid lecture', and she found another ally in the secretary, Robert Weare, the factory worker who had welcomed a guilt-stricken Katharine St John Conway with Carpenter's *England's Ideal*.[3] Opposition came in April 1891 when the Marxist engineer, James Watt Treasure, maintained that if women gained the vote 'the tendency would be reactionary'. Quoting Laurence Grönlund, he insisted that women's economic subjection had to be tackled first. Such procrastination caused a furore. The minutes record 'a marked divergence of opinion'; so marked indeed that it was agreed to resume the following week with Gertrude, who no doubt had been a vociferous opponent of Treasure, introducing the discussion.[4]

Gilliard records that Gertrude read from a 'pamphlet' by Havelock Ellis, claiming 'a wider sphere for women than that to which conventional ideas of what was proper to the sex had confined her'.[5] This sounds like Ellis' 1889 article on 'The Changing Status of Women' from the *Westminster Review*, reproduced as a pamphlet, *Women and Marriage: Evolution in Sex*, which outlined the theories of evolutionary anthropologists on the family and commended Mary Wollstonecraft, Robert Owen, William Thompson, Anna Wheeler and George Sand as exponents of women's emancipation. A close reading also reveals a fond mention of Ellis' love, 'Miss Olive Schreiner', the South African new woman novelist.[6]

Gertrude was introducing the Bristol Socialist Society to a writer branded as *dangerously* modern in the early 1890s. Ellis' first book, *The New Spirit* (1890), had acclaimed Whitman's celebration of the body and approved Ibsen's belief that an 'aristocracy of character' was to be found among women and workers. Such views caused Ellis to be reviled not simply as a 'socialist' who defied all authority, but as a 'neo-pagan' and 'Epicurean' who wanted unbridled sexual relations.[7] Despite being an advocate of simple associative living, the Greek philosopher Epicurus had given his name to the aesthetics of pleasure associated with fin-de-siècle bohemia. Undaunted by Ellis' reputation, Gertrude was impressed.

Ellis and 'a wider sphere for women' were to be Gertrude's swan song in the Bristol Socialist Society, for she was leaving home to study nursing. Gilliard, who was taking the chair as well as the minutes, expressed sadness upon losing another member, one who had 'worked in the cause' and to whom they had become 'attached'. He evidently admired the intrepid young speaker, braving her opponents, just as his beloved Miriam had done. The Bristol Socialist Society members gave her their blessing, convinced she 'would become an influence in the right direction wherever she went'.[8]

Leaving home was still relatively unusual for young single women like Gertrude, and she was turning her back on a close-knit family. Born on 12 December 1867 to Juliet and William Chatterton Dix, she was the couple's first child.[9] Grandfather John Ross Dix had named his son after the Bristol poet, Thomas Chatterton, whose biography he wrote. A heavy drinker, John Ross had deserted his wife, the daughter of a Bedminster soap manufacturer, and travelled to America. In marked contrast, his sober son, William Chatterton, worked at the soap factory and attended the High Church, St Raphael's, where he began composing hymns. After marrying Juliet Wartnaby in 1864, he became a clerk for the post office and then an accountant.[10] At the time of the 1871 census they were living at Colston Cottage in Hampton Road, Redland, and were still there in 1881, by which time Gertrude had four brothers and three sisters.[11]

Gertrude recalled apple trees, Sweet Williams and snapdragons in the garden and a house filled with her father's books and pictures of the Holy Family. Both parents' all-consuming interest was the Anglican Church. Thomas Chatterton Dix's reputation as a hymn-writer was enhanced by his devotional works. Curates arrived in flocks to discuss questions of theology on the lawn, architects called round with propositions for church designs. Gertrude, raised amid a haze of piety, struggled to explain her religious upbringing to her modern, twentieth-century daughters: 'Angels were very close. They surrounded our beds at night and guided and guarded us by day. When I saw one on the roof, my mother did not explain that a workman in a white jacket was mending the roof.'[12]

Gertrude did not want to be dependent on her parents and at twenty-three, galvanised by Plato, Ellis and socialism, she made her break. While a minority of young educated women like Conway and Stacy were going on to university, Florence Nightingale's reforms had made nursing a respectable career choice and middle-class women were flocking into one of the few occupations available to them. Gertrude trained on the job for a year as a nurse probationer; the experience was sobering and left her critical of the long hours and bad conditions. Lack of staff could mean that after a twelve-hour shift nurses had to cover for an even longer period. Rest was difficult because their sleeping accommodation was often badly ventilated and noisy.[13]

After completing her training, Gertrude was aghast to find herself on night duty and responsible for a wing of sixty-four beds on two floors. The brutal reality of nursing was a shock. She wrote feelingly of 'running from ward to ward, upstairs and down, all night, with hardly time to snatch for meals'.[14] It was not just the arduous physicality of the work that wore her down, but being deprived of solitary contemplation:

> Only those who have fully realised the real hardship of never being alone, or free from other eyes and tongues for one minute out of the twenty-four hours, can have full measure of sympathy for the probationer who used to go to a public library for seclusion.[15]

After a few months Gertrude gave up and simply researched conditions. She documented long hours in Harrogate and nurses scrubbing and cleaning windows in Rhyl. Predictably, she found the Poor Law infirmaries were the worst; at Bethnal Green 'twenty nurses, some of whom are over sixty-five years of age, ... supplemented by 80 paupers' were responsible for 600 impoverished patients. In contrast, an exemplary King's College Hospital had reduced nurses' hours and secured around one nurse for every three patients, leading the matron to remark 'that the nurses did not "break down" as formerly'.[16] Mining her own experience, Gertrude commented:

> Only one who has actually lived among nurses, as one of them, can perhaps realise all the suffering summed up in that one phrase – the long and weary struggle for weeks and months against failing strength; the dreaded day when perforce work has to be relinquished; the final verdict of 'unfit'; the dismissal and going away, handicapped with broken health, to compete once more in the labour market, or to return to a dreaded dependence.[17]

Gertrude's heartfelt protest coincided with a campaign for state registration and with the rebellious stirrings of a fellow-spirit who was similarly critical of nurses' conditions, Honnor Morten. Morten, who had also trained as a nurse probationer wrote and spoke on a wide range of issues from progressive infant care to women writers.[18] Gertrude, too, was not content with nursing reform; she wanted to write.

*   *   *

On 7 November 1891, when Keir Hardie's *Labour Leader* published an article by 'Gertrude Dix' entitled 'Liberty', she found a national outlet. The newspaper was committed to the cause of independent labour representation with which she had been associated in Bristol. It was later linked to the Independent Labour Party, formed in 1893. But in 1891, all was flux; the *Labour Leader* reported on Bernard Shaw's talk to the Fabians on 'The Difficulties of Anarchism', carried one of Katharine St John Conway's poems, critiqued the Theosophists' interpretation of symbols of the 'Serpent and the Cross', engaged with Annie Besant on Theosophy, and advertised the works of Thomas Lake Harris on 'Theo-socialism'.[19]

Sardonic about the claim that Britons never 'shall be slaves', Gertrude defined the 'essence of slavery' as 'the power to use another as a means to his own ends'; an adaptation of Kant circulating in Fellowship of the New Life circles. Detailing the profits of the Midland Railway Company to demonstrate inequality, she was adamant 'There is no freedom where poverty and starvation compel.'[20] As in Carpenter's *Towards Democracy*, outcasts from the system lurk in the shadows: a 'loafing rough' scorns the empty show of freedom; a young woman worker's face reveals 'intelligence', but she is denied 'a beautiful and joyous body' by being reduced to a 'machine' to turn out 'button holes'. Her fate leads a Platonic Gertrude to conclude that women's low-paid work required protective legislation, otherwise the victims of sweated labour would become incapable 'of bearing and educating strong children for the State'.[21]

In April the following year the *Bristol Mercury* reports Gertrude speaking in Bristol with two Fabians, Enid Stacy's brother Paul, and a Cambridge graduate, paid to organise lectures, William S. de Mattos. She urged the organisation of a May Day demonstration in Bristol and argued the need for a 'Labour Party'.[22] Gertrude's socialist movement contacts saved her from 'the dreaded dependence' on family that was the fate of many middle-class women.[23] By June 1892, she had found work looking after and teaching the two daughters of Sydney and Margaret Olivier. Olivier, one of the central figures in the Fabian Society, was working his way up in the Colonial Office, though he entertained literary ambitions as a playwright. Margaret's brother, Harold Cox, had been at Tonbridge School with Sydney Olivier, and both families knew Edward Carpenter. After an unsuccessful attempt at farming and the simple life in a country cottage, Cox had gone to teach in India, returning with the Kashmiri sandals that became the prototype for versions issued from Millthorpe by Carpenter.[24]

Margaret, too, inclined towards the simple life. Country cottages were coming into vogue and, upon Sydney Olivier's return from British Honduras in 1891, he and Margaret, who was expecting a third child, began to renovate a cottage, 'The Champions', in Limpsfield, Surrey, overlooking the Weald of Kent. The Fabian secretary, Edward Pease, and the housing reformer, Octavia Hill, whose campaigns to preserve the commons and public footpaths the Oliviers supported, lived nearby.[25]

When Gertrude arrived in 1892, Brynhild Olivier was five and her sister Daphne three. Their new nurse approached her two young charges with advanced theories of childcare. Gertrude's lofty aim was 'to bring them up on principles of freedom. If they run into a pond with their boots on, I do not like the ordinary nursemaid cuff them and call them naughty. I tell them to do what they desire & show them by precepts & example they should take their boots off first.'[26] That summer, the Olivier offspring and twenty-four-year-old Gertrude, with her freckles and red curly hair, ran barefoot through the mossy countryside around Chart Woods. A rebel Gertrude rejoiced that the new generation would enjoy greater freedom than her own, though occasionally the enlightened nursemaid buckled: 'I sometimes wonder if all socialist infants are so exhausting. "If these are only socialist" I say to myself, "what must anarchists be?"'[27]

Working at 'The Champions' was nevertheless intellectually and politically stimulating. As well as figures like Pease and Bernard Shaw from the centre of the Fabian Society, their friendship networks included Carpenter and his fellow simple lifers, Henry and Kate Salt, along with the Dublin-born anarchist and Fabian, Nannie Dryhurst.[28] Gertrude regarded her with awe because she had 'kept a school for young anarchs [sic] and survived it'.[29] The anarchists' commitment to changing consciousness made them early advocates of learning through play, and Dryhurst worked at the child-centred International School, started by the former Paris Communard, Louise Michel. Infiltrated by an agent provocateur, it was forced to close in 1892, when bomb-making equipment was found in the basement. Nevertheless, Michel's opposition to authoritarian rote-learning influenced other progressive educators.[30]

Nannie Dryhurst sometimes helped another Olivier visitor, the Hampstead anarchist, Charlotte Wilson, edit the anarchist-communist journal *Freedom*. In a joke aimed at the popular physiological type-casting of criminals, anarchists, artists and advanced women, Wilson decreed that Fabian Gertrude had 'Anarchist Ears'.[31]

*   *   *

Gertrude's reflections on anarchistic child-care are recorded in a notebook kept by a group of young, enquiring Fabians like herself. Early in
1891, just before she left Bristol, Sam Hobson, from Cardiff, had joined
the Bristol Socialist Society. Described by Katharine St John Conway as
'six foot high and desperately good to look at', Hobson initiated 'Our
Fabian Circle' in March 1892.[32] Each member wrote their contribution
in the notebook and then posted it to the next contributor. Hobson,
who came from a Quaker background and admired Whitman, wanted
the Circle to 'cultivate a spirit of loving comradeship' which could renew
and sustain their efforts for 'the cause'. The notebook was to be a psychological and political 'nerve centre', and he instructed contributors to be
honest and direct: 'No titles, such as Mr, Miss or any other like nonsense
to be used.'[33]

At the outset Hobson hoped they might be able to discuss the Carpenterian conviction that socialism would bring a more 'natural life' and
discover how this might be squared with 'the Epicurean philosophy of
other socialists'.[34] This guarded comment alluded to the Fabians' lecture
organiser, William S. de Mattos, and hinted at a disturbing clash of mores
within which Gertrude was soon to be embroiled. De Mattos moved in
London bohemian avant-garde circles that embraced sensation, flux and
excess as sources of creativity.[35] Not only did De Mattos criticise marriage
and advocate divorce, he believed in 'free love' and had a reputation in
Fabian circles as a philanderer. He was hardly alone; his problem was that
he saw no reason to conceal his opinions.

Gertrude and De Mattos had met by early April, having spoken
together in Bristol on 'The Idea of a Labour Party' for the Clifton and
Bristol Fabian Society.[36] In 1892, though Sidney Webb favoured per-
meating the Liberals, sections of the Fabian Society wanted a distinct
Labour Party. This was hardly Epicurean, but when the ever-hospitable
Stacys put up the visiting speaker, he upset Mrs Stacy by asserting that
'to be a socialist and "free lover" was one and the same thing'.[37] He then
further annoyed daughter Enid by assuming she agreed with him. In fact,
she strongly disapproved of the influence De Mattos was acquiring over
her emotional and impressionable friend, the delicate beauty, Katharine
St John Conway. A divisive fracas ensued, in which Gertrude, by aligning
with De Mattos, clashed with both Enid and Paul Stacy.

Early in April, when Hobson chose her to follow his contribution to the Circle, Conway wrote melodramatically from the 'Gulf of
Dark Despair'.[38] She had left her post at Redland High School for a

Katharine St John Conway
(Bristol Reference Library)

working-class Board School, but was 'at home on sick leave', daunted by 'the huge classes & the deadening cram system'.[39] She was also ethically troubled. Should one be directed by 'principle' and come out for 'freedom & be comfortable, or does it injure the cause'. It was a question she 'fought over at least five times a day' and she believed Gertrude was struggling with the same dilemma.[40]

That April, driven by guilt and duty, Conway confided her woes to De Mattos. Not only was she miserable at the Board School, she was exhausted by lodging at Dan and Clara Irving's. Conway was running the household, caring for the invalid Clara, as well as wage earning and propagandising. She was near to collapse. De Mattos rode to the rescue with a series of paid Fabian lectures and Conway began a tour in the North.[41] He was delighted by her 'magnetic influence' and her popularity among provincial Fabian audiences.[42] However, frantic telegrams from Enid Stacy and Dan Irving caused her to break off her engagements and rush back to Bristol to care for Clara Irving.[43] Conway claimed the invalid had been made dangerously ill by rumours coupling her 'name with that of Mr De Mattos'.[44] She informed Edward Pease that she and Enid Stacy could no longer lecture for the Fabian Society 'while we run such painful risks'.[45]

De Mattos' view of the risks she faced differed. As he saw it Conway had not just been made a 'house drudge' by the Irvings, 'she was being led headlong to utter ruin' by Dan Irving, and was under an 'insane infatuation' when 'in his company'. De Mattos expressed contempt for Irving as 'a narrow uneducated workman', who had convinced Conway that De

Mattos harboured an 'impure motive'.[46] He told Pease that the Irvings hated 'Gertrude Dix & myself who have been trying to rescue K.C. like poison and I hear are saying everything devilish about me in Bristol'.[47] Away from Irving, De Mattos described Conway as the 'kindest and purest hearted woman that ever lived'. He and Gertrude Dix, being well aware of her abilities, had become 'too fond of her'; now, however, an irate De Mattos was beginning to think they 'should leave her to her fate'.[48] It sounds as if Gertrude pleaded for further rescue attempts, for the following day De Mattos reported that 'Miss Dix' would confirm Conway was deluded by Dan Irving's 'evil influence' and 'a narrow prudish idea of "spirit wife" and ascetic duty'.[49] Gertrude presumably decided that the in-situ Irving constituted a greater threat than De Mattos to her supposedly helpless friend.

Enid Stacy's distrust of the London Fabian was unrelenting; De Mattos incarnated 'Epicurean' sensuality and she abhorred 'an undercurrent by which some of the Fabians are influenced'. At the same time Stacy denied any suggestion that she and the Bristol Socialists were 'conventional' in outlook.[50] Indeed the Irvings and Conway described their relationship in terms of Whitmanite loving comradeship and 'spirit unions' redolent of Thomas Lake Harris. The difference was that these forms of heterodoxy were couched in terms of a superior morality and hence acceptable.

The letters pounded into Pease's post box from Bristol. Conway regarded the Irvings as her 'best friends' and insisted the three of them believed in purity and self-control.[51] Yet in practice, these ideals of denial do appear to have been under stress, for, on May 17th, an exasperated De Mattos informed Pease that Katharine had confided in him that Irving did not love his wife and was 'violently in love with Miss Conway'.[52] Pease, bombarded by letters and emotionally out of his depth, accused Katharine of flirting with De Mattos, before being taken ill himself and vanishing into hospital.[53] Meanwhile, Katharine, grateful to De Mattos for speaking engagements and openings with editors, but with her feelings of affection and respect towards the Irvings now marred by embarrassment, became fearful that her letters were about to be exposed to the Fabian executive. Like other young women in the socialist movement who assumed a public role, she found herself in a vulnerable position in which overt attitudes and covert prejudices clashed. She took refuge that May under Enid Stacy's confident, protective wing.

Who had what intentions and who flirted with whom remained unresolved, but the conflagration had political and personal consequences.

Irving belonged to the Marxist Social Democratic Federation as well as the Bristol Socialist Society, and on 13 July, a scathing Bernard Shaw, who was friendly with both De Mattos and the Stacys, urged Paul Stacy to detach the Bristol Fabians from the influence of the S.D.F. Three days later Paul complained to Pease about the S.D.F's influence within the B.S.S.[54] Pressure upon socialist unity in Bristol combined with personal rifts. Gertrude snapped at Conway and came out against Paul and Enid Stacy's views on free love in 'Our Fabian Circle'.

Conway had introduced Gertrude to 'Our Fabian Circle' in April as a figure of supreme probity, wilting under her nursing responsibilities: 'If a clear vision of truth living is in any of us it is in her. Only she is not strong as the rest of us in body, & has not been able to get away from her hospital work hitherto to join hands with other comrades.'[55] By June 4th, when it was Gertrude's turn to contribute to the notebook, she was at 'The Champions' in Surrey, amid sophisticated Fabians; Conway's breathless religiosity clearly irritated her and 'truth living' was not a self-image she desired. Denying that she was a 'truthful person', Gertrude let rip against Enid and Paul Stacy's contributions.[56] Like De Mattos, Gertrude argued that restraints were 'unnecessary when people love each other and absolutely wicked and cruel where they don't'.[57] Characterising conventional 'external restraints' as 'harmful & immoral', she wished women who were 'the slaves of contracts' would realise this and fight the 'damnable system' by 'refusing even to walk up the back stairs of a registry office'.[58]

Invoking Carpenter, Gertrude opposed 'the impure hush' about sex, adding in an allusion to the gossip circulating about De Mattos in Bristol that 'prurient garrulity' about the 'sex question without honest purpose' was just as bad.[59] 'I don't see why a man should be scouted for holding unorthodox opinions on sex relations any more than on religious questions.'[60] Instead, she put forward an alternative approach to ethics: 'The sooner we get to understand that right & wrong does not consist in acting or refraining from acting in certain ways & that actions are neither moral or immoral per se or to be judged apart from spirit & intention the better for us.'[61]

Mentioning the 1890 divorce case involving the Irish leader, Charles Parnell, and Katherine O'Shea, Gertrude asks whether socialists were to join the Liberals in supporting a hypocritical external moral code? Following Carpenter's dictum, 'The Outcast of one age is the Hero of another', Gertrude asked rhetorically, 'What about the "outcasts" Jesus had chosen?'[62] Intent on a thorough sweep, Gertrude announced that Christianity's preoccupation with sin had 'mentally hypnotised the world too long'.[63] The reference to hypnotism was up to the minute. In Paris, Jean-Martin Charcot's scholarly interest in hypnotism had stimulated psychological theories of the unconscious which coincided with a cultural exploration of similar themes in literature, philosophy and art.[64]

A defiantly modern Gertrude declared, 'Art is the test of personality & personality is the test of everything.'[65] In place of the altruistic stress upon 'character', which involved discipline and of self-restraint, the term 'personality' implied experience and expression.[66] 'Believe in yourself and others', advised Gertrude.[67] Reaching back to Romanticism, Gertrude pointed out how great artists like George Sand, Heine, Shelley and many others had defied the conventions. Creative plenitude was the aim, 'there is no limit to the possibilities of our humanity'.[68] People must be free to 'do as they like' and 'to act as they <u>chose</u>', regardless of whether their choices proved destructive. The crux lay in discovering the consequences of freedom for oneself. Citing Plato, 'Browning (some of him) & Ibsen' in support of her position, Gertrude insisted the essential problem was a lack of active 'feeling' and 'passion' in human relations.[69]

An alarmed Sam Hobson intervened. He was personally drawn to Conway, but hardly knew Gertrude and his attitude towards 'Epicureanism' had hardened. He decided they should stand above the 'indiscriminate debauchery', which seems so dear to the heart of a De Mattos'.[70] Dismissing the Neo-Platonist 'cloudland' of 'some of the Esoteric members' of the Fabian Circle, he called for the topic of free love to be banned.[71] It was to no avail; the young Fabian contributors held forth regardless.

The majority shared Hobson's wariness and backed the Stacy line. However, Gertrude's ethical iconoclasm gained two supporters, both slightly older men in their mid thirties. Jim Kennedy, whom De Mattos had made responsible for protecting Conway's virtue on her tour of the North, wrote from Carlisle, congratulating 'Comrade Gertrude Dix' on her 'brave and outspoken expression of opinion', pointing to a contradiction in Hobson's endorsement of 'Nature' and rejection of free love.[72] Eschewing any hint of Neo-Platonism, Kennedy adopted a materialist approach, arguing that repression was harmful because the sexual organs required 'due exercise'.[73]

Gertrude's other ally, H. Russell Smart, a failed actor turned commercial traveller, was a free thinker from Clapton, East London. He also considered that she had 'the clearest and noblest ideas on the subject', though he teased Kennedy for treating sex as 'a method of exercise'.[74] Smart thought marriage should be 'without formalities and dissoluble at will' when it ceased to be a 'union of body, mind & spirit' and that women (especially actresses) would bring the sexual 'revolution'.[75] Smart declared: 'Expediency never accomplished anything great & noble. Moderation has ever been the enemy of progress.'[76] Nevertheless, he, along with other members of the Fabian Circle, including Conway, opted for the Independent Labour Party in 1893, entering an arena of electoral politics in which expediency necessarily figured. In 1900, Gertrude pursued the dilemma in her second novel, *The Image Breakers*.

Yet another reel was still to run on these tensions within Bristol socialism which further fractured the little band of 'sister women'. While Gertrude was not an active protagonist in an attempt to create a community at Starnthwaite in the Lake District in 1892, events that occurred there affected her nevertheless and feature significantly in the plot of *The Image Breakers*.

Conway wrote her last contribution for the Fabian Circle's notebook in the summer of 1892 from Lancashire, when she was about to leave for Starnthwaite, near Kendal. Revd Herbert V. Mills, a Unitarian Liberal Unionist she had impressed on her Northern lecture tour, had proffered a welcome escape from her Bristol morass.[77] Mills believed that 'Home Colonisation' provided the solution to unemployment for the 'able bodied poor', rather than poor relief or emigration.[78] Money was donated from socially concerned figures, including the renowned editor of the *Manchester Guardian*, C.P. Scott. But Starnthwaite's supreme benefactress was the Countess de Noailles, a supporter of women doctors and an opponent of vaccination and vivisection, with bizarre views on alternative health. Her contribution was a staggering £1,000.[79]

Mills appointed Conway as secretary and she brought in Dan and Clara Irving to the Home Colony, as well as Enid Stacy, who had been organising with the striking Sanders 'sweet girls'.[80] Few of the settlers knew much about agriculture, and the colony predictably lost money. In Spring 1893, Mills replaced Irving with another foreman, quelling all opposition, whereupon Irving and Stacy led a revolt. Mills responded by besieging the colonists' houses and, to Stacy's fury, the rebels were violently evicted, regardless of Clara Irving's heart disease.[81] A shaken Stacy denounced the Home Coloniser as 'an autocrat' and lost all patience with

Conway, who had sided with Mills.[82] When the controversy went public, the Bristol socialists sympathised with Enid Stacy and the Irvings, and an angry Dan Irving began to show people letters from Conway. At this point, Shaw stepped in to try and minimise scandal, urging Enid Stacy, 'Pray let everybody fall on everyone's neck without further delay.'[83] He also wrote to Conway and managed to salvage Irving's personal reputation. But he was not able to stop litigation between Irving and Mills.[84]

By June 1893, the apparently fragile Conway, who possessed a capacity to renew herself with the moon, was in love with the Independent Labour Party member, John Bruce Glasier, confiding about the 'black agonies' before they had met: Dan Irving had 'nearly killed the spring of my life'; Herbert Mills had 'utterly' loved her.[85] Glasier successfully batted off the black agonies, along with various other aspirant suitors, including spirit-husband and Bolton Whitmanite, James William Wallace, and a somewhat half-hearted Bernard Shaw. The couple married on June 21st at Rough Firth on the Dumfriesshire sea-shore, by declaring before two witnesses, a custom accepted by Scottish law.[86]

Though Gertrude was not at Starnthwaite, the difficulty of prefiguring communal alternatives within capitalism, along with a recognition that unity between advanced women could not necessarily be assumed, resonate painfully in *The Image Breakers*. The three 'sister-women', who had seemed, early in 1891, to have so much in common, were within two years travelling along dissimilar paths.

In June 1893 Gertrude made an appearance at a Bloomsbury dinner party given by two friends of the Oliviers, Eustace and Margaret Hartley. Hartley, a wealthy tea merchant, was a Fabian sympathiser who cultivated an 'advanced' ethos. The Hartley's offered an agreeable source of literary gossip and their flat in Museum Mansions, Great Russell Street, conveniently faced the British Museum.[87] Bloomsbury had become an intellectual and artistic hive where socialists, anarchists, radicals, new women, decadents and émigré revolutionaries were all to be found. Dinners at the Hartleys would have been exactly where Gertrude wanted to be.

Her presence was recorded by Olive Garnett. The twenty-two-year-old diarist lived even closer to the British Museum, because her father, Richard Garnett, was the Library's Keeper of Printed Books. Reared amid paper and ink, she adopted a world-weary tone towards Gertrude – the Bristol parvenu was evidently trying too hard to impress. 'Miss Dix was of an extreme socialist, modern young woman type, dress, hair, eyeglasses & all. I expect she is very worthy, but she was ten times more affected than Mr Wallas.'[88] The retiring and scholarly Fabian, Graham Wallas, was just beginning his research into the effect of human psychology on politics. After the Hartley's 'excellent' dinner and a look at the Museum from the roof of the Mansions, the company set off to a huge meeting organised by the Theosophical Society at St James Hall, to hear the former Marxist and Fabian, Annie Besant, put the case for Theosophy. Three thousand people had crammed in for the debate, and they only just found seats up in the gallery. Wallas gave up half-way through, but the others stayed on, fanning themselves with Theosophical Society pamphlets, 'thoughtfully provided … in great abundance'.[89]

Despite this unpromising first encounter, Gertrude and Olive Garnett remained in contact, enabling Gertrude to savour the wide-ranging spectrum of the Garnett circle. Richard Garnett was a friend of William Michael Rossetti, the brother of the Pre-Raphaelite artist. In 1891 the precocious Rossetti children started the anarchist magazine *The Torch* from their home and, by 1893, the magazine had declared for anarchist communism.[90] Olive Garnett was critical of *The Torch*, but an enthusiastic supporter of the Friends of Russian Freedom and an admirer of the Nihilists. Russian revolutionary émigrés were frequent visitors at the Garnetts, as were Shaw and Olivier, who hoped to have one of his plays performed.[91] This Bloomsbury milieu no doubt appeared more intriguing to Gertrude, the aspiring writer, than her own earnest lecture circuit. In September 1894 she was due to speak on Plato's Republic in Poplar Co-operative Hall.[92]

The ice broke between Gertrude and Olive Garnett at a play reading at the Hartley's on 16 November 1894. Gertrude solemnly rendered the Second Act of Dorothy Leighton's new woman play, *Thyrza Fleming*, but, when Garnett's turn to deliver the Third Act came, she 'giggled' at her own falsetto. Her laughter proved infectious; 'After that one could not save the play.' The reading proceeded with 'continued bursts of hilarity'.[93] Both young women were at the Hartley's Twelfth Night party in January 1895, playing games 'until twelve o'clock' with several doctors who were Fabian sympathisers; Anna Nordgren, a radical Swedish woman artist; and a sister of Margaret Olivier who Gertrude may have already met at 'The Champions'.[94]

*   *   *

In June 1895, Gertrude's first novel, *The Girl from the Farm*, was published by John Lane in his daring 'Keynotes' series. Both the publisher and the series sent out signals. Lane, who also published the avant-garde journal, *The Yellow Book*, marketed controversy with panache. Keynotes had been named after an 1893 collection of short stories by 'George Egerton' (Mary Chavelita Dunne), celebrating woman's 'eternal wildness', and Grant Allen's startling *The Woman Who Did* was on the Keynotes list in 1895. Although Lane's authors were inclined to reject conformity from the highest of motives, the Keynotes covers were designed by Aubrey Beardsley. Virtually unknown when Lane commissioned him in 1893, the panic over sexual decadence following the conviction of Oscar Wilde in 1895 propelled the artist into notoriety.[95]

A hint of Gertrude's 'Our Fabian Circle' dissidence precedes *The Girl from the Farm*, obliquely folded into a quote from Hegel, informing readers how 'unconscious moral habit' conflicts with 'the claim of the consciousness of the reason, creating a world out of itself – the claim to eat of the tree of knowledge of good and evil'.[96] The book's central character is Katharine, the academically brilliant daughter of the Marchants, who returns from 'Nuneham', Cambridge, to her family home in the sleepy cathedral town of Allington, where her father, Cuthbert Marchant, is Dean.[97]

At university, Katharine has acquired 'new woman' style ideas of earning her own living. She walks 'with the long swinging strides of the woman whom healthy athleticism has taught to discard unnecessary draperies'.[98] In contrast, her mother, Ellen Marchant, fussy and concerned with appearances, disapproves of Katharine's loose, cool gowns and her 'plainly-coloured' room with its bare 'polished floor'.[99] Gertrude, in an affectionate dig at Carpenter, depicts Mrs Marchant as distrusting the ideas of her daughter's friend, 'Mr Gardener', about 'Nature and simplification of life'. Not only did he write books on the subject, the man, himself, went 'to *absurd* extremes'. He dwelt with 'quite poor people in their *hugger-mugger* way ... and earns a living by market-gardening – or was it making sandals? Calls himself a socialist, and positively declines to live on some property which was left him.'[100] A friend of Mrs Marchant's had been 'surprised to find him quite a gentleman', making his odd behaviour 'all the more regrettable'.

The character of Katharine's father is less caricatured than that of her mother. Intellectually estranged from his wife, he is wrapped up in ruminations about faith and reason and writing a work of abstruse philological scholarship. His sight is deteriorating and he assumes his well-educated

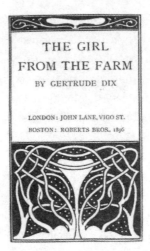

Cover for *The Girl from the Farm*

daughter will remain cloistered with him as his amanuensis. In contrast, younger brother Hilary, destined for the law but unable to concentrate on his studies, is adored by his mother and left unconstrained by his father.

Duty leads Katharine to reject an offer of a socially useful and intellectually stimulating position as the librarian for the Woman's Literary and Scientific Association.[101] Her mysterious London friend, 'Mary Field', has the post lined up for her and urges Katharine to come in time for 'Story's new play', promising, 'There are many delights into which I shall have the pleasure of initiating you.'[102] For the Epicurean 'Mary Field' the choice is clear: 'health, happiness and growth' versus the 'rendering up of yourself and all your powers for the selfish satisfaction of an old man'.[103]

Katharine, however, feels she cannot break from her family and her father's need for her. 'The Girl from the Farm', as the title indicates, acts as the catalyst. Pregnant and homeless, she is discovered in Allington's cathedral and ejected. Katharine comes across the suicidal young woman rushing towards the river and brings her home to bed at the Deanery. 'Think of the servants, what will people say!' exclaims Mrs Marchant.[104] Then, as Katharine's mother hustles the unwanted guest out of the house, younger brother Hilary arrives. When he and the pregnant young woman regard one another 'with a mute stare of horrified recognition', Hilary is exposed as the seducer and the Marchant's Christian morality uncovered as sham.[105] Katharine's rebellion is thus ethically legitimated.

Echoes of Gertrude's own experiences can be seen in the novel. 'Nuneham' is an obvious allusion to Katharine St John Conway's scholarship days at Newnham, and 'Mary Brown', who 'is exceedingly good to poor people' in Barton Mills, evokes the philanthropic Mary Clifford.[106] 'Mary Field', who offers freedom and initiation into the delights of literary London, hints at 'Michael Field' of whose work Gertrude, like Miriam, would certainly have been aware.

Gertrude herself understood the complex obstacles preventing a young woman from self-determination, but her heroine's predicament was not literally autobiographical for, while Gertrude's parents may have cohabited with angels, dismissed Darwin and been unaware of Marx, they appear to have been relatively tolerant towards their children's choices in life. Juliet Wartnaby Dix may well have favoured mid-Victorian fussy decoration, but Gertrude would later portray her as a spirit of fun who made everyone 'gay' when she entered a room.[107] It was the broader philosophical and psychological implications of the dialectic between conscious individual choice and the pull of family loyalties that provide the tension in Gertrude's depiction of Katharine.

Reviewers registered the cues of the Hegel quote and the Keynotes series. The *Saturday Review* deemed the book 'decidedly clever'. The liberal *Manchester Guardian* proclaimed 'her figures live and act with individuality as well as naturalness'. In contrast, the conservative *Morning Post* deplored the predominance of the author's 'doctrines', while the *Standard*'s reviewer was suspicious of the Hegel quote, 'the mystic twirls on the cover' and a story replete with 'modern facts'. The *Glasgow Herald* considered that the Dean and his wife were needlessly caricatured; the *Western Daily Press* regretted her choice of such 'a singularly disagreeable and selfish family' while observing how the character of the 'girl from the farm' was never developed. It compared Gertrude's 'girl' unfavourably with Thomas Hardy's *Tess of the D'Urbervilles* (1891) and George Moore's *Esther Waters* (1894).[108] It was true that seduced working-class women were outside Gertrude's range, but for a woman writer to explore even the high-minded rebellion of her middle-class heroine invited vilification.

Nevertheless, as John Lane realised, aspersion assisted sales and within a year a second edition had appeared in Britain. Moreover, the novel was published in America by the prestigious Roberts Brothers, whose 'Famous Women Series' included George Sand and Louisa May Alcott. The review in the *New York Times* in July 1895 dismissed 'another variation on the jarring theme of the dissatisfied woman, to whom the old idea of honouring your father and mother is not deemed worthy of consideration'. But Gertrude would have taken heart from the *Brooklyn Eagle*'s demand for a 'sequel' headed 'The Very Latest Woman'. Best of all, she was hailed by the *Chicago Times and Herald* as 'A modern of moderns'.[109] This was precisely the persona Gertrude was aspiring to attain.

When the 'modern of moderns' turned up at Edward Carpenter's home Millthorpe with Raymond Unwin in October 1895, she might well have been entertaining the idea of a speaking trip to the United States. One of the other guests, a charming young enthusiast of enthusiasts from Philadelphia, called Phillip Dalmas, who knew Horace Traubel, would undoubtedly have encouraged her. He was a favoured presence among the British Whitmanites, drifting round the Northern countryside carrying a 'baize bag' filled with vegetables. Not only was Dalmas setting some of Carpenter's poems to music, he had aroused passions among Bolton Whitmanites and had enlisted Kate Salt's help with contacts such as Shaw to promote his compositions.[110]

Gertrude was staying with Raymond and Ethel Unwin who lived nearby, and appeared in bloomers, which Carpenter described to his former lover, George Hukin, as 'ballet costume knickers'.[111] While he allowed infinite leeway to bohemian male visitors, Carpenter was inclined to bouts of primness in relation to young assertive heterosexual women. He had been left reeling from the hostile climate of fear towards same-sex love after Wilde's trial, making it impossible for him to write, even obliquely, on homosexuality. However, that evening Carpenter was surrounded by some of his closest friends. He was at ease with Kate Salt, who acted as Shaw's secretary, and her sister-in-law, Bessie Joynes. His blunt lover George Merrill and burly Jim Shortland, a local socialist, were people he trusted completely. But Gertrude rather overstayed her welcome, leading Carpenter to grizzle, 'Miss Dix cd not tear herself away till nearly 10 pm.'[112] Now a bohemian Londoner, Gertrude probably saw 10 p.m. as relatively early.

The apparently unexceptional gathering at Millthorpe that autumn evening ricocheted through Gertrude's life, for Carpenter, who was corresponding with Robert, happened to mention that Gertrude was interested in getting in touch.

If visiting America did flit through Gertrude's mind she put it on hold, for her immediate preoccupation was the promotion of her novel in Britain. Cultural conservatives might suspect new women writers like herself of aiding and abetting moral subversion, but a substantial audience existed for their work. *The Girl from the Farm* brought Gertrude a modest celebrity in advanced circles while her journalism and investigative research on nursing earned her praise and requests to speak. The radical *Reynolds's Newspaper* announced that Gertrude Dix, 'an authoress', was guest of the evening at the Socialist Club on 'St. Andrews Street, in London' on 7 March 1896.[113]

The Socialist Club was part of an attempt at unity, involving Christian Socialists, the Independent Labour Party, Fabians and the Marxists in the S.D.F. By the mid 1890s Gertrude's networks spanned literary bohemians, journalists, new women and new lifers, along with anarchists, Fabians, I.L.P. members, Christian Socialists and the Humanitarian League, a group formed by the Salts to secure reforms in civil society. She shared the honours as guest of the evening with a close friend of Carpenter's, Isabella Ford. Ford's novel, *On the Threshold* (1895), also explored women's search for individual freedom, stressing the importance of friendships between women and a compassionate social commitment. She had grown up in a family of radical Quakers and internationalists who had entertained the American feminist, Susan B. Anthony, as well as the Russian exiles, Stepniak and Kropotkin, in their large house in Adel, outside Leeds. Their daughters were encouraged to study and think independently. Teaching young women factory workers led Isabella to reject Radical Liberal philanthropy for a libertarian socialism, which stressed the need to listen to women workers themselves. She became a member of the I.L.P., formed in 1893, as well as the suffrage movement.[114]

Despite 'a downpour', *Reynolds's Newspaper* records that the two women novelists attracted quite a crowd, 'members turned up in goodly numbers and enjoyed themselves till a late hour'.[115] Among them was the Fabian, Ramsay MacDonald. Having realised the Liberals would never accept him as a candidate because of his working-class background, he had finally joined the I.L.P. in 1894, and was rising rapidly within its ranks. The anti-militarist, J.F. Green, a member of the Humanitarian League who had contributed to 'Our Fabian Circle', rubbed shoulders with Paul Campbell, active in the London Labour Church and editor of the Christian Socialist. The Garnett's Russian revolutionary friend, Felix Volkhovsky was also present; he was editing the Friends of Russian Freedom magazine, *Free Russia*, dodging both the Russian Secret Service and the British Special Branch.[116]

The Fabian nursing reformer, Honnor Morten, took the chair. Accustomed to speaking and chairing meetings, Morten's manifold causes embraced child development, the municipalisation of hospitals, prison reform and working-class education as well as nursing. She well understood the individual fight for independence that featured in Gertrude and Isabella Ford's novels. Demanding a latch-key from her father had been her first 'great fight for liberty'.[117] Never afraid to shock, when she formed a small social settlement with a group of friends in Hoxton, East London, she had terrified the local curate with her Chianti, cigarettes and unorthodox religious views. Contemporaries remarked on her striking black hair, pale complexion and steady gaze as well as her silver cigarette case and barbaric jewellery. In 1889 Morten had founded the Women Writers' Club, which, like Gertrude's fictional 'Woman's Literary Association' led by 'Mary Field', aimed to foster women's skills and confidence through networking.[118] She and Gertrude were thus linked by their interest in writing as well as the Fabian Society and social reform.

Though ensconced in these progressive London literary circles, Gertrude remained close to her family. The Dixes had moved to Cheddar, and in February 1897 Gertrude's younger siblings Phyllis, Helen and Clement performed in a pantomime she had written, to raise money for a local Girls' Club. The Dix family was turning out to be a highly creative bunch; brother Frank had become a popular writer, actor and director; sister Hilda was showing promise as an artist, specialising in black-and-white drawing. When Gertrude herself had a short story, 'The Portrait of Daphne', printed in the cycling magazine the *Wheelwoman* in December 1897, Hilda did the pictures.[119]

Gertrude was, however, worried that her younger brother Clement seemed rather aimless. Since that visit to Carpenter, she and Robert had been corresponding and she encouraged Clement to visit Robert in America. Though Gertrude would have remembered Robert as an intransigent firebrand, it appears that Robert had presented himself in his letters as a suitably wise and enlightened guide for the drifting Clement. Clement sailed from Liverpool on the Britannic to New York on March 17th.[120]

It is impossible to know the extent to which Gertrude and Robert exchanged thoughts and confidences in a correspondence that has not survived. But they were, albeit in differing contexts, pursuing recognisable preoccupations: new forms of personal life and relationships, inner rather than external ethics, the fusion of body and spirit, egoism versus altruism. Perhaps these common quests comprise the psychological truth behind Robert's romantic assertion as an old man that nothing could keep Gertrude and he apart.[121] Robert was pressing time concertina-like in his memory and erasing other events in both their lives; it would be some years before the couple met in the flesh.

TWELVE

Cosmic Vibrations: 1894–1897

It was to be several months before Robert could bring himself to sort through the few belongings Miriam had left at White-nights ranch. The pain was still sharp in September 1894 when he wrote to Carpenter admitting he had cried while 'folding up her dainty little gowns'. Raised to regard weeping as a mark of weakness, he sought reassurance from the older man: 'You don't mind me making my moan to you often, I must, to someone who understands for it is sore, sore.'[1] He need not have worried; a non-judgemental Carpenter absorbed the anxieties of innumerable correspondents, who, like Robert, sought his spiritual and psychological counsel.

Robert had been copying Miriam's poems onto the only paper he could find at the ranch, apologising for the 'old scraps' with 'ragged edges and ink spots'. Her words left him troubled, driving him out into the night, where he sought release by starting to clear a waterway in preparation for the winter rains. Yet he felt he could sense her still, 'deep in the night and clear above all sights and sounds'.[2]

Like Miriam he associated communion with nature to a heightening of perception. Sometimes, he told Carpenter, he thought he could hear 'a great breathing like prolonged music' in the 'whisperings of the gentle mountain winds' among the pine forests that enveloped the ranch. Trying to assuage his grief through Thomas Lake Harris' idealised 'Woman', Robert fancied this was 'like the sweet breathing – the swaying, rising and falling of Miriam's bosoms: mother bosoms'.[3]

Loftily he informed Carpenter, 'it is foolish to weep for the mere

appearance of a loved one'. Nevertheless, Miriam, the woman he had
desired, lingered. Clumsily Robert struggled to explain: 'But the girlie
was very dear in her little body – so brave, and so able to do good work
for the world.' Nor was it just her physical presence that eluded him:
'I only wish I who have not the hundredth part of her power had been
taken. I was not worthy of such a good heart – and am not now, though
it would be grand to stand together in the fight again for freedom and
Love.'[4] Without the forceful older woman, Robert at twenty-six felt
himself to be abandoned and adrift. He fixed on a passage in the same
1894 pamphlet by Carpenter that Helena had been reading, *Marriage
in Free Society*, about the indivisibility of a union based on love, within
which each partner dreaded remaining without the other. Robert, who
had also read Carpenter's *Sex-Love in a Free Society* (1894), greeted the
two pamphlets' tidings of companionate democratic unions and frank
acceptance of the body with gusto.[5]

He was similarly full of praise for Carpenter's critique of capitalist
values and western science, *Civilisation: Its Cause and Cure*, published in
America in 1891, recounting how it had been lauded in the prestigious
Twentieth Century, and gained popularity during the Homestead Steel-
workers' Strike of 1892. Carpenter's book did not deal directly with labour
struggles, but by challenging the ethical basis of capitalism it affirmed the
unease many Christian Socialists and supporters of the Bellamy Nationalist movement felt about the Carnegie Steel Company's violence against
the strikers. Robert proposed acting as Carpenter's agent and distributor
in America, listing contacts he and Miriam had made, including Underwood's *Religio-Philosophical Journal* along with *The Arena*, edited by the
Boston reformer and spiritualist, Benjamin O. Flower, who tapped into a
zeitgeist of heart hunger among opinion formers.[6]

Despite his sage-like demeanour, Carpenter was sufficiently worldly
wise to know that the young, isolated and paperless Robert was hardly
in a position to promote his publications. But the 'sex' pamphlets and
Civilisation: Its Cause and Cure had provoked vehement criticism from
some of his socialist acquaintances in Britain, and Robert's unstinting
adulation must have been gratifying.

Inspired by Carpenter's belief that Kashmiri-style sandals offered liberation from the constraints of civilisation, Robert alighted upon another
entrepreneurial scheme, sandal-making, enquiring if Carpenter could
send him the patterns he used? Robert intended to obtain an alternative
to leather, which was just being marketed in Philadelphia, to prevent the

'killing of animals for their skin', and planned to make sandals for children as well as adults.[7]

Responding to a remark in Carpenter's letter about Cecil Reddie's innovative boys' school, Abbotsholme, Robert, who had not heard from the educationalist since Bristol, expressed regret about his dislike of Miriam. The mention of Abbotsholme prompted Robert to ask, 'What about starting a girl's [*sic*] school?' Envisaging Sunrise attending a progressive girls' school, Robert declares, 'I wish I could help start such a school. It will hasten the dawn of a better day if we can educate and unfold the beautiful woman in England.' As he closed his letter, Alexander Ellis returned from 'fig picking & preparing' and Sunrise wandered in from playing in the wood. Robert closed his letter explaining he was about to take his daughter out with him 'for the milk'.[8]

Committed to education through nature, in his next letter on December 28th, Robert described presenting Sunrise with a 'beetle, (called a "weevil")'. Holding the 'emerald green' insect in her hand '"to love it"', the little girl had cried when it bit her, but was reluctant to leave it on the grass. Instead she wanted to 'take it to the house, to give it something to eat', insisting, '"Its [*sic*] hungry".' Despite her father's reverence for animal life, he considered this an excess of altruism, comparing it to loyal workers thanking their exploiters.[9]

Robert Allan Nicol with Sunrise at White-nights ranch in
Weimar (Courtesy of Georges Rey, Private Collection)

This letter is addressed to his 'Dear Comrades', 'E.C. & R.U. & wife'. Raymond and Ethel Unwin had sent Sunrise a Christmas present of Rudyard Kipling's *The Jungle Book*. It had just come out that year with its dark purply-blue cover, embossed with three gold elephants. A delighted Robert, who believed that nurturing his daughter's imagination should be paramount, assured them 'I am careful not to stimulate her brain too much.'[10]

After a friend at the ranch, Will Russell, had shown Sunrise the illustrations, and she was asleep in bed, Robert had begun reading, declaring the book 'glorious … for young and old'. He thought Kipling, through Mowgli raised by wolves, bridged the gulf 'in this progressive scientific age' between human beings and the natural world. Dipping breezily into Eastern mysticism and the ancient Pythagorean quest for harmony, Robert proclaimed his desire to shed the 'rags of civilization', commune with Nature 'and vibrate in accord with the music of the Spheres'.[11]

Despite living in the wilds of Placer County, Robert had acquired a circle of fellow experimental lifers:

> I wish I could give you some idea of our neighbors in these blue mountains. Curiously enough everybody in this State seems infected with occultism. We are cut off from the rest of the U.S. by great deserts and if you ever came here you would imagine you were coming to a different place altogether from those in the Eastern States. The 'feel' of the place is quite different.[12]

Amid these 'uncanny' neighbours was, of course, the relatively recent settler, Hiram E. Butler, whose 'colony of Esoterics' at Applegate was about nine miles south of White-nights ranch. Butler's esoterics created quite a psychic bustle around Applegate; 'people are always coming and going', Robert explained.[13] Though small, the settlement had generated such a flurry of correspondence and propaganda that Applegate had acquired its own post office to cope with the volume of esoteric communication.

Butler, originally a Congregationalist, had developed his notions of 'Solar Biology' by mixing esoteric spirituality with a 'can-do' cult of individual perfectionism. Astrology, Thomas Lake Harris' emphasis on breathing, 'yoga philosophy' and American alternative health diets all figure in his publications. Butler's own preoccupations about the 'senses' also loom large. Like other nineteenth-century sexual prophets, he believed that physical desires 'exhaust the vital fluids and leave us depleted, and whilst we are ruled by them, we are jostled here and there', hence the punctilious admonition that sexual intercourse should occur only once every eighteen months.[14] Butler stressed the blessings of physical abstinence for women and promised intriguing compensations to the initiated. These included an 'harmonious exchange of magnetism' between members 'of the opposite sex', evoking 'such a feeling of exhilaration, that their bodies seemed to have no weight, but seemed to float along without effort'.[15] Butler's nudges towards tantalising magnetic delight caused much controversy in esoteric circles.

Robert was in two minds about Butler's colony. Despite sending one of their books to his friends, he had become aware that the exacting community did have its critics: 'some claim that Butler is side-tracked – like Lake Harris but I don't know'. Wary for once, Robert took to the fence: 'Colonies are difficult things to run owing to the transition state most people are in.' However, one beneficial effect of the controversies disrupting the meditative peace of Applegate's esoterics, was that 'some of those who differ from Mr Butler's inmost ideas settle around us. Thus we come in contact with all kinds & grades of Spiritualists. Theosophists, Xtian [*sic*] Scientists etc., and it is a rich experience.'[16]

Alternative belief systems like these promised fulfilment through the enhancement of personality and a dissolution of constraining boundaries. They held a particular attraction for women by proffering a recognition and power society denied. Robert was impressed by the 'plucky' clusters of occult women in the neighbourhood. Sara Thacker lived 'down at the other end of the canyon close to the American River'. Not only had this former pupil of Butler just issued a booklet, *Reflections from the Sun*, she had successfully 'vibrated' two threatening rattle snakes on a mountain path with her compelling 'Peace and Love'.[17] Then there was an alluring group of advanced women who had escaped from unhappy marriages and were living just two miles away in Little Codfish Canyon. Robert was careful to explain that one of these 'students of the occult', who was teaching music in the nearby towns of Auburn and Newcastle, was 'no mere spiritualist'.[18] Although spiritualism attracted many supporters of women's rights, female mediums' power was commonly associated with their supposed female receptivity.[19] In contrast, Robert's musical occultist was teaching him 'about the use and control of bodily forces'.[20] Controlling 'bodily forces' could well have embraced the practice of sex without male orgasm, which circulated in free love and alternative health circles as a form of birth control. Perhaps this explains why the young men at White-nights ranch were all 'receiving lessons from her'.[21]

Whitman and Carpenter's body-affirming writings on spirituality offered a congenial release from sexual guilt. 'One begins to own one's body at last', declared Robert, exulting in his newly made sandals based on the pattern Carpenter had sent him. While an idealistic Robert believed his new footwear enhanced the earth's magnetism and did away with 'the unclean fears' of Victorian priggish hypocrisy, he could not help but notice the sandals 'skinned' and wrenched his ankles on the rough mountain terrain.[22] Controlling one's body and connecting to the earth clearly carried a measure of discomfort; still, sales looked promising – a woman neighbour had already placed an order.

Surrounded by the vast, blue mountains covered with green pines, their snowy peaks 'pale rose' in the late December sunlight, Robert sensed infinite possibility. At night, the stars seemed so close it felt as if 'lovers and comrades' were present.[23] Robert had shed conventional Christianity, yet still yearned for personal immortality. His thoughts were with Miriam, but also with Carpenter and that strange, 'sweet' walk down Fox Lane and the road from Chesterfield, on a summer evening, with Carpenter's arm in his.[24]

It had undoubtedly been 'sweet' too for Carpenter. By the time he received Robert's December letter, copies of his pamphlet, *Homogenic Love*, on same-sex love, would have at last arrived from the Labour Press in Manchester. He posted bundles out to friends and subscribers, for it could only be issued for private circulation. Its first lines were:

> Of all the many forms that Love delights to take, perhaps none is more interesting (for the very reason that it has been so inadequately considered) than that special attachment sometimes denoted by the word Comradeship.[25]

'Love' has many meanings and so too does 'comradeship'. Had there been something more than walking arm and arm when Robert visited Carpenter at Millthorpe? They had met on only a few occasions, yet these letters reveal Robert repeatedly laying claim to a close and loving intimacy. Unlike Carpenter, Robert was not exclusively attracted to men, but in his letters to the older man he expressed an effusive attachment that flirts with eroticism.

When Robert next wrote to Carpenter in July 1895, he had read *Homogenic Love*. Moreover, he had come across the 1892 edition of *Towards Democracy*, which contained several passionate love poems, as well as 'The Secret of Time and Satan', the poem that had so impressed Helena. 'Of course your poems are strong meat', Robert told Carpenter, 'I have to go slow and let them suffuse thro' me. Breathe them into my being so to speak.' 'But after all', he added, 'I care for you, dear one, before anything you've written. You contain all: though I am glad you can utter so well for the people.'[26]

Reporting in excitement on the startling effect of his deep breathing exercises upon his mental energy, Robert enquired if Carpenter knew 'of Lake Harris and "inward breath"'.[27] At a loss without Miriam, Robert needed psychological communication with an empathetic intellectual and spiritual guide. However, he was also seeking to recover that sense of mission he had known with Miriam. Carpenter's name was becoming known in California beyond the left and the experimental new lifers. Robert was beginning to realise that his special access to the charismatic older man provided a kind of kudos. He was chuffed about finding a customer for the sex pamphlets, including *Homogenic Love* – a 'Dr Hawver', who Robert described as a 'decent chap'.[28] The open-minded dentist who ordered Carpenter's works was a sceptical and inquiring intellectual with broad interests. Dentistry was a newly technologised profession that attracted searching, 'modern' spirits, and Hawver was a figure in Auburn's small cultural enclave. A keen photographer and palaeontologist, interested in evolution, Hawver would later acquire celebrity by finding dinosaur bones in a local cave.[29]

Arrogant and jejune in his compulsion to express every stray fleeting impression, Robert did worry that his letters might be 'boring': 'I know I am beastly selfish down at bottom to presume to waste your time talking of my needs, desires & hopes.' Eager to please, he tells Carpenter he was going 'to give up vampiring'; resolving not to want things for himself, he had decided to go 'out as a beacon to folk'. Still pursuing the role he and Miriam had marked out for themselves, Robert saw himself as carrying some special destiny to serve and had come to believe this required a renunciation of self and rigorous spiritual training as an adept. Yet, conversely, he longed to experience 'the sorrow and joy of life and love'. Moreover, while he felt fatally attracted to the extremes that feature in Carpenter's 'The Secret of Time and Satan', Robert's desire to be 'as "bad" as the baddest and "good" as the best' muddled his evangelical aspiration to serve as a 'beacon'.[30] The annihilation of customary moral boundaries in pursuit of an ethics based on self-knowledge was not unusual among those struggling to cast off Victorian constraints. Havelock Ellis and Raymond Unwin, as well as Carpenter, had drawn upon similar ideas in the writings of the unconventional mystic James Hinton, and the trans-valuation of values was in vogue during the 1890s.[31] But Robert, who tended to pick up ideas jackdaw-like, was spinning in confusion.

In 1895 Alexander Ellis had left Robert to his own devices by departing to Philadelphia. According to Robert, Ellis was liking 'the change much'.[32] Maybe he found city life more restful than Robert's indefatigable quests for cosmic enlightenment. In his friend's absence the gregarious enthusiast was doing his best to fill the wild open spaces. Robert's younger brother Davie was over from Scotland. Unlike Robert, Davie's head seems to have been well screwed on; his dour response to Robert's mystical wish to be like a 'mountain' was, 'I wouldn't be that.' Carpenter was informed that friends were expected for an alternative Independence Day celebration on July 4th; the menu was 'Yankee Cake', fruit and cocoa. Robert confided that the most exciting guest was 'my artist boy'. This was Harris Osborn, the young man Robert and Miriam had befriended. 'He is a quiet great eyed chap – & paints & yet <u>knows</u>. He has been taught much by an old Boston artist who is also a Spiritualist. Someday Harris will live here.' They were having a wonderful time 'up and down canyons', bathing and taking 'sun baths', amid 'lots of laughter'.[33] Carpenter had adopted Walt Whitman's habit of taking naked sunbaths, and now Robert, an elderly twenty-seven, could be the wise older companion.

Another friend, Sim E. Hyde, a former medical student from Oakland, was also at the ranch that summer. The mountain air in the foothills of the Sierras was beginning to attract convalescents and Hyde suffered from weak lungs. Robert described Hyde as a 'sweet chap', an 'enthu-siast of course'.[34] Hyde's particular enthusiasm was a curious project, the Ralston Health Club. Its mastermind was Albert Webster Edgerly, who adopted the pseudonym, 'Edmund Shaftesbury'. After practising law, Edgerly began to write about oratory and breathing, moving on to advise on personal magnetism. For Robert, already adept at persuasion, Ralstonism offered system and status. He was not alone. The promise of magnetic powers, combined with dietary instruction on wholegrain cereals, proved exceedingly popular and Edgerly/Shaftesbury prospered. Indeed, the cereals were eventually to be marketed by the owner of Purina animal feeds. In November 1895 Robert wondered whether Carpenter had received the 'Ralston Book' from Hyde.[35]

Carpenter appears to have maintained a characteristically tactful silence on Ralstonism as well as on the Esoteric Christian, Edward Maitland, whose work Robert similarly admired. Unbeknown to Robert, though sympathetic to Maitland's criticism of vivisection, Carpenter was wary of the Hermetic Society and Maitland's Esoteric Christian Union, inspired by the mystical Anna Kingsford. Moreover, Carpenter's friend, Henry Salt, whose Humanitarian League campaigned against cruelty to animals, opposed Kingsford's extreme approach to vivisection and found Maitland exasperating.[36] Innocent of these tensions in the anti-vivisectionist cause, Robert was delighted when Dr Albert Leffingwell, a moderate American anti-vivisectionist, sent him a copy of Henry Salt's *Animal Rights*.[37]

Robert maintained links with British anarchists and socialists. He was reading Henry Seymour's *The Anarchist*, and asked Carpenter to send him copies of two pamphlets to sell, Morris' *Art and Socialism* (1884), which William Bailie had bought in Belfast before he left, and Kropotkin's *Appeal to the Young* (1889), which called upon students to recast culture in the interests of the people.[38] Robert corresponded too with Robert Weare, now living near Liverpool, and was in touch with Robert Sharland and his delicate son Harold in Bristol, who he wished could come and stay for a year: 'I am very poor or would have him at once. It would give him a splendid body and rescue him from that old age in youth, which the dear little fellow may have amid such intense life as Bob and the rest create in Bristol.'[39]

The body and the curative power of nature had become a quasi-religious cause.

A blissed-out Robert wrote in November 1895:

> Things are going wonderfully here. Oh if you only knew what joy is coming to me, utter intoxication of Love. I can only say as you once said 'Joy, Joy I have found.' Words are helpless. How beautiful Love is! And if one will only have faith, perfect trust, all things are delivered unto him. May strength be given to me to hand on what is entrusted to me. Do not mind my vagueness. <u>You understand</u> for you know.[40]

Robert could feel 'the descent to the earth of wonderful forces'; he considered 'the old order doomed to pass away'. 'Words' were so halting and he longed 'To be Light'. He wanted to 'take the wretched, sick poor' to his heart. Then, in a flicker of self-doubt, he assured Carpenter, 'I'm in splendid health – mentally & physically so don't think I'm going mad.' Despite being 'helped nobly thro' by an old doctor', who he describes as 'a gem', he insists his ecstatic excitement was simply because 'experiences follow hard on one another'.[41]

By that November, Robert had adopted tones of gushing intimacy:

'Dear one, I received your lovely letter and it gladdened my heart unutterably. How dear you are. Why should I love you so much? It is so sweet to have you. Ah! I cannot express my feeling to you.'[42] Eager to disseminate Carpenter's writing, Robert asked for two copies of *Towards Democracy*, photos of himself and two 'copies of H.L.?' (*Homogenic Love*).[43] There was, however, a catch. Carpenter's amorous correspondent was now offering to pay *after* they had been sold.

What is more, Carpenter now had a rival celebrator of male comradeships. Robert was enamoured by a new correspondent, Edmund Russell, the New York populariser of François Delsarte's theories of combined breathing, voice and movement. Influenced by the Theosophists, Russell translated the quest for spiritual harmony into the promise of a perfected self and ideal life-style. Instead of wholegrain diets, he offered aesthetic savoir-faire by advising on colours and textures. Dressed either as Prince Siddhartha or clad simply in tights, with a red handkerchief serving as a loincloth, he created himself as a glamorous, outré celebrity through well-publicised demonstrative readings. A dazzled Robert announced, 'Another comrade for us'.[44]

Through Russell, Robert came to feel that he embodied 'Young America' and consequently took a dim view of Robert Gilliard's son, Sydney, who was visiting, working for his board on a nearby ranch. 'He's a regular John Bull, eating all the time.'[45] Far more welcome of course was Harris Osborn. Whether he and Robert were actually lovers or simply erotic comrades is not clear, but 'my young Yankee Artist comrade' is graced with unstinting adoration in Robert's missives to Millthorpe.[46]

In November 1895 Robert expressed himself as bounteous and accepting, 'men & women come & want me – and I give gladly so that they in turn may give also'.[47] In the midst of so much polymorphous creative energy, an extra contact was neither here nor there. Carpenter must have mentioned Gertrude, for Robert responds, 'Gertrude Dix! Yes, I remember her well. Tell her if she cares to I would like to hear from her.

You know I like women as much as men.'[48] And thus, cosmic, anarchical Robert and the Fabian new woman Gertrude resumed contact.

Robert continued his search for mystical revelation over the winter. In a letter dated March 1896, he reported to his 'dear Comrade' that 'a few days ago' a '"clear feeling"' had come to him:

> For the first time in my life I could distinguish myself as something apart from, and superior to my brain & intellect. There swept thro' me a power of mastery over my body – not an attitude of rejection, but self- realization – something I have long known & believed but never up till now realised.[49]

It was the state of perception for which he had been struggling, but he still could not yet enter it 'to order'. Robert wrote that he wanted 'to realize my body & all its faculties – to be sound and tested & pliant in every part'. To accomplish this, he believed he needed balance and harmony, to thwart the 'usurpation of the brain or stomach'. He aspired to 'limpid clarity', but had not attained 'that fine consciousness where one vibrates with universal music and pours it into an exquisite intellectual & artistic mould'. He explained to Carpenter that dwelling in this 'transitional stage' made it difficult to find words. No longer believing 'in cold intellect' and experiencing 'flashes of the future' that he could not articulate, he was longing for the 'walls' restricting his 'path' to melt away. Echoing Miriam, he wanted to emerge 'once more into Light and Liberty'. Standing 'on a mountain side', it felt sometimes that he had only to open his arms to 'breathe in the Life' in order to gain the strength to 'heal' those who were 'sick' or 'sorrowful'. But he knew it could not be 'just yet'.[50]

Robert's struggle for cosmic consciousness and social redemption was tailed by his combat with sexual guilt. By spring 1896 he had become convinced, 'No longer can <u>priest</u> or <u>anyone</u> cast obloquy on the sexual act or on woman – on the testes or vagina – or womb or the sweetness of coition.'[51] Yet, like Miriam, he dreaded 'animalism' as a weakness, concluding honesty was the key. 'To me impurity simply consists in knowingly abandoning reality for illusion.' But how was such authenticity to be authenticated? He had been reading Kingsford and Maitland's *The Perfect Way* (1882), and the thought had occurred to him that in order for a man to attain the perfect union it might be necessary 'to "marry" again and again'. Now convinced marriage was a symbol, Robert puzzled over 'what the sexual act symbolises exactly'.[52]

Disingenuously Robert told his 'dear lover' that none of his insights came 'from books'. Awareness was gleaned 'from the mountains, the over-arching dazzling blue sky – the silence – my pines – my comrades'. He did encounter fellow spiritual searchers in the mountains and mentions a woman visitor, 'a beauty', 'a healer' who 'travels in the spheres', but Robert was, of course, constantly dipping into books.[53] Snatched gobbets from Kingsford, Maitland, Harris, Butler, Whitman and Carpenter, along with Russell and the French Symbolists, swirled around in his head. Helena was about to add to the confusion by sending him that translation of Desjardins with its message of humanity and love.

He had come to agree with Carpenter that he could do little alone: 'I long for a glorious comradeship – a band of brothers, men & women … who could … sing the glad day which dawns & lead the people to the re-construction of society & humanity.' The socialism and anarchism he had previously embraced goes cosmic in California. It seemed to him 'the nucleus of the new society' was 'gathering in Young America'. Robert was convinced, 'To my house on the hillside from North and South, East and West, come invisible wires innumerable with messages of Love, & hope & joy.'[54] Some wires arrived in a more everyday manner at Weimar's post office; Russell, an accomplished networker, wanted Robert to ask Carpenter to 'receive' him when he visited England. Explaining that Russell's heart was so great, Robert feared 'few people will understand him'.[55]

Robert's 'glorious comrades', or 'the other boys' as he calls them, Will Russell and Sim Hyde, were scattered now in various parts of America, and Alexander Ellis was working as a reporter on the *Philadelphia Ledger*, a high-minded Republican paper. Robert includes among his 'boys' two women: 'Helena Born, (Boston, proof-reading)', and Ellen Creelman, who had trained at the California Kindergarten Training School in San Francisco, before meeting Robert in the Sierras.[56] By 1896, Creelman was in Seattle, pioneering progressive kindergarten education, where, according to Robert, she was wielding a great influence over others and had been 'helped very much' by *Towards Democracy*.[57]

They had all moved on, apart from 'Douglas Hotchkiss (in Applegate teaching mental science & divine healing)'.[58] This is Robert's first reference to Hotchkiss, who in 1892 had been attracted to Butler's community, testifying in *The Esoteric* on the 'ineffable peace' he experienced from subduing his carnal nature.[59] He appears to have been among those who wandered from 'Solar Biology' to join the other alternative healers who were beginning to cluster in the area. Ideas of 'mental science' and 'divine healing' came to be associated with the famous Mary Baker Eddy, the founder of Christian Science, but during the mid 1890s there were many less authoritarian currents flowing into the broad movement of New Thought, influencing Malinda E. Cramer's Divine Science Church and her journal *Harmony*.[60] They wafted around a receptive Robert who relayed snippets from California to Carpenter in the Cordwell Valley.

Carpenter was no doubt gratified to hear that Hotchkiss was reading *Towards Democracy*. Sadly, actual *cash* did not travel along any of the wires, postal or telepathic. Robert, ever in need of more copies of *Towards Democracy* for 'comrades', states, 'I wd. willingly pay if you will let me, tho' I am glad to accept them if you can afford it as we are not rich just now.'[61] Perhaps Carpenter could add a copy of his book on India and Ceylon, *From Adam's Peak to Elephanta* (1892). Ralstonism and Russell seem to have taught Robert ways of asking for favours that were difficult to refuse.

He was also inclined to announce grandiose schemes. Robert and Harris Osborn were 'entering into partnership as "Makers for America"' of the Kashmiri-Millthorpe sandals. But in order for them to improve their workmanship could Carpenter send a pair for Sunrise? He promised her

Edward Carpenter in sandals at Millthorpe, near Sheffield, by
Alf Mattison (Carpenter Collection, Sheffield Archives)

foot size and a postal order.[62] The sandals were needed for an extraordinary expedition. Robert, Harris Osborn and Sim Hyde were planning 'a trip to San Francisco soon on foot. We shall haul Sunrise in a little wagon.'[63] The journey they proposed making was one of around 100 miles.

The next letter, sent in April 1896, reported on the 'sweet time' they had spent in San Francisco and Oakland. Welcomed by Sim Hyde's hospitable mother in Oakland and conveniently able to leave Sunrise with her German maid, the two young men headed off for San Francisco. 'I'm sure you would love San Fran. and Oakland', Robert enthused to Carpenter, 'The bay is noble, dotted with islands, and San Francisco rises steeply from the shore on numerous hills.'[64]

In 1896 San Francisco was the eighth largest city in the United States and renowned for inventiveness and pleasure. Nothing seemed impossible in a financial centre where money was easily made and lost, and a judge could be found dancing at a bifurcated bloomer-ball with a 'saucy-eyed' partner with 'buff hair'.[65] Robert revelled in the cosmopolitan flux of the city: 'It is a curious place – you meet all types there – for it is a sea-port – the great outlet from the States, & the great inlet from China, Japan, India, Australia. China-town is quite a sight. I like such a motley crowd.'[66] Such empathy was in the romantic spirit of Carpenter's all-embracing *Towards Democracy* and his account of his travels in India and Ceylon (Sri Lanka), *From Adam's Peak to Elephanta*, which Robert had borrowed. But while Chinatown might have appeared exotic to an exploratory tourist, anti-Asian prejudices were rife, not only on the right, but in the labour movement.

Robert mentions the socialists in passing: 'I looked up the Socialists in S.F. but did not see much of them. Everybody seems to be expecting a break-up in the U.S. in a year or so. Certainly things seem to be tending that way. But I'm not afraid.'[67] The feeling of apocalyptic disintegration could have arisen not simply from the state of American capitalism but from the socialists' internal disputes, exacerbated by the schismatic leader of the Socialist Labor Party, Daniel DeLeon.[68]

All this acrimony was a far cry from Robert's cosmic questing at Whitenights ranch, but if he had lingered in Oakland he might well have found the spiritually inclined 'laureate of labor', Edwin Markham, more congenial. The poet, who admired Carpenter and had been influenced, like Robert, by Thomas Lake Harris, was in contact with local occult groupings who saw California as the 'cradle' of a new spiritually evolved race on the lines of Robert's 'Young America'. And Markham also happened to know Donna Brooks Beaumont, the woman who utterly bowled Robert over when he and Harris Osborn were introduced to her in San Francisco that spring.[69]

Under the pseudonym of John G. Claxton, Beaumont's *She of the Holy Light* had been issued in 1893 by the Western Authors' Publishing Association. It told the story of an exoticised Native American Indian, Garangula, whose dark face combined 'the strength of the Anglo Saxon with the grace of the oriental'. The convoluted plot hinges on his meeting with Zalona, a woman of mysterious powers, 'with the mouth of Cleopatra', whose child he saves.[70] A bizarre fantasy, the book nevertheless criticised white domination and plunder.

Robert dilates at length in his letter to Carpenter in April 1896 on the 'wonderful meeting' with Donna Brooks Beaumont. The novelist was then in her early sixties, and Robert describes a woman, 'small in stature, palish complexion, blue eyes, flaxen hair, calm face and demeanor, flute-like voice – lulling & pleasant to listen to for a long while'. He was utterly fascinated. 'Madame I fancy very much. She strikes me not so much as a woman as a sexless unity. When I look at her I am not conscious of sex – rather I feel to be in the presence of one who includes man & woman.'[71] Not only did 'Madame Beaumont' transcend gender, Robert announced, 'I found that she was actually working out the great sex question along the same lines you have – sane, simple, clear, scientific, all from the spiritual basis.'[72] Edmund Russell was now rapidly demoted.

Robert enthused on the symbolical importance of a woman with the capacity to discard 'the shackles of custom, prejudice, & slavery to man, and resume her throne as queen'. 'Madame Beaumont' was, moreover, surrounded by other 'splendid women'. Robert, having assumed that being close to nature was crucial 'if one were <u>aware</u>', found it a 'revelation' to meet such 'calm, stately, beautiful women who were cognisant of occult powers & actually possessors of them living so happily in a great city & doing such splendid work'.[73]

Indeed, everything was so splendid, that he had decided to leave Sunrise in Madame's care at her home in Pine Street! It sounds as if Robert's five-year-old daughter was beginning to display a will of her own: 'Daughter is beautiful, and has a finely strung nature & so needs someone who is very well balanced & knowing to guide her unfoldment. God has been very good to me in sending Madame.'[74] Sunrise may well have had other views about her father and the Almighty conspiring to deposit her with a woman she hardly knew in order to be unfolded.

Robert's trip to San Francisco induced a transcendent millenarian mood: 'I know that our bodies and all material expressions will some day soon be resolved into pure white vibration like unto God.' He felt young people in America were seeking to understand 'the unity of all things … the without beginning & without end'. They needed 'someone or some group – the Theban band to outline the new synthesis'.[75] Carpenter's 'Theban band' had been an ideal of male comradeship within a broader socialism, but Robert's was energised by the empathetic women at Pine Street, breathing 'in & out the Divine breath'. He was convinced Walt Whitman's 'great race' would derive from America, unencumbered by custom.[76]

On his trip Robert had found many 'young fellows' interested in Carpenter's books and could report how the 'Theosophists felt very kindly to you'. He was introduced as the 'Gentleman who knows Ed Carpenter, and I felt as tho' you were my dress coat'.[77] In Oakland and in San Francisco, the Theosophists had espoused ideas of the 'Brotherhood of Humanity', working with the Nationalists in the early 1890s. From 1896 under the new leadership of Katherine Tingley they were beginning to shift towards a purely spiritual evolution, but it seems they could still embrace Carpenter.[78]

The mounting demand for both *Towards Democracy* and for Carpenter's other writings was resulting in a balance of payments problem. Hinting there were yet other books he needed, Robert asserts, 'I will not get you to send them to me till I can pay. For I will degenerate if I accept so much.'[79] Spiritual enlightenment was proving beyond Robert's material means and the grand plan of becoming Carpenter's distributer was crumbling.

Nevertheless, he was looking forward to the publication of Carpenter's *Love's Coming of Age*, happily envisaging that a readership of prostitutes, despised 'old maids', high society American and European women, as well as Chinese, Japanese, African and Hindu women, would 'thrill with the touch of Universal democratic (as well as aristocratic) … love'. Robert, having come to believe in an aristocracy of 'the soul', now considered that Carpenter was not sufficiently 're-constructive' for the American context where it was possible to 'pitch right in', rather than having to waste time destroying what existed. Somewhat tactlessly he explained, 'Madame Beaumont's work will include your "Love's Coming of Age".'[80]

Robert was unaware of the difficulties Carpenter had faced in finding a publisher for the book, even without the inclusion of *Homogenic Love*. The trial of Oscar Wilde in 1895 had given rise to moral panic about

same-sex love, leaving only the small Labour Press in Manchester prepared to take the risk in 1896.[81] Nevertheless, over the next decade,
Carpenter's cautious assertion of the 'immense *variety* of love' would
reach an international readership and his work would be translated into
many languages.[82] It appealed partly because of his skill in presenting
radical ideas as self-evident but also because his writing on love bridged
spiritual exploration and 'modern' psychological approaches to self-hood
and desire.

When Robert opened his copy of *Love's Coming of Age* he would have
found two short extracts from 'Miriam Wheeler Nicol', part of the material he had posted to Carpenter in 1894. In one she asserted her belief in
the superiority of the kind of love that involved 'the subtler intercourse of
the soul and the affections, or … a comradeship in work for Humanity'.
She believed 'The energy degrades to sensualism if it has only the individual channel for expression.'[83]

In the other extract, she outlined her ideals of women and men, different, yet transformed. Her future women were to be 'beautiful … athletic,
free, able in mind and logic, great in love and in maternal instincts,
unashamed of their bodies and of the sexual parts of them, calm in nerve,
and with a chronic recognition of Spiritual qualities'. Her future men are
depicted as 'gentle, strong, courageous, continent, affectionate, unselfish,
large in body and mind, full of pluck and brawn, able to suffer, clean
and honest in their animal necessities, self-confident, with no king or
overseer'.[84] Miriam spoke out from the pages of *Love's Coming of Age* of
the ideals she had sought to live, amid an imposing supporting cast that
included the sex psychologist, Havelock Ellis, and Geddes' friend, James
Mavor, who became a professor in Canada.

Her legacy shadows Robert. Between September 1894 and April 1896,
the letters to Carpenter reveal Robert's frantic efforts to fit an image he
had derived from Miriam, while finding his own individuality. His search
for harmony and balance resembles a one-man band with a juggling act.
He attempts everything at once, understanding the universe, knowing
himself, expanding without boundaries. He wants to achieve the light
of spiritual revelation in order to become a democratic beacon, while
cultivating that little notch of snobbery, an aristocratic soul. He is unsure
whether to aim at ascetic detachment or sensuous connection. Robert's
lofty muddles are characteristic of the spiritual quests of his era, in which
conventional religious beliefs were being called into question. His preoccupation with personal energy, will and infinite cosmic possibility also

tallied with an America in traction to become a major economic and political power.

Robert next surfaces, somewhat mysteriously, on 9 February 1897, purchasing the ranch and eighty acres of the surrounding land from Alexander Ellis who was still living in Philadelphia.[85] Of course the ranch yielded fruit, but no doubt Robert, like many others in California, hoped a fortune lay hidden, waiting to be discovered. Gold had been pretty well exhausted in Placer County, but the possibility of other minerals was alluring. Land also provided a form of security; small tracts could be parcelled out to cover debts.[86] Gertrude's brother Clement, who arrived in the United States in March 1897, may well have been drawn towards mining by Robert's enthusiasm.

It was shortly after Robert became a landowner that Helen and Helena started planning their visit. But the journey westwards was not to be. Helen recorded in her journal on April 23rd, 'We have given up the California trip', adding, 'Too many obstacles in the way'.[87] A few months later, three considerable sums of money passed from Helena's account to Robert. On August 31st, she transferred $50 to him at Weimar through Wells Fargo by telegraph; then, on September 15th a further $50 went by American Express to Robert who was in Marysville, Yuba County, about forty miles from Sacramento. The third payment of $350 went to a 'Mr Ryan', possibly a solicitor, at 313 E. Street, Marysville, during October.[88] Incredibly Helena had, over the course of three months, handed over to Robert an amount that was more than her year's salary.

The next surprising transaction occurred on December 10th, when Robert transferred the ranch to 'Miriam S. Nicol', now just seven years of age. It was witnessed by a notary in Yuba County and, on December 14th, it was 'Filed for record' at the request of none other than 'Donna B. Beaumont'.[89] Why did Robert need hundreds of dollars from Helena, and what induced her to give it to him? The most likely reason would be to benefit Sunrise in some way. And, indeed, Robert and Sunrise's lives were about to change dramatically. No sooner had Robert become a landowner, when he and Sunrise moved to San Francisco.

THIRTEEN

Love, Pure Food and the Market: 1897–1899

Whatever motives Helena might have had for handing over so much money to Robert, she surely knew him well enough to see it was not wise. But at thirty-seven, Helena, usually so circumspect, was betraying an uncharacteristic recklessness. In the summer of 1897 with the Tufts once again at Squibnocket in Martha's Vineyard, she terrified everyone by getting lost on the lagoon in a boat. A search party set off with lanterns and a megaphone to rescue her, only to find she had walked home over the fields and along the road barefoot.[1] Squibnocket provided Helena with copy for an article denouncing the contrast in male and female attire at 'summer resorts', 'The Last Stand Against Democracy in Sex'.[2] Russell immortalised Helena and his sister in their swimsuits by a rock on the beach; Helen glowing and luxuriant, Helena looking at the camera as if surprised by unexpected happiness. It was not to last, for upon her return a vindictive manager at Ginn & Company sacked her without giving any reason. Helena was back setting type at a printers that autumn.[3]

On 4 September 1897 Helen recorded that 'William Lloyd, whom Miss Holmes knows', was corresponding with Helena and had sent her a volume of his poems.[4] J. William Lloyd had been part of the Liberty anarchist network before clashing with Tucker over Egoism. In 1897, Lloyd's pamphlet, *The Red Heart in a White World: A Suggestive Manual of Free Society Containing a Method and a Hope*, outlined his 'free socialist' proposals for balancing 'Human Equal Liberty' and 'Voluntary Recip-rocal Co-operation' through associations of free spirits seeking the simple

L. to R.: Helen Tufts Bailie and Helena Born, 1897 (Helen
Tufts Bailie Papers, Sophia Smith Collection, Smith College)

life, supported by mutual farming, 'Labor Exchanges' and a free currency.
Lloyd believed in 'natural social rights' and, like Helena, his ideal was an
equilibrium between self-affirmation and altruism.[5]

Lloyd's utopia included equality in daily life; he recommended a combination of the socialisation of domestic labour and each partner living
in separate dwellings. As for sex, while advising 'those who wished to be
life-companions' to marry 'legally' until the 'free society' was achieved,
his 'Comradeship of Free Socialists' (C.F.S.) offered a startling freedom to
experiment: 'What relation of the sexes seems to you ideal reader? There
is nothing whatever to prevent you realising it in the CFS. Provided it
does not invoke force and that you can find a mate to agree with you.'[6]

Scrupulous not to be authoritarian in his proposals for 'free socialism',
when it came to organisation Lloyd was an obsessive, devoting several
pages to an elaborate structure. The 'Association' was to be the 'Comradeship of Free Socialists'; the Federation was composed of 'Comrades of the
Free Society'. The small band required not only the customary secretaries
and treasurers, but several layers of local and general leaders, topped by a
'Directing Liberator'.[7]

Lloyd's C.F.S. resulted in irreparable rifts within the Tufts family. A
firm believer in individual choice, William Tufts was unfazed by his

J. William Lloyd (Labadie, Special
Collections Library, University of Michigan)

daughter attending lectures by the Theosophist, Besant, and the anarchist communist, Kropotkin.[8] But he was *appalled* to hear that Helena and
Helen had 'signed the comradeship paper' of the C.F.S. 'Papa thinks
William Lloyd may be Satan himself, and that we have signed away our
souls.'[9] Nevertheless, Helen remained in the Comradeship and Helena
continued her correspondence with Lloyd. When Helena took over as
'Directing Liberator', Helen became 'General Secretary'.[10]

'Satan himself' was a working-class grassroots intellectual who had left
school at fourteen, learning about self-sufficiency as a homesteader, cow-
puncher, poultry man and sawmill worker. Also a drugless physician and
masseur, Lloyd had lived in two communities in Tennessee and Florida.
In December 1897, Lloyd, who was a widower with two children, began
to urge his Directing Liberator to visit him in New Jersey.[11]

Helena's austere blast against female adornment, 'The Last Stand
Against Democracy in Sex', was due to appear in the next issue of *The Conservator*, and she was apt to joke about herself as 'fearless and repellent'.[12]
Her strong emotional relationships had all been with women. Perhaps
she felt that, unlike most men, who 'regarded women as adjuncts, objects
of use or pleasure, or both', here was a man interested in 'soul' rather than

'body'.[13] On January 10th, she set off for Lloyd's home in Westfield, New Jersey.[14]

It was a disaster. The romantic feelings aroused by their correspondence withered upon meeting. According to Helen, the brutal truth was that when Lloyd saw Helena his ardour 'cooled'. A good friend and a fierce hater, she expressed outrage in her journal: 'I detest this William Lloyd. He got so emotional about Helena; he wanted her to come to Westfield … as soon as he saw her, she wasn't what he wanted.' While Helen remonstrated against shallowness, Helena's account was apparently guarded. 'This is not the way she told it. She is too high minded to blame him, but I know what I think about it.'[15] Whatever happened in New Jersey, Helena was severely jolted. Helen described her as 'rocked back on herself, and her eyes betray the shock'.[16]

However, the two women remained in the C.F.S. Amid ominous signs of America's deteriorating relations with Spain and the rise of an imperialist mood, the little band of utopians in the C.F.S. were pondering how to combine self-sufficiency with co-operation. Their members lacked practical skills; but this did not deter a dreamy Helen from transplanting Boston into the wilds: 'We would like to improve ourselves and have Whitman societies, and take the magazines. And we would be artistic. Helena would be great on that.'[17] Some favoured settling in the Gulf of Mexico, but a former Unitarian, James Haworth, was lobbying for the mountains of North Carolina. Being individualists, they rejected the idea of a community but could not decide whether to live in clusters or in isolation.

Helena meanwhile resumed her round of meetings and organising. She was impressed by the socialist feminist writer, Charlotte Perkins Stetson (later Gilman), at the Massachusetts Suffrage Association, and renewed her Edinburgh friendship with the freethinker, John M. Robertson, visiting Boston for a lecture.[18] With pride, she informed Traubel of a new recruit for the Boston Walt Whitman Fellowship, the artist James S. Campton, and five English members in Liverpool.[19]

Shortly after her trip to Lloyd in Westfield, Helena had started thinking about studying agriculture. She then found a practical way of turning herself into a farmer *and* making a self-sufficient getaway. Through the C.F.S. she had come into closer contact with the free-love campaigners, Flora and Josephine Tilton, who were part of the Individualist anarchist network. When Josephine decided to run the family farm in Epsom, New Hampshire, complementing its earnings by taking in boarders, Helena offered to help her.[20]

Early in April, Flora Tilton and Archibald Simpson held a farewell party for Josephine and Helena in their Boston home at 84 St Botolph Street, at which Simpson's friend from the Boston Anarchist Club, William Bailie, arrived with a present of one of his baskets for Josephine to take to Epsom.[21] The man with the basket was going to have a profound impact upon Helena's life and Helen's too.

Over the previous decade he and Helena had been following such parallel courses it was curious they had not already come across one another. Not only had William Bailie met Miriam and Robert, Helena would have heard of his *Liberty* articles during the early 1890s. Even before then, she and William had been moving in very similar socialist circles in Britain. Despite the differences in their backgrounds, they shared a voracious love of reading and knew people in common, including Edward Carpenter and Raymond Unwin.

Helen describes Helena and William's first 'encounter' at St Botolph Street as 'electric'.[22] Immediately after they met, he wrote to Helena enclosing a precious book by William Morris with passages marked for special attention. However, the prospects of closer intimacy were bleak. Helena was about to depart; William was married with six children. William had glimpsed joy and she was about to vanish to Epsom. He must have explained something of his former life, for when Helena wrote to him on April 7th, she urged, 'Be not depressed or embittered by the past, sad friend.'[23]

In 1892, William had complained in 'The Martyrdom of the Soul' that 'Family life is a pretence, a shadow, hardly ever a pleasant reality', and grumbled away about 'Visits, entertainments, shopping and other indifferent locomotory functions' being 'always dull and often positively abhorrent'. Was he thinking of Ellen when he wrote 'the unconscious martyrdom enwraps in tighter folds the whole character of woman'?[24] For Ellen, bitterly resentful towards the man who was hardly ever there, her children must have seemed her only hold on William, but a family of six overwhelmed her. William had moved them from Chelsea out to Scituate, a small fishing town half way between Boston and Plymouth, connected by train Monday to Saturday and by horse and phaeton on Sundays. Perhaps he thought the sea air would benefit the children, but it would have left Ellen even more stranded.

By the time William met Helena at the Tiltons' party in 1898, he had fled the miserable, fractious marriage and was squatting in his basket workshop. In Helen's remorseless account, he was driven out by Ellen's 'thriftlessness, … nagging hostility' and 'the squalor of his home'.[25] William proffered material support, but could not feel affection for his wife and escaped from her misery and rage by staying away from home. How he must have envied the intellectual loving companionship of the Schumms and Simpson's happiness with the 'easeful' Flora Tilton.[26] The unexpected encounter with a calm, empathetic and rational Helena caught him off guard. He had found a woman who could comprehend his political passions and intellectual searching.

At first William must have felt thwarted, for Helena's initial response after receiving the Morris book on April 6th was, 'Circumstances unknown to me when I saw you necessarily change my attitude.'[27] Did he explain about Ellen? Or did friends warn her? Nevertheless on April 7th Helena observed:

> Nothing that I know alters my feeling towards you, but on any hypothesis it seems to me; and it seems so still, there could not be complete unity between us. I may be mistaken. I do not judge. I am the last person to make enquiries concerning the home life of another.[28]

A steely Helena told William, 'In such matters the opinions of others weigh little with me.' A lofty Helena informed him, 'I have yet hope that our fellowship may be to high ends.' Then a pragmatic Helena proposed a trip out into the country for a picnic, assuring William, who was no doubt sorely confused, 'I can meet you as frankly & simply as I have hitherto. I am grateful for your belief in me.'[29]

They picnicked in Arlington and their lives turned over. William even took up his pen to write a romantic poem to his beloved 'Lena'. 'Nor time, nor space nor circumstance/Can part two souls knit close by spirit ties'. And, as he worked weaving baskets, his thoughts were of her, 'Sustained in hope and trust'.[30] By the time he sent his verse dated April 20th to Helena, however, William's new love, being a woman of resolute principles, had joined Josephine Tilton in Epsom. Helena had given her word and she kept it. William had fallen for a would-be, self-sufficient, new-woman farmer, digging salsify and parsnips.[31] His one consolation was Helena's announcement that she no longer intended to join the C.F.S. member, 'James Haworth', in his North Carolina settlement.[32] Alone with his wicker work, William may well have reflected that at least

Helen Tufts Bailie on the stone wall at Epsom, New Hampshire, 1898
(Helen Tufts Bailie Papers, Sophia Smith Collection, Smith College)

a woman of this ilk would be unlikely to require his presence on those
abhorrent shopping trips.

Epsom was a small settlement in remote rural New Hampshire. The
Tiltons' farm stood near the summit of a hill, and when Helena arrived
in the April of 1898, storms made the wind whistle around her room at
the top of the house.[33] There, on a table between two windows, she composed her careful response to the heartfelt emotions in William's poem:
'Your lines to me are very sweet – they are dear to me, and I love the
spirit in which you wrote them.'[34] Again she had contrived her own little
world: 'I have Morris' portrait on the wall, and Emerson's and Whitman's
conspicuous.'[35]

Unaccustomed to farm work, Helena found clearing land, burning
brush on the hillside, ploughing, tending her newly arrived hens and
helping to build an old-style stone wall, exacting. She was so busy and
so weary that she recycled parts of her letters to friends. Emma Schumm
('E') and J. William Lloyd were both firmly warned, 'I am a farmer first

and a correspondent afterwards.'[36] Defying Helen's strictures on 'vegetarian gloves', she appealed to 'E' for a discarded pair of strong leather ones to protect her hands from cuts.[37] In her letter to Lloyd she informed him that his copy of Alice B. Stockham's *Karezza: Ethics of Marriage* (1896) (a book advocating sex without orgasm) had been left with a 'friend' in Boston, and then just could not help mentioning 'Wm. Bailie' as a possible C.F.S. speaker.[38] Regardless of her exhaustion, William was favoured over Helena's other correspondents. For the six long months of their separation letters flew back and forth between Epsom post office and Boston. Neither was experienced in matters of romance. Helena explained to William that she had known 'comradeship and friendship', but now meeting him had awakened so many feelings and thoughts that she found it difficult to sort 'them out line by line'.[39] Nevertheless, adept in self-denial, she sought to curb William's impatience, 'We have the sustenance of pleasant memories.'[40]

An epistolary love affair came rather easier to Helena than to William. Unlike Helena, William had known a physical sexual relationship, but the lengthy animadversions on emotional conduct emanating from Epsom were uncharted territory to him. Squatting in his dusty basket-making workshop, perhaps with Alice B. Stockham's manual on non-penetrative love-making close to hand, William laboured away at his missives. Playing safe, he copied out quotations from Robert Browning and Arthur Hugh Clough, careful to avoid appearing 'over-sentimental' before this intellectual woman. Helena's response must have confused him; she rebuked his distrust of emotion, which she suspected derived from the 'Secularistic or Anarchistic' tendency to 'apotheosize Reason'. Echoing Miriam's dispute with him in *Liberty* on 'Enthusiasm', she insisted 'natural spontaneous expression' had its place. William had no cause to fear he would injure her 'morals' by 'too much love – or even a little praise now and then'.[41]

She had left him with Edward Carpenter's *Love's Coming of Age* (1896) for guidance. Ironically Carpenter's volume of essays, which could not include his most personally felt writing on 'homogenic love', was becoming a guide for 'modern' heterosexual lovers. Helena set the terms: 'I see things so much from his (Carp.'s) point of view that your appreciation of his utterance will conduce greatly to our mutual understanding without tedious discussion.'[42] Concurring with both Carpenter and the free lovers who discouraged all-consuming Romantic passion, Helena declared, 'A great love should be a central fire radiating its warmth and glow in all directions.'[43] Yet, she and William, lover-like, still scanned one another's letters for the personal expressions of longing neither found it easy to pen. Of course, grizzled a tetchy Helena, she did not want 'sentimental verbiage or protestations, but in aiming at self-control I wished to avoid an excessive reticence'.[44]

To William, who was inclined to think in straighter lines, Helena seemed to shift stances while holding his letters up to judgement. He was dismayed to read how she had perused them, 'lest I should find the discordant note, for I know if it were there, I should have to give you up – for we couldn't make-believe, you know that'.[45] It was if he were on trial. William rebelled, and, by May 8th, it was Helena who was sorry her letters did not 'please' him. She did not mean to 'preach' but he must not mind her 'being a little exalted at times'.[46] Exaltation was, indeed, second nature to Helena, but meeting William had revealed what she called her 'many sidedness'. Had he forgotten 'the me you picnicked with at Arlington'? She was not 'above human love'.[47] This surely would have been what William *really* wanted to hear.

Helena's circumlocutory writing style, formed in those early addresses at the Oakfield Unitarian Church, obscured raw emotion in a fog of high-minded spirituality. Nevertheless, her ingrained habit of reflection enabled her to acknowledge, 'I am not proficient in the art of love of the "unique" type, any more than your-self.' Although transfigured by a love that was both physical and spiritual, they were both ever 'on the look out for all kinds of dangers and pit falls' and afraid of taking 'the joy within our reach'. She suggested this was because of their 'maturity'.[48] They were hardly aged, Helena about to turn thirty-eight and William thirty-one, but their ration of personal joy had been meagre, and both, for different reasons, had learned to bury their feelings. They were miles apart, connected only by the memory of a brief encounter, which was a secret even from their closest friends, apart from a sympathetic George Schumm.[49] The scope for misapprehension was immense.

Amid the mood swings of distanced desire and the psychological impact of physical fatigue, Helena strove to maintain her routines of reading. In her letters to William that spring she mentions Emerson, Whitman and Thoreau along with two British socialist journals, *The New Age*, then close to the Independent Labour Party, and the S.D.F.'s, *Justice*.[50] She learned of the death of Eleanor Marx from *Justice*'s May Day issue, which included a drawing by Walter Crane, 'FLOWERS FOR MAY DAY'. The flowers surrounded a wreath for 'EMA' – Eleanor Marx had committed suicide that March.[51] Helena wrote effusively to Helen about the San Francisco based 'paper', *The Coming Light*, 'devoted to higher thinking, higher living'. This may well have been the 'paper' she mentions as having been sent by Robert from San Francisco without any accompanying letter.[52] Keen now to vindicate the 'reforming power of love', she was pleased by an article in a new publication from Chicago, *The Individual*, and quoted it to William: 'Love demands no covenants, requires no conditions, asks for no favouring circumstance … It waits not upon social or political changes. It creates them. Love is the great equalizer … Equality is in essence and not in things.'[53]

On May 13th Helena described to William waiting for the 6.30 mail at the post office and reading his letter as she walked back up the hill, regardless of the rain. Joyously she picked sprays of wild cherry blossom as she went.[54] She had come around to William's materialist view; love required proximity. Thus, the couple applied their considerable organisational skills to planning a secret tryst en route to the Walt Whitman Fellowship commemoration due to be held in Walden Woods, Concord on May 31st. The prospect of meeting brought a great release. On May 18th Helena wrote, 'The self you reveal is my other self, we belong to each other.' She had cherished dreams of such a union for many years, 'with never a hope – hardly a thought of their personal realization'. At last, her anxious self-consciousness dissolved; they were 'in unity with each other'. For once the assiduous letter-writer felt unable to respond adequately on 'paper', telling him simply, 'What you give I joyfully and reverently accept.'[55] For an antinomian like Helena, who obeyed the inner voice, this subjective covenant was the equivalent to marriage vows.

As secretary of the Boston Branch of the Walt Whitman Fellowship, Helena continued to organise from her Epsom outpost. On May 18th she told Helen she had stayed up until 11 p.m. and then risen at dawn, 'getting off the Whitman notice to the printer'.[56] Her report records the fostering of a freer, more spontaneous structure within the Fellowship and the introduction of group-led discussions, involving as many female speakers as male. 'Miss' and 'Mrs' were no more. Helena lists the women lecturers simply by name, just like the male Whitmanites: Helena Born, Charlotte Porter, Arathena B. Drake, Mary D. Davenport, Mary D. Hicks, Helen A. Clarke. The branch boasted forty-three members, nine of whom were new, and it had attracted many visitors.[57] She was evidently chuffed to tell Traubel that Franklin Benjamin Sanborn was to accompany the Boston Branch's Whitman Memorial excursion to Walden Woods.[58] Sanborn brought his fame in the movement against slavery as well as his deep knowledge of Transcendentalism to the Whitmanite cause. In her greeting on behalf of the Boston Branch to the W.W.F. gathering to remember Whitman in New York, Helena stressed the importance of 'inclusive unity with the universal' rather than 'sectarianism', urging them to honour Whitman as 'pioneers' rather than 'followers'.[59]

Nominally still the 'Directing Liberator' of the Comradeship of Free Socialists, she viewed the elaborate rules in Lloyd's second edition of *The Red Heart in a White World* (1898) with some apprehension, but told William she thought the 'spirit' and comradeship of the Boston C.F.S. were, nonetheless, positive.[60] Ever inclusive, she busied herself gathering together freedom seekers in the C.F.S. as well as the W.W.F. so they could intermingle at Whitman's birthday celebrations on May 31st, badgering William for the address of a Harvard undergraduate, Walter Leatherbee Leighton, whom he had introduced to Helen at the C.F.S., in order include him in the gathering.[61]

Walter Leatherbee Leighton had adopted the older man as his mentor, though the contrast in their backgrounds was extreme. Both the Leatherbees and the Leightons were descended from British seventeenth-century settlers. Moreover, Walter's father, George, was Vice-President of the major building firm, Woodbury and Leighton, which was reconstructing Boston. The firm's contracts included not only the resplendent Public Library, but the First Church of Christ, the Christian Scientists' new $200,000 base.[62] George Leighton intended his sons to be educated so they could take their place as gentlemen, hence Walter had been sent to Harvard, where, inspired by Transcendentalism, he had wandered towards anarchism and the idealistic free lovers in the C.F.S.

Accustomed to fashionable socialites, Walter rapidly developed a reverential attachment to the earnest, impecunious Helen. Indeed, by May 27th Helena was admonishing William, suddenly over-protective, not to let his 'imagination mislead' him about Walter and Helen.[63] She was right; Helen found she enjoyed being admired by her eligible beau, but could not help comparing him unfavourably with 'Mr Bailie', so wise on social and political topics – especially anarchism. Helen admired and respected William, intuitively trusting him as a confidant. His company was at once reassuring and fun, so much so that she somehow contrived to overlook the fact that he was an Irishman – albeit a Protestant one. An amused Helena chuckled at this 'great headway in the way of friendship' between William and 'my dear reticent, liberal, semi-puritanical, brave-hearted Helen'.[64]

While Helen disdained Walter Leighton's ignorance of 'progressive ideas', the differing tendencies, overlain by deep personal loyalties, were often hard for her to comprehend.[65] She was, however, making friend-ships through the Walt Whitman Fellowship and the Comradeship of Free Socialists. When Helena introduced her to James F. Morton, Jr Helen recalled a previous sighting of this striking young man, with his shock of red hair and a 'face squeezed under a towering forehead', block-ing the entrance to the Hollis Theatre by reciting Shakespeare at length.[66] Helen, who fretted so much about how to conduct herself in the daily details of living, gasped at his insouciance. Morton was connected to the group of free lovers around Moses Harman's journal *Lucifer*, and knew the Tiltons. While Helen found the young man's laconic confidence beguiling, she 'burned up' when he visited her at Houghton Mifflin and held forth on free love.[67]

The nonchalant poise derived from Morton's self-confessed 'Boston Brahmin' background.[68] His grandfather, Revd Samuel F. Smith, had written the renowned hymn 'America', and young Morton took his mem-bership of the 'noble free' for granted. Reading Plato at Harvard had led him to question his family's liberal Baptist faith and, after exploring Spiritualism, Theosophy and Occultism, he had become an agnostic and an anarchist. Despite these diversions, Morton was a Harvard Phi Beta Kappa who had graduated 'cum laude' in 1892.[69] Helen regarded such intellectual prowess with nervous awe, reminding herself that because he was a keen philatelist they could always discuss stamps.[70] Over the years she lost the shyness but retained a soft-spot for the red-haired icono-clast who disregarded the mundane proprieties she could never, herself, discard.

Helena had been studiously vague about her travel plans for the Whitman Memorial celebration on May 31st, telling her 'semi-puritanical' Helen simply that she had some 'friends to visit' along the way.[71] William had taken charge of logistics, blocking Helena's idea of staying with Josephine Tilton's friends in tiny Tyngsboro in favour of the extra night together in Lowell, a manufacturing town where he would have been aware an odd couple could be less conspicuous.[72]

After contriving a night together without raising anyone's suspicions, the two secret lovers duly met up with Helen and Walter Leighton on the 31st and rode their bicycles towards Concord. At the Library they found Morton holding a telegram from the Poet-Lores, who had missed the train. Next a frantic Simpson was sighted, waving his handkerchief to attract attention; Walter Leighton had borrowed Simpson's bicycle and absent-mindedly pocketed the key. Helen recorded how poor 'Mr Simpson' had not only been forced to carry his bicycle from Sleepy Hollow, but had nearly been 'arrested for stealing it'.[73] It would have been an ignominious clash with the state for a serious revolutionary like himself!

In contrast, the contingent of C.F.S. members from Wellesley, William Denton Jr, his sister Carrie, and Clarence Lee Swartz, arrived at Walden Pond without misadventure. To Helen's delight, the two men produced ice creams for the hot and panting cyclists and Denton deftly improvised scoops from tree bark.[74] Innovation came easily to the Dentons, whose family history exemplifies the entwining strands of radicalism in nineteenth-century America. William Denton Sr was a naturalist who had left England in the turmoil of 1848, marrying Elizabeth M. Foote in 1854. Both were abolitionists as well as supporters of women's rights and sex reform. He was a freethinker; she was a spiritualist who wore bloomers. William Sr transmitted his passion for natural history to his children and the result was to be a truly remarkable collection of butterflies from many lands.

When his son, Sherman, devised a system for preserving, mounting and exhibiting them the family's fortunes were secured. The butterflies, along with radical nonconformity, had been passed on to William Jr, who formed a free union with the imposing and intellectual May Clifford Hurd.[75] Clarence Lee Swartz helped them with the butterflies. He, too, moved in freethinking anarchist circles. By 1898 Swartz had adopted an Egoist philosophical position, and was about to launch a new magazine, called, appropriately, 'I'.[76] In its first issue in July, Swartz announced how he edited it purely out of 'desire'.[77]

Helen found them invigorating and fun, she could hardly remember a more enjoyable outing.[78] She was, however, perplexed to find herself so frequently with Walter Leighton and Archibald Simpson on the way home. Helena and William kept vanishing, 'they weren't looking where we were going and turned off on the wrong road'.[79] The lovers made bids for freedom three times, hurtling off along the secluded country lanes in jubilant, stolen delight; on each occasion, Helen and Walter Leighton conscientiously rounded them up.

Their destination was the Tufts' home at Arlington where William –
who unlike Helena still thought Papa Tufts could be persuaded into anarchism by reason – conversed amiably with the older man. It was Helen
who wrecked the contrived harmony by announcing that Archibald
Simpson had introduced a lecture by the anarchist, Lucy Parsons, whose
husband Albert had been accused of the Haymarket bombing and executed in 1887. The Tufts parents' tremor of horror was suppressed by
a veneer of politeness. The following day, when Helen's father erupted,
Helena urged tact; but Helen, like her father, was *not* tactful.[80]

Nevertheless, when Helena confided at last in Helen, the impetuous
younger woman decided upon discretion. On June 2nd Helen wrote
in her journal that her friend 'and Mr Baillie [*sic*]' were 'fearfully and
wonderfully in love'. Hugging this huge romantic secret to herself, she
resolved not to tell her parents: 'If they knew all they wouldn't like it.'[81]
Proud that Helena trusted her, Helen wrote on June 7th, 'I do not feel
jealous. I am sure of Helena's love. I shall back them up, though I feel as if
I were standing on a mine. People are so easily horrified.'[82] This was 1898
and Helen, who was so fastidious about inconsequential propriety, displayed a courageous loyalty to Helena and William about a relationship
that shocked even free lovers.

On June 7th, as Helen watched them being swept up in the sociability
of the C.F.S. meeting at Flora Tilton's Boston home, she felt solicitous
because the loving couple could spend so little time alone. Keyed up by
romantic danger, she found Simpson's peroration on the 'Idea of Individualism', packed with quotes from Josiah Warren, exceedingly tedious,
and grumbled that the speaker 'was not auditory'. When Simpson maintained 'disintegration is the secret of progress', Helena, who had pondered
long on abstruse Hegelian dialectics, and evidently knew her Proudhon,
managed to interpolate 'that disintegration and assimilations are working
together all the time'. Helen complained: 'Some of us wanted to ask for
explanations, but couldn't get a word in edgewise, for Mr. Simpson was
always so sure he knew what we wanted to ask that he would start on an
explanation before words were out of our mouth.'[83]

At this meeting Individualism trumped Comradeship. Helen noted
that Walter Leighton wanted to be 'the center of the universe', while
Morton and Simpson locked horns at such length, they had to be disen-
tangled in order for the date of the ncxt gathering to be fixed. In Helen's
eyes, William was the only male without hubris. Cannily, he knew
how to play his cards close to his chest; it was agreed he would be the

next speaker on the topic of 'The Evolution of the Individual in Social Ideas' and that Helen would host the gathering at the Tufts' home in Arlington.[84]

The 'creed' her father had so distrusted was now assembling under his roof, for with Helena in Epsom and no instructions forthcoming, Helen had taken charge of the C.F.S. Stepping into her friend's shoes, she positioned Helena's reclining 'steamer chair' to display Miriam's aesthetic 'snake panel' and her own 'little bamboo book case', spreading 'folded quilts on the floor' of her room, instead of chairs. An eager Walter Leighton arrived first with a German anarchist communist, Jacob Vest. William and 'Mr Haworth' (planner of the abandoned North Carolina settlement) came next, talking earnestly with William Tufts. Russell had gone into disgruntled hiding, but when James F. Morton was introduced to 'Mama' and 'Papa', the rebel Brahmin conducted himself with his customary aplomb, amazing Helen by 'freely admitting that he has been called a lunatic'.[85]

Though Helen had prepared a press release, a somewhat garbled version of William's grand historical sweep of the growth of Individualism found its way into the *Boston Sunday Herald*, referring to the 'communism' of the middle ages and the 'socialism' of the present day. Still, Herbert Spencer, Karl Marx and Josiah Warren were mentioned, while the headline, 'Human Equal Liberty', caught William's gist.[86]

Helen continued to condescend towards Walter Leighton for showing off, for depending on theories in books, and expressing traditional views about women.[87] She was furious when Russell, who regarded her C.F.S. friends as dangerous subversives, approved because he had 'lots of money behind him'.[88] Only when her woebegone suitor confided to having been driven by power, competition and the 'almighty dollar', before meeting people with 'ideals that have stood the buffetings of the world', did Helen relent sufficiently to apply herself to rescuing Walter Leighton from Mammon.[89]

Helena, the seasoned politico, noting potential competition, warned William that the '*Lucifer* people' were making a bid for the wealthy young would-be anarchist and indicating that this would not be 'beneficial' for Walter.[90] Her concern was personal as well as political. She wanted Helen to be happy and hoped the affinity between the young couple would develop. Moreover, since starting a relationship with William, Helena had grown somewhat anxious about the devoted dependence Helen displayed towards her: 'She is miserable if she fancies herself left out of my plans for the future.'[91] Walter Leighton created a convenient foursome out of a slightly awkward threesome.

Early in June Helena was back in Epsom; the 'cyclometer registered 58 miles', but she had actually carried her 'wheel' further along the sandy roads from Tyngsboro. Her limbs were aching, but she told William how she cherished the memory of their 'little honeymoon in May' – her birthday month.[92] The undemonstrative William had not proposed another meeting, but now they were parted, he was keen to visit Epsom. While they were apart their worries loomed. William's despair about his predicament led a brisk Helena to threaten using 'a scrubbing-brush' on his 'pessimism'.[93] Yet Helena, too, was aware how vulnerable a woman like herself who broke with convention could be, and scolded William for 'talking about the "undue prolongation of love's suspense"'. Reminding him that three months before they had not even seen one another, he was firmly told, 'You must be less dependent on my bodily presence.'[94]

Nevertheless, after William visited Epsom, 'bodily presence' surged experientially and William was her 'sweetheart boy'. Declaring her 'thoughts' were 'mostly unutterable', she simply says, 'The memory of our days and nights are sweet.' A sensually assured Helena felt she had taught William 'something of love', declaiming, 'Love cancels all obligations, levels all distinctions and is the passport to an unsuspected world. We have entered it hand in hand, dear love.'[95] But their brief encounters did not assuage the physical desire, which Helena now experienced too. On July 10th, trying to calm William, she admitted being 'a little appalled' at the intensity of these 'disturbing' feelings, 'It makes self-mastery somewhat harder.' She concluded that 'The reconciliation of love and freedom is a problem for us to solve.'[96] The endeavour proved 'a trying ordeal' even for Helena. 'I don't always know how I'm going to hold out myself', declared the one who had departed to live the self-sufficient simple life. [97]

Momentarily, Helena's composure wavered upon reading William's account of 'a little lunch' with Helen at his workshop. 'Not that I grudge Helen – only I want to take a turn – and my turn is a long time coming', responded a petulant Helena. The emotions awakened by William evoked contradictory wishes. She wanted her close friend to be complicit in her secret love for William and relied more and more upon Helen's support; but the independent friendship between Helen and William evoked a flicker of doubt: 'I like to hear of your chats together. I wish you told me more.'[98] Helena struggled to make sense of these unfamiliar and troubling fears and desires. 'I should be a terrible person with my "principles" were it not one of my principles to follow my impulses.' On impulse she 'slept in the barn … No moon and no Willie-boy, but lots of little birdies for company.'[99]

By July 21st she had taken herself off for a holiday in West Buxton, Maine, where unfortunately the post proved slower and less regular than Epsom. Somehow she managed a review of Charlotte Perkins Stetson's (later Gilman) *Women and Economics* (1898) and Traubel rushed it into the July *Conservator*. Long an admirer of Stetson's deft satirical verse, Helena approved her call for the reorganisation of domestic life and labour, along with the simplification of life. But the two women disagreed on monogamy. Helena argued that Stetson's 'ideal' of a 'lifelong, expansive, continent, complete union', was not something most men and women could attain. She believed they needed the opportunity to grow into it through 'experience' and should not face restriction in acquiring this.[100] Even among the liberal Whitmanites, such a statement from a woman was extremely bold.

William shared Helena's interest in Stetson's synthesis of a material and social case for women's emancipation but was beginning to chafe against Carpenter and Whitman as set texts, grumbling they were 'tedious'.[101] Helena wanted him to read William Blake's 'Love's Secret' in order to see how some feelings resisted explicit expression. A Romantic sensibility towards the 'unsaid' did not convince her rationalistic correspondent. William joked about himself as her '"somewhat materialist lover"'. He did concede though that he was '"growing spiritually toward"' her.[102]

When Helena returned to Epsom early in August, the farmhouse was overflowing with guests. Among the visitors were the Tufts who, after much dithering, had decided to vacation at Josephine Tilton's, so Helena and Helen were able to take long secluded walks in the hills, clambering up Catamount, Sanborn and McCoy Mountains. In an unexpected symbiosis, Josephine Tilton took to Isabel and Helen, Russell's photography was a great hit, and their new dry-stone wall was immortalised on camera. Reassured about the infamous Josephine Tilton, William and Isabel Tufts were both delighted by her friend, Lucy Colman, a veteran abolitionist in her eighties.[103]

Colman embodied the extraordinary radicalism that flowed into several emancipatory movements from abolitionism. She was associated with the minority who had questioned religion, women's inequality and conventional sexual attitudes. A veteran of the first women's rights

Helen Tufts Bailie with a group of family and friends, Epsom, New Hampshire, 1898. L. to R. (rear): R.D.G., Flora Tilton, F's brother, Josephine Tilton, Helena Born, Helen Tufts Bailie, William Tufts. R. to L. (front): Maria, Lucy Colman, Mrs Ruggli. L. to R. (seated on ground): Leslie Swartz and unnamed woman (Helen Tufts Bailie Papers, Sophia Smith Collection, Smith College)

convention at Seneca Falls in 1848, she had, like the Bristol Women's Liberal Association, backed the radical suffrage International Council of Women in 1888. Colman believed in openness about sexual relations and frank honesty in the sex education of children. Like the Heywoods and the Tiltons, Colman's commitment to sexual freedom was guided by a concept of 'self-sovereignty'. Their application of this conviction to sexual relations was controversially extreme even in radical individualistic and freethinking circles.[104]

Knowing she would need allies when she returned to Boston, Helena was consequently depressed to discover that Flora Tilton was critical of William and began to despair of anyone's empathy.[105] A childless Helena could never inwardly comprehend William's relations with his family, yet she sensed that his evasive desire to avoid conflict would make things worse in the long run: 'I wish I knew more exactly the actual state of affairs at Scituate, beneath the surface, I mean, so that I might advise ... Be as honest as you can and not too diplomatic. Find some human meeting place if possible.'[106] Usually full of counsel she was uncertain what to suggest. One thing was sure though – her love. Just before William was due to visit again she signed off her August 28th letter, 'With the love that grows only on the tree of Equality'.[107]

Neither of the illicit lovers really knew how to handle Helena's return to Boston; they discussed running a Gilman-style 'kitchen restaurant' offering 'Pure Food' and living together as though they were married. After William left, Helena revealed to Tilton and Colman the truth they had undoubtedly surmised about her relationship with William. To her consternation both women opposed the plan of pretending to be married, a course which they explained could lead to imprisonment. Eight decades of self-sovereignty had endowed Colman with political and psychological sagacity. She warned deceit could bring 'discredit on the cause of freedom' and advised Helena against relying on any promises William's wife Ellen might make.[108] Conscious that she was out of her depth in circumnavigating conventions, Helena put Josephine Tilton's suggestion to William: they could be 'known as simply friends cooperating in a business partnership'.[109] They decided that Helena would rent accommodation and sublet to William.

A distressing rift was opening up between the lovers on what constituted 'Pure Food'; against Helena's dandelion salads and vegetarian soups, William expressed a partiality for beefsteak. After conferring with Josephine and Flora on catering, Helena reluctantly concluded that there would not be sufficient vegetarian customers, so a compromise was struck.[110] A characteristically thorough Helena began to study the storing of produce, while William and Helen looked for suitable premises. At last, early in October 1898, the harvest over, Helena returned to Boston with barrels of potatoes as well as mushrooms, tomatoes, cucumbers, cottage cheese and cream for the Pure Food Kitchen.[111]

On October 21st, filled with apprehension, Helen revealed Helena and William's relationship to her parents. Their response amazed her. A perceptive Isabel Tufts had already guessed and, though she disapproved, regarded the couple as 'responsible to themselves'. William Tufts surprised his daughter by expressing sympathy 'with the love they have for each other'.[112] Nor did they object to Helen's proposition of renting a room at the couples' Gainsborough Street apartment. So Helen, in a replay of Helena's role with Miriam and Robert, provided a degree of respectability for the unmarried woman and her male lodger.

The apartment was not far from the Pure Food Kitchen on Norway Street, a narrow alley off Falmouth Street. The wealthy Boston liberal reformer, Edward Atkinson, who believed in healthy nutrition for the poor, had donated them some of the 'Aladdin ovens' he had invented to cook cheaper cuts of meats slowly over a kerosene lamp.[113] The Pure Food Kitchen's menu extended to cold meats, fried fish, beef and oyster stew along with macaroni cheese, baked beans, vegetable hash, potato and vegetable croquettes and potato salad. Poultry could be 'cooked to order'; custard and milk puddings were offered as dessert.[114]

By November 16th, the Kitchen was taking $12 to $15 a day, but Helena and William were doing a seven-day week because they were short of staff; moreover, the clientele were stealing the crockery and the Aladdin ovens proved inadequate.[115] The restaurant, being close to the large Christian Science Church built by Woodbury and Leighton on Falmouth Street, enjoyed a brief boom just after Christmas when the Christian Scientists were conducting their Examination for certificates. But these religious consumers were unreliable, as was the labour force. In the New Year Helen noted grimly that the waitresses were 'either leaving on short notice or are unsatisfactory'.[116] In May 1899, when Helen dropped in with her mother, 'The dishwasher and the waiter both had left suddenly. Mama and I washed and wiped till 8 o'clock.' Within a few days Helen was back there again helping, admitting in her journal, 'Got tired and mad and ended up with a howl.'[117]

Helena and William were learning a hard lesson; it was far easier to dream a Pure Food Kitchen than to run one.

In contrast, Helen's working life at Houghton Mifflin was relatively fulfilling despite her lack of editorial responsibility. Apart from Helena and William's restaurant, Helen's main anxieties focused on Walter Leighton and the Tufts' family finances.

Her troubling relationship with Walter lurched up and down. He responded to Helen's firm insistence on 'comradeship pure and simple' by courting her with theatre tickets.[118] It appeared so easy and obvious for Walter to take Helen to see The Bostonians in *Robin Hood* in October or the renowned Ada Rehan in *The Taming of the Shrew* in November, but such largesse filled Helen with doubt: 'I don't believe I can go on taking so many things from Walter. I would enjoy being with him if I could pay for my tickets myself. There is an element of patronage in it, and I often wound his very sensitive Ego.'[119] Ruefully, she decided 'Walter really loves me', but she was not at all sure that she loved *him*, 'I have horrible hours of reaction, but hope it will come out all right. And yet, what faintness of spirit and sinking of heart come over me!'[120]

On November 16th they were due to attend a lecture on 'The Westward Movement of the American People' by Theodore Roosevelt, just back in autumn 1898 from his 'rough riding' in the war in Cuba. Thousands were clamouring for tickets, eager for triumphalist tales of American expansionism. Walter and Helen failed to go, owing to 'a bad falling out'.[121] However, in January 1899, the theatre trips were resumed – with a significant modification. When Helen and Walter went to see the statuesque Australian, Nellie Melba, and the elegant bewhiskered French bass singer, Pol Plancon, in *Faust*, Helen, who was wrestling with her own Faustian compact, made sure they perched on the cheap rush seats.[122]

Now the main earner at home, Helen's genteel proof-reading barely supported the four of them. On January 8th she confided in her journal, 'If I marry Walter, it will all be easier', only to add, 'but I hate to think of being dependent on him, and I don't believe we shall ever marry, anyway'.[123] That spring Helen's savings from her time at Riverside enabled the Tufts to move from their damp, draughty house in Arlington back to Cambridge. The new home at 84 Wendell Street was blessed with gas, heat from a furnace, a bathroom, a back piazza and a new thick rug in the front room which delighted William Tufts; 'He says his feet sink in so far he can hardly pull them out again', recorded his daughter fondly.[124] Nevertheless, Helen did wish her exhausted mother would make him do more housework.[125]

While Helena had been closeted at Epsom, the General of the Philippine Army, Emilio Aguinaldo, had declared independence from Spain. However, President McKinley bypassed America's former allies in the revolutionary movement and negotiated with Spain. When the Filipinos resisted, the American mainstream press reviled them, invoking America's civilising mission. In response, dissident liberals and leftists formed the Anti-Imperialist League, which had a strong base in Boston and appointed the Aladdin-oven donator, Edward Atkinson, as its Vice-President. Conflict over American intervention in Cuba and the Philippines started to disrupt the Walt Whitman Fellowship. On 17 January 1899 Helen reported an outbreak of hostilities when the Revd B. Fay Mills supported 'Expansion', on the grounds of progress and civilisation, while Charlotte Porter and Helen Clarke retorted sharply that it was wrong to treat Filipinos as 'children'. After Clarence Swartz roundly condemned American foreign policy, the liberal Rabbi Charles Fleischer rose staunchly to its defence.[126]

But there was discord not only over the war; to Helen's dismay her radical friends no longer seemed to agree on anything at all. Helena, William and Helen had formed a small discussion group at 3 Joy Street with the Poet-Lores, their lodger Sarah MacDonald, Helen's friend Ella Davis, the Schumms and a C.F.S. member, George Coffin. Early in March the topic was 'liberty, equality and fraternity'. While William and George Schumm insisted 'liberty' was the key, the Poet-Lores insisted competition blocked any possibility of individual growth. Helena and Ella Davis asserted the supremacy of love, Helen advocated 'knowledge'. Then the Stirnerites, Schumm and Coffin, outraged the egalitarian democrats, the Poet-Lores, Helena and Ella Davis, by arguing for the superiority of some individuals over others.[127]

On March 28th William spoke with admiration about Robert Owen's belief that changing the external environment would foster co-operative values. But Helen, reflecting on her own dealings with Walter, felt privately sceptical, making the un-Owenite observation in her journal, 'We can't be very different from what we are.'[128] She had her doubts too about Kropotkin's *Fields, Factories and Workshops*, which Houghton Mifflin were to publish the following year. How could rent, interest and profit be abolished, wondered Helen? And even if they were what was to prevent them coming back?[129]

On April 18th, William, who assumed a star role in the Joy Street discussions, introduced the theme of 'Liberty and Authority'. In his opinion 'voluntary co-operation' was the answer. But while he and George Schumm agreed in opposing the need for 'government', the socialistic Poet-Lores scorned his faith in 'the individual boss'. Their defence of the state touched a raw nerve when they argued that the Goths had progressed as a result of Roman imperial rule, causing William, the Irishman, to insist there was no knowing *what* the Goths might have made of themselves without the Romans.[130] Helen describes the May 15th session on 'the cost principle' as petering out when they meandered onto 'Mutual Banking' because, 'Only W. and Mr Schumm knew anything about it.'[131] The two men were left discoursing alone over Josiah Warren's proposition that the cost of making and distributing goods should decide prices rather than any subjective value to the consumer, and Proudhon's view that mutual banking could break financial monopoly.[132]

Amid the disputes about liberty, love, the individual and collectivism, Helena was gathering together her own thoughts. Two essays were the result in 1899, 'Individualism versus Organisation' in *The Conservator*, and 'Whitman's Ideal Democracy' in *Poet-Lore*. In *The Conservator* she argued for a balance between egoism and altruism. 'Some people guard their freedom so jealously they love only themselves.'[133] Others, however, were apt to over-emphasise the need for union 'regardless of compatibility'.[134] She thought there was as much danger in overreacting against the type of individualism that fostered 'self-seeking and greed' as in rebelling against the coercive forms of social organisation.[135] Her synthesis sought to transform the dichotomies. She wanted a form of 'association so infused with the free spirit that opinions of assent and dissent are treated with equal respect, in which individual variation and unconventionality in word and act meet with frank unreserved welcome'.[136]

Helena considered the *Poet-Lore* article to be 'the best expression' of her 'beliefs'.[137] In this she returned to altruism and individualism, but was primarily preoccupied with democracy in personal relations. Helena's 'Democracy' required freedom and equality for all, including between the sexes. This involved inward as well as external changes. She wanted a 'well-poised self-hood' to fuse with a loving reciprocity, new forms of being and relating which could nurture the full expression of individuality.[138] She outlines the 'directing posts' she saw in Whitman's writing.[139] They pointed towards fostering the power of love in human relations, the 'full expression' and acceptance of 'individuality', a 'copiousness of life' and 'mutual helpfulness'. Only then could the dynamic, spontaneous adjustment to needs of 'non-governmental organization' be ensured.[140]

Helena prioritised changing consciousness over changing structures. Whitman had been her revelatory inspiration, but she had also glimpsed the politics of the personal in the Quaker and Unitarian influences upon the Bristol women's movement, in the warm fellowship of the Bristol Socialist Society, and in the yearning for union in Carpenter's *Towards Democracy*. When Helena tries to express *how* this 'Ideal Democracy' is to be inaugurated she invokes a 'natural leadership' and a 'Brotherhood of Lovers'. She envisages them on Whitman's 'roads of the universe', combining Carpenter's dreams of a 'Theban band' with an image familiar within the British labour movement, that of democratic heroes marching along a broad highway.[141] Her procession was spectacularly all-encompassing – an ideal of 'America'. In Helena's mind's eye, a motley advance-guard marshalled in their 'various sections': 'Socialism,

Individualism, Communism, Anarchism, Egoism, Mysticism, Universal Brotherhood, Idealism, Sex Reform, Evolution, Revolution etc.' Just in case this line up was not sufficiently inclusive, even with the 'etc.', she added 'other respected groups which as yet are disinclined to claim kinship'.[142] Could she have had William Tufts in mind, hastening after the 'banner of Democracy'?

While Helena dwelt in generalities of transfiguration, Helen was more alert to the issues of the day. When Edward Atkinson sent three pamphlets against the war through the mail to soldiers in the Philippines to test free speech, they were stopped in San Francisco as seditious. He was caricatured in the press and there was talk of the seventy-two-year-old being accused of treason. Helen was anxious on his behalf, clashing with William Tufts who 'snorted' at her fears. Edward Atkinson, he assured her, was far too well connected to be charged with sedition.[143] In this instance her father proved to be correct.

Helen was desperate for independence. After battling for several years with her father, she now sometimes found her mother's protective concern irksome too. Even her relationship with Helena had shifted:

> I used to hurt her, and now she hurts me. With neither has it been intentional. I love her so, and she loves me, but to her I am a child, which is natural I suppose, for I am immature, but I resent it. This is a very unhappy time in my life – I am so mixed. I want to go on growing forever, but it's blind work.[144]

William alone could put Helen at her ease. He seemed to accept her and was 'one of the very few with whom I can feel myself'. On Memorial Day in 1899, Helen, her mother and William 'wheeled' to Mount Auburn Cemetery in search of the grave of the famous actor, Edwin Thomas Booth. Helen and William set out to find it, got lost and, on a vacant lot, with nobody looking, William 'turned a somersault'.[145] With Helen he could experience a youth he had never known.

In contrast to this uncomplicated friendship, Helen was rent by vacillating 'passions' towards Walter. One moment she was in 'a quiver that enthrals me', but the next she was shrinking from what the quiver might entail. Helena's tutoring in self-determination had not been in vain; 'I know I can do what I will, and I will', wrote Helen after a 'mad letter' arrived by extravagant special delivery on June 3rd.[146] As the June heat in

Boston intensified to what Russell called 'sizzle sazzle', a restless, naked Helen mused 'Am I I?'[147] On June 7th, due to meet Walter, she remained in her room at home, her 'heart falling lower and lower'. A distraught Walter 'vibrated' between Norway Street and Gainsborough Street, eventually dragging William off to the park 'to have it out' with him. William dutifully arrived at Helen's home to negotiate. Assuring her that Walter loved her, he seized her hand and talked a long time, declaring that he too loved her like 'his little Viola'. Helen concluded from this that William took Walter's side, whereas Helena, though 'flabbergasted', sympathised more with her. Unable to wait until their next meeting Walter sent yet another special delivery letter. This provoked Helen to compose her final 'goodbye', adding a bland 'blessing for the future', whereupon Walter consulted a 'swami' and uncovered a loathing for Helen. When he came round in person to announce this, Helen firmly 'chucked him out'.[148]

That August, going over Walter's letters, Helen noted how often he had expressed contempt for William. Dismissing the self-taught intellectual as nothing but a '"walking encyclopedia"', Walter opined that William was not a 'gentleman' because he did 'not care for his clothes and his nails'. William was further demeaned for being 'brusque'.[149] How was Walter to know that in working-class Belfast and Manchester, smooth talkers who wore their hearts on their sleeves were dismissed as insincere?

Sniping at William did Walter no good at all in Helen's eyes. On the contrary, she delighted in working with Helena on a manuscript of the book William was now painstakingly writing on Josiah Warren, copying the text, sub-editing, and pitching 'into him on grammar' – William's Achilles Heel.[150] He had remembered Tucker's criticism and set out to learn more about the libertarian thinker and community builder.

Keen to help William, Helen agreed to pay a visit to Ellen and the children, whereupon a watchful Isabel Tufts offered to accompany her. The two women envisaged combining their diplomatic mission with cranberry picking, which Helen had heard was well paid. They imagined their trip to Scituate would provide a good 'week's rest'; needless to say, it did not go as planned. The cranberry picking left them with raw fingers, burning ears from the language they heard, and derisory earnings of around '$2 a piece'.[151] Contact with the Bailie children, 'be-slapped' and behind with their education, horrified the two philanthropic Tufts so much that they returned resolved to adopt the whole family. William and Russell Tufts were predictably horrified, but a compromise was struck, and, early in October, a twelve-year-old Annie Bailie arrived in Cambridge.[152]

Helen embarked on improving outings. Having been a historically minded child herself, she wrongly assumed Annie would share her interest in the revolutionary past, and began with Boston Common. Ironically only Russell could joke naturally with Annie, who predictably became homesick and soon opted to return to what Helen described as 'the old demoralized ways'.[153] It was incomprehensible to Helen why the familial chaos at Scituate might be preferable to the starchy friends of a remote father the children hardly knew; all she could see was William's depressed misery each time he returned from Scituate.

An indefatigable Walter had meanwhile devised a bizarre plan to win Helen back through Benjamin Tucker. Helen met the editor of *Liberty* that October with Helena and William at the Schumms. She notes that Tucker was on a 'money raising trip' and 'much jollier' than she expected.[154] That autumn he had cause for cheer; unbeknown to Helen, Walter had pledged $100 to Tucker and hoped to persuade George Leighton for more. Tucker informed the wealthy anarchist Henry Bool, 'I think from his talk that he expects through me to work into the movement.'[155] It seems unlikely that George Leighton would have regarded investing in anarchy as an attractive proposition, but Walter, consumed by jealousy, wanted to undermine Helen's hero, William.

On December 5th Helen noted, 'Walter says to William that I shall have to come back to him; that my Ideal, when I find him, will pass me by. William got into a rage over this, and was disagreeable.'[156] So, by the end of 1899, Walter was angry, William was angry, and a disgruntled William Tufts was beginning to shift his allegiance in Walter's favour.

Oddly, this swing was partly triggered by the arrival in Boston that December of Enid Stacy, on a speaking tour for the American Fabians and Church Social Union.[157] Stacy, now a prominent figure in the British socialist movement, was pursuing, in a very different context, the same dilemma as Helena – how to combine individual freedom and egalitarian social collectivity.[158] Helen had reported to Traubel how they were arranging for Enid Stacy to give a special lecture on 'British Socialism and its work', adding that 'Miss Born knew her in Bristol'.[159] But when Isabel Tufts returned home full of enthusiasm about Stacy's lecture on socialism, her irate husband criticised 'Enid Stacy's morals'.[160] Had some distorted Unitarian gossip about Stacy's rebellion with Irving against Mills at Starnthwaite reached him? Whatever the source, upon meeting Helena at Josiah Royce's lecture on 'The Conception of Immortality', William Tufts 'gave her a look calculated to penetrate her to the soul'.

Increasingly erratic, Helen's father had come to the conclusion that not only his daughter, but *all* women, were 'eccentric'.[161] Bristol women, like Helena and Enid Stacy, were particularly suspect, spreading their contagious eccentricities first to his beloved Helen and then threatening even dear Isabel.

Helena had troubles enough of her own. The Kitchen finances had reached such 'a low ebb' she had been forced to look for 'proof-reading'.[162] Boston might harbour a plethora of dissidents seeking an 'Ideal Democracy', but they were just not consuming enough Pure Food to keep the Norway Street restaurant going. The year was not ending well. The only flash of hope was a message that the piano Helena had asked Richard Born to ship over was on its way.[163]

FOURTEEN

Family Ructions and Political Exploration: 1900

J anuary 1900 found William Tufts in high spirits; upon inheriting shares from his mother, he had, in Helen's words, 'plunged into speculation'. Each day he did the rounds of his brokers, returning tired but happy, and 'drenched in tobacco smoke'.[1] However, by February, he was again consumed with anxiety about his daughter. Helen and Flora Tilton had been to see *Zaza*, a popular social problem melodrama about a music hall performer. Played by Leslie Carter, Zaza breaks off her love affair with a young married man from the suburbs, Bernard, after meeting his child. Zaza's renunciation left Helen so moved, tears streamed down her face. Helen and Flora departed from the theatre rejecting the conventional moral message, convinced that only they and Leslie Carter understood the inner dignity of the heroine's love.[2]

William Tufts was not to be bamboozled; detecting vice, and yet another eccentric woman liable to disrupt his home, he paid a secret visit to Flora Tilton, declaring his resolve to 'shoot' any man who 'joined' with his daughter without marriage. Of course, Helen found out, and a row ensued, whereupon he informed her that girls went 'astray' and he was going to keep her 'respectable'. Embarrassed by her father and resentful of her parents' vigilance, Helen wrote, 'If only they could understand how little Sensuality appeals to me. I have a great deal to say on the subject, sometimes and I suppose they think I am morbidly inclined that way.'[3] Helen's cerebral commitment to free love was driven by concepts of honesty and reason that her parents had instilled in her from childhood, and she was exasperated at how her frankness was incomprehensible to them: 'Papa says as we get down to the body we get to vulgarity and he is mortified and outraged when I go about the house without my clothes on.' As intransigent as her father, she insisted, 'Nothing ... will turn me from what is right'; the stubborn pair simply diverged on how they defined right and wrong.[4]

When another 'problem' play, *Sapho*, was banned that February, and the lead actor, Olga Nethersole, arrested on a charge of indecent behaviour, an indignant Helen penned a protest against censorship and, encouraged by Helena and William, sent it to Horace Traubel.[5] Nethersole, a British actor with strong views on women's sexual freedom, played the heroine not as a repentant victim, but as a woman actively seeking sexual pleasure. The pother was compounded by Nethersole's see-through Grecian drapery and a scene in which the amorous couple mounted a spiral staircase.[6]

In her article for the March *Conservator*, Helen insisted on the purity of Nethersole's motives: *Sapho* presented 'a serious side of existence with honest realism'. Instead of seeking to 'educate people by repressing them', Helen believed 'They must learn to lead themselves.'[7] The New York jury appears to have agreed; on April 6th they acquitted Nethersole, a decision that marked a shift in what could be portrayed on the American stage. Diplomatically, however, Helen did not mention *Sapho* at home.[8]

William Tufts was anyway distracted by jotting 'down charts and memoranda' on financial opportunities.[9] Energised and excited by winning $15, he dreamed of a new home, a library, his own horse and carriage. Meanwhile, his daughter, who possessed a better grasp of figures, noted that his capital was going down and he was borrowing from Russell and herself.

Debt surrounded Helen on all sides. William and Helena, still saddled with the Kitchen, were struggling to pay off creditors.[10] Even though Helena had been accustomed to constant work at the farm and the Pure Food Kitchen, the return to wage labour taxed her. In a letter to the Koopmans in February she complained of tiredness caused by the 'mental strain' of proof-reading. Nevertheless, she had been busying herself collecting clothes from the Koopmans for the Bailie children, and her thoughts turned to Sunrise. She told the Koopmans she had no news of the little girl, who was now nine years old.[11] On March 3rd Helen wrote in her journal, 'I have never seen my Helena so depressed.'[12]

Despite so many set-backs, William and Helena were still politically engaged. President McKinley's support for the British against the
Boers *and* the American suppression of the Filipino rebels made opposition especially urgent, and a broad coalition was emerging around his
old opponent, William Jennings Bryan. Bryan's Bostonian supporters
spanned the Irish community and the Anti-Imperialist League, which
included many members of the 'Mugwump' dissident elite.[13] In January
1900, when Bryan came to speak at Boston's Mechanics Hall, Helena and
Helen 'pressed to pancakes' reached the gallery, but William managed to
scramble into a seat near the platform. William Tufts went too, though
the former Mugwump had started to cheer British victories in the hope
that his stocks would rise.[14]

William, whose political awareness had been ignited by Home Rule,
was galvanised by the atmosphere of war-fever and imperialism. In February he urged resisting taxation to the Boston Anarchist group as a
means of demonstrating opposition to the war in the Philippines. To
his dismay, civil disobedience was dismissed as 'too half-hearted and
half-way'.[15] William began to cast around for a more pragmatic arena of
political engagement.

Helena remained resolutely utopian; the vision of enhancing individuality through co-operative association constituted the crux of her political
outlook. Her organisational and intellectual influence was evident in the
Boston Walt Whitman Fellowship. Several members of the old guard
were still in evidence, including Percy Wiksell, now Traubel's secret
beloved, and Laurens Maynard, back from a trip to Europe, sporting a
new padded coat. But Helena had encouraged newcomers, among them
James S. Campton, the artist Helena had recruited; young Amy Wellington, a friend of Charlotte Perkins Gilman; Clarence Swartz; and Emma
Heller Schumm, who was about to leave Boston for New York, where
George Schumm was to manage Tucker's print shop.[16] James F. Morton
puffed the Boston W.W.F. in the March issue of the anarchist communist paper *Free Society* 'as one of the liveliest literary societies of the city',
maintaining that nearly half its members were 'declared anarchists'.[17] This
was Morton in hyperbole; though anarchists were a vocal, if argumenta-
tive, contingent.

On January 18th when the Individualist anarchist, Clarence Swartz,
delivered his lecture on 'Whitman the Egoist: Nietzsche, Schopenhauer', Helen records how his defence of 'selfishness' was 'countered'
by William.[18] Swartz had perhaps held forth at some length for, when

Helena followed him on February 15th with a lecture on 'Whitman & Nature: Thoreau', her manuscript notes contain a flinty reference to a speaker having difficulty in checking 'the flame of his thought' when dealing with 'burning problematical questions of the hour'.[19]

Over the first half of 1900 Helena was developing her own theories about radical association. She had come to envisage the W.W.F. as prefiguring, in microcosm, alternative forms of organising and relating. The manuscript notes for that February address include an interesting preamble which is not included in the two printed versions. Regarding the *process* of radical politics as vital, and firmly opposed to 'the oracular, and the methods of the pulpit', Helena wanted a co-operative dynamic that could enable every individual to contribute 'differentiated experience to the common fund' and, in turn, be enriched by others.[20] Convinced that developing one's individual 'power of vision' could 'help to illumine the social whole of which we are a part', she imagined the Boston branch as a living expression of autonomy and union.[21]

This conception of the individual in active relationship with a wider collectivity, contributing to and benefitting from association, was compounded by the approach to knowledge she had encountered at the 1892 Edinburgh Summer School, with its emphasis upon original enquiry rather than rote-learning: 'Most people are what Prof Geddes calls "ear-minded" rather than eye-minded – they take things at second and third hand. The nature-lover derives his knowledge direct from the source.'[22]

As an athletic and modern new woman, Helena's individualism was not simply intellectual, but about physical freedom. She recommended long bicycle and motor-car rides for 'oxygenizing' the blood. She also criticised fashionable attire:

> Ordinary clothes are apt to be an impediment to the appreciation of nature. For women the disqualifications of dress have been very serious, – happily becoming less so, not so much from a saner view of the dignity of the body as from the demands of locomotive improvements.[23]

Convinced of an integral connection between matter and spirit, Helena moreover approved of Thoreau and Whitman's distrust of physicians who disregarded the effect of the mind upon the body.

Her critique of capitalism combined her ideals of human solidarity and a life close to nature with social justice. In speaking and writing on Thoreau, Helena praised the writer's rejection of luxury and material

acquisition, which fostered inequality. Again she focuses on consciousness, highlighting how the externals of capitalist production were
internalised, not simply in the workplace but in society and in culture.
Stressing Thoreau's rejection of alienating, soul-destroying labour and of
the 'quiet desperation' this engendered, she argued that capitalism created
'a tendency to value things at cost and therefore to set little store by things
that are free to all. Simple pleasures, like weeds, are often despised.' She
was at one with Whitman and Thoreau on the virtues of loafing and
leisure, 'The desire for tangible results eclipses the desire to *be*…'.[24]

In Helena's original notes for her talk she states that 'Only yesterday' a
young pressman had told her that after ten years in the print, he wished
the inventor of printing had been shot. The young pressman does not
appear in the printed text entitled 'Thoreau's Joy in Nature'.[25] However,
Helena's critique of labour under capitalism is retained. Though she
admits the 'severity' of workplace conditions had been mitigated by the
provision of 'stools and chairs', ergonomics were not enough for Helena.[26]
She was all too familiar with the psychological costs of yielding *time* to
competition and profit, and had experienced working under 'an overseer
… whose estimate of skill' was 'purely financial'. She regretted how 'we
learn to acquiesce in conditions in which our desire for self-expression is
irrevocably thwarted'.[27]

She had assimilated two harsh lessons. Firstly, 'The qualities possessed
by idealists are not those which make for material prosperity.'[28] Secondly,
in pursuing concerns that *really* mattered, every individual had to find
their own course and follow it alone.[29]

Helena had remained in contact with Dan Irving, now in Burnley,
Lancashire, and active in the Social Democratic Federation. On May 3rd
she finished 'A Message from Over the Sea' for the Burnley S.D.F. magazine, *The Pioneer*. Sent with 'fraternal greetings', it is the clearest, most
succinct summary of her political views to appear in print. Offering her
thoughts on the 'individualistic side of socialism', Helena stated:

> Society at present denies us freedom to realize ourselves, to enrich the
> world by such contributions as the full development of our powers
> would afford. All our energies are concentrated on supplying our bodily
> needs; our varied talents are lying fallow, and society is the loser.[30]

Drawing on her own working life, she described how occupations
which might be joyful were distorted by hierarchy and the drive for

profit. She elaborates again on managerial control that only takes profit into account, thwarts creativity and distorts human consciousness of labour. Capitalism's failure to allow individuals to fulfil their potential was at the root of Helena's critique – and she recycles the young press-man mentioned in her manuscript notes for the lecture on Thoreau, now encountered 'only last week'. She also returns to a theme in this lecture: the 'present system' brought no 'joy' even to the 'capitalist'.[31]

Rejecting the deterministic interpretations of Marxist theory which prevailed in the S.D.F., Helena argued:

> To quote Marx to the effect that conditions make men what they are is to utter a partial truth. Every institution originated as an idea in the human mind, and the fact that men create their conditions is as important to remember as that conditions re-act on men and help to make them what they are.[32]

Like Carpenter, she believed socialism could 'remove the external obstacles', but individuals had to struggle with the inner emotional bond-ages themselves. Helena stressed the existential self-activity of human beings, 'Socialism ... Will merely enable us to attain things for ourselves', insisting that 'Socialism must be made neither a prop nor a peg.'[33]

Because she did not think it possible to 're-model ourselves all at once', Helena emphasised the need to nurture 'a loving and fraternal spirit' in the here and now. Inner consciousness was the active vital force: 'I am not greatly concerned about systems nor about the methods by which they are to be introduced.'[34] However, she did say that she did not consider co-operation incompatible with private enterprises or 'fear that to accept reform in instalments will postpone the social millennium'. She added: 'I am willing to go step by step if there are no forces ahead of me, for I do not regard any predicted social system as a goal.'[35]

Her S.D.F. readers would no doubt have derided her sympathy for the capitalist and acceptance of private enterprise, as well as the mix of Ideal-ist and Vitalist influences in her thought. Nevertheless, a few crossing points could be found; though S.D.F. Marxists saw socialism as preced-ing a *communist* future, like Helena's, it was hazy in outline. Also, despite thundering against 'palliatives', the S.D.F. did put forward municipal candidates. Dan Irving himself served on the Burnley School Board and on the Board of Guardians, responsible for poor relief.[36] With his Liberal Radical background, Irving must have recognised Helena's statement,

'My main hope is in freedom and the preservation of the balance between self interest and social interest.'[37] The problem lay of course in how the balance was to be *weighted*.

Helena's handwritten notes for a talk on 'Socialism' include much of the same material that appeared in the Burnley *Pioneer* in June 1900. They are undated but presumably predate May 3rd when she completed her article for Irving. In these she mentions attending socialist meetings 'week after week', and refers to a discussion about the Socialist Labor Party Programme two weeks before.[38] Commenting on the conflict within 'this Section' between 'Socialists' who desired simply public ownership of the land and means of production and 'Communists' who advocated 'the entire abolition of private property', Helena states that she inclined 'to the former side', while regarding the 'abolition of rent, interest and profits' as fundamental.[39]

In 1900 the S.L.P. was in meltdown and Daniel De Leon was losing his grip on the organisation. Early that year moves were afoot for unity between the Social Democrats and a group of S.L.P. dissidents, nicknamed the 'Kangaroos', who, like Helena, accepted the possibility of changing capitalism 'step by step'. On May 11th Helena, William and Helen went to hear Eugene Debs, and all three were 'stirred' by the trade unionist's 'idealism and sincerity'.[40] Debs, a Whitmanite friend of Horace Traubel, had founded the Social Democratic Party in 1898 and was prepared to accept the need to struggle for immediate reforms. In 1901, he brought the Kangaroos and the Social Democrats together in the formation of the American Socialist Party.

In her notes for the lecture on 'Socialism', Helena argues that struggling for reforms was an educational process which enabled people to envisage alternatives. Stating that socialism was 'the thing to work for at present', she declared with evident feeling that it offered an escape from 'this quagmire where we are jostled and pushed back continually and where barbed wires cross our path at every turn'.[41] She deftly forestalled criticism by observing that the S.L.P. programme was not sufficiently 'radical' for her. Insisting that socialism was much wider than economics, she took her stand on the ground where she felt most assured, human relations.[42] For Helena, the most powerful aspect of socialism was 'comradeship between equals', and she reiterated her conviction about the need to prefigure values and relationships based on love and tolerance by living them in the present.[43] Her socialism was inclusive. She believed in being 'tolerant with those who differ from us. (I do not think we may even exclude Anarchists or Fabians) in our Co-operative Commonwealth'.[44]

In her lecture notes, Helena did not specify *how* socialism could be achieved in America, but she did not see it as simply evolving inevitably, arguing that it would require 'reconstruction'. Repeating the admonition about educating the rich that appears in the article for Irving, she adopts a more Populist hot gospel style for the American meeting. 'The altars' on which the wealthy had sacrificed 'human flesh & blood' to the 'God' of 'profit' were to be torn down.[45] Reconstruction required agency, and the memory of the radical Garrisonian wing of anti-slavery is evident when she argues that an unprepared 'multitude' would find themselves without 'chart or compass' and calls for a movement of 'new abolitionists' to 'put an end to wage slavery'.[46] Conceiving these 'new abolitionists' as 'men & women at the helm, strong in self-control, of inflexible purpose and incorruptible will', she endowed them with the duty of 'self-criticism'.[47] But she warned against taking pride in belonging to such an elect: 'It is not sufficient to pat ourselves on the back because we are in a minority and because new truths always originate with minorities.'[48]

As in her *Pioneer* article, she stresses the role of individuals.[49] Socialism should not to be regarded as 'a peg', she says; 'It is a means, – not an end'.[50] Like many on the left, Helena saw socialism as a transitional stage not as *the* goal. However, instead of defining the utopian future as being communist, anarchist or anarchist communist, she echoed Edward Carpenter's less specific but inclusive phrase, 'Transitions to Freedom'. The promise of socialism was thus 'freedom to attain heights which we cannot yet see'.[51]

No evidence survives on how Helena came to be at these weekly meetings of what she describes as a 'Section' consisting of 'Socialists' and 'Communists'.[52] But it shows she was aware of schisms in the Socialist Labor Party, possibly through Martha Moore Avery, who, along with her close ally, the cigar maker, David Goldstein, had deserted De Leon and attached themselves to the rival Social Democratic Party, playing what the De Leonites described as 'a very ambiguous role'.[53]

Broader movements also gained Helena's support. At the end of May, she and Helen attended the annual gathering of the Massachusetts Woman Suffrage Association at Faneuil Hall where the national President, Carrie Chapman Catt, declared women were going to 'purify politics' from 'the great vice trust'.[54] A politics based on superior female purity appealed to Helen, but differed from the claim for emancipation on the grounds of women's equality that Helena endorsed. After the meeting Helena greeted the Radical Liberal from Britain, Helen Bright Clark, who was on the platform.[55] Only a few days later, Helena and Helen, resolutely anti-war and anti-imperialist, were lining up to shake the hands of Boer leaders touring to raise money. The Boers had strong Irish-American allies and attracted an enthusiastic crowd in Boston, but were unable to alter President McKinley's foreign policy. 'Not a very satisfactory meeting. Too much gas'; was Helen's verdict.[56]

While attending these public political gatherings of protest, Helen was beset by personal worries about her father, who, having predictably 'lost everything', was in a state of acute agitation. Before long he was desperately borrowing again; Helen sighed as she drew out another $100 from her savings, making her total losses mount to $170.[57]

Walter too was taking revenge by stirring up trouble for her at home. On May 28th Helen noted grimly that he had sent her father a copy of the British novelist, Grant Allen's controversial article, 'The New Hedonism', along with a letter from May Hurd to Walter discussing free love. Far from evangelising for sensuous excess, Grant Allen was merely arguing for the acknowledgement of sexual feelings and the need for bodily fulfilment. Such sentiments were not particularly pleasing to Helen's parents, but May Hurd's letter horrified them. When Helen eventually persuaded her parents to let her read it, she pointed out that her friend was arguing *against* Walter's assertion that love was simply physical; but for William and Isabel Tufts it was unconscionable that a young woman should be writing to a man on such a topic at all.[58]

Next Walter's unwitting mother was despatched 'to effect a reconciliation'. Helen 'stuck' to her 'guns', asserting their 'incompatibility', but exploded in her journal, 'what trouble that insignificant boy does make'.[59] Before long Walter had found a new channel for his hurt by writing articles in *Free Society* proposing 'bachelordom' as the answer to 'enchainment'. In Helen's view he was going public with an account of their relationship that 'suited' him, and indeed Walter later confessed ruefully to Horace Traubel that 'again and again' he had been 'scorched' by jealousy.[60]

Walter's intervention caused Helen to try to clarify her own views on 'free love' to her father. She explained to a bemused William Tufts that while freedom for a great and noble love was acceptable, she disagreed with 'those who advocate variety'.[61] 'Varietists' advocated sexual experimenting and Helen was currently entangled in a dispute with other members of the C.F.S. over a particular varietist, George F. Morong. The anarchist teacher had joined both the C.F.S. and the W.W.F., voicing opinions so distasteful to Helen that she had not invited him to the Whitman Memorial celebration that year. 'Miss Tilton' disapproved of this undemocratic action and the Wellesley group concurred. By June, Helen and May Hurd were 'threshing out the Morong question'. It was particularly distressing for Helen because she so enjoyed the company of the unconventional Wellesley radicals and had come to like and respect the 'thoughtful reserved' May Hurd.[62]

Helen resented Morong for breaking up the comradeship of the C.F.S. by talking 'of nothing but free love'.[63] She does not elaborate, but Morong was inclined to enjoy offending the idealism of the free lovers by waxing enthusiastically about the pleasures of 'sex gratification' and the 'sexual virility' of prostitutes.[64] Her loathing was visceral – Morong had a 'nasty look' and a 'nasty way'.[65]

By autumn, rumours of a 'row' led J. William Lloyd to enquire what was happening. In response Helen explained she had 'simply stopped going and said nothing' because she found it impossible to discuss free love 'with Tom, Dick and Harry who may, and generally do not, feel as deeply as I'.[66] It was not just a matter of differing interpretations of free love, for Lloyd, and indeed Helena in writing on Gilman, had argued for varietism as an aspect of self-development. It sounds as if Morong's innuendos of lust had provoked Helen's disgust and reduced her to a humiliated silence.

'There is a fearful lot of trash written about love', Helen wrote in her journal that summer.[67] Despite her proclivity towards moral principles, Helena and William's love affair had made her aware how difficult it was to impose theories upon personal emotions. She was disconcerted because both Emma Heller Schumm and Sarah Holmes remained intractable: 'Theoretically these two are the most anarchistic of anarchists claiming no one can judge for another, and demanding that each shall be allowed to do as he considers best.'[68] Both Schumm and Holmes had experienced motherhood with its powerful emotions of attachment and bonds of interdependence. Even though such an empathetic knowing did not fit neatly with an abstracted Anarchist Individualism, it meant they could see Ellen Bailie as a person. In contrast, Helen, despite having met Ellen, remained resolutely impervious to her. Helen considered that 'pity' had warped the judgement of the two women Helena held so dear, and was distressed on Helena and on William's behalf, musing anxiously that 'William's best side does not appear in public'.[69]

Perhaps William, accustomed to male company through work and politics, may have not been comfortable in the company of highly cultured women like Emma Heller Schumm and Sarah Holmes. He had been inspired by William Morris, the libertarian socialist who linked hand and brain, and he cherished precious pamphlets by Morris still engrained with 'dirt and grime' from the hands of workers who had borrowed them.[70] His close friends tended to be men who combined an interest in ideas with craft skills – Simpson, George Schumm and the designer-poet, William Walstein Gordak in Scituate. William did not show his feelings readily; his love for Helena and his protective friendship with young Helen were, however, effecting a change.

In autumn 1900 all three of them were still involved in the W.W.F. But Helen missed her C.F.S. Wellesley friends, and the polite smiles at a W.W.F. 'at home' that autumn, held by 'Mrs Dana Hicks Prang', made her uneasy.[71] After Louis Prang's wife Rosa died, Dana Hicks had married the innovative exile from the 1848 revolution in Germany who had made his fortune by introducing America to Christmas cards. Helen found herself gravitating towards him, and was surprised at how George Schumm's name acted as an 'open sesame'.[72] Unknowingly she had touched on close affiliations, for in his youth Schumm had set the type for books by Prang's friend, the revolutionary exile and opponent of Marx, Karl Heinzen. When Prang introduced Helen to Heinzen's widow, Henriette Schiller Heinzen, the young American encountered a gentle survivor from a distant European milieu of revolutionary turmoil and exile.[73]

Helen's impression of Boston Marxism was more negative. Upon attending a meeting with Helena and William organised by 'Mrs Avery and Goldstein', she was bewildered by the Marxist theory crashing about the room. But her sharp eyes spotted how they 'ran the meeting to suit themselves though it is supposed to be a debate'. Of course they did, for they were veterans of the S.L.P. When William intervened, Helen noticed 'Mrs Avery hates him.'[74] Not only could William cut through her abstruse interpretations of Marx, he had acquired plenty of experience in disrupting managed meetings. Having bashed his way out of the Marxist S.D.F. and the anarchist communist wing of the Socialist League, William would not have been easily squashed by Avery and Goldstein.

*   *   *

Opposition to imperialism had made William restless in discussions with small groups, and that autumn he decided to align himself with William Jennings Bryan who had been chosen as the Democratic candidate for the Presidency.[75] Early in November, William sat on the platform at a rally for Bryan in Faneuil Hall as a member of the Bryan Club.[76] Bryan's opposition to the bloody suppression of the movement for independence in the Philippines led to his vilification in the press. A movement of Bryanite Democrats, anti-war Republicans and socialists had converged through the Anti-Imperialist League.[77] Dressed up in his best clothes and wearing a new hat, William distributed anti-imperialist leaflets and wrote 'An Appeal to the Working Man' for Bryan's campaign. An admiring Helen read it out loud to her distinctly unBryanite parents.[78] But it was to no avail; on November 7th a devastated Helen announced in her journal, 'McKinley re-elected'.[79]

On November 11th, William returned to familiar political turf, addressing the Boston Anarchist Club on 'The Chicago Martyrs'. His speech was reported in *Free Society*, with which James F. Morton was associated. The men accused of the Haymarket bombing were totemic figures for William and outrage over their execution had led him towards anarchism. In the religious idiom common on the left in the period, William linked the executed men symbolically to the sufferings of Christ, the early Christian Martyrs, and to Irish Republicans. All were 'victims of murder ... in the name of law and order'. Thirteen years after their death he depicted their sacrifice as being for 'broader opportunities, more culture; a chance to live a freer, healthier fuller life' – his own thwarted longings.[80]

For William the central state that had judicially murdered the Chicago anarchists could never be benign. The state socialism of the Bellamy Nationalists and the Fabians was anathema to him. However, the bitter politics of Ireland had left him equally opposed to those anarchists who called rhetorically for 'armed resistance'.[81] Instead, William now placed his hopes on the slow accretion of economic reforms. This long-view, sustained by a social evolutionary faith in progress and by a residue of deterministic Marxism, did not go down well with his anarchist comrades at the meeting, still eager for revolution.

By 1900, though absolutely certain about rejecting socialism, William had discovered that he was not in complete affinity with the Boston anarchists. His problem as a left-wing activist was twofold: he tended to dig out ideological problems within every tendency he encountered, yet was ever on the lookout for forms of pragmatic action. William had arrived at an impasse; how were workers to turn the long-term economic changes he predicted to their advantage under the beady eyes of their alert employers? As a businessman, albeit a small and reluctant one, William was well aware that 'The propertied class' would 'forcibly resist any effort to despoil them'.[82] Indeed, labouring away over his basket-making accounts over all those years had hardened his own outlook. William took a much tougher line than Helena on ownership, opposing socialists who assumed they 'could confiscate private property under the guise of "instruments of production"'.[83]

Property was a sore point for them both in 1900. The Pure Food Kitchen finally closed that December. Helen records that 'the milk and cream man' bought 'the furnishings'.[84] Helena and William had lost a great deal of money, along with their dream of creating a mini-utopia. Helen shuddered in her journal because William was 'working with ward politicians to get a job with the city'.[85] He was desperate.

Helena did what she had always done. She started a new job, proof-reading at Spurrell Printers.[86] Materially she was defeated and her small-scale utopia in ruins, yet she could cherish the inner happiness she and William had found through their love. At the end of December, she affirmed it in a letter to Virginia E. Graeff, the friend from the Edinburgh Summer School, now in Philadelphia:

> I am not sure that you would be in perfect sympathy with my course, but I think you might. But I am sure you will like to know that a great and supreme love has come into my life. You know something of my ideals and that they were conceived quite impersonally. I never thought of the possibility of realizing them in my own experience.[87]

Helena's vindicatory letter draws on eclectic approaches towards emancipatory intimacy. By invoking 'a great and supreme love', she is able to transcend conventional morality and to conceive the possibility of new forms of human relationships.[88] The 'great love' was an idea rooted in Romanticism and was to exert an important influence upon early twentieth-century women seeking sexual freedom and fulfilment. Helena combines it with echoes of the free lovers' appeal to a higher morality when she tells Graeff that she has found a union greater than ordinary marriage. Whitman imparted yet another way of describing loving connection, through 'comradeship'. Helena explained to Graeff how, before meeting William, her 'ideal soul', she had been 'happy and content' in her 'Comradeships which were an outlet for my intensity. I loved and was conscious of no further desire.'[89] The most intense of those affectionate 'comradeships' had, of course, been with women friends. And one of these, the ruck-sack carrying Beatrice Taylor from Oakfield Unitarian days, sent New Year greetings to say how she was looking forward to a promised visit from Helena and Helen in 1901.[90]

FIFTEEN

'Separation': 1901–1902

Early in 1901 Helena, who had been experiencing spasmodic pain since election day in November, was finally forced to abandon her customary mind control and consult Dr Fanny Berlin, who lived with the Prangs.[1] Born Stefanija Berlinerblau and of Russian Jewish parentage, the enlightened doctor had been part of a radical colony of Russian women studying medicine in Zurich and then qualified in Bern. She had then made her way over to the United States and specialised in obstetrics.[2]

When she examined Helena, Dr Berlin diagnosed 'a tumor' and warned that the operation to remove it would be 'risky'.[3] Within a few days Helena was in the Vincent Memorial Hospital for sick and indigent working-class women.[4] Lying in bed, Helena, ever the organiser, occupied herself by scrutinising how the regimented routines might be improved, clashing with the nurses over her knowledge of hygiene, vegetarian diet and alternative health views about wool next to the skin. In a letter to Helen she described Vincent as 'no sort of a place for a person with reformed ideas'.[5] She asked for her knitting and her sewing basket, requesting Helen, her mainstay, to copy the poem Miriam had written when she returned from Scotland in 1892.[6] On January 12th she prepared a list of 'Friends to be notified of my death'. Along with Richard Born, were 'Miss Southcombe', Robert Sharland, Dan Irving, Beatrice Taylor, Virginia E. Graeff, a correspondent in South Africa called 'Nurse Camp', 'Mrs Schumm', Sarah Holmes, 'Mr and Mrs Koopman' and Helen's workmate, Ella Davis. Meticulously Helena also remembered her new employers, Spurrell Printers.[7]

On the same day she composed 'Last words to my darling, about the least important concerns'. She told William she would like him to have her books and bookcase and Helen her clothes. 'The other tag-rags divide as you please'. With her usual attention to detail she noted friends might want mementos and her father would inform him on what to do with the piano. Helena wanted William and Helen to split her 'savings-bank money between them', adding, 'The California money in pocket-book (both in trunk in kitchen) is for you.'[8] This is a mystery. Helena had not *made* any money while in California herself and the plan to visit had been abandoned in 1897. Had she started saving for another trip? Was the money intended for Sunrise? Or had Robert uncharacteristically paid back part of the debt, which Helena had not yet banked?

Lying in her hospital bed, Helena worried about William whose old leg wound was causing him considerable pain. Similarly consumed with anxiety and barely able to work on his baskets in the basement he had rented, William was dragging himself back and forth to Vincent Hospital. Apparently he disguised the severity of his pain with some success; 'Tell him to get a hot-water bag', Helena told Helen.[9]

The operation on January 21st revealed the cancer had spread. Dr Berlin, aware of what this meant, was nearly in tears when she told Helen that 'Tumors along with uterine ligaments had softened, and all the parts around were broken and decayed.' The doctor said if she were in Helena's position she would prefer 'to die now' rather than go through the 'misery' to come.[10]

Helen faced the prospect of breaking the news to William before he was admitted to Massachusetts General Hospital for an operation on his leg.[11] Confined in a separate hospital William was unable to visit Helena, nor could she answer all of his letters because the hospital doctors kept her lying down, making writing difficult. Helena was trying to pump them for information but with little success.[12] Dr Berlin had convinced a stricken Helen that after the operation Helena should go into a Convalescent Home in Roxbury. But the recalcitrant patient rebelled against being 'incarcerated', informing William, 'as long as I retain my reason I shall try to avoid being prescribed for on General Principles. My individual characteristics are of paramount importance.'[13]

Separated from William, Helena reassured him, 'We are one now and always.'[14] The visitors queuing downstairs were not all *entirely* welcome at the bedside. Helena confided that while she was glad of Josephine Tilton's 'basket of fruit & cracked walnuts', she feared 'it was given more in a spirit of charity than of love'.[15] They had grown estranged since Epsom. Helena, did, however, make a point of asking for Sarah Holmes, who was living in Providence. She was a friend too close to lose.

After February 15th, when Helena was brought back to 21 Gainsborough Street according to her wishes, Holmes proved a quiet source of strength. Helen had found a nurse, and a core of faithful friends clustered round. Flora Tilton, Helen and Isabel Tufts bathed her, Archibald Simpson sat up with her during the nights to relieve Helen. Initially shaken by the news that the cancer was not cured, Helena had swiftly regained her composure.[16] Indeed she had been preparing herself for the worst and had somehow embroidered a piece of cloth with jagged enigmatic words:

> Did we think
> Victory
> great
> so ++++
> Death
>   and
> Dismay
> are Great[17]

She sought to console Helen, 'our nearest truest friend', by saying 'My life has been good and death will be good too.'[18]

But before long she could not eat and the pain became intolerable; Helen started to give her friend heroin to alleviate the agony. On February 23rd Archibald Simpson brought William in 'the hack' to visit, waiting downstairs while they spent a precious hour together. William then had to return to hospital for another operation. Helen recorded tersely, 'Pus had gathered, and he nearly lost his leg.'[19]

After William's visit, Helena had two days' respite. She could talk with her visitors and carers Charlotte Porter, Helen Clarke, Mary Stevens, Flora Tilton and Sarah Holmes. Helen notes, 'she was radiant, her brain clear and very active'.[20] When Isabel Tufts came, Helena said thoughtfully, 'Tell Mr Tufts not to worry about Helen.'[21] Insisting that Helen stayed close by her, Helena related how intense memories of her life were passing at great speed through her mind as if in a dream. Helen wrote down her words for William, 'My life is so concentrated now.'[22] She retained an awareness of how hard under normal circumstances separation from William would be. Yet as her sense of the material faded it came to seem 'William and I are one.'[23] Helen observed how Helena 'withdrew into herself, strove to marshal the thoughts that thronged into her mind'.[24]

The following day, February 26th, she was barely conscious. On the morning of February 27th, she briefly recognised Dr Berlin, smiled and stretched out her hand. She died that day at one o'clock and Helen placed daffodils on her friend's breast. Her body was removed by the undertakers who were affronted by the simple pine box Helen had chosen.[25] Dr Berlin's post mortem verified 'Carcinoma of right ovary' and 'Degeneration of peritoneum and lymphatic glands' as the cause of death.[26]

On March 1st Helena was cremated at the cemetery in Forest Hills, near to the Schumms' former home where, four years before, she and Helen had wandered by Daniel Chester French's monumental 'Death Staying the Hand of the Sculptor'.[27] Walter Leighton learned from Archibald Simpson that the funeral was attended by about twenty 'dear and intimate friends'.[28] William Tufts had never visited the woman he blamed for stealing his daughter from him, but he did go to see William in hospital on that day.[29]

Throughout March Helen assuaged her grief in a frenzy of activity, clearing the Gainsborough Street apartment and finding a new room for William. She emptied a frozen tank at his workplace and sent Mary Stevens with William's letter to Kropotkin, who was speaking again in Boston, though owing to 'bungling' it was never read out.[30] She also took on the task of writing to Richard Born, Beatrice Taylor, the Sharlands, Dan Irving, as well as the Wallasey Whitmanites near Liverpool, Robert Weare and the young working-class socialist, Will Young, with whom Helena had corresponded on the need for inner as well as outer change.[31]

When a somewhat lukewarm Horace Traubel wrote saying 'his personal relations with Helena Born were very slight', Helen responded by informing him the Poet-Lores intended to contact him about Helena. Moreover she sent the summary she had written of her friend's life not simply to Traubel but also to his wife, Anne Montgomerie. In this she alluded openly to William, though not by name: 'Helena had always claimed great things for love. Three years ago began deepest fulfilment – and supreme cost.' Requesting recollections, Helen announced, 'Sometime I and One Other – will write her life.'[32] In a later undated letter to Traubel she described Helena as her 'heart companion'.[33] Helen's resolve ensured that Helena, so often overlooked in life, became a minor celebrity after her death. While Helen constituted the driving force, she could not have created space for this process of remembering without support from the networks around the Boston branch of the Walt Whitman Fellowship and the Boston Anarchists. The Poet-Lores were compelling allies, and after a small group met at Joy Street it was announced that the Boston W.W.F. were to hold a meeting in memory of Helena on 17 March 1901.[34]

The speakers included Helen herself, Emma Heller Schumm, Mary Stevens, Archibald Simpson and a Jewish anarchist from France, David Mikol, a tailor with a syndicalist faith in the general strike, who had been befriended by Helena.[35] Helen stressed how Helena had combined 'self-poise' and service to others.[36] Praising a 'fearless independent spirit', Emma Heller Schumm observed: 'Her's was certainly the experimental life: there were no rut marks on her. She always lived never vegetated.' True to her conscience, Schumm added that being 'human', Helena was 'liable at times to succumb to the delusions of our all too human limitations'.[37]

William, still in hospital, did not intend to be side-lined as an aberrant 'delusion', sending a letter that did not shilly-shally with surface gentilities. Even though 'The sense of personal loss is to me still too sharp-edged for calm expression' and words were such 'halting instruments', William wanted Helena's 'moral courage' and their love affair to be acknowledged and affirmed at the memorial, asserting overtly that 'the fullness' and 'completeness of love' had been hers. None could 'miss her' as he did, 'to whom she was life and love'.[38]

Among those who heard his letter read aloud were more than forty signatories of the tribute to 'the equal comrade ... A natural free person, who hated shams and pretence'. They included W.W.F. friends Clarke, Porter, Wiksell, Laurens and Gertrude Maynard, Amy Wellington, the artist James S. Campton, and the Prangs. The C.F.S friends William Denton and May Clifford Hurd also signed. Anarchists of varying persuasions were well represented, including Holmes, Simpson, Mikol, the Tilton sisters, Swartz and of course the Schumms; new additions were the homeopathic doctor, Arathena Drake, and K.A. Snellenberg, the agent for *Free Society*.[39]

The Bristol socialists took longer in mobilising, but on May 7th they, too, commemorated Helena's 'noble life'. Robert Gilliard forwarded a copy of their resolution, sending 'greetings and fraternal comradeship' to her American friends.[40] It was apt that even after her death, Helena's rebel spirit crossed geographical and political boundaries. Gilliard, the

Christian Socialist, wrote feelingly of Helena's concealed strength and 'self-abnegation' in her loving friendship with Miriam:

> When we meet Miriam in the spiritual world she will have her arms around the neck of Helena, and declare she was the best friend, the most helpful companion, the person who knew her more, than all others put together, <u>and Helena will not believe it</u>.[41]

Gilliard mentioned that Dan Irving and Robert Weare were planning to write down their memories of Helena. Helen, meanwhile, was intent on producing *her* version of her friend's 'noble' exemplary life.

In her obituary in *Free Society* she stated that Helena had been a member of the Social Democratic Federation in Bristol.[42] This is most probably a misunderstanding, for though Dan Irving and Robert Sharland were personally connected to the S.D.F., the Bristol Socialist Society was an autonomous body when Helena was active in 1889 to 1890.[43] In another article in *The Conservator*, Helen simply describes Helena's commitment as being to the 'socialists in Bristol', whose politics she describes as based on 'love', 'solidarity' and 'social endeavor'. She added that Helena subsequently 'grew' into the principles of Philosophical Anarchism 'through her reading of Herbert Spencer' and her 'disinclination to sacrifice individuality'.[44]

Friendly with the Individualist (or Philosophical) Anarchists around *Liberty*, Helena did, indeed, share their emphasis upon 'individuality'. Her political roots had, after all, been in Radical Liberalism. However, Helena's emphasis upon individual self-development drew more broadly on the Romantic and Transcendentalist cultural valuing of self-realisation which was also a vital element in some strands of British and American socialism in the late nineteenth century.

J. William Lloyd's assertion in his publication, *The Free Comrade*, that Whitman and Carpenter were Helena's inspiration is confirmed in her writings.[45] Whitman's celebration of self was emancipatory, vindicating her desire for autonomy. In Whitman, Helena found an idiom for that freedom of 'being' that promised new forms of relating in the here and now. Carpenter offered her a balance of the personal and the social, the spiritual and the material, and Helena, who followed him in imagining a future society defined by freedom, embraced his eclectic tolerance towards differing paths for change. Consequently, she could find an affinity with anarchists and with socialists, be stirred by Eugene Debs, support

women's suffrage, attend anti-imperialist meetings and Bryan's campaign
for election as president. This openness to differing currents is reflected
in Helena's article for the Burnley *Pioneer* and in her notes for the lecture
on socialism in which she identifies as a socialist concerned to allow space
for individual development and personal comradeship.

Intellectually Helena strongly resisted 'being prescribed for on General
Principles'. She took Geddes' castigation of scholastic specialisation to
heart, reading economists and sociologists, Idealist philosophers, Comte-
ans and Vitalists, along with Shelley, Thoreau, Whitman and Carpenter.
Labouring over her lectures and her essays, she never really did justice
to the breadth of her understanding. Her arguments meandered and
her style was often contorted. Traubel, who had tried to edit her, sensed
'something seemed inarticulately hers' that she was 'not able to utter'.[46]
Helena, so committed to self-expression, found *actually* expressing herself
a difficult matter. Her elusive crab-like manner of communicating made
it easy to miss the startling radicalism of her thinking.

Throughout 1901, Helen and William assembled the collection of Helena's writings which would be published the following year as *Whitman's
Ideal Democracy and Other Writings by Helena Born*. In preparing the short
biographical introduction, Helen diligently contacted Minnie Southcombe in Devon, Helena's Bristol friends, and even the organiser of the
1892 Edinburgh Summer School, Kate Crooke. Yet, while Geddes had
made a lasting impression on Helena, Crooke could not recall 'people
who were interested' in Helena apart from 'Miss Graeff'.[47] In contrast,
Helen's visit to the Koopmans in April did yield a great deal of information, though not exactly of the kind that was compatible with her
aim of publishing an account that would be 'an inspiration' others could
live by.[48]

Money was collected by subscription and donation for 500 copies of
Whitman's Ideal Democracy to be produced. Early in 1902 Helen had
pre-publication copies to send off. Several were mailed to Robert Gilliard
and members of the Bristol Socialist Society. One went to Helena's cousin
Minnie, but not to her father; Helen explained to Gilliard that she feared
Richard Born, who was 'bitter toward Miriam, whom he blames for all
Helena's actions … would not wish to see the book'.[49] On January 27th,
posting off three more books for 'William Sharland, William Boster
[*sic*] and E.J. Watson', Helen expressed relief at Gilliard's response to her
biographical introduction: 'You deal gently with the omissions.'[50]

Helen explained how she found it 'grievous' not to speak of Helena's 'sane and sweet, rounded and unending' love, explaining that few even of her close friends had understood it and thus Helena had been unable to 'share her joy with the world'. The omission of William was because she had wanted to protect Helena from 'mauling by the public'.[51] Helen was well aware how women who defied conventional moral standards were reviled and that those with radical opinions stood in double jeopardy.

Another missing man, however, was Robert, who was not directly linked to Helena. Helen acknowledged, 'I foresaw that Miriam's friends would be puzzled.' She told Gilliard, 'it seemed better to essay a general effect than to enter details that could give rise to endless controversy'.[52] As a result, odd blips confuse Helen's narrative in the 'Biographical Intro-duction'. By discarding the 'detail' of Robert, Sunrise enters apparently by virgin birth and the two women are persuaded by an anonymous mystery man to travel out to the ranch in California. Inconsistent specificities were of no concern to Helen; she was portraying Helena's life as an ideal.

A tension is evident in Helen's characterisation of Miriam. Because Helena had loved Miriam, Helen had to present her as spiritually noble, if not of equal stature. Consequently, she could not appear as the lover of Robert or the mother of a child out of wedlock. Helen Koopman had described Miriam's ultimate harsh condemnation of Helena; thus to reject Helena, Miriam must be flawed and Helena's judgement in trusting such a friend could seem questionable. Hence several suppressed suspicions lurk around the margins of Helen's account and flicker briefly in a depic-tion of an ambivalent Miriam. She is described as a sensitive 'dreamer' wandering through the world with 'her head in the clouds', perceiving with 'acute vision' the 'reasons' for 'human suffering', while also being an imperious, doomed, heroic figure, 'Dominating the many, loved by the few, she moved in isolation of spirit, fulfilling a destiny in which mingled the grey and gold of tragedy and passionate enthusiasms.'[53]

Gilliard, who bore no hostility towards Miriam's lover, was notified by Helen that Robert 'appears to have been a negative quantity, and hardly has place in the narrative of Miriam and Helena'.[54] She told Gilliard, somewhat lamely, that 'Helena had lost track of him' and hence she did not 'feel justified in bringing his name and personality into the narrat-ive without his knowledge and consent'. She added, though how she could have known this is unclear, that 'painful aspects ... in the end pre-dominated' between Miriam and Robert.[55] Helen could not completely eradicate her resentment towards two people she had never met, Miriam and Robert. And so, Robert, the 'negative quantity', was decisively erased from Miriam and Helena's life. All three continued to be remembered by the Bristol Socialists, but in public no mention was made of Robert and Miriam's relationship.

Nevertheless, *Whitman's Ideal Democracy* made Helena's writing accessible, while Helen's Biographical Introduction, despite its omissions and eulogistic intent, provides a treasure trove of valuable material which otherwise would have vanished. It reveals too the profound impression the older woman made upon her. Their friendship meant that Helen, who was by inclination forthright and clear-cut in her views and affiliations, came to recognise ambiguities below the surface of politics. So while repeating that Helena 'grew into the principles of philosophical anarchism', she also states that Helena always 'accepted the name of "socialist" in its widest sense', even though 'socialism, as it worked through customary channels, had less and less of her sympathy'.[56] Helen also emphasises Helena's constant quest for political understanding, quoting her friend as saying:

'With me social effort is (somewhat as love is) its own fulfilment, irrespective of success ... In bringing about the new order, I am willing to further any of the plans that commend themselves to diverse adherents of the several schools of thought, if they are born of the love of liberty, if I find myself in accord with the spirit in which they are conceived, and if I can do so without being bound.'[57]

Helena's antinomianism led her to resist confinement and boundaries. As Helen says, 'The spirit of an undertaking was always more to Helena than the name it went by.'[58]

The 500 copies of *Whitman's Ideal Democracy* were published in 1902 on Helena's birthday, May 11th, by the comradely Everett Press. After Emerson's poem, 'Give all to love;/Obey thy heart'; came Helen's introduction and a portrait of Helena by James S. Campton from a photograph. They were followed by nine articles of Helena's written between 1895 and 1900: 'Whitman's Ideal Democracy' (1899); 'Thoreau's Joy in Nature' (1900); 'Poets of Revolt: Shelley, Whitman, Carpenter' (1896); 'Whitman's Altruism' (1895); 'Individualism versus Organization' (1899); 'Ingenuities of Economic Argument' (1897); 'Inequality in Divorce' (1896); 'Marriage Safeguards' (c. 1895); and 'The Last Stand Against Democracy in Sex (1898).

Helen utilised what she had learned about publishing at Houghton Mifflin, systematically working through a list of contacts in the mainstream as well as the radical press. Considering she was promoting a book of essays by an unknown woman with far-left politics, she did an effective job. The responses from both the *Boston Globe* and the *Chicago Evening Post* were largely favourable. However, J.E. Chamberlain on the *New York Mail and Express* sneered knowingly that 'Between the lines' of Helena's love for Miriam one could read a 'pathetic longing for affection'.[59] By cutting William out, Helen had inadvertently exposed Helena to scorn as the unfulfilled spinster. Women like Helena could be condemned if they did *and* if they didn't.

In contrast, the anarchist, Mary Hansen, praised Helena's advocacy of an athletic, natural open-air life in *Free Society*, while in *The Free Comrade*, Lloyd argued that she had possessed a dual 'nature' which was 'masculine in its analysis and logic, tenderly feminine in its loyalty and personal sympathy'.[60] For him, Helena presaged the androgynous woman of the future. Lloyd's friend, Leonard D. Abbott, who moved in both socialist and anarchist circles, similarly hailed Helena in *The Socialist Spirit* as 'a woman of the ages that are to be' who had been 'born out of her due time'.[61]

In July a more critical review, signed 'J.S.', appeared in the socialist monthly *The Comrade*. John Spargo, the editor, had recently arrived from Britain and had joined the newly formed American Socialist Party in 1901. In Britain he had been active in the S.D.F. and wrote fondly of Dan Irving, 'Bob' Gilliard, John and Robert Sharland. He had met Miriam twice, recalling her as 'brave, impetuous and loveable', but he had never known Helena and was dismissive of her fears of 'losing her "individuality" in the organized movement'. While he detected in her essay, 'Individualism and Organization', a recognition that 'the fullest individuality is most possible in organization for common support', he maintained that she had failed to live this out in practice. Spargo concluded that though Helena described herself as a 'Socialist', since coming to America she seemed to have 'drifted away from, and to have distrusted the Socialist *movement*'. Unjustly, he claimed this was because she thought herself 'too great to conform'.[62]

Spargo was right, Helena had not participated in an American socialist grouping as she had in Bristol, but then she had discovered no equivalent to the comradely politics of the Bristol Socialist Society in 1890s Boston. As a Victorian woman reared to sacrifice her individuality, achieving personal autonomy *was* certainly vital for her, but she did not dismiss social solidarity. She found it possible among the Boston Whitmanites to balance her own self-development with service to a community of fellow searchers questioning relationships, culture and daily life. She envisaged the Boston W.W.F. as prefiguring a non-hierarchical structure, and her involvement in it resulted in a good deal of organising. She hoped the C.F.S., too, could foster bonds of comradeship. Both constituted forms of radical 'organization for common support', though not ones Spargo was willing to recognise in 1902.

Coming from an opposing perspective, Emma Heller Schumm, writing in *Liberty* as 'E.H.S.', believed Helena 'was gradually ripening into a perfect comprehension of the ideals of Anarchism'.[63] Again this is partially true, Helena did comprehend the 'ideals of Anarchism'. Her anti-statist vision of free association was close to anarchism, but had also been present in libertarian strands of British socialism during the 1880s, before the two wings of left politics were irrefragably severed. Observing how the *process* of living was, for Helena, synonymous with her politics, Schumm invokes a wonderful German word: 'She was "eine Lebenskünstlerin" in the true sense of the word, – an artist of life.'[64] This captures Helena's rooms with their carefully assembled objects marking out an alternative space for personality, her new woman clothing and bicycling. Yet Helena was not simply practising a politics of personal life, she was also a conscientious organiser, an inveterate committee-woman, an attender of meetings, large and small. Schumm had observed at the W.W.F memorial meeting in March 1901 that Helena gave 'full expression to her individuality', but this was always configured through a commitment to the common weal.[65] Many-sided Helena was not easy to compress.

Helen's loyalty to the friend she had loved so much did ensure that Helena's impact on those around her and her example as an advanced woman survived. But this loyal remembering tended towards a quasi-religious reverence, which froze Helena the woman into Helena the Ideal. At the 1902 Whitman Memorial, the homeopath, Arathena Drake, too, placed Helena up in the pantheon with Whitman and his mystical acolyte Dr Bucke, the author of *Cosmic Consciousness* (1901). It was a paradoxical fate for a woman who had warned against Whitman worship.[66]

The messy anomaly in Helen's air-brushed portrayal of Helena's life was Robert Allan Nicol, still over in California. On 26 July 1902, Edward Carpenter wrote to Helen saying that his friend, Leonard Abbott, had forwarded him 'the little book about Helena Born'.[67] He enclosed two dollars and requested a second copy, adding that he had not yet had time to read more than the first few pages of her biographical 'sketch'.[68] Despite being constantly busy, Carpenter was in contact with Robert and would have only had to peruse four pages in order to notice his absence from the narrative. Adept at gentlemanly tact, the sage of Millthorpe added a little sting to his careful diplomacy. By employing the term 'sketch' he hints at the possibility of gaps in Helen's version.

Robert lingered as the elephant in the room within Helen's psyche. Long afterwards, in 1930, she revealed that she was aware he and Helena had continued to correspond 'almost up to the time' of her friend's death. So she had not been precisely truthful to Gilliard about the difficulties of tracing him, and it appears she was 'criticised' by those who knew Robert in Britain.[69] Still profoundly uneasy about the man in California she had never met, Helen justified her decision to conceal his connection to Miriam and Helena. She 'had' to omit him: not only had he borrowed $500, which Helena 'never saw again', he was also 'jealous' and disliked Helena, depriving her of contact with Sunrise. Helen's animus against Robert remained undiminished. Helena might never have spoken 'ill of him', but a protective Helen believed she had the measure of the man. The 'Shelley type' was inwardly warped; 'Robert looked well, but did not wear well.'[70]

PART 3

ECHOES

SIXTEEN

'Clues and Meanings': 1898–1902

During 1898 Robert had made two big changes in his life. He left White-nights ranch for San Francisco and married Marie Terry Jutie (short for Jerusha) Coan. Robert was her fourth husband. When they met, Jutie Coan, the daughter of a tavern keeper, was in her late forties and the mother of a teenage son, Raymond. Jutie seems to have been a resourceful survivor, handy with a needle as well as a hammer. A good singer, she earned her living as a music teacher.[1]

Her arrival in Robert's life enabled him to fulfil that long-held dream of establishing a school for Sunrise to attend, designed according to his own theories. 'Robert A. Nicol' and 'Marie T. Nicol' appear in the San Francisco *Crocker-Langley Directory* for 1899, as respectively Secretary and Principal of Harmony School, on Larkin Street.[2] It is possible Helena's $500 had gone towards the school. The name, 'Harmony', may simply indicate that it specialised in music, Jutie's forte. But a preoccupation with harmony had featured in Robert's mystical fascination with the harmony of the spheres, and was a recurring theme in the overlapping circles of spiritual enlightenment, mental healing and New Thought with which he was familiar; indeed, Malinda E. Cramer's Divine Science magazine was called *Harmony*.[3]

Meanwhile, Gertrude had left London and was working on her new novel in the village of Witley in Surrey. On the outer circumference of London, Witley was attracting clusters of literary and aesthetic migrants, and Gertrude had set up an 'associated home' with an interesting group of writers and artists in a beautiful sixteenth-century, steep-roofed, high-chimneyed farm called 'The Fowl House'. True, the windows were somewhat small for writers and illustrators, but there was plenty of light and space outside. It was an idyllic retreat, and the artistic tenants renamed the old house, 'Godspeace'.[4]

On 17 September 1898, Arnold Bennett, just beginning his novel-writing career, visited. He noted that the 'Godspeace' dwellers were 'vegetarians and teetotallers – and they wear sandals. They have an air of living the higher life.' He met Esther Wood, 'a writer on art', 'C.E. Dawson, a young artist', and 'Morris, a journalist who writes on the connection between Whitman and architecture'. Though he had evidently heard of Gertrude, whom he refers to as 'the novelist', she was not there.[5] William Chatterton Dix had recently died after a long illness, so presumably she was still with her family at Cheddar.[6]

Gertrude's housemate, Esther Wood, was a new woman writer and speaker for whom Dante Gabriel Rossetti epitomised 'the reconciliation of the physical with the spiritual'.[7] In December 1894, reviewing Katharine St John Conway's novel, *Husband and Brother*, for the Independent Labour Party's *Labour Leader*, she approved its perspective: 'every woman has the same right as a man to order and dispose of her own life and person' and 'should be economically free to do so'. Wood defended divorce, adding, 'a loveless marriage is nothing less than prostitution without the opportunity of escape from it'.[8]

By April 1895, Wood was a member of the I.L.P. in bohemian Chelsea.[9] Moving, like Gertrude, in both I.L.P. and Fabian circles, she participated in the unity initiative that created non-sectarian Socialist Clubs, like the one Gertrude graced in March 1896.[10] In 1897, when Wood divorced her violent husband (a temperance lecturer), the case was widely reported in the press.[11] *Reynolds's Newspaper* reported that she was 'well known in London Socialist circles as an active propagandist and an able writer', describing her as 'quite a young woman, wears her hair cut short, holds advanced views relating to marriage'.[12] Not only did Wood inhabit a similar political milieu to Gertrude, they both cultivated an ultramodern image and shared a rebellious outlook on personal behaviour.

Gertrude's other sandal-wearing friends at 'Godspeace' were exponents of a Carpenter-style simple life and engaged in practical crafts. Wood and the Whitmanite, George Llewellyn Morris, applied arts and crafts ideals of simplicity to book design and architecture. They later collaborated on a guide to converting country cottages, *The Country Cottage*

(1906), which translated the Carpenterian rejection of the trappings of Victorianism into a life-style choice for the modern middle class.[13] Like Gertrude's sister Hilda, Charles Edwin Dawson did drawings for *The Wheelwoman* and had also worked on 'posters', which sound ominously like advertisements.[14]

The 'Godspeace' friends networked. When William Heinemann and his partner, Sidney S. Pawling, accepted Gertrude's new novel, *The Image Breakers*, they agreed that Dawson should design the cover. He outlined two lovers in white against a black background. They face one another across a raging sea of passion, but on the spine he drew the female figure as assertive and the male as receptive. Esther Wood lauded the simple black and white lines of his cover in the *Studio's* special issue on bookbinding in Winter 1899–1900.[15] It was a good opening for Dawson. He went on to collaborate with Wood and Morris and became established as an illustrator for publishers, despite grumbling about how many of them 'could not distinguish' between 'a lithograph or a pull from a half-tone block'.[16] In the 1900s he also provided drawings for socialist papers and was an ardent supporter of militant suffrage.

In July 1900, the month before *The Image Breakers* was due to appear, Gertrude's short story, 'Veronica's Mill', appeared in the *Pall Mall Magazine*. Backed by William Waldorf Astor, the prestigious magazine serialised novels by George Meredith and Robert Louis Stevenson, charting a careful course between 'advanced' and mainstream writing. Gertrude's story adopts a light touch towards the live issue of relations

Cover for *The Image Breakers*

between the sexes. Veronica and Edmund, a young married couple living in an old mill in France, fall out over whether Edmund's bohemian artist friend should leave his wife. When Edmund dismisses his friend's wife as 'the usual butterfly, who wanted to gad about, and had no interest in his work', Veronica took it personally. She accuses male artists of wanting to marry 'models – dummies who would sit perfectly still even if there were black-beetles crawling over them'.[17] The combination of the beetles and news that her husband had invited his bohemian friend to join them arouses Veronica's feminist fury.

A disillusioned Veronica flees dramatically back to the Paris hotel where the lovers had known only happiness. A repentant Edmund follows her, unfortunately in a new pair of fashionable but quite unsuitable boots, which he is forced to discard en route. He arrives in Montparnasse in the early hours of the morning, exhausted, with bleeding feet. Veronica is reconciled to her wounded and contrite love, and Edmund, having abandoned his penchant for bohemian artists, now just wants a honeymoon in the Old Mill.

Gertrude was no doubt pleased that 'Veronica's Mill' was republished in America that August. But by then the reviews of her novel – her big book – *The Image Breakers* (1900) were beginning to appear.

Whereas *The Girl from the Farm* examines the clash between duty and the desire for independence, Gertrude's far more ambitious second book asks when reason has created a world out of itself how life is then to be lived. Her account pursues clues and meanings through both outward circumstances and through her characters' submerged and fleeting emotions. In *The Image Breakers* she relates how two 'new women', Rosalind Dangerfield and Leslie Ardent, engage in left politics, adopt advanced lifestyles, and yet still confront dilemmas in combining love and freedom.

Rosalind, troubled by social inequality, starts a class for young working-class women in 'Burminster' and begins writing for the London-based revolutionary socialist paper *The Lantern*, edited by Justin Ferrar. She becomes active in the socialist movement, supporting women workers on strike at a sweet factory, 'Sampson's'. Eventually she abandons her protected and privileged life as the wife of the mill owner, Herbert Dangerfield, for a free union with Ferrar. Nevertheless, her former High Church religious faith means she remains dogged by guilt.

The younger woman, Leslie, an artist, is from a very different background. She lives with two maiden aunts in an old red-brick house screened by white muslin curtains. This quiet world of 'Respectability, grown threadbare', is disrupted when socialists begin to hold open-air meetings in the square outside on a garish 'red and yellow bandstand' erected by the 'Municipality'.[18] An animated Leslie misquotes Georges Jacques Danton to her startled Aunt Letitia, 'L'audace de l'audace, et toujours de l'audace' and embarks on 'Socialistic designs'.[19] She is drawn into the labour uprising in Burminster and meets the local socialists. Inspired by a Fabian speaker, Leslie resolves to pursue her art in London, which she sees as 'the bourne of all wisdom'.[20] Just before she leaves, she meets John Redgold, a seasoned journalist able to provide her with contacts for her artwork and with whom she falls in love.

The two 'image breakers' are together in an old Priory when the novel opens. Leslie, who reveres Rosalind as a 'goddess', is delighted when an intimately sensuous Rosalind tells her to 'nestle close' on the bed.[21] Rosalind sends Leslie to collect a young anarchist, Charles Whiston, sent by a protective Justin Ferrar because he has been drawn into a 'scrape'.[22] After Leslie takes him to a safe address, she learns with a shock that he had put a lead pipe filled with gunpowder into a post box. Nevertheless, the anarchist is characterised humorously in his 'knickerbocker suit, low turn-down collar and unconventional tie', tenderly carrying a pet marmoset wrapped in a bundle.[23] His hero-worship of Ferrar runs counterpoint to Leslie's adulation of Rosalind.

The ascetic Ferrar adopts a succession of causes: first he is a revolutionary socialist; then a Tolstoyan community builder committed to personal transformation. Later he seeks spiritual enlightenment through Christian Science and then switches to a lesser known alternative cult. Ferrar assails 'selfishness', insisting sex must be 'redeemed and purified as Love and Intelligence'. Gertrude describes how he fixes Leslie with a gaze of 'magnetic intensity', saying '"I see ... great possibilities in you waiting to be unfolded."'[24]

Though Rosalind is initially the dominant figure, Leslie subsequently breaks away, and the two women characters are wrenched apart, partly because they make differing political choices and partly because they come to love utterly opposing men. Absorbed in Ferrar, Rosalind follows each of his perfectionist quests in the belief that their relationship is not based on 'the hateful selfishness à deux people mistake for love'.[25] She tells Leslie that she and Ferrar 'have broken the laws of the world, not merely for our own selfish indulgence, but in obedience to something higher'.[26]

In contrast, Gertrude depicts John Redgold as the 'soldier' type, 'powerful, full fleshed, genial, easy, tolerant, acceptable to the rank and file because the rank and file was acceptable to him'.[27] Leslie meets him at Culver, which its founder Harvey Hargood had conceived as a colony for unemployed workers, but Rosalind and Ferrar see as a refuge from 'a rotten and corrupt civilisation'.[28] According to Rosalind, under the influence of the 'unscrupulous lecturer', Daphne Lester, Hargood has become 'a pope and a despot' who would brook no criticism.[29] War was raging in utopia and Hargood's main benefactress, Miss Branwhite, appalled by rumours of free love, sends for the journalist John Redgold to smooth over the conflict and squash the scandal.

Culver constitutes a turning point in the novel, for it there that Leslie meets Redgold and rejects the influence of Rosalind and Ferrar. She first sees Redgold's face lit by the moon, and 'the cloud upon her spirit was riven as though with a golden flash'. From this moment, 'the whole world … suddenly changed'.[30]

The pragmatic journalist arrives too late to prevent the violent eviction of the rebels, but carries one of the colonists – a distressed, ailing 'Minnie Hare' – to safety and Leslie revives her with his 'spirit-flask'.[31] Redgold reflects sardonically on the fracas that if Hargood had established a 'monastery for men only', they might have slaved away making 'a melancholy living out of the soil'. But the presence of 'lovely woman' was bound to stir up scandal. His message to Leslie is that 'The real fight is with the world as it is, not with some figment of our own brains we can never realise.'[32]

In contrast, Ferrar and Rosalind have come to the opposite conclusion. Culver had failed because 'it brought into itself all the evils of the society outside'. Ferrar has decided that 'the deep basic questions of religion and sex' could not be ignored. His conclusion is ascetic: 'a colony of communists' required a 'spiritual foundation'.[33] Leslie defies both Ferrar's derision and Rosalind's incomprehension by announcing she is going to London to make her own way in life, 'as an artist in black and white'.[34]

Redgold personifies an important theme in the novel: living in and confronting the world as it is, rather than dreaming of utopia. Yet, through her characterisation of Leslie, Gertrude interrogates this outlook by demonstrating its downsides. Emotionally linked to the sensuous man of action, Leslie realises she disagrees with many of his views. Opposed to married women working, he regards love in Ruskinian terms as a haven of 'rest and reliance'.[35] He would have the 'charming' but dependent wife in a little house with the man in charge, 'It's he who pays the piper calls the tune.'[36] When Redgold considers a position as secretary to a wealthy Liberal MP called Lupton, who shows signs of conceding to the 'loud-voiced' sexual purity lobby, dreadful images of a villa with bay-windows in provincial Sheerborough and attendance at a Unitarian church loom before Leslie.[37]

Worse, lured by Lupton's excellent wine and beautiful niece, Redgold betrays Leslie with a kiss. There is personally felt venom in Gertrude's description of her heroine's rival, the 'well-poised head, red and gold at once', her 'coat of rich crimson brocade', the 'ivory gown' matching her white skin. 'Dress was one of her weapons', writes Gertrude through clenched teeth.[38]

Gertrude's portrayal of Leslie and Rosalind exposes the complex undertows of new womanhood. Both experience painful conflicts around ideals and actuality, physicality and emotion, autonomy and love, security and danger. Leslie makes a cathartic break from Redgold, realising she had sunk her being into his, yet she is left drifting, feeling worthless, and doubting the value of her own work. At her most vulnerable, Leslie meets an older woman, called 'Miss Fear', who had abandoned her aspiration to be an artist. The manifestation of defeat, she haunts Leslie 'like some curious riddle'.[39]

Rosalind is left perilously exposed by clinging to her relationship with Ferrar, and eventually recognises that 'she had burned her bridges behind her; drifted out into the open', for a man who had never loved her.[40] She had lost herself in him, simply to be an aid to his 'work'.[41] In despair she makes her way into a church, where she meets Ferrar's brother who is an Anglican priest. A repentant Rosalind sits among empty benches half-way up the nave, to reflect on the course her life has taken. Gertrude tells us, 'She went over the past, reviewing it for clues and meanings.'[42] Rosalind's gloomy fate is to care for the disturbed anarchist, Whiston, and work in a stained-glass factory.

The book ends with Leslie going back to Burminster. She tracks down the new secretary of the Socialist Society who shows her a copy of Walt Whitman's *Leaves of Grass*, given to his wife by Rosalind. She learns how Rosalind (like Miriam Daniell, Helena Born, Enid Stacy and Katharine St John Conway) was remembered locally as a heroine of labour. Hearing that Redgold has been searching for her, she goes to a meeting in support of Parnell, where an acquaintance of his is speaking. Rescued by Redgold from a violent 'scrimmage' there, they are reunited.[43] While Rosalind can only run through her life in her mind, Leslie is allowed the opportunity to make an actual return and start again.

Rosalind's love for the remote idealist Ferrar, and Leslie's affair with his antithesis, the pragmatic man of action Redgold, drive the narrative. Yet, while the men's actions define the course of the women's lives, neither Redgold nor Ferrar examine their inner motivation in any depth. The aloof Ferrar is in complete denial of personal emotion, while Redgold resembles Carpenter's 'Man The Ungrown', in *Love's Coming of Age* (1896), who deals with the outer world and leaves his inner self-unexamined.

The Image Breakers explores sex and power through the eyes of the *women* characters. Gertrude has Rosalind employing the physiological typecasting popular at the time. Bemused by the 'strange power' of men like Redgold 'to attract women', she warns Leslie in a letter, 'the heavy jaw; the mouth hidden by the moustache … those thick fleshy lobes to the ears. They are signs which speak infallibly of the sensual type engrossed on material planes.' Leslie never wrote back, but contends with an imaginary Rosalind, 'You do not understand, … He is a *real* man.'[44]

When Rosalind hears Ferrar speaking at a socialist meeting in Burminster, he reminds her of the idealised portraits of Christ driving the money lenders from the Temple. She is fascinated by 'His face, a long oval, with high forehead and pointed beard'. Later we learn he is a 'mystic' type, 'proud, yearning, narrow, sensitive, with mingled brooding bitter sweetness, remote from the crowd with its crude common needs, uncomprehended and uncomprehending'.[45]

Nevertheless, passionate female friendship creates a powerful undertow to the male-female dynamic. Rosalind writes to Leslie as, 'My Sister – My Dear Girl', and when the two women meet again at Culver, Gertrude describes how they looked searchingly at one another and 'met in a swift, tremulous kiss'.[46] Even as Leslie rejects the older woman's charisma, the sight of Rosalind's head close to Justin Ferrar's evokes a surge of grief, 'Tears that she did not understand welled into her eyes.'[47] 'It is the men', reflects Leslie, 'who make all the horrid complications.'[48] However, Rosalind's assertion of women having a special mission, 'together with the men who see with us', to cure the 'sickness' of the world, along with her call to Leslie as 'Dear sister woman', go unheeded.[49] Gertrude's message is neither evangelical duty, sensuous sisterhood or female bonding, but one of women taking differing paths and making autonomous choices. Rosalind is fatally drawn towards extreme absolutes. Leslie, too, searches for truth, but in a more pragmatic manner in which her own personal fulfilment is paramount.

Gertrude endeavoured to express the manifold complexities faced by women like herself who sought an independent and sensuous life. She was able to draw not only on her knowledge of contemporary psychology through Havelock Ellis, but on the literary Symbolism that had emerged alongside it in late nineteenth-century Europe and was in vogue among novelists as a means of uncovering unconscious influences. Redgold and Leslie's first outing together is splattered with fire, storm and 'naked sword-thrusts'.[50] Gertrude wedges allegorical names as signals into the text. Leslie is indeed 'Ardent', Rosalind 'Dangerfield' courts disaster, while 'Miss Fear', the haunting 'riddle', abandons her creative work.

While *The Image Breakers* examines Leslie and Rosalind's inner emotions, it also presents political protagonists and debates in realistic settings. Gertrude translates her own experience as a politically active woman into her fiction. The novel reveals Gertrude in conversation with the revolutionary socialism of her Bristol days, differing strands of anarchism and the left reformism she later encountered among the Fabians and sections of the I.L.P. Like her two heroines, Gertrude had struggled for self-expression, while retaining a yearning for a wider social communion that was not simply individualistic. Her High Church upbringing had led her to the Bristol and Clifton Christian Socialists, the Bristol Socialist Society, the strike upsurge, to an idea of a Labour Party, and eventually to the London Fabians and the I.L.P. She had challenged male prejudice in the Socialist Society, but had not been in accord with her socialist 'sister women' (a term also used by both Miriam and Katharine St John Conway). She had disagreed with her obvious ally, Enid Stacy, over free love, and taken De Mattos' side in the conflict around Irving and Conway's 'spirit marriage'. Sisterhood had been fractured again at the Starnthwaite community when Conway sided with Mills, and Stacy joined Irving in rebellion.

Gertrude situates her plot in recognisable places, evoking milieus and people familiar to her. 'Burminster' borrows from Bedminster, a working-class suburb in Bristol. The Burminster socialists are closely observed; Gertrude details their disagreement over tactics during the 'Sampson's' (Sanders') sweet girls' strike in a 'blue-washed coffee-room with a long counter' topped with metal urns, which could well have been the Quaker-owned British Workman Coffee House where the socialists often met. She describes too in the novel, how, as the 'girls' come and go with

Robert G. Tovey (Bristol Reference Library)

their collection boxes, the socialists argue in the committee room.[51] Enid Stacy was involved with the actual Sanders' strike in 1892, but Gertrude herself would have observed similar scenes while in Bristol.

Some of the activists Gertrude knew are partially recognisable. Robert Gilliard makes a brief appearance as 'Thomson – a burly shopkeeper' with 'almost ascetic habits', who holds forth on immortality.[52] Gertrude teases with 'almost'; for, though interested in spirituality and linked to the Tolstoyans, Gilliard, with ten children, must have been ascetic only in parts! A mischievous Gertrude describes Silas Lambrick, 'a little man who might have been a shopkeeper, and wore black mutton-chop whiskers' (just like Robert Tovey), urging compromise in the sweet girls' strike.[53]

A victory is won at Sampson's (unlike the actual outcome of the Sanders' sweet women's strike), but before long dissension erupts over how to achieve socialism. This is when the 'prominent Socialist' from London, 'Alan Russell', elaborates a Fabian strategy of working with the Liberals.[54] Why use the word socialism? Why not simply permeate the body politic?

'Give them the thing without the name. Descend upon them like wolves in sheep's clothing. The one real thing that matters is that you should impress upon them the fitness of your ideas, and get something done. Lay yourselves out to discover points of unity rather than of difference, and work from *them*. Don't despise the day of small things. Take a nibble where you cannot get a bite.'[55]

Russell's speech draws upon Sidney Webb's policy of permeation and Unwin and Carpenter's focus on small projects in the late 1880s. It invokes too the mid 1890s attempt at a broad alliance between Radical Liberals, I.L.P. socialists and Fabians, familiar to Gertrude through the Socialist Clubs and the *Labour Leader.*

Gertrude gives her herald all the best lines and an impressed Leslie concludes:

> He was a human being of delightful newness of cut, as it were, unlike all the rest. And he had power. She could imagine him as holding a clue in his hand and pointing to the right path unwaveringly, while the men of Burminster blundered in dark places, knocked their heads against stone walls, and confidently predicted revolutions which failed to come off.[56]

Of course, Russell's perspective of permeation is anathema to the Burminster socialists and he is doubly suspect as coming from London. However, Gertrude, familiar with the lanterns that appeared on socialist demonstrations in Bristol during the evenings, contrasts the clear signal of the London Fabian with the lantern of the Burminster socialists, 'a curious parchment thing, painted with mottoes'.[57]

Though Gertrude was not herself at the Starnthwaite community, the dramatic rift there clearly troubled her. Several characters are drawn directly from life: 'Hargood' is Mills; the lecturer 'Daphne Lester', Katharine St John Conway; and the evicted 'Harcs', the Irvings. Gertrude moves them to Manchester, whereas they were in nearby Burnley when she was writing the book. 'Miss Branwhite' stands in for Starnthwaite's chief donor, the Countess de Noailles, whose many causes did, indeed, include diet reform.

In reality, of course, it was Bernard Shaw who intervened to patch up the mess at Starnthwaite, smothering any potential damage caused by the circulation of the letters from Katharine St John Conway and enabling a rehabilitated Dan Irving to speak for John Trevor's Labour Church.[58] Redgold's emphasis upon engaging with the world as it is instead of pursuing dreams is in accord with Shaw's fulminations against the 'Illusions of Socialism' in Carpenter's *Forecasts of the Coming Century* (1897), in which he endorses 'Acuteness of intellect, political experience, practical capacity, the strength of character which gives a man power.'[59] Shaw later claimed to have warned Henry Salt and Carpenter that 'the socialist colonies in America failed except when they were monastically celibate'.[60]

The Image Breakers is crowded with cascading echoes upon echoes, many of which derive from the efforts within Gertrude's own circles to change personal relations and consciousness. Rosalind's dream of a small associated home, in which she and Ferrar would live with Charles Whiston and his sister Lucy, resembles 'Godspeace'. Not only Gertrude's housemates, but Carpenter, Henry and Kate Salt, Havelock Ellis, Robert Gilliard, and indeed Robert over in California, were all in differing ways preoccupied with inner prefigurative change and the small-scale utopias that abounded in the 1890s. Gertrude is likely to have known about J.C. Kenworthy's Tolstoyan community at Purleigh, Essex, which had split in 1898 partly over Tolstoy's ascetic rejection of sexuality. A William Hare happened to be with Kenworthy at Purleigh, and Gertrude may have transplanted the name to the Irvings at Culver in *The Image Breakers*.[61]

Gertrude's bohemian Fabian friendships brought her into contact with a series of overlapping networks, which included Russian revolutionaries and anarchists. William Rossetti's children's incendiary paper, *The Torch*, is transposed into Ferrar's paper, *The Lantern*.[62] Gertrude's version signals light rather than ignition, though doubtless Shaw, who expostulated over 'the damned Bohemian anarchism which never succeeds anywhere', would have excoriated her softness towards Ferrar's acolyte, the whimsical Whiston.[63]

Gertrude tells us Whiston is associated with the insurrectionary wing of the anarchist movement. This had never gained a significant following in Britain, though she would have known of the 1892 case of the Walsall anarchists' 'plot', encouraged by an agent who had also been associated with Louise Michel's children's school. However, violent direct action in Spain had made headlines in 1897, when a bomb was thrown into a religious procession. A protest committee, supported by the anarchist journal *Freedom*, as well as by the Salts and Carpenter, through the Humanitarian League, had publicised the savage reprisals taken against the anarchists.[64]

Initially Whiston is a sketchy figure of fun, but he assumes a symbolic import as the novel progresses. Gertrude relates how, when he reads out the poems of an anarchist called 'Barlow', Leslie 'enters' the 'Utopian visionary's golden world' in a semi-dream state. Allegorically she imagines a fragile ladder stretching 'upward to the heaven of illusion', which is 'balanced fearfully on the edge of an abyss'.[65] Gertrude plants clues through names, and her reference to 'Barlow' resonates with the fate of the anarchist poet, John Barlas, whose work was admired by Henry Salt. In November 1891 Barlas had been arrested for shooting in the air outside the House of Commons and was subsequently confined to a mental asylum.[66]

Gertrude's understanding of the travails of self-supporting women like Leslie also comes directly from her own and her friends' experiences. The 'dingy registry office for governesses', with its 'grimmest of recording angels' (another Shavian echo) insisting on 'irreproachable references' simply for 'tutelary and domestic servitude', was all too familiar.[67] Gertrude had seen how her designer friends at The Fowl House, as well as her sister Hilda, struggled with the imperatives of commercial art by designing the posters for 'temperance' groups or advertisements for 'hair-wash' mentioned in the novel.[68] As a writer herself, she knew all about market pressures, low rates and financial insecurity. Delays in payment from *Fire-Fly*, loss of work for 'carelessness and want of method' on the *Ladies' Gazette*, spelt disaster for Leslie.[69]

The pell-mell manner in which *The Image Breakers* is written makes it confusing to read. Characters and events are often barely introduced or explained. Some of Gertrude's allusions are open to differing interpretations. For instance, Rosalind recoils from 'Madame Belmont', an American exponent of Christian Science. We are told that Ferrar admires her message, the new spirituality of 'the *Divine Wholeness*' that leads from within, but a suspicious Rosalind traces 'the curve of the woman's jaw on the counterpane', convinced its prominence 'spelled sensualism writ large'.[70] Was Gertrude smuggling a secret message to Robert or simply drawing on a news item? In November 1898 an actual Christian Scientist, Mrs Mills, acquired notoriety in a manslaughter trial after the death of a sick patient.[71] Sure enough, the court sketch reveals a woman with a jaw like Desperate Dan's.

Gertrude's mix of realistic reportage, ironic humour and melodrama, combined with her probing for psychological meanings, produces a vertiginous effect. Not only do the symbols, signs and clues come thick and fast, the reader is presented with a series of submerged discordant dialogues Gertrude appears to be having with herself. Despite her iconoclastic cultural radicalism, her thoughtful characters are all middle class. Plato's natural aristocracy is eugenically manifested in the superior physical attributes of Redgold, towering over the 'under-sized' common man.[72] She never depicts workers taking self-directed action, pessimistically conjuring instead the fin-de-siècle crowd as 'a huge feline monster'.[73] A snobbish Gertrude disdains trade; looking like a 'shopkeeper' is code for obdurate stupidity. While she fights the gendered class war on behalf of self-supporting women against Lupton's niece, snobbery peeps through in relation to another potential rival for Redgold's affection, who is branded as 'common-looking'.[74] Gertrude's habitat, like Leslie's, had been one of gentility laced with bohemianism, making the cottage acceptable but not the provincial villa.

The novel also reveals an interesting aesthetic ambivalence which echoes the unease that had emerged in the 'Our Fabian Circle' correspondence. Leslie considers it 'a sort of heresy to admit that elaboration could be enthrallingly attractive'. Rosalind, in contrast, sets off her 'ivory face and crisp, lightless, dark hair with ample draperies of flame-coloured silk and gauze'.[75] Gertrude, like Leslie, espoused simplification, but perhaps hankered after more hedonistic display. Initially she allows Leslie only one aesthetic luxury, an embroidered dressing gown of cobalt blue, closeted in the bedroom, before relenting by equipping her heroine with a tasteful and personalised dress style – dark-blue open coat and skirt with soft green silk vest.[76]

Gertrude graces her heroine with a reconstituted hero. '"The villa's all in ruins now,"' Redgold tells her, '"and you and I are on the open road!"'[77] A calm, fulfilled Leslie waits for him to return from a six-month trip to America. She has work in a 'Black and White Exhibition', just like Gertrude's sister Hilda, and is living in a country cottage.[78] One evening, while lighting the candles on each side of a mirror, she sees the face of 'the man' reflected next to her own, 'rosy with the wind and the sun'. Gertrude is careful to tell us that the mirror's frame is 'carved in the rude semblance of a snake'. In case the reader misses the clue, Gertrude tells us that the snake is 'Eternity'.[79]

But a mirror image is transient and the harmonious denouement is at variance with Leslie's earlier restless independence. It also plasters over the cultural and political polarities in the text which make it so fascinating, if frustrating, to read. *The Image Breakers* is a novel pulling in several contradictory psychological and ideological directions at the same time.

Hidden amid the overt 'clues and meanings' are more deeply buried perplexities which perhaps Gertrude herself was experiencing. Rosalind Dangerfield's identification with a cause or a faith that transcends self is presented as a false trail. In contrast, Leslie Ardent's impulses lead her to seek freer, more equal personal relationships. Is Gertrude shedding an earlier aspect of her self through the demise of Rosalind, and embodying in Leslie her own powerful wish to connect with 'life'? *The Image Breakers* is, indeed, a 'propagandist romance', but the propaganda is not for political and social commitment.[80] Instead it expresses an exhaustion with collective utopianism,[81] anticipating the early twentieth-century themes of H.G. Wells' *Kipps* (1905) and *Ann Veronica* (1909), and, in a very different way, E.M. Forster's vindication of personal connection. Gertrude is cutting loose as an individual.

The cultured and cosmopolitan William Heinemann was not averse to 'new women' novelists and took a gamble on Gertrude's labyrinthine second novel.[82] *The Image Breakers* was assiduously promoted and reviewed in a wide range of newspapers and journals, including local ones. However, the frisson of the 'new woman novel' had dulled by 1900, and the book evoked some predictable yawns. *The Saturday Review* enquired, 'Are we not a little disgusted with and tired of stories of girls who are too pure to wear wedding-rings?'[83] In *The Graphic*'s opinion, 'The various persons of both sexes' who were portrayed as 'trying to smash what they consider mere fetishes, such as marriage, property, and so forth', met with the common fate of iconoclasts: 'the only damage they do is to themselves'.[84]

Nonetheless the *Bookman* thought it 'very clever', *The Athenaeum* was relieved to find its author a 'fervid romancer', and the *Daily News* opined that the book was 'full of promise'.[85] The reviewer in *The Academy* disliked the theme, but praised the writing and pondered on the meaning of a 'novel, upon which so much artistic feeling and technique have been expended'. *The Outlook* deemed it 'almost a great novel'.[86]

Three reviewers displayed special insight. Arnold Bennett was writing a column, 'A Gossip about Books', in *Hearth and Home: An Illustrated Weekly Journal for Gentlewomen*. He explained to his gentlewomen readers that the socialist and anarchist characters in the novel were 'for ever trying to find out what in life is real and what is unreal', and, while 'ridden by convictions, theories, fads, ideals', he nevertheless found them 'human'. As a novelist himself, he noted the lack of 'shape, cohesion and logic' in the book's structure and thought the story '*de*presses where it ought to *im*press'. Some readers 'may call it annoying, disappointing', but Bennett expressed admiration for a book he considered to be 'Interesting as a novel and even more interesting as the revelation of a personality'. Pronouncing 'Miss Dix … a literary artist', he predicted the book would be 'the forerunner of some really notable work'.[87]

A young G.K. Chesterton, who had just embarked on his literary career and was reviewing in *The Speaker*, a liberal publication set up to counter *The Spectator*, picked up on 'the pervading sense of colour and form' in *The Image Breakers*; reading Gertrude through the novel, he observed that these revealed 'more of an author than the author knows'. Chesterton loved the romance of Leslie and Redgold and admired the opening description of Leslie lying in her bed in the Priory. To the young High Church man it was 'as graceful as a mediaeval tomb'. For him, the book evoked 'that austere loveliness of "plain living and high thinking" which marks the best of these modern revolutionaries'. The Whiston character was the exception, being 'a sanguinary young noodle' in Chesterton's eyes.[88] Otherwise he waxed enthusiastic:

> We wish that all novels of Socialism and vague unconventionality were as good as Miss Gertrude Dix's work, in which she shows a genuine sense of beauty and delicacy and a comprehension of that nameless aesthetic hunger which has so little to do with Socialism in formula and so much in fact.[89]

In contrast, the anonymous reviewer in the *Modern Review* thought that the tragic fate of the idealists rang true, but not the happy romance: 'We doubt very much whether the impulsive, passionate Leslie would have been happy with an earthly, good-natured Philistine like Redgold, and we believe in our heart Miss Dix also shares our doubts.' This reviewer grasped the novel's élan vital, remarking how Gertrude should have quoted Mephistopheles' observation to Faust, '"Dear friend all theory is so much grey ash, but the golden tree of life is still green!"' Once again came the forecast: Gertrude could 'write a novel which will be really great'.[90]

Gertrude may have been disappointed to find herself still placed in the 'shows promise' category, yet, with a stash of generally favourable reviews in Britain, and an American edition produced by Frederick. A. Stokes, a publisher with the celebrated Stephen Crane on his list, she could feel pleased with herself. Across the Atlantic her novel was greeted with American spin as a 'new realistic study of modern socialism' by an author who 'has lived for many years in socialistic colonies and has experimented with various communal ideas'.[91]

*   *   *

While Gertrude's writing provoked literary and political speculation, biographical details of her actual life and ideas at the turn of the century are sparse indeed. Tantalisingly she makes two appearances in the 1901 census, but on both occasions is listed as a visitor. Gertrude is described as 'Novelist and Journalist', at the home of Sidney Filmore, a 'draughtsman (artistic)' who worked on books and newspapers, and his wife Fanny in Kingston-on-Thames. They lived in Cheady Cottage, a late Victorian villa, at 65 Cobham Road.[92] It was an artistic street, for the Holdens, devotees of white-washed walls and the Carpenterian simple life, were close by. Charles Holden, then a Whitmanite architect's assistant, was soon to design Bristol Central Library and later Senate House in London.[93] The other entry on Gertrude is equally intriguing. She was recorded as visiting the home of Margaret Olivier's younger brother, Oswald Cox, at Rosslyn Hill, Hampstead Heath.[94]

In both entries Gertrude's income is categorised as 'Own Account', and on each occasion she declared that she was twenty-nine. Born in December 1867, Gertrude was, in fact, thirty-three in the spring of 1901. *The Literary-Year Book* for 1901 gives an address for her at 61 Chancery Lane.[95] But this was a site for safe-deposit boxes, storing legal documents and manuscripts. Gertrude's daughter Margot later recalled being told that her mother had lived in Chelsea and was 'friends with George Bernard Shaw and Gordon Craig'. Her sister Amaryllis, too, believed Gertrude was 'a great friend' of Shaw's and knew the 'socialist crowd'.[96]

An elusive Gertrude, accompanied by clues, meanings and mottoes on lanterns, seems to have been living on the cusp of many causes, mixing with utopian idealists and with worldly politicians and journalists, Liberals as well as socialists. *The Image Breakers* suggests that she had grown somewhat ambivalent politically, but, as an advanced woman, remained hopeful about creating more democratic sexual relationships between men and women.

In the spring of 1902, something made Gertrude turn her back on socialist clubs, communal cottages, Bloomsbury dinner parties and Chelsea artistic circles to join Robert in an old mining town in California. Did she set off across an ocean and a continent to promote her book, or hope to cash in on the craze for tales of the Wild West? Or was she drawn by a lantern glimmer of the aloof young revolutionary turned rancher and mining prospector, who finally wrote proclaiming his love?

Harmony School had not lasted long; no entry appears in the *Crocker-Langley Directory* for 1900. Instead, the 1900 census reveals Robert, aged thirty-one, living with Jutie T. Nicol, aged forty-eight, in Los Angeles' Ward 7. Sunrise was with them and entered as 'Elenor Nicol', aged nine. Robert's occupation is recorded as being a 'News Correspondent'.[97] By 1902 they had parted amicably. 'Mrs Marie T. Nicol' stayed in Los Angeles; Robert and Sunrise moved back north.

The medical student-cum-organiser-cum-rancher-cum-newspaper-man proceeded to reinvent himself as a mining engineer. Mining suited the pattern of dreams and contrivance that had come to define Robert's existence. In 1902 he was working for the largest copper-producing business in California, the Mountain Copper Company at Keswick, in Shasta County. After sulphide copper was found at Iron Mountain in 1896, the company had introduced a smelter and built a railway to transport ore. Keswick, named after the British Company's President, Lord William Keswick, a Conservative MP and businessman, mushroomed into a settlement of around 1,600 people, with cottages, bunkhouses and a store. When Robert was there, eight roaster stalls were belching forth sulphur dioxide turning the 'roaster stiffs'' whiskers green and poisoning the atmosphere. Complaints that the fumes were damaging vegetation led to a series of enquiries and the miners unionised, striking unsuccessfully at the end of 1902. But the Mountain Copper Company brought employment, and its commanding presence extended through the area around Keswick, imprinting itself upon the lived as well as the natural environment. Taylor, a community to the south of Keswick, took its name from a forceful Mountain Copper Company lawyer, Clay Taylor.[98]

Taylor was graced with a post office, where, on 11 June 1902, Robert posted a grandiloquent love letter to Gertrude. Surely a sly smile was playing on Carpenter's lips when he inserted an apparently extraneous comment in his letter to Helen on July 26th: 'I had a letter from Robert Nicol a few weeks ago, from Shasta City. As doubtless you know, Gertrude Dix has joined him out there; & they seem happy.'[99] 'Happy' was an understatement. They were ecstatic.

That June Gertrude had mysteriously become Robert's 'sweet-blessed darling woman'. He was up at the Copper Mine and she was awaiting the return of her lover from Keswick. They had only been parted a few days, but Robert was aching to cover 'thy beautiful Grecian body with light laughing kisses, courting and compelling thee to throw me about and kiss me back'.[100] Rather conveniently, Gertrude, the subject of all these poetic 'thys' and 'thees', was looking after Sunrise down in Shasta City. Sunrise's views go unrecorded; aged eleven, she had already observed several women idealised by her father come and go.

Did Gertrude invest in Robert the idealistic, mystical yearning of Farrar and the commanding sensual man of action she had created in Redgold? And how did Robert envision Gertrude? All that is certain is that sexual explosion chronicled in Robert's purple prose and posted from Taylor on 11 June 1902. Henceforth it would be Gertrude and Robert who were on 'the open road'.

SEVENTEEN

A New Beginning: 1901–1903

Helen's journal entries become clipped in the months follow-ing Helena's death. After scattering her thoughts so fluently, grief gripped hold of her words. On 11 May 1901, Helena's birthday, she states, 'Wm. and I went to Forest Hills and got the ashes.'[1] They sat silently under the trees in the cemetery, watching a squirrel capering. On May 24th, when an unwelcome Walter disturbed them huddled together at William's lodgings in Columbus Avenue, she writes, 'W.L.L. called at 305, and delayed our supper two hours.' A long, lectur-ing letter followed. 'Returned it as usual', grimaced Helen.[2] Incapable of dignified retreat, Walter could not comprehend the powerful bond con-necting Helen and William. The day before Whitman's birthday, Helen ruminated, 'Helena much with us'.[3] Then, on June 17th, they went to Helena's beloved Walden Pond. Helen noted tersely, 'Scattered Helena's ashes. Read Whitman.'[4]

At the 1901 Whitman Memorial Gathering, Helen testified that 'the spirit of loving fellowship' which had endeared Helena to them all remained 'as a joy and inspiration forever'.[5] But was a memory sufficient? The loss of Helena had tested even William's secular rationalism. Lying helpless in Waverley hospital on February 27th he had felt convinced that 'he knew when Helena died' and, in his letter to the Memorial Meeting, imagined Helena at 'one with the Universal'.[6] Within a few months, however, his habitual scepticism reasserted itself.

That May, perhaps at William's instigation, Helen began reading Ernst Haeckel's *The Riddle of the Universe* (1901). Haeckel's fierce critique of religion, combined with his commitment to material and evolutionary explanations for humanity's presence on earth, seemed so sombre. Finally, in July, she finished it with the comment, 'Terrible. What to think?', noting bleakly, 'Wm. has said if there is immortality, Helena would surely have let us know.'[7] She also turned to *The Grammar of Science* (1892) by the British mathematician, Karl Pearson. Pearson is mainly known as a statistician and eugenicist, however, in this book he argues for a 'world beyond sense'. Careful to distinguish his theory from metaphysics, Pearson suggested that what appeared to be the material world was simply a fluke of human perception. Hence space and time, rather than being 'realities of the phenomenal world' were 'the modes under which we perceive things apart'.[8]

Such an approach would later have an important impact on physics, but it was too abstract for a distressed Helen. Her confusion is evident in an article for *The Conservator* in August, 'Progressive Tendencies in Religion'. For Helen, religion was not confined 'to one prophet', and the truly free religions were to be found 'outside the Church'. Like William she placed her faith in human 'brotherhood'. Yet she retained the residual imprint of her childhood Unitarian faith, and could not accept an absolute extinction after death, settling instead for a 'blending and unifying of idealism and physical well being'.[9]

The love that grew between Helen and William while mourning Helena was a kind of legacy. Neither could let go of the woman they both had loved. Moreover, a dying Helena, worrying over what would become of William, had been assured by her younger friend that she would 'look out' for him. Upon Helen's admission that she loved William, 'for his goodness and his sufferings', Helena's wistful response had been, 'but it can't be like my love'. Acknowledging this to be true, Helen had then said she wanted 'to help him through this great trial'.[10] In later life, Helen told her daughter, Helena Bailie, that she had taken William over after Helena's death; while Helena Bailie describes her father as having been 'turned ... over' by Helena Born to her mother.[11]

Though Helen and William's love developed symbiotically in relation to their feelings for Helena, it must also have been driven by an independent empathy and attraction. Just one undated letter from Helen to William has survived from 1901, in which she addresses him as, 'My dear true love'.[12] Helen undoubtedly experienced a range of complicated emotions in those early years of their relationship; but the journal retains its silence. From September 1901 the entries cease altogether. When Helen

James F. Morton (Labadie, Special
Collections Library, University of Michigan)

was typing the journal in 1951, she inserted only a brief retrospective
summary of her life between autumn 1901 and February 1904.

Consequently Helen tells us very little about her and William's association with the anarchist journal *Free Society*, in which Walter Leighton
had extolled the virtues of bachelordom. Its editors, Abe and Mary Isaak
and their children, were closer to the anarchist communism of William's Manchester days than the Individualist Anarchists around *Liberty*.[13]
Nevertheless James F. Morton provided a link with the journal and two
Free Society sympathisers had signed the W.W.F. Memorial for Helena:
the anarchist David Mikol, who advocated the syndicalist tactic of the
general strike, and *Free Society*'s Boston agent, F.A. Snellenberg.

During 1899 and 1900, Morton's lively accounts in the paper of his
travels across America had made Emma Goldman laugh about the elite
itinerant's ability to regard 'a dish of Boston baked beans and two slices of
bread a day' as a feast.[14] She and Helen did not always see eye to eye, but
they did share a liking for the irrepressible, cheery Morton. In November
1900, Helen observed to J. William Lloyd that *Free Society* was much
improved since Morton 'took it up …. He seems the right man in the
right place.'[15]

Helen's debut in *Free Society* was an article in March 1901 on 'Walt
Whitman's Love of Comrades'. Writing on the 'Calamus' poems, she

described the 'bitter-sweet flag-root' Calamus 'with its earthy fragrance, and the penetrating tang it leaves in the mouth'. Empathetic towards the concealment imposed upon Whitman by convention, she said his life was 'full of the most delightful friendships some of which he could not talk about because they meant so much to him'. For Helen these 'companion-ships' were 'with men and women who loved him'.[16] She did not probe Whitman's cover any further.

William, too, appears in *Free Society* in June 1901, using as his pseud-onym the name of the 1381 leader of the English Peasants' Revolt, 'Wat Tyler', to excoriate 'Robber Barons Old and New'. It was a safe topic; his anarchist readers were unlikely to be fans of Carnegie, Morgan or Rockefeller. Pouring scorn on official hypocrisy towards the use of violence, William commented how the anarchist Gaetano Bresci, who assassinated King Umberto I of Italy, was regarded by the mainstream media with horror, while a lieutenant who killed two striking workers during a street-car strike at Albany, N.Y. was being celebrated as a hero.[17]

William was writing in a period of rapacious capitalist develop-ment when the United States was transporting the violence previously employed against Native and Black Americans into a global scenario. Linking the imperialism of the western powers in China and Amer-ica's brutal suppression of independence movements in Cuba and the Philippines, William held out no hope for an anti-imperialist foreign policy because he regarded international diplomacy as simply an integral part of capitalism.[18]

Mass immigration made organising difficult in industries employing large numbers of unskilled and semi-skilled workers, so the leaders of the American Federation of Labor (A.F.L.), accommodated by focusing on wage rises for skilled white male workers.[19] But William's reading of economics made him doubtful of the ability of workers to make real gains through trade unions. He expressed an equal scepticism about efforts to curb big business and protect workers through state legislation, which he argued was likely to 'boomerang' and be used against them.[20]

Though he believed in 'Spontaneous, non-political, industrial re-organisation', he did not endorse the tactic of the general strike advoc-ated by Mikol and other anarcho-syndicalists.[21] Instead William called for education, the fostering of new values of 'solidarity' and 'self-reliance'.[22] Only an inner change in individuals could effect any viable social transformation. Without such preparation, William warned, the consequences of rebellion would be disastrous, while talk of 'a forcible attack' was 'criminal folly'. William had become convinced that 'An abortive revolution is even more to be feared than a continuance of existing society.'[23]

Profoundly gloomy about labour's capacity to resist, the only action he proposed to his readers was studying 'the laws of development' of social and industrial life.[24] Though overtly critical of the 'determinism' of the followers of Marx, William retained habits of thought from his youthful days in the Marxist S.D.F., observing in 'The Growth of Wealth' on 14 July 1901 how capitalism's colonial wars, trusts and the decline in the rate of interest were 'disintegrating the old forms of society'.[25] He maintained that 'the unthinking mass becomes slowly modified by the unconscious changes which will finally bring economic equality'.[26] With his hopes pinned upon changing culture and consciousness through evolutionary progress, the transition William envisaged was clearly going to be a very long haul indeed.

An article by Walter Leighton in defence of government as a necessary evil disrupted William's perorations.[27] Gloves off, class hackles up, he took a bad-tempered swipe at the 'ponderous persiflage' and 'labored effusion' of the 'Harvard senior'.[28] Morton pitched in, endorsing William's critique of the state with a graphic metaphor, 'At best, government is the wolf which lives off the fox, to render the sheep more surely its own prey.'[29]

Through the summer William laboured doggedly on, resolved to grasp the modern forms capitalism was assuming and follow through their implications. Instead of focusing on the direct exploitation of the workers' capacity to labour and its alienating consequences, as Helena had done, William's gaze shifted to the interest acquired through the accumulation of capital, 'The one class saves what the other class creates.'[30] As capital accumulated, he argued, 'the aggregate share of the product falling to capital is ever increasing'.[31] He observed too how the worker was 'fleeced not only as a wage earner, but also as a consumer',[32] and pointed out that 'national and racial animosities', stoked by 'the ruling classes', affected workers' consciousness.[33]

Unremitting reasoning took him to some unpalatable propositions. On September 8th, in Social Darwinian mode, William remarked: 'The most energetic, intelligent, and resourceful members of the class are constantly moving from it into the ranks of the master class.'[34] Recognising the power of capital was penetrating deep into society, he observed: 'The needs of industrial competition which in its acutest stage means war, demand the most effective organization, politically and economically, the cheapest methods both of administration and of production, and collectivism.'[35] Yet the use of violence to combat such strategies was anathema to William as an anarchist committed to individual freedom and hounded by a dread of revolution leading not to 'a free society but to a collectivist economic despotism'.[36]

Readers of *Free Society* were likely to accept William's critique of capitalism and imperialism and agree with his scepticism about the impact of both state reforms and trade unions. Yet William's long-term perspective was hardly arousing and his extreme caution about all forms of immediate action must have been exasperating. His apprehension and his logic led him towards a series of impasses which he never could break through.

Sensing he was not making converts, in his September 8th article William protested, 'let none suppose I am pessimistic'. Aware he was assailing shibboleths, he bared his breast and declared, 'I anticipate criticism and await it in the spirit of truth-seeking and fraternity.'[37] Sure enough, the attacks rolled in. For one anarchist-communist reader, he displayed 'arrogant superiority towards the Communists', while A.L. Ballou, sniffing Individualist infiltration, grumbled, 'Comrade Tyler ... floods us with an "Anarchist Economics"' that implied 'Anarchist Communism is authoritarian'.[38] He wondered whether 'Tyler' and his associates were motivated by a hope they might 'mount the ladder of wealth'.[39] It was an unkind cut at a group who bore little resemblance to robber barons.

William's pursuit of absolute truth made it difficult for him to settle comfortably in any particular group or tendency. In Manchester he had doubted 'Communism', then in *Liberty* he had detected flaws in Individualist Anarchist thinking; now he was at loggerheads with the anarchist communists around *Free Society*. His predilection for nosing out potential problems made this intensely political man ill-suited to politics in practice – even libertarian left politics.

On 6 September 1901, William's Cassandra-like fears about the adoption of violent means were tragically borne out when a young worker from the wire factories at the edge of Cleveland, Leon Czolgosz, shot President McKinley.[40] Repression followed; Helen's journal entry that day was, 'The "Free Society" Isaaks arrested in Chicago.'[41] The following day she wrote, 'Cussedness supreme. Great outcry against the anarchists.'[42]

Czolgosz was from a poor Polish immigrant farming family. Both his own life and his reading contributed to an interest in socialist and anarchist ideas. In May 1901 he may have been inspired by hearing Emma Goldman's speech at the Franklin Liberal Club in Cleveland where she had opposed violent methods, but praised the 'high and noble motives' of the perpetuators of propaganda by deed.[43] Goldman's defence of anarchists who adopted violence against authoritarian rulers was not dissimilar from the sympathetic response of many liberals to the Russian 'Nihilists' in an earlier era. The difference was, of course, one of context, and the fact that the young Polish-American took such remarks literally.

An agitated Czolgosz, expressing admiration for the Italian assassin Gaetano Bresci, alarmed anarchists in Cleveland who took him for an agent provocateur. Indeed, a warning against him as 'a police spy' went into *Free Society*, leading Emma Goldman, who had met Czolgosz at the Cleveland meeting, to send an angry riposte in his defence.[44] On September 8th, Helen announced, 'Hunt for Emma Goldman'.[45] The police found her on September 10th, attired in 'a jaunty white sailor hat, white waist, blue skirt, belt and neck-tie'.[46] Carrying a copy of Edward Carpenter's *Towards Democracy* in her hand, Goldman was led to jail.

A worried Archibald Simpson, reliving the paranoia and persecution surrounding the Haymarket bombing, called round on September 11th to confer with Helen and William. On the 14th Helen documented McKinley's death; on the 19th she 'wrote letters to Chicago', presumably on behalf of the Isaaks.[47] To her evident relief, on September 23rd Helen could state: 'The Isaaks and the rest of Free Society's editors, 9 in all – freed. They had been visited by Czolgosz, thought him crazy, and had warned their readers about him.'[48] The journal entry on the 24th was, 'Emma Goldman released. Police admit no case against the anarchists.'[49] Despite being tortured, Czolgosz insisted he had acted alone and would not implicate others. He was executed on October 29th.[50]

Instead of going by the propaganda-by-deed scrip and rousing the supine masses, the attack on McKinley fed hostility towards anarchists, enabling the extreme right to brand them all as potential terrorists. The notorious private detective, Robert A. Pinkerton, recommended that an island in the Philippines should be turned into a prison to detain every anarchist in America. Only those who informed on others were to be spared. An enraged William retaliated with a defence of free speech in *Free Society*, denouncing the 'lynx-eyed Pinkerton' for proposing to recruit Secret Service agents from the ranks of 'peaceable Anarchists'.[51] His warning of more extensive suppression proved correct; the panic and suspicion spilled over to include socialists and immigrants. It also strained links between liberals and the left, weakening the vital protective buffer created by networks of alliances that had arisen from a series of campaigns.

Most painful for William and Helen was the sharpening of divisions among anarchists over 'propaganda by deed'. After Czolgosz' torture and execution, the initial suspicion towards him had dissipated; while criticising his action, Emma Goldman, along with other anarchists, praised the principles and courage of the frail and sensitive young assassin. To William and Helen, in contrast, Czolgosz was dangerously deranged. At first Helen tried invoking the transcendental tolerance inherited from Helena. In *Free Society* on 10 November 1901, remembering the Chicago anarchists, she sought to assuage the 'wounds of conflict' that periodically afflicted anarchism:

> Let us at once realize that differ though we may among ourselves, we agree in one common ideal, the emancipation of the human race. Let us ever remember the higher aspect of the Great Idea; and let us sink petty differences, … in our struggle to embody that Truth which is vaster and more inclusive than any one individual's range of thought.[52]

She had been going through Miriam's writings, and, in December 1901, *Free Society* reprinted 'In Robes of Anarchy', which began with the apt lines, 'Truth came to me oft in varying dress,/And still she stood revealed in loveliness'.[53] Helen wanted a libertarian left that could agree to disagree.

Like Helena, she also yearned for a broad, experiential fellowship: 'beyond all teaching and preaching is actual living'.[54] Morton had settled in the anarchist community in Home, near Tacoma in Washington State, where he was producing their paper *Discontent*. It offered Helen a congenial outlet, and she sent him a long extract from an article by Joseph Dana Miller, which had been published in the November issue of *The Arena*. The Boston-based journal challenged social ills while calling for new moral and spiritual values, and Helen commended Miller's call for reformers to show themselves 'superior to the faults and foibles' of existing society.[55] Helen linked this personal witnessing to the communality fostered at Home.

In a similar vein she welcomed a new left cultural magazine, *The Comrade*, informing *Free Society* readers that the common root of both socialism and anarchism was 'Love'. Singling out poems by three socialistic Carpenter enthusiasts – Edwin Markham, famous for his poem against the inhuman consequences of harsh labour, 'The Man with the Hoe'; Ernest Crosby, a Tolstoyan pacifist; and the Christian Social-ist, George D. Herron – Helen predicted the socialists' 'Co-operative Commonwealth' and the anarchists' 'Voluntary State' could grow 'side by side, mingling ... leafage and ... blossoms'.[56]

Helen's hopes of libertarian left commingling proved rather too optimistic. However, Traubel's *Conservator* continued to be an important non-sectarian space, and in December 1901, Helen sent him Miriam's moving last poems with an explanatory letter.[57] Not only did Traubel reprint them, he also ran Helen's review of Charles W. Chesnutt's *The Marrow of Tradition*. Based on the testimonies of African-American sur-vivors of a racist attack by whites in Wilmington, North Carolina in 1898, Helen found it 'burns into the soul'.[58] Impressed by Chesnutt, the son of 'free persons of color', his book convinced her that 'negroes them-selves' would effect their 'emancipation'. Her conclusion was that race, as well as class injustice, had to be challenged through a wide 'brotherhood of man'.[59] This review, which marked a significant shift in Helen's atti-tudes to race, placed her out on a limb, for *The Marrow of Tradition* was regarded by critics as 'bitter'.[60]

Over the course of 1901, Helen was submitting articles, working on her collection of Helena's writings, withstanding the conflicts following Czolgosz' assassination of McKinley, and seeking to assuage her own sorrows. Moreover, she was holding down an increasingly demanding full-time job at Houghton Mifflin. At last she had achieved her ambition of reading manuscripts, and was laboriously sorting and typing Thoreau's manuscripts and scrapbooks for publication.

In the meantime, the Tufts' family home in Cambridge was imploding. William Tufts speculation mania had resumed, and Helen was digging once again into her savings to keep her parents afloat. She notes in her journal that her father was 'venturing on margin and losing'.[61] William Tufts was taking himself off to his brokers and investing borrowed money, only to incur yet more debt.

Defending her father to her 'dear true love', Helen insisted, 'His motives are all good; it is his judgment that is lacking.' Deciding that the only way to stop the disastrous financial gambling was to find her seventy-year-old father a new career in journalism, Helen begged William to use his newspaper contacts: 'What I think you may be able to do is to get the right sort of Irish pull and work him in as a literary man who will favor the democrats, Ireland, and Catholic benevolent work etc. Perhaps you don't think he will fit that bill – but you leave it to me.'[62] William might love Helen, but he was not a prestidigitator who could convince hard-bitten Irish Bostonian newspapermen they needed William Tufts! It was an ironic turn of events. When her father had been a young man, the Irish were immigrant outsiders; now they held political power and cultural influence in Boston and a previously haughty Helen was pleading for 'Irish pull'. She escaped from the 'dreadful' atmosphere at home to William's room at 305 Columbus Avenue whenever she could.

Just before Christmas 1901, William Tufts suffered a heart attack while he was in his 'broker's office'. Sent home in a hack, he was told by the doctor he had not long to live; the Moloch of finance was about to claim its victim. Conscious to the end, he sat in a 'rocking chair, wrapped in a quilt', until Helen heard him say to her mother, 'Oh, Belle, I'm falling away.'[63] Isabel and Helen rushed to him and he died in their arms. On December 29th they buried him in the Tufts' family lot at Mount Auburn Cemetery – where long ago William had somersaulted amid the graves.

The family might retain its lot, but Helen's father's death marked the end of any semblance of parental authority. William's landlady, 'Miss Cheney', was a woman of advanced views and Helen was able to move in with William.[64] Despite leaving home, Helen's familial responsibilities continued, for after the death of Grandfather Terrill in 1902, Isabel Tufts also took a room with Miss Cheney, and Russell, who had begun to drink heavily, was frequently there. The two of them clustered around Helen, as if she had morphed into head of the household. One emotional weight, however, had removed himself. Walter had given up. He now confined himself to ruminating on jealousy in letters to an empathetic Horace Traubel, and pursuing his studies.[65] In 1908 Walter's thesis from the University of Virginia was completed on *French Philosophers and New England Transcendentalism*.[66]

Helen's own working relationship with Traubel as an editor had continued to be easy and affectionate, and she was particularly fond of his wife, Anne Montgomerie, with whom she also corresponded. She must have felt she had established a niche when an unexpected hitch occurred in her previously uncomplicated dealings with Traubel. On 27 May 1902 Helen sent *The Conservator* an unsolicited review of Edward Carpenter's compilation, *Ioläus: An Anthology of Friendship*, asking Traubel to send it back if he could not use it. The bookseller, Charles Eliot Goodspeed, who was helping Traubel, gave it an automatic go ahead, then abruptly reversed the decision, stating the book had 'already been sent out for review'.[67]

Traubel, aware that Carpenter was concerned about the American response to his collection of accounts of same-sex love through the ages, must have intervened. Although Carpenter diplomatically describes its theme as 'comrade attachment' and 'romantic friendship', the lovers speak for themselves in *Ioläus*.[68] Traubel's short review of Carpenter's book intimates his own feelings for the Whitmanite dentist, Wiksell. 'We are always talking of love and brotherhood but any attempt to add to either in unusual ways is met with persecution.' He knew from his own experience, 'You meet love in the unexpected ... You see how men ache for love they dare neither give nor accept ... It is a love full of sex yet greater than sex.'[69]

A distracted Traubel forgot to return Helen's spiked review and she had to claim it back for *Free Society*, where it was published in September 1902.[70] Needless to say, Helen's take on the book was somewhat different. Recognising it as 'a companion' to Carpenter's 1894 pamphlet *Homo-genic Love*, Helen distinguished between the unsuitable passions of 'the ancients', marked by 'what we would term grossness', though no doubt existing 'on purely spiritual planes', and 'the comrade-love' celebrated by Whitman. Helen believed that modern 'Friendship' expressed that 'craving of the human soul for love and for loving which is differentiated from sex-love'. Helen, herself, had known such love through her friendship with Helena; but she misunderstood what Carpenter was about.[71]

William continued to slug it out with critics of his attempts to develop anarchist economic theory in *Free Society*; but the decisive rift came early in 1902 over Czolgosz. In February, William stated bluntly that McKinley's assassin was clearly mad. As Czolgosz' action resulted from his delusions, it followed that it could not be regarded as politically motivated, or as in any way related to anarchism. William's case was based on the evidence of two doctors who disagreed with the initial diagnosis of Czolgosz which had decreed him sane. He argued the insanity of the assassin not only took 'the wind out' of Teddy Roosevelt's 'blustering sails', but would 'bury the anti-Anarchist bills of congressional busy bodies in a cloud of everlasting ridicule'.[72]

William ignored two crucial emotional and political factors. Czolgosz alive might have been regarded suspiciously by anarchists, but Czolgosz executed was a very different matter. Moreover, the definition of insanity was ideologically loaded, for late nineteenth-century social theorists had devised elaborate typologies that transposed radical beliefs into mental illness. *Free Society* contributors pointed out that Czolgosz' 'madness' was defined by his opposition to government, the law, marriage and God, because such opinions were associated by a conservative criminology with social degeneration. Abe Isaak Junior, who helped his parents produce *Free Society*, remarked wryly that 'Wat Tyler' himself 'would surely qualify' for the same categorisation.[73] One of William's harshest critics was the anarchist Kate Austin. Despite being seriously ill with consumption, Austin wrote a vigorous rejection of the claim of insanity and its concomitant implication that anarchists were 'socially diseased'.[74] Austin was deeply respected, and her words carried even greater force because she was so ill.[75] Emma Goldman, too, denied Czolgosz' insanity, despite having received death threats for defending him.[76]

Propelled by his own conscience to engage in political controversy, William, who was increasingly engrossed in his history of the life and ideas of Josiah Warren, was showing signs of battle fatigue. The essay on Warren he contributed to George Lockwood's *The New Harmony Communities* (1902) provides a model for internal disputes among comrades. William briskly informs us that Warren left the Owenite's New Harmony, 'not like so many others, as an embittered reactionary, but as an earnest, hopeful student who had spent his time to good purpose'.[77] Unfortunately, political splits had a tendency to be more messy.

It would be Helen who reopened the dispute over Czolgosz' action in the columns of *Free Society* on 21 December 1902. Angrily, she denounced the comparisons being made in the paper between him and the 'Chicago Martyrs' as 'eulogies on the act of a lunatic'. Pointing out that McKinley had not been regarded as a 'tyrant' by the 'great mass of the people' in the United States, she insisted it was folly to think they would see any point in his murder. On the contrary, his assassination had enhanced his reputation.[78]

Kate Austin had died and it was her friend, the anarchist lawyer, William T. Holmes, who took up Czolgosz' defence. Along with his wife Lizzie, Holmes had been closely associated with the British Socialist League, sending reports from America to *Commonweal*. Holmes, who had known the men executed for the Haymarket bombing, was confident they might have 'condemned the deed itself as unnecessary and unwise', but would not have endorsed Helen's 'feelings of indignation and abhorrence of Czolgosz himself'.[79] Helen responded by trying to deny that the Chicago Martyrs had advocated armed resistance, before metaphorically packing her bags and retreating with the declaration that the 'divergences' between 'Comrade Holmes' and herself were 'irreconcilable'.[80] The 'higher aspect of the Great Idea' had bit the dust.

Helen's intervention was partly fired by the fallout from the assassination of McKinley at Home, where the anarchists had been subjected to a sustained witch-hunt. In 1902, one of the residents, the veteran campaigner for free love and women's rights, Lois Waisbrooker, had been arrested along with the local post mistress, Mattie D. Penhallow, and accused of disseminating obscene material. Waisbrooker's article, 'The Awful Fate of Fallen Women', published in her anarchist paper, *Clothed with the Sun*, was deemed obscene and Waisbrooker was found guilty. Mattie D. Penhallow was acquitted, but the Postmaster General closed Home's post office. Undaunted, in 1903 Morton started a new paper, *The Demonstrator*, from Lakebay, the site of the nearest post office.[81]

Penhallow spent the winter of 1902 to 1903 in Boston, forming a warm friendship with Helen. Helen was sorry when she had to leave, sending an account to *The Demonstrator* of their delightful 'long talks', with feasts of 'oranges, crackers, and wine' as well as meals of 'chop suey and chow mein' in Chinatown. She mentions their rush to the gallery at Ibsen's *Ghosts*, with the comment, 'in which at least one of your present number was wont to indulge years ago in Boston'. Morton, evidently remembering the hold up caused by his Shakespeare recitation, inserted '[Guilty – J.F.M]'.[82]

The two women grew very close, personally and politically, that winter. Helen gazed longingly at Penhallow's photographs of distant Home, 'the bay and the cluster of houses fringing the shore, all encircled by the forest'. She, in turn, brought out her precious pictures of Helena at Epsom. They both attended meetings of the newly formed Boston Social Science Club, which gathered 'on Sunday afternoons to discuss social and economic questions from the Anarchist stand point'.[83] Similar clubs had begun to appear in other American cities and were open to participants who were not necessarily anarchists. At a time when anarchists were being vilified, they offered lectures and broad discussion; Penhallow went to hear William, as well as Archibald Simpson and the anarchist defender of free speech, Adeline Champney. The former Home postmistress also attended William's 'reminiscences and estimate' of William Morris at the

Walt Whitman Fellowship, along with Ernest Crosby on Tolstoy and the Unitarian writer on Transcendentalism, George Willis Cooke, whom Helen describes as 'a close and earnest student of sociology, and an enthusiastic recent convert to Socialism (In its broader Spiritual significance)'.[84]

Helen could accommodate spiritual socialists. Like Helena, she placed great emphasis upon encouraging new forms of relating and the *processes* of radical politics, valuing the Social Science Club and the Walt Whitman Fellowship for the ethos of freedom in which '"the other side"' was respected and all radical views were recognised as having 'a bearing'. In her 'Boston Letter' to the *Demonstrator* she stated that 'both groups were run on lines of anarchism'.[85] Penhallow and Home helped Helen to keep faith with Helena's desire to prefigure democratic co-operation through fellowship.

Conversely, William kept a foot in mainstream politics. In October 1902 he chaired a rally on Tariff Reform where the Democratic candidate for the House of Representatives, John A. Sullivan, spoke along with Boston municipal politicians.[86] Adversity had taught William to suppress utopianism. He had acquired lower expectations about personal relationships within radical groups and was prepared to make strategic alliances. His own experience, combined with his research into the history of American utopian social movements, had bred caution. Aware of the slip between cup and lip, William observed in his essay for Lockwood that dwelling in 'Communist' New Harmony had convinced Josiah Warren that 'any theory of reform, however perfect or plausible, should be put to the test before being offered to the world as a remedy for existing evils'.[87]

Yet William's youthful attraction to imagining what might be was not completely extinguished. In his essay on Warren, he describes the Modern Times community:

Broad avenues, tree-shaded streets, pretty cottages surrounded by strawberry-beds and well-tilled gardens, formed the outward appearance of Modern Times. The occupants were honest, industrious and had learned to mind their own business, while readily co-operating with their neighbors for mutual advantage. They were free from sectarian dissensions, law-courts, jails, rumshops, prostitutes, and crime. No one acquired wealth save by his own industry.[88]

A virtual Modern Times lurked within William's own mind's eye.

EIGHTEEN

Romancing the West: 1902–1908

The town of Shasta, the site of Robert and Gertrude's passionate tryst, was the ideal spot for a writer looking for a nostalgic West. Placed on three converging rivers, it had grown up as a supply centre for the miners during the gold rush of the 1840s and, apart from the women who worked the saloons, had initially been a male town. When a minority of resourceful female 'respectables' first appeared, they adapted to carrying small 'muff' guns and using rifles against burglars, unruly menfolk and a species of local giant rats.[1] It may not have been coincidental that several of its women-folk went on to embrace moral reform causes and later suffrage.

By the late nineteenth century Shasta's decline had set in and its growth halted when the Southern Pacific Railroad built a terminus at nearby Redding, which became the county seat. Residents of Shasta might sneer at the suffocating temperature of Redding in the summer, contrasting it with their 'healthy mountain Eden', but in modern Redding, Shasta was disdained as a 'has-been' town. Despite a brief spurt of optimism in 1901, when gold was found nearby, most of the old sites had been exhausted.[2] Fading Shasta did, however, hold an allure for artistic adventurers. The town could offer visitors and residents alike a smattering of culture through Literary Society events and musical theatrical performances in the old courthouse, while its boom-town legacy ensured a plentiful supply of elegant hotels.[3]. Robert's reference in his June letter to their 'little home in Shasta' sounds more like lodgings than a hotel, and the couple appear far too preoccupied with 'caresses and dear wide envelopings' to be sampling Shasta's literary evenings.[4]

Robert casts himself in courtly terms, kneeling 'to my White Lady', kissing 'her feet', and announcing he was 'born to love a woman – to worship, to serve, yea, to be equal mate of a great dear woman, my Gertrude Mary'. When he tosses her 'a kiss' from the Copper Mine, he writes, 'Not a vacant recognition of your lips, but a cool, fiery darting, gently descending kiss – and you cannot, Oh you cannot push it away for I insist.' His workaday trip to the Mountain Copper Company is elevated into his need to withdraw in order 'to see thee, as we saw Mt. Shasta last eve, in all your amorous red-hearted beauty. To learn that my life was encircled by thine and that I had penetrated into thy secret place.'[5]

Robert promises to 'descend … on Wednesday evening' and, after reporting somewhat bathetically on his lunch of hot tea, mutton chops and stewed rhubarb pie, muses, 'How is it that one individual becomes so utterly merged with another so that everything, – eating, sleeping, having babies and novels, … romping and chasing one another, are of intimate concern and delightful, delicious concern too! Ah, it is like wine-nectar.' With a nod to Carpenter's *Towards Democracy*, he imagines bending Gertrude's body back, gathering up her 'loins and bosoms and tender limbs' so that he could fly with her 'naked as Adam … thro the canyons and forests'.[6]

He sends his 'love to Bopeep Sunrise', now denoted as 'one of our progeny', and imagines the arrival of a 'darling boy – from out thy ruddy womb and pearly sheath of thy body. A kiss to thy fiery top-knot.'[7] As it turned out, Robert spoke too soon, Gertrude was not pregnant, which was probably just as well, as he was still technically married to Jutie.

Gertrude the novelist might have composed along more literary lines, but Gertrude the woman was in love with the tall, handsome Californian Scot and prepared to apply a lover's willing suspension of disbelief to the letter from 'The Mine'. She preserved and cherished Robert's ardent, magniloquent missive all her life – through the thick and the thin of their relationship.

Gertrude's passionate love for Robert took her to White-nights ranch, Weimar, Placer County, and a life that was utterly different from any-thing she had known before. Though the railway was extending its reach into the Sierras, small communities like Weimar and other nearby former mining settlements were mainly still dependent on horse-drawn stagecoaches and covered wagons. Otherwise, walking or going on horse-back were the only means of transport on offer. By the early 1900s the Placer West and County Improvement and Development Association was trying hard to attract settlers and tourists, promoting not simply property and commerce, but Californian hope. From its base in Auburn, it extolled 'Earliest and best oranges' as well as 'Choicest Extensive Mining'. Gold was only to be found on rare occasions, but quartz was plentiful, and mining, with its promise of quick fortunes, encouraged those with a gambling spirit. The 'snow clad peaks' and 'yawning canyons' of the Sierras had also begun to gain a reinvigorating reputation, and the area around Weimar was now well stashed with alternative healers and psychic seers.[8] They, too, were gambling with hope.

Robert, unlike Gertrude, was truly at home at White-nights. In old age he described himself as 'aching for the Sierras'. He missed the 'warm days', the dry air and the cold nights of the mountains' foothills. Most of all he missed the 'brightness of the stars'.[9] Amid the wildness of the countryside Robert attached himself symbolically to the traces left by earlier inhabitants. In the canyon near the ranch stood a 'big Live Oak under which the Indians used to pound their acorns in the pot-holes in the big Rock from which the Oak sprang'.[10] He was fascinated too, by the tunnels left by the gold miners and later by the railway tunnel burrowing under the ground near the ranch.[11]

Robert Allan Nicol (Courtesy of Georges Rey, Private Collection)

In contrast, in 1903 Gertrude was on Robert's terrain, pregnant and contriving to bond with twelve-year-old Sunrise, who, as a wild child Californian, was unlikely to have relished being domesticated by the literary English woman. Gertrude, with her English voice, elaborate manners and learned references, must have seemed a bizarre figure to Sunrise. Strain was likely on both sides.

On 9 February 1903, Robert and Jutie M. Terry Coan Nicol had divorced by mutual consent in Placer County, leaving Robert free to marry Gertrude, though the marriage licence was not issued until April 8th. Gertrude and Robert's first child, a girl, was born on November 6th. They called her 'Margaret', like Robert's mother and sister.[12] Gertrude, still adjusting to life in the ranch, faced the anxieties of being a first-time mother far from her life and friends in London. Her own knowledge of nursing and whatever Robert could recall from his medical student days would have been their main practical recourse.

Confronted by an alien habitat, a step-daughter and motherhood all at once, Gertrude faced a tough challenge. Her response was to do what she had always done, write. Once baby Margaret became a toddler, Gertrude found her own pathways through the foothills of the Sierras by romancing the West. Surrounded by the vast, craggy, deserted landscape, she mined it metaphorically, along with her relationship with Robert.

In February 1905 she sold 'The Cry on the Trail: How it Wrought a Great Change at Lone Pine Ranch' to the *San Francisco Argonaut*, and, thanks to the wonders of the American system of syndication, it was later reprinted in several other newspapers. The tale opens with a Robert-style character, Gerald Geraldson, on a ranch in the middle of nowhere: 'In the high, bare sitting-room of a lonely ranch house, with brown, unpainted walls, and doors and windows open to the pine-clad mountain side, a man sat at a small deal table reading over a pile of cherished letters.'[13] We learn these had been sent from Beacon Street, Boston, by a woman called Elsie Vining who wrote about books, music and art. Gerald longs for the intellectual treasure-house she communicated, and also for something simpler, a home, a fireside, the woman herself.

Gertrude explains to the reader how Lone Pine ranch was so isolated that no visitors appeared for weeks. A tiny child of three, called Margery, adopted after her father died, was Gerald's only companion. After corresponding with Elsie Vining for several years, he finally threw restraint aside and confessed his love. For years he had wanted to ask her to come out to be with him but poverty had made this impossible.

Gertrude Dix, c. early 1900s (Courtesy
of Georges Rey, Private Collection)

His hopes had been raised by a recent prospecting venture. But this
had failed.

However, before he could post the letter Gerald collapses from malaria.
His last desperate act before passing out is to tell the child to go down the
trail and call out. There, by good fortune, she is found by Elsie Vining
who has travelled all the way from Boston and usefully happens to be a
nurse. She also happens to possess the most beautiful white hands and
to move in ways the semi-conscious patient notes are quite unlike those
of a local mountain woman. The face of his unknown rescuer, however,
remains concealed by a large blue sun bonnet – just the kind of bonnet a
red-haired and freckled Gertrude would have needed to shield her from
the Californian sun. The precocious Margery gives the visitor the letter
Gerald never sent, declaring she must be 'the lady daddy talks about that's
coming to be my muvver'.[14] Assuming Margery to be a child from a
marriage he has not disclosed, Elsie Vining embraces the chubby three-
year-old nonetheless.

When, at last, Gerald identifies his nurse, 'She dropped on her knees
beside him. She gave him her hands and her face.'[15] Gertrude portrays
Gerald as helpless, passive and adoring, which may well have been how,
in part, she wished Robert to be. Her own passion for Robert pervades
the story; like Elsie Vining she, too, had written 'intellectual' letters

to her Californian, and several years had apparently passed before she or Robert came to reveal their attraction towards one another. Had it 'seemed' to Gertrude, as it did to Elsie, that 'so much had passed without words between them', when she had met Robert in Bristol? Echoing Rosalind Dangerfield and Justin Ferrar, the Elsie character had found Gerald's letters 'cold' and feared she was 'no more than an abstraction' to him.[16] Despite Robert's excessive expressions of love, perhaps Gertrude had already encountered an aspect of his character which was noted later by his children and grandchildren.

Gertrude acquired glory and $50 in April 1905, when her short story, 'Pardners', was awarded a prize by the *San Francisco Call*. The newspaper plugged Miss Dix's 'widely read novels', explaining that although English by birth, she had spent 'many years in a close study of California mining'. This was, of course, pure hype, though her story does include a reference to the Chinese who continued panning for gold after the rush subsided. The by-line announcing 'Pardners' as 'highly literary and very human' was more accurate. Gertrude's account of the jealousy and eventual rec- onciliation of two old gold prospectors, Brand and Gilbert, who had both loved the same woman, Juanita, is well-crafted. It also features 'the great oak tree' from White-nights ranch.[17]

In June 1905, Gertrude's 'A Flight into the Mountains' was accepted by the prestigious *Munsey's Magazine*, which catered for an aspiring middle- class readership. In the early 1890s, technological advances in paper and photography had enabled *Munsey's* to lower its price and gain a mass readership with a mix of short stories, features and advertisements. The magazine catered for a yearning for excitement, glamour and a distinct- ive individualised fantasy self. Readers could wash with Pears' soap, pass through 'The Portal to Beauty' and 'leave hopeless homeliness behind', or cross the frontiers of the Wild West with writers like Gertrude.[18]

'A Flight into the Mountains' tells of an escaped convict, Lawson, who stops to save the life of a man hurt when debris falls on him from the roof of a tunnel. Unlike the wounded man and his companions, Lawson is 'ascetic' from 'over-study'. He cares for the wounded man, working 'with all the knowledge of a clever medical student'.[19] When his identity is revealed the teamsters demonstrate a rough justice in allowing him to escape rather than claiming the reward on his head. Gertrude's sympath- ies are with the fugitive; Robert, along with his haunts, the tunnels and the nearby Codfish Canyon, provides the copy.

*   *   *

Gertrude was thirty-seven when a second daughter, Amaryllis, was born on 31 July 1905. Robert was close at hand, for as an old man he told her:

> As soon as you were born you were handed to me and I gave you your very first bath in Olive Oil. I can see you in my arms and all the doors and windows were open as the night was very warm. The stars were shining brightly as they always do in the Sierras and the night was completely calm and absolutely quiet. Not a coyote gave a single yelp.[20]

A decade before, when Robert was writing to Carpenter, White-nights had been predominantly male. Now, however, Robert was surrounded by femininity, and an adolescent Sunrise had two small half-sisters. Robert's earnings continued to be sporadic. In later life, his eldest daughter, Margaret, having changed her name to the more exotic sounding 'Margot', explained to a friend, Edna Eldred, that Robert 'inclined toward philosophy and had inherited small money'. A puzzled Eldred concluded that a meagre private income enabled the British to regard being 'a Gentleman' as sufficient.[21] Robert, the scion of the Dunfermline clothes shop, was mysteriously gentrified by his life on a California ranch; he continued to be convinced he had prospects, even though they never quite materialised.

In contrast, Gertrude resolutely wrote on. Robert recalled 'how she would come down the trail from the Post Office when she had sold a story shouting, "Another story sold"'.[22] She abandoned Hegel and psychological novel writing to join the ranks of writers churning out dramatic stories for a burgeoning popular market. The timing was right. The population was expanding; basic literacy and wages were both relatively high, while the railroad meant speedy distribution was possible on a mass scale. America was becoming the home of spin, and, spotting a lucrative market, advertisers were keen to cash in. The magazine *Out West* announced itself as 'For the Out Door Life', marketing 'Gold Pans, Pocket Smelters, … Guns, Ammunition, Fishing Tackle' with literary kudos.[23] Its writers included the spiritual socialist, Edwin Markham, bohemian 'poet of the Sierras', Joaquin Miller, and Charlotte Perkins Gilman, whose ideas on women's social and economic freedom Helena had admired.

Gertrude's story, 'The Passing of the Forty-Niner', appeared in *Out West* in May 1906. A stronger reworking of the 'Pardners' theme of overcoming deep antagonisms, it also features two old prospectors. Ropes, 'the outcast of the river', cares for Featherstone, his prosperous and formerly aloof neighbour, wounded by a rock fall in a tunnel where he had been working. As the dying man's mind wanders to past claims – Lone Star, Black Oak, Brown Bear – Ropes mentions a tale of treasure being buried under 'the big oak at the head of the cañon where the Indians used to meet', but Featherstone tells him not to mention Indians for they had killed his child.[24] The old prospector explains he had remained not for the gold but because his wife was buried 'under the oak tree at the back of the cabin where the white stone lies'.[25] Fearful of facing Featherstone's death, Ropes nonetheless suppresses his impulse to flee and waits until two hunters come by from Yankee Jim's (the staging post from gold rush days which was a favourite of Robert's). Ropes is resolved to ensure that the dying man will be buried beside his wife, '"I'm no coward"' he keeps saying to himself. Ropes finds dignity and pride in service, muttering, 'But I stayed … I was no deserter.'[26]

By 1906 Gertrude was becoming established as a writer of Western short stories as well as novels. Her 1906 entry in *The Literary Year Book*, published in New York as well as London, shows that 'Dix, Gertrude (Mrs Nicol)' of 'Weimar, California', was acquiring a reputation in America.[27] Moreover, that December she was being promoted as one of the 'best' of the 'well-known writers' to be published by *The People's Magazine*, puffed as 'decidedly the strongest short-story magazine sold for 10 cents'.[28] Its cover that month may well have contributed to its buoyant sales by featuring 'an unusually pretty girl, in a broad brimmed felt hat, secured by a flowing automobile veil tied under her chin'.[29] Gertrude was being packaged as part of the dream driving a new mass culture in America – personal freedom.

But her story 'The Wandering Angels', also published in *The People's Magazine*, evoked another America, the grim Frankenstein of raw human energy fuelling material wealth. Set in 'the smelter camp of Kendal', it is surely based on Robert's accounts of Keswick. Gertrude relates how a clergyman, Peter Chalfont, reaches the camp searching for his lost brother Arnold. He had travelled from his church in Chelsea, London, and had met the general manager of the Western Mining Company, the 'Massive, leonine, dominant, Hawkins', at a shareholders' meeting in London's Lombard Street.[30]

Gertrude stresses the grotesque symbiosis between the two worlds; one cultivated and genteel, the other monstrous and inhuman. Coughing in the camp's 'sulphurous smoke', the refined Chalfont is dazed by the 'great wheels' spinning 'in a white glare' in 'a power-house', while the 'red gleam' of the furnaces seem like the 'eyes of wakeful beasts lurking in the shadows'. Far below, in 'a sort of pit', men run 'to and fro like ants' creating the capital that an appalled Chalfont realises flows into his church. He discovers his brother Arnold 'sleeping in the bunk-house – built of rough lumber', the tiers of bunks covered only by dirty cotton wool quilts.[31] Their mother arrives just as Arnold is injured; nursed back to health, his memory conveniently wiped, the prodigal is reclaimed for an English middle-class life. The deaths and maiming of the other miners are quickly forgotten, and new, despised immigrants, Slavs and Italians, take their place. 'The Wandering Angels' went global, appearing in the New Zealand *Star* in 1908, and Burnley's *Express and Advertiser* in Britain the following year.

Gertrude's romanticised tale, 'The Last Flicker of the Candle', published in *Out West* early in 1907, was in a different vein. Monsieur De la Roche, a 'natural leader' in 'the revolutionary epoch of '48', had become the owner of a Californian orange-grove. Now confined to a wheelchair, he is attended by Armitage, 'the strangest of orange-pickers. The texture of his skin had the softness of fine breeding. The material of his negligée shirt was a flat contradiction to the clumsy stiffness of new overalls.'[32] Madame De la Roche suspects Armitage of being the secret suitor of her granddaughter Yvonne, and is determined that she should be speedily married to the wealthy Joseph Fernandez. Fortune, however smiles on true love, for at the eleventh hour, Fernandez is revealed to be the descendent of a terrible Mexican bandit who had been shot by De La Roche in the 1860s. Yvonne is able to marry her well-bred Armitage, and the diplomatic priest, 'Father Russell', presents her with a glass of wine, 'with the reflection that he was glad he had not been obliged to marry her to the Mexican'.[33] The old world's ethnic hierarchies were reproduced in the apparent wilderness, 'out west'.

Early in 1907, Gertrude's brother Clement, perhaps exploring the prospects of mining as a career, paid a second trip to the United States, presumably visiting his sister and her husband, whom he had inadvertently helped to bring together. He is on record as arriving back in Liverpool on 4 May 1907. That October, Gertrude too was back in Britain, leaving Margaret and Amaryllis with Robert and Sunrise; journeying via Boston, she reached Glasgow on October 28th. Gertrude would have been in the early stage of pregnancy when she left. She was forty when her third child, a boy this time, Robert Dix Nicol, was born on 16 June 1908.[34]

In the same year, Gertrude had two stories published in *Out West*, 'The Apples of Hesperides' and 'The Mystery of Miranda'. Peace and quiet must have been rare, and Gertrude had resorted to working in one of the huts near the ranch house. Familiar with the chaos of a young family, in 'The Apples of Hesperides', she describes the children of a Mexican miner, Martinez, running and shouting 'in so many places at once that they appeared to multiply themselves into unaccountable numbers'.[35] 'Mr Martinez' is portrayed as a natural aristocrat who plays the violin 'with the air of a Spanish grandee', nevertheless, the children are reviled as 'greasers' at the local school. Again an outsider acts as a catalyst. When an old Captain from the gold rush returns, Martinez greets him with a hopeful march on the violin, before switching empathetically to a sad refrain, for the survivor has returned from his wanderings to find 'only the ghosts of dead friends and half-forgotten things'.[36]

The sailor skilfully makes wooden brigs and schooners for the children, which little Joe Martinez thoughtfully sells to help the penniless old man. Moreover, the visitor has brought with him the seeds of a very special kind of golden apple from the mountains of Washington, and plans to create an orchard. 'It is better to grow things', he tells the boy's father, 'Mining's dangerous' – a view with which Gertrude concurred.[37] The orchard he envisions is a magical place where 'a dryad', or perhaps an 'angel', like those who had been part of Gertrude's childhood, greets him. Joe Martinez finds the 'Capitano' lying on the grass and drops the gold he has brought for him from the sale of the ships. In death the old man finds eternal youth with the mythical 'Apples of Hesperides'.[38]

In 'The Mystery of Miranda', Gertrude more successfully makes fun of the middle-class literary milieu she knew. 'Miss Margaret Arden' arrives in New York, having left a Californian ranch. She had been 'suffering from want of success and will-power' and had found ranch-life not 'at all conducive to literature' because it was so noisy and full of distractions. In New York she attends a lecture on Christian Science by 'Miss Eddystone' and moves in with her and 'Miss Forsitt', a novelist writing on 'The Eternal Womanly'.[39] She explains to the sympathetic pair that her main problem at the ranch had been a friend who was constantly out in 'the open air ... riding, hunting, fishing'. This evokes a scornful sniff from Miss Forsitt, 'A regular athletic type entirely on the physical plain'.[40]

Miss Arden relates with a blush how this vigorous 'Randy ... Miranda I mean', could never understand her need to write, 'She said it was a waste of life. She could not leave me alone. She was a continual temptation – a merry, whistling, singing Temptation, striding in and out of the house.'[41] Miss Arden's problems were compounded because she was a slow worker who could take a whole day on a page, only to tear it up as no good, sometimes destroying months of work that had cost her 'a great effort'. An empathetic Miss Forsitt interpolated, 'like Henry James and myself', while Miss Eddystone urged positive thinking and a stop for ten minutes every hour to tell herself she was a 'perfect success'.[42]

Nevertheless, as Miss Arden's rejected manuscripts pile up, Miss Eddystone fears she is 'haunted' by the friend in California, and finally, 'her eyes ... ringed with dark circles', Miss Arden leaves New York. She returns to California without collaborating with Miss Forsitt on her novel about the 'Domestic Servant Problem', an issue of great moment for middle-class America faced with a shortage of young white women servants because of plentiful opportunities for employment offering higher wages.[43]

Two years later, literary New York is humming with news of an unknown writer who has acquired star status. Margaret Arden's short stories about the Sierras were being greeted with acclaim. Rescuing a few remaining pages from their former lodger's rejected novels, the Misses Eddystone and Forsitt set off to find her, eventually arriving at Linden, in Eldorado County. Stumbling awkwardly over the rough, hilly countryside, they come across 'a pleasant little flat surrounded by gentle grassy slopes'. There, instead of the rough farmhouses they had passed earlier, lay 'a peaceful dwelling', with 'white curtains' and 'a terraced garden'. Flowering vines, roses and wisteria climb its walls and surround the porch, 'inviting paths' wind to its doors. 'Smoothing their crumpled shirt-waists and pluming their disordered locks they passed through a painted gate', whereupon the two dishevelled literary new women notice 'Margaret Arden with a babe in the lap of her many-folded gown'.[44]

When she calls out to 'Randy', the visitors hear 'footsteps too vigorous to belong to the most athletic girl who ever existed'. To their amazement, 'a tall man with commanding shoulders' emerges, and bends over mother and child to observe the baby catching his mother's fingers with his toes. 'Randolph' declares the boy to be a 'wonder' and the best thing that could possibly have happened to them, 'better than all the novels and stories in the world'. Shocked by such heresy, the two New Yorkers sink down behind the manzanita bushes, until hunger drives them to knock on the door. As they cross the 'matted floor' of the ranch house, a beaming Margaret Arden invites them in for supper. Breezily she introduces them to her 'husband, Randolph Burton, and our last production – he's the cunningest sweetest thing you ever saw'.[45]

In 'The Mystery of Miranda', Gertrude returned to one of the stylistic devices of *The Image Breakers* – gentle irony. The story springs from a world she actually knew, as a writer and mother, rather than a pastiche of local colour. Not only Robert, but baby Bob Dix Nicol, make bows, and the manzanita, which had fascinated Miriam, also figures. Gertrude seems to have made her mark upon the wild, for instead of the bare wooden ranch house depicted in 'The Cry on the Trail', the New York visitors are greeted by vines, roses and wisteria. When the eldest daughter, Margot, drew on her childhood memories of the ranch in an unpublished novel, *Her Father's Daughter*, she mentioned tiny wild pink and white baby roses, entwined with honeysuckle climbing up the logs of the porch. The 'matting' in 'The Mystery of Miranda' becomes 'Japanese grass matting' in Margot's account, in accord with the arts and crafts simple life aesthetic.[46] Margaret Arden's 'many folded gown' in the short story sounds Gertrude-like; Margot related to her friend Edna Eldred how, 'when other ladies wore mutton sleeves and high pompadours and pinched waists, her mother wore bangs and a long bob and Grecian cut robes'.[47]

To Margot, and possibly to Sunrise, too, Gertrude, never a conventional mountain woman, seemed incongruous at White-nights. Margot has her fictionalised Sunrise character, 'Anita', declare in *Her Father's Daughter*, 'She belongs to another world.'[48] Her only consolation was, 'There's no one of her sort here, soon she'll be longing for London.'[49] Perhaps the returning old timers, the ghosts, outcasts and outsiders in her short stories, indicate a further source of Gertrude's unease. Miriam had spent only a few months at the ranch, but she had lived on in Robert's memories. The presence of Sunrise, growing to be a proud beauty like her mother, was an inescapable reminder for Gertrude of a ghostly rival. Nevertheless, she appears to have gritted her teeth like Ropes in 'The Passing of the Forty Niner', muttering to herself 'I'm not a deserter'.

Gertrude's love for Robert had brought her to White-nights; he and the children kept her there. She romanced her destiny, turning the orchard into a magical place in the 'Apples of Hesperides'. But, unlike Robert and the children, who were accustomed to life in Placer County, a bookish

Gertrude worried constantly about the dangers of tunnels and mining, regarding the untamed countryside and its inhabitants alike as potentially threatening.

Gertrude's discomfort gives her western stories an edge that makes their romancing more interesting. There is an evident irony in this awkward, intellectual English woman contributing to a popular nostalgia for rough prospectors and noble escaped convicts. Meanwhile the *actual* inhabitants of Placer County were inclined to foreground the prevalence of 'law and order', 'thrift' and 'perseverance'.[50] Theirs was a less lively narrative; but then they were not trying to sell magazines in a competitive market place.

NINETEEN

Bundles of Contradictions: 1903–1907

'Do you know that Tucker's *Liberty* is launched again?' enquired Helen in a letter to Horace Traubel on 2 January 1903.[1] *Liberty* had resurfaced after a break of two years and that February saw William back in the fold, denouncing the 'gigantic monopolies' dominating America and ridiculing the idea that big business could be tamed by 'sloppy sentimentalism'. Tucker's prodigal had returned, exposing a contradictory 'state' that produced 'the very evils which many well-meaning people' were vainly calling for it to suppress.[2] William agreed with the socialist W.J. Ghent, whose *Our Benevolent Feudalism* (1902) challenged socialists who believed the trusts could serve as a basis for nationalised public ownership. Instead Ghent predicted the concentration of capital would produce an oppressive oligarchy, and William concurred, observing, 'The Munseyizing of the magazines is no less marked than the Morganization of industry.'[3] Little did he know that his former comrade in the Boston Anarchist Club, Robert Nicol, was living with a minor player in this 'Munseyizing'.

The tensions in William's politics had become more pronounced. He was emotionally driven by anger against the thwarting of individual freedom and fulfilment, while inclining to theoretical pessimism. With American capitalism at full throttle, William's sober assessment was that the possibility of achieving beneficial change had to be deferred. The only remedy he could countenance was absolute: the workers' rejection of government.[4] In March he noted cynically how the big railroad companies were improving wages, only to recoup by increasing costs, or forestalling labour militancy.[5]

That May, William posited that the 'diffusion of capital' through shareholding in the Steel Corporation refuted 'Marxian dogma' predicting concentration.[6] He insisted that attacking the 'governmental system' rather than some deterministic economic process was the real key to change, a point reiterated in his article on the British civil service, 'The Senile State', that September.[7] Yet William was all too aware of the interpenetration of state, economy and society.

Throughout 1903, beset by harrying theses and antitheses, William tussled away over determinism and human agency along with the relative significance of political and economic factors. He expresses respect for the 1656 treatise by James Harrington, *The Commonwealth of Oceana*, which had pioneered the connection between economics and politics. Moreover, he hails Archille Loria's *The Economic Foundations of Society* (1903) as following Proudhon in combining 'free spontaneous associations of laborers and unprivileged producers of industrial capital' with 'individual liberty and practical equality of condition'. William saw securing 'competition between economic equals, and an egoistic basis of individual conduct' as 'a possible, rational, and desirable social ideal' and maintained it was in accord with 'economic evolution'.[8] Concurring with Loria's critique of the existing capitalist state as the 'political expression' of economic systems, William also approved his term, 'Inverted Darwinism', to describe how politics fostered the rise of the most unfit. He argued that 'The dominant class' wanted governments strong enough to 'check' the 'masses', but not efficient enough 'to curb their own power of exploitation and accumulation'.[9]

A lingering determinism remained deeply rooted in William's theoretical approach, a legacy of the dogmatic Marxism he had imbibed from the S.D.F. in the 1880s. Nevertheless, by 1903 he was aware of the subtlety in Marx's own thinking. While praising Marx as the founder of the 'economic interpretation of history', William recognises that this did not mean Marx saw economic factors *alone* as creating change.[10]

A driving force in William's life as a self-taught scholar was his love of ideas. He was at his happiest trundling through the theories of Harrington, Loria, Proudhon, Marx and Warren, or alluding to works by the evolutionary anthropologist, Lewis H. Morgan, and pioneering economic historians such as Thorold Rogers and William Cunningham.

However, early in 1904, he forced himself to make a determined effort to reorganise his business. Helen, who had resumed her journal, recorded that 'William was staining the walls and oiling the wood work' at his bas-ket-making workshop. Noting with approval that the owner of the Bailie Basket Co. had 'moved his stuff … and fenced off a corner for an office', she joked, 'When he gets a swivel chair he will be made.'[11] Announcing that they had 'pretty much done with "meetings"', on March 7th Helen stated, 'Wm. says that for the first time in his life he is going to concen-trate.' Worldly-wise at thirty, she mused, 'you have to go through with meetings to find out how much a waste of time and energy they are'.[12]

It was not to be *quite* so clear-cut, but a change was certainly occurring.

Three years into their relationship Helen felt she and William had attained an ideal balance of autonomy and connection. Still transcribing Thoreau at Houghton Mifflin, she was convinced 'I shall always want to earn my own living, get out everyday into the world, bring home at night fresh news to share with Wm.'[13] Even though it was cramped in the room at Miss Cheney's, Helen delighted in returning to their precious space: 'William comes home to me every night, boyish and simple as ever.'[14] On some evenings they ventured out for little treats in a newly cosmopoli-tan Boston. Having discovered chop suey and chow mein with Mattie Penhallow, they started going to Chinatown for supper, or wandering through the open-air markets for a mug of Italian wine at 'Scarino's'. In the warm days of June they sat listening to a Chinese band or canoed on the river, spying a muskrat as evening drew in.

William had come to share Helen's love of the theatre. They went to see Louise Closser, who was staying at Miss Cheney's, perform in Shaw's *Candida*, and the intense and imposing Nance O'Neil in Ibsen's *Hedda Gabler*. Drama seared through William's emotional reserve. Helen watched him fondly taking 'a long time to undress', because he was so 'full of ideas about actors and plays'. When she teased him for talking to himself, Irish William quipped, 'And what if I am? I'm having a sensible crack with a sensible man, and that's one I don't meet every day.'[15]

Helen and William's intimacy was kept even from friends. Their discretion could result in confusion, however, as the bizarre entry of a Whitmanite young woman called Louise Heald into their lives revealed. It was Helen who had met her at Houghton Mifflin in the winter of 1903, and introduced her to William. According to Helen's account, the impressionable Louise Heald, having been told by an astrologer that she would meet a lover capable of unlocking the powers of her mind if only she were to prostrate herself before him, overheard Horace Traubel and 'Percy Wiksell' describing William as 'beautiful' and decided he was the one. Heald sent an urgent appeal to William to come to her home in Medford.[16]

William chivalrously set off on the long journey after leaving work. His version of what ensued is recorded by Helen in tightly pursed prose: 'She greeted William completely nude. She threw herself into his arms with a wild outburst of weeping and revealed her feelings.' The combination of a naked young woman, seduction and excessive emotion caused pronounced shock to the reticent William. So pronounced indeed that it took some considerable time before he could 'delicately' extricate himself from 'the exhausted and unmanageable girl'. It was 12 o'clock before William could get away and he had to walk all the way home. When he 'turned up at 2 o'clock in the morning' he was faced with a distraught Helen who 'thought he had broken his neck'. A non-communicative William collapsed exhausted into bed, 'too tired to talk'.[17]

Discretion had embroiled them in a comedy of errors. It appears William had failed to make things completely clear, for Louise Heald was unable to grasp his failure to respond. Moreover, she was relaying embarrassing confidences to Traubel and Wiksell, and felt no qualms about publicising her disappointment. To Helen's horror, at Whitman's birthday celebration an offended Heald read out a poem directed at William about awakening from a futile love to the sorrows of the world and a wider social purpose – she had started work in a brush factory.[18] Before long she announced her engagement to an artist, seeking Helen's opinion because 'Percy Wiksell' did not approve of him. Helen advised her to follow her heart, concluding icily that Louise Heald had once again fallen in love with herself.[19]

Helen still earned $9 a week at Houghton Mifflin, despite having acquired a broad range of skills, and her aspiration for full editorial responsibility remained on hold. William realistically pointed out how she would be forever undercut by young men from college, confident enough to take low wages on the assumption they would be promoted. He convinced her to learn the Isaac Pitman system of shorthand and qualify as a stenographer, a practical skill that would enable her to earn more.[20]

Helen found the course difficult, all the more so because she developed appendicitis during it and was hospitalised. In September 1904 she resumed her training, but aware of losing her tiny toe-hold among the literati, her spirits were low. She tried to remind herself there was 'plenty to live for right here in the present', but admitted, 'something of the zest of life is gone'.[21] That winter, still weak after her operation, Helen steadfastly made her way with William through Edward Gibbon's *The Decline and Fall of the Roman Empire*, Volume II, ingesting from it the fatal consequences of military rule. They were also searching Thorold Rogers' *The Economic Interpretation of History* (1888) for facts about the 'life of the masses'.[22] However, Helen no longer believed in religion, her political ideals had been shaken, her dream of an editing career abandoned.

She cheered up that December when May Hurd asked her to sign a calendar she was making for William Denton's birthday. Helen had kept the birch bark ice-cream spoon from that carefree celebration of 'Walt's birthday' in 1898; in her message to the butterfly collector she remembered the 'gathering of comrades now scattered, some gone forever'.[23] Helen no longer experienced the fellowship she had known back in the late 1890s. But her love for William sustained her. He was her joy, 'Altogether, he satisfies me.' The woman who had believed she was not sensuous when courted by Walter, now expanded on the strength of her beloved's features, his chin, his forehead, the dark brightness of his eyes, the beauty of his mouth, 'like a woman's'.[24] While conceding his nose was a little too thick, Helen opined that it balanced his face. She made no mention of William's ears, surely burning, despite the sobering nature of their reading that winter.

The New Year saw Helen ruminating on how at first she and William had taken their love only 'from day to day'. Still committed to existential freedom, she realised that imperceptibly, over time, a shift had occurred:

> William and I once had a great deal to say to each other about freedom in our love. We prized our love for its entire spontaneity: it was good while it lasted, and we would never hold the other mortgaged to the future. That was our foundation; – it is the foundation of our love. But what a structure we have reared on it. Nested in a city room, we are yet, as in limitless space, – we have made our world. There are no walls between us; there are no walls anywhere.[25]

Love at Columbus Avenue could not curb all buffetings from the workaday world. Helen proudly brought her certificate in shorthand and stenography home in January 1905 to William and her mother, only to miserably report in February that she was only able to find 'substitute work'. Moving from job to job was stressful, 'Each new assignment means setting my teeth and preparing for the worst.' She now looked back upon her 'literary' connections with cynicism, feeling Houghton Mifflin's had known all too well 'how to trade on the mistaken notion' of what was on offer.[26] Yet her wages were just $10 a week as a casual stenographer and the work so unrewarding she took pleasure only in her lunch breaks. By early April she was wondering if she could 'keep' her 'end up'. William's response was 'why do you say such things'?[27] He, after all, had done unfulfilling work from the age of eleven.

Luckily, Helen bumped into Ida Ruggli, a friend she had made while visiting Josephine Tilton's farm in Epsom. Ruggli was working for the prominent lawyer, George Read Nutter, one of the senior partners in a firm with the social reformer, Louis Brandeis. She told Helen a position was available as secretary to one of the younger lawyers, a Harvard graduate, Edward Francis McClennen. Taken on at Brandeis, Dunbar and Nutter, ironically Helen found herself doing demanding and interesting work in a firm led by Brandeis, a prominent proponent of state regulation of the trusts.[28]

Meanwhile Helen relates how William was 'straining uphill, pushing the business before him'.[29] Yet neither of them could accommodate easily to worldly 'money-getting', in and for itself. While Helen moralised about 'honest dealing' and endeavour, William saw himself as a protagonist in a desperate battle, confiding:

> The one thing I dread above all else, … is to be a failure, whether it be a moral, intellectual, or an economic failure. I would rather be a success in the small average affairs of life than a failure in high-flung ambitions. I had to live more than 35 years before I learned to give up my dreams and grub at making a living.[30]

After sprucing up his workshop, he had started to diversify by producing willow furniture, which Helen tried to promote to Horace Traubel. In May 1905, she gleefully reported two new advances at Bailie Basket Co., the introduction of 'a typewriter' and 'a stenographer'.[31]

However, William was coming 'home with his hair damp on his brow, his head buzzing'.[32] They both knew he was caught in the kind of economic and social contradiction he had spent so many years analysing. Basket making as a craft was a relic. Modern basket makers no longer created the whole basket, they turned out the same piece of work already cut out. Few wanted to enter an unprofitable trade and William's employees were apt to desert for better prospects. Often, with only two or three basket makers, William had to resort to bringing work home himself, 'fagged out with the cussedness of his men'.[33] Subtlety, William and Helen's social and political outlook was becoming more pessimistic.

Helen had begun 1905 weeping for the peaceful Russian demonstrators, fired upon for protesting against Nicholas II. She had waved her red sweater when 'The Boston Russian Jews paraded ... carrying red flags', but the fundamental tenets of her radicalism were being eroded.[34] It was no longer her belief that society caused 'the ills of the working class'. By June 1905, Helen had decided these were 'inherent in humanity', sharing William's fatalistic conviction that 'the few' were 'able to take advantage of the rest'. Helen's dilemma was that she wished to belong to the 'few', while ethically disapproving of taking 'advantage' of the weak.[35] She kept catching herself asserting attitudes held by conservatives, while not sharing their premises.[36] The gradual erosion of their former assumptions accentuated the emotional significance of their continuing association with the Walt Whitman Fellowship and *Liberty*. Both networks also assumed a new practical significance, because, at last, William had completed his manuscript on Josiah Warren.

Josiah Warren: The First American Anarchist had been long in the making, but it finally appeared, early in 1906, dedicated 'To the memory of H.B.' In the first chapter, William traces the early nineteenth-century context in which Warren's ideas developed, noting the influence of Robert Owen and the co-operator's son, Robert Dale Owen, Warren had known at the New Harmony community in Indiana. Venturing into a newly emerging field, the history of radical utopianism in America, William mentions, too, the outspoken advocate of sexual and racial equality, Frances Wright, as well as reformers such as Stephen Pearl Andrews and Moncure Conway.

But it was Warren himself who really intrigued him. William admired the founder of the libertarian community, Modern Times, for his conviction that individual freedom and initiative were crucial elements in social harmony, his rejection of a top-down approach to change, and his insistence on investigating actual needs before seeking to meet them. He also concurred with Warren's theory that labour time, including the time taken in selling articles in the community's 'time-store', scanned by its large clock, should decide the value of goods.

But most of all he had come to feel a personal empathy with his subject:

> Like all earnest workers for righteousness in human relations, Warren
> was doomed to many a disappointment, to see many a hope unfulfilled,
> many a promising scheme nipped in the bud, ere time and circum-
> stance converged to carry out his aspirations.[37]

Despite presenting a gruff, tough analytical front to the world, William
was inwardly far from confident and could identify with Warren's
testimony:

> Having spent a long life in trying to find the roots of human miseries,
> and believing that I have succeeded, I freely admit that I am very sensi-
> tive to the manner in which the results of a long life's labor are received
> and treated by the public – not so much for my own, as for their sake.[38]

Josiah Warren starts with 'The Anarchist Spirit', in which William dis-
tilled his own ideas with much greater clarity than in his contributions
to *Liberty* and *Free Society*. Defining anarchism as 'primarily a tendency
– moral, social and intellectual', rather than a cult, party, organisation
or even a movement, William said it questioned 'the supremacy of the
State, the infallibility of Statute laws, and the divine right of all Authority,
spiritual or temporal'.[39] Tolstoy was right, evil was inherent in the state.
Brutal despotisms gave rise to violent opposition but state control could
also be hegemonic, whereby 'Laws in the interest of property' were presented 'as the will of the people'.[40] Government, regardless of the efforts
of reformers, would always entail the abuse of 'social justice'; hence, for
William, like Warren, 'the individual' must be 'sovereign'.[41]

Though he wrote respectfully of the radical liberal tradition exemplified
by Herbert Spencer, William believed Spencer's writings did not confront economic and social inequality. Conversely he thought 'socialistic'
demands for the state to provide 'work for the unemployed and enact a
legal eight-hour day' sacrificed 'individual liberty for a chance to establish
economic equality'.[42] Acknowledging connections between 'Socialism'
and 'Anarchism', William considered anarchism to have avoided the
subordination of the individual to the collective by recognising 'political
and industrial freedom as indispensable steps toward economic equality'. Unlike statist forms of 'Socialism', William argued, 'Anarchism …
would maintain complete equality of rights and opportunities'.[43] Instead

of public ownership, he advocated voluntary associations, pointing to the churches as models. William's ideal was a society in which 'each person, singly or in association with others', would be able 'to work out his own destiny in accordance with his capacities, temperament and desires'.[44]

'The Anarchist Spirit' and the study of Warren appeared when William's own thinking was in flux, but they reveal his underlying loathing of authoritarian patronage and restraint, along with a compelling desire for the release of human capacity which he personally had been denied. Besides Warren, he mentions Proudhon, Nietzsche, Tolstoy and Kropotkin as thinkers he admired, adding the lesser known anarchist geographer, Elisée Reclus, and his brother, the anthropologist, Elie, who challenged the contempt in which 'primitive' peoples were held. William Morris is not mentioned, though the Tory, John Ruskin, whose vision of a social economy was paternalistic, receives a surprisingly favourable reference. William also displays a love of literature that never figures in his political and economic writings: dramatists, novelists and poets such as Ibsen, Hauptmann, Shaw, Meredith, Gissing, Hardy, as well as Whitman and Thoreau, all receive mention. The last two were surely William's way of thanking Helena and Helen for all that devoted sub-editing and proofreading.

William expresses a belief in science, characteristic of working-class radicals of his generation. True to this spirit of enquiry, he had consistently refused to take any system of thought on trust. His book on Warren was no exception, for, while still identifying as an Individualist Anarchist, William praises 'the Metropolitan Park System of Massachusetts'.[45] Boston's string of parks had been initiated by a campaign for green spaces in the early 1890s, but they were funded and administered through the State legislature. Donning his civic cap, William conceded the community could benefit from taxation imposed on individuals. The implication was that while individuals might well take a short-term perspective, the Metropolitan Park System of Massachusetts safeguarded the long-term common good.

In December 1905 William was still putting the final touches to his manuscript while running his workshop and thinking up new articles. Unsurprisingly, the pressure upon him resulted in some fatal errors, and on February 6th he had to apologise to Tucker for failing to acknowledge 'Liberty and its mission', assuring the man who had spent his life studying Warren's ideas that he had made a last minute amendment.[46]

The February 1906 issue of *Liberty* announced that the book was 'very prettily gotten up' and 'of high interest to every Anarchist'. A review was promised describing its abundant 'merits', adding ominously, 'and its demerits, from which unhappily, it is not free'.[47] On March 12th, perhaps in an effort to mollify Tucker, William described having heard 'Rabbi Fleischer speak in his church on "Anarchy and Anarchists"', quoting 'copious passages from the Introduction to Warren'.[48] Fleischer, the successor of Solomon Schindler at Temple Adath Israel synagogue, was a supporter of Reform Judaism. A believer in political democracy, the charismatic Rabbi shared the Boston Brahmins' distrust of rule by the majority, while asserting the importance of individual rights. A gratified William observed, 'His address was quite in harmony with the principles of the book', and added that a 'member of the audience' also had a copy and cited it 'during his remarks'.[49]

Helen's rather different journal account explains their late arrival at the event – they had forgotten to put in the pudding. She, too, was delighted by praise from the handsome, cultured Fleischer for William's book on Warren. However, while her tolerance could graciously extend to the distinguished liberal Rabbi, it was abruptly withdrawn from 'a little bullet-headed Jew' who rose to 'demolish' a passage from *Josiah Warren*.[50] Helen's old prejudices resurfaced in the face of opposition. Though her *political* sympathies were with Jews, Filipinos and Black Americans as oppressed peoples, emotionally she regarded them as outsiders. In a flicker of unease over her racism, she maintained that her objection to 'darkies' was not a matter of skin colour, but a result of her dislike of 'bad manners'.[51] Before long she had found another outsider group to castigate, 'the scoundrel Poles employed by William'.[52] Helen's identification with an enlightened minority strengthened her fortitude in backing unpopular causes, but it also invested in her a feeling of superiority as part of a WASP moral elite.

In April 1906 the promised review of Josiah Warren appeared in *Liberty*. Tucker had given the book to Clarence Swartz. Recognising it as 'a work of love', Swartz lauded 'the fullness' of the author's 'sympathy for his subject', as well as the book's 'lucid and entertaining' style.[53] However, Swartz, the arch-individualist, honed in mercilessly on William's momentary 'lapse' into 'collectivism' on the Metropolitan Park System: 'Mr Bailie' was denounced as 'a special pleader for State Socialism'.[54] Swartz also rebuked William for omitting those who had ensured the *'continuation'* of Warren's politics.[55] Notable among these was, of course, Tucker, the very man who had encouraged William.

Josiah Warren had not been an easy book to write and Helen would later reveal that Swartz's review 'cut William terribly', especially as he had sent Swartz the manuscript, requesting notes on 'omissions' as well as 'comments and criticism'.[56] Swartz had returned it without any word of correction: for William this must have seemed a betrayal of trust from a man within his own circle. But, as a Stirnerite Egoist, Swartz presumably set no store on sentiment.

In the April issue of *Liberty* William had contributed 'Murder Entirely Satisfactory', a blistering attack on Theodore Roosevelt and his ally, 'Butcher-General Wood', who had brutally crushed the Filipino rebels.[57] But when Tucker asked him to contribute to *Liberty* in September 1906, William declined: 'I am compelled to give such close attention to my business nowadays that I feel as if I could not write anything worthwhile.' It was true he had little leisure to think. But Tucker may well have raised an eyebrow on reading, 'My Sundays are necessarily spent out of doors, except in winter.' Insisting his 'interest in Liberty' was 'no less keen', William enclosed a catalogue for the 'Bailie Basket Company' which was now refurbishing 'cane and rush chairs', and retired into his shell.[58]

Though William was far too proud to admit he had been wounded, Swartz left a scar which never quite healed. That autumn William reflected to Helen that 'character' was a better measure of integrity than 'principles'; 'Scalawags', he declared, were to be found on the left as well as the right.[59] All those years of principled theorising had not equipped William for 'scalawaggery', or, indeed, for an attack from a man he had assumed was an ally and a friend.

Helen did write a short article for *Liberty* in June 1906. Entitled 'What is a Mob?', it was her response to the Brooklyn crowd that menaced the visiting Russian writer, Maxim Gorky, after it was revealed he was not married to his woman companion. Helen echoes a dread of the 'mob' as a 'primal horde', prevalent among contemporary middle-class commentators. Through a 'homage' to Helena's mix of individual expression and altruism, she also conveyed an oblique reminder to Swartz of the disagreement over his lecture on Egoism for the Walt Whitman Fellowship; it was 'the highly individualized member of society who feels most sensitively the rights of others and his obligation towards them'.[60]

*   *   *

The year 1906 saw a crucial change in Helen and William's personal circumstances. Ellen agreed to a divorce and, in March, William 'put through' his application. It meant that in two years' time he would be free to marry. Nevertheless, a defiant Helen insisted she needed no 'authority' or ceremony for her love.[61] Cocooned at Miss Cheney's, they lived as lovers still; 'I hear him springing on the stairs, so eager to reach me he stumbles.' One evening he arrived bearing 'strawberries, eggs and a loaf'.[62] Picking over the berries, talking and talking, they washed up and then drew their chairs under the light to read William Morris' epic poem from an Old Norse legend, 'Sigurd'. Only when they were going to bed did William discover their omelette lying cold and forgotten in the pan.

In her early thirties, Helen could not help wondering 'how a child of William and me would turn out'.[63] Pregnancy was, however, inadmissible. Twice she had conceived and on both occasions they had appealed for help from Miss Cheney. A woman friend of their resourceful landlady had performed two abortions. Helen knew they were in no position to have a child, and instead was resolved to help William with his own family. She could only envisage marrying in order to ensure the legality of her relationship with William in respect to the Bailie children.

With the prospect of the divorce before them, they fantasised about living in a six-room house with a 'porch and dormer windows and an orchard yielding barrels of apples and pears'.[64] Instead William found a scrubland lot available for sale on Lake Cochituate in Natick, which they could now reach by trolley.[65] Electrification had made an area previously accessible only to rich holiday-makers, possible to visit from Boston. The waters of the great lake supplied the city with water, but to William and Helen their patch constituted an idyll of nature. Happily they nurtured the little trees they had planted and watched their 'cottage' going up. William had moved his family out to Scituate to be away from city life; now, once again, he and Helen imagined the children transformed by this new rural paradise.

But the children remained 'a heavy problem', and that autumn when young Willie was discovered lying, Helen recorded in dismay how 'William harangues him endlessly'. Despite her resolution, she found herself dreading 'the days when the children are brought here'.[66] A year later she was still baffled by her own inability to teach them orderly habits, motivate them at school or gain their trust. Helen admitted that in dealing with the young Bailies, 'patience is not one of my shining attributes'.[67]

A further blow occurred in autumn 1906 when their lake-side cottage burned down. Aware that she and William were regarded with fear and hostility as 'pariahs' by the local people, Helen wondered whether living close to nature was quite so simple as it had seemed.[68]

Since 1901, glaring inequality, the power of big business, violent industrial confrontations and unease about rampant materialism had contributed to the growth of the Socialist Party.[69] In 1905 a militant grouping, the Industrial Workers of the World (I.W.W.), emerged, opposing the exclusionary practices of craft unions and emphasising the need for workers to take direct control in the workplace. It was supported by Debs on the left of the Socialist Party, but in 1906 its key organiser, 'Big Bill' Haywood, was accused of ordering the assassination of the former Governor of Idaho, Frank Steunenberg. Thousands of Bostonians demonstrated in support of Haywood, but the press was fiercely hostile towards him.[70] In July 1907, Helen, who had acquired an insider's scepticism towards law as 'a game of chess', was all the more impressed when the labour lawyer, Clarence Darrow, won Haywood's acquittal.[71]

The rise of socialism and the I.W.W. increased William's political isolation. The Individualist Anarchists, always a minority, were losing cohesion and becoming side-lined even as a theoretical presence. Gritting his teeth, William struggled to expand the Bailie Basket Co. His 1907 trade catalogue now offered not just baskets and furniture, but modern 'automobile trunks'.[72] Ever on the lookout for creative designs, William had become interested in ethnological studies of Native American basketry, and, making contact with the United States National Museum in Washington, he began a correspondence with Otis Tufton Mason.

Despite an evolutionary perspective that placed white people at the apex of development, Mason admired the craft skills of American Indian men and women. Arguing that 'Nothing common is trivial', his epistemology acknowledged 'the lore of the uneducated'.[73] One of his areas of interest was basket making, and on 5 December 1907 William sent him a detailed summary of materials and craft terminology.[74] In his letter William explained that when he was a boy, journeymen could still 'elaborate original designs', but regrettably those days were gone, and even the memory of older techniques had been lost. He did not believe that basket makers in England or America could any longer express 'artistic skill' or 'pride and pleasure in the work'.[75] William's voracious appetite for knowledge embraced ethnology, archaeology and geology, and he confided to Mason his efforts to connect them through his 'particular hobby … Sociology'.[76] The anthropologist, too, sought a means of synthesising ethnological findings, devising the concept, 'culture –history'.[77]

William's study of Josiah Warren brought a welcome rapport with a group of academic social reformers examining the historical culture of labour and cognisant of the connection between knowing and doing. Among them was the Progressive economist, Richard T. Ely, who had visited Boston in the spring of 1907. Ely, who had helped to found the Society of Christian Socialists back in 1889, opposed class conflict and advocated reforms in labour relations which seriously upset powerful interests. Unlike William however, Ely's Protestant social gospel endowed the state with a moral authority that justified not simply welfare, but imperial expansion.[78]

Nevertheless, from differing vantage points, both men stressed the need for an inner change of heart and were aware of the problems in reconciling individual freedom with greater social equity. Ely's favourable review of *Josiah Warren* in the November 1907 issue of *The American Political Science Review* noted how Warren's ideas on the sovereignty of the individual had influenced John Stuart Mill, and summarised Warren's theories of costing goods on the basis of the time taken in both producing and selling them. Emphasising that the book was a key text for 'the careful student of social movements' in the United States, Ely commented, 'It should be scarcely necessary to tell the intelligent reader that there are anarchists and anarchists.'[79]

Ely was linked to a group of researchers in the American Bureau of Industrial Research who were studying labour, socialist and anarchist movements. Based at the University of Wisconsin, they included Professor John R. Commons and a researcher, John B. Andrews. Though secular in outlook, they shared Ely's view that historians and social scientists needed to examine social movements, radical groupings and utopian communities in order to comprehend what could or could not be done.[80] Their interest and approbation was confirming and encouraging to William at a time when he was isolated.

In 1907 Andrews made contact with William, as well as with other anarchists, including Emma Goldman, *Free Society's* C.L. James, and the former Socialist Labor Party activist, Joseph Labadie, who was a supporter of *Liberty*. It must have been bizarre for them to be consulted by academics when anarchists had been regarded as pariahs only a few years before. On 4 December 1907, an enthusiastic William responded zealously to

Andrews' question about anarchists' attitudes towards competition. In explaining that his opinions were those held by 'individualistic and philosophic Anarchists', William remarks how his 'pen and thoughts' ran away with him, 'launching out into an exposition or at least the draft of an essay' rather than a letter.[81] William was in his element, piloting these earnest academic researchers through the unpredictable currents and submerged shoals of anarchist social movements.

It was Helena's friend, Beatrice Taylor, who prompted Helen to fulfil her promise of a visit to England. She arrived on 14 August 1907 for a six-week vacation, and the two women rambled across London to the medieval Inns of Court, exploring the Knights Templar Church. Along with memories of Helena, they shared an interest in the libertarian educationalist, Francisco Ferrer, and Taylor introduced Helen to the *Boletin de la Escuela Moderna*.[82] A free interpretation of this 'Modern School' of Ferrer's was soon to be created by American anarchists in New Jersey.

In Bristol, Helen met her tactful correspondent, Robert Gilliard, who had recently published a book, *The Divine Basis of Society* (1906), in which he argued that socialism started not with economics, but with the 'birth of a new consciousness'.[83] Still active in the Bristol Socialist movement and living at the same house in Lower Eastville, he was in contact with Robert Sharland, and with Robert Weare, who had moved north in 1894. Sharland took Helen on 'a round trip through Cheddar, Glastonbury and Wells', and on an exciting excursion to 9 Louisa Street in St Philips, where she 'peeped in at the window of the house where they lived'. In an attempt to heal old wounds, Robert Sharland brought Richard Born to meet her. 'Not a pleasant visit', noted Helen tersely; Helena's father appears to have repented, hurrying 'back to invite me to his home'.[84] However, by then Helen had departed for Liverpool, taking the long, slow train journey up through Wales to meet Weare.

The Weares, along with their daughter Lily, her Whitmanite socialist husband Will Young and baby Doreen, lived in a communal house called 'Walden' at St Hilary's Brow, Wallasey, where Whitman and Thoreau were household names. The bustling commune was accustomed to visitors; Carpenter, Gilliard, Sharland, Irving, Katharine and Bruce Glasier all went there.[85] Weare accompanied Helen on her visit to Manchester, especially interesting because of William's life there.[86] She was also keen to meet members of the Whitmanite group in Bolton, the Lancashire mill town where the socialist J.W. Wallace had founded an informal network

Robert Weare, September 1905
(Bristol Reference Library)

of Whitman enthusiasts, 'The Eagle Street College'. Wallace was away, so Helen never encountered Katharine Glasier's former 'spirit lover', but she was able to report to 'Horace and Anne' that she had seen other Whitmanites.[87]

In the village of Adlington, just outside Bolton, Helen stayed at the home of Charlie and Lucy Sixsmith. There among the Lancashire hills, rills and waterfalls, she formed a warm bond with Charlie Sixsmith, 'a loveable fellow'. Mindful of Traubel's amour-propre, she assured him that his picture was on the Sixsmiths' mantelpiece amid the memorabilia. The Traubels were informed that she and Charlie Sixsmith talked 'for a long time of things Whitmanite' and he showed her his treasured collection of books, including a first edition of *Leaves of Grass*.[88] Profoundly influenced by Carpenter as a young man, Sixsmith had risen to become a manager of a cotton mill, but retained his love of Whitman.[89] He expressed profound dismay to Helen about Bliss Perry's 1906 book, *Walt Whitman: His Life and Works*.[90] Although this heralded Whitman's entry into the newly institutionalised field of 'American Literature', Perry, the cool man of letters, had derided the Walt Whitman Fellowship as a 'cult' of 'Hot little prophets'.[91] Evangelically, Helen urged Traubel to denounce Perry and 'put the truth in black and white in The Conservator'.[92]

Sixsmith visited her in Liverpool, and as they walked around the reservoir with Weare, he held forth on municipal mismanagement, reminding her of William, who had found a new cause – the purification of Boston's municipal water. After she returned to America, Helen wrote Sixsmith an affectionate letter and sent him a copy of *Josiah Warren*, explaining to the Independent Labour Party member and parish councillor that the 'little volume' was 'by my friend William Bailie whose point of view may interest you'.[93]

Helen's spirits were lifted by the visit. It was as if she had by-passed time, telling the Traubels, 'Among Helena's old comrades I felt as if she were again living with me.'[94] Reflecting in her journal, Helen wrote, 'They were dear people, Helena's old Socialist friends, lovely types.'[95] Henceforth, every May Day, Robert Sharland posted the special issue of the Social Democratic Federation paper, *Justice*, across the Atlantic to Helen in America. It joined all the other bundles of contradictions jostling for space in Helen and William's lives in the first decade of the twentieth century.

TWENTY

Political Reorientation and a
New Arrival: 1907–1914

In December 1907, William, the man who so recently had abjured meetings, was enquiring whether Professor John R. Commons might speak at 'our *Boston City Club*, a young but large and active body of men'.[1] William's participation in the Boston City Club, a group of businessmen and social reformers, and his admiration for Commons, indicate how much his political outlook had shifted. After projecting his hopes for revolutionary transformation further and further into the future, by 1907 William was branching off into social amelioration. The pragmatic aspect of his character had come to the fore, though the habits of organising remained.

He moved into a milieu pulsating with reform agendas. 'Economics' had become a quarrelsome terrain and the supposed 'laws' of the market were being challenged on several fronts. Some were maintaining that increased productivity, higher wages and mass consumption should be the aim, a perspective still regarded as an heretical denial of the virtues of thrift. Others sought to introduce values of love and human well-being into economic models, arguing that competitive individual interests could tally with the wider social good.

Like their mentor Ely, Commons and Andrews connected individual realisation with the creation of a good society, but instead of Ely's social gospel based on Christian altruism, they sought a secular basis for ethical reform. Commons endorsed Ely's historical approach and proposed that the new discipline of 'sociology' should be the foundation of the social sciences, including economics.

Commons' socio-historical heterodoxy was compounded by his studies of conflicts between workers and employers, which advocated learning from trade unionists. Academic orthodoxy hit back; in 1899 he was dismissed from his post as a Professor at Syracuse University on the grounds of radicalism. Exiled from academia, he spent his time research-ing for the U.S. Industrial Commission and the U.S. Bureau of Labor, reading Marx, along with the Webbs' massive tome *Industrial Democracy* (1897). The leader of the American Federation of Labor (A.F.L.), Samuel Gompers, convinced him that unions could play a crucial economic role against the trusts, and Commons argued that labour movement influence should be complemented through social legislation. In 1904, Ely, who was planning to write a history of industrial democracy, had managed to bring Commons to the University of Wisconsin as his key collaborator.[2]

Their efforts to uncover the source of class conflicts, find alternatives to the violence of American labour relations, and to estimate the potential strengths and weaknesses of differing forms of working-class institutions and social movements appealed to William. Moreover, their objective of improving workers' lives tallied with that of the founder of the Boston City Club, Edward Filene. The owner of one of Boston's most successful department stores, with its popular and innovative 'Automatic Bargain Basement', Filene believed in industrial democracy, co-operation, rel-atively high wages and the integration of politically conservative trade unionism. Like the Wisconsin academics, he was not afraid of conflicting views, encouraging debate in the City Club and fostering a congenial atmosphere by providing good food at subsidised rates. Among his allies were Helen's employers, Louis Brandeis and George Read Nutter, both of whom were involved in the Good Government Association (G.G.A.), determined to rectify waste and corruption in Boston.[3]

Boston's finances in the 1900s were in serious disarray. The cost of running the city had steadily mounted; debts had been incurred and these had accrued interest. While inefficiency and corruption added to the city's budgets, so did new projects such as transport, parks and water systems, while state taxes also put pressure on accounts. As the wealthy moved out to the suburbs, the income from business premises in the centre became crucial and property taxes went up. The G.G.A. led a campaign for a Finance Commission to vet expenditure, in the belief that the mobili-sation of honest citizens, scrutinising and reorganising services, would reduce costs. The G.G.A. was not an overtly political body; nonetheless, they viewed the Democratic Mayor, John F. Fitzgerald, with suspicion as the corrupt tool of the ward bosses. In Nutter's opinion Fitzgerald had accepted the establishment of a Finance Commission to avert legislative investigation.[4]

Known as 'Honey Fitz', Fitzgerald was a dynamic publicist, who, having speeded up his 1906 campaign for office with modern auto-mobiles, had contrived to circumvent municipal fiefdoms by appealing to the electorate over their heads. While Fitzgerald did pad his ability to spin a narrative with political patronage, during his first year in office, expenditure had actually declined, only to leap up dramatically during 1907, mainly owing to the increased city debt. In 1908 Fitzgerald lost to the Republican, George A. Hibbard, and some economies in depart-ments affected by political patronage were introduced. However, the 'good government' lobby was not necessarily synonymous with extending democracy, and Hibbard looked kindly on demands for the city council to be replaced with rule by the Mayor and the Finance Commission. Instead, a compromise was reached, by which the layers of representa-tion were streamlined and the powers of the Mayor's office strengthened through a new City Charter.[5]

On 30 November 1908, Helen notes that William was out discuss-ing the City Charter at a gathering of the 'Economic Club', a branch of the National Economic League based at Boston's Beacon Hill.[6] The Economic Club's membership, which included Brandeis and Nutter, overlapped with that of the Boston City Club and the G.G.A. Osten-sibly educational, its members shared a broad opposition to socialism, but were prepared to countenance reforms. The Club's meetings debated municipal affairs, along with wider economic and social issues, such as housing and public ownership of the railways.

William appears to have joined around January 1908, for he was out hobnobbing at the Economic Club when Helen came home on the evening of the 21st and was touched to find 'three chocolates laid out in a row on a piece of white paper'. She considered preserving these small symbols of luxury, but ate them 'as he had intended'.[7] William's basket business was struggling after several large outlays, and perhaps it was his new contacts that enabled him to obtain a $400 loan from the 'Merchant Co-op'.[8] But his attachment to the City and Economic Clubs was ideological rather than commercial: they appeared to proffer viable alternatives to violent class conflict and they created new contexts for William's advocacy of vol-untary association, as opposed to the state. Later in the year he was to be found at the Economic Club's discussion of 'Socialism', led by Harvard

President, Charles William Eliot (whose defence of scabs had so enraged Helena), along with John Graham Brooks from the National Consumers' League, and J.G. Phelps Stokes, the millionaire member of the Socialist Party, recently married to the former cigar maker and rousing speaker, Rose Pastor.[9]

William had entered a gradualist political environment. Not only had his faith in working-class revolutionary struggle and a future utopia of absolute freedom worn thin, his former Individualist Anarchist base was eradicated. In January 1908, a fire at Benjamin Tucker's New York book-shop and office destroyed his publishing ventures, and soon Tucker, his young love, Pearl Johnson, and new-born baby Oriole would move to France. The Individualist Anarchist group around him had already been shrinking, and his departure left those who held on to their beliefs in predominantly personal networks pursuing a range of causes.[10]

William's trajectory into civic affairs was unusual. Yet amid the shift in his political orientation, he was still searching for that elusive com-bination of individual freedom and the social good. His resolute wish for self-improvement also persisted, along with a tendency to take on too much. In 1908 William and Helen started a geology course at the Teacher's School of Science, where an exhausted William was wont to fall asleep.[11]

Two other constants remained in William and Helen's lives: the room at Miss Cheney's, and family problems. Russell and Isabel Tufts had moved to New York, but early in 1908 Russell's employers, Eagle Spirits, were absorbed into another company and he was laid off. That March, when her brother, who was still drinking heavily, announced that he wanted to work for William, Helen wrote in trepidation, 'Mama and he are coming back to Boston.'[12] Always a worrier and a saver, she feared Russell's spendthrift ways and, sure enough, before long she was drawing on her savings.[13] Helen had continued dutifully to escort the Bailie chil-dren on educational outings to theatres and museums. Hopes were raised when the youngest child, Viola, showed interest in learning the violin; William bought a fiddle and arranged for lessons. But the young Bailies were recalcitrant. Willie, allowed to help at Bailie Basket Co., retaliated by stealing from the safe.[14]

When Helen received a letter from Sarah Holmes in June remonstrat-ing over William's failure to provide for Ellen and his family, she lashed out in fury, 'It is true she never has anything; that the house is bare of comfort; that the food is always running low.' But the reason was 'not lack of adequate means, but common thriftlessness'. Contrasting Ellen with Emma Schumm, who had managed a family on very little, Helen asserted the Bailie children were fed 'on bakery stuff'.[15] Moreover they were left unwashed and verminous, treated violently, kept from school and taught to lie, while Ellen went to the theatre every week. An unrelenting Helen went on: 'She was born sickly. Her girlhood was sickly. Her unhappiness with her relatives and her ailments were worked upon to bring about the marriage at a time when William had not a friend in the world to tell him he was making a mistake.'[16]

Incensed by Holmes' accusation that Ellen was 'the instrument' of William's 'passion', Helen insisted that the rift between William and his wife had already occurred before 'they came to America'. Ellen had wanted the children, 'Their babyhood has given her probably the only real comfort she has ever had.' William had tried for years 'to nurture harmony', and thus had left himself open to misunderstanding and criticism. It sounds as if Ellen Bailie was overwhelmed, unhappy, erratic and chaotic, rather than consistently harsh or vicious. But in Helen's view, Ellen was 'cunning enough'. She insisted Ellen 'has no enemy but herself', and that her 'wrongs' existed only in Sarah Holmes' imagination. Through her wrath Helen managed to remember her friendship with Holmes, sending 'loving greetings' and telling the principled free lover, 'I have called you "Dear" and you are dear to me. Write again sometime if and when you can write of other things.'[17]

Though estranged from Holmes, Helen and William maintained their friendship with Traubel and Wiksell in the Walt Whitman Fellowship, as well as with May Hurd and William Denton, now making fashionable butterfly jewellery. Occasionally they had supper in Chinatown and went to see Shakespeare and Ibsen plays.[18] But their chief source of relaxation was their retreat at the rebuilt cottage, 'Lakeledge', where Helen had started to grow vegetables and flowers. Yet the peace of Lakeledge was apt to be encroached upon either by the Bailie children or by Russell and Isabel Tufts. Despite having sold his house in New York, Russell never had any money. He had found lodgings for 'Mama', but the discovery that these were being used by prostitutes meant they had to be hurriedly vacated. So, in the summer of 1908, Helen noted tersely that the expanded cottage was 'pretty crowded'.[19]

With little time ever to be alone, far less for romance, a June canoe trip with William on Lake Cochituate under a 'fine moon' was sufficiently notable to be mentioned in Helen's journal.[20] Nonetheless, that autumn, Helen and William *did* manage to snatch two whole days for themselves. On October 30th, Helen wrote, 'Left B.D. & N. [Brandeis, Dunbar and Nutter] forever. $50 from firm $25 from the girls.' The following day she added 'Wm. and I to Wrentham for the night – Viola ransacked our room.'[21]

This was their backwards way round honeymoon; they were married on the 31st in a hall decorated with yellow chrysanthemums. In the antinomian spirit inherited from Helena, Helen continued to sign herself 'Helen Tufts'. It was the inner freedom that mattered, not the external ceremony, and she assured May Hurd, 'I can truly say that marriage has no fetters for us. We are still united by what defies the sanction of society and which will persist despite it.' She insisted that she and William remained 'still at school to life, and will not, I hope, ever become exclusive or wooden'.[22]

In January 1909, as another year began, Helen copied out an adage, reminding herself, 'If the main thing in one's life is right and true, sorrows can but bruise, not crush.'[23]

William, the 'right and true', was immersed in his water purification cause, triggered unwittingly by Russell. In June 1908, upon taking the boat out onto Lake Cochituate, Russell had been ignominiously towed back, because William was the sole licensee. On July 3rd, Helen reported that the Metropolitan Water Board had revoked William's canoe licence. Indignant over bureaucrats interfering in his right to canoe, William lobbied members of the Board, only to find its chairman, Henry H. Sprague, according to Helen, 'Fussy and unreasonable'.[24] He did, however, gain a local ally; 'Mr Whitney of Natick' was at odds with the Board over a bay near his property, which he believed was a potential source of typhoid.[25] Embarking on their own survey, the two amateur investigators detailed three graveyards and a piggery draining into the Lake providing Boston's water. Unconvinced by the Board's claim that the intake pipe was sufficiently far from any dangers of infection, an outraged William then found the water from Lake Cochituate was not being filtered, whereupon he decided to write on 'Boston's Water Supply'.[26] Bizarrely, his fondness for his canoe had led into the deeps of local politics.

On 3 January 1909, William's pamphlet was at the printers with the cumbersome title, *An Inquiry into Boston's Water Supply and Its Relation to the Public Health, with some startling Facts about the Pollution of Sources of Supply.* A strapline announced that it offered a solution to the 'Dead-lock' of high costs, waste and inefficiency caused by 'divided authority and irresponsible control'.[27] Though one element in William's case against the Metropolitan Water Board was the unnecessary loss of water through leaks, the main thrust of his argument was the danger of pollution from far more sinister sources than canoes. William revealed that Lake Cochit-uate was not just affected by the piggery and graveyards, but by a public dump, drainage from a shoe factory, sewage as well as coal dust and oil from trains.[28] Why, he asked, did the Metropolitan Water Board ignore all these but shut off the inoffensive and 'time-honoured privilege of boating and fishing'?[29] Venting his frustration upon the inefficiencies of overlap-ping responsibility and 'well-paid public servants devoting their time to their own private business', William expostulated that honest citizens, submitted to 'a burdensome system of taxation', were denied 'the right to protest' and lacked the time to gain an understanding of the issues.[30]

In the early 1900s research was underway into microscopic algae and there were proposals to disinfect drinking water with chemicals, along with sand filters to purify water; William opted for filtration. Elaborating on the social cost of water-borne diseases, he argued for investment in a large main from the Weston aqueduct to add water from the Nashua River.[31] However, not only were such measures costly, they would require more decisive centralised powers.

Helen, who had corrected the proofs, was indignant when the Boston papers rejected an article from William on the water supply. Worse, 'Almost everyone asks Wm. what his interest is behind it all, – as if no one could conceive of public-spirited endeavor without thought of self.'[32] She had evidently forgotten the canoe license.

In January 1909, William and Helen, with 2,000 water-supply pamphlets to distribute, resolutely stuffed 300 into envelopes at Miss Cheney's. Making sure one reached 'Mr Brandeis', Helen diplomatically 'lunched' with the wife of her former boss, 'Mrs McClennen at the Tou-raine'. Initially the City Club would not allow them to circulate copies to members, but the Economic Club proved more compliant. Helen mailed a large batch from its office, and eventually William brought the City Club round. By the end of January, Helen and William's combined organisational skills had resulted in 2,000 denunciations of the Metro-politan Water Board being despatched.[33]

*   *   *

William's investigation into Boston's water coincided with the outcry over waste, inefficiency and corruption initiated by the Finance Commission. Moves were afoot for a new City Charter, and Filene was hoping to regenerate Boston by bringing together a taskforce of business leaders, lawyers and social reformers, with a remit extending beyond the governance of the city to economic and social conditions. Recognising the value of publicity, he approached the brilliant, 'muck-raking' journalist, Lincoln Steffens. Offered the handsome salary of $10,000 by Filene and the Good Government Association, Steffens' well-publicised arrival in Boston towards the end of 1908 was hailed by Filene, Brandeis, Nutter and their associate, James J. Storrow, a philanthropic investment banker with political ambitions.[34] Early in 1909, Steffens came across William at the Economic Club and a purring Helen reported his interest in the book on *Josiah Warren*.[35] Steffens' investigative journalism had convinced him that corruption was as likely to come from the top as the bottom of the social scale. Moreover, he had realised that simply revealing what was wrong did not offer any alternative to a tooth-and-claw capitalism.[36]

That January, William managed to see their ward representative, Malcolm Nichols, a Republican in the Massachusetts House of Representatives. Nichols agreed to put forward a bill drafted by William, proposing that Lake Cochituate should be abandoned as a source of water. It looked as if the press silence was about to be broken when the *Boston Herald* sought an interview with William, but the journalist had not bothered to read the pamphlet and was ominously preoccupied with human-interest material on its author.[37] During February, when William arranged a hearing on the water supply at the City Club, the apathetic response dismayed him.[38] With the Club overflowing with proposals for reform, William and his water were bypassed.

By March, rumours that William had some mercenary interest in filtration were circulating widely, while the Secretary of the Metropolitan Water Board, William N. Davenport, asserted that William's preoccupation with the water supply derived solely from his desire to go out in his canoe. When boating was permanently prohibited on the lake, some local residents blamed William.[39] Over the summer William managed to arouse anxiety about 'wigglers', and, in July, jars of the creatures were presented to the Board and the *Boston Globe*.[40] However Davenport had staying power; William's evidence of pollution was squashed. In August 1909, Helen raged, 'Every newspaper in Boston is throttled.'[41]

Nevertheless, buried in the bureaucratic miasma of the Board's Ninth Annual Report for 1909 was an admission that, during September, the water in Lake Cochituate had 'acquired an objectionable taste and odor, due to a growth of microscopic organisms'.[42] One source of contamination, Dug Pond, was, moreover, cut off from the lake and responsibility for it handed over to Natick. William and Helen's efforts had several other consequences. William was put on the 'Committee of 100', the group working for a new City Charter, and Filene agreed to put the water problem before the Boston-1915 Committee – a group that included Brandeis and Storrow.[43]

Filene's Committee were responsible for the 'Boston-1915 Plan'. The liberal businessmen, lawyers, settlement workers and reforming journalists around Filene envisaged changes on a much shorter time-scale than the distant futures to which William had grown accustomed. The Boston-1915 Plan proposed that by 1910, expert financial accounting would be in place to assess waste in both public services and the social skills of citizens, accompanied by improvements in working conditions, economic development, workers' insurance and old-age pensions. It was envisaged that by 1915 Boston would enjoy superior public health and

HER MASTERPIECE.

Boston-1915 Movement,
Sunday Herald, 4 April 1909

education services, more public libraries, co-ordinated transport and music in the parks.[44]

Filene's comprehensive Plan was developed when a great swathe of reform initiatives was sweeping through American cities, propelled by combinations of socialists and reformers, as well as by some liberal employers like Filene, seeking a more inclusive capitalism.[45] In January 1909, William and Helen went to hear the settlement worker, Raymond Robins, who had played a key role in the overthrow of a corrupt ward boss in Chicago. Radicalised by Henry George, he had campaigned vigorously in defence of the Isaaks, the editors of *Free Society*. An inveterate protester, and married to the wealthy activist in the Women's Trade Union League, Margaret Dreier, Robins had defended efforts by Chicago's Teachers' Federation and radical School Board to improve schools. Helen was impressed by his 'enthusiasm for justice and single minded generosity' and approved of his accounts of people mobilising in Chicago to clean the streets and distribute pure milk. But Robins' 'inextricable mixture of idealism and expediency' puzzled her, and she was sceptical about his politics, 'he believes in the People, calls that Democracy'.[46] Robins had opposed Chicago's centralising City Charter, insisting on democratic controls over municipal finance.

In contrast, the agitation over the water supply was to align William with the push for vesting *more* power with the Mayor through Boston's City Charter. By the summer of 1909, William was not just a Charter member on the Chamber of Commerce, he also belonged to the City and Economic Clubs, the Chamber of Commerce, the South End Improvement Society, the United Improvement Association, the American Economic Association, the American Association for Labor Legislation, the Single Tax League and Filene's Boston-1915 movement.[47] The former anarchist was festooned with a plethora of bodies favoured by the liberal establishment; amid so many meetings, Annie Besant on Theosophy, in September, probably felt like light relief.[48]

In November 1909, the new City Charter was approved by voters and the Boston-1915 movement mounted an impressive exhibition at the old Museum of Fine Arts on Copley Square. It depicted the city as it might be, using 'steroptican [*sic*] slides and moving pictures'. Parks, model tenement housing and visions of the City Beautiful all featured.[49] The Boston-1915ers and the G.G.A. were now overtly in the political arena, pinning their hopes on Storrow becoming Mayor. But in January 1910 their candidate was trounced by Fitzgerald. The new Democratic Mayor smoothly adopted the language and methods of the reformers. And, irony of ironies, it was Honey Fitz who inherited the extended powers created by the new Charter.[50]

Helen, too, was busily attending meetings. In 1909 the National American Woman Suffrage Association (N.A.W.S.A) was backing an Equal Suffrage Bill in Massachusetts, and on February 22nd, Helen and her mother went to hear N.A.W.S.A. President, Anna Howard Shaw, speak for it at Faneuil Hall.[51] Attempts to gain suffrage state by state were, however, being repeatedly defeated, and the ethos of temperance and self-help Shaw personified no longer appealed to many dissatisfied rank-and-file members. The following day, when Helen and Isabel went to the State House for the hearing, they were lucky to get in, for the suffrage contingent was augmented by a large, new crowd of socialist women. Dressed in white, the women marched together, but again the bill was defeated.[52]

Helen was heartened by a mass meeting in March addressed by Charlotte Perkins Gilman, Leonora O'Reilly and Charles Edward Russell, because they voiced 'splendid revolutionary ideas bigger than votes for women'.[53] Gilman turned conservative ideas of women's domestic sphere on their head by declaring 'home should mean the whole country and not be confined to three or four rooms, or a city or state'.[54] O'Reilly, a former shirtwaist maker, had not only organised women garment workers, she supported the Socialist Party women's initiative for the National Woman's Day in 1909, which claimed social as well as political citizenship. Moreover, along with the muck-raking enemy of the Trusts, Charles Edward Russell, O'Reilly was a founding member of the National Association for the Advancement of Colored People.[55] Nationally a range of movements were being linked by interconnecting radical networks like these.

In Massachusetts, the younger generation of suffrage campaigners started to adopt evangelical tactics, selling papers and buttons at street meetings, perched on soap boxes with 'Votes for Women' banners on their shoulders. Their enthusiasm reinvigorated the women's movement. A new kind of feminist direct action quickened the tempo, as news of the British militant 'suffragettes' crossed the Atlantic.[56] In July, Helen was delighted when 'a copy of Mrs Pankhurst's Votes for Women' arrived through the post from Beatrice Taylor's mother: 'she seems to think I like them – which indeed I do. Wm. says they are sure to win. They have won respect from many in this country and have given wonderful impetus to the movement here.'[57] Emmeline Pankhurst was given an overwhelming welcome in Boston that October.[58]

Helen acknowledged one could not expect a 'revolution' to follow women's 'suffrage', but she was nonetheless roused by an heroic cause, 'one must take a stand'.[59] That September, in an upbeat mood and convinced that progress in the workplace accompanied by 'saner views on the sex question' were fast-approaching, she wrote a paper herself on 'equal suffrage', stressing the importance of 'the will to be free'. Helen maintained that if a woman acted 'as though her rights were equal to man's in business, in public affairs, in society, in marriage, there are few men who would fail to respect her claims'.[60] Such voluntarism had not exactly been borne out by her own experience in the publishing world! Just one little troubling gripe disturbed her – William, the staunch supporter of women's rights – possessed a blind spot: 'Wm. hardly ever wipes the dishes but he says, "I can't understand where all these dishes come from!" My dearest would like to forget dishes after he has used them.'[61]

In summer 1909 Helen and William read with horror of the bloody suppression of an anarchist uprising in Barcelona.[62] This was followed by the arrest and execution of Francisco Ferrer, whose Modern School and International League for the Rational Education of Children was anathema to the Spanish Catholic hierarchy. Though Ferrer was not in Barcelona in late July during the 'Tragic Week' of the rebellion, as a supporter of the anarchist movement, he was condemned as its instigator on the basis of his influence. Beatrice Taylor sent a file of his writing on the Modern School to Helen, who also obtained from Spain a copy of the will of 'Mlle Meunier', the benefactress who had enabled Ferrer to found the school, thus countering aspersions on his personal character.[63]

Hostile press reports of the international demonstrations against Ferrer's execution provoked a protest from Helen to *Harper's Weekly* early in 1910. Whereupon Leonard Abbott, the libertarian socialist friend of Carpenter, Lloyd and Goldman, responded by sending her the outline of a book he was compiling on Ferrer's work. Helen impulsively offered him access to the material she had been collecting in Spanish, French and English, and agreed to help.[64] But that June, when Abbott proposed handing the project over to Emma Goldman, Helen responded proprietorially, 'I convinced him she is not the one to do it. I like her nerve.'[65] In fact, Goldman was hardly an opportunistic interloper, she had a long-standing interest in libertarian education, spoke frequently against

Ferrer's execution, and would play a key part with Abbott in creating the New York Modern School. A tactful Abbott proposed that Helen might organise a meeting in Boston, and went ahead with the book himself.[66]

Helen proceeded to book Faneuil Hall and organise the speakers, who included Edwin D. Mead, founder of the Twentieth Century Club and the Anti-Vivisectionist journalist, Edward Henry Clement. Helen was delighted by the direct action of David Mikol's young Jewish anarchist friends. When 'the fellow on guard at Faneuil Hall' banned the sale of the booklet she had prepared on Ferrer, her allies 'cleverly passed [it] around in the crowd', disposing of nearly all the copies in the packed 'stuffy' hall and bringing her the dimes.[67] The meeting just broke even and Helen studiously ignored demands for receipts from New York.

The two essays Helen translated from the French on Ferrer's life for the Boston meeting both appeared in *Francisco Ferrer: His Life, Work and Martyrdom* (1910). She and Abbott also wrote 'The Trial of Ferrer' for the book, critically examining the evidence brought against him. Emma Goldman reflected on the implications of the anarchist educator's death, and tributes came from internationally known writers, including Ernst Haeckel, Jack London, Upton Sinclair, Edward Carpenter and Havelock Ellis. Abbott, a natural networker, displayed an eclectic list of 'Francisco Ferrer Association' advisers in the book. It included Goldman, Charles Edward Russell, J.G. Phelps Stokes and Rose Pastor Stokes, along with Helen herself.[68]

However, Helen's personal faith in children's innate inclinations for enlightenment was dealt a blow in June 1910, when fourteen-year-old Viola, William and Helen's last hope, rebelled against high culture, abandoning the fiddle. Helen logged 'agony all round'.[69]

Though William's links with his former anarchist networks had loosened, Helen was aware that her beloved was not completely at ease in the new milieu. In February 1910, she reflected, 'Wm. is not built like the men he meets. He has always been and will be unable to take the selfish point of view, the view of special interest, of individual interest. It cuts him off.'[70] William still searched for truth and held by principles. But now he was close to the world of mainstream politics and business lobbies, nothing was quite as it sounded. William's previous socialist and anarchist politics had been about exposing; in the circles he now entered, much effort was devoted to concealing.

While campaigning against Storrow, Fitzgerald had refused to concede the reforming high ground to his opponent. His slogan, 'Manhood against Money', branded his wealthy and well-connected rival as effete, padded by capital and hen-pecked by women social reformers. Nevertheless, upon emerging victorious, Fitzgerald adopted certain elements of Boston-1915's programme, such as improving co-ordination between municipal departments. Equably, he wrote for the Boston-1915ers publications, opened their pageants and enthused about planning, while retaining his support among Boston's Irish community. In June 1910, when Fitzgerald took the chair at a meeting addressed by the moderate Irish Nationalist MP, John Redmond, Helen and William were in the great crowd that attended. Acclaiming the man who was seeking Home Rule through the Westminster Parliament, Helen recoiled from the cheers of the 'Hibernian audience' for Fitzgerald.[71] The opinions of the Hibernian by her side go unrecorded.

Boston proved far harder to change than the reformers around Boston-1915 had imagined. At the close of 1910, Steffens had still not finished the report Filene and the G.G.A. had hoped would prepare for Storrow's victory. Predictably, he had uncovered 'interests' not simply among the tough ward leaders, but in the leafy suburbs represented by the United Improvement Association, which backed Storrow. Filene's entrepreneurial skills were thwarted by great blocs of resistance that congealed against his schemes for a 'better' Boston.[72] Owners of businesses wanted lower property taxes, and few ordinary citizens were prepared to pay more for civic improvement. Boston-1915, with its disparate bases of support and its lack of any effective means of carrying out its plans, floundered on William's dilemma over how individuals' immediate short-term interests were to be coaxed towards longer-term projects that could yield a broad social good.

Early in 1911, however, William found an issue which married utopianism with pragmatism – social housing. Efforts to clear slums and allow space for healthy recreation were fusing with an aesthetic enthusiasm for the 'City Beautiful' among reformers, though they were divided on whether state funding should complement voluntary contributions. Filene's schemes for co-operative housing were supported by his ally in the Boston-1915 network, the pioneering landscape architect and planner, John Nolen, who happened to be in contact with William's former acquaintance from the Socialist League, Raymond Unwin. By 1911 Unwin had become internationally known in planning circles for

transplanting the visions of Morris and Kropotkin into community projects at Letchworth Garden City and Hampstead Garden Suburb.[73]

In May 1911 Unwin visited the United States, where he was to give
a paper in Philadelphia at the Third Annual Conference on City Planning, and an excited William went to New York to escort him to Boston.
Helen relates how William 'was up till past midnight among the group of
Boston's progressives who dined Unwin'.[74] Staunchly promoting Unwin's
work and ideas in the *Boston Evening Transcript*, William described him
as closely associated with the 'philosophic writer', Edward Carpenter, and
at the forefront of 'an organized social movement' of enlightened town
planners founded by Ebenezer Howard and Patrick Geddes. Stressing
Morris' influence on Unwin's aesthetic, William praised the co-operative voluntarism of the garden cities and their acknowledgement of the
need for individual privacy, contrasting them favourably with European
socialist communal phalansteries and with the 'formal piles' erected as
tenements in U.S. cities.[75] But a sharper-eyed Helen detected that the
'cool, practical' Unwin did not share William's interest in going back over
'the old Morris days in Manchester'.[76] Despite his libertarian socialist past,
Unwin had moved towards Fabianism and municipal socialism, though
he continued to support co-operation and residents' participation.

After Mayor Fitzgerald attended the 1911 Philadelphia Town Planning Conference, Boston was buzzing with plans. Having widened
his scope from water pollution, William was now writing for Boston-
1915's magazine, *New Boston*, on planning. In the July issue he noted
that despite Boston's excellent Metropolitan Parks System, in contrast
to British co-operative projects, the city had been somewhat backward
on planning.[77] That November William maintained that 'Comprehensive
City Planning' in Boston required a Planning Board as a clearing-house to
overcome the conflicting responsibilities of the city's departments.[78] The
libertarian who wished to reduce the state was now calling for additional
machinery in order to curb the inefficient usage of public resources.

After a swipe at waste in Boston's water supply, William asserted that
a city's real greatness was based on the 'standard of living, the degree of
contentment'.[79] Convinced that civic improvements should be for the
benefit of all classes, he also called for a social audit of the 'racial and
social characteristics' of Boston's 'citizens with a view to finding out their
special needs', an approach in accord with that of the African-American Organisation secretary of Boston-1915, C. Bertrand Thompson,
as well as with Nolen and Unwin.[80] William argued for a survey that

would take into account the *human* dimensions of planning and development; invoking Patrick Geddes' dynamic approach to planning based on needs, he wrote, 'A city is *always* in the making; it is never completed.'[81] Co-operative schemes and planning seemed to offer a feasible utopia, and William expressed unstinting admiration for Unwin as 'a dreamer whose dreams come true'.[82] Helen observed protectively, 'Wm's emotions played about memories of his old friend Unwin.' The utopian yeast was at work and, to Helen's delight, William came back to life: 'Ideas flow; he is writing again.'[83]

In November 1911 Helen and William went to a performance of *The Blue Bird* by a defender of Ferrer, the popular Belgian symbolist playwright, Maurice Maeterlinck. Maeterlinck believed the natural world was pervaded by divinity and that humanity could, through contemplation, attain enlightenment. The elusive Blue Bird metaphorically embodies the Neo-Platonic quest. It aroused Helen's Idealism and she was filled with 'regrets' by the play. She wished she could recover her 'old beliefs – such convenient barricades against despair, these guileless propositions'.[84]

Regardless of a mutual scepticism towards mystics, both she and William carried the Blue Bird, along with their memories of Helena, buried within them. Helen felt flickers of nostalgia for the years of her unique closeness to Helena and reflected that 'if Wm. should die, he would be joined again with Helena'.[85] William was always cautiously oblique, but when one of John B. Andrews' protégées wrote in 1911 asking William's advice on how to combine 'intellectual pursuits' with family obligations, he advised her to read the book about Helena Born by Helen Tufts.[86]

Andrews visited them again in 1912 and collected their copies of *Liberty* and *Free Society* to take to Wisconsin. It was at once an indication of their trust in him, and a sober acknowledgement that the journals belonged to a past they were laying to rest.[87] While William mused on city planning, Helen had become an advocate of 'sex hygiene' and was soon to join the philanthropic Women's City Club, presided over by 'Mrs James Storrow'.[88]

Yet, of course, the past lingered on in the present. Helen experienced remorse about her estrangement from her parents. In November 1912 she wrote, 'It is no use going to Wm. He doesn't know how to allay ghosts, and it only reminds him of his own torments.'[89] William was tortured by his feelings of failure as a father. The grim toll of disappointment

had continued. By 1913, the second daughter, Nellie, had had an illegiti-
mate baby, cared for by Ellen; and bashed around, incorrigible Willie had
finally overstepped the mark after stealing Ellen's pocket book. The other
daughters had not continued with their education and could find only
low-paid work.[90]

Early in 1913 Helen asked Abbott to remove her name from the mailing
list of the New York Modern School because she disapproved of the
educational approach she thought it represented. Perhaps with the
Bailie children in mind she had concocted her own secular version of
original sin:

> Children are groping, wayward and erratic, full of sinister impulses as
> well as of impulses that are lovely. Discipline is essential in the forming
> of character, for their own protection and the protection of society –
> enlightened discipline of course, not despotism.[91]

She informed Abbott sternly, 'This is sound anarchism.'[92] The mild
and gentle Abbott, who could entrance children from poor immigrant
backgrounds with his lessons on science and was remembered fondly for
letting them feast on his cherry trees, no doubt begged to differ. The
Modern School encouraged the inner capacity to discipline oneself,
rather than Helen's censorious pessimism.

Helen's decision to sever her connections with the School was not
simply about whether or not the theories of Ferrer were being followed.
She distrusted its connections to anarchists such as Emma Goldman
and believed it was inspired by 'the Jewish temperament'.[93] Helen's anti-
Semitism manifested itself selectively according to her personal likes and
dislikes. Mikol's young comrades were on her approved list, as was the
eminent Brandeis; however, Dr Antoinette Konikow, a Jewish immigrant from Russia and a socialist advocate of birth control, was not. A
testy Helen complained that Eugène Brieux's daring play about venereal
disease, *Damaged Goods*, was ruined by 'Dr Konikow and a string of Jews'
who sat in the balcony and talked through the performance.[94]

Helen's opinions on socialists were subject to similar discrepancies.
When the would-be femme fatale, Louise Heald, made contact in June
1912, she was dismissed with the wrathful comment, 'She has gone
over to Socialism … Natures like hers not only do not expand, – they
deteriorate.'[95] In contrast, the Bristolian socialist, Robert Sharland,

being Helena's friend, escaped Helen's opprobrium. In 1913 the usual May Day issue of *Justice* arrived from him with a newspaper clipping announcing the death of 'Mr Edward Tuckett Daniell'. This led Helen to ruminate:

> I never rightly understood his actions in regard to Miriam. He really intended no harm to her or to Robert in seeking evidence for a divorce. Miriam's panic and the flight to California were but part of her unhinged impulses. Would that Helena had never gone with them on that distracted flight – or that Robert Nicol had been left behind! Sunrise knows little of the great and loving soul that nurtured her in babyhood and sacrificed so much for her mother and father. Robert has seen to that.[96]

Despite being obstinately inclined to hang on to old antipathies, she did send Richard Born Campton's portrait of Helena. He responded by apologising belatedly for not inviting her to his home when they had met, with the etiolated excuse that his wife's aunts did not like 'social-ists'.[97] Little did they know they had escaped taking tea with an anarchist!

During 1913 Helen became seriously interested in her family's history. From her childhood she had loved to hear her relative, Cora Brown, in Concord, relate stories of Anne Adams Tufts tearing up her linen sheets to bandage the wounded at Bunker Hill. Helen set about systematically investigating the part played by the Tufts family in the War of Independence against the British, thrilling with pride when the Daughters of the American Revolution erected a memorial plaque to the revolutionary heroine on Winter Hill.[98]

William, who distrusted all forms of romantic patriotic zeal, poured scorn on such effusive excitement about forebears. He regarded much of his own heritage askance. After they saw a play about Protestant and Catholic bigotry in Ireland, called *Mixed Marriage*, William asked did she wonder why he had wanted to escape the country by the age of sixteen.[99] Through the enlightened Unitarian, Revd Street, in Belfast, William had been offered an alternative to sectarian hatred – reason. He had held on to it, often at the expense of expressing his emotions. Helen, too, had been reared most rigorously to live by reason, but her feelings, like those of her father, were liable to erupt as high-handed assertions that trumped dispassionate analysis.

*   *   *

In the early summer of 1913, when William was planning a trip to Europe in search of skilled basket makers, Helen, at thirty-nine, discovered she was pregnant again. At last, they felt in a position to care for a child. When Helen visited May Hurd (now May Denton) that June with a basket of strawberries, her friend happened to remark that it was 'a mistake for parents to expect gratitude from their children who had not asked to be brought into the world'.[100] Full of expectant baby-thoughts, Helen spontaneously communicated her secret, adding how she relied on May Hurd for 'moral support'. In a flash of self-knowledge, Helen admitted a fear that 'I would count too much on what I want the baby to be.'[101]

But Helen's tendency to try and exert control over every contingency remained in the ascendency. Just before William had left for Europe, she nobbled him for what she describes as one of her serious 'talks'. It appears that Helen did the talking, presenting William with a comprehensive long-term plan: 'In all respects, spiritual, mental, material, our Baby, whether boy or girl, shall have that care and provision that it has ever been Wm's purpose to give all his offspring, – nurture, and an education directed to independence at 21.'[102] Babies being arguably even less amenable to planning than cities, it goes without question that this project was to hold some surprises.

In William's absence, Helen worried about bills, then she worried about worrying in case she caused the baby stress. The doctor instructed her to get out into the sunshine at their Lakeledge cottage and relax.[103] Though Helen never really did stop worrying, all went well. On 6 January 1914 Helen recorded the arrival of a baby girl, 'with fat little toes'.[104] They named her Helena, after the woman they both had loved.

TWENTY-ONE

Elusive Realities: 1908–1914

In 1908 the Southern Pacific Railroad was reconstructing the line northwards up to the old mining town of Colfax. When they built a vast roundhouse in Roseville, a small town in Placer County to the south of Auburn, a great influx of itinerant railway workers, the 'boomers', arrived. Soon everyone was renting rooms to the 'boomers'; when the rooms ran out they slept in tents and the saloons expanded into 'drinking emporiums' catering for the thirsty men. Roseville became a city – thanks to the railway.[1] By the following year, the mighty Southern Pacific was heading towards White-nights and buying up land around Weimar. On 24 June 1909, a newly qualified notary, Raglan Tuttle, destined to become a judge, 'affixed the official seal' to a document confirming that Robert Allan Nicol, Gertrude Dix Nicol and Miriam S. Nicol had sold a parcel of land to the railway company through Wells Fargo.[2]

The expanding reach of the railway coincided with a dramatic change in eighteen-year-old Sunrise's life. Leaving the familiar foothills of the Sierras, she made the long journey to New York, where she boarded the *Arabic* for England, arriving in Liverpool on 27 September 1909.[3] Sunrise's trip to England may have been funded by the land sale to Southern Pacific. But why did she have to go to a school so far from home? Could tension between Gertrude and Sunrise have been a factor? Did Sunrise rebel against playing nursemaid while Gertrude wrote? Or was Robert's long-standing dream of Sunrise studying at an English boarding school the reason for her drastic uprooting. And who exactly was responsible for her in Britain?

Sunrise with Margot and Amaryllis
(Courtesy of Georges Rey, Private Collection)

The only clues come from the oral testimony of Robert and Gertrude's children. They were young when Sunrise left, so their memories must be mainly based upon what they gleaned later from their parents. Amaryllis recalled hearing that Sunrise had been given 'all kinds of wonderful addresses' but 'she didn't like any of their friends', including the Fabian Webbs.[4] Margot felt resentful that her half-sister had been given money by Robert to travel around Europe, chaperoned by a Scottish aunt who Sunrise disliked as much as the socialist intellectuals.[5] Despite embracing his new homeland, Robert affected bizarre puffs of snobbish superiority amid the wilds of Placer County, and according to Margot, Sunrise was 'sent abroad to be educated and to travel' because Robert 'felt that America was no place to receive your culture'.[6] Margot was only five when her half-sister left, but as she grew older she came to envy Sunrise as 'something of a beauty who was given every advantage'.[7] It was a verdict Sunrise might well have contested.

After Sunrise's departure, life at the ranch resumed its familiar pattern. Despite Gertrude's terror of the mines, Robert appears to have worked sporadically on mining projects and received some money from the Nicol family.[8] Gertrude, with three young children, still endeavoured to write. In 1911, her poem, 'Manzanita', appeared in *Sunset*, the magazine published by the Passenger Department of the Southern Pacific Company.[9] She had established a modest reputation with her short stories in popular magazines such as *Out West* and *The Red Book Magazine*. Danger lurks in hidden places in these tales; black sheep return to haunt the prosperous, fortunes are precarious, money is made and lost, rewards are arbitrary. Even so Gertrude managed small subversions; in 'Van Velsor's Apotheosis' she has a reactionary old-timer pronouncing, 'The women, young man, are too much on top in this Western country.' Her women continue to display inner resolution despite constricting circumstances, like 'Mrs Redfield Scott' in 'One Touch of Nature' who, having contributed to her husband's wealth by scrubbing work clothes in tin cans on 'a little hot porch' in Nevada, sells the diamonds he has given her and insists that he recognises their disowned artist son and grandchild.[10]

Gertrude and Robert were at one on women's rights. On 10 March 1910 Robert's letter in support of the British militant suffragettes appeared in the avant-garde left journal *The New Age*:

> In the Western States of the U.S., where even now women hold the suffrage in some States, I can speak from actual knowledge of how keenly women in the remotest districts follow the battle in England. The American newspapers chronicle the moves made by the English suffragettes fully as they occur, and as the newspapers and cheap ten cent magazines are the great media of American education when school days finish, it follows that the average man and woman of the States is kept well posted about the struggle. America is a great woman's country – woman is coming to her own rapidly out here – and the press is, on the whole, sympathetic, even with the militancy of the British sisters.[11]

From 1909, the Liberal Government in Britain had responded to the window-smashing militants in the Women's Social and Political Union with imprisonment and the forcible feeding of hunger strikers. But after the leader of the W.S.P.U., Emmeline Pankhurst, announced a change of tactics on 31 January 1910, a truce was effected by an all-party Conciliation Committee. Far away at White-nights, Robert was keeping abreast of events. Noting that the *New York World* of February 7th had welcomed the truce, an unabashed Robert took it upon himself to advise the suffragettes that perhaps the time had come 'to drop the forcible methods', pronouncing with customary bravura, 'the thanks of all women are due to the noble fighters who suffered violence that in the end all the race should gain'.[12]

Robert was intervening in a controversy that had been running for several months in *The New Age*. Despite the journal's attachment to extreme radical causes, its prominent woman contributor, Emily Alice

Haigh, writing under the pseudonym, 'D. Triformis', supported the constitutionalist wing of the suffrage movement rather than the militants. Before Emmeline Pankhurst put militant tactics on hold, 'D. Triformis' had declared, 'Militant tactics have proved a failure.'[13] Haigh, a journalist from South Africa, maintained multiple selves; 'D. Triformis' was just one of several names she adopted. Appearing often as 'Beatrice Hastings', Haigh also signed herself 'Beatrice Tina'. Haigh's opposition to the W.S.P.U. derived not only from their adoption of violent direct action, but because they had boycotted a book by 'Beatrice Tina', *Woman's Worst Enemy, Woman* (1909), demanding women's sexual freedom. She regarded the W.S.P.U. as 'puritanically opposed' to the 'sex revolt'.[14]

Through *The New Age*, Robert and Gertrude imported vehement iconoclasms fermented in a small office in London to the foothills of the Sierras. Since 1907, the journal had been edited by a former school-teacher, Alfred Orage, whose interests encompassed Theosophy, Fabianism and anti-statist Guild Socialism. Its contributors included writers familiar to Robert and Gertrude: Carpenter, Geddes, Bennett and Sam Hobson from Fabian Circle times. By 1910 it was extending to Nietzscheans and anarchists. Ultra-modern in its cultural coverage and politically inclined to veer left, *The New Age* pursued dichotomies that preoccupied Robert and Gertrude: rationalism and romanticism, sex and spirit, individual and social transformation.[15]

Gertrude's younger sister, Phyllis Snaith, who followed Clement Dix westwards in 1910, no doubt relayed news of Sunrise, still in exile across the Atlantic. The following year, Sunrise's whereabouts emerge through the 1911 British Census, conducted in April. The young woman who had roamed freely in the canyons and hills of the Sierras was to be found in Bournemouth, the balmy South Coast resort favoured by sufferers from tuberculosis and the elderly rich. 'Miriam Sunrise Nicol', aged twenty, is listed as living in a boarding house at 29 Suffolk Road along with nine other young women students and four teachers. She is described as a 'House Training Student'.[16]

This address was the School of Domestic Management attached to Bournemouth High School. Sunrise's lodgings were only a short walk from the School's main site in Norwich Avenue, consisting of three large houses, connected by a basement corridor.[17] Training Sunrise to manage a household appears at first sight a curious educational choice on the part of her unconventional father with his extravagant ideals. Yet her formal academic education had been so interrupted it may have been the only option.

Moreover, Bournemouth High School announced itself in 1905 as 'on the modern plan'. It specialised in languages, mathematics and 'Physical Training' and girls were offered not simply hockey, cricket and tennis, but dancing, swimming and 'Swedish gymnastics'.[18] Its athletic, fun-loving head mistress, Mary Broad, sought to help young minds grow spontaneously and believed in 'free discipline' methods – fixing the recalcitrant with her penetrating eyes. She disliked competition and discouraged individual prizes; instead her school was committed to social citizenship and the fostering of free-spirited women.[19] A photograph of her with the staff suggests that she, too, was something of a rebel with her short hair brushed back and a 'new woman' tie and blouse.[20]

Any one of Gertrude and Robert's acquaintances could have recommended the Bournemouth school. But an obvious suspect was Edward Carpenter, who used to visit a group of Tolstoyans living in austere simplicity nearby at Tuckton House. An offshoot of the Purleigh Tolstoyan community, while Sunrise was studying at Miss Broad's they were smuggling Tolstoy's manuscripts into Russia, printing pamphlets in English, debating Marxism, practising vegetarianism and running a football team.[21]

Within a few months of the Census being taken, Sunrise was gone. Aged twenty, she returned to New York from Liverpool on the *Baltic*, arriving in the United States on 18 August 1911. Presumably she returned to the ranch. However, a 'house-trained' Sunrise was not to settle. In November 1912, an indenture exchanging land for a loan of $1,500 in gold coins was signed solely by 'Robert A. Nicol' and 'Gertrude Mary Nicol, his wife'.[22] 'Miriam Sunrise Nicol' never appeared in any subsequent legal documents relating to the property.

Sunrise's exodus constituted a traumatic familial crisis and many accounts coiled around it. Margot told her friend, Edna Eldred, that Sunrise 'eloped with a farm hand'. In a later account she described him as 'Harvey Lee', a 'section hand'. Several narratives wafted their way down to the next generation: Barbara Donnelly, the daughter of Robert and Gertrude's son, Bob Nicol, heard a rumour that Sunrise had vanished on a ship in Southern California; Bob Nicol reassured her, however, by saying that he had seen Sunrise in later life. Robert's grandson, Georges Rey, whose grandmother, Nora Keating, began a relationship with Robert around the time of the First World War, was told that 'Sunrise fell in love with a railway worker (a "lineman") of whom RAN strongly disapproved and forbade her marrying.'[23]

In the decades following 1912, the missing Sunrise acquired a mythical presence in family memory. Margot described to her friend Edna Eldred how 'her father washed his hands of the whole affair and indeed the affairs of the whole family and returned to his books'.[24] The Nicol children, Margot, Amaryllis and Bob, testify to the dramatic effect upon Robert, who became depressed and withdrawn, and describe the upheaval this caused between him and Gertrude.[25] After Sunrise left, he would go into the railway tunnel near the ranch and sometimes took the children with him. On one occasion, Amaryllis relates how, as he held forth about the Whitmanite dancer, Isadora Duncan, whom he and Gertrude admired, a freight train came through and they only just got out.[26]

Though Margot's memories were inclined to be chronologically jumbled and subject to flights of fancy, she remained acutely attuned to the strong emotions swirling through her childhood. The mystery of her half-sister's desertion and the subsequent psychological retreat of her father haunted her, forming the core of the unpublished novel, *Her Father's Daughter*, which combines a melodramatic plot with insightful speculation about her parents' relationship and the impact of Gertrude's arrival upon Sunrise.

It seems to have been shortly after Sunrise left home that Gertrude took Margaret (Margot), Amaryllis and Bob on a trip to England. When Bob was interviewed by Georges Rey, he stated that Gertrude went without Robert because she was exasperated with him. However, Amaryllis thought Gertrude went because she was anxious to see her mother.[27] In 1912 Juliet Wartnaby Dix, aged seventy-five and ailing, had just moved from a large house with ten rooms in Chislehurst, Kent, where she had been living with her two oldest sons and a niece. She was independently wealthy and her new home, 2 Broadway, Littleham Cross, Devon, must still have been sufficiently capacious for Gertrude and the three grand-children. Amaryllis retained vivid memories of the stiff formality of Littleham Cross, and how she winced when Bob cried and Grandmother Dix sardonically remarked, 'There goes Robert turning on the water works.'[28] He would be removed to the nursery to be comforted.

In contrast, Margot writes fondly of the visit to Littleham Cross. The ancient church in the village, so unlike anything she had previously seen, remained in her memory and features in the manuscript of *Her Father's*

L. to R.: Hilda and Juliet Wartnaby Dix
(Courtesy of Georges Rey, Private Collection)

Daughter. She was evidently intrigued by the panache of her grandmother's orderly domain, referring to the cook being summoned to 'discuss' meals by an intriguing foot-bell embedded in the carpet. Unlike Amaryllis, Margot does not seem to have been intimidated by her grandmother, though like the church, she must have seemed exceedingly old, for Margot makes her eighty-four in the novel, adding nearly a decade to Grandmother Dix's actual age.[29]

Details relating to the visit to England which appear in the novel are recognisably ones that would have been of special interest to an eight-year-old: 'currant buns', 'scones', 'sponge cakes', along with 'yellow primroses' and 'pink and white daisies'. Various quintessentially British food items also apparently made their way to the ranch and feature in *Her Father's Daughter*: 'Scotch shortbread', Keelers (Keiller's) marmalade, 'Cheddar cheese' and 'Ridgways English Breakfast' tea.[30]

According to family memory, Gertrude needed to sort out what Amaryllis describes as 'tangled' business affairs in England. The tangles appear to have arisen from Robert; Amaryllis recalled 'Aunt Hilda' remarking, 'Look how your father squandered your mother's income.'[31] Amaryllis says Gertrude went to see a 'solicitor' called 'Sir Richard Garnett' in London. Sir Richard worked for the British Library and died in 1906;

so this would have been his solicitor son, Robert Singleton Garnett.[32] Gertrude stayed away longer than she intended and was evidently short of cash, for various Dix uncles contributed towards their return home.[33] They had visited just in time. Juliet Wartnaby Dix died in 1913.[34] Gertrude and the children arrived in New York on 11 April 1912. Upon reaching the ranch they found Robert in bed sick and everything in 'disarray' in the house.[35] It was left to Gertrude to hold daily life together.

The crisis over Sunrise, lack of money, looking after three young children and writing the potboilers had all taken their toll. Gertrude's literary reputation was fading. Her name is included in *The Literary Year Book* for the last time in 1912.[36] Nevertheless she was being published and earlier work was still circulating. One story, 'The Metamorphosis of a Toy Soldier', syndicated in Australia in 1910, was reproduced in the *Taunton Courier and Western Advertiser* in Britain in 1914. It is set not in the American West, but in the workers' uprising in Moscow during 1905. Gertrude writes with sympathy of a young officer who is appalled at finding himself among troops who were killing 'workmen and students and young women'. Tearing 'the facings from his uniform', he is 'thrown like a torch into the burning city'.[37]

It was not simply the scandal surrounding Sunrise's departure that distanced Gertrude and Robert from their neighbours, but also their opinions and outlook. They retained a habitual air of haughty disdain towards American culture as 'the kingdom of mediocrity'.[38] Moreover, Gertrude's disregard for convention, her clothes, her choice of décor, her writing, combined with Robert's icy disengagement, placed them apart.

As the children grew older they gradually became aware of their parents' nonconforming difference. Amaryllis recalled how, one time when Robert was away, a kindly Gertrude had sheltered an old German lace maker who was lost. In the morning, he gave her a beautiful piece of lace and she took him to the railroad.[39] Her parents' books and her mother's literary connections were imprinted upon Margot's mind. She remembered seeing Schopenhauer by the soap rack and copies of Goethe and Nietzsche about the house.[40] In *Her Father's Daughter*, she refers to the Richard character's interest in *Thus Spake Zarathustra* and *Beyond Good and Evil* and to bookshelves stacked with Carpenter's *Towards Democracy*, Whitman's *Leaves of Grass*, Henry James' *The American* and *The Wings of the Dove*, as well as *The Martyrdom of Man*, an 1872 secular history of the world by Winwood Reade, admired by H.G. Wells. Gertrude's novels, *The Girl from the Farm* and *The Image Breakers*, also appear in *Her*

Father's Daughter, ostensibly written by the character closely resembling Gertrude, 'Sarah Lake'.[41] Margot lists Sarah Lake's literary and Fabian acquaintances as including Wells, Ellis, Shaw, Garnett, Beardsley, Annie Beasant [*sic*] and Olive Shriner [*sic*].[42] These all appear to have been lifted from actuality.

Margot seems to have experienced an ambivalence towards the intellectual world she saw her parents as inhabiting. It fascinated her, yet she could not understand or share it. However, while Bob was critical of both parents, and especially of Robert, Margot, like Amaryllis, adored her distant father and continued to defend him. Interviewed by Georges Rey, all three children testify to Robert's detached reserve. In contrast to the effusive man bursting with schemes for social change and self-perfection or the hyperbolic lover of Gertrude in Shasta, the Robert his children portray was coldly remote. They recall how he disdained common-place civilities, helping to bury a neighbour without simulating grief. This same indifference enabled him to coolly face down an angry neighbour with a gun who was threatening to shoot him for leaving his gate open and allowing bulls to stray.[43] Margot confirmed the danger was real, describing how disputes between neighbours did become violent: 'A lot of people there just went crazy. They hadn't talked to anyone for years.'[44]

The unbounded enthusiasm Robert had shared with Miriam, and the frantic spiritual quests that followed her death, had flowed towards Sunrise. Her loss seems to have locked Robert into a cynical protective shell. Henceforth, the transformative hopes were channelled into the gambler's dreams of a lucky break. Yet, while Robert's search for a new life was compressed, it was not entirely eradicated. Reflecting fondly on her father's 'idealism', Amaryllis observed, he 'thought the human body was so beautiful'.[45] This much remained from Robert's herculean struggle to reject the Victorian society into which he had been born.

Margot's desire to understand her father, probe the mystery of the family's break with her half-sister, and retrace the unfamiliar cultural and political influences that had shaped her parents, tumble through the pages of *Her Father's Daughter*. The inchoate, packed manuscript is replete with childhood memories and snippets of information which seem to have been mainly gleaned from Gertrude, embellished with her own vivid delight in the dramatic.

The plot, set just after the First World War, is a thinly disguised reworking of her own family's story. Phyllis, aged fourteen, arrives with her mother, Sarah Lake, from England, at the ranch where Richard Mac-Donald and his daughter Anita live in California. Phyllis is told by her mother that she and Richard had been active together in the socialist movement and had become very close, before Anita's mother, Lady Anne Crothers, 'from a noble family in Spain', had treacherously snatched him away. Sarah, who Grandmother Lake describes as 'unbecomingly affected by men', had married a 'cad', called Bert, who had rejected Phyllis.[46] She was told this was because he disdained girls, but Phyllis later learns that Richard was actually her father. Reared by her old grandmother, Phyllis saw little of Sarah until Bert, the cad, is conveniently killed in the War. Sarah and Richard had never forgotten one another, and in response to a letter from him, Sarah, at an impasse in her life, decides to join him.

Lady Anne has died and Richard lives alone 'in a wilderness of solitude' with their daughter Anita.[47] Margot's plot requires Phyllis to be the elder, but Anita is described as already a young woman with golden curls and high heels, confident in her sensuous beauty. She resents the intrusion of the English visitors; they disrupt her exclusive relationship with Richard. Phyllis, too, longs for him to notice her but cannot compete with her half-sister. In Margot's narrative, neither can Sarah Lake, and the three women jockey for the attention of the withholding Richard.

Margot's physical description of Richard, ostensibly spied 'out of the corner' of Phyllis' eye, tallies with photographs of Robert:

> His abundant brownish hair, marked by a light streak, curled in the shape of a question mark above his dark arc of meeting brows. On the taut sun tanned face the morning light revealed, almost imperceptible lines of melancholy which appeared graven into the flesh by self-imposed denials.[48]

Margot laboured over the graphic image of her brooding hero, crossing out and amending the typescript to add how the 'muscular contours of his body' appeared to strain beneath his shirt.[49] At another point in the novel, Richard expresses a sense of kinship with a local mountain woman neighbour who possesses 'the misty soul of a dreamer and the constitution of a rock'.[50] He recognises what it is to be at once elusive and hard as stone. Margot makes Anita remark upon how he 'preferred nature to human beings'.[51]

Margot relates that Richard's interest in America had first been awakened by Andrew Carnegie's visits to Dunfermline, though he had emigrated not after a fortune, but in pursuit of the ideals of Whitman and Thoreau.[52] His radical politics had been tempered by his American experiences, but she represents him as still expressing sympathy with the immigrant section hands from Mexico, China and India labouring on the railway. Richard remarks on the irony of their search for 'Liberty' in America, only 'to find slavery in a capitalist heirarchy [*sic*] bent on monopolizing the fruits of the new industrialism'.[53]

In the novel Richard is said to have arrived at the ranch in order to establish a Tolstoyan utopia. This is the only reference to Tolstoy as the inspiration for White-nights and may have been transplanted from Gertrude's interests and connections. Unlike the romantic Richard, Sarah Lake, the character based on Gertrude, is portrayed as eccentric, dowdy and tedious. A misfit in the mountains, Sarah, with her 'crisp bird-like' English voice, her long quilted grey gowns, her advanced woman cigarettes and her aesthetic of simplification, personifies gloom.[54] She hangs up a dark, sombre painting of London Bridge in fog over the Thames by James McNeil Whistler, and plasters 'white calcimine' over the red roses on the dining room wallpaper. Anita, who revels in bright colours, triumphantly points out how the roses persist as 'soft pink shadows'.[55] The glamorous young woman mocks Sarah's readiness to don Richard's trousers, despising the English woman's utilitarian approach to dress. Contemptuous of Sarah's fearfulness about mine shafts, vagrants and the wild countryside, she clashes furiously with the unwelcome intruder's efforts to restrain her by sending her away to school. Phyllis finds herself divided between her anxious mother and her growing friendship with Anita.

This is initiated after Anita pushes the English girl into the railway tunnel, and then shields her from the 'shower of sparks that sputtered from the fire box of a passing locomotive'. Anita puts her arm around Phyllis' waist as they stumble out, calming her terror. After washing their dresses in the pool, they lie naked on the 'warm rock' until their clothes dry, and Anita confides how as a small girl she had been rescued from the tunnel by the railway workers' 'section boss' who is part Spanish, 'Luis Diaz'.[56]

Anita had acquired from her father the idea that 'only when in danger' was one 'truly alive'.[57] Though she admires Richard, she confides to Phyllis that she finds herself held at a distance by her father. As a child she had been physically close to him and felt utterly adored, but, as she entered early adolescence, 'He who had taught me to regard the human body as the sacred temple of the soul; he who had preached against the hypocrisy of people who hid their nakedness in bathing suits, he went and bought us both black bathing suits.'[58] After the advent of the bathing suits, Anita relates how Richard would push her away if she climbed onto his knee or even blew in his ear. In the novel, Margot depicts Richard's body worship crashing head on with his own unconscious desires for his daughter who, as she grew older, seems to incarnate her mother. Anita too recognises that Richard loves her as he had her mother, 'She lives in me.'[59] In the eyes of Sarah Lake, this was a sinister, 'unbalanced' inheritance.[60]

Margot's portrayal of Anita's mother, the aristocratic 'Lady Anne', shifts into farcical melodrama. Green-eyed, auburn haired, bewitching and untrustworthy, she was 'a destructive force, a creature touched with madness whose pursuit of the male amounted to a fever of the blood'.[61] Lady Anne had come between Sarah and Richard, bringing free love ideals into discredit with her sensual attraction to 'adolescent youth'. A callow Presbyterian Richard is represented as just one of the many victims of this 'morbidly passionate creature'. Instead of acknowledging Lady Anne's depravity, Richard expresses guilt for snatching her away from 'a rich and distinguished husband' and then, after becoming 'disenchanted with the class struggle', being persuaded by his friend to build the Tolstoyan utopia in California.[62]

Margot's account of Lady Anne's tragic nemesis belies Richard's faith in her. In *Her Father's Daughter*, true to her supposedly rampant sensuality, Lady Anne runs away with a Mexican track worker – doubly despised for his ethnicity and his class. She drowns in a whirlpool and is found Ophelia-like by Richard, who miraculously saves baby Anita. Nevertheless, to Sarah's exasperation, he admits that he feels bound to the place where the wicked Lady Anne died. Margot's negative portrayal of Miriam was possibly composed from hints dropped by Gertrude, embroidered into a ghoulish vampire. In the novel, all three women are competing with a ghost.

The denouement is similarly melodramatic. Anita, flattered by the compliments of the married womaniser, Luis Diaz, begins a secret affair. She vanishes; her seducer leaves the area. A distraught Richard searches for his daughter, pacing through the tunnels in vain. Cursing Diaz as a 'mongrel brute', he sinks into a depression, which the doctor diagnoses as a 'morbid paralysis of the mind', which 'often ran in families'.[63] But Richard denies he is ill; he wants his wife to leave and take Phyllis, so that if Anita returns they will not be there. Sarah begins to suspect that his love for Anita was more than a father's love. She reaches the devastating conclusion that he had married her only to 'liberate Anita'.[64] She tells Richard he is emotionally affected by his daughter as he had been by Anne, 'Her ardent nature breaks through your emotional frigidity.'[65]

Margot's desire to comprehend her father's inner psychology drives the dense, often inconsistent plot of *Her Father's Daughter*. Her overriding impulse is to plumb his concealed inner feelings. However, the novel also reveals a puzzled interest in her parents' politics and intellectual culture. We learn that Sarah, the Fabian, was distressed when Richard, like Justin Ferrar in *The Image Breakers*, had 'joined in with the Anarchists', believing them to be 'pure minded and idealistic'. She scolds, 'there was a streak of the fanatic in you then'.[66] Sarah is appalled by the lack of purpose in Richard's life in the wilds. What has happened to his '"desire to struggle for a better world"?' But for Richard, 'The present is the forecast of the future. There's nothing else. And I've lost interest in the working classes with their lowbred minds and materialistic aims that lead them only to the avarice and greed of their exploiters.' All he could cling onto was the individual's 'personal destiny'. He declares, 'It is better to be alone and doomed than doomed with the herd.' When Sarah opines that isolation had changed him 'into a Nihilist', Richard replies it was not the place, but his 'inability to cope with the elemental forces of my own nature'. His existential individualism combines with a quasi-religious quest: 'Rationalism is a failure. We must seek harmony through a unification of the physical and the spiritual. The separation has resulted in Puritanism – a denial of nature.'[67]

Margot echoes the actual views of a younger Robert in this rejection of rationalism. Being a twentieth-century modern, she regarded the contorted efforts of her Victorian parents to escape from their repressive heritage with a degree of condescension, yet she cannot distance herself from the consequences for these had marked her own childhood. She gives Sarah lines that no doubt she had always longed for Gertrude to voice. After Anita's disappearance, Sarah confesses to Richard:

Even you, I don't think you feel my love. But then, you yourself are in grown. Your feelings aren't really alive. Perhaps we are both too mental, Richard. Our roots are buried in puritanism. We've freed our minds. We perceive the ideal of freedom, but our emotions never flower. We live and feel by concepts.[68]

Margot depicts Sarah and Richard as conscious of themselves as fail-ures. Earlier in the novel, Sarah tells Richard he is a 'visionary', but he thinks he is 'nothing', adding, 'I failed as a social reformer. Failed in medicine. Failed with love.' He decides, to Sarah's horror, that he 'might as well court failure once again' by mining Green Immigrant Hill.[69] A fortune would free him from dependence, and a rich man with imagina-tion could do much good. Mining to Sarah is yet another manifestation of his 'fanaticism'.

After pouring such intense emotion into her highly charged elabora-tion upon her parents' lives, perhaps Margot herself wondered whether she had succeeded in taking hold of the characters who loomed so power-fully within her own psyche. Perhaps they were at once too close and too remote, making words an inadequate means of breaking through the reserve that rested uneasily between the generations. Mystified by hints about Miriam, and intrigued by her half-sister Sunrise, Margot dives through layers of familial concealment. As her character Richard rumin-ates, 'Reality is very elusive.'[70]

Margot *did*, however, know the name of the man with whom Sunrise eloped, 'Harley D. Lee'. In February 1914, 'Maria Sunrise Nicol' married 'Harle D. Lee' in a Methodist chapel in Auburn. Harle or Harley D. Lee was not a ranch hand, but a boiler man on the railway. The couple settled in the Southern Pacific Company town of Roseville. That was also the year Robert and Gertrude sold some of their ranch land on Prospect Hill to Aubrey L. Wisker, a mining engineer.[71] But Robert, like Margot's fic-tional Richard, had contracted the fortune-seeking 'fanaticism'. He never could shake off the conviction that tunnelling through the earth would somehow lead him to Eldorado.

TWENTY-TWO

Loose Endings

Reality proved particularly elusive in relation to Sunrise. After her marriage in 1914, she next surfaces in the Census of 1920, this time entered as 'Marian', with 'Harley' Lee, boiler man on the railroad, aged thirty-three, from Indiana. They are still in Roseville, Placer County, and have a daughter, 'Marie Lee' born in Colorado.[1] The entry is unclear but appears to give her age as nine. This would mean she had been conceived when Sunrise was still subjected to the penetrating gaze of Miss Broad in Bournemouth! Margot provides a credible explanation: the couple 'adopted a little girl'.[2] Later that year they had left Roseville; Harley and 'Miriam' Lee are recorded in the City Directory of Cheyenne, Wyoming, where he worked for the Cheyenne Light Fuel & Power Co.[3]

Sunrise's nomenclature is mercurial; 'Sunrise', then 'Elenor' (or 'Eleanor'), followed by 'Miriam' or 'Marian S. Nicol'. After the Cheyenne entry, she and Marie Lee elude the records, vanishing into the vast ambiguity of America. Margot was aware that 'Sunrise walked out on Harley Lee and the child', but knew nothing about what became of the 'little girl'.[4] Harley Lee can be traced. He married again and rose to be an Inspector of street cars in Indianapolis.[5] But Sunrise and Marie fade from the official data.

Instead, the stories *about* Sunrise moved in to occupy the blank spaces. Margot was the main source. She absorbed facts and spun fictions, making it hard to unravel one from the other. The tale Barbara Donnelly heard of Sunrise's perishing on a ship in Southern California most probably derived from Margot. A variant was printed in the *Soho News'* Poetry

Column in 1975. It cites Margot in an interview declaring how despite her parents being 'advocates of free love', when they found her 'sister was fucking the gardener', they 'promptly shipped her off to France to stay with relatives'. Margot fantasises Sunrise disappearing during the channel crossing, concluding she had committed suicide by leaping into the sea.[6] For Margot 'Imagination' was 'a bird that flies'.[7]

Not only did Margot elaborate upon reality, she is vague on chronology, fusing Sunrise's departure with a later more extensive break up in the Nicol family, when Robert abandoned the home and Gertrude followed him. While Robert seems to have been quite frequently away because of his mining projects, Gertrude's absence made for a crisis. Bob was boarded out and Margot and Amaryllis left Mill Valley for San Francisco and eventually New York. Quite *when* all this happens is not completely clear.

Bob Nicol told his daughter, Barbara Donnelly, that they moved from the ranch to Mill Valley around 1919, when he was eleven. In January 1920 when the Census was taken, the whole family were, indeed, living in rented accommodation in Mill Valley Town. Initially a summer retreat for San Franciscans, by 1920 it had acquired paved roads and a population of 2,554 – quite a contrast from White-nights' forty acres, sold along with the wooden ranch house, complete with basic furniture on 30 April 1920.[8]

'Miss Margaret Nicol' was certainly still in Mill Valley early in May that year, for her performance of Isadora Duncan-style dancing at the Boy Scout Benefit caused a divisive furore in the community. When sixteen-year-old Margot's 'gauzy garb' was condemned as likely to have a 'demoralizing' effect on children and young people by the Women's Society of the Congregational Church, Mill Valley's artistic women sprang to her defence, pointing out how her mother accompanied her on the piano. Husbands were wheeled in, including the painter and art teacher Ray Boynton, along with an attorney, Arthur Brand, who issued a statement on behalf of his wife and himself about the religious significance of Greek dances in ancient times. The Brands were neighbours, and he described 'Miss Nicol' as 'a very modest and proper little girl'.[9] This was possibly not the image Margot was after, but she would have been delighted with the beautiful photograph of her dancing in the 'gauzy garb' on the front page of the *San Francisco Examiner*.

Duncan's associations with San Francisco had fostered enthusiasm for 'expressive dance' in the Bay area. François Delsarte, whose ideas had interested Robert, also had an impact, and a group was formed at 'The Temple of the Wings', a studio set in the Berkeley Hills. The *San*

Francisco Examiner reported how the craze was evident among 'young gals' on all the California beaches.[10] Margot, however, had resolved to become a professional. She later claimed to have had lessons with the famous dancer, Ruth Saint Denis, who incorporated ballet, eurhythmics and Delsarte-style movements into vaudeville dancing.[11]

Presumably Robert and Gertrude's desertion occurred shortly after Margot's performance in May 1920. Margot described to Barbara Donnelly how, when Gertrude followed Robert, she and Amaryllis ate every bit of food that was at hand. Amaryllis also told Georges Rey how they used all the dishes in the house because, while they had light, the water was turned off. Eventually the food ran out and they made off to San Francisco, where an enterprising Margot found them clerical jobs by pretending Amaryllis was older. Margot was subdued about doing boring work for the Shipping Board, but enjoyed telling Edna Eldred that she and Amaryllis joined a vaudeville dance team. She was particularly proud of her belly dance. Margot exulted in her time in San Francisco's early 1920s bohemia when she was 'so young and unafraid' as a wonderful freedom, claiming she quickly climbed from artists' model to becoming the mistress of an 'opera singer'.[12]

Margot by Edward Weston (Courtesy
of Georges Rey, Private Collection)

Amaryllis by Edward Weston (Courtesy
of Georges Rey, Private Collection)

Both sisters posed for the well-known photographer Edward Weston in San Francisco, folding easily into its bohemia. Money was scarce, creativity was plentiful, and the cheap dives where bohemians met, drank and ate were full of people who could talk the talk. Margot, reared to despise conventional jobs, was not unique in spinning drama around her life. Young and beautiful women occupied a precarious position in a milieu that had apparently discarded all prejudices, but in which male artists were far more likely to be recognised. Embellishing one's past constituted a means of making oneself unforgettable, hence letting imagination fly was common practice. Margot developed it into a way of life.[13]

The disintegration of the Nicol family was decisive. Margot and Amaryllis did not return and eventually moved on to New York. They appear to have regarded leaving Mill Valley with equanimity. Margot was desperate to get away and Amaryllis, retrospectively at least, took the view that Gertrude had 'made a choice. We could get on by ourselves and daddy couldn't.' She, like Margot, looked out on the world in the Romantic manner of her parents, 'Life ought to have a passion.'[14] In contrast to his two older sisters, Bob, who spent several years living with two other families, resented his parents' defection and disapproved of their irresponsibility. He remained angry with Robert all his life, 'He didn't do what a father should do.'[15]

*   *   *

Margot and Amaryllis believed that Robert had suffered a bout of 'amnesia'.[16] This may well have been a metaphorical rather than a medical condition, conceived by a humiliated Gertrude as a way of explaining to her daughters that Robert, in his early fifties, had put them all out of his mind.

For several years Robert had been wrapped up in a love affair with a young woman called Honora (Nora) Keating. It is not certain when they became involved with one another, though a letter to her from Robert dated 1 March 1922, suggests it was around 1916, as he refers to her sticking by him for six years.[17] Their relationship could explain Margot's impressions of Robert as so distant during her early adolescence.

The Keatings had emigrated from Burnley, Lancashire, where Nora's grandfather, a printer called George Frankland, ran a Conservative newspaper. Her father was of Irish descent and her parents emigrated when she was a child. Proud, beautiful, intelligent and independent, Nora graduated from dental school in San Francisco in 1913, aged thirty-two. Dentistry, still relatively new as a profession, offered openings for women, and she established a successful practice, first in the Sierras, then later in San Francisco. Robert and Nora appear to have met because he was a patient of hers.[18] Georges Rey describes his grandfather as 'her only, but awful weakness'.[19]

On 22 August 1920 Nora gave birth to a daughter, who she and Robert named Tamara Jean Nicol.[20] With Nora, Robert rediscovered his effusive, amative self. The first surviving letter to 'My Own Darling Girl' is dated 24 January 1921, with the address 'Fort Steamer Sutter'. 'Fort Sutter' was the passenger steamer connecting San Francisco with Sacramento and, full of his happiness with Nora and 'our lovely daughter', he refers to their meeting 'down at the boat'. Characteristically Robert packs in the promises; he will 'bend every nerve' to 'make money', he feels his 'power coming', soon 'I shall really rule & run things'. They had experienced such 'pleasure', but he announces portentously, 'our real work now lies ahead of us'. This mission statement is accompanied by advice to Nora to buy herself 'chops or steak'. She cooked them so nicely and she needed 'meat'.[21] A vegetarian no more, chops, steak and sex commingle in Robert's love affairs.

In November a somewhat furtive Robert writes from Yankee Jim's; being not far from Weimar, he urges Nora to seal her letters with wax because 'this is the country & you know the curiosity'. Robert presents himself as an epic figure in the wilds, hitching to Forest Hill, then walking five miles through the night to Yankee Jim's. The pioneer hero sent 'oceans of love and kisses', while badgering her and her sisters to invest in a mining venture.[22]

On 1 March 1922 he was again at Forest Hill and missing Nora and Jean.[23] On April 24th he mentions a visit to the Esoteric Colony at Applegate; Butler had died and it now consisted only of four elderly men led by a 'Miss Crow'. Robert plays on Nora's sympathy, relating how he had been injured in the woods and had wrapped his handkerchief around the cut. He refers to mining deals, but somehow can never quite get the money due. Remembering his paternal obligations, and turning to Fate for sustenance, he announces he has arranged a horoscope for Jean.[24] In an undated note to his 'Darling Jean', he enquires if she can walk and whether her shoes are all right. Otherwise it is promises, promises for his toddler daughter, 'Daddy wants to see you so much and he will be down soon.'[25]

As Tamara Jean grew older she remembered her father visiting inter-mittently. Robert does seem to have been genuinely fond of his little daughter. His grandson Georges Rey recounts that Robert set about encouraging her to read books, imparting 'his own ferocious cultural/ intellectual snobbism, and this led her to display scorn and contempt toward her peers and teachers, who, following her father, she referred to as "hoi polloi"'.[26] Tamara recalled her father as 'cool & aloof & always in control of himself'.[27] Robert was capable of bringing the shutters down on himself and never spoke of his past life to her.

Over time Nora became increasingly disillusioned with Robert's prot-estations of devotion and demands for money. When she grew angry, an icy Robert would observe sardonically, 'look at the little Mick perform-ing'.[28] With Nora as with Gertrude, Robert appears to have oscillated between florid passion, a state of pent-up imminence, cutting deri-sion and cold withdrawal. However, Nora responded differently from Gertrude. Their relationship eventually ended around 1930.

Just one burst of fury is on record from Gertrude in response to a sug-gestion from Robert that the two households should merge. It seems that Gertrude really thought she was about to lose him; Barbara Donnelly believes Gertrude abandoned the children and pursued Robert 'to save her marriage'.[29] Perhaps for Gertrude, Robert was 'the great love' that romantically inclined emancipated women in the early twentieth century viewed as transcending everyday morality. Or perhaps she simply dreaded being utterly alone. Only her poems hint at her feelings. In 'To An Ide-alist', published in *The New Age* in 1919, the poet is 'the earth-child', the Idealist the 'miraculous iceberg'. In the day 'clear as crystal', by night the Idealist becomes terrible, 'with the chill of dissolution and death'.[30]

Another unpublished poem by Gertrude to 'R.A.N.' begins:

> When I am very old and in my room
> I sit alone and ponder on things sped,
> I shall remember those dark hours of gloom
> When I would listen for your tread;
> and when I heard your knock upon the door,
> it was as though you knocked for the first time
> and I was twenty-one and loved you more
> Than anything in reason or in rhyme...[31]

Had she then desired Robert long ago back in Bristol?

The cache of papers Georges Rey preserved reveal Gertrude and Robert together during the 1940s, surviving on small amounts of money left by Robert's relatives and whatever he could scrounge. Bob, a probation officer in San Francisco, who must have borne the main brunt of their care, regarded his father without any illusions. In August 1943, Gertrude, still protective towards Robert, wrote to Amaryllis saying it was difficult to meet Bob without 'friction'. She complained, 'He insists that Dad should get a job but Dad is seventy five and begins to feel his age.' She added, 'besides he is working hard on one of his projects'.[32] Gertrude never did stop believing in Robert. In old age her eyes began to fail, and in an evocative poem entitled 'Once More' she wrote of 'this death/of darkness, slowly closing on the eyes'.[33] She conjures the early days of their love at the ranch:

> Once more
>   Could I but see again
> the lush and fragrant meadow in the April light,
> so far from travelled roads it was unknown,
> an Eden that was ours and ours alone,
> made for Love's solitude and Love's delight.
> A ring of mountains guarded it, like white
> and silent sentinels. It was our own,
> our very own, our own...

Once more
   to rest, to sleep, as then in the warm grass, thigh over thigh:
my foot to seek your foot, your fingers pass to where my hair streams
down across my breast…

Once more
to stand apart, to watch you search in vain,
your fingers, no more tangled in my hair,
groping across the grass where I had lain,
perturbed in dream, because I was not there.
And then to see you, leaping to full height,
taut as an arrow that is poised for flight,
vivid and golden in the mellow light,
to hear your cry,
and in a moment, swifter than a sigh,
be in your arms again,
in ecstasy
near pain.[34]

Gertrude exults in his male beauty. He is 'supreme', a 'sculptured solitude'.[35] Without doubt, Gertrude loved Robert, and he, after his fashion, loved Gertrude.

In later life Robert and Gertrude's politics were broadly on the left. Both were fiercely anti-fascist and appalled by the treatment of the Jews in Germany. The former mystical anarchist and the Fabian new woman became staunch supporters of the Soviet Union. During the Second World War, Robert describes reading the Soviet writer, Ilya Ehrenburg's *The Fall of Paris* (1941), as well as novels by the radical American, Sinclair Lewis, pronouncing, 'The whole competitive system is rotten to the core.'[36] In 1947 he was chiliastic, imagining post-war America as 'a new civilization, possibly along Russian or Marxist lines'. As ever, Robert declaimed with unquestioning confidence. But his politics consisted of a series of disconnected extreme stances. Alarmed by the influx of 'darkies' into San Francisco, he wished they could be 'placed in enclaves'.[37] Robert saw no inconsistencies between his socialism and his racism, or indeed his snobbery. He was finally naturalised as a citizen in capitalist America in May 1950, still supported by money from the Nicols he trounced as capitalists.[38]

Gertrude seems to have been more politically coherent, supporting Henry A. Wallace who had backed Franklin D. Roosevelt's New Deal and served as Vice-President until 1944. Progressives of various hues rallied around Wallace for President in 1948, but he was not successful. From the late 1940s, the mood changed abruptly and Senator Joe McCarthy spread fear and repression until the mid 1950s. Regardless of the Cold War, Gertrude remained an unperturbed fellow traveller, maintaining contact with Jessica Smith, the editor of *Soviet Russia Today*.[39] Smith, the author in 1928 of *Women in Soviet Russia*, became a leading figure in building support for Communism through Friends of the Soviet Union.[40]

Towards the end of 1949, despite her loss of sight, Gertrude finished a long poem, 'One World or None', about the dangers of atomic warfare and state secrecy. Though she had hopes of finding a publication with a 'wider circulation', it appeared in the January 1950 issue of Smith's *Soviet Russia Today*, a magazine revealing the contradictions facing American leftists like Gertrude who supported the Soviet Union. The copy in which the poem appeared carried a letter from 'Up-state New York'. The anonymous sender explained she was enclosing a cheque for *Soviet Russia Today* signed by someone else, because her husband was a postmaster and she feared for his job if it was discovered. The red scares of the late nineteenth and early twentieth centuries were once more resurgent, and this message from a frightened woman expresses the good faith and sacrifice of thousands of Americans who believed in the Communist Party. At the same time, *Soviet Russia Today* endorsed a grim real politick, and its January issue also included a loyal birthday message to Stalin, neither pacific nor transparent as a ruler.[41] Later that year Gertrude signed a Communist-backed Peace Petition.[42] It was no longer a popular cause to follow, but she was oblivious to danger. 'Swings wide the gate before me', she had written, 'I must go/where the road leads, so be it up or down.'[43] Gertrude died on 30 October 1950, aged eighty-two.[44]

Robert remained at their home in 1440 Sutter Street and proceeded to eulogise Gertrude. 'How I miss Mother', he declared to Amaryllis, 'She was a darling girl with never a grudge about life.'[45] He continued with his 'projects', announcing intentions of visiting a speculative mining venture in Peru in November 1950 and the ranch near Weimar in August 1951. He had high hopes for Bob's daughter Barbara, and his friend, the astrologer Carl Bodding, had done her chart.[46] Decrying the Cold War 'hysteria' in the U.S., Robert decreed that Stalin was 'a very able man'.[47]

In old age Robert's attitudes towards the modest securities of daily life shifted a little and he expressed pride in Bob's job as a probation officer.[48] The man who had always lived in the present, also began to dwell on his youth. But he does not mention Sunrise in the extant clutch of letters.

When the end came, it was Bob who assumed responsibility. On 8 July 1956 he wrote to Amaryllis and Margot (or Margaret as he continued to call her) to say that Robert was dead, adding that in the last few months Robert had been 'low for some time' and contracted 'double pneumonia' from which he never recovered. Towards the end he had been put on 'sedatives'.[49] At eight-eight, the idealist, the organiser, the lover, the Nietzschean, the inveigling spinner of multiple selves went out quietly at the last.

In differing ways Margot and Tamara continued Robert, Gertrude and Nora's defiance of convention. During the Depression, Margot married a Chilean writer, Alvaro de Silva. A bohemian and full of charm, he was friendly with the left-wing poet, Pablo Neruda. At the time of the Spanish Civil War, de Silva and Margot became active in the American anti-fascist movement. Then, after the Second World War, Margot settled in New York's East Village, reading poetry in bohemian clubs. In 1974, a booklet of her poems, *A Geography of the Erotic Body*, was published and one of her poems appeared in the collection *For Neruda, For Chile* in 1975.[50]

Like Gertrude, she lied about her age, and, like Robert, enjoyed inventing personas. Among the announcements she issued about herself was the claim of having been born in Sierra Leone with a diplomat as a father. The stories kept on shifting; in the words of a friend, Peggy Garrison, 'One saw Margot like one looked at a piece of cut crystal in the sun, illusion after illusion cancelled with the slightest turn of the glass.'[51] Yet certain aspects of Margot remained more real than 'real', her love of dancing, her love of writing and her love of love. Margot, the woman who had never wanted to grow old, died in 1983.

Tamara Nicol Rey Patri did not share Margot's unstinting admiration for Robert, but nevertheless she wanted to understand him. She, too, lived an exploratory life. Dropping out of college during the Depression, she worked for the National Youth Administration Art Project. A series of dead-end office and sales jobs turned her into an active trade unionist, featuring as the 'Member of the Month' in the December 1945 issue of the *Retail Unionist*. In 1945 she married Noël Rey, an accordionist and linotype setter, who became the heir and manager of the *Courier Français des Etats-Unis*. Her second husband was Giacomo Patri,

the Bauhaus-influenced radical artist who taught at the California Labor
School and then ran his own School. Tamara studied at the Labor School
and won a scholarship to the California School of Fine Arts, moving in
San Francisco's radical art world. Patri encouraged her as an artist, but
was also a demanding figure. After his death in 1978, when Tamara was
in her sixties, she was finally able to focus on her own art work – sculpt-
ing.[52] Tamara died in 2001, leaving, in the words of her son Georges Rey,
'heavily weathered, discarded timbers' and 'pieces of old metal' in stark,
arresting forms.[53] He had become friendly with Amaryllis and Margot
during the 1970s, while all three were living in New York, and through
taped interviews and written material brought together a record of the
two wings of the bifurcated family.

Robert's blundering quest for inner power and Gertrude's fascination
with psychological motivation contrast with William and Helen's faith
in individual reason. After a box luncheon with Emersonians, a sceptical
Helen's response was, 'mystics depress me'.[54] Neither she nor William
regarded reality or truth as at all elusive, though their views of what constituted these were to shift over the decades. Yet the past echoed on in
their lives too. Just as Miriam Daniell hovered edgily around Robert and
Gertrude's psyches, Helena Born never quite left William and Helen's.
   All four supported the allies in the First World War, though their later
political trajectory diverged. In August 1917, William wrote an article
for the *Boston Sunday Globe*, 'Ireland and Common Sense', explaining
Irish Americans' unease about allying with Britain. He reminded Americans how Home Rule had been blocked by Sir Edward Carson, and the
'ultra loyalist faction in the North', while the repression that followed
the Easter Rising in 1916 had further strengthened the separatist wing
of Irish nationalism. His appeal to Irish-Americans combined pragmatism and idealism. Convinced that complete separation from Britain by
'force' was a 'chimera' and that the Irish were a 'practical' people, William
pointed out that Britain constituted the main market for their agricultural
produce. Stressing Prussia's record of anti-democratic authoritarianism,
he reminded Irish readers how, historically, Ireland had backed struggles
against autocratic power.[55]
   Those socialists and anarchists who, unlike Helen and William, took
an anti-war stand faced harsh reprisals after America entered the war in
1917. Meetings were disrupted, presses closed down, 'reds' were imprisoned, and others, including Emma Goldman, were deported to Russia.

William and Helen found themselves at variance with their old friend, Archibald Simpson, who not only opposed the war but was enthusiastic about the Bolshevik revolution.[56]

By the post-war era the transformatory hopes of both Individualist Anarchism and the Walt Whitman Fellowship had been elided. Traubel, seriously ill from 1914, died in 1919. That year William and Helen attended the memorial for Rosa Luxemburg and Karl Liebknecht, murdered after an abortive rising in Germany, but they remained wary of 'Marxian Socialism'.[57] Having come to regard reform as the only option, they transferred their habits of campaigning to single-issue agitations. One of their daughter Helena's earliest memories was of her parents speaking on soap-boxes for women's suffrage – finally secured in 1920.[58] William renewed his youthful connection to the Unitarian Church and discovered a congenial discussion group in the Ethical Culture Society. Established by Felix Adler, this sought a secular foundation for ethics and social action. Helena viewed her father in his later years as 'basically a pragmatist' whose interests were broader than anarchism, adding that he 'saw himself in the tradition of Jefferson'.[59]

William continued to admire Filene's efforts to reform capitalist economic relations. The collapse of Boston-1915 had convinced an undaunted Filene that a city's problems could not be resolved in isolation. Filene's book, *The Way Out: A Forecast of Coming Changes in American Business and Industry* (1924), inspired a long review by William in the Unitarian *Christian Register*, endorsing Filene's faith in 'Fordizing', mass production and distribution in a high-wage economy. Loyally, William pointed out that Edward Atkinson (the philanthropic anti-imperialist who had donated the Aladdin stoves to the Pure Food Kitchen) had long ago predicted that 'the present industrial system was bound to go on increasing the real wages of labor, and at the same time continually lower costs of production'. William never discarded his predilection for teleological economic analyses, and, like Filene, now believed the new American economic model could end 'class distinctions' and 'class war'.[60] Nevertheless, a cautious William did modify Filene's optimistic claim that this would occur in ten to twenty years, suggesting it would more likely take fifty or a hundred. As it happened, of course, capitalism proved more contrary; William's 'Fordizing' was accompanied by other unforeseen variables.[61]

William, who had seen such amazing transformations in production and consumption within his own lifetime, reflected upon the expanding character of needs:

Human wants, desires and ambitions are endless. The more they are satisfied, the more they stretch out toward new wants and more pressing needs ... The well-paid wage-earner has for a generation demanded a house with a bathroom and a piano for his daughters. Now he must have the latest radio installation, a garage in the rear and at least a Ford masterpiece to convey him to lodge meetings or the factory. Under the new industrial regime a few years hence, he will demand a college education for his children, just as the professional man or merchant does to-day.[62]

For William, as for Filene, in 1925 it seemed there was nothing that capitalism could not provide. Filene was delighted with William's review, greeting him at a performance of Ian Hay's light comedy *Happy-Go-Lucky* in April that year.[63]

Now in his late fifties, William had begun to display an unexpected hedonism himself. In the summer of 1925 the Bailies went on holiday to Cape Cod. While they were visiting friends called 'the Snows' in tiny Truro, a mystified Helen records that William went off dancing in a barn at nearby Wellfleet. These were prohibition times, but according to 'Mr Snow' the place was 'a booze center'. William's embrace of 'jazz-music' and the Roaring Twenties was utterly incomprehensible to Helen.[64] In June 1927, when William was sixty, she remarked how he 'refuses to be old'.[65] Having worked since the age of eleven, he probably felt he had been allowed little enough time for being young.

William and Helen, whose opinions on personal conduct in the late 1890s and early 1900s had positioned them on the nether edge of respectability, were being overtaken by the mainstream. At a discussion on 'Companionate Marriage' at a Community Church in 1927, Helen was flabbergasted to hear birth control being taken for granted. William's was the solitary nineteenth-century voice reminding everyone of the need for 'the perpetuation of the race'.[66]

In July 1927 a flicker of concern appears in Helen's journal about William's 'business troubles', but her attention in the late 1920s was focused upon the far right's encroachment on personal political freedoms rather than on the economy.[67] In 1929, the crash hit them like a tsunami; William's business contracted. In 1930, after they were forced to move, a horrified Helen was reporting rats and bed bugs in their apartment. By 1931 William was virtually bankrupt.[68]

*   *   *

Helen was ever a worrier; but she did have sufficient cause. Not only
had economic insecurities dogged her life, so had personal tragedies.
When, in 1919, her three-year-old son Terrill, nicknamed 'Sonny', died,
Helen was so consumed with grief that Helena grew up convinced that
her mother blamed *her* for her little brother's death. This strain in their
relationship was compounded by Helen's excessive anxiety about Helena.
She sought to impose her will upon her daughter, worrying over her
behaviour, her schoolwork, then about her views, boyfriends, make-up
and clothes. Helen's own thwarted aspirations drove this incessant pressure on Helena, but to her daughter it must have seemed as if Helen
could never be satisfied. In response to her fuss-budget mother, Helena
withdrew in exasperation, regarding Helen as 'neurotic and unhappy'.[69]

In February 1926 Helen remarked, 'Helena goes her own way – like
her father.'[70] William and Helena were, indeed, close to one another and
Helen could see that young Helena adored him.[71] Meanwhile, William
and Helen were growing apart, and, from the mid 1920s, Helen records
William's bouts of irritability; she reacted with cold silences, which
Helena remembered as more painful than her parents' rowing: 'when
mad she wouldn't speak to us for weeks'.[72] In July 1927 an isolated Helen
felt William was 'so changed' towards her that she often 'feared he was
lost'.[73] In her fifties Helen no longer idealised William, even though she
did still love him.

During 1927 Helen was disquieted by the wave of right-wing panic
about 'reds' fanning demands for the execution of two anarchists, Nicola
Sacco and Bartolomeo Vanzetti, despite contradictory and inconclu-
sive evidence against them. In March she ridiculed warnings from the
headquarters of the Daughters of the American Revolution against the
subversive nature of the song 'America the Beautiful' on the grounds
that it was supported by radical groups and approved by Trotsky and
Lenin. 'Are American women such boobies?' asked Helen[74] William then
learned from an associate at the City Club that 'a man called Hunter' was
distributing a blacklist against liberal and left speakers for the D.A.R.[75]
Indignantly, Helen protested in a letter to D.A.R. President, Grace H.L.
Brosseau, who ignored her. Realising that Edward H. Hunter's activities
were condoned by the leadership and supported by prominent right-
wing militarists, Helen organised a 'Committee of Protest' and, in Spring
1928, published *Our Threatened Heritage: A Letter to the Daughters of
the American Revolution*. The pamphlet denounced the blacklisting of

members of such bodies as the Association of University Women and the Women's International League for Peace and Freedom (to which Helen herself belonged), along with sundry bishops and rabbis, as profoundly 'un-American'. Helen poured particular scorn on a ban placed on Mrs Lucia Ames, an advocate of the League of Nations, because the Episcopalian clergyman who arranged her lecture happened to hail from Moscow – in Idaho!.[76]

Two opposing visions of American patriotism clashed. For Grace H.L. Brosseau, it meant absolute loyalty – there was no half-way house. Subversion extended far beyond the usual suspects – Bolsheviks, socialists and anarchists – out towards a great host of social reformers, pacifists, liberals, church people, trade unionists and radical do-gooders whose 'rose-colored spectacles' towards sedition amounted to collusion.[77] In contrast, Helen thought the revolutionary daughters should be safeguarding an America that upheld liberty of conscience, free speech and enlightened discontent. She deplored the 'complacent "patriotism"' that maintained, '"My country always right"', stating bluntly, 'If that is patriotism I'll have none of it.'[78]

Helen's rebellion became national news. Amid the exhilaration of a just fight her confidence surged back. When William, the opinionated politico, butted in while she was being interviewed by a reporter, Helen threatened to 'shut him out of the room next time'.[79] However, it exposed both of them to publicity and the press started digging into William's socialist and anarchist past; the links to William Morris, the book on Josiah Warren. Helen had underestimated the forces against her and the power base of her right-wing opponents. Her protests were swept aside and the blacklist denied. By June 1928 she had been expelled from the D.A.R. Brosseau's wing of the movement emerged victorious, though the national publicity caused damage and led to subsequent resignations.[80]

Helen had braced herself against the possibility of defeat, without comprehending how isolated and exposed it would leave her; 'I felt sure we wd be steamrollered, but never dreamed it wd be so raw.'[81] A photograph from this period reveals a woman of fifty-four, with severely cropped hair, gazing short-sightedly through uncompromising round spectacles. Her large eyes droop with an air of disappointment, but her lips are resolved and her chin set in defiance. The severe-looking impeccably W.A.S.P. woman did not fit the stereotype of a subversive; nevertheless Helen became suspect. A sympathiser sent her an ironic cutting from the *New York Times*:

The fate of Mrs Bailie
Is oh! a very sad one.
They've put her on the black list
Because she said they had one.[82]

The stressful fall-out from her stand over the D.A.R. blacklist con-
trasted with a warm encounter in October 1929 at Boston's Ethical
Society with R.H. Minshall, a member of the Sheffield Independent
Labour Party. A friend of Edward Carpenter, who had died earlier that
year, Minshall could tell them about William's former comrade from
the Manchester Socialist League, Alf Barton. He had moved to Sheffield
with his wife Eleanor, sampling Marxism before settling for the Labour
left. Minshall had also known Dan Irving, who had served on Burnley
Council before becoming a Labour MP in 1918 until his death in 1924.
To Helen's regret, Minshall could give them no news of other 'dear
Bristol people'.[83] She was in touch with Robert Sharland, but the roll of
1880s activists was diminishing, Robert Weare and Robert Gilliard both
were dead.

In 1930 another visitor, the American Will S. Monroe, who was research-
ing the lives of Whitman and Carpenter, activated those old connections.
Like Minshall, he contributed to Gilbert Beith's collection, *Edward Carpenter: In Appreciation* (1931), mentioning Helena in his essay, 'Walt
Whitman and other American Friends of Edward Carpenter'.[84] He had
begun work on a larger study, *Whitman and his Contemporaries*, which he
was never able to complete. Helen was impressed by 'Dr Monroe's' scholarship, finding him 'a man of deep feeling and generous impulses'; she
was perplexed: 'How he ever remained unmarried is a mystery.'[85] But she
stiffened with dread when he sought information about Robert.

After Robert Sharland died in 1931, Helen reflected on what she called
the 'three Bob committee', Sharland, Weare and Gilliard. Robert Nicol's
presence was erased, along with Robert Tovey who was apparently off
Helen's radar. Even when Monroe returned in 1937 with welcome news
of Charlie Sixsmith and Will Young, Helen remained unrelenting.[86]

A good correspondent, Helen had maintained contact with Beatrice
Taylor until February 1937, when her letter was returned marked
'Deceased'.[87] Helen also kept up with Archibald Simpson, who had
returned to England after Flora Tilton died. Haunted by memories of
Flora, Simpson attended meetings as ever, but was unable any more to
make friends. His great sadness was that no one would remember Flora

and the freethinking Individualist circles to which she had belonged. Helen felt sympathy for the lonely man, stranded by the loss of his love, but his Trotskyist leanings mystified her. In June 1943, an incredulous Helen observed that 'Mr Simpson' still looked to a revolution by 'Labor ... as if the proletariats were not of the same human stuff as the rest of us'.[88] He, meanwhile, was scathing to George Schumm, who was working on the left-wing magazine, *The Nation*, about the 'anti-Marxists" faith in President Roosevelt: 'I heard from Helen Bailie "hoping & <u>trusting</u>" so much that Roosevelt will save the nation (& capitalism) & William doing his bit to help.'[89]

Although the little grouping of Individualist Anarchists had long scattered, personal friendships persisted. Pearl Tucker's sister, Bertha Johnson, stayed in touch with Helen in the 1940s. Both women contributed papers and material to the Labadie collection which the exemplary archivist, Agnes Inglis, was nurturing at the University of Michigan. Inglis possessed a rare understanding of the significance of these informal networks, encouraging her correspondents to communicate information about the present as well as the past. As a result, the remarkable archive she accumulated documents not just political engagement but what happens to people personally in its aftermath — stories history often misses. 'What an interwoven mesh society and friendship make', Johnson reflected to Inglis.[90]

Over the course of the 1930s and '40s, Helen's political views grew more ambivalent. On a practical level she supported Roosevelt, nevertheless, anarchism remained her ideal. She found Kropotkin's co-operative vision attractive and her daughter Helena describes her as 'a friend and admirer of Emma Goldman's', with 'strong sympathies for ... the anarchist-communists'.[91] Despite Helen's earlier mistrust, she and William had come to admire Emma Goldman in exile, and were in agreement with her critique of the Soviet Union. When she read Goldman's autobiography, *Living My Life* (1931), Helen raised metaphorical eyebrows at the lovers, but respected the writer and campaigner.[92]

In 1938, Helen began campaigning for a cause Goldman had pioneered, birth control.[93] Over time, changing circumstances, combined with constant challenges from Helena, somewhat modified Helen's prejudices towards non-British immigrants, Jews, Irish Catholics and African Americans. Yet her daughter's assertion in December 1940 that homosexuality was a matter of 'chromosomes' proved a step too far. A shocked Helen produced an irrefutable authority as ally, 'Wm won't accept the excuse about they can't help it.'[94] As far as she was concerned that should have been that – but of course it was not. In June 1942, Helen was devastated by the suggestion that Walt Whitman's 'Calamus' expressed sexual feelings towards men. A distressed Helen simply could not square this with what Whitman had 'meant to Helena'. The idea of Whitman being 'homosexual' left her feeling betrayed, 'Horace Traubel never lisped a word about anything like that'.[95] Helen avoided what she did not wish to see.

The underlying disharmony between Helen and William broke out into the open in 1939, damaging Helen and Helena's relationship too. When William became involved in an affair and left Helen, she suspected Helena had encouraged him to obey 'his impulse'.[96] Helen was thus estranged from the two people she loved above all others. As she grew older the devoted reader's eyesight declined, and, in 1943, she went into hospital for a cataract operation. William visited every day. She was too proud, and too much of an individualist, to ask him to come back; nor was he adept at expressing fond emotion. Instead, Helen records he simply announced that 'he would take care of me'.[97] They were reunited.

During the Second World War William had recovered from bankruptcy by making ships' fenders; they also bought property and became landlords in Cambridge. In 1945, with William still doing heavy work aged seventy-nine, Helen, with a sigh that 'along with my dreams has gone some of my rebellion', started to plan a new life – their retirement in Nantucket.[98] Reflections upon the past flicker through her journal. She expresses her happiness when her daughter remembered 'Aunt Helena's birthday' that May, and pleasure when a Labour government was elected in Britain, urging William to write down his experiences of Manchester.[99]

However, with so many anarchist and Whitmanite friends dead, it was Helen who was encircled by memories. She dwelt increasingly on her early life, her parents, her ancestry, old friends. So much seemed unfinished, so many lost. When William finally retired, and they moved to a cottage in Nantucket in 1946, she found herself arranging objects redolent of times past; a round table belonging to her parents, 'Grandma's dinner set', 'Helena's china'. The books had to wait for shelves.[100] Always so fascinated by history, Helen came to realise her generation had become part of it. Carefully she sent her Whitman collection to Stanford, her Ferrer collection and typed interview with the Schumms to Agnes Inglis for the Labadie. The D.A.R material went to Smith College.[101] She wondered at her own obsessive chronicling. Why did she keep a journal?

Whoever would read it? Should she burn it?[102] Instead on she went.

By 1954 her sight and hearing were in serious decline and William had begun to display symptoms of dementia. After Helen fell and injured her leg they moved from Nantucket to live with Helena and her husband, Walter Jolly, in Ohio; to Helen's great regret, she was forced to leave behind Helena's piano, never reclaimed by Richard Born.[103]

Helen did what she had always longed to do. In 1956, her novel, *Darling Daughter: A Satire*, was published. Despite the disclaimer in bold type that 'Any resemblances between its characters and actual persons living or dead' were 'unintended' and coincidental, the wretched 'Mr Trailer', with his lists of subversives, and the machinations of the narrow-minded women in the 'Patriotic Patrol', were not exactly unrecognisable. Yet the book is not strictly a 'satire', for while Helen pulled no punches in the portrayal of her right-wing characters, they are nuanced and not simply caricatured. *Darling Daughter* is a humane and humorous account of the clash between supporters of idealistic reforming America and their fearful and repressive right-wing opponents.[104] By 1956 those old D.A.R. battles of the late 1920s had assumed a new relevance because of McCarthy.

The book was dedicated to William; but his dementia meant he could no longer recognise Helen. He died in a nursing home in 1957.[105] At his memorial service she recalled the man she had so respected when they met in the 1890s, who had overcome adversity to become a 'thinker' and a 'scholar'.[106] Helena and Walter Jolly took William's ashes to Mount Auburn Cemetery where the Tufts were buried and where, on Memorial Day 1899, William had so gleefully somersaulted.[107]

Helen still pondered the meaning of life and wondered whether after all there might be 'the other side'.[108] Yet, running counterpoint with the high-minded, well-mannered, self-restrained Helen, there remained that sharp-edged rebel. On 23 April 1959, upon reading an obituary of her former adversary, Mrs Grace Lincoln Hall Brosseau, in the *New York Herald Tribune*, Helen noted grimly that 'Mrs Boss Patriot' was dead.[109] Helen was not one for crocodile tears.

Helen herself died in 1962. Her ashes were placed next to William's at Mount Auburn in the Tufts' lot.[110] She left a strange modern world in which John F. Fitzgerald's grandson was President and new social movements were stirring in America. Despite all Helen's anxieties about her daughter, the young Helena became a college professor and Civil Rights supporter. Helen's granddaughter, Christine Ann Bailie Jolly, declared proudly of Helena in 2009, 'My mother was a pistol.'[111]

Acknowledgements

Many people helped me to research and write *Rebel Crossings*. I owe an enormous debt to David Sachs who, in 2009, encouraged me to embark on this book and has contributed his time with true generosity, providing innumerable references to books, along with information on the history of American anarchists, esoteric spiritual groups and alternative health advocates. He helped me through the wonderful Labadie Collection at Michigan University, as well as contributing his own research on J. William Lloyd, the Boston Anarchist Club, William Bailie's pamphlet on water, and Jutie Coan. Moreover, it was he who traced Sunrise's marriage and located Robert Allan Nicol's granddaughter, Barbara Donnelly, and his grandson, Georges Rey. He also painstakingly checked an early version of the manuscript for errors.

I am similarly profoundly indebted to Georges Rey, who found letters from Nicol to Geddes in the National Library of Scotland and allowed me access to the Private Collection of Rey Papers, including taped interviews he had conducted with family members. As well as copying written material and photographs for me, he has followed my slow and sometimes painful process of research with interest and offered comments and corrections.

I was fortunate in being able to conduct two interviews with Barbara Donnelly about Robert Nicol and Gertrude Dix; Leslie Gelb kindly provided material on Margot Nicol; while Christine Ann Bailie Jolly gave me material relating to her grandfather, William Bailie, including a typed manuscript written by Helen Tufts Bailie, and urged me on when I flagged. David Stockton emailed information on his grandfather, the Manchester anarchist, Herbert Stockton. Ed Folsom and Michael Robertson provided me with vital references on the Walt Whitman Fellowship. Magdalena Modzejewska shared information on the Individualist Anarchists, and Steve Wootton on the Bristol Socialist Society. Theresa Moriarty contacted Revd Chris Hudson, who was able to throw light on Unitarianism in Belfast in the 1880s; Michael Herbert and Bernadette Hyland investigated Salford pubs used by the Social Democratic Federation in the 1880s; Martin Kenner explained borrowing on margin; and Mike Seifert perused the White-nights ranch land deeds. Cynthia Haggard spared time from her novel-writing to type out Robert Allan Nicol's letters in Sheffield's Carpenter Collection. Judy Greenway sent me her article on Gertrude Dix. From Kumari Jayawardena came information about the Wallasey Whitmanites via Doreen Wickremasinghe (Robert Weare's granddaughter who settled in Sri Lanka). Barry Pateman, from the Emma Goldman Papers, copied William Bailie's *Josiah Warren*; he and Candace Falk, the late Rosalyn Baxandall, Robin Blackburn, Paul Buhle, Linda Gordon, Temma Kaplan, Riley Linebaugh, Carole Turbin, Barbara Winslow and Joey Cain have all generously shared their knowledge of American radical history with me.

American friends put me up on the six research trips I made to several places in the U.S., and Joey Cain, who I met through my work on Edward Carpenter, drove from San Francisco to Placer County, tramping with me along the old railway line and climbing the hills surrounding the valley where White-nights ranch had been. He helped me to take photographs of the land deeds, check newspaper files and explore the museum at Auburn. Outings with dear friends have been highlights. Sheli Wortis took me to Concord. On one memorable day in the summer of 2014, Nigel Fountain drove Georges Rey, Monica Henriques, Mike Richardson and myself to Surrey in search of the Oliviers' cottage, 'The Champions'. After a freak storm, much searching, and inspired map reading by Monica, we arrived, and to George's amazement and awe, were kindly welcomed.

My partner, Mike Richardson, accompanied me on several similar exploratory trips: to the International Institute for Social History in Amsterdam, and to Hatherleigh, Devon, where Kathleen Sanders, sheep-shearer and local historian, took us in and told us about Minnie Southcombe. We also went to Bournemouth in search of Sunrise's school (greatly helped by the Heritage Team at the local library), and then to Dunfermline and Edinburgh in pursuit of Robert, as well as many walks around Bristol. Mike has guided me through the local labour and business history of his native city and provided me with innumerable references and source material relating to the Bristol Socialist Society and the Organising Committee, becoming so interested he wrote on the 1889–90 strike wave, the cotton workers and Hugh Holmes Gore himself. He then moved on to tracking down information on Gertrude Dix, coming up with her work on nursing, her involvement with the London Socialist Club, her amateur dramatics, and her tenancy of Fowl House, as well as several of her stories not in the Rey Papers – all vital clues about a woman who has left remarkably few traces. Since 2010 he has read several drafts, given me unflagging support and displayed an unshaken belief in *Rebel Crossings*.

My heartfelt thanks to my agent, Faith Evans, who also read the manuscript, offering invaluable suggestions for cuts and changes. She has been subjected to various moans and groans, as I struggled away, bearing the brunt of a writer's woes with brisk confidence. My skilful editor, Leo Hollis grappled manfully with many thousands of words and his incisive criticisms have enhanced the book's clarity and structure. Thanks to all the workers at Verso and to Tim Clark for scrupulous and often inspired copy editing. Thanks also to Richard Grove for resurrecting and photographing forgotten visual material relating to Bristol's radical history.

Thanks for help and encouragement to the late Swasti Mitter, Juliet Ash, Lucy Bland, Mary Cunningham, Angela John, Stuart Maclennan, Aneez Esmail, Anna Ford, Allen Hunter, Jonathan Ned Katz, Stephanie Tailby, Madge Dresser, June Hannam, Derek Clarke, Hilary Wainwright, Lynne Segal, Nancy Krieger, Tony Garnett, Trevor Griffiths, Collette Swietnicki, Lisa Vine, the Morgan Centre for Research into Everyday Lives, Atmospheres Conference, July 2015, the modern-day Bolton Whitmanites, members of Bristol's Radical History Group, Bauhaus Hairdressers and Inks R' Us, Bedminster. (The latter sadly closed in 2015.)

I am grateful to all the people who successfully urged Manchester University to enable me to continue working part-time as a Research Professor for three years after my retirement in 2008, making it possible to begin the project and to colleagues in Social Science at Manchester who put me forward as an Honorary Fellow, which, since 2011, has allowed me to retain access to the resources of the wonderful John Rylands Library. Sincere thanks to Lord Alliance for his generous donation which convinced me research in the U.S. would be possible. Similarly, an Honorary Fellowship at the University of Bristol between 2011 and 2012 allowed me helpful access to the library. I would also like to thank the Eccles Centre for American Studies, for selecting me as a Writer in Residence at the British Library in 2012. This opened up the Library's impressive collection of American historical sources, which constituted invaluable background for *Rebel Crossings*. Moreover, members of the Eccles Centre displayed unfailing interest in my writing, enabled me to do talks and blogs which seeded this book, while the funding I received made it possible for me to complete my research in America. My thanks also to the Society of Authors' Authors' Foundation and K. Blundell Trust Awards for a grant towards research costs and to the Lipman–Miliband Trust for a grant towards the cost of the photographs.

Two brilliant physios, Nicola Shaw in Manchester and James Ross in Bristol, saw me through problems in writing caused by RSI and vertigo, for which I will be for ever grateful. Similarly my thanks go to Anne Morrow, who typed the monster handwritten text with a remarkable good cheer and many observations on the characters and their doings. Without Anne I cannot see how any book would have emerged at all.

Profound thanks to the many archivists and librarians who have helped me in my searches, and especially to those who went beyond the bounds of duty, digging into their invaluable *memories* of material as well as online catalogues. I am grateful to the following for access to material in their possession cited in *Rebel Crossings*: Andover-Harvard Theological Library, Harvard Divinity School, American Unitarian Letterbooks (bMS571); Bristol Record Office (Bristol Socialist Society and Workers Organising Committee Minutes); Bristol Reference Library (Bristol Socialist Society); Georges Rey (Rey Papers, Private Collection); Brown University, Special Collections (Harry Lyman Koopman Papers, Ms 79-2); International Institute for Social History, Amsterdam (Socialist League Papers); Library of Congress (Horace and Anne Montgomerie Collection, Gustave Percy Wiksell Collection and the Walt Whitman Papers in the Charles E. Feinberg Collection); London School of Economics (Fabian Papers); National Archives (Daniell Divorce Minutes); National Library of Scotland (Nicol's letters to Geddes); National Anthropological Archives and Human Studies, National Museum of Natural History, Smithsonian Institution (William Bailie's letters to O.T. Mason); New York Public Library, Manuscripts and Archives Division, Astor, Lenox and Tilden Foundations (William Bailie's letters in Benjamin R. Tucker

Papers); Placer County Museum and Archives (Deeds); Princeton University Library, Manuscripts Division, Department of Rare Books and Special Collections (Charles Hodge Papers, CO261, and Henry Van Dyke Family Papers, CO276); Sheffield Archives (Carpenter Collection); Smith College, the Sophia Smith Collection (Helen Tufts Bailie Papers); Tamiment Library/Robert F. Wagner Labor Archives, New York University (Helena Born Papers); the University of Bristol Special Collections (John Gregory Papers); the University of Liverpool, Special Collections (Glasier Papers); the University of Michigan, Special Collections Library (Joseph A. Labadie Collection); the University of Strathclyde, Department of Special Collections (Geddes Papers); Wisconsin Historical Society (Boston Anarchist Club); the Working Class Movement Library, Salford (Angela Tuckett Papers, including the library's edited version of the manuscript on Enid Stacy).

Thanks are also due to Special Collections, University of Michigan for allowing me access to *Free Society*, *The Word*, *The Demonstrator* and *Discontent*, and to Harvard Theological Library for allowing me to consult their complete run of *The Conservator*; to *Poet-Lore* for their online archive and to the Libertarian Labyrinth for putting *Liberty* online; to the British Library's Newspaper Library, Bristol Reference Library, the Bodleian, Oxford, and Goldsmiths, Senate House and University of Bristol Special Collections for access to manuscript copies of daily newspapers and left journals. The text from newspapers online is reproduced courtesy of the British Library Board (All Rights Reserved) and the Library of Congress. For permission to quote I am indebted to Christine Ann Bailie Jolly, Georges Rey and the Society of Authors (George Bernard Shaw).

For permission to reproduce images I am grateful to Bristol Reference Library; Georges Rey; the Joseph A. Labadie Collection, University of Michigan; the Sophia Smith Collection, Smith College; Tamiment Library/Robert F. Wagner Labor Archives (PHOTOS 003, box1, folder1); and Sheffield Archives.

Notes

Abbreviations Used in Notes

A.T.P.	Angela Tuckett Papers
B.I.	Biographical Introduction (in Helen Tufts, ed., *Whitman's Ideal Democracy and Other Writings by Helena Born*)
B.R.O.	Bristol Record Office
B.S.S.	Bristol Socialist Society
B.W.L.A.	Bristol Women's Liberal Association
c.	container (at Library of Congress)
C.C.	Carpenter Collection
G.P.	Glasier Papers
G.W. & G.L.U.	Gas Workers and General Labourers' Union
H.B.P.	Helena Born Papers
H.F.D.	*Her Father's Daughter* (by Margot de Silva)
H.L.K.	Harry Lyman Koopman Collection
H.T.B.P.	Helen Tufts Bailie Papers
H.T.J.	Helen Tufts Journal (in Helen Tufts Bailie Papers)
H.V.D.F.P.	Henry J. Van Dyke Family Papers
I.B.	*The Image Breakers* (by Gertrude Dix)
I.I.S.H.	International Institute for Social History
L.C.	Labadie Collection
L. of C.	Library of Congress
L.S.E.	London School of Economics
N.L.S.	National Library of Scotland
R.P.	Rey Papers
W.I.D.	*Whitman's Ideal Democracy*
W.O.C.	Workers' Organising Committee
W.S.P.U.	Women's Social and Political Union
W.W.F.	Walt Whitman Fellowship
W.W.Q.R.	*Walt Whitman Quarterly Review*

Introduction

1. Helen Tufts, 'Biographical Introduction' (B.I.), in Helen Tufts, ed., *Whitman's Ideal Democracy and Other Writings by Helena Born*, Boston: The Everett Press, 1902, pp. xii–xxx.
2. See Sheila Rowbotham and Jeffrey Weeks, *Socialism and the New Life: The Personal and Sexual Politics of Edward Carpenter and Havelock Ellis*, London: Pluto, 1977; Sheila Rowbotham, *Edward Carpenter: A Life of Liberty and Love*, London: Verso, 2008.
3. Helena Born to 'A cousin in rural Devon', Spring 1890, Tufts, B.I., pp. xvi–xxiii. The original letter in the Helena Born Papers (H.B.P.) Tamiment Library and Robert F. Wagner Labor Archives, is addressed to 'Minnie'. This was the nickname of Elizabeth Southcombe – information from Kathleen Sanders. The date of January 25th is in accord with the timing of Carpenter's lectures in Bristol; see Mike Richardson, 'The Bristol Strike Wave of 1889–1890', in Dave Backwith, Roger Ball, Stephen E. Hunt and Mike Richardson, eds, *Strikers, Hobblers, Conchies and Reds: A Radical History of Bristol, 1880–1939*, London: Breviary Stuff Publications, 2014, p. 132.
4. Helen Tufts Bailie, *Journal* (H.T.J.), 31 December 1954, p. 75. The typed manuscript is in Helen Tufts Bailie Papers (H.T.B.P.), Sophia Smith Collection, Smith College.
5. See Samson Bryher (pseudonym of Samuel Bale), *An Account of the Labour and Socialist Movement in Bristol*, Part 2, Bristol: Bristol Labour Weekly, 1929, pp. 7–8; James J. Martin, *Men Against the State*, Colorado Springs: Ralph Myles, 1970, pp. 5, 257–8, 285; Geoffrey C. Goldberg, *The Socialist and Political Labour Movement in Manchester and Salford, 1884–1914*, MA History thesis, Manchester University, 1975, p. 31; Paul Avrich, *Anarchist Voices*, Edinburgh: AK Press, 2005, pp. 14–15; Martin Henry Blatt, *Free Love and Anarchism: The Biography of Ezra Heywood*, Urbana: University of Illinois Press, 1989, p. 58; William Bailie's *Problems of Anarchism* and Miriam Daniell's *Songs of Struggle and Sorrow* have been issued in pamphlets by the Alliance of the Libertarian Left in their Anarchist Classics Zine series in 2011 and 2013.
6. On Dix see Eileen Sypher, *Wisps of Violence: Producing Public and Private Politics in the Turn-of-the-Century British Novel*, London: Verso, 1993; Ann Ardis, '"The Journey from Fantasy to Politics": The Representation of Socialism and Feminism in *Gloriana* and *The Image-Breakers*', in Angela Ingram and Daphne Patai, eds, *Rediscovering Forgotten Radicals: British Women Writers 1889–1939*, Chapel Hill: The University of North Carolina Press, 1993; Sally Ledger, *The New Woman: Fiction and Feminism at the fin de siècle*, Manchester: Manchester University Press, 1997; Judy Greenway, 'No Place for Women? Anti-Utopianism and the Utopian Politics of the 1890s', *Geografiska Annaler Series B, Human Geography*, Vol. 84, Issue 3–4, October 2002; Matthew Beaumont, *Utopia Ltd: Ideologies of Social Dreaming in England, 1870–1900*, Chicago: Haymarket Books, 2009 (1st edition 2005); Christine Bayles Kortsch, *Dress Culture in Late Victorian Women's Fiction: Literacy, Textiles, and Activism*, Farnham: Ashgate, 2009; Diana Maltz, 'Ardent Service: Female Eroticism and New Life Ethics in Gertrude Dix's The Image Breakers (1900)', *Journal of Victorian Culture*, Vol. 17, No. 2, 2012; Christina Murdoch, '*A Large and Passionate Humanity Plays About Her*': *Women and the Social Problem Novel*, PhD, University of Glasgow, 2012. On Tufts see Kim E. Nielsen, *Un-American Womanhood: Anti-radicalism, Anti-feminism and the First Red Scare*, Columbus: Ohio State University, 2001; Kirsten Marie Delegard, *Battling Miss Bolsheviki: The Origins of Female Conservatism in the United States*, Philadelphia: University of Pennsylvania Press, 2012; Anissa Harper and Kathryn Kish

Sklar have collected and interpreted relevant documents, in *Pacifism vs. Patriotism in Women's Organizations in the 1920s*, State University of New York at Binghamton, August 1998, online at womhist.alexanderstreet.com, accessed 14/05/2012.

7. Helen Tufts, 'Our Threatened Heritage: A Letter to the D.A.R.', 4-5-28, Document 20, in Harper and Sklar, *Pacifism vs. Patriotism*, http://womhist.alexanderstreet.com; 'D.A.R. Drops Mrs Bailie, Accused of Injuring Good Name of Body in Blacklist Charges', *New York Times*, 23 June 1928, reproduced online in Women's History Primary Source Documents, at greenstone.org, accessed 14/05/2012.

8. Helen Tufts Bailie Papers (H.T.B.P.) Sophia Smith Collection, Smith College; Helena Born Papers (H.B.P.), Tamiment Library Robert F. Wagner Labor Archives, New York; Rey Papers (R.P.), San Francisco; Helen Tufts Bailie, 'Notes For Helena About Her Father', Typed MS, no date. Donated to the author by Christine Ann Bailie Jolly.

1. Radical Endeavour: Helena Born

1. 1851 England Census, Coham, Black Torrington; Births Registered in April, May, June 1860, Holsworthy; 1871 England Census, Moor Head, Hatherleigh; the 1881 England Census, Westbury-upon-Trym, reveals Helena's birthplace.

2. 1871 England Census; Minnie is Elizabeth Mary Southcombe, born circa 1872 Hatherleigh. Her gravestone gives her age in February 1949 as seventy-six; Tufts, B.I. pp. xvi–xvii.

3. Hatherleigh Parish Council and towns people, *The Story of Hatherleigh*, *Hatherleigh Millennium 981–1981*, Pamphlet, Hatherleigh Millennium Committee, May 1981, pp. 1–10.

4. Tufts, B.I., p. xi; Helena Born, 'A Chat about Bazaars', January 1885, MS notes, H.B.P.

5. Tufts, B.I., p. xi.

6. Elm Villa, Stoke St Mary, *Exeter Flying Post*, 16 February 1876.

7. On Bristol, Kenneth Morgan, 'The Economic Development of Bristol', in Madge Dresser and Philip Ollerenshaw, eds, *The Making of Modern Bristol*, Bristol: Redcliffe Press, 1996, pp. 48–75; Charles F. Harvey and Jon Press, 'Industrial Change and the Economic Life of Bristol since 1800', in Charles E. Harvey and Jon Press, eds, *Studies in the Business History of Bristol*, Bristol: Bristol Academic Press, 1988, pp. 1–32.

8. 1881 England Census; on Clifton see H.E. Meller, *Leisure and the Changing City 1870–1914*, London: Routledge & Kegan Paul, 1976, pp. 36–7; Derek Winterbottom, *Clifton After Percival: A Public School in the Twentieth Century*, Bristol: Redcliffe Press, 1990, pp. 11–17.

9. Moira Martin, 'Managing the Poor', in Dresser and Ollerenshaw, *The Making of Modern Bristol*, p. 161; Ellen Malos, 'Bristol Women in Action, 1839–1919', in Ian Bild, ed., *Bristol's Other History*, Bristol: Bristol Broadsides Co-op, 1983, pp. 97–114; Emma Hopley, *Campaigning Against Cruelty: The Hundred Year History of the British Union for the Abolition of Vivisection*, London: BUAV, 1998, pp. 2–3; Lorna Bradley and Helen Reid, '*Go Home and Do the Washing*': *Three Centuries of Pioneering Bristol Women*, Bristol: Broadcast Books, 2000, pp. 11–35, 63–5, 144–8; Madge Dresser, ed., *Women and the City: Bristol 1373–2000*, Bristol: Redcliffe Press and the Regional History Centre, University of the West of England, 2016, pp. 92–136.

10. Helena Born Scrapbook from 1880, H.B.P. On William and Jane Hargrave, 'The Contagious Diseases Acts', *Bristol Mercury*, 16 March 1872; 'Women Suffrage',

Bristol Mercury, 5 November 1880, and 'National Union of Working Women', *Bristol Mercury*, 2 May 1879; Richardson, 'The Bristol Strike Wave', in Roger Ball et al., *Strikers, Hobblers, Conchies and Reds*, pp. 98–9. See also Walter L. Arnstein, *The Bradlaugh Case: Altruism, Sex and Politics Among the Late Victorians*, Columbia: University of Missouri Press, 1983, and Laura Schwartz, *Infidel Feminism, Secularism, Religion and Women's Emancipation, England 1830–1914*, Manchester: Manchester University Press, 2013.

11. John Gregory, 'Beauty's Choice' and 'Reward of Labour', Born, Scrapbook, 1880, H.B.P.

12. John Gregory, Draft of an Election Address, no date, John Gregory Papers, University of Bristol. On Gregory's life, Gerrard Sables, 'John Gregory and William Morris: Two Socialist Poets', *William Morris Society Newsletter*, Summer 2008, p. 16; William J. Watson, 'John Gregory: A Bristol Poet', *Western Graphic*, Vol. vi, No. 11, 5 September 1903.

13. Richardson, 'The Bristol Strike Wave', pp. 99–100; Bryher, *Labour and Socialist Movement in Bristol*, Part 1, pp. 13–22; 'The Bristol Socialist Society', *Justice*, 10 April 1924, Cutting, in Bristol Socialist Society (B.S.S.) Album, Samuel Bale Collection, B19560, Bristol Reference Library. Funeral of John Sharland, Cutting, no reference, in B.S.S. Scrapbook, Samuel Bale Collection, B19561, Bristol Reference Library. On Robert Sharland, see *The Social-Democrat*, February 1931, Cutting in B.S.S. Album, Bristol Reference Library, and 'A Life Devoted to his Fellows: Tributes at the Funeral of R. Sharland', unnamed newspaper cutting dated 10 July 1931, in John Gregory Papers, Bristol University. W.W. Young, *Robert Weare*, pamphlet, Manchester: Cooperative Wholesale Society, no date, Bristol Reference Library, is a biography of Weare which describes the B.S.S. See also Sally Mullen, 'The Bristol Socialist Society, 1885–1914', in Bild, *Bristol's Other History*, pp. 36–7.

14. B.S.S. flyer, no date, B.S.S. Scrapbook, B19561; Bryher, *Labour and Socialist Movement in Bristol*, Part 1, pp. 24–5.

15. On Gilliard, Bryher, *Labour and Socialist Movement in Bristol*, Part 1, p. 20; 'The Late Mr Gilliard', *Western Daily Press*, 22 November 1921, Cutting B.S.S. Album, B19560.

16. J. Ramsay MacDonald, quoted in Bryher, *Labour and Socialist Movement in Bristol*, Part 1, p. 32; on Bristol's radical coffee houses see Stephen E. Hunt, 'Intermezzo: Coffee Taverns', in Backwith et al., *Strikers, Hobblers, Conchies and Reds*, pp. 185–95.

17. Born, Scrapbook, January 1883, 'The Female Apostle of Anarchy', Cutting, no date, H.B.P. On Michel's visit, Edith Thomas, *Louise Michel*, Montréal: Black Rose Books, 1981, p. 203.

18. Born, Scrapbook, 1883–1884, H.B.P.

19. Tufts, B.I. pp. xi–xiii; 1881 England Census.

20. Beatrice Taylor is cited as 'an early friend', Tufts, B.I. pp. xi–xii.

21. Taylor quoted in Tufts, B.I., p. xii.

22. Taylor quoted in Tufts, B.I., p. xii.

23. Helena Born, 'Bias', MS, Notebook, no page numbers, H.B.P.

24. Tufts, B.I., p. xii.

25. Bristol Women's Liberal Association (B.W.L.A.) Report for 1885 (1886), pp. 2, 8–9; B.W.L.A. Report for 1886 (1887), p. 10, Bristol Reference Library; *Bristol Mercury*, 10 March 1886.

26. B.W.L.A. Report for 1881 (1982), p. 3.

27. Anna Maria Priestman quoted in Sarah A. Tooley, 'The Woman at Home; Ladies of

Bristol and Clifton', offprint of article, no date, no publisher, Bristol Central Library, p. 454.

28. Sandra Stanley Holton, *Suffrage Days: Stories from the Women's Suffrage Movement*, London: Routledge, 1996, pp. 56–8.

29. Elizabeth Crawford, Priestman Sisters, *The Women's Suffrage Movement: A Reference Guide, 1866–1928*, London: UCL Press, 1999, pp. 565–7, 671. See also correspondence on C.D. Acts and Suffrage between Margaret Tanner, Miss M. Priestman and Josephine Butler, 1882–1891, Josephine Butler Letters, Women's Library, L.S.E.

30. June Hannam, '"An Enlarged Sphere of Usefulness": The Bristol Women's Movement, c 1860–1914', in Dresser and Ollerenshaw, *The Making of Modern Bristol*, p. 189.

31. Sandra Stanley Holton, *Quaker Women: Personal Life, Memory and Radicalism in the Lives of Women Friends, 1780–1930*, London: Routledge, 2007, pp. 178–9.

32. Elizabeth Cady Stanton, *Eighty Years and More: Reminiscences 1815–1897*, New York: Schocken Books, 1971 (1st edition 1898), pp. 364–5; see Sandra Stanley Holton, '"To Educate Women into Rebellion": Elizabeth Cady Stanton and the Creation of a Transatlantic Network of Radical Suffragists', *The American Historical Review*, Vol. 99, No. 4, October 1994.

33. Crawford, Sturge Sisters, *The Women's Suffrage Movement*, pp. 661–2; Brierly and Reid, '*Go Home and Do the Washing*', p. 57, Patricia Hollis, *Ladies Elect: Women in English Local Government, 1865–1914*, Oxford: Clarendon Press, 1987, pp. 157–8; B.W.L.A. Report for 1885 (1986), p. 10.

34. Crawford, Mary Anne Estlin, *The Women's Suffrage Movement*, pp. 209–10; Hannam, '"An Enlarged Sphere of Usefulness"', pp. 186–7; for links between Estlin and U.S. radicals, the Garrisons, Stanton and Susan B. Anthony, see letters to Estlin from Frank J. Garrison and letter from Sarah Pugh, 19 June 1876, Estlin Papers, Dr Williams Library.

35. B.W.L.A. Report for 1885 (1986), p. 5. See Moncure D. Conway, *Autobiography, Memories and Experiences*, London: Cassell & Co., 1904.

36. The Women's Suffrage Movement, Clifton Conference, *Bristol Mercury*, 17 December 1886.

37. Holton, *Suffrage Days*, pp. 40–1.

38. B.W.L.A. Report for 1887 (1888), p. 9; H.T.J., 6 September 1897, p. 65.

39. Helena Born, 'Pro Bono Publico', MS, no page numbers, H.B.P.

40. B.W.L.A. Report for 1887 (1888), p. 10.

41. On the pervasive influence of 'altruism', a concept partially deriving from the French Positivist Auguste Comte, see Thomas Dixon, *The Invention of Altruism*, Oxford: Oxford University Press, 2008.

42. Maria Colby, 'Woman's Mission', Cutting from *Bristol Mercury*, 13 July 1886, Born Scrapbook, H.B.P.

43. Emily Sturge, 'Am I My Sister's Keeper?', December 1887, B.W.L.A. Report for 1887 (1888), pp. 10–11; see also Miss A. Macdonnell, 'Women's Political Work', *The Liberal and Radical*, Vol. 3, No. 31, 7 January 1888, p. 12.

44. J.M.B., 'British Factory Girls', Cutting from *The New York Sun* (no date), Born, Scrapbook, 1887, H.B.P.

45. Letter to the International Council of Women at Washington, B.W.L.A. Report for 1888 (1989), pp. 12–13.

46. Letter to the International Council, p. 13.

47. Report of the International Council of Women assembled by the National Woman

Suffrage Association, Washington, U.S.A., March 25 to April 1, 1888, online at https://archive.org, accessed 20/10/2011.

48. Bristol Women's Liberal Association leaflet 1888, H.B.P. On the background to the measures see G.R. Searle, *A New England? Peace and War 1886–1918*, Oxford: Clarendon Press, 2005, pp. 125–6, 204–5.

49. 'Marlborough Workmen's Flower Show', *Western Daily Press*, 27 July 1887; 'Flower Show in St. James', *Bristol Mercury*, 1 August 1888; 'Marlborough Workmen's Show', *Western Daily Press*, 1 August 1888.

50. B.W.L.A. Report for 1886 (1887), June 1886, p. 8.

51. 'Bristol Women's Liberal Association, 'Soiree and Meeting at the Victoria Rooms', *Western Daily Press*, 2 February 1888.

52. Mr H.T.M.C. Gwynn, quoted at 'Liberal Meeting in Clifton', *Bristol Mercury*, 28 February 1888.

53. 'Liberal Meeting at Bedminster', *Western Daily Press*, 27 February 1888; 'Liberal Meeting at Montpelier', *Bristol Mercury*, 28 March 1888.

54. Helena Born, quoted at B.W.L.A. meeting in Montpelier, *Bristol Mercury*, 14 March 1888.

55. 'Women's Liberal Association, Wells Division', Cutting, no reference, Born, Scrapbook, 1888, H.B.P.

56. Robert Tovey quoted in *The Liberal and Radical*, 18 August 1888. On Tovey, see Bryher, *Labour and Socialist Movement in Bristol*, Part 1, pp. 39, 43 and Part 2, pp. 8–9.

57. On Irving see Bryher, *Labour and Socialist Movement in Bristol*, Part 2, pp. 10–11; David Howell, 'Irving, David Daniel [Dan] 1854–1924', *Oxford Dictionary of National Biography*, online, October 2009, accessed 24/03/2010; Martin Crick, *The History of the Social Democratic Federation*, Keele: Ryburn Publishing, 1994, p. 308.

58. Hugh Holmes Gore, 'Socialism. An Explanation', *Bristol Mercury*, 11 September 1886; Hugh Holmes Gore, 'Socialism. A Rejoinder', *Bristol Mercury*, 28 August 1886. On Gore see Bryher, *Labour and Socialist Movement in Bristol*, Part 1, p. 42 and Part 2, pp. 12–14, and Mike Richardson, *The Enigma of Hugh Holmes Gore: Bristol's Nineteenth-Century Christian Socialist Solicitor*, Bristol: Bristol Radical History Group, 2016.

59. Born, 'Pro Bono Publico', 1887, MS, no page numbers, H.B.P.

60. Born, 'Insincerity', 1888, MS, no page numbers, H.B.P.

61. See Royden J. Harrison, *The Life and Times of Sidney and Beatrice Webb*, London: Palgrave, 2000, p. 97; Mark Francis, *Herbert Spencer and the Invention of Modern Life*, Stocksfield: Acumen, 2007, p. 335; William Sweet, 'Herbert Spencer (1820–1903)', *Internet Encyclopedia of Philosophy*, online, accessed 15/07/2015.

62. Dixon, *The Invention of Altruism*, p. 195.

63. Herbert Spencer, *The Man Versus the State*, Williams & Norgate 1888 (1st edition 1884), pp. 31–2; see H.W. Taylor, *Men Versus the State: Herbert Spencer and Late Victorian Individualism*, Oxford: Clarendon Press, 1992, pp. 5, 25, 71.

64. 'Marriage of Sir Joseph Weston', *Western Daily Press*, 12 October 1888.

65. Tufts, B.I., p. xii.

66. B.W.L.A., Report for 1888 (1889), p. 15.

67. Tufts, B.I., p. xiii.

68. Tufts, B.I., p. xiv.

69. Tufts, B.I., p. xiii.

2. *Subversive Intimations: Miriam Daniell*

1. Birth Certificate, Elizabeth Miriam Wheeler, Clifton, Bristol, 1861.
2. 1851 and 1871 England Census; Sir Mortimer Wheeler, *Still Digging*, London: Michael Joseph Ltd., 1955, p. 13; Advertisements, 'Jellies', *Bristol Mercury*, 17 November 1877.
3. Minute Book of the Committee Meetings, Pembroke Chapel, Register, 1866–1915, Bristol Record Office (B.R.O.).
4. Wheeler, *Still Digging*, pp. 13–14; the name of the governess was Susanna Elizabeth Weinmann; 1871, England Census.
5. Wheeler, *Still Digging*, p. 16.
6. Wheeler, *Still Digging*, p. 14; on John Stuart Blackie, David and Emily Rosaline Masson, see Wikipedia and Elizabeth Ewan, Sue Innes, Siân Reynolds, eds., *The Biographical Dictionary of Scottish Women*, Edinburgh: Edinburgh University Press, 2006, pp. 258–9.
7. Wheeler, *Still Digging*, p. 14; Robert Mark Wenley, *The University Extension Movement in Scotland*, Glasgow: Glasgow University Press, 1895, p. 53.
8. 'Bazaar at the Victoria Rooms', *Bristol Mercury*, 4 November 1880.
9. Minute Book, Pembroke Chapel, B.R.O.
10. *Bristol Mercury*, 16 July 1881; *Bristol and Clifton Directory*, Bristol: J. Wright & Co., 1880, p. 14.
11. Copy of Marriage Register, Edward Tuckett Daniell and Elizabeth Miriam Wheeler, 13 July 1881; on James Livett Daniell and Sophie Day Baynes' marriage, *Bristol Mercury*, 15 January 1870.
12. On James Livett Daniell, *Bristol Mercury*, 22 October 1880, *Western Daily Press*, 23 January 1883, *The Shield*, 7 June 1884; on Sophie Daniell, Bristol and Clifton Association for Home Teaching of the Blind and Industrial Employment of Blind Women and Girls, 28th Annual Report, Bristol, 1886; B.W.L.A. Report for 1884 (1885), p. 10; Clifton branch of the Ladies National Association for the Abolition of Government Regulation of Vice, Annual Meeting, 1886, Bristol Central Library.
13. 'Pictures at the Bristol Academy', *Bristol Mercury*, 7 April 1884 and 31 March 1884; Richardson, 'The Bristol Strike Wave', in Backwith et al., *Strikers, Hobblers, Conchies and Reds*, pp. 96–7.
14. Tufts, B.I., p. xiii.
15. Angela Tuckett, Henry Stacy, Exercise Book, Box 10, Angela Tuckett Papers (A.T.P.), Working Class Movement Library; Bristol Savages, 'Stacy, Henry Edward', online accessed 08/08/2012; June Hannam, 'Stacy, Enid' (1868–1903), *Dictionary of National Biography*, online, 24/03/2010; B.W.L.A. Report for 1884, (1885), p. 11.
16. Bryher, *Labour and Socialist Movement in Bristol*, Part 1, pp. 26–8; William Morris, *Art and Labour*, pp. 1, 14, online at marxists.org, accessed 27/01/2016.
17. Bryher, *Labour and Socialist Movement in Bristol*, Part 1, pp. 26–8; Gore on 'Socialism', *Bristol Mercury*, 28 August, 11 September 1886; on Grönlund's influence, Enid Stacy to Julia (? Dawson), 27 May 1899, E.S., Box 9. On Morris' visit, Tuckett MS on Enid Stacy, Box 24 xi, 7; 6 xi 7, A.T.P.
18. 'E Miriam Daniell', Letter, 'The Sheep on the Downs', *Western Daily Press*, 27 July 1885.
19. 'E.T.D.', Letter, *Western Daily Press*, 28 July 1885.
20. 'A Bristol Divorce Suit, Socialism and Free Love', *Bristol Mercury*, 1 May 1894.
21. Tufts, B.I., p. xx.

22. *Reynolds's Newspaper*, 6 May 1894; on the operation see *Yorkshire Evening Post*, 30 April 1894; *St James's Gazette*, 1 May 1894; *Morning Post*, 1 May 1894; *Manchester Courier and Lancashire General Advertiser*, 1 May 1894; *Cheshire Observer*, 5 May 1894.

23. 'Women's Liberal Associations', *Englishwomen's Review*, 15 March 1889, p. 123; B.W.L.A. Report for 1889 (1890), p. 8.

24. Tufts, B.I., p. xiii.

25. On the background to the rise of socialist groups in the 1880s see Peter d'A. Jones, *The Christian Socialist Revival, 1877–1914*, Princeton: Princeton University Press, 1968; E. P. Thompson, *William Morris: Romantic to Revolutionary*, London: Merlin Press, 1977 (1st edition 1955); Mark Bevir, *The Making of British Socialism*, Princeton: Princeton University, 2011.

26. On Gore and Christian Socialism, Jones, *The Christian Socialist Revival*, pp. 308–9, 325–6; on the Clifton and Bristol group, Richardson, *The Enigma of Hugh Holmes Gore*.

27. 'Memorial to the Docks Committee', *Bristol Mercury*, 11 December 1888.

28. Path Preservation Society Meeting, *Bristol Mercury*, 6 June 1888; on Henry Stacy's membership, Angela Tuckett MS on Enid Stacy, xi/45/5, A.T.P.; on F. Gilmore Barnett, Bryher, *Labour and Socialist Movement in Bristol*, Part 1, p. 18, and Obituary, *Western Daily Press*, 19 March 1908; George Hare Leonard, *Some Memories of Dr Lloyd Morgan and Old Days in University College, Bristol*, pamphlet, March 1936, Bristol, Bristol Reference Library; on Francis J. Fry, see Frenchay Village Museum, *J. S. Fry and Sons: A Rough Gide to the Family and the Firm* (booklet), Bristol, 2010, pp. 34–9; on the Footpath Preservers' direct action tactics see Mike Richardson, *The Enigma of Hugh Holmes Gore*, pp. 41–2.

29. Emily Guest, 'The Religious Basis of Socialism', *Western Daily Press*, 28 November 1887.

30. Tufts, B.I., p. xiii.

31. Tufts, B.I., p. xiv.

32. Tufts, B.I., p. xiii–xiv.

33. Tufts, B.I., p. xiv.

34. Tufts, B.I., p. xiii.

35. Tufts, B.I., p. xii. On the impact of *Towards Democracy*, see Sheila Rowbotham, *Edward Carpenter: A Life of Liberty and Love*, London: Verso, 2008, pp. 71–4.

36. Rowbotham, *Edward Carpenter*, pp. 89–96, 130–1.

37. Bryher, *Labour and Socialist Movement in Bristol*, Part 2, pp. 9–12.

38. *Commonweal*, Vol. 3, No. 76, 25 June 1887, p. 203.

39. *Commonweal*, Vol. 3, No. 72, 28 May 1887, p. 176.

40. Robert Gilliard to Helen Tufts, 9 May 1901, H.B.P.

41. Bryher, *Labour and Socialist Movement in Bristol*, Part 2, p. 30; Young, *Robert Weare*, pp. 27–8.

42. Bryher, *Labour and Socialist Movement in Bristol*, Part 2, p. 30; First Annual Report of the Bristol Sunday Society, A.T.P., Box 10, p. 8.

43. Bryher, *Labour and Socialist Movement in Bristol*, Part 2, pp. 30–1; on Irving, p. 10.

44. Young, *Robert Weare*, pp. 28–9.

45. 'Bristol Socialist Society, List of Lectures', Leaflet, H.B.P.

46. 'Bristol Women's Liberal Association', *Women's Penny Paper*, 23 February 1889; 'Toilers in the Chain Trade', Cutting, no references, Born, Scrapbook, circa Spring 1889, H.B.P.

47. 'The Deluge at Bristol', *Bristol Observer*, 16 March 1889, in Reece Winstone, *Bristol in the 1880s*, Bristol: Reece Winstone, 1962, pp. 35–6.

48. 'The Deluge at Bristol', Winstone, *Bristol in the 1880s*, p. 35.

49. Revd T.W. Harvey quoted in James M. Wilson, *An Autobiography, 1836–1931*, London: Sidgwick & Jackson, 1932, p. 142. (I am grateful to Clifton College Archive for this reference.)

50. Wilson, *An Autobiography*, pp. 142–3.

51. *Western Daily Press*, 14 March 1889.

52. *Western Daily Press*, 15 March 1889.

53. Tufts, B.I., pp. xiv–xv

54. *The Liberal and Radical*, Vol. vii, No. 98, 20 April 1889, Special Collections, University of Bristol.

55. B.W.L.A. Report for 1889 (1890), p. 14.

3. Awakenings: Robert Allan Nicol

1. William Blake, 'Eternity, Gnomic Verses', *The Poetical Works of William Blake*, ed. John Sampson, London: Oxford University Press, 1934, pp. 196–7; Walter Pater, unsigned review, *Westminster Review*, October 1868, reprinted in the Conclusion to *The Renaissance: Studies in Art and Poetry* (1873), online at morrisedition.lib.uiowa.edu, p. 6, accessed 28/04/2013.

2. On the Nicol shop see *Fife Traders*, Typed MS, Dunfermline Public Library, p. 125 and Sheila Pitcairn, *The Old 'Fitpaths' and Streets of Dunfermline, Then and Now*, Dunfermline: Pitcairn Publications, no date c. 2000. On the economic background see E. Patricia Dennison and Simon Stronach, *Historic Dunfermline: Archeology and Development*, The Scottish Burgh Survey, Third Series, Dunfermline: Dunfermline Burgh Survey Community Project, 2007, pp. 62–4, and 'Linen and Damask Trade in Dunfermline', *Dundee Courier and Argus*, 30 April 1875.

3. 'Notes on Fife', *Dunfermline Journal*, 6 April 1878, p. 51.

4. *Fife Traders*, p. 125.

5. *Dundee Courier*, 28 November 1882.

6. Family Tree and US Naturalization Record Indexes, 1791–1992 record for Robert Allan Nicol, Date of Action, 15 May 1950, R.P.

7. 1881 Scotland Census. The house is now knocked down but a photograph is online, Dunfermline, Cousins Lane, Railside Cottage, at ScotlandsPlaces.gov.uk, accessed 18/06/2014. On the factory workers, Pitcairn, *The Old 'Fitpaths' and Streets*, p. 302.

8. *Reynolds's Newspaper*, 25 April 1886.

9. *Dunfermline Saturday Press*, 24 September, 1 October, 10 December, 17 December 1887.

10. James J. Trotter, *Royal High School, Edinburgh*, Edinburgh: Pitcairn & Son, 1911, pp. 1, 45–9, 68–9; Robert Nicol to Urry (Cabell), 27 June 1955, R.P.

11. Nicol to Urry (Cabell), 27 June 1955, R.P.

12. J. Arthur Thomson quoted in Amelia Defries, *The Interpreter Geddes: The Man and his Gospel*, London: Routledge, 1927, p. 120. On Geddes' impact, Philip Mairet, *Pioneer of Sociology: The Life and Letters of Patrick Geddes*, London: Lund Humphries, 1957, p. 39; Helen Meller, *Patrick Geddes: Social Evolutionist and City Planner*, London: Routledge, 1990, p. 16.

13. Douglas Sutherland, 'Education as an Agent of Social Evolution: The Educational Projects of Patrick Geddes in Late-Victorian Scotland', *History of Education*, Vol. 38, Issue 3, May 2009, pp. 349–65.

14. Robert Nicol to Patrick Geddes, 7 September 1884, National Library of Scotland (N.L.S.), copy of letter from 'PG' to 'Robert' is inserted (no date).

15. Patrick Geddes, *On the Conditions of Progress of the Capitalist and the Labourer* (pamphlet), Edinburgh: Co-operative Printing Co., 1886, pp. 105–9.

16. Quoted in Defries, *The Interpreter Geddes*, p. 124.

17. 'Matriculation' 1884–1888, University of Edinburgh. (I am grateful to Archives and Manuscripts, University of Edinburgh for this information); Robert Nicol to Patrick Geddes, 9 March 1886, N.L.S.

18. Nicol to Geddes, 9 March 1886, N.L.S.

19. Robert Nicol to Amaryllis (Nicol Cabell), 2 June 1955, R.P.

20. Nicol to Geddes, 9 March 1886, N.L.S.

21. Helen Meller, 'Geddes, Sir Patrick', *Oxford Dictionary of National Biography* online, accessed 24/03/2010, p. 3; on Anna Morton see Tanya Cheadle, *Realizing a 'More Than Earthy Paradise of Love': Scotland's Sexual Progressives, 1880–1914*, PhD, School of Humanities, University of Glasgow, 2014.

22. Philip Boardman, *The Worlds of Patrick Geddes*, London: Routledge & Kegan Paul, 1978, pp. 86–7.

23. Peter Kropotkin quoted in Boardman, *The Worlds of Patrick Geddes*, p. 87.

24. James Mavor, *My Windows on the Street of the World*, London: J.M. Dent, 1923.

25. George Eyre-Todd, 'The Genius of the Outlook Tower', *Scots Observer*, Edinburgh, 30 July 1931, quoted in Boardman, *The Worlds of Patrick Geddes*, p. 105.

26. Nicol to Amaryllis (Nicol Cabell), 2 June 1955, R.P.

27. Edward Heron-Allen, Obituary, John Arthur Thomson, *Journal of the Royal Microscopical Society*, Vol. 53, Issue I, March 1933, pp. 35–8.

28. Nicol to Amaryllis, 2 June 1955, R.P.

29. Isabella Thomson 1871, 1891, Scotland Census.

30. Nicol to Amaryllis (Nicol Cabell), 2 June 1955, R.P.; on the offer of assistance see copy of letter from 'P.G.' to Robert Nicol enclosed in Nicol to Geddes, 7 September 1884, N.L.S.

31. Nicol to Amaryllis (Nicol Cabell), 2 June 1955, R.P.

32. Matriculation, 1884–1888, Information from Archives and Manuscripts, University of Edinburgh.

33. See James Bradley, Anne Crowther, Marguerite Dupree, 'Mobility and Selection in Scottish Medical Education, 1858–1886', *Medical History*, Vol. 40, 1996, pp. 15–24.

34. Nicol to Geddes, 9 March 1886, N.L.S.

35. William Kenefick, *Red Scotland: The Rise and Fall of the Radical Left, c. 1872–1932*, Edinburgh: Edinburgh University Press, 2007, pp. 56–68; Megan C. Ferguson, *Patrick Geddes and the Celtic Renascence of the 1890s*, PhD, University of Dundee, 2011; Jane Rendall and Sue Innes, 'Women, Gender and Politics in Scotland 1701–2000', in Lynn Abrams, Eleanor Gordon, Deborah Simonton and Eileen Yeo, eds, *Gender in Scottish History*, Edinburgh: Edinburgh University Press, 2006.

36. Mavor, *My Windows on the Street of the World*, pp. 178–81; Bruce Glasier, *William Morris and the Early Days of the Socialist Movement*, London: Longmans, Green and Co., 1921, pp. 10, 18, 21–4; Jonathan Hyslop, *The Notorious Syndicalist J.T. Bain: A Scottish Rebel in Colonial South Africa*, Johannesburg: Jacana Media, 2004, pp. 66–75;

see also correspondence 1884–89, Socialist League Papers, International Institute of Social History, Amsterdam.

37. Edinburgh University Socialist Society, *Beauty for Ashes: An Appeal*, Edinburgh, 1884, p. 15.

38. Edinburgh University Social-Reform Society, Report for 1885–86, Edinburgh, pp. 13–14, 16.

39. *Commonweal*, 5 March 1887.

40. Patrick Geddes, *Co-operation versus Socialism* (pamphlet), Manchester: Co-operative Printing Society, 1888, pp. 14, 19, 24.

41. Chris Renwick, 'The Practice of Spencerian Science: Patrick Geddes's Biosocial Programme 1876–1889', *Isis*, Vol. 100, No. 1, March 2009, Figure 3, p. 54.

42. Renwick, 'The Practice of Spencerian Science', pp. 48–54; Elaine Thomson, 'Physiology, Hygiene and the Entry of Women to the Medical Profession in Edinburgh c. 1869–c. 1900', *Studies in the History of Philosophy, Biology and Biomedical Science*, Vol. 32, No. 1, pp. 111–12, 116–20; Eileen Janes Yeo, *The Contest for Social Science*, London: Rivers Oram, 1996, pp. 197–8; Cheadle, *Realizing a 'More Than Earthly Paradise'*, pp. 130–8.

43. Quoted in Renwick, 'The Practice of Spencerian Science', Figure 3, p. 34.

44. Meller, *Patrick Geddes*, p. 83; Renwick, 'The Practice of Spencerian Science', p. 51.

45. The newspaper reports vary on the date of their meeting; for example, *Bristol Mercury*, 1 May 1894, opts for 1886; *Western Daily Press*, 1 May 1894, for 1889. On the networks, Wheeler, *Still Digging*, p. 14; Robert Mark Wenley, *The University Extension Movement in Scotland*, printed at the University Press by Robert Maclehose & Co., Glasgow, 1895, pp. 52–3; Meller, *Patrick Geddes*, p. 55, note 57; Thomson, 'Physiology, Hygiene and the Entry of Women to the Medical Profession', pp. 119–20, note 16.

46. Pater, unsigned review, *Westminster Review*, October 1868, online at morrisedition.lib. uiowa.edu, p. 6, accessed 28/04/2013.

4. Exaltation: Autumn 1889

1. *Bristol Mercury*, 1 May 1894.

2. *Cheshire Observer*, 5 May 1894.

3. *Daily News*, 1 May 1894.

4. *Daily News*, 1 May 1894.

5. *Reynolds's Newspaper*, 6 May 1894; *London Standard*, 1 May 1894.

6. *Western Daily Press*, 1 September 1889.

7. Richardson, 'The Bristol Strike Wave', in Backwith et al., *Strikers, Hobblers, Conchies and Reds*, p. 106.

8. Sheila Rowbotham, *Hidden from History*, London: Pluto, 1973, p. 61; on the match women, see Louise Raw, *Striking a Light*, London: Continuum, 2011; on new unionism, Yvonne Kapp, *Eleanor Marx*, Vol. 2, London: Lawrence & Wishart, 1976, pp. 270, 318–34.

9. Brian Atkinson, *The Bristol Labour Movement, 1868–1906*, PhD, University of Oxford, 1969, p. 205.

10. Kapp, *Eleanor Marx*, Vol. 2, p. 320.

11. Vickery quoted in Richardson, 'The Bristol Strike Wave', p. 102.

12. Schwartz, *Infidel Feminism*, pp. 52–4; Kapp, *Eleanor Marx*, Vol. 2, p. 348.
13. Richardson, 'The Bristol Strike Wave', p. 104.
14. *Daily News*, 1 May 1894.
15. Richardson, 'The Bristol Strike Wave', p. 104.
16. *Commonweal*, 19 October 1889, p. 334.
17. Miriam Daniel [*sic*], Robert Nicoll [*sic*], *The Truth about the Chocolate Factories or Modern White Slavery its Cause and Cure*, Facts for the Times, Vol. 1, Second Edition, Bristol, no date, p. 3, Wood Collection, University of Huddersfield.
18. Frenchay Village Museum, *J.S. Fry & Sons*, pp. 37, 43.
19. Daniel, Nicoll, *The Truth about the Chocolate Factories*, pp. 3–9.
20. Daniel, Nicoll, *The Truth about the Chocolate Factories*, p. 9.
21. Daniel, Nicoll, *The Truth about the Chocolate Factories*, pp. 3–11.
22. Daniel, Nicoll, *The Truth about the Chocolate Factories*, pp. 10–11.
23. Daniel, Nicoll, *The Truth about the Chocolate Factories*, p. 12.
24. Frenchay Village Museum, *J. S. Fry and Sons*, pp. 34–8.
25. Ibid., pp. 39–40.
26. Daniel, Nicoll, *The Truth about the Chocolate Factories*, p. 13; see Lawrence Grönlund, *The Co-operative Commonwealth*, Boston: Lee and Shepard, 1884, p. 83.
27. Daniel, Nicoll, *The Truth about the Chocolate Factories*, p. 14.
28. Daniel, Nicoll, *The Truth about the Chocolate Factories*, p. 14.
29. Daniel, Nicoll, *The Truth about the Chocolate Factories*, p. 14.
30. On Thomas Lake Harris, see Herbert W. Schneider and George Lawton, *A Prophet and a Pilgrim*, New York: Columbia University Press, 1942, pp. xv–xvi, 276–309; Fountain Grove is examined in Robert V. Hine, *California's Utopian Colonies*, New Haven: Yale University Press, 1966 (1st edition 1953), pp. 12–32. For examples of the poems see Thomas Lake Harris, *Star-Flowers: A Poem of the Woman's Mystery*, Privately Printed, 1886, reproduced by Biblio Bazaar, Lightning Sources Milton Keynes, no date; on God as male and female see Mary Farrell Bednarowski, 'Outside the Mainstream: Women's Religion and Women Religious Leaders in Nineteenth-Century America', *Journal of the American Academy of Religion*, Vol. XLVIII, No. 2, 1980, pp. 207–31; Mary Farrell Bednarowski, 'Harris, Thomas Lake', *American National Biography*, online, pp. 1–3, accessed 25/03/2010.
31. Schneider and Lawton, *A Prophet and a Pilgrim*, p. 459; Thomas Lake Harris summarised his ideas of spiritual and political change in *The Brotherhood of the New Life. Its Fact, Law, Method and Purpose*, London: E. W. Allen, 1891, and in *The New Republic*, London: E. W. Allen, 1891.
32. Cheadle, *Realizing a 'More than Earthly Paradise of Love': Scotland's Sexual Progressives*, provides a comprehensive historical study of Harris' British following which was based in Glasgow.
33. *Reynolds's Newspaper*, 6 May 1894.
34. *Morning Post*, 1 May 1894.
35. Bristol Socialist Society (B.S.S.) Minutes, February 1886–May 1891, 3 October 1889. Handwritten minute book in B.R.O.
36. Robert Gilliard to Helen Tufts, 20 June 1901, H.B.P.
37. Gilliard to Tufts, 20 June 1901, H.B.P.
38. *Western Daily Press*, 21 October 1889.
39. Richardson, 'The Bristol Strike Wave', p. 108.
40. Daniel, Nicoll, *The Truth about the Chocolate Factories*, p. 15.

41. Richardson, 'The Bristol Strike Wave', p. 108.
42. Bryher, *Labour and Socialist Movement in Bristol*, Part 2, p. 16.
43. Bryher, *Labour and Socialist Movement in Bristol*, Part 2, pp. 16–17.
44. Bryher, *Labour and Socialist Movement in Bristol*, Part 2, p. 17.
45. Strike Committee Minutes, 26 October 1889, in Workers' Organising Committee (W.O.C.) Minute Book, October 1889–July 1892, B.R.O.
46. Strike Committee Minutes, 27 October 1889, in W.O.C. Minute Book; Tufts, B.I., p. xv.
47. On the background see Kieran Kelly and Mike Richardson, 'The Shaping of the Bristol Labour Movement, 1885–1985', in Dresser and Ollerenshaw, *The Making of Modern Bristol*; S.J. Jones, 'The Cotton Industry in Bristol', *Transactions and Papers: Institute of British Geographers*, Vol. 1, No. 13, 1947; Garry Atterton, *Cotton Threads: The History of the Great Western Cotton Factory* (pamphlet), Bristol: Barton Hill History Group, 2015; for the first comprehensive account of workers' conditions, discontent and resistance see Mike Richardson, *The Maltreated and the Malcontents: Working in the Great Western Cotton Factory, 1838–1914*, Bristol Radical History Group, 2016.
48. Helena Born to Professor Beesly, 25 November 1889, H.B.P.
49. Spafford, quoted in Richardson, 'The Bristol Strike Wave', p. 111.
50. Daniell, Strike Committee Minutes, 28 October 1889, in W.O.C. Minute Book.
51. Gilmore Barnett, Strike Committee Minutes, 28 October 1889, in W.O.C. Minute Book.
52. Strike Committee Minutes, 29 October 1889, in W.O.C. Minute Book.
53. Strike Committee Minutes, 30 October 1889, in W.O.C. Minute Book.
54. Strike Committee Minutes, 4 November 1889, in W.O.C. Minute Book.
55. Daniel, Nicoll, *The Truth about the Chocolate Factories*, p. 13.
56. Lesser Columbus, *Greater Bristol*, London: The Pelham Press, 1893, pp. 29, 32; see also Madge Dresser, 'People's Housing in Bristol, 1870–1939', in Bild, *Bristol's Other History*.
57. Tufts, B.I., p. xvi.
58. Tufts, B.I., p. xvii.
59. Edward Tuckett Daniell in *Bristol Mercury*, 1 May 1894 and *Daily News*, 1 May 1894; Strike Committee Minutes, 2 November 1889, in W.O.C. Minute Book, record Mary Wheeler's participation.
60. Gilliard to Tufts, 9 May 1901, H.B.P.
61. Robert Allan Nicoll to Edward Carpenter, 16 September 1894, MS 271–53, C.C. Sheffield Archives; Charles Helton Tuckett, Letter, *Western Daily Press*, 31 October 1889; Miriam Daniell quoted, *Western Daily Press*, 1 November 1889.
62. Gilliard to Tufts, 20 June 1901, H.B.P.
63. *Western Daily Press*, 1 November 1889.
64. Memorial to the R. Hon. J. Morley MP, *The Women's Penny Paper*, 9 November 1889.
65. *Commonweal*, 2 November 1889, p. 350, and 9 November 1889; Bryher, *Labour and Socialist Movement in Bristol*, Part 2, pp. 19–20.
66. *Commonweal*, 9 November 1889, p. 358.
67. Strike Committee Minutes, 11 November 1889 and 22 November 1889, in W.O.C. Minute Book.
68. Richardson, 'The Bristol Strike Wave', p. 115. On the Carters' donation, *Western Daily Press*, 2 November 1889.
69. Richardson, 'The Bristol Strike Wave', p. 114.

70. Laurence Thompson, *The Enthusiasts: A Biography of John and Katharine Bruce Glasier*, London: Victor Gollancz, 1971, pp. 65–6.
71. Katharine St John Conway quoted in Thompson, *The Enthusiasts*, p. 66.
72. Enid Stacy quoted in Bryher, *Labour and Socialist Movement in Bristol*, p. 22.
73. Strike Committee Minutes, 19 November and 25 November 1889, in W.O.C. Minute Book.
74. Strike Committee Minutes, 6 November, 7 November and 8 November 1889, in W.O.C. Minute Book.
75. A.O., *Western Daily Press*, 7 November 1889.
76. Strike Committee Minutes, 19 November 1889, in W.O.C. Minute Book.
77. Strike Committee Minutes, 11 November 1889, in W.O.C. Minute Book.
78. Strike Committee Minutes, 22 November 1889, in W.O.C. Minute Book.
79. Revd James M. Wilson, *Western Daily Press*, 22 November 1889.
80. Richardson, 'Bristol Strike Wave', p. 116.
81. Robert Weare, *Western Daily Press*, 22 November 1889.
82. Born to Beesly, 25 November 1889, H.B.P.
83. Ibid.
84. Ibid.
85. Mary Clifford to Blanche Piggott, 28 November 1889, in Gwen Mary Williams, *Mary Clifford*, Bristol: J.W. Arrowsmith, 1920, pp. 144–5; on Clifford, see Ellen Malos, 'Bristol Women in Action, 1839–1919', in Bild, *Bristol's Other History*, pp. 115–16; Hollis, *Ladies Elect: Women in English Local Government 1865–1914*, pp. 233–4.
86. Mary Clifford, *The Relation of Women to the State* (1894), quoted in Hollis, *Ladies Elect*, p. 234.
87. Richardson, 'The Bristol Strike Wave', pp. 117–18.
88. Clifford to Piggott, 28 November 1889, in Williams, *Mary Clifford*, p. 145.
89. Liselotte Glage, *Clementina Black: A Study in Social History and Literature*, Heidelberg: Carl Winter Universitätsverlag, 1981, pp. 24–35.
90. 'The Women's Trades Association', leaflet, H.B.P; Glage, *Clementina Black*, pp. 35–7; Ellen Mappen, *Helping Women at Work 1889–1914*, London: Hutchinson, 1985, p. 13.
91. Glage, *Clementina Black*, p. 35.
92. Helena Born, handwritten notes on 'The Women's Trades Association' leaflet, H.B.P.
93. 'Bristol Socialist Society, List of Lectures', leaflet, H.B.P.
94. Born, handwritten notes on 'The Women's Trades Association', leaflet, H.B.P.
95. Friedrich Engels to F.A. Sorge, 7 December 1889, quoted in Richard Hyman, *Marxism and the Sociology of Trade Unionism*, London: Pluto, 1971, p. 9.
96. Emily Sturge quoted in *Western Daily Press*, 17 December 1889.
97. Tufts, B.I., p. xviii.
98. Strike Committee Minutes, 10 November 1889, in W.O.C. Minute Book.
99. Richardson, 'The Bristol Strike Wave', p. 122.
100. Helena Born to a 'cousin in Devon' [Minnie Southcombe], 25 January 1890, in Tufts, B.I., p. xvii.

5. Seekers: 1890

1. W.O.C Minutes, 4, 19, 24 January, 1890.

2. W.O.C. Minutes, 4 January 1890.

3. W.O.C. Minutes, 19 January 1890. On the idea of a federation, see Logie Barrow and Ian Bullock, *Democratic Ideas and the British Labour Movement, 1880–1914*, Cambridge: Cambridge University Press, 1996, pp. 51–63.

4. B.S.S. List of Lectures, H.B.P.

5. Bryher, *Labour and Socialist Movement in Bristol*, Part 2, p. 24.

6. W.O.C. Minutes, 24 January 1890.

7. *Bristol Mercury*, 13 January 1890.

8. Richardson, 'The Bristol Strike Wave', in Backwith et al., *Strikers, Hobblers, Conchies and Reds*, pp. 126–7.

9. *Reasons Why Tailoresses Should Join a Union*, leaflet, H.B.P.

10. *Reasons Why Tailoresses Should Join a Union*, leaflet, H.B.P.

11. The correspondence is in the *Western Dairy Press*, 17, 20, 22 January 1890; see Richardson, 'The Bristol Strike Wave', pp. 127–8; *The Women's Penny Paper*, 22 February 1890.

12. Sidney and Beatrice Webb, *The History of Trade Unionism, 1666–1920*, Printed by the Authors, London, 1920, note 1, pp. 336–7; Malos, 'Bristol Women in Action', in Bild, *Bristol's Other History*, pp. 114–15; Gerry Holloway, 'United we Stand: Class Issues in the Early British Women's Trade Union Movement', in Mary Davis, ed., *Class and Gender in British Labour History*, London: Merlin, 2011, pp. 134–41.

13. Kapp, *Eleanor Marx*, Vol. 2, p. 395; Richardson, 'The Bristol Strike Wave', pp. 129–30.

14. *Rules of the Bristol Tailoresses' Branch of the Bristol District of the National Union of Gas Workers and General Labourers of Great Britain and Ireland*, pamphlet, H.B.P. The initial intention had been to form a branch of the National Union of Working Women, see *Bristol Mercury*, 14 January 1890.

15. Richardson, 'The Bristol Strike Wave', pp. 128–30; *Reasons Why Tailoresses Should Join a Union*, leaflet, H.B.P.

16. Kapp, *Eleanor Marx*, Vol. 2, p. 320; Masthead of *Monthly Record*, April 1890; quoted Tom Mann and Ben Tillett, *The 'New' Trades Unionism*, 21 June 1890, pamphlet, London, p. 16, Wood Collection, Huddersfield University. The quote is a slightly modified version of Percy Bysshe Shelley, 'The Revolt of Islam', Canto V, 1818.

17. Helena Born to Minnie Southcombe, 25 January 1890, extract in Tufts, B.I., pp. xvi–xvii, original letter, H.B.P.

18. *The Peoples Press*, 26 April 1890.

19. Tufts, B.I., p. xxi. The identity of Alice Willway is revealed in Born to Southcombe, 25 January 1890, H.B.P.

20. W.O.C. Minutes, 19 January, 6 February, 28 March 1890, B.R.O.

21. Born to Southcombe, 25 January 1890, H.B.P.

22. Born to Southcombe, 25 January 1890, H.B.P., also in extract quoted Tufts, B.I., pp. xvi–xvii.

23. Born to Southcombe, 25 January 1890, H.B.P.

24. Edward Carpenter to Helen Tufts, 26 July 1902, H.B.P.

25. Richardson, 'The Bristol Strike Wave', pp. 130–2.

26. *Bristol Mercury*, 28 January 1890; Edward Carpenter, 'Breakdown of Our Industrial System', Lecture notes, Bristol, January 1890, MS 258, C.C.

27. Richardson, 'The Bristol Strike Wave', p. 133.

28. Richardson, 'The Bristol Strike Wave', pp. 133–4; Miriam Daniell quoted in *Bristol Mercury*, 3 February 1890.
29. Elizabeth Cady Stanton, *Eighty Years and More: Reminiscences 1815–1897*, New York: Schocken Paperback, 1973 (1st edition 1898), p. 408. On the Russian exiles' reception, see Alex Butterworth, *The World That Never Was: A True Story of Dreamers, Schemers, Anarchists and Secret Agents*, London: The Bodley Head, 2010, pp. 272–3.
30. Robert Nicol, B.S.S., *The Labour Song Book*, pamphlet, circa 1889–90, p. 1, Wood Collection, University of Huddersfield.
31. B.S.S., A List of Lectures, leaflet, H.B.P.
32. Miriam Daniell and Robert Allan Nicol, *The New Trade Unionism: Its Relation to the Old; and the Conditions of Its Success*, pamphlet, Bristol, 1890, L.S.E., p. 13.
33. Daniell and Nicol, *The New Trade Unionism*, pp. 12–13.
34. Daniell and Nicol, *The New Trade Unionism*, pp. 13, 5.
35. Daniell and Nicol, *The New Trade Unionism*, p. 13.
36. Daniell and Nicol, *The New Trade Unionism*, p. 10.
37. Daniell and Nicol, *The New Trade Unionism*, p. 13.
38. Thomas Lake Harris quoted in Daniell and Nicol, *The New Trade Unionism*, p. 4.
39. Daniell and Nicoll, *The New Trade Unionism*, p. 15.
40. Daniell and Nicol, *The New Trade Unionism*, p. 7.
41. Daniell and Nicol, *The New Trade Unionism*, p. 15.
42. Daniell and Nicol, *The New Trade Unionism*, p. 15.
43. Daniell and Nicol, *The New Trade Unionism*, p. 14.
44. Daniell and Nicol, *The New Trade Unionism*, p. 14.
45. See Alex Owen, *The Place of Enchantment: British Occultism and the Culture of the Modern*, Chicago: University of Chicago Press, 2004; Joy Dixon, *Divine Feminine: Theosophy and Feminism in England*, Baltimore: John Hopkins University, 2001.
46. On James Hinton, see Dixon, *The Invention of Altruism*, pp. 81–9; Seth Koven, *Slumming: Sexual and Social Politics in Victorian London*, Princeton: Princeton University Press, 2004, pp. 14–18.
47. Robert S. Gilliard quoted in Daniell and Nicol, *The New Trade Unionism*, p. 3.
48. Gilliard to Tufts, 9 May 1901, H.B.P.
49. Kapp, *Eleanor Marx*, Vol. 2, p. 366.
50. Miriam Daniell and Helena Born, Report of Bristol Strike Committee, *The People's Press*, 22 March 1890.
51. Bristol Labour Notes, *The People's Press*, 22 March 1890.
52. Bristol Labour Notes, *The People's Press*, 29 March 1890.
53. The Bath Gasworkers, *The People's Press*, 29 March 1890.
54. The Bristol Labour Party, *The People's Press*, 29 March 1890.
55. Raymond Unwin, *Commonweal*, 10 May 1890, p. 151. His talks are noted in *The People's Press*, 19 April 1890.
56. W.O.C. Minutes, 4 January 1890; Cotton Operatives' Branch, *The People's Press*, 29 March 1890; on the miners' discontent, *The People's Press*, 22, 29 March 1890; on Gertrude and Robert's visit to the miners, Amaryllis Nicol Cabell interviewed by Georges Rey, Tape, R.P.
57. W.O.C. Minutes, 16 April 1890.
58. Robert Nicol, *The People's Press*, 12 April 1890; on the idea of a labour union federation see W.O.C. Minutes, 19 January 1890.

59. *Bristol Mercury*, 28 April 1890.
60. Kapp, *Eleanor Marx*, Vol. 2, pp. 374–6; John Quail, *The Slow Burning Fuse: The Lost History of the British Anarchists*, London: Paladin, 1978, pp. 90–1.
61. Richardson, 'The Bristol Strike Wave', pp. 138–9; Don Bateman, 'The First Bristol May-Day, 1890 – Eleanor Marx Aveling on The Downs', Copy of typed manuscript, no date. Mike Richardson Private Collection.
62. Henry Stacy quoted in Bryher, *Labour and Socialist Movement in Bristol*, Part 2, p. 24.
63. *Bristol Times and Mirror*, 5 May 1890.
64. 'Robert' (Nicol) to 'Amaryllis' (Cabell Nicol), 31 December 1947. He claims to have shared the platform with Eleanor Marx at the London May Day demonstration, but it is more likely to have been in Bristol where other local labour activists and socialists spoke.
65. Receipts of Demonstration Committee, May 1890, in W.O.C. Minutes; Richardson, 'The Bristol Strike Wave', pp. 139–40.
66. On Helena Born see W.O.C. Minutes, 6 May 1890.
67. Bryher, *Labour and Socialist Movement Bristol*, Part 2, p. 27.
68. Minutes of the First Yearly Conference of Delegates of the National Union of Gas Workers and General Labourers' of Great Britain and Ireland, 19 May to 21 May 1890, John Levy, London, 1890, Working Class Movement Library; Yvonne Kapp, *The Air of Freedom: The Birth of the New Unionism*, London: Lawrence & Wishart, 1989, p. 88.
69. Robert Nicol, G.W. & G.L.U. Conference Minutes, 20 May, pp. 5–6.
70. 'Bro Vickery', G.W. & G.L.U. Conference Minutes, 20 May, p. 6.
71. Robert Nicol, G.W. & G.L.U. Conference Minutes, 21 May, p. 13.
72. G.W. & G.L.U. Conference Minutes, 20 May, p. 7, 21 May, pp. 10–11.
73. G.W. & G.L.U. Conference Minutes, 21 May, p. 14.
74. Yearly Report and Balance Sheet National Union of Gas Workers and General Labourers of Great Britain and Ireland, 1889–94, p. 44, Working Class Movement Library.
75. Gilliard to Tufts, 9 May 1901, H.B.P.
76. Gilliard to Tufts, 9 May 1901, H.B.P.
77. Gilliard to Tufts, 9 May 1901, H.B.P.
78. Miriam Daniell to Edward Tuckett Daniell, no date, 1893, quoted in *Bristol Mercury*, 1 May 1894.
79. Gilliard to Tufts, 9 May 1901, H.B.P.
80. *The People's Press*, 21 June and 5 July 1890.
81. *Bristol Mercury*, 14 June 1890.
82. Gilliard to Tufts, 9 May 1901, H.B.P.
83. Helena Born quoted in Tufts, B.I., p. xviii.
84. Born quoted in Tufts, B.I., p. xviii.
85. Born quoted in Tufts, B.I., p. xviii.
86. Tufts, B.I., p. xix.
87. Gilliard to Tufts, 9 May 1901, H.B.P.
88. *Bristol Mercury*, 2 June 1890; Bristol Labour Emancipation League, 11 July 1890, leaflet, H.B.P.
89. *The People's Press*, 21 June 1890.
90. *Bristol Mercury*, 14 June 1890.
91. *Bristol Mercury*, 3 July 1890.
92. *The People's Press*, 2 August 1890.

93. Robert Nicol to Edward Carpenter, 28 December 1894, C.C.

94. The address of the Ellis's at the Gynsills is in Edward Carpenter, Address Book, C.C. Biographical material on Alexander Ellis is from the Library of the Religious Society of Friends, London. 'Alexander Ellis', *Bootham School Register*, New and Revised Edition, printed Scarborough, 1935, p. 148; 'Deaths', Alexander Ellis, *The Magazine of Bootham School*, Volume Six, 1912–1914, printed London, 1914, p. 52; on his family, Andrew Moore, *Ellis of Leicester: A Quaker Family's Vocation*, Leicester: Laurel House, 2003, pp. 47–9. On the local background, Bill Lancaster, *Radicalism, Cooperation and Socialism: Leicester Working-Class Politics 1860–1906*, Leicester: Leicester University Press, 1987, pp. 70–3.

95. Miriam Daniell quoted in *Reynolds's Newspaper*, 5 May 1894.

96. Tufts, B.I., pp. xx.

97. Tufts, B.I., pp. xxi; Helen Tufts, Speech at Memorial Meeting for Helena Born, Walt Whitman Fellowship, Boston Branch, March 1901, H.B.P.

98. On William Sloane Kennedy and the supposed letter from Carpenter for Whitman, H.T.J., 4 June 1930, p. 245b.

99. Gilliard to Tufts, 9 May 1901, H.B.P.

100. U.K. Outward Passenger Lists, Liverpool, August 1890, New York; U.S. Passenger Lists, August 1890.

101. Copy of *Pilgrim's Progress*, H.B.P.

102. *The People's Press*, 30 August 1890.

103. Tufts, B.I., p. xix.

6. New Bearings: America 1890–1894

1. Majestic (1). Floating Pontoon Hire, White Star Line History website, whitestar history.com, accessed 11/09/2012.

2. Helen Tufts, Speech at Memorial Service for Helena Born, Walt Whitman Fellowship, Boston Branch, March 1901, H.B.P.

3. Tufts, B.I., p. xxi.

4. Cambridge Historical Commission, *Brief History of Cambridge, Mass.*, online at cambridgema.gov, accessed 12/09/2012.

5. Miriam Daniell quoted in *Western Mail*, 1 May 1894.

6. Births Registered in the City of Cambridge, U.S. 1890.

7. Tufts, B.I., p. xxv.

8. Tufts, B.I., p. xxv.

9. Tufts, B.I., p. xxii; Carroll D. Wright, *The Working Girls of Boston*, Boston: Wright & Potter, 1889, pp. 77–81.

10. Helena Born to Minnie Southcombe, no date, quoted in Tufts, B.I., p. xxii.

11. Tufts, B.I., p. xxv.

12. Born to Southcombe, no date, quoted in Tufts, B.I., p. xxii.

13. Born to Southcombe, no date, quoted in Tufts, B.I., p. xxii; on the electric trolleys see Stephen Puleo, *A City So Grand: The Rise of the American Metropolis, Boston 1850–1900*, Boston: Beacon Press, 2010, pp. 224–5.

14. Born to Southcombe, no date, quoted in Tufts, B.I., p. xxiii.

15. Tufts, B.I., p. xxiv.

16. Helena Born, 'Give all to Love', Emerson, Notebook, H.B.P.

17. Miriam Born, 'To H. Born', handwritten poem, H.B.P.
18. Nicol to Carpenter, 16 September 1894, C.C.
19. Tufts, B.I., p. xxiii.
20. Robert Nicol to Amaryllis (Nicol Cabell) no date, R.P.
21. Robert Nicol to Edward Carpenter, no date, March 1896; Robert Nicol to Edward Carpenter, November, no date, 1895.
22. Tufts, B.I., p. xxiv.
23. Angela Tuckett, Enid Stacy, original manuscript, 8/xii/9/XL, A.T.P.; W.O.C. Minutes, 28 January 1891.
24. B.S.S. Minutes, 13 February 1891; Tuckett, Enid Stacy, original manuscript, 21X, A.T.P.
25. Miriam Daniell to Enid Stacey [*sic*], no date, October 1891, A.T.P.
26. Daniell to Stacey, no date, October 1891, A.T.P.
27. Daniell to Stacey, no date, October 1891, A.T.P.
28. Dixon, *Divine Feminine*, pp. 164–7; Owen, *The Place of Enchantment*, pp. 41, 86–8.
29. See H.E. Butler, *The Seven Creative Principles*, Boston: Esoteric Publishing Company, 1887; on the move to California, *The Esoteric*, Vol. V, no.1, 21 June to 22 July 1891, pp. 6, 24.
30. Daniell to Stacey, no date, October 1891, A.T.P.
31. Daniell to Stacey, no date, October 1891, A.T.P.
32. 'R.A. Nicol, 256 Green St.', List of Names, Boston Anarchist Club, Wisconsin Historical Society. (I am grateful to David Sachs for this information.)
33. Wendy McElroy, *The Debates of Liberty: An Overview of Individualist Anarchism, 1881–1908*, Lanhan: Lexington Books, pp. 2–4; Michael E. Coughlin, Charles H. Hamilton and Mark A. Sullivan, eds, *Benjamin R. Tucker and the Champions of Liberty*, St Paul: Coughlin and Sullivan, 1986, pp. 1–6.
34. Hamilton, 'Introduction' and Carl Watner, 'The English Individualists as They Appear in Liberty', in Coughlin, *Benjamin R. Tucker*, pp. 4–9, 194–211; McElroy, *The Debates of Liberty*, pp. 124–6; see also Martin, *Men Against the State*.
35. W.W Gordak to George Schumm, 31 July 1898, Schumm Box, Labadie Collection (L.C.); see Max Stirner, *The Ego and His Own: The Case of the Individual Against Authority*, London: Verso, 2014.
36. Shoshana Edwards, 'The Worthy Adversaries: Benjamin R. Tucker and G. Bernard Shaw', in Coughlin et al., *Benjamin R. Tucker*, pp. 92–100; Wendy McElroy, 'The Culture of Individualist Anarchism in late Nineteenth-Century America', *The Journal of Libertarian Studies*, Vol. V, No. 3, Summer 1981, pp. 293–7. Benjamin R. Tucker to the Editor, *Commonweal*, 13 March 1887, Socialist League Papers, International Institute for Social History (I.I.S.H.), Amsterdam; William J. Lloyd, *Memories of Benjamin Tucker*, Mises Daily, prepared by Wendy McElroy, online at https://mises.org/daily/697, accessed 24/4/2011.
37. Elroy, 'The Culture of Individualist Anarchism', pp. 293–4; Sharon Presley, 'Feminism in Liberty', in Coughlin, et al., *Benjamin R. Tucker*, pp. 161–2; Martin, *Men Against the State*, p. 269; Martin Blatt, 'Ezra Heywood and Benjamin R. Tucker', in Coughlin et al., *Benjamin R. Tucker*, pp. 28–43.
38. Presley, 'Feminism in Liberty', p. 161; Charles A. Madison, 'Benjamin R. Tucker, Individualist and Anarchist', *The New England Quarterly*, Vol. 16, No. 3, September 1943, p. 449; on Mackay see Thomas A. Riley, 'Anti-Statism in German Literature as Exemplified by the work of John Henry MacKay', *PMLA*, Vol. 62, No. 3, September 1947, pp. 828–43.

39. Miriam Daniell to Helena Born, 'Stumpy and Me', handwritten note, H.B.P.

40. Richard Born, Maria Jane Born, England Census, 1891.

41. Malos, 'Bristol Women in Action', in Bild, *Bristol's Other History*, pp. 119–21; see Also Ball, 'The Origins and an Account of Black Friday, December 23, 1892', in Backwith et al., *Strikers, Hobblers, Conchies and Reds*, pp. 153–4.

42. Edward J. Watson, 'The Croak', Katharine St John Conway, 'For All or for None', Born, Scrapbook, 1892, H.B.P.

43. Edward Carpenter, 'To Thine Own Self Be True', *Towards Democracy*, Part III, complete edition, London: George Allen and Unwin, 1915, pp. 352–3, copied in Born, Notebook, 1892, H.B.P.

44. Edward Carpenter, 'The Secret of Time and Satan' (1888), *Towards Democracy*, Part III, complete edition, p. 363, copied in Born, Notebook, 1892, H.B.P.

45. Carpenter, 'The Secret of Time and Satan', p. 362, copied in Born, Notebook, 1892, H.B.P.

46. Tufts, B.I., p. xxiv; Sutherland, 'Education as an Agent of Social Evolution', *History of Education*, Vol. 38, No. 3, May 2009, p. 361; R.M. Wenley, *The University Extension Movement in Scotland*, booklet, Glasgow: Glasgow University Press, 1895, pp. 37–43.

47. Harriet [*sic*] Stanton Blatch, 'University Extension in England', July 1892, in George F. James, ed., *University Extension: The Official Organ of the American Society for the Extension of University Extension*, Vol. 2, July 1892–June 1893, printed in Philadelphia, p. 97; 'Nora' quoted in J. Arthur Thomson, 'A Summer School of Art and Science', *The Monthly Packet*, 1 June 1892, p. 646.

48. Anon., 'The Edinburgh Summer Meeting', in James, *University Extension*, p. 123.

49. Tufts, B.I., pp. xxiv–xxv.

50. Edinburgh, Report, *The University Extension Journal*, 1 October 1892, p. 99.

51. Virginia E. Graeff, 'The Edinburgh Summer Meeting', in James, *University Extension*, pp. 389–91.

52. Kate Crooke to Anna Geddes, 23 August 1901, Geddes Collection, University of Strathclyde Library, Department of Special Collections.

53. J.M. Robertson, *The National Reformer*, 24 April 1892, newspaper cutting, MS 25, C.C. Helen Tufts records Helena's meeting him while in Britain, H.T.J., 27 January 1898, p. 67.

54. Carpenter, 'To Thine Own Self Be True', *Towards Democracy*, Part III, complete edition, p. 352, copied in Born, Notebook, 1892, H.B.P.; Review of 'Prince Kropotkin, *La Conquête du Pain*', cutting, no reference, Born, Scrapbook, 1892.

55. Tufts, B.I., p. xxiv; on Tucker's move to New York see Martin, *Men Against the State*, p. 270.

56. Miriam Daniell, 'A Daughter of the Gods', *Liberty*, 9 January 1892, pp. 3–4.

57. Miriam Daniell, 'An Un-Henly Hen', *Liberty*, 6 February 1892, pp. 3–4.

58. Miriam Daniell, 'The Black-Caps', *Liberty*, 14 May 1892, pp. 2–3.

59. Daniell, 'The Black-Caps', pp. 3–4.

60. Miriam Daniell, 'From the Spirit', *Liberty*, 21 May 1892, p. 4. (Miriam's poems from *Liberty* and *Free Society* are reprinted in the pamphlet, Miriam Daniell, *Songs of Struggle and Sorrow*, ed. Charles Johnson, Alliance of the Libertarian Left, Auburn, Alabama, 2013.)

61. Miriam Daniell, 'Epigram', *Liberty*, 25 June 1892, p. 1.

62. Miriam Daniell, 'The Price of Love', *Liberty*, 25 June 1892, p. 4

63. Miriam Daniell, 'Toleration', *Liberty*, 2 July 1892, p. 1; see Lucy Delap, *The Feminist Avant-Garde*, Cambridge: Cambridge University Press, 2007, pp. 122–38.

64. Miriam Daniell, 'The Bandit', *Liberty*, 23 July 1892, p. 1; 'The Coach and Four', *Liberty*, 30 July 1892, p. 4; 'Modern Trade', *Liberty*, 6 August 1892, p. 1; 'Any Worker to Any Strikers', *Liberty*, 3 September 1892, p. 1. For an account of the range of themes and forms in this period, see Robert H. Walker, *The Poet and the Gilded Age: Social Themes in Late 19th-Century American Verse*, Philadelphia: University of Pennsylvania Press, 1963.

65. Miriam Daniell, 'In Robes of Anarchy', *Liberty*, 10 September 1892, p. 1.

66. Miriam Daniell, 'Pastures', *Liberty*, 6 August 1892, p. 1.

67. Miriam Daniell, 'Chains', *Liberty*, 13 August 1892, p. 1.

68. Miriam Daniell, 'The Gothic Minster' (review), *Liberty*, 2 July 1892, pp. 3–4. On Harry Koopman see the catalogue to Harry Lyman Koopman Papers, Brown University.

69. Miriam Daniell, 'Not in Hell', *Liberty*, 11 June 1892, p. 2.

70. Miriam Daniell, 'You Positively Must', *Liberty*, 30 July 1892, p. 1; 'You Must Not', *Liberty*, 6 August 1892, p. 1.

71. Miriam Daniell, 'Conjugal Bliss', *Liberty*, 24 September 1892, p. 3.

72. Daniell, 'Conjugal Bliss', p. 3.

73. Helen Tufts, Notes for Helena About Her Father, Typed MS, pp. 1–13, from Christine Ann Bailie Jolly.

74. William Bailie, 'Bursting a Bubble', *Liberty*, 25 June 1892, pp. 2–3.

75. Miriam Daniell, 'Enthusiasm', *Liberty*, 20 August 1892, p. 4.

76. See Walter E. Houghton, *The Victorian Frame of Mind*, New Haven: Yale University Press, 1957, pp. 263–304.

77. Benjamin Tucker, 'On Picket Duty', *Liberty*, 20 August 1892, p. 1.

78. Wendy McElroy, *Individualist Feminism of the Nineteenth Century*, Jefferson, NC: McFarland & Company, 2001, pp. 135–63; Presley, 'Feminism in Liberty', in Coughlin et al., *Benjamin R. Tucker*, pp. 158–65.

79. Miriam Daniell, 'Enthusiasm Again', *Liberty*, 10 September 1892, p. 3.

80. Daniell, 'Enthusiasm Again', p. 3.

81. Daniell, 'Enthusiasm Again', p. 3.

82. Daniell, 'Enthusiasm Again', p. 3.

83. On Michael Field, *Callirrhoë*, see T.D. Overton, 'Libidinous laureates and lyrical maenads: Michael Field, Swinburne and erotic Hellenism', online at thefreelibrary .com, accessed 02/10/2012.

84. Emma Donoghue, *We Are Michael Field*, Bath: Absolute Press, 1998, pp. 33–8; Diana Maltz, 'Katharine Bradley and Ethical Socialism', in Margaret D. Stetz and Cheryl A. Wilson, *Michael Field and Their World*, High Wycombe: Rivendale Press, 2007, pp. 191–5; 'An Anti-Vivisection Society for Bristol', *Bristol Mercury*, 1 February 1883.

85. Daniell, 'Enthusiasm Again', p. 3.

86. Editor Liberty [Benjamin Tucker], in response to letter from Miriam 'Enthusiasm Again', *Liberty*, 10 September 1892, p. 3.

87. Miriam Daniell, 'Enthusiasm and Tranquility', *Liberty*, 17 September 1892, p. 1.

88. Harry Lyman Koopman, 'To Miriam Daniell', *Liberty*, 17 September 1892, p. 1.

7. 'Knotty Points': William Bailie

1. Helen Tufts, Notes for Helena About Her Father, Typed MS from Christine Ann Bailie Jolly. The account of William's Belfast childhood that follows is based on this document, pp. 1–7.

2. Tufts, Notes, p. 5. On Street, see Roger Courtney, *Second Congregation Belfast, 1708–2008*, All Souls' Non-Subscribing Presbyterian congregation, Belfast, 2008, pp. 48–5; William Morris, *Art and Socialism*, London and Manchester: W. Reeves and Heywoods, 1884.

3. Tufts, Notes, p. 8.

4. Andrew Davies, *The Gangs of Manchester*, Preston: Milo Books, 2008, p. 128.

5. Tufts, Notes, p. 8. William and Helen's daughter, Helena Tufts Bailie, gives a slightly different version. She says her father 'married his landlady's daughter'; see Avrich, *Anarchist Voices*, p. 14.

6. Birth, Marriage and Death Indexes for England and Wales, William Bailie, 1885; England Census, 1891.

7. Tufts, Notes, p. 9.

8. *Justice*, 1 May 1886, p. 120. On George Smart, see Geoffrey C. Goldberg, *The Socialist and Political Labour Movement in Manchester and Salford*, MA History Thesis, Manchester University, 1975, p. 18.

9. *Justice*, 18 September 1886, p. 4.

10. Tufts, Notes, p. 9; on J. Hunter Watts, see Crick, *The History of the Social Democratic Federation*, p. 318.

11. See John Ivor Rushton, *Charles Rowley and the Ancoats Recreation Movement*, PhD Thesis, Manchester University, 1959. The Cherubic Christmas card is in H.B.P.

12. William Morris, '2nd Annual Lecture to the Sunday Society at Ancoats', *Commonweal*, 15 December 1888, p. 396. See also Edmund and Ruth Frow, *William Morris in Manchester and Salford*, pamphlet, Working Class Movement Library, Salford, no date.

13. Tufts, Notes, p. 9.

14. *Commonweal*, 20 April 1889, p. 127. On Ritson and Marshall, see Goldberg, *The Socialist and Political Labour Movement*, pp. 21, 30–1; William Bailie to the Secretary of the Socialist League, 12 August 1889, Socialist League Papers, I.I.S.H., Amsterdam. On the impact of the executions, see Thompson, *William Morris*, pp. 500–7.

15. On Alf Barton and Herbert Stockton, see Nick Heath, '1893: The Manchester Anarchists and the Fight for Free Speech', online at https://libcom.org, accessed 25/09/2010; Sarah Irving, 'Manchester's Radical History Anarchists on Ardwick Green 1893', online at https://radicalmanchester.wordpress.com, accessed 25/09/2010; Jerome Caminada, *Twenty-Five Years of Detective Work*, Manchester: John Heywood, 1895, pp. 329–39. I am grateful to David Stockton for information on the Bartons and the Stocktons.

16. H.T.J., 6 August 1945, pp. 177–8.

17. J.B.S., 'A Revolutionary Reminiscence', *The Co-operative News*, 5 August 1905, p. 945.

18. J.B.S., 'A Revolutionary Reminiscence', p. 944.

19. 'Reports, Manchester', *Commonweal*, 26 October 1889, p. 343.

20. 'Reports, Manchester', *Commonweal*, 18 January 1890, p. 23.

21. J.B.S., 'A Revolutionary Reminiscence', p. 945.

22. Socialist League Functionaries, no date, Socialist League Papers (S.L. Papers), I.I.S.H.

23. J.B.S., 'A Revolutionary Reminiscence', pp. 944–5.

24. William Bailie to Secretary of the Socialist League, 12 August 1889, S.L. Papers; on

McCormack see Newspaper Cutting, S.L. 2060/3, S.L. Papers, I.I.S.H., and Quail, *The Slow Burning Fuse*, pp. 114–15.

25. Tufts, Notes, p. 10; on Kropotkin's visit see 'Reports, Manchester', *Commonweal*, 9 November 1889, p. 358.

26. William Morris to William Bailie, November 1889, H.B.P.; see Tufts, Notes, p. 10.

27. 'Reports, Manchester', *Commonweal*, 7 December 1889, p. 391.

28. J.B.S., 'A Revolutionary Reminiscence', p. 944.

29. 'Reports, Manchester', *Commonweal*, 30 November 1889, p. 383.

30. Goldberg, *The Socialist and Political Labour Movement*, pp. 29–31; 'Reports, Manchester', *Commonweal*, 2 November 1889, pp. 350–1, 9 November 1889, p. 358, 16 November 1889, p. 367, 21 December 1889, pp. 404–5.

31. Goldberg, *The Socialist and Political Labour Movement*, pp. 31–2.

32. *Workman's Times*, 18 July 1890, p. 1.

33. 'Manchester Club', *Commonweal*, 1 March 1890, p. 71.

34. John Marshall quoted in Goldberg, *The Socialist and Political Labour Movement*, pp. 52–3.

35. See Thompson, *William Morris*, pp. 565–73.

36. 'Reports, Manchester, Edward Carpenter, The Present and Future Society, 31 March 1890', *Commonweal*, 12 April 1890, p. 119; Edward Carpenter, 'The Future Society', Lecture Notes, MS 48, C.C.

37. WB, 'Reports, Manchester', *Commonweal*, 28 June 1890, p. 203.

38. WB, 'Reports, Manchester', *Commonweal*, 28 June 1890, p. 203.

39. Tufts, Notes, pp. 9–10.

40. 'Street Obstruction by Socialists', *Manchester Evening News*, 4 August 1890.

41. Tufts, Notes, p. 10; Irving, 'Manchester's Radical History Anarchists on Ardwick Green 1893'.

42. *Commonweal*, 30 August 1890, p. 275, 20 September 1890, p. 300.

43. George Cores, *Personal Recollections of the Anarchist Past* (1947), pamphlet, London: K.S.L. Publications, 1992, p. 9.

44. 'Propaganda. The Midlands', *Commonweal*, 5 September 1891, p. 107.

45. I am grateful to Herbert Stockton for this information. On Alf and Eleanor Barton, see also Helen Eliza Mathers, *Sheffield Municipal Politics 1893–1926*, PhD Sheffield University, 1979, pp. 197–205.

46. 'Reports, Manchester', *Commonweal*, 22 November 1890, p. 373.

47. Tufts, Notes, p. 10.

48. 'Lecture Diary, Manchester', *Commonweal*, January, no date, 1891, p. 7.

49. 'Lecture Diary, Manchester', *Commonweal*, January, no date, 1891, p. 7.

50. Tufts, Notes, p. 10.

51. John Trevor, *My Quest for God*, London: Labour Prophet Office, 1897, pp. 233–4; William Bailie is named in John Trevor, 'The Founding of the Labour Church', *Labour Prophet*, March 1893, p. 18.

52. Trevor, *My Quest for God*, pp. 241–2.

53. 'A Manchester Labour Church', *Manchester Times*, 9 October 1891; England Census, 1891, and Manchester Directory, 1891, Manchester Reference Library.

54. Tufts, Notes, p. 10; Helen Tufts to Agnes Inglis, 24 April 1947, L.C.

55. Tufts, Notes, p. 10; the Chelsea address is in List of Names, Boston Anarchist Club, Wisconsin Historical Society. I am grateful to David Sachs for this information.

56. William Bailie, 'Notes from the United States', *Labour Prophet*, June 1892, p. 46.

57. William Bailie, List of Names, Boston Anarchist Club, Wisconsin Historical Society. (Sachs).

58. 'A', 'An Afternoon with Anarchists', Newspaper Cutting, *The Congregationalist*, no date, 1888, Wisconsin Historical Society (Sachs).

59. William Bailie, 'The Martyrdom of the Soul', *Liberty*, 6 February 1892, p. 3.

60. Benjamin R. Tucker, 'Has Had a Similar Experience' (Letter), *Printers' Ink*, Vol. 6, No. 6, 10 February 1892, pp. 187–8; online at http://blog.libertarian-labyrinth.org, accessed 19/11/2013.

61. Tufts, Notes, pp. 10–11; Helen Tufts, George Schumm, Interview, Typed MS, 1941, p. 26., L.C.

62. Helen Tufts to Agnes Inglis, 24 April 1947, L.C.

63. Tufts, Notes, p. 11.

64. Tufts, Notes, p. 11.

65. Bailie, 'The Martyrdom of the Soul', p. 3.

66. Bailie, 'The Martyrdom of the Soul', p. 3.

67. William Bailie, 'A Mighty Consultation and a Multitude of Diagnoses', *Liberty*, 28 May 1892, pp. 1–4.

68. Bailie, 'Bursting a Bubble', *Liberty*, 25 June 1892, pp. 2–4; William Bailie, 'The Production of Crime', *Liberty*, 30 July 1892, pp. 2–3.

69. William Bailie, 'Notes from the United States, the Other Side of the Gospel of Wealth', *Labour Prophet*, September 1892, pp. 69–70.

70. William Bailie, Letter, *Liberty*, 3 September 1892, p. 1.

71. William Bailie, 'Ireland's Need for a Free Currency', *Liberty*, 24 September 1892, p. 2.

72. 'Subscription List', *Liberty*, 1 October 1892, p. 2.

73. 'T' (Benjamin Tucker), 'An Important Work', *Liberty*, 7 January 1893, p. 2.

74. William Bailie quoted in 'T', 'An Important Work', p. 2.

75. 'T', 'An Important Work', p. 2.

76. William Bailie, 'Problems of Anarchism', *Liberty*, 7 January 1893, p. 1; 14 January 1893, p. 1. (Extracts from the articles are reprinted in William Bailie, *Problems of Anarchism: Property, Labor and Competition*, 1893, booklet prepared by Charles Johnson Alliance of the Libertarian Left, 2011 and 2013, Las Vegas, Nevada.)

77. Bailie, 'Problems of Anarchism', *Liberty*, 28 January 1893, p. 1.

78. Bailie, 'Problems of Anarchism', *Liberty*, 11 February 1893, p. 1; 18 February 1893, p. 1; 25 February 1893, p. 1.

79. Bailie, 'Problems of Anarchism', *Liberty*, 15 April 1893, p. 1.

80. 'T' (Benjamin Tucker), *Liberty*, 22 April 1893, p. 3.

81. Bailie, 'Problems of Anarchism', *Liberty*, 13 May 1893, p. 3.

82. Bailie, 'Problems of Anarchism', *Liberty*, 13 May 1893, p. 1.

83. Bailie, 'Problems of Anarchism', *Liberty*, 13 May 1893, p. 3; on Walker, Bailie, 'Problems of Anarchism', *Liberty*, 20 May 1893, p. 1.

84. Bailie, 'Problems of Anarchism', *Liberty*, 20 May 1893, p. 1.

85. 'T' (Tucker), 'An Important Work', p. 2; 'Editor Liberty', *Liberty*, 3 June 1893, p. 1.

86. Bailie, 'Problems of Anarchism', *Liberty*, 17 June 1893, p. 1.

87. Helen Tufts Bailie to Agnes Inglis, 10 May 1945, L.C.

8. *Wanderers: 1892–1894*

1. Subscription List, *Liberty*, 1 October 1892, p. 2.
2. Miriam Daniell, 'To Any Natural Child', *Liberty*, 8 October 1892, p. 1; 'Lullaby', p. 4.
3. Miriam Daniell, 'To Each His World', *Liberty*, 8 October 1892, p. 4.
4. Daniell, 'To Each His World', p. 4.
5. Miriam Daniell, 'The Bottom of the Sea', *Liberty*, 22 October 1892, p. 1.
6. 'M.D.' (Miriam Daniell), 'Lena, the equinoxial gales are near', handwritten poem, H.B.P.
7. 'M.D.', 'Lena', H.B.P.
8. Helena Born, New York Incoming Passenger Lists, 1820–1957, October 1892.
9. Tufts, B.I., p. xxv; Tufts, Interview with George Schumm, p. 26, L.C.
10. Tufts, B.I., p. xxv.
11. Miriam Daniell to 'Mr Koopman', October, no date, 1893, Box 10, folder 3, Harry Lyman Koopman Collection (H.L.K.). (Miriam is catalogued as 'Miriam D. Nicol'. To prevent confusion I use her actual name 'Daniell'.)
12. Daniell to Koopman, October, no date, 1892, Box 10, folder 3, H.L.K.
13. Miriam Daniell, 'In Robes of Anarchy', *Liberty*, 10 September 1892, p. 1.
14. Daniell to Koopman, October, no date, 1892, Box 10, folder 3, H.L.K.
15. Daniell to Koopman, October, no date, 1892, Box 10, folder 3, H.L.K.
16. Interview with Helen Koopman, H.T.J., no date, c. 1901, p. 110.
17. Interview with Helen Koopman, H.T.J., p. 110.
18. Interview with Helen Koopman, H.T.J., p. 110.
19. Interview with Helen Koopman, H.T.J., p. 110.
20. Interview with Helen Koopman, H.T.J., p. 110.
21. Interview with Helen Koopman, H.T.J., p. 111.
22. Interview with Helen Koopman, H.T.J., p. 111; 230 Pearl Street is the address on Miriam Daniell's letter to Harry Lyman Koopman, December, no date, 1892, Box 10, folder 5, H.L.K.
23. Blatt, *Free Love and Anarchism*, pp. 100–18, 148–58; Hal D. Sears, *The Sex Radicals: Free Love in High Victorian America*, Lawrence: The Regent Press of Kansas, 1977, pp. 74–6 110–17, 128–34; Sheila Rowbotham, *Dreamers of a New Day*, London: Verso, 2010, pp. 58–69.
24. Owen, *The Place of Enchantment*, pp. 97–100; Thomas Lake Harris, *God's Breath in Man and in Humane Society*, Published by the Author, Fountain Grove, Santa Rosa, California, 1891, pp. 62–4, 297–8; Cheadle, *Realizing a 'More Than Earthly Paradise of Love'*, pp. 72–5; H.E. Butler, 'Eighth Lecture Sensation', in *The Seven Creative Principles*, Boston: Esoteric Publishing Company, 1887, pp. 135–48. On sex every eighteen months see H.E. Butler, 'Practical Methods', *The Esoteric*, 23 September to 23 October 1891, p. 102; H.E. Butler, *Practical Methods to Insure Success*, Applegate, California: The Esoteric Fraternity, 1907 (1st edition 1893), p. 59.
25. Miriam Daniell to 'H. Lyman Koopman', December, no date, 1892, Box 10, folder 5, H.L.K.
26. Interview with Helen Koopman, H.T.J., p. 110.
27. Interview with Helen Koopman, H.T.J., p. 111.
28. On the Schumms' lives and characters, Tufts, Interview with George and Emma Heller Schumm, p. 26, L.C.; Bertha F. Johnson to Agnes Inglis, 2 April 1941, quoted in Agnes Inglis to Beatrice [Schumm] Fetz, 5 October 1941, L.C.; Bertha F. Johnson to Agnes Inglis, 23 April 1942, L.C.

29. Emma Heller Schumm, Speech at Memorial Meeting for Helena Born, Walt Whitman Fellowship, Boston Branch, March 1901, H.B.P.

30. George Schumm to Gretchen Smith, 9 August 1925 (I am grateful to David Sachs for this reference).

31. See Tufts, Interview with George and Emma Heller Schumm, L.C.; Martin, *Men Against the State*, p. 226, Carl Wittke, *Against the Current: The Life of Karl Heinzen*, Chicago: University of Chicago Press, 1945, p. 233; Agnes Inglis cards, Schumm, 1196, 4052, 4053, 4054, 4055, 4059, 4060, 4061, 4067, 4068, L.C.

32. Stirner, *The Ego and His Own*, 'Owness', pp. 143–58; on Nietzsche see Christopher Janaway, *Schopenhauer: A Very Short Introduction*, Oxford: Oxford University Press, pp. 67, 122–3, and Christopher Janaway, 'Beyond Selflessness in Ethics and Inquiry', *Journal of Nietzsche Studies*, No. 35/36, Spring–Autumn 2008, pp. 136–7.

33. Daniell to the Koopmans, 2 October 1893, Box 10, folder 17, H.L.K. Mackay's visit to Schumm is recorded in Agnes Inglis card 3566 as being in September 1893. On Robert in Harvard Yard, see Tufts, Interview with George and Emma Heller Schumm, p. 26., L.C.

34. Emma Heller Schumm, Speech at Memorial Meeting for Helena Born, Walt Whitman Fellowship, Boston Branch, March 1901, H.B.P.

35. 'A Bristol Divorce Suit', *Bristol Mercury*, 1 May 1894; on Hughes, *Cheshire Observer*, 5 May 1894; *Morning Post*, 1 May 1894.

36. Daniell to the Koopmans, no date, July 1893, Box 10, folders 13–14, H.L.K.

37. Daniell to the Koopmans, 2 October 1893, Box 10, folder 17, H.L.K.

38. Interview with Helen Koopman, H.T.J., p. 111.

39. Daniell to the Koopmans, no date, July 1893, Box 10, folders 13–14, H.L.K.

40. Tufts, B.I., p. xxvi; on Alexander Ellis see Ellis Family Papers, Friends House.

41. Tufts, B.I., pp. xxv–xxvi.

42. Daniell to the Koopmans, no date, July 1893, Box 10, folders 13–14, H.L.K.

43. Daniell to the Koopmans, no date, July 1893, Box 10, folders 13–14 H.L.K.

44. Daniell to the Koopmans, no date, July 1893, Box 10, folders 13–14, H.L.K.

45. Daniell to the Koopmans, 2 October 1893, Box 10, folder 17, H.L.K.

46. Daniell to the Koopmans, 2 October 1893, Box 10, folder 17, H.L.K.

47. Wheeler, *Still Digging*, p. 13.

48. Daniell to the Koopmans, 2 October 1893, Box 10, folder 17, H.L.K.

49. Tufts, B.I., p. xxvi.

50. Daniell to the Koopmans, 23 November 1893, Box 10, folder 18, H.L.K.

51. Daniell to the Koopmans, 23 November 1893, Box 10, folder 18, H.L.K.

52. Tufts, B.I., p. xxvi.

53. Helena Born to the Koopmans, 20 December 1893, Box 10, folder 19, H.L.K.

54. Tufts, B.I., p. xxvi.

55. Helena Born quoted by Helen Tufts in 'Memo' inserted in interview with Helen Koopman, H.T.J., no date, p. 110.

56. Interview with Helen Koopman, H.T.J., p. 110.

57. Extract from letter quoted in Interview with Helen Koopman, H.T.J., p. 110.

58. Daniell to the Koopmans, 8 November 1893, Box 10, folder 18, H.L.K.

59. Daniell to the Koopmans, 8 November 1893, Box 10, folder 18, H.L.K.

60. Daniell to the Koopmans, 8 November 1893, Box 10, folder 18, H.L.K.

61. Daniell to the Koopmans, 8 November 1893, Box 10, folder 18, H.L.K.

62. Daniell to the Koopmans, 8 November 1893, Box 10, folder 18, H.L.K.

63. Daniell to the Koopmans, 23 November 1893, Box 10, folder 18, H.L.K. For a more pessimistic account of the ranch see Tufts, B.I., p. xxvi.

64. Daniell to the Koopmans 28 November 1893, Box 10, folder 18, H.L.K.

65. Daniell to the Koopmans, no date, December 1893, Box 10, folder 18, H.L.K.

66. Born to the Koopmans, 20 December 1893, Box 10, folder 19, H.L.K.

67. Daniell to the Koopmans, no date, December 1893, Box 10, folder 18, H.L.K.

68. Miriam Daniell, 'In a Cañon', *The Conservator*, March 1902, p. 5.

69. Born to the Koopmans, 20 December 1893, Box 10, folder 19, H.L.K.

70. Tufts, B.I., p. xxviii; Born to the Koopmans, 20 December 1893, Box 10, folder 19, H.L.K.

71. Born to the Koopmans, 20 December 1893, Box 10, folder 19, H.L.K.

72. See Arthur Summers, *Auburn*, Charleston, SC: Arcadia Publishing, 2008; Pat Jones, *The Colfax Connection: A History of Colfax*, Colfax Historical Society, 1980, reprinted with additions by Placer County Historical Society, 1997. On Weimar, see W.B. Lardner and M.J. Brock, *History of Placer and Nevada Counties, California*, Los Angeles: Historic Record Co., 1924, p. 77; 'Auburn Opens its Fine New Opera House', *Daily Evening Bulletin*, 20 November 1891; 'In the Foothills. Horticulture Replacing Mining from Auburn to Placerville', *Daily Evening Bulletin*, 23 July 1891.

73. Miriam Daniell quoted in Tufts, B.I., p. xxvii.

74. Born to the Koopmans, 20 December 1893, Box 10, folder 19, H.L.K.

75. Daniell to the Koopmans, no date, December 1893, Box 10, folder 19, H.L.K.

76. Miriam Daniell, 'Bohemia', *Free Society*, 30 March 1902.

77. Daniell to the Koopmans, no date, December 1893, Box 10, folder 19, H.L.K.

78. Daniell to the Koopmans, no date, December 1893, Box 10, folder 19, H.L.K.

79. 'New Occasion', *Boston Investigator*, 12 April 1893. See also B.F. Underwood, *Essays and Lectures*, New York: D.M. Bennett, Liberal Publisher, no date.

80. Miriam Daniell, 'Letter from San Francisco', quoted in Tufts, B.I., p. xxviii. No indication is given on the recipient of this letter.

81. Helena Born quoted in Tufts, B.I., p. xxviii.

82. Daniell, 'Letter from San Francisco', quoted in Tufts, B.I., p. xxviii.

83. Interview with Helen Koopman, no date, H.T.J., p. 110.

84. Miriam Daniell, 'Bohemia', *Free Society*, 30 March 1902; Miriam Daniell, 'Cross-Roads', *Free Society*, 11 May 1902.

85. Daniell to the Koopmans, 17 February 1894, Box 10, folder 20, H.L.K.

86. Daniell to the Koopmans, 17 February 1894, Box 10, folder 20, H.L.K.

87. Daniell to the Koopmans, 17 February 1894, Box 10, folder 20, H.L.K.

88. Daniell to the Koopmans, 17 February 1894, Box 10, folder 20, H.L.K.

89. Daniell to the Koopmans, 15 April 1894, Box 11, folder 21, H.L.K.; Charles Kelley, a labour organiser, led the unemployed from San Francisco. They were part of a wider movement; see Benjamin F. Alexander, *Coxey's Army: Popular Protest in the Gilded Age*, Baltimore: John Hopkins University Press, 2015. On Miriam's death on 19 April 1894, see Tufts, B.I., p. xxviii.

90. Daniell Edward Tuckett v Daniell Elizabeth Miriam and Nicol Robert Allan, Decree Nisi on the grounds of 'Adultery with the Co-Respondent', 30 April 1894, 15935, Public Record Office, London.

91. Tufts, B.I., p. xxvii.

92. Helen M. Tufts to Horace Traubel, 18 December 1901, Traubel, Library of Congress (L. of C.), c. 104.

93. Miriam Daniell, 'I AM', Typed MS enclosed in Tufts to Traubel, 18 December 1901, Traubel, L. of C., c. 104.

94. Daniell, 'I AM', Traubel, L. of C., c. 104.

95. Miriam Daniell, 'REFORM', Typed MS enclosed in Tufts to Traubel, 18 December 1901, Traubel, L. of C., c. 104.

96. Miriam Daniell, 'To the Earth', *The Conservator*, February 1902, p. 181.

97. Miriam Daniell, 'So Long!', *The Conservator*, December 1901, p. 149.

98. Daniell, 'So Long!', p. 149.

9. Revolutionary Lineages: Helen Tufts

1. The term derives from Mark Twain and Charles Dudley Warner, *The Gilded Age: A Tale of Today*, Hartford, CT: American Publishing Company, 1873.

2. H.T.J. Introductory, p. 1b, Hand Genealogy, MS, Box 1, H.T.B.P.

3. Helen Tufts, Notes re some Revolutionary Ancestors, Typed MS, no page numbers, 1956, H.T.B.P.

4. 'About the Author', in Helen Tufts Bailie, *Darling Daughter: A Satirical Novel*, New York: Greenwich Book Publishers, 1956.

5. Helen Tufts Bailie, Joseph Tufts, Highlights from his Journals, being offered to Widener Library, Typed MS, H.T.B.P.; on the Whittemores, Helen Tufts Bailie to 'Mary', 8 March 1951, H.T.B.P.

6. H.T.J., Introductory, p. 1. On the splits, see David M. Robinson, 'The New Epoch of Belief', *The New England Quarterly*, Vol. 79, No. 4, December 2006, pp. 557–79.

7. H.T.J., Introductory, p. 1.

8. 'Tufts' American and Foreign Literary Agency and Agency for Libraries', Charles Hodge Papers (C0261), Box 19/F15, Manuscripts Division, Department of Rare Books and Special Collections, Princeton University Library.

9. H.T.J., Introductory, p. 1.

10. W.W. Tufts to Dr John Maclean, 10 December 1855, Henry Van Dyke Family Papers, H.V.D.F.P. (C0.276); Manuscripts Division, Department of Rare Books and Special Collections, Princeton University Library.

11. W.W. Tufts to Henry J. Van Dyke, 18 March 1862, H.V.D.F.P.

12. H.T.J., Introductory, p. 1.

13. Dr Maclean quoted in W.W. Tufts to Henry J. Van Dyke, 16 June 1862, H.V.D.F.P. Helen was unaware of Maclean's intervention, believing her father declined a Presbyterian ministry, H.T.J., Introductory, p. 2.

14. H.T.J., Introductory, p. 2.

15. H.T.J., Introductory, p. 2.

16. Hand Genealogy, MS Box 1, H.T.B.P.

17. H.T.J., Introductory, p. 2. See Elmo Arnold Robinson, *American Universalism*, New York: Exposition Press, 1970; Ernest Cassara: *American Universalism*, Boston: Beacon Press, 1972; David Robinson, *The Unitarians and the Universalists*, Westport, CT: Greenwood Press, 1986.

18. H.T.J., 7 December 1926, pp. 128–9.

19. H.T.J., Introductory, p. 3; Hon. Jonathan Blake, *History of the Town of Warwick, Mass.*, Boston: Noyes Holmes & Co., 1873, pp. 152–3; H.T.J., 29 August 1929, p. 233.

20. H.T.J., 7 December 1926, p. 128; 1 December 1937, p. 159.

21. H.T.J., Introductory, p. 4.
22. H.T.J., Introductory, p. 4.
23. H.T.J., Introductory, pp. 5–6.
24. H.T.J., Introductory, p. 3.
25. H.T.J., Introductory, pp. 4, 6.
26. H.T.J., 7 December 1926, p. 129; Introductory, p. 4.
27. H.T.J., Introductory, p. 7.
28. H.T.J., 7 December 1926, p. 28; Introductory, p. 7.
29. H.T.J., Introductory, pp. 7–8.
30. H.T.J., Introductory, p. 9.
31. H.T.J., Introductory, pp. 8–9. ·
32. H.T.J., Introductory, p. 8. On the Mugwumps, see Hugh Brogan, *The Penguin History of the United States*, London: Penguin Books, 1990 (1st edition 1985), pp. 424–5; Gordon S. Wood, 'The Massachusetts Mugwumps', *The New England Quarterly*, Vol. 33, No. 4, December 1960, pp. 435–40.
33. W.W. Tufts to Grindall Reynolds, 27 March 1884, Andover-Harvard Theological Library, Harvard Divinity School Archives.
34. H.T.J., Introductory, p. 10.
35. H.T.J., Introductory, p. 10.
36. H.T.J., 28 June 1888, p. 23.
37. H.T.J., 20 July 1888, p. 23.
38. H.T.J., 7 April 1886, p. 7; 23 August 1886, p. 12.
39. H.T.J., 29 November 1887, p. 22.
40. H.T.J., 10 November 1931, p. 284.
41. H.T.J., 17 November 1886, p. 12; on the anarchists see H.T.J., 11 November 1887, p. 21.
42. H.T.J., 22 June 1888, p. 23.
43. H.T.J., 4 April 1890, p. 26.
44. H.T.J., 23 June 1892, p. 29; 28 May 1892, p. 29.
45. H.T.J., 27 June 1892, p. 30.
46. H.T.J., 18 August 1892, p. 30.
47. H.T.J., 22 October 1892, p. 33.
48. 'Rapid Transit' discussed at a meeting of the Twentieth Century Club, *Boston Daily Advertiser*, 28 June 1894; Sam Bass Warner Jr, *Street Car Suburbs: The Process of Growth in Boston 1870–1900*, Cambridge, MA: Harvard University Press, 1978, pp. 22, 53–60; Mona Domosh, 'Shaping the Commercial City', *Annals of the Association of American Geographers*, Vol. 80, No. 2, June 1990, pp. 268–84.
49. H.T.J., 10 March, 13 March, 14 March 1893, p. 34.
50. H.T.J., 26 June 1893, p. 35.
51. H.T.J., 27 June 1893, p. 35; 6 July 1893, p. 36; 26 July 1893, p. 36; 2 August 1893, p. 36.
52. H.T.J., 14 August 1893, p. 36.
53. H.T.J., 22 August 1893, p. 36.
54. On Rabbi Schindler, see Arthur Mann, *Yankee Reformers in the Urban Age: Social Reform in Boston, 1880–1900*, New York: Harper & Row, 1966 (1st edition 1954), pp. 54–72.
55. H.T.J., 16 March 1893, p. 34.
56. H.T.J., 29 May 1894, p. 47.

57. See Richard D. Brown and Jack Tager, *Massachusetts: A Concise History*, Amhurst: University of Massachusetts Press, 2000, pp. 203–17, 227–9; Barbara Miller Solomon, *Ancestors and Immigrants: A Changing New England Tradition*, Chicago: University of Chicago Press, 1972, pp. 101–6; on Most, see Candace Falk, Barry Pateman and Jessica Moran, eds, *Emma Goldman: A Documentary History of the American Years, 1890–1901*, Volume 1, Berkeley: University of California Press, 2003, pp. 544–6.

58. H.T.J., 7 February 1894, p. 39; Sharon Hartman Strom, 'Leadership and Tactics in the American Woman Suffrage Movements: A New Perspective from Massachusetts', *The Journal of American History*, Vol. 62, No. 2, September 1975, pp. 298–300.

59. H.T.J., 9 January 1895, p. 48.

60. H.T.J., 10 May 1894, p. 46.

61. 'Women Cyclists', *Boston Daily Advertiser*, 11 August 1894.

62. H.T.J., 19 April 1894, p. 44.

63. William Whittemore Tufts, *A Market for an Impulse*, General Books, 2009 (1st edition 1897), p. 77.

64. H.T.J., 9 April 1894, p. 41; for a report see 'Bimetallism. An Address by General Walker', *Boston Daily Advertiser*, 9 March 1894; on the background see Barry Eichengreen, 'Introduction', in Barry Eichengreen, ed., *The Gold Standard in Theory and History*, New York: Methuen, 1985, pp. 16–17.

65. H.T.J., 10 May 1894, p. 45.

66. H.T.J., 1 May 1894, p. 45.

67. On Coxey, see Alexander, *Coxey's Army: Popular Protest in the Gilded Age*; on Lease, see Robert C. McMath Jr, *American Populism: A Social History, 1877–1898*, New York: Hill and Wang, The Noonday Press, 1993, pp. 125–7; Jo Buhle, *Women and American Socialism, 1870–1920*, Urbana: University of Illinois Press, 1983, pp. 82–90. See also Mary Elizabeth Lease, 'Wall Street Owns the Country', speech circa 1890, online at historyisaweapon.com, accessed 28/1/2016.

68. Howard H. Quint, *The Forging of American Socialism: Origins of the Modern Movement*, Indianapolis: The Bobbs Merrill Co., 1953, pp. 72–102, 142–74; Henry F. Bedford, *Socialism and the Workers in Massachusetts, 1886–1912*, Amherst: University of Massachusetts Press, 1966, pp. 11–45.

69. Joshua Freeman et al., eds, *Who Built America?* Volume 2, New York: Pantheon, 1992, pp. 140–4.

70. H.T.J., 12 December 1894, p. 46.

71. H.T.J., 12 December 1894, p. 48.

72. H.T.J., Note added, 1895, p. 50.

73. H.T.J., 4 April 1895, p. 50. On Morrison I. Swift, see Mann, *Yankee Reformers*, pp. 155, 173, 194–5.

74. Lease, 'Wall Street Owns the Country'; Buhle, *Women and American Socialism*, pp. 88–9.

75. H.T.J. 4 April 1895, p. 50.

76. H.T.J., Note added, 1895, p. 50.

10. *Whitmanites and New Women: 1894–1897*

1. Tufts, B.I., pp. xxviii–xxix.

2. Sarah Deutsch, *Women and the City: Gender, Space and Power in Boston, 1870–1940*,

New York: Oxford University Press, 2000, pp. 170–9; Freeman et al., *Who Built America?* Volume 2, pp. 137–52; 'To Stamp out Anarchy', *Boston Daily Advertiser*, 27 June 1894.

3. Tufts, B.I., pp. xxviii–xxix.

4. Helen Tufts, Speech at Memorial Meeting for Helena Born, Walt Whitman Fellowship, Boston Branch, March 1901, H.B.P. Helena rented at least two rooms in Beach Street, as her addresses were 53 and 47.

5. Items preserved in H.B.P.

6. Tufts, B.I., p. xxix.

7. Tufts, B.I., p. xxix.

8. Born, Notebook, no date, H.B.P. (Helena's version contains small inaccuracies); Sculley Bradley and Harold W. Blodgett, eds, Preface, *Leaves of Grass* [1855], in Walt Whitman, *Leaves of Grass*, New York: W.W. Norton, 1973, pp. 716–17.

9. On the formation of the Boston branch, see Laurens Maynard, 'Organization of the Boston Branch', Walt Whitman Fellowship Papers, 11, Philadelphia, January 1895, pp. 67–8, L. of C., c. 185; 'Boston Branch of the Walt Whitman Fellowship', *The Conservator*, November 1894, p. 141; Charlotte Porter to Horace Traubel, 9 November, 1894, L. of C. c. 96.

10. On Traubel and the Walt Whitman Fellowship, see Michael Robertson, *Worshipping Walt: The Whitman Disciples*, Princeton: Princeton University Press, 2008, pp. 234–50; Ed Folsom, 'Walt Whitman's Disciples', and Joann P. Krieg, 'Without Walt Whitman in Camden', *Walt Whitman Quarterly Review* (W.W.Q.R.), Vol. 14, No. 2, Fall 1996; Bryan K. Garman, '"Heroic Spiritual Grandfather": Whitman, Sexuality, and the American Left, 1890–1940', *American Quarterly*, Vol. 52, No. 1, March 2000.

11. Maynard, 'Organization of the Boston Branch', L. of C., c. 185, pp. 67–8.

12. Helen A. Clarke and Charlotte Porter, 'A Short Reading Course in Whitman', *Poet-Lore*, Vol. 6, November 1894, p. 645. (Reprinted in Walt Whitman Fellowship Papers, 13, Philadelphia, February 1895, L. of C., c. 185.)

13. Clarke and Porter, 'A Short Reading Course', p. 645.

14. Charlotte Porter, 'Some of the Pros and Cons of Socialism', *The Conservator*, October 1894, pp. 117–18.

15. Laurens Maynard to Horace Traubel, 9 November 1894, L. of C., c. 87.

16. On Helen Abbott Michael, see Margaret W. Rossiter, *Women Scientists in America*, Baltimore: John Hopkins University Press, 1982, p. 38; Robertson, *Worshipping Walt*, p. 267.

17. Helen Abbott Michael, 'Woman and Freedom in Whitman' (Read before the Walt Whitman Fellowship, Boston, 19 November 1896), *Poet-Lore*, Vol. 9, 1897, p. 235.

18. Maynard to Traubel, 9 November 1894, L. of C., c. 87.

19. Mary Stevens, Speech at Memorial Meeting for Helena Born, Walt Whitman Fellowship, Boston Branch, March 1901, H.B.P.

20. Tufts, B.I., p. xxx.

21. H.T.J., Note, Spring 1895, p. 50.

22. H.T.J., Note, Spring 1895, p. 50.

23. Tufts, B.I., p. xxx.

24. H.T.J., Note, Spring 1895, p. 50.

25. Helen A. Clarke to Horace Traubel, 14 April 1895, L. of C., c. 59.

26. Helen A. Clarke to Horace Traubel, 22 May 1895, L. of C., c. 59.

27. Helen A. Clarke to Horace Traubel, 19 November 1895, L. of C., c. 59.

28. Krieg, 'Without Walt Whitman in Camden', p. 107; Clarke to Traubel, 22 May 1895, L. of C., c. 59.

29. Krieg, 'Without Walt Whitman in Camden', p. 107.

30. Helen A. Clarke to Horace Traubel, 29 May 1895, L. of C., c. 59

31. Laurens Maynard to Horace Traubel, 25 July 1895, L. of C., c. 59.

32. Walt Whitman Fellowship, Boston, 1895–1896, L. of C., c. 183–4.

33. Helena Born, 'Whitman's Altruism', *The Conservator*, September 1895, reprinted in Tufts, ed., *Whitman's Ideal Democracy* (W.I.D.), pp. 56–7; see Bernard Schmidt, 'Whitman and American Personalistic Philosophy', W.W.Q.R., Vol. 7, No. 4, Spring, 1990.

34. Born, 'Whitman's Altruism', ed. Tufts, W.I.D., p. 59.

35. Born, 'Whitman's Altruism, ed. Tufts. W.I.D., p. 60

36. Born, 'Whitman's Altruism', ed. Tufts, W.I.D., pp. 59–60.

37. Helena Born, 'Marriage Safeguards', c. 1895, ed. Tufts, W.I.D., pp. 87, 85. On Carpenter's *Marriage in Free Society* (1894), see Rowbotham, *Edward Carpenter*, pp. 211–12.

38. Born, 'Marriage Safeguards', ed. Tufts, W.I.D., p. 88.

39. Born', Marriage Safeguards', ed. Tufts, W.I.D., p. 87.

40. Helena Born to Horace Traubel, 10 December 1895, L. of C., c. 53.

41. *The Conservator*, December 1895, p. 138.

42. Helen A. Clarke to Horace Traubel, 14 February 1896, L. of C., c. 59.

43. Helena Born, 'Poets of Revolt', Walt Whitman Fellowship Boston, Programme Second Session, 1895–1896; reprinted in *The Conservator*, March, April, May, 1896 and in ed. Tufts, W.I.D.

44. On Wiksell and Traubel see Robertson, *Worshipping Walt*, pp. 268–72.

45. Born, 'Poets of Revolt', ed. Tufts, W.I.D., pp. 39, 41, 37.

46. Born, 'Poets of Revolt', ed. Tufts, W.I.D., p. 42.

47. Born, 'Poets of Revolt', ed. Tufts. W.I.D., 45–7.

48. Born, 'Poets of Revolt', ed. Tufts, W.I.D., p. 54.

49. Edward Carpenter, 'England Arise', in Edward Carpenter, ed., *Chants of Labour*, London: George Allen & Unwin, 1888, p. 19.

50. Born, 'Poets of Revolt', ed. Tufts, W.I.D., pp. 51–2.

51. Helena Born to Horace Traubel, 5 March 1896, L. of C., c. 53.

52. Helena Born to Horace Traubel, 28 April 1896, L. of C., c. 53.

53. Helena Born to Horace Traubel, 28 April 1896, L. of C., c. 53.

54. Krieg, 'Without Walt Whitman in Camden', pp. 101–5.

55. Helena Born to Horace Traubel, 27 May 1896, L. of C., c. 53. On Desjardins and Geddes, see Siân Reynolds, *Paris-Edinburgh: Cultural Connections in the Belle Epoque*, London: Routledge, 2007, pp. 89–92.

56. Helena Born, 'Inequality in Divorce', published in *The Conservator*, July 1896, reprinted in ed. Tufts, W.I.D., p. 79.

57. Born, 'Inequality in Divorce', ed. Tufts, W.I.D., p. 81.

58. Born, 'Inequality in Divorce', ed. Tufts, W.I.D., p. 82; H.T.J., 31 May 1896, p. 51.

59. Born, 'Inequality in Divorce', ed. Tufts, W.I.D., p. 83.

60. H.T.J., June, no date, 1896, p. 52; 24 July 1896, p. 52.

61. H.T.J., 1 August 1896, p. 52.

62. H.T.J., 22, 23, 24, 27 August 1896, p. 52.

63. H.T.J., 21 October, 29 September 1896, p. 54.

64. H.T.J., 29 September 1896, p. 54.

65. H.T.J., 25 September 1896.

66. 'Bryan in Boston', *Boston Daily Advertiser*, 26 September 1896; Rebecca Edwards, *New Spirits: Americans in the Gilded Age*, Oxford: Oxford University Press, 2006, pp. 85–7.

67. H.T.J., 25 September 1896, p. 54.

68. H.T.J., 1 December 1896, p. 57; 19 November 1896, p. 55; 17 December 1896, p. 57. On Gilchrist, see Marion Walker Alcaro, *Walt Whitman's Mrs G.: A Biography of Anne Gilchrist*, New Jersey: Associated University Presses, 1991.

69. *Boston Herald*, no date, cutting enclosed in Elizabeth Porter Gould to Horace Traubel, 2 June 1896, L. of C., c. 74.

70. See correspondence from Elizabeth Porter Gould to Horace Traubel, 1893–1903, L. of C., c. 74. Laurens Maynard to Horace Traubel, 9 December 1896, L. of C., c. 87.

71. H.T.J., 26 November 1896, p. 57.

72. H.T.J., 24 and 28 December 1896, p. 57.

73. Helena Born, 'Ingenuities of Economic Argument', *The Conservator*, February 1897, reprinted in ed. Tufts, W.I.D., p. 68.

74. Laurens Maynard to Horace Trauble, 9 December 1896, L. of C., c. 87.

75. Helen A. Clarke, 'Ideal Womanhood', II, *The Conservator*, January 1897, p. 164.

76. Helen A. Clarke to Horace Traubel, 27 May 1897, L. of C., c. 59.

77. Laurens Maynard to Horace Traubel, 5 June 1897, L. of C., c. 87.

78. Helen A. Clarke to Horace Traubel, August, no date, 1897, quoted in Robertson, *Worshipping Walt*, p. 268.

79. Emma Heller Schumm, Speech at Memorial Meeting for Helena Born, Walt Whitman Fellowship, Boston Branch, March 1901, H.B.P.

80. On A.H. Simpson, see Paul Avrich, *The Haymarket Tragedy*, Princeton: Princeton University Press, 1984, p. 105; Agnes Inglis Cards 4163–4177, 4396, 11369, L.C.; A.H. Simpson, Letter, *The Word*, July 1889, pp. 3–4; he also wrote in *The Individualist*, *Liberty* and *Free Society*.

81. McElroy, *Individualist Feminism of the Nineteenth Century*, pp. 19–47, 78–82.

82. Josephine Tilton quoted in McElroy, *Individualist Feminism*, p. 80.

83. List of members, Boston Anarchist Club, Wisconsin Historical Society (I owe this information to David Sachs). Agnes Inglis to Beatrice Fetz, 13 October 1942, mentions 'Mr Simpson – who loved Joan Flora Tilton so much', L.C.

84. McElroy, *Individualist Feminism*, pp. 135–63; Agnes Inglis Cards 1782–1785, 1787, 1789, 1790, 1793, 1798, L.C.

85. Beatrice Fetz in Avrich, *Anarchist Voices*, p. 12; See McElroy, *Individualist Feminism*, for reprints of some of these articles, pp. 143–63; on Holmes, see also, Rowbotham, *Dreamers of a New Day*, pp. 58–9, 61–2.

86. Bertha T. Johnson to Agnes Inglis, September, no date, 1942, L.C.

87. William J. Lloyd, Story of my Life, Typed MS, L.C.

88. Fetz in Avrich, *Anarchist Voices*, p. 12.

89. Johnson to Inglis, September, no date, 1942, L.C.

90. H.T.J., 17 March 1897, p. 60; on the Y.W.C.A. gym and the enthusiasm for exercise, see Martha H. Verbrugge, *Able-Bodied Womanhood: Personal Health and Social Change in Nineteenth-Century Boston*, New York: Oxford University Press, 1988.

91. H.T.J., 17 March 1897, p. 60.

92. H.T.J., 21 January 1897, p. 58. 'Franklin Benjamin Sanborn 1831–1917', *American National Biography*, Vol. 19, New York: Oxford University Press, 1999, pp. 237–8.

93. H.T.J., 21 January 1897, p. 58. On Avery, see 'Martha Moore Avery', in Edward T. James, ed., *Notable American Women: A Biographical Dictionary, 1607–1950*, Cambridge, MA: Harvard University Press, 1971, pp. 69–70; Buhle, *Women and American Socialism*, pp. 73–4; Bedford, *Socialism and the Workers in Massachusetts*, pp. 143–7.

94. H.T.J., 25 April 1897, p. 61.

95. H.T.J., 18 February 1897, p. 59.

96. H.T.J., 15 May 1897, p. 62.

97. H.T.J., 25 April 1897, p. 62.

98. H.T.J., 19 April 1897, p. 61.

99. H.T.J., 22 February 1897, p. 59.

100. H.T.J., 6 April 1897, p. 60; H.T.J., 1 April 1897, p. 60; H.T.J., 2 June 1925, p. 65.

101. H.T.J. Note added 1 September 1897, p. 64.

102. H.T.J., 11 May 1897, p. 62; H.T.J., 11 March 1897, p. 60.

103. H.T.J., Note added 1 September 1897, p. 64.

104. 'Life in Boston. Boston's Latin Quarter', *The Daily Inter Ocean* (Chicago, Illinois), 4 April 1896.

105. H.T.J., 1 March 1897, p. 59. On Anagarika Dharmapala, H.T.J., 11, 12, 16 April 1897, pp. 60–1.

106. H.T.J., 21 March 1897, p. 60.

107. H.T.J., 21 March 1897, p. 60.

108. H.T.J., 6 April 1897, p. 60.

109. H.T.J., 21 January 1897, p. 58; '"Inappropriate", Say Authorities Who See the Bacchante Exhibition', *Boston Daily Advertiser*, 17 November 1896; 'Bacchante Withdrawn', *Boston Daily Advertiser*, 29 May 1897. See also the Wikipedia entry for 'Bacchante and Infant Faun'.

110. H.T.J., 24 February 1897, p. 59; H.T.J., 11 March 1897, p. 60.

111. H.T.J., 16 March 1897, p. 60.

112. H.T.J, 4 June 1930, p. 245b.

11. Fabianism and Free Love: Gertrude Dix

1. Jones, *The Christian Socialist Revival*, pp. 99–120, 308–11.

2. B.S.S. Minutes, February 1886–May 1891; 9, 16 January 1891 (no page numbers), Bristol Record Office.

3. B.S.S. Minutes, 16 January 1891; 27 February 1891.

4. B.S.S. Minutes, 10 April 1891.

5. B.S.S. Minutes, 17 April 1891.

6. Havelock Ellis, *Women and Marriage; or, Evolution in Sex*, pamphlet, London, 1889, pp. 3–8.

7. Havelock Ellis, *The New Spirit*, London: Bell, 1890, p. 139. On Ellis' reputation, see Phyllis Grosskurth, *Havelock Ellis: A Biography*, New York: New York University Press, pp. 129–30.

8. Sam Hobson's arrival is noted in B.S.S. Minutes, 17 April 1891.

9. Gertrude Mary Dix, Certified Copy of an Entry of Birth, General Register Office.

10. 'John Ross Dix', Wikipedia; Gordon Giles, 'Dix, William Chatterton', *Oxford Dictionary of National Biography*, online, accessed 14/10/2013.

11. England Census, 1871 and 1881.

12. Gertrude Dix, Letters to my daughter, Typed MS, R.P.
13. Gertrude Dix, 'Hard Labour in the Hospitals', *Westminster Review*, Vol. 140, No. 1, July 1893, p. 631.
14. Dix, 'Hard Labour', p. 631
15. Dix, 'Hard Labour', p. 632.
16. Dix, 'Hard Labour', p. 632.
17. Dix, 'Hard Labour', p. 632–3.
18. Ellen Ross, 'Morten (Violet) Honnor', *Oxford Dictionary of National Biography*, online, accessed 07/01/2013; Ellen Ross, *Slum Travellers: Ladies and London Poverty, 1860–1920*, Berkeley: University of California Press, 2007, pp. 161–3.
19. Gertude Dix, 'Liberty', *Labour Leader*, 7 November 1891; see also *Labour Leader*, 24 October, 14 and 21 November, 5 December 1891.
20. Dix, 'Liberty', *Labour Leader*, 7 November 1891.
21. Dix, 'Liberty', *Labour Leader*, 7 November 1891.
22. 'Labour Party's Programme', *Bristol Mercury*, 4 April 1892; on Williams S. de Mattos, see Paul Thompson, *Socialists, Liberals and Labour*, London: Routledge & Kegan Paul, 1967, p. 140.
23. Dix, 'Hard Labour', p. 633.
24. Sydney Olivier, 'Not Much: A Fragment of Autobiography', in Margaret Olivier, ed., *Sydney Olivier: Letters and Selected Writings*, London: George Allen & Unwin, 1948, pp. 31–6; on Harold Cox see Rowbotham, *Edward Carpenter*, pp. 98–9, 150–1.
25. Olivier, *Sydney Oliver*, pp. 92–4.
26. Gertrude Dix, 'Our Fabian Circle', 4 June 1892, Notebook, Glasier Papers (G.P.), 3/3/3, p. 143.
27. Dix, 'Our Fabian Circle', p. 141.
28. See Rowbotham, *Edward Carpenter*, pp. 90, 98, 176, 252; Angela V. John, *War, Journalism and the Shaping of the Twentieth Century: The Life and Times of Henry W. Nevinson*, London: I.B. Tauris, 2006, pp. 85–90.
29. Dix, 'Our Fabian Circle', p. 141.
30. On Louise Michel's School see John, *War, Journalism and the Shaping of the Twentieth Century*, pp. 90–1; Alex Butterfield, *The World That Never Was: A True Story of Dreamers, Schemers, Anarchists and Secret Agents*, London: The Bodley Head, 2010, pp. 292–3; Edith Thomas, *Louise Michel*, Montréal: Black Rose Books, 1981, pp. 318–19; Carolyn Steedman, *Childhood, Culture and Class in Britain: Margaret McMillan 1860–1931*, New Brunswick: Rutgers University Press, 1990, pp. 128–30.
31. Dix, 'Our Fabian Circle', p. 141. On Charlotte Wilson see Nicolas Walter, 'Introduction', in Nicolas Walter, ed., *Charlotte Wilson, Anarchist Essays*, London: Freedom Press, 2000, pp. 7–17; Mark Bevir, 'The Rise of Ethical Anarchism in Britain 1885–1900', *Institute of Historical Research*, Vol. 69, No. 169, 1996, pp. 147–8.
32. B.S.S. Minutes, 9 January 1891; Katharine St John Conway quoted in Thompson, *The Enthusiasts*, p. 83.
33. S.G. Hobson, 'Our Fabian Circle', pp. 5–7.
34. Hobson, 'Our Fabian Circle', p. 15. For the broader cultural context see Terry Eagleton, 'The Flight to the Real', in Sally Ledger and Scott McCracken, eds, *Cultural Politics at the Fin de Siècle*, Cambridge: Cambridge University Press, 1995, pp. 11–21.
35. Holbrook Jackson, *The Eighteen Nineties: A Review of Art and Ideas at the Close of the Nineteenth Century*, London: Penguin Books, 1950 (1st edition 1913), pp. 17–20; Regenia Gagnier, 'Is Market Society the *Fin* of History"', in Ledger and McCracken,

Cultural Politics at the Fin de Siècle, pp. 302–3.

36. 'Labour Party's Programme', *Bristol Mercury*, 4 April 1892; see Anne Fremantle, *This Little Band of Prophets: The Story of the Gentle Fabians*, London: George Allen & Unwin London, 1960, pp. 94–6.

37. Enid Stacy, 'Our Fabian Circle', 5 April 1892, p. 79.

38. Katharine St John Conway, 'Our Fabian Circle' (no date), p. 17.

39. Conway, 'Our Fabian Circle', pp. 17, 23.

40. Conway, 'Our Fabian Circle', p. 22.

41. W.S. de Mattos to Edward Pease, 10 May 1892. This correspondence is in the Fabian Papers, L.S.E. A/8/2.

42. De Mattos to Pease, 13 May 1892.

43. De Mattos to Pease, 10 May 1892.

44. Katharine St John Conway to Edward Pease, 12 May 1892, Fabian Papers, L.S.E. A/8/2.

45. Conway to Pease, 12 May 1892.

46. De Mattos to Pease, 10 May 1892; 12 May 1892.

47. De Mattos to Pease, 12 May 1892.

48. De Mattos to Pease, 12 May 1892.

49. De Mattos to Pease, 13 May 1892.

50. Enid Stacy to Edward Pease, 12 May 1892, Fabian Papers, L.S.E. A/8/2.

51. Conway to Pease, 12 May 1892.

52. De Mattos to Pease, 17 May 1892.

53. Conway to Pease, 14 May 1892.

54. George Bernard Shaw to Paul Stacy, 13 July 1892, A.T.P., Box 9. Paul Stacy to Edward Pease, 16 July 1892, Fabian Papers, L.S.E., A/8/2.

55. Conway, 'Our Fabian Circle', pp. 22–3.

56. Dix, 'Our Fabian Circle', pp. 141, 143.

57. Dix, 'Our Fabian Circle', pp. 147–9.

58. Dix, 'Our Fabian Circle', p. 149.

59. Dix, 'Our Fabian Circle', pp. 145–7.

60. Dix, 'Our Fabian Circle', p. 143.

61. Dix, 'Our Fabian Circle', p. 145.

62. Edward Carpenter, *Civilisation: Its Cause and Cure*, London: Swan Sonnenschein, 1893, p. 100; Dix, 'Our Fabian Circle', p. 145.

63. Dix, 'Our Fabian Circle', p. 152.

64. Henri F. Ellenberger, *The Discovery of the Unconscious: The History and Evolution of Dynamic Psychiatry*, London: Allen Lane, 1970, pp. 278–9, 314–15.

65. Dix, 'Our Fabian Circle', p. 150.

66. On 'personality' see Roger Smith, *The Fontana History of the Human Sciences*, London: Fontana, 1997, pp. 600–1; Owen, *The Place of Enchantment*, pp. 113, 125, 145, 176.

67. Dix, 'Our Fabian Circle', p. 151.

68. Dix, 'Our Fabian Circle', p. 151.

69. Dix, 'Our Fabian Circle', p. 147.

70. Hobson, 'Our Fabian Circle', 19 June 1892, p. 159.

71. Hobson, 'Our Fabian Circle', p. 159.

72. James (Jim) Kennedy, 'Our Fabian Circle', 26 June 1892, p. 189.

73. Kennedy, 'Our Fabian Circle', p. 192.

74. H. Russell Smart, 'Our Fabian Circle', 13 October 1892, pp. 204–5.

75. Smart, 'Our Fabian Circle', pp. 204–5.
76. Smart, 'Our Fabian Circle', p. 211.
77. Conway, 'A Lancashire Cotton Town', 'Our Fabian Circle', 13 June 1892, pp. 167–9.
78. 'Mr. Mills', quoted in 'Home Colonisation Conference', *Bristol Mercury*, 3 May 1888.
79. 'A Home Colonization Experiment', *Pall Mall Gazette*, 1 April 1892.
80. Angela Tuckett, 'Our Enid', Original typed MS 23XI, A.T.P.; Malos, 'Bristol Women in Action', in Bild, *Bristol's Other History*, pp. 119–21; Ball, 'The Origins and an Account of Black Friday', in Backwith et al., *Strikers, Hobblers, Conchies and Reds*, pp. 147–84.
81. On Starnthwaite, see Angela Tuckett 'Our Enid', edited MS, Chapter Four, A.T.P.; Thompson, *The Enthusiasts*, pp. 76–7.
82. Enid Stacy quoted in 'The Last 24 Hours', *Bristol Mercury*, 4 April 1893.
83. George Bernard Shaw to Enid Stacy, 6 May 1893, quoted in Tuckett, 'Our Enid', edited MS, Chapter Four, A.T.P.
84. George Bernard Shaw to Enid Stacy, 4 and 17 May 1893, quoted in Tuckett, 'Our Enid', edited MS, Chapter Four, A.T.P.
85. Katharine St John Conway to Bruce Glasier, 3 June 1893, G.P.
86. Thompson, *The Enthusiasts*, pp. 79–83.
87. Barry C. Johnson, ed., *Tea and Anarchy: The Bloomsbury Diary of Olive Garnett, 1890–1893*, London: Bartletts Press, 1989, pp. 28, 154.
88. Garnett, *Diary*, 30 June 1893, in Johnson, ed., *Tea and Anarchy, 1890–1893*, p. 205.
89. Garnett, *Diary*, 30 June 1893, in Johnson, ed., *Tea and Anarchy, 1890–1893*, p. 205.
90. Hermia Oliver, *The International Anarchist Movement in Late Victorian London*, Croom Helm, London 1983, pp. 120–122.
91. Garnett, *Diary*, 2 December 1891, in Johnson, ed., *Tea and Anarchy, 1890–1893*, pp. 58–9; Barry C. Johnson, ed., 'Introduction', *Olive and Stepniak: The Bloomsbury Diary of Olive Garnett, 1893–1895*, London: Bartletts Press, 1993, pp. 162–3; Richard Garnett, *Constance Garnett: A Heroic Life*, London: Faber and Faber, 2009 (1st edition 1991), pp. 73–110.
92. 'Sunday Lectures, Co-operative Hall, 70 Brunswick–road, Poplar, 8, Miss Gertrude Dix, "Plato's Republic",' *Reynolds's Newspaper*, 9 September 1894.
93. Garnett, *Diary*, 16 November 1894, in Johnson, ed., *Olive and Stepniak, 1893–1895*, p. 133. In note 22, p. 139, Johnson observes that 'Dix' is spelt 'Dicks'. He also records that after the Garnetts moved from Bloomsbury to Hampstead Gertrude and Olive Garnett frequently met to discuss their writing. As the move occurred in 1899 this was the period in which Gertrude was writing her second novel.
94. Garnett, *Diary*, 6 January 1895, in Johnson, ed., *Olive and Stepniak, 1893–1895*, p. 142.
95. Wendell V. Harris, 'John Lane's Keynote Series and the Fiction of the 1890s', *PMLA, Modern Language Association*, Vol. 83, No. 5, October 1968, pp. 1407–13; Margaret Diane Stetz, 'Sex, Lies and Printed Cloth: Bookselling at the Bodley Head in the Eighteen-Nineties', *Victorian Studies*, Vol. 35, No. 1, Autumn 1991, pp. 72–3; Elaine Showalter, *Daughters of Decadence: Women Writers of the Fin-de-Siècle*, London: Virago, 1993 p. xii.
96. Hegel, *Geschichte der Philosophie*, Vol. II, p. 102, quoted in Gertrude Dix, *The Girl from the Farm*, London: John Lane; Boston: Roberts Bros, 2nd edition 1896 (1st edition 1895).
97. Dix, *The Girl from the Farm*, p. 62.
98. Dix, *The Girl from the Farm*, p. 101.
99. Dix, *The Girl from the Farm*, pp. 93–6.

100. Dix, *The Girl from the Farm*, pp. 30–1.

101. Dix, *The Girl from the Farm*, p. 165.

102. Dix, *The Girl from the Farm*, p. 123.

103. Dix, *The Girl from the Farm*, p. 174.

104. Dix, *The Girl from the Farm*, p. 211.

105. Dix, *The Girl from the Farm*, p. 226.

106. Dix, *The Girl from the Farm*, p. 33.

107. Dix, Letters to my daughter, Typed MS, R.P.

108. *Saturday Review*, 13 July 1895; *Manchester Guardian*, no date, quoted in 'Novels by Gertrude Dix', Notice, R.P.; *Morning Post*, 4 October 1895; *Standard*, 16 August 1895; *Glasgow Herald*, 27 June 1895; *Western Daily Press*, 19 August 1895.

109. *New York Times*, 20 July 1895; *Brooklyn Eagle*, 28 July 1895; *Chicago Times and Herald*, no date, quoted in 'Novels by Gertrude Dix', Notice, R.P.

110. On Dalmas, see Rowbotham, *Edward Carpenter*, pp. 198–9, 203, 226.

111. Edward Carpenter to George Hukin, 8 October 1895, MS 361/22, C.C.

112. Carpenter to Hukin, 8 October 1895, MS 361/22, C.C.

113. 'The Socialist Club', *Reynolds's Newspaper*, 8 March 1896. On the unity campaign, see Barrow and Bullock, *Democratic Ideas in the British Labour Movement*, pp. 83, 85.

114. See June Hannam, *Isabella Ford*, Oxford: Basil Blackwell, 1989; Rowbotham, *Dreamers of a New Day*, pp. 22, 28, 37, 49, 172–3, 228–9; Chris Waters, 'New Women and Socialist Feminist Fiction: The Novels of Isabella Ford and Katharine Bruce Glasier', in Ingram and Patai, eds, *Rediscovering Forgotten Radicals*, pp. 25–42.

115. 'The Socialist Club', *Reynolds's Newspaper*, 8 March 1896.

116. Jane Cox, ed., *A Singular Marriage: A Labour Love Story in Letters and Diaries, Ramsay and Margaret MacDonald*, London: Harrap Ltd., 1988, pp. 42–55; J. Fred Green, *Socialism and Militarism*, Fabian Society, 10 December 1897, Fabian Papers, L.S.E.; on Paul Campbell, see Bevir, *The Making of British Socialism*, p. 280; David Saunders, 'Volkhovsky, Felix Vadimovich (1846–1914)' *Oxford Dictionary of National Biography*, online, accessed 02/01/2013.

117. Honnor Morten quoted in Arthur Porritt, *The Best I Remember*, London: Cassell & Co., 1933, p. 135.

118. Ellen Ross, 'Morten, Violet Honnor, 1861–1913', *Oxford Dictionary of National Biography*, online, accessed 07/01/2013; Ross, *Slum Travellers*, pp. 161–71; Honnor Morten, 'Municipalization of Hospitals', Fabian Society Members Meeting, Fabian Society, Vol. C. 39.

119. 'Cheddar Entertainment', *Bristol Times and Mirror*, 17 February 1897; 'Sketch Exhibition, Miss Hilda Rose Dix', *Western Daily Press*, 17 September 1895; Gertrude Dix, 'The Portrait of Daphne', *The Wheelwoman*, 25 December 1897.

120. Gertrude Dix to Amaryllis (Cabell), no date, 1947, R.P.; Clement Dix, 17 March 1897, Outward Passenger Lists, 1890–1960.

121. 'R.A.N.' to Amaryllis (Nicol Cabell), 22 April 1951, R.P.

12. Cosmic Vibrations: 1894–1897

1. Robert Nicol to Edward Carpenter, 16 September 1894, MS 271–53, C.C. Excerpts from Nicol's letters are reprinted and his sexual ambiguity discussed in Jonathan Ned Katz, *Gay/Lesbian Almanac*, New York: Harper Row, 1983, pp. 250–4.

2. Nicol to Carpenter, 16 September 1894, MS 271–53, C.C.

3. Nicol to Carpenter, 16 September 1894, MS 271–53, C.C.

4. Nicol to Carpenter, 16 September 1894, MS 271–53, C.C.

5. Nicol to Carpenter, 16 September 1894, MS 271–53, C.C. See Marcus Collins, *Modern Love*, London: Atlantic Books, 2003, pp. 13–34.

6. Nicol to Carpenter, 16 September 1894, MS 271–53, C.C. On Flower, see Mann, *Yankee Reformers in the Urban Age*, pp. 163–71.

7. Nicol to Carpenter, 16 September 1894, MS 271–53, C.C.

8. Nicol to Carpenter, 16 September 1894, MS 271–53, C.C.

9. Robert Nicol to Edward Carpenter, 28 December 1894, MS 271–54, C.C.

10. Nicol to Carpenter, 28 December 1894, MS 271–54, C.C.

11. Nicol to Carpenter, 28 December 1894, MS 271–54, C.C.

12. Nicol to Carpenter, 28 December 1894, MS 271–54, C.C.

13. Nicol to Carpenter, 28 December 1894, MS 271–54. On the post office, see Lardner and Brock, *History of Placer and Nevada Counties*, p. 206.

14. Butler, *The Seven Creative Principles*, p. 146; H.E. Butler, 'Practical Methods', *The Esoteric*, Vol. v, No. 4, 23 September to 23 October 1891, p. 100; H.E. Butler, *Practical Methods to Insure Success*, Applegate, California: The Esoteric Fraternity, 1907 (1st edition 1893), p. 59.

15. Butler, *Practical Methods to Insure Success*, p. 78; on Butler, see Timothy Miller, *The Quest for Utopia in Twentieth-Century America, Volume 1, 1900–1960*, New York: Syracuse University Press, 1998, p. 29.

16. Nicol to Carpenter, 28 December 1894, MS 271–54 C.C. On the background, see Howard Kerr and Charles L. Crow, eds, *The Occult in America: New Historical Perspectives*, Urbana: University of Illinois, 1983; Arthur Verhuis, *The Esoteric Origins of the American Renaissance*, New York: Oxford University Press, 2001.

17. Nicol to Carpenter, 28 December 1894, MS 271–54, C.C.

18. Nicol to Carpenter, 28 December 1894, MS 271–54, C.C.

19. Mary Farrell Bednarowski, 'Outside the Mainstream', *Journal of the American Academy of Religion*, Vol. XLVIII, No. 2, 1980, pp. 213–17; Ann Braude, *Radical Spirits: Spiritualism and Women's Rights in Nineteenth-Century America*, Bloomington: Indiana University Press, 2001, pp. 195–7.

20. Nicol to Carpenter, 28 December 1894, MS 271–54, C.C.

21. Nicol to Carpenter, 28 December 1894, MS 271–54, C.C.; see Ida Craddock, 'Heavenly' (1894), in Vere Chappell, ed., *Sexual Outlaw, Erotic Mystic: The Essential Ida Craddock*, San Francisco: Weiser Books, 2010, pp. 129–32; Sears, *The Sex Radicals*, pp. 207–20.

22. Nicol to Carpenter, 28 December 1894, MS 271–54, C.C.

23. Nicol to Carpenter, 28 December 1894, MS 271–54, C.C.

24. Nicol to Carpenter, 28 December 1894, MS 271–54, C.C.

25. Edward Carpenter, *Homogenic Love, and its Place in a Free Society*, pamphlet printed for Private Circulation, Manchester: The Labour Press, 1894, p. 1, see Rowbotham, *Edward Carpenter*, pp. 189–95.

26. Robert Nicol to Edward Carpenter, 2 July 1895, MS 271–55, C.C.

27. Nicol to Carpenter, 2 July 1895, MS 271–55, C.C.

28. Nicol to Carpenter, 2 July 1895, MS 271–55, C.C.

29. On J.C. Hawver see Arthur Sommers, *Auburn*, Charleston: Arcadia Publishing, 2008, p. 39. I am grateful to Auburn Museum for further information on Hawver, and to the

Sindecuse Museum of Dentistry's Exhibition, 'Inside the Dental Practice, 1860–1940', University of Michigan, June 2012, for insights into the history of dentistry.

30. Nicol to Carpenter, 2 July 1895, MS 271–55, C.C.

31. On Hinton see Havelock Ellis, Notes from Hinton's diaries, Havelock Ellis Papers; Mrs Havelock Ellis, *Three Modern Seers*, London: Stanley Paul & Co., no date, c. 1910; Dixon, *The Invention of Altruism*, pp. 81–9, Grosskurth, *Havelock Ellis*, pp. 98–100; Rowbotham, *Edward Carpenter*, pp. 90, 117. On transvaluating values, see Jackson, *The Eighteen Nineties*, p. 130.

32. Nicol to Carpenter, 2 July 1895, MS 271–55, C.C.

33. Nicol to Carpenter, 2 July 1895, MS 271–55, C.C.

34. Nicol to Carpenter, 2 July 1895, MS 271–55, C.C.

35. Robert Nicol to Edward Carpenter, November, no date, 1895 (postcard), MS 375–25, C.C.; on Albert Webster Edgerly and the Ralstonism, Wikipedia.

36. Edward Carpenter, *My Days and Dreams*, London: George Allen & Unwin, 1916, pp. 240–5; Henry Salt to Edward Carpenter, 9 February 1892, MS 356–8, C.C.; on Salt and Maitland, Rowbotham, *Edward Carpenter*, pp. 176–7.

37. Robert Nicol to Edward Carpenter, November, no date, 1895, MS 375–26, C.C.

38. Nicol to Carpenter, November, no date, 1895 (postcard), C.C., MS 375–25, C.C.

39. On Unwin and Weare, Robert Nicol to Edward Carpenter, March (no date), MS 271–561896, C.C.; on the Sharlands, 2 July 1895, MS 271–55, C.C.

40. Nicol to Carpenter, November, no date, 1895, MS 375–26, C.C.

41. Nicol to Carpenter, November, no date, 1895, MS 375–26, C.C.

42. Nicol to Carpenter, November, no date, 1895, MS 375–26, C.C.

43. Nicol to Carpenter, November, no date, 1895, MS 375–26, C.C.

44. On Edmund Russell see, Nancy Lee Chalfa Ruyter, *The Cultivation of Body and Mind in Nineteenth-Century American Delsartism*, Connecticut: Greenwood Press, 1999, pp. 8, 35–3; Frederic Sanburn, Edmund Russell, *A Delsartean Scrap-Book*, New York: The United States Book Company, 1891 (1st edition 1890); 'Society Listens to Him', *Inter-Ocean* (Chicago, Illinois), 23 December 1894; 'His Décolleté Clothes', *The Milwaukee Journal*, 23 February 1895; Nicol to Carpenter, November, no date, 1895, MS 375–26, C.C.

45. Nicol to Carpenter, November, no date, 1895, MS 375–26, C.C.

46. Nicol to Carpenter, November, no date, 1895, MS 375–26, C.C.

47. Nicol to Carpenter, November, no date, 1895, MS 375–26, C.C.

48. Nicol to Carpenter, November, no date, 1895, MS 375–26, C.C.

49. Robert Nicol to Edward Carpenter, March, no date, 1895, MS 271–56, C.C.

50. Nicol to Carpenter, March, no date, 1896, MS 271–56, C.C.

51. Nicol to Carpenter, March, no date, 1896, MS 271–56, C.C.

52. Nicol to Carpenter, March, no date, 1896, MS 271–56, C.C.

53. Nicol to Carpenter, March, no date, 1896, MS 271–56, C.C.

54. Nicol to Carpenter, March, no date, 1896, MS 271–56, C.C.

55. Nicol to Carpenter, March, no date, 1896, MS 271–56, C.C.

56. Nicol to Carpenter, March, no date, 1896, MS 271–56, C.C.

57. On Ellen Creelman and her work from 1896 in developing kindergartens in Seattle, see 'Seattle Public Schools 1862–2000: Bailey Gatzert Elementary School', online at historylink.org, Essay 10511, accessed 29/01/2016. Nicol to Carpenter, March, no date, 1896, MS271–56, C.C.

58. Nicol to Carpenter, March, no date, 1896, MS 271–56, C.C.

59. Douglas F. Hotchkiss, *The Esoteric*, Vol. v, No. 9, 19 February to 21 March 1892, p. 296.

60. See Beryl Satter, *Each Mind a Kingdom: American Women, Sexual Purity and the New Thought Movement, 1875–1920*, Berkeley: University of California Press, 2001, pp. 97–9, 162–75; Charles S. Braden, *Spirits in Rebellion: The Rise and Development of New Thought*, Dallas: Southern Methodist University Press, 1963, pp. 18, 150–271, 323–6.

61. Nicol to Carpenter, March, no date, 1896, MS 271–56, C.C.

62. Nicol to Carpenter, March, no date, 1896, MS 271–56, C.C.

63. Robert Nicol to Edward Carpenter, April, no date, 1896, MS 271–57, C.C.

64. Nicol to Carpenter, April, no date, 1896, MS 271–57, C.C

65. On the dancing judge, 'Again the Bloomers', *Morning Oregonian*, 3 August 1895. On bloomers, 'To Chicago in Bloomers: A Party of Women to Ride From San Francisco', *The Milwaukee Sentinel*, 23 October 1895. On the background, see Dick Muscatine, *Old San Francisco: The Biography of a City from Early Days to the Earthquake*, New York: G.P. Putnams, 1975, pp. 326–46.

66. Nicol to Carpenter, April, no date, 1896, MS 271–57, C.C. On anti-Chinese racism, see Alexander Saxton, *The Indispensable Enemy: Labor and the Anti-Chinese Movement in California*, Berkeley: University of California Press, 1971, pp. 113–37.

67. Nicol to Carpenter, April, no date, 1896, MS 271–57, C.C.

68. Ira Brown Cross, *A History of the Labor Movement in California*, Berkeley: University of California Publications in Economics, 1935, pp. 224–5; Mari Jo Buhle, Paul Buhle and Dan Georgakas, eds, *Encyclopedia of the American Left*, Chicago: University of Illinois, 1992, pp. 760–5.

69. On Markham see Louis Filler, *The Unknown Edwin Markham*, Yellow Springs, OH: Antioch Press, 1966, and William R. Nash, 'Modern American Poetry: Edwin Markham's Life and Career, A Concise Overview', online at english.illinois.edu, accessed 27/9/2014. Leonard D. Abbott, 'Edwin Markham: Laureate of Labor', *The Comrade*, Vol. 1, No. 4, 1902; Edwin Markham to Donna Brooks Beaumont, 6 May 1894. (I am grateful to David Sachs for sending me a copy of this letter.)

70. John G. Claxton (Donna Brooks Beaumont), *She of the Holy Light*, San Francisco: Western Authors' Publishing Association, 1893, pp. 9, 18.

71. Nicol to Carpenter, April, no date, 1896, MS 271–57, C.C.

72. Nicol to Carpenter, April, no date, 1896, MS 271–57, C.C.

73. Nicol to Carpenter, April, no date, 1896, MS 271–57, C.C.

74. Nicol to Carpenter, April, no date, 1896, MS 271–57, C.C.

75. Nicol to Carpenter, April, no date, 1896, MS 271–57, C.C.

76. Nicol to Carpenter, April, no date, 1896, MS 271–57, C.C.

77. Nicol to Carpenter, April, no date, 1896, MS 271–57, C.C.

78. Robert V. Hine, *California's Utopian Colonies*, New Haven: Yale University Press, 1966 (1st edition 1953), pp. 41–2.

79. Nicol to Carpenter, April, no date, 1896, MS 271–57, C.C.

80. Nicol to Carpenter, April, no date, 1896, MS 271–57, C.C.

81. Rowbotham, *Edward Carpenter*, p. 194.

82. Edward Carpenter, *Love's Coming of Age*, Manchester: Labour Press, 1896. pp. 104–5. On the book's reception, see Rowbotham, *Edward Carpenter*, pp. 218–22.

83. Miriam Wheeler Nicol, Appendix, in Carpenter, *Love's Coming of Age*, p. 157.

84. Nicol, Appendix, in Carpenter, *Love's Coming of Age*, pp. 162–3.

85. Indenture, 9 February 1897, between Robert Allan Nicol and Alexander Ellis, Land Deeds, Archives & Research Center, Auburn, Placer County.

86. See Dan Plazak, *A Hole in the Ground with a Liar at the Top: Fraud and Deceit in the Golden Age of American Mining*, Salt Lake City: University of Utah Press, 2010, p. 8.

87. H.T.J., 23 April 1897, p. 61.

88. The receipts are in H.B.P.

89. Indenture, 8 December 1897, between Robert Allan Nicol and Mariam [*sic*] S. Nicol. Filed for record at request of Donna B. Beaumont on 14 December 1897. Land Deeds, Archives & Research Center, Auburn, Placer County.

13. Love, Pure Food and the Market: 1897–1899

1. H.T.J., Note after August holiday, 1897, p. 64.

2. Helena Born, 'The Last Stand Against Democracy in Sex', *The Conservator*, January 1898. Reprinted in ed. Tufts, W.I.D., p. 75.

3. H.T.J., Note after August holiday, 1897, p. 64.

4. H.T.J., 4 September 1897, p. 65; the 'volume' may have been *Wind-Harp Songs*, Buffalo: The Peter Paul Book Co., 1895.

5. J. William Lloyd, *The Red Heart in a White World: A Suggestive Manual of Free Society Containing a Method and a Hope*, pamphlet, 1st edition, Holland Publishing Company, February 1897, Koopman Papers, pp. 2–3, 19–21, 41–3.

6. Lloyd, *The Red Heart*, p. 39

7. Lloyd, *The Red Heart*, pp. 22–5.

8. H.T.J., 6 September 1897, p. 64, 13 November 1897, p. 66.

9. H.T.J., 6 October 1897, p. 65.

10. H.T.J., 13 November 1897, p. 66; H.T.J., 1 April 1898; Appendix attached to the first edition of *The Red Heart in a White World* and reproduced in the second edition, dated 1898, pp. 52–3.

11. For a list of J. William Lloyd's writings see http://libertarian-labyrinth.org/archive/J._William_Lloyd, accessed 04/04/2012. His Auto-biographical essay is archived online at http://wendymcelroy.com/blog/00000933.html, accessed 07/09/2011. A longer account is J. William Lloyd, 'Story of My Life', Typed MS, L.C. I am grateful to David Sachs for allowing me to see copies of his biographical notes on Lloyd.

12. Extract from a letter by Helena Born, 1897, quoted in Tufts, W.I.D., p. xxxi.

13. Born, 'The Last Stand Against Democracy', *The Conservator*, January 1898. Reprinted in ed. Tufts, W.I.D., p. 74.

14. H.T.J., 10 January 1898, p. 66.

15. H.T.J., 18 January 1898, p. 66.

16. H.T.J., 18 January 1898, pp. 66–7.

17. H.T.J., 1 April 1898, p. 68.

18. H.T.J., 27 January 1898, pp. 66–7.

19. Helena Born to Horace Traubel, 10 March 1898, L. of C., c. 53. A card from Will Young and the Liverpool Walt Whitman Foundation (W.W.F.) Branch to Horace Traubel, 6 August 1898 reveals the link to Robert Weare, L. of C., c. 53 (see Chapter 19).

20. H.T.J., 27 January 1898, p. 67; 3 March 1898, p. 67; Tufts, 'Notes for Helena about Her Father', Typed MS, p. 12.

21. Tufts, 'Notes for Helena about Her Father', p. 12.

22. Tufts, 'Notes for Helena about Her Father', p. 12.

23. Helena Born (from 47 Beach St.) to William Bailie, 7 April 1898, H.B.P.

24. Bailie, 'The Martyrdom of the Soul', *Liberty*, 6 February 1892, pp. 2–3.

25. Tufts, 'Notes for Helena about Her Father', p. 12.

26. William Bailie speaking at 'Services for Joan Flora Tilton at the Crematory', Walk Hill Street, Forest Hills, 25 November 1918, Denton Family Papers, L.C.

27. Helena Born (from 47 Beach St) to William Bailie, 6 April 1898, H.B.P.

28. Born (from 47 Beach St) to Bailie, 7 April 1898, H.B.P.

29. Born to Bailie, 7 April 1898, H.B.P.

30. William Bailie, 'To Lena', Handwritten MS, 20 April 1898, H.B.P.

31. Helena Born to William Bailie, no date (postmark 22 April), 1898, H.B.P.

32. Helena Born to William Bailie, 28 April 1898, H.B.P.

33. Born to Bailie, no date (postmark 22 April), 1898, H.B.P.

34. Born to Bailie, no date (postmark 22 April), 1898, H.B.P.

35. Helena Born to William Bailie, 1–3 May 1898, H.B.P.

36. Helena Born to 'E', 24 April 1898, in Tufts, B.I., p. xxxii; Helena Born to J. William Lloyd, 25 April 1898, L.C.

37. Born to 'E', Tufts, B.I., p. xxxii.

38. Born to Lloyd, 25 April 1898, L.C.

39. Born to Bailie, 28 April 1898, H.B.P.

40. Born to Bailie, no date (postmark 22 April), 1898, H.B.P.

41. Born to Bailie, 28 April 1898, H.B.P.

42. Born to Bailie, 1–3 May 1898, H.B.P.

43. Born to Bailie, 1–3 May 1898, H.B.P.

44. Born to Bailie, 1–3 May 1898, H.B.P.

45. Born to Bailie, 1–3 May 1898, H.B.P.

46. Helena Born to William Bailie, 8 May 1898, H.B.P.

47. Born to Bailie, 8 May 1898, H.B.P.

48. Born to Bailie, 8 May 1898, H.B.P.

49. Born to Bailie, 8 May 1898, H.B.P.

50. Born to Bailie, 1–3 and 8 May 1898, H.B.P.

51. Helena Born to William Bailie, 13 May 1898, H.B.P.

52. Helena Born to Helen Tufts, 4 May 1898 (mistakenly dated 4 April), H.B.P.

53. Quoted from *The Individual*, no date, Born to Bailie, 1 May 1898, H.B.P.

54. Born to Bailie, 13 May 1898, H.B.P.

55. Helena Born to William Bailie, 18 May 1898, H.B.P.

56. Helena Born to Helen Tufts, 18 May 1898, H.B.P.

57. Helena Born, Report of Boston Branch of W.W.F., May 1898, handwritten MS, H.B.P.

58. Helena Born to Horace Traubel, 23 May 1898, L. of C., c. 183.

59. Helena Born, 'To all Whitman-lovers glad greeting', May 1898, handwritten MS, H.B.P.

60. Born to Bailie, 13 May 1898, H.B.P.

61. Helena Born to William Bailie, no date (postmark 20 May), 1898, H.B.P.

62. Walter L. Leighton, *The Leighton Family*, Privately Printed, Newton Center, Mass. 1940, pp. 2, 16–17. On the Christian Science Church in Boston, see Arthur Meier Schlesinger, *The Rise of the City, 1878–1879*, New York: Macmillan, 1933, p. 338.

63. Helena Born to William Bailie, 27 May 1898, H.B.P.

64. Born to Bailie, 13 May 1898, H.B.P.

65. H.T.J., 8 May 1898, p. 69.

66. H.T.J., 18 March 1898, p. 69.

67. H.T.J., 1 April 1898, p. 69.

68. James F. Morton, 'Fragments of a Mental Autobiography', in David E. Schultz and S.T. Joshi, eds, *H.P. Lovecraft: Letters to James F. Morton*, New York: Hippocampus Press, 2011, p. 425.

69. D. Ivan Lee, 'Memorial of James F. Morton', in Schutlz and Joshi, *H.P. Lovecraft*, pp. 429–31.

70. H.T.J., 18 March 1898, p. 68.

71. Born to Tufts, 18 May 1898, H.B.P.

72. Born to Bailie, 18 May 1898, H.B.P.

73. H.T.J., 2 June 1898, p. 70.

74. H.T.J., 2 June 1898, p. 70.

75. Beth Hinchliffe, 'Borne on the Wings of History', *Wellesley Weston Magazine*, 19 May 2011, online at wellesleywestonmagazine.com, accessed 07/05/2012. See also William D. Denton, 3rd son of William and Elizabeth Foot Denton, Subject Vertical File, L.C.

76. Clarence Lee Swartz, Biographical data compiled by Agnes Inglis, L.C.

77. Clarence Lee Swartz, *I*, July 1898, Agnes Inglis Note, Box 31, L.C.

78. H.T.J., 2 June 1898, p. 70.

79. H.T.J., 2 June 1898, p. 70.

80. H.T.J., 2 June 1898, pp. 70–1.

81. H.T.J., 2 June 1898, p. 71.

82. H.T.J., 7 June 1898, p. 71.

83. H.T.J., 7 June 1898, p. 71.

84. H.T.J., 7 June 1898, p. 71

85. H.T.J., Saturday, no date (June), 1898, p. 72.

86. 'Human Equal Liberty. William Bailie Defines it to Comrades of Free Society', *Boston Sunday Herald*, 20 June 1898.

87. H.T.J., 10 June 1898, pp. 71–2.

88. H.T.J., 16 June 1898, p. 72.

89. H.T.J., 20 June 1898, p. 72.

90. Helena Born to William Bailie, 8 June 1898, H.B.P.

91. Helena Born to William Bailie, no date (Sunday), 1898, H.B.P.

92. Born to Bailie, 8 June 1898, H.B.P.

93. Born to Bailie, 8 June 1898, H.B.P.

94. Helena Born to William Bailie, Friday, no date (postmark 16 July), 1898, H.B.P.

95. Helena Born to William Bailie, no date (Thursday), 1898, H.B.P.

96. Born to Bailie, 10 July 1898, H.B.P.

97. Born to William Bailie, no date Friday (postmark 16 July), 1898, H.B.P.

98. Born to Bailie, Friday, no date (postmark 16 July) 1898, H.B.P.

99. Born to Bailie, Friday, no date (postmark 16 July) 1898, H.B.P.

100. Helena Born, 'Women and Economics', *The Conservator*, July 1898, p. 77.

101. Helena Born to William Bailie, 10 August 1898, H.B.P.

102. Helena Born (quoting William Bailie) to William Bailie, 22 August 1898, H.B.P.

103. Helena Born to William Bailie, Monday night, no date (postmark 16 August) 1898, H.B.P.

104. Lucy Colman, *Reminiscences*, Buffalo: H.L. Green, 1891, pp. 51–5; Braude, *Radical*

Spirits, pp. 62–3; *Report of the International Council of Women, 1888*, p. 359; Blatt, *Free Love and Anarchism*, p. 173.

105. Helena Born to William Bailie, 4 August 1898, H.B.P.
106. Helena Born to William Bailie, 10 August 1898, H.B.P.
107. Helena Born to William Bailie, 28 August 1898, H.B.P.
108. Lucy Colman quoted in Helena Born to William Bailie, 16 September 1898, H.B.P.
109. Born to Bailie, 16 September 1898, H.B.P.
110. Born to Bailie, 16 September 1898, H.B.P.
111. Helena Born to William Bailie, 2 October 1898, H.B.P.
112. H.T.J., 22 October 1898, p. 76.
113. H.T.J., 27 October 1898, p. 76.
114. 'Cooked Food for Home Use', Pure Food Restaurant Menu, H.B.P.
115. H.T.J., 16 November 1898, p. 77.
116. H.T.J., 8 January 1899, p. 78.
117. H.T.J., 26 May 1899, pp. 81–2.
118. H.T.J., 7 September 1898, p. 74
119. H.T.J., 10 October 1898, p. 76.
120. H.T.J., 1 November 1898, p. 77.
121. H.T.J., 10 December 1898, p. 77; on the clamour, see 'Col. Roosevelt's Lectures', *Boston Daily Advertiser*, 25 November 1898.
122. H.T.J., 24 January 1899, p. 78.
123. H.T.J., 8 January 1899, p. 78.
124. H.T.J., 9 March 1899, p. 79; on William Tufts, H.T.J., 11 April 1899, p. 79.
125. H.T.J., 8 January 1899, p. 78.
126. H.T.J., 17 January 1899, p. 78; see Michael Patrick Cullinane, *Liberty and American Anti-Imperialism, 1898–1909*, New York: Palgrave Macmillan, pp. 17–28; on Rabbi Charles Fleischer, see Mann, *Yankee Reformers*, p. 71.
127. H.T.J., 7 March 1899, pp. 78–9.
128. H.T.J., 28 March 1899, p. 79.
129. H.T.J., 7 March 1899, p. 79.
130. H.T.J., 18 April 1899, pp. 79–80.
131. H.T.J., 15 May, 1899, p. 81.
132. On the background, see McElroy, *The Debates of Liberty*, pp. 124–54.
133. Helena Born, 'Individualism versus Organization', *The Conservator*, June 1899. Reprinted in ed. Tufts, W.I.D., p. 64.
134. Born, 'Individualism versus Organization', ed. Tufts, W.I.D., p. 62.
135. Born, 'Individualism versus Organization', ed. Tufts, W.I.D., p. 64.
136. Born, 'Individualism versus Organization', ed. Tufts, W.I.D., p. 65.
137. Helena Born to J. William Lloyd, 26 June 1900, L.C.
138. Helena Born, 'Whitman's Ideal Democracy', *Poet-Lore*, Vol. xi, No. 4. Reprinted in ed. Tufts, W.I.D., p. 8.
139. Born, 'Whitman's Ideal Democracy', ed. Tufts, W.I.D., p. 18.
140. Born, 'Whitman's Ideal Democracy', ed. Tufts, W.I.D., p. 18.
141. Born, 'Whitman's Ideal Democracy', ed. Tufts, W.I.D., pp. 8, 18.
142. Born, 'Whitman's Ideal Democracy', ed. Tufts, W.I.D., pp. 18.
143. H.T.J., 28 April 1899, p. 80.
144. H.T.J., 26 May 1899, p. 82.
145. H.T.J., 1 June 1899, p. 82.

146. H.T.J., 3 June 1899, p. 82.
147. H.T.J., 6 June 1899, p. 83.
148. H.T.J., 7 June 1898, p. 83.
149. H.T.J., 10 August 1899, p. 83.
150. H.T.J., 14 September 1899, p. 84.
151. H.T.J., 14 September 1899, p. 84
152. H.T.J., 26 September 1899, p.84.
153. H.T.J., 10 October 1899, p. 85; 16 October 1899, p. 85; 6 November 1899, p. 86.
154. H.T.J., 23 October 1899, p. 85.
155. Benjamin Tucker to Henry Bool, 30 October 1899, Bool Correspondence, L.C.
156. H.T.J., 5 December 1899, p. 86.
157. Enid Stacy, First tour, A.T.P., 26/11/121, 27/11/123–12.
158. Enid Stacy, 'A Century of Women's Rights', in Edward Carpenter, ed., *Forecast of the Coming Century*, Manchester: The Labour Press, 1897, p. 100.
159. Helen Tufts to Horace Traubel, 27 November 1899, L. of C., c. 104.
160. H.T.J., 5 December 1899, p. 86.
161. H.T.J., 5 December 1899, p. 86.
162. H.T.J., 16 December 1899, p. 86.
163. H.T.J., 16 December 1899, p. 86.

14. *Family Ructions and Political Exploration: 1900*

1. H.T.J., 10 January 1900, p. 86.
2. H.T.J., 31 January 1900, p. 87; on 'Zaza' see Montrose J. Moses, 'David Belasco and the Psychology of the Switchboard' (1917), in Sharon K. Hall, ed., *Twentieth-Century Literary Criticism*, Volume 3, Detroit: Gale Research, 1980, and Katie N. Johnson, '"Zaza": That "Obstructing Harlot" of the Stage,' *Theatre Journal*, Vol. 54, No. 2, May 2002.
3. H.T.J., 15 February 1900, p. 88.
4. H.T.J., 15 February 1900, p. 88.
5. H.T.J., 28 February 1900, p. 88; Helen Tufts to Horace Traubel, 14 March 1900, L. of C., c. 104. For Traubel's own correspondence with Olga Nethersole see Traubel Papers, L. of C., c. 91. His interview with her is in *The Conservator*, November 1899, p. 137.
6. On *Sapho* (play), Wikipedia.
7. Helen Tufts, 'The Censor and the Play', *The Conservator*, March 1900, p. 8.
8. H.T.J., 28 February 1900, p. 88.
9. H.T.J., 27 March 1900, p. 89.
10. H.T.J., 3 May 1900, p. 90.
11. Helena Born to the Koopmans, 20 February 1900, H.L.K.
12. H.T.J., 3 March 1900, p. 89.
13. Alan Dawley, *Struggles for Justice: Social Responsibility and the Liberal State*, Cambridge, MA: Belknap Press, Harvard University, 1991, pp. 51–4; Cullinane, *Liberty and Anti-Imperialism*, pp. 48–9, 79–91; see also Ryan D. Dye, 'Irish-American Ambivalence Toward the Spanish-American War', *New Hibernia Review*, Vol. 11, No. 3, Autumn 2007.
14. H.T.J., 31 January 1900, p. 87. On William Tufts, H.T.J., 10 January 1900, pp. 86–7.
15. H.T.J., 19 February 1900, p. 88.

16. Boston Members of the Walt Whitman Fellowship, Lists of members, no date, c. 1900. Gustave Percy Wiksell Collection, L. of C., c. 185. On Wiksell, see Robertson, *Worshipping Walt*, pp. 268–72; on Maynard's new coat and monocle, H.T.J., 2 May 1899, p. 80; on Amy Wellington, see Charlotte Perkins Gilman Papers, Catalogue on correspondence, Schlesinger Library, Radcliffe.

17. James F. Morton, 'Across the Continent', *Free Society*, 25 March 1900, p. 2.

18. Clarence Swartz, 'Whitman the Egoist: Nietzsche, Schopenhauer', Boston Branch of the Walt Whitman Fellowship, Programme, Sixth Session, 1899–1900, L. of C., c. 185.

19. Helena Born, 'Whitman and Nature: Thoreau', MS Notes, p. 1, Folder 3, H.B.P.

20. Born, 'Whitman and Nature', MS Notes, p. 1.

21. Born, 'Whitman and Nature, MS Notes, p. 1.

22. Born, 'Thoreau's Joy in Nature', ed. Tufts, W.I.D., pp. 22–3. An edited version of Helena Born's 'Whitman and Nature: Thoreau', MS Notes, was published without the preamble as 'Thoreau's Joy in Nature' in *The Conservator*, May/June 1900. This article was then reprinted in Tufts W.I.D collection. When the quotations are in both the MS and the book I have referred to the printed version in the notes that follow.

23. Born, 'Thoreau's Joy in Nature', ed. Tufts, W.I.D., p. 26.

24. Born, 'Thoreau's Joy in Nature', ed. Tufts, W.I.D., pp. 24, 28–9.

25. Born, 'Whitman and Nature: Thoreau', MS Notes, p. 8, H.B.P.

26. Born, 'Thoreau's Joy in Nature', ed. Tufts W.I.D., p. 28.

27. Born, 'Thoreau's Joy in Nature', ed. Tufts, W.I.D., p. 24.

28. Born, 'Thoreau's Joy in Nature', ed. Tufts, W.I.D., p. 25.

29. Born, 'Thoreau's Joy in Nature', ed. Tufts, W.I.D., p. 29.

30. Helena Born, 'A Message from Over the Sea', *The Pioneer*, June 1900, p. 3 (Article is dated 3 May 1900).

31. Born, 'A Message from Over the Sea', pp. 3–4.

32. Born, 'A Message from Over the Sea', p. 4.

33. Born, 'A Message from Over the Sea', p. 4.

34. Born, 'A Message from Over the Sea', p. 4.

35. Born, 'A Message from Over the Sea', p. 4.

36. Crick, *The History of the Social Democratic Federation*, pp. 298, 308. David Howell, 'Irving, David Daniel [Dan], 1854–1924', *Oxford Dictionary of National Biography*, online, accessed 24/03/2010; Jill Liddington, *The Life and Times of a Respectable Rebel: Selina Cooper 1864–1946*, London: Virago, 1984, pp. 113–18.

37. Born, 'A Message from Over the Sea', p. 4.

38. Helena Born, (Socialism), MS Notes, p. 1, Folder 3, H.B.P.

39. Born, (Socialism), MS Notes, p. 7.

40. Helen recalls hearing Debs on Helena's Birthday, 11 May 1900, in H.T.J., 11 May 1923, p. 11. On the S.L.P. see Quint, *The Forging of American Socialism*, pp. 336–8, 368–72; Bedford, *Socialism and the Workers in Massachusetts*, pp. 144–72; on Debs see Charles A. Madison, *Critics and Crusaders: A Century of American Protest*, New York: Frederick Ungar, 1959 (1st edition 1947), pp. 453–5; Robertson, *Worshipping Walt*, pp. 253–6.

41. Born, (Socialism), MS Notes, p. 7.

42. Born, (Socialism), MS Notes, pp. 2–3.

43. Born, (Socialism), MS Notes, p. 1.

44. Born, (Socialism), MS Notes, p. 7.

45. Born, (Socialism), MS Notes, p. 7.

46. Born, (Socialism), MS Notes, pp. 7–8.
47. Born, (Socialism), MS Notes, p. 8.
48. Born, (Socialism), MS Notes, p. 3.
49. Born, (Socialism), MS Notes, pp. 3, 5.
50. Born, (Socialism), MS Notes, p. 5.
51. Born, (Socialism), MS Notes, p. 7.
52. Born, (Socialism), MS Notes, p. 7.
53. On Avery, see James, ed., *Notable American Women*, pp. 69–70; Bedford, *Socialism and the Workers*, pp. 146–7; see also *Proceedings of the Tenth National Convention of the Socialist Labor Party*, New York City, 21 June to 8 July 1900, New York Labor News Co., 1901, p. 65; Henry Kuhn, Report of the S.L.P. National Committee, June 1900, p. 24, online at marxists.org, accessed 04/03/2012.
54. H.T.J., 8 June 1900, p. 93; Catt's speech is reported in *Boston Evening Transcript*, 31 May 1900. On the suffrage movement in 1900, see Nancy Woloch, *Women and the American Experience*, New York: Overture Books, The McGraw-Hill Co., 1996, pp. 216–17.
55. H.T.J., 8 June 1900, p. 93.
56. H.T.J., 8 June 1900, pp. 92–3; on the Boers visit, see Charles T. Strauss, 'God Save the Boer: Irish American Catholics and the South African War, 1899–1902', *U.S. Catholic Historian*, Vol. 26, No. 4, February 2008, p. 23.
57. H.T.J., 3 May, 15 May 1900, pp. 89–90.
58. H.T.J., 28 May 1900, pp. 90–1; William Greenslade and Terence Rodgers, 'Resituating Grant Allen', in William Greenslade and Terence Rodgers, eds, *Grant Allen: Literature and Cultural Politics in the Fin de Siècle*, Aldershot: Ashgate, 2005, pp. 10–11.
59. H.T.J., 28 May 1900, p. 91.
60. Walter Leighton, 'Bachelorism', *Free Society*, 23 December 1901; H.T.J., 31 December 1900, p. 105; Walter Leighton to Horace Traubel, 20 November 1901, L. of C., c. 84.
61. H.T.J., 28 May 1900, p. 91.
62. H.T.J., 26 June 1900, p. 94.
63. H.T.J., 26 June 1900, p. 94.
64. 'G. Morong Replies', *Discontent*, 28 August 1901, p. 3.
65. H.T.J., 26 June 1900, p. 94.
66. Helen Tufts to J. William Lloyd, 27 November 1900, L.C.
67. H.T.J., 26 June 1900, p. 94.
68. H.T.J., 28 August 1900, p. 99.
69. H.T.J., 28 August 1900, p. 99.
70. William Walstein Gordak to Henry Bool, May 18, 1899, L.C.
71. H.T.J., 1 November 1900, p. 101.
72. H.T.J., 1 November 1900, p. 101; see Agnes Inglis, Notes on the career of Louis Prang, Typed MS, Box 3, L.C.
73. Wittke, *Against the Current: The Life of Karl Heinzen*. pp. 33–4, 104–5, 316–17.
74. H.T.J., 1 October 1900, p. 100.
75. H.T.J., 1 November 1900, p. 102.
76. H.T.J., 2 November 1900, p. 103.
77. Cullinare, *Liberty and American Anti-Imperialism*, pp. 3–4.
78. H.T.J., 2 November 1900, p. 103; 5 November 1900, p. 105.
79. H.T.J., 7 November 1900, p. 105.
80. William Bailie, 'The Chicago Martyrs', *Free Society*, 2 December 1900, p. 1.

81. H.T.J., 13 November 1900, p. 105.
82. Bailie, 'The Chicago Martyrs', p. 1.
83. Bailie, 'The Chicago Martyrs', p. 1.
84. H.T.J., 20 December 1900, p. 105.
85. H.T.J., 20 December 1900, p. 105.
86. H.T.J., 31 December 1900, p. 105.
87. Helena Born to Virginia Graeff, 29 December 1900, H.B.P.
88. Born to Graeff, 29 December 1900, H.B.P.
89. Born to Graeff, 29 December 1900, H.B.P.
90. H.T.J., 31 December 1900, p. 105.

15. 'Separation': 1901–1902

1. H.T.J., 7 January 1901, p. 106.
2. Judith Chasin, 'Fanny Berlin', Jewish Women's Archive, online at http://jwa.org, accessed 23/10/2015.
3. H.T.J., 7 January 1901, p. 106.
4. H.T.J., 7 January 1901, p. 106.
5. Helena Born to Helen Tufts, no date, c. 13 January 1901, H.B.P.
6. Born to Tuffts, no date, c. 13 January 1901, H.B.P.
7. Helena Born, 'Friends to be notified of my death'; 12 January 1901, H.B.P.
8. Helena Born, 'Last words to my darling, about the least important concerns', 12 January 1901, H.B.P.
9. Born to Tufts, no date, c. 13 January 1901, H.B.P.
10. H.T.J., 22 January 1901, p. 106.
11. H.T.J., 23 January 1901, p. 108; 29 January 1901, p. 108.
12. Helena Born to William Bailie, 'Vincent Memorial', no date, H.B.P.
13. Born to Bailie, 'Vincent Memorial', no date, H.B.P.
14. Helena Born to William Bailie, 'Dearest Love', no date, H.B.P.
15. Born to Bailie, 'Vincent Memorial', no date, H.B.P. Her reference to Sarah Holmes is in Helena Born to William Bailie, Vincent Memorial Hospital, Sunday, no date, postmark 3 February 1901.
16. H.T.J., Note written later, p. 107; 'Diary at the Time', 15, 19, 20, 21, 22 February 1901, p. 108.
17. Embroidered piece of cloth in H.B.P.
18. Helena Born to Helen M. Tufts, no date, 'Dear Helen, our nearest, truest friend', H.B.P.
19. H.T.J., Note written later, p. 107, 'Diary at the Time', 23 February 1901, p. 108.
20. H.T.J., Note written later, p. 107.
21. Helena Born quoted in Helen Tufts to William Bailie, 25 February 1901, H.B.P.
22. Born quoted in Tufts to Bailie, 25 February 1901, H.B.P.
23. Born quoted in Tufts to Bailie, 25 February 1901, H.B.P.
24. Tufts to Bailie, 25 February 1901, H.B.P.
25. H.T.J., Note added later, p. 108, 'Diary at the time', 26, 27 February 1901, p. 109.
26. Helena Born, Massachusetts Death Records, 1841–1915, February 1901.
27. H.T.J., 1 March 1901, p. 109; on the visit to the Schumms, H.T.J., 25 April 1897, p. 61.

28. Walter Leighton to Horace Traubel, 9 March 1901, L. of C., c 84.

29. H.T.J., 1 March 1901, p. 109.

30. H.T.J., 5, 6, 10, 13, 16, 23, 25 March 1901, p. 109.

31. H.T.J., 3 March 1901, p. 109.

32. Horace Traubel to Helen Tufts, 1 March 1901, H.B.P., Helen Tufts to Horace Traubel, 3 March 1901, L. of C., c. 104; Helen Tufts to Anne Montgomerie, with note added to 'Dear Anne Montgomerie and Horace Traubel', Sunday, 3 March 1901, L. of C., c. 23.

33. Helen Tufts to Horace Traubel, no date, 1901, L. of C., c. 23.

34. Helen Tufts to Horace Traubel, 3 March 1901, L. of C., c. 23; Helen A. Clarke to Horace Traubel, no date, 1901, L. of C., c. 59; Helen A. Clarke to Horace Traubel, 16 March 1901, L. of C., c. 59; H.T.J., 6 March 1901, p. 109.

35. On David Mikol see Michel Cordillot, ed., *La Sociale en Amérique, Dictionnaire Biographique du Mouvement Social Francophone aux États-Unis (1848–1922)*, Paris: Les Editions de L'Atelier, 2002, pp. 315–16.

36. Helen Tufts, Speech at Memorial Meeting for Helena Born, Walt Whitman Fellowship, Boston Branch, March 1901, H.B.P.

37. Emma Heller Schumm, Speech at Memorial Meeting for Helena Born, Walt Whitman Fellowship, Boston Branch, March 1901, H.B.P.

38. William Bailie, Letter to W.W.F. Memorial Meeting for Helena Born, dated 16 March 1901, H.B.P.

39. Copy of the memorial read and adopted by the Boston Branch of the Walt Whitman Fellowship at meeting held in memory of Helena Born, 17 March 1901, H.B.P.

40. Copy of a Resolution passed at a meeting of the Bristol Socialist Society, 7 May 1901, H.B.P.

41. Robert Gilliard to Helen Tufts, 9 May 1901, H.B.P.

42. H.M.T., 'Helena Born', *Free Society*, 7 April 1901, p. 4.

43. Richardson, 'The Bristol Strike Wave', in Backwith et al., *Strikers, Hobblers, Conchies and Reds*, p. 100.

44. Helen Tufts, 'Helena Born', *The Conservator*, May 1901, p. 38.

45. J. William Lloyd, *The Free Comrade*, 1 May 1901, p. 8.

46. On 'General Principles', Helena Born to William Bailie, Vincent Memorial, no date, H.B.P., on Helena's style, Traubel to Tufts, 1 March 1901, H.B.P.

47. Kate Crooke to Anna Geddes, 23 August 1901, T-GED 9/359, Geddes Papers, University of Strathclyde, Department of Special Collections.

48. H.T.J., Notes on visit to the Koopmans in Providence, 1901, pp. 110–11.

49. Helen Tufts, extracts from my letter to Robert Gilliard, 27 January 1902, H.T.J., p. 112.

50. Tufts to Gilliard, 27 January 1902, H.T.J., p. 111.

51. Tufts to Gilliard, 27 January 1902, H.T.J., p. 112.

52. Tufts to Gilliard, 27 January 1902, H.T.J., p. 111.

53. Tufts, B.I., p. xxvii.

54. Tufts to Gilliard, 27 January 1902, H.T.J., p. 111.

55. Tufts to Gilliard, 27 January 1902, H.T.J., pp. 111–12.

56. Tufts, B.I., p. xxxi.

57. Helena Born quoted in Tufts, B.I., pp. xxx–xxxi.

58. Tufts, B.I., p. xxx.

59. List of review copies and newspaper cuttings from *The Boston Globe*, 12 June 1902;

The Chicago Evening Post, 2 August 1902; J.E. Chamberlain, *The New York Mail and Express*, 2 August 1902, H.B.P.

60. Mary Hansen, 'Whitman's Ideal Democracy', *Free Society*, 26 October 1902, H.B.P.; J. William Lloyd, *The Free Comrade*, July 1902, p. 4.

61. Leonard D. Abbott, 'Helena Born's Testament', *The Socialist Spirit*, August 1902, p. 12, H.B.P.

62. J.S. (John Spargo), 'Views and Reviews', *The Comrade*, July 1902, H.B.P.

63. E.H.S. (Emma Heller Schumm), 'Helena Born and Her Book', *Liberty*, April 1903, p. 4.

64. E.H.S., 'Helena Born and Her Book', p. 4.

65. Emma Heller Schumm, Speech at Memorial Meeting for Helena Born, Walt Whitman Fellowship, Boston Branch, March 1901, H.B.P.

66. Arathena B. Drake, To the Whitman Fellowship, Whitman Memorial, May 1902, L. of C., c. 183.

67. Edward Carpenter to Helen Tufts, 26 July 1902, H.B.P.

68. Carpenter to Tufts, 26 July 1902, H.B.P.

69. H.T.J., 4 June 1930, p. 245b.

70. H.T.J., 4 June 1930, p. 245b.

16. *'Clues and Meanings': 1898–1902*

1. I am grateful for information on Jutie Biggs Spear Coan Nicol Hambly from David Sachs' research on the Coans at the Library of Congress and the New York Historical Society.

2. *Crocker-Langley Directory for 1899, US City Directories, 1821–1989*, San Francisco, p. 1299.

3. Satter, *Each Mind a Kingdom*, pp. 98–9; Charles S. Braden, *Spirits in Rebellion: The Rise and Development of New Thought*, Dallas: Southern Methodist University Press, 1980 (1st edition 1963), pp. 270–1, 323–4.

4. Arnold Bennett, Saturday, 17 September 1898, in Newman Flower, ed., *The Journals of Arnold Bennett, 1896–1910*, London: Cassell and Co., 1932, p. 80.

5. Bennett, Saturday, 17 September 1898, in Flower, ed., *The Journals of Arnold Bennett*, p. 80.

6. *Bristol Mercury*, 10 September 1898; *Bristol Mercury*, 13 September 1898.

7. Esther Wood, *Dante Rossetti and the Pre-Raphaelites*, London: Sampson, Low, Marston, 1894, p. 309; on Wood, see 'Lily Bell', 'Matrons and Maidens', *Labour Leader*, 26 May 1894.

8. Esther Wood, 'The New Woman', *Labour Leader*, 1 December 1894.

9. 'I.L.P.', *Labour Leader*, 1 December 1894.

10. Esther Wood represented 'the women Socialists' at the 'Nationalist Social Club' where William Morris addressed Fabians, I.L.P. and S.D.F. members, *Reynolds's Newspaper*, 6 October 1895.

11. For example, *Daily News*, 27 October 1897; *Manchester Evening News*, 26 October 1897; *Leicester Chronicle*, 30 October 1897.

12. Esther Wood represented 'the women Socialists', *Reynolds's Newspaper*, 31 October 1897.

13. Esther Wood and G.Ll. Morris, 'The Architecture of the Passmore Edwards Settlement',

reported in *Nottingham Guardian*, 25 February 1899; it was published in *The Studio*, No. 16, 1899, pp. 11–16.

14. Charles E. Dawson's work is in *The Wheelwoman*, 25 December 1897; see also Esther Wood on Charles E. Dawson in 'British Trade Bookbindings and their Designers', *The Studio*, Special Winter Edition 1899–1900, p. 30.

15. Wood, 'British Trade Bookbindings and their Designers', p. 30.

16. Charles E. Dawson, 'Modern Book Covers: From the designers' point of view, 1908–1909', Part 1, *Penrose's Pictorial Annual*, Vol. xix, 1908–1909, Reprinted in *Trade Bindings Research* (T.B.R.), Newsletter, Spring 1991, p. 6.

17. Gertrude Dix, 'Veronica's Mill', *The Pall Mall Magazine*, July 1900, p. 316.

18. Gertrude Dix, *The Image Breakers* (I.B.), New York: Frederick A. Stokes Co., 1900, p. 12.

19. Dix, I.B., p. 18. Danton is reported to have said, 'L'audace, et encore de l'audace, et toujours de l'audace'.

20. Dix, I.B., p. 51.

21. Dix, I.B., p. 3.

22. Dix, I.B., p. 4.

23. Dix, I.B., p. 10.

24. Dix, I.B., p. 101.

25. Dix, I.B., p. 101.

26. Dix, I.B., p. 275.

27. Dix, I.B., p. 93.

28. Dix, I.B., p. 82.

29. Dix, I.B., p. 83.

30. Dix, I.B., pp. 90–1.

31. Dix, I.B., p. 92.

32. Dix, I.B., p. 95.

33. Dix, I.B., p. 100.

34. Dix, I.B., p. 102.

35. Dix, I.B., p. 237; Leslie's relationship with Redgold is discussed in Ann Ardis, '"The Journey from Fantasy to Politics"', in Ingram and Patai, *Rediscovering Forgotten Radicals*, pp. 50–2.

36. Dix, I.B., p. 210.

37. Dix, I.B., p. 234.

38. Dix, I.B., pp. 245, 320–1. On dress, class and gender in *The Image Breakers*, see Kortsch, *Dress Culture in Late Victorian Women's Fiction*, pp. 169–78.

39. Dix, I.B., p. 342.

40. Dix, I.B., p. 279. On Rosalind, see Ann Ardis, *New Women, New Novels*, New Brunswick: Rutgers University Press, 1990, pp. 134–5, 159–60.

41. Dix, I.B., p. 103–4.

42. Dix, I.B., p. 277.

43. Dix, I.B., p. 356.

44. Dix, I.B., p. 105–6.

45. Dix, I.B., pp. 31, 93.

46. Dix, I.B., pp. 105, 81. On Rosalind and Leslie's relationship, see Sypher, *Wisps of Violence*, p. 137; Christine Murdoch, '*A large and passionate humanity plays about her*': *Women and Moral Agency in the Late Victorian Social Problem Novel*, PhD, University of Glasgow, 2012, pp. 174–5.

47. Dix, I.B., p. 105.
48. Dix, I.B., p. 80.
49. Dix, I.B., p. 274. On Rosalind and Leslie's divergent choices and the contrasting aesthetic symbolism employed in depicting them, see Kortsch, *Dress Culture*, pp. 174–7.
50. Dix, I.B., p. 204.
51. Dix, I.B., pp. 22–3.
52. Dix, I.B., p. 44. On Gilliard's family, 1891 England Census, Stapleton, Gloucester, Robert G. Gilliard.
53. Dix, I.B., p. 23.
54. Dix, I.B., p. 42. On the political background, see David Howell, *British Workers and the Independent Labour Party, 1883–1906*, Manchester: Manchester University Press, 1985, pp. 221–5, 366–9.
55. Dix, I.B., p. 46.
56. Dix, I.B., p. 50.
57. Dix, I.B., p. 30. Unwin's report of speaking at the Haymarket mentions the Bristol socialists' flag and their 'lamp bedecked with mottoes', *Commonweal*, 10 May 1890, p. 151.
58. Bernard Shaw to Enid Stacy, 4, 6, 17 May 1893, A.T.P.
59. Bernard Shaw, 'Illusions of Socialism', in Carpenter, ed., *Forecasts of the Coming Century*, p. 161.
60. Bernard Shaw, 'Preface' to Stephen Winsten, *Salt and his Circle*, London: Hutchinson & Co., 1951, p. 13.
61. On J.C. Kenworthy, see W.H.G. Armytage, *Heavens Below: Utopian Experiments in England 1560–1960*, London: Routledge and Kegan Paul, 1961, pp. 336–9, 349–53. 'R.S. Gillard' [*sic*] is mentioned as a supporter of Kenworthy and Wallace's Tolstoyan Brotherhood Trust, p. 345. On Tolstoy's influence upon Purleigh, see Dennis Hardy, *Alternative Communities in Nineteenth-Century England*, London: Longman, 1979. Diane Maltz, 'Ardent Service: Female Eroticism and New Life Ethics in Gertrude Dix's *The Image Breakers* (1900)', *Journal of Victorian Culture*, Vol. 17. No. 2, 2012, pp. 147–13, infers Hintonian and Tolstoyan influences from the text of the novel. Of course both were familiar to people within Gertrude's political and literary circle, but I have not been able to find any historical reference to their influence upon her during the 1890s.
62. On *The Torch*, see Judy Greenway, 'No Place for Women? Anti-Utopianism and the Utopian Politics of the 1890s', *Geografiska Annaler* 84B, 2002, pp. 202–3; Oliver, *The International Anarchist Movement in Late Victorian London*, pp. 120–5; Johnson, ed., *Olive and Stepniak*, pp. 245–87; Isabel Meredith (Helen and Olivia Rossetti), *Girl Among the Anarchists*, Marston Gate: Aeterna, 2010 (1st edition 1903).
63. Shaw, 'Preface', Winsten, *Salt and His Circle*, p. 13.
64. See Rowbotham, *Edward Carpenter*, pp. 165–7, 247.
65. Dix, I.B., p. 265.
66. George Henrick, *Henry Salt, Humanitarian Reformer and Man of Letters*, Urbana: University of Ilinois Press, 1977, pp. 118, 128; Gutala Krishnamurti, 'Barlas, John Evelyn', *Oxford Dictionary of National Biography*, online, accessed 03/03/2014; Henry S. Salt, 'The Poetry of John Barlas', *The Yellow Book*, October 1896.
67. Dix, I.B., p. 108; 'The Recording Angel' appears as the name of a book for recording faults at a girl's school in Bernard Shaw, *An Unsocial Socialist*, London: Constable and Co., 1950, pp. 4–8 (published in serial form in the S.D.F.'s *To-Day*, March–December 1884).

68. Dix, I.B., p. 127.
69. Dix, I.B., pp. 304, 248.
70. Dix, I.B., pp. 375–6.
71. 'Christian Science: Mrs Mills the Faith Healer', *Reynolds's Newspaper*, 6 November 1898.
72. Dix, I.B., p. 92.
73. Dix, I.B., p. 355.
74. Dix, I.B., p. 129.
75. Dix, I.B., pp. 64–5.
76. Dix, I.B., pp. 133, 377; on the symbolism of Leslie's clothes see Kortsch, *Dress Culture*, pp. 171, 174.
77. Dix, I.B., p. 367; see Ledger, *The New Woman*, p. 58.
78. Dix, I.B., p. 378; 'Sketch Exhibition – Miss Hilda Dix', *Western Daily Press*, 17 September 1895.
79. Dix, I.B., p. 392; see Carol L. Hale, 'Gertrude Dix', *Dictionary of Literary Biography*, 2005–2006, p. 5, online, accessed 6/9/09.
80. George Goschen quoted in Beaumont, *Utopia Ltd*, p. 5.
81. Beaumont, *Utopia Ltd*, pp. 118–19.
82. Linda Marie Fritschner, 'Heinemann, William Henry', *Oxford Dictionary of National Biography*, online, accessed 13/01/2013.
83. *The Saturday Review*, 27 October 1900.
84. *The Graphic*, 13 October 1900.
85. *The Bookman*, March 1900, p. 166; *The Athenaeum*, 6 October 1900, p. 438; *Daily News*, quoted on 'Novels by Gertrude Dix', flyer, no date, R.P.
86. *The Academy*, 3 November 1900, p. 418; *The Outlook*, 24 November 1900, p. 536.
87. E.A. Bennett, 'A Gossip About Books', *Hearth and Home: An Illustrated Weekly Journal for Gentlewomen*, 25 October 1900, p. 940.
88. G.K.C., *The Speaker: The Liberal Review*, 13 October 1900, pp. 50–1.
89. G.K.C., *The Speaker*, p. 50
90. Anon., *The Modern Review*, quoted on 'The Novels of Gertrude Dix', flyer, no date, R.P.
91. See 'THE IMAGE BREAKERS', Advertisement, Frederick A. Stokes Company, *The Sun*, 22 September 1900; *The Times*, Washington, 27 May 1900.
92. England Census 1901, Gertrude Dix, Kingston-on-Thames.
93. On Holden, see Anthony Beeson, *Bristol Central Library and Charles Holden: A History and Guide*, Bristol: Redcliffe Press, 2006, p. 9; Fiona MacCarthy, *The Simple Life: C.R. Ashbee in the Cotswolds*, London: Lund Humphries, London, 1981, pp. 146–147.
94. England Census 1901, Gertrude Dix, Hampstead. On Oswald Cox's friendship with Henry Nevinson and Nannie Dryhurst, see John, *War, Journalism and the Shaping of the Twentieth Century*, p. 89.
95. Herbert Morrah, ed., *The Literary Year-Book and Bookman's Directory*, London: George Allen, 1901, p. 161.
96. Edna Eldred, 'People Are More Important Than Happenings', Typed MS, p. 6, Leslie Gelb and R.P. (I am grateful to Leslie Gelb for enabling me to see this manuscript of recollections about Margot de Silva, born Margaret Dix.); Amaryllis Nicol Cabell, interviewed by Georges Rey, Tape, R.P.
97. *Crocker-Langley Directory, 1900*; Twelfth Census of the United States, Ward 7, Los Angeles Township, California.

98. Dottie Smith, *Historic Data Inventory of the Shasta County Interlakes Recreation Management Area*, Report prepared for Bureau of Land Management, Cultural Resources Publications History, Redding CA, 1995, pp. 55, 57–8, 79; Dottie Smith, Shasta County History, online at http://shastacountyhistory.com, accessed 26/02/2014; 'William Keswick', Wikipedia; on the strike, see *San Francisco Call*, 12 December 1902; *Los Angeles Herald*, 18 and 31 December 1902.

99. Edward Carpenter to Helen Tufts, 26 July 1902, H.B.P.

100. Robert Nicol to Gertrude Dix, The Mine, Monday Noon, no date, postmark 11 June 1902, R.P.

17. *A New Beginning: 1901–1902*

1. H.T.J., 11 May 1901, p. 112.

2. H.T.J., 24 May and 27 May 1901, p. 112.

3. H.T.J., 30 May 1901, p. 112.

4. H.T.J., 17 June 1901, p. 112.

5. Helen Tufts, Speech at 'Whitman: 1901', *The Conservator*, July 1901, p. 72.

6. H.T.J., 28 February 1901, p. 109; Bailie Letter to W.W.F. Memorial Meeting for Helena Born, 17 March 1901.

7. H.T.J., 27 July 1901, p. 112; see Ernst Haeckel, *The Riddle of the Universe*, London: Watts & Co. London, 1929 (1st edition 1901).

8. Karl Pearson, *The Grammar of Science*, London: Adam & Charles Black, 1900 (1st edition 1892), pp. 179, 191.

9. Helen Tufts, 'Progressive Tendencies in Religion', *The Conservator*, August 1901, p. 89.

10. H.T.J, Note added later relating to the death of Helena Born in 1901, pp. 107–8.

11. Tufts, Notes for Helena About Her Father, Typed MS; Helena Bailie in Avrich, ed., *Anarchist Voices*, p. 14.

12. Helen Tufts to William Bailie, no date, H.B.P., Folder 7.

13. Falk, Pateman, Moran, eds, *Emma Goldman, 1890–1901*, Volume 1, pp. 565–6.

14. Emma Goldman, 'Some More Observations', *Free Society*, 29 April 1900, in Falk, Pateman, Moran, eds, *Emma Goldman, 1890–1901*, Volume 1, p. 400.

15. Helen Tufts to J. William Lloyd, 27 November 1900, L.C.

16. Helen Tufts 'Walt Whitman's Love of Comrades', *Free Society*, 31 March 1901, pp. 4–5.

17. Wat Tyler (pseudonym of William Bailie, abbreviated as W.T.), 'Robber Barons Old and New', *Free Society*, 30 June 1901, pp. 1–2; William's use of the pseudonym is revealed by J. William Lloyd, 'Gordak, The Poet', *The Demonstrator*, 10 June 1903, p. 3.

18. W.T., 'Robber Barons', pp. 1–2.

19. See Neville Kirk, *Labour and Society in Britain and the USA*, Volume 2, Aldershot: Scolar Press, 1994, p. 59.

20. W.T., 'Strikes and Labor Unions', *Free Society*, 16 June 1901, p. 1; on the attempts to regulate, see Philip Jenkins, *A History of the United States*, London: Macmillan, 1997, pp. 168–78; Martin J. Sklar, *The Corporate Reconstruction of American Capitalism, 1890–1916*, New York: Cambridge University Press, 1988, pp. 100–32.

21. W.T., 'Strikes and Labor Unions', p. 1.

22. W.T., 'Strikes and Labor Unions', p. 1.

23. W.T., 'Strikes and Labor Unions', p. 2.
24. W.T., 'Financial Methods of Appropriation', *Free Society*, 4 August 1901, p. 2.
25. W.T., 'The Growth of Wealth', *Free Society*, 14 July 1901, p. 1.
26. W.T., 'The Growth of Wealth', p. 2.
27. Walter Leighton, 'The Curse of Government?' *Free Society*, 14 July 1901, pp. 2–3.
28. W.T., 'The Curse of Government Again', *Free Society*, 21 July 1901, p. 4.
29. James F. Morton Jr, 'Certain Comment', *Free Society*, 4 August 1901, p. 4.
30. W.T., 'The Source of Exploitation', *Free Society*, 11 August 1901, p. 2.
31. W.T., 'Profit, Rent and Interest', *Free Society*, 18 August 1901, p. 1.
32. W.T., 'The Source of Exploitation', p. 2.
33. W.T., 'Anarchism and Revolution', *Free Society*, 8 September 1901, p. 1.
34. W.T., 'Anarchism and Revolution', p. 1.
35. W.T., 'Anarchism and Revolution', p. 2.
36. W.T., 'Anarchism and Revolution', p. 2.
37. W.T., 'Anarchism and Revolution', p. 2.
38. 'Notes and Comments', *Free Society*, 25 August 1901, p. 4; A.L. Ballou, 'An Era of Transition', *Free Society*, 8 September 1901, p. 5.
39. Ballou, 'An Era of Transition', p. 5.
40. Candace Falk, 'Introduction', in Falk, Pateman, Moran, eds, *Emma Goldman, 1890–1901*, Volume 1, pp. 73–4; Buhle, Buhle and Georgakas, *Encyclopedia of the American Left*, p. 172.
41. H.T.J., 7 September 1901, p. 112.
42. H.T.J., 7 September 1901, p. 112.
43. Emma Goldman, 'Defends Acts of Bomb Throwers', *Cleveland Plain Dealer*, 6 May 1901, in Falk, Pateman, Moran, eds, *Emma Goldman, 1890–1901*, Volume 1, p. 453.
44. Emma Goldman, 'Tragedy at Buffalo', *Free Society*, 6 October 1901, in Falk, Pateman, Moran, eds, *Emma Goldman, 1890–1901*, Volume 1, pp. 471–7.
45. H.T.J., 8 September 1901, p. 112.
46. 'Story of the Arrest of Anarchist Queen', *New York World*, 11 September 1901, in Falk, Pateman, Moran, eds, *Emma Goldman, 1890–1901*, Volume 1, p. 466.
47. H.T.J., 11, 14, 19 September 1901, p. 112.
48. H.T.J., 23 September 1901, p. 112.
49. H.T.J., 24 September 1901, p. 112.
50. Emma Goldman, *Living My Life*, Volume 1, London: Pluto, 1988, (1st edition 1933), p. 317.
51. W.T., 'Stamping Out Anarchism?' *Free Society*, 24 November 1901, pp. 2–3, in response to Robert A. Pinkerton, 'Detective Surveillance of Anarchists', *The North American Review*, November 1901, pp. 727–45, online at http://theanarchistlibrary.org, accessed 04/02/2013; on the impact, see Sidney Fine, 'Anarchism and the Assassination of McKinley, *The American Historical Review*, Vol. 60, No. 4, July 1955, pp. 780–93.
52. Helen Tufts, 'Through Solidarity', *Free Society*, 10 November 1901, p. 4.
53. Miriam Daniell, 'In Robes of Anarchy', *Free Society*, 15 December 1901, p. 1; on Miriam's poems, Helen Tufts to Horace Traubel, 18 December 1901, L. of C., c. 104.
54. Tufts, 'Through Solidarity', p. 4.
55. Helen Tufts, 'Holding up the Glass', *Discontent*, 11 December 1901, p. 3; On *The Arena*, see Mann, *Yankee Reformers*, p. 167; on B.O. Flower's rejection of the anti-anarchist hysteria, see Fine, 'Anarchism and the Assassination of McKinley', p. 789, note 55.

56. Helen Tufts 'Welcome "Comrade"', *Free Society*, 17 November 1901, p. 3; on Markham, Crosby and Herron, see Rowbotham, *Edward Carpenter*, pp. 352–4.

57. Helen Tufts to Horace Traubel, 18 December 1901, L. of C., c. 104.

58. Helen Tufts, 'The Emancipation of a Race', *The Conservator*, December 1901, p. 155.

59. Tufts, 'The Emancipation of a Race', p. 155.

60. William Dean Howells in Charles W. Chesnutt, *The Marrow of Tradition*, ed. Werner Sollors, New York: W.W. Norton & Co., 2012 (1st edition 1901), pp. 383–4.

61. H.T.J., Section added later summing up the years 1901–1904, p. 113.

62. Tufts to Bailie, no date, H.B.P., Folder 7.

63. William Tufts quoted in H.T.J., Section summing up 1901–1904, p. 113.

64. A 'Mrs M.E. Cheney' advertised rooms at 305 Columbus Avenue for those seeking 'quiet quarters' in *The Word*, January 1893, p. 3.

65. Leighton to Traubel, 20 November 1901, L. of C., c. 84.

66. Leighton, *The Leighton Family*, pp. 16–17.

67. Helen Tufts to Horace Traubel, 27 May 1902, L. of C., c. 104; on her affection for Anne Montgomerie, see Helen Tufts to Horace Traubel, 1 October 1902, L. of C., c. 104; C.E. Goodspeed to Helen Tufts, 12 June 1902, L. of C., c. 104.

68. Edward Carpenter, *Ioläus: An Anthology of Friendship*, London: Swan Sonnenschein, 1906 (1st edition 1902), pp. 3, 42. Traubel was chivied about a review by Leonard Abbott on January 8 and 18, L. of C., c. 104.

69. 'T' (Horace Traubel), '*Ioläus: An Anthology of Friendship* by Edward Carpenter', *The Conservator*, May 1902, in Gary Schmidgall, ed. *Conserving Walt Whitman's Fame*, Iowa: University of Iowa Press, 2006, pp. 328–9.

70. Helen Tufts to Horace Traubel, 16 June 1902, L. of C., c. 104.

71. 'H.T.' (Helen Tufts), *Free Society*, 28 September 1902, p. 7

72. W.T., 'Was Czolgosz Insane?', *Free Society*, 16 February 1902, p. 73; on the background see Fine, 'Anarchism and the Assassination of McKinley'; Robert Bach Jensen, 'The United States, International Policing and the War Against Anarchist Terrorism', 1900–1914; *Terrorism and Political Violence*, Vol. 13, No. 1, Spring 2001, pp. 369–74.

73. Abe Isaak Junior, 'Excommunication Rejected', *Free Society*, 9 March 1902, p. 2.

74. Kate Austin, 'The Experts and their "Facts"', *Free Society*, 9 March 1902, p. 4.

75. Falk, Pateman, Moran, eds, *Emma Goldman, 1890–1901*, Volume 1, p. 517.

76. Candace Falk, 'Introduction', in Falk, Pateman, Moran, eds, *Emma Goldman, 1902–1909*, Volume 2, Berkeley: University of California Press, 2008, pp. 12–13.

77. William Bailie, 'Josiah Warren', in George B. Lockwood, ed., *The New Harmony Movement*, New York: D. Appleton and Co., 1905 (1st edition 1902), p. 295.

78. Helen Tufts, 'The Chicago Martyrs and After', *Free Society*, 21 December 1902, p. 2.

79. William Holmes, 'Comment', *Free Society*, 21 December 1902, p. 3; on William and ·Lizzie Holmes, see Falk, Pateman, Moran, eds, *Emma Goldman, 1890–1901*, Volume 1, p. 535.

80. Helen Tufts, 'In Reply to a Comment', *Free Society* (fragment, no date, c. January 1903).

81. Sears, *The Sex Radicals*, pp. 233–4; Falk, Pateman, Morn, eds, *Emma Goldman, 1902–1909*, Volume 2, pp. 535, 537, 550.

82. Helen Tufts, 'Boston Letter', *The Demonstrator*, 20 May 1903, p. 3.

83. Tufts, 'Boston Letter', p. 3.

84. Tufts, 'Boston Letter', p. 3.

85. Tufts, 'Boston Letter', p. 3.
86. 'Which Rules?' *The Boston Globe*, 29 October 1902.
87. Bailie, 'Josiah Warren' in Lockwood, *The New Harmony Movement*, p. 296.
88. Bailie, 'Josiah Warren' in Lockwood, *The New Harmony Movement*, p. 304.

18. Romancing the West: 1902–1908

1. Al M. Rocca, *Old Shasta*, Charleston, SC: Arcadia, 2005, pp. 7–8, 20, 67, 76.
2. Rocca, *Old Shasta*, pp. 113–14.
3. Rocca, *Old Shasta*, pp. 114–16, 123.
4. Nicol to Dix, The Mine, Monday noon, no date (postmark 11 June 1902), R.P.
5. Nicol to Dix, (postmark 11 June 1902), R.P.
6. Nicol to Dix, (postmark 11 June 1902), R.P.
7. Nicol to Dix, (postmark 11 June 1902), R.P.
8. 'Placer County, California', *Placer County Improvement and Development Association, Bulletin and List of Lands for Sale*, No. 4, 1 April 1903.
9. Robert Nicol to Amaryllis Nicol Cabell, 7 November 1950, R.P.
10. Robert Nicol to Amaryllis Nicol Cabell, 21 August 1951, R.P.
11. Amaryllis Nicol Cabell interviewed by Georges Rey, Tape, R.P.
12. Biographical details from: Decree of Divorce, County of Placer, U.S. Copy issued, 1950, R.P.; Marriage Licence, Robert Allan Nicol & Gertrude Mary Dix, 8 April 1903, California County Marriages, R.P.; Margot de Silva, Certificate of Death, Brooklyn, New York, 14 November 1983, P.R.; Nicol Family Tree, R.P.
13. Gertrude Dix, 'The Cry on the Trail', *The Roanoke Beacon*, 1 August 1905, p. 1. First Published in *The San Francisco Argonaut*, February 1905.
14. Dix 'The Cry on the Trail', p. 1.
15. Dix, 'The Cry on the Trail', p. 1.
16. Dix, 'The Cry on the Trail', p. 1.
17. Gertrude Dix, 'Pardners', *The San Francisco Call*, 30 April 1905.
18. 'Pears Soap Advertisement', Frontispiece, *Munsey's Magazine*, April 1905, University of California, Haithi Trust Digital Library; see Stuart Ewen, *P.R. A Social History of Spin*, New York: Basic Books, 1996, pp. 52–4.
19. Gertrude Dix, 'A Flight into the Mountains', *Munsey's Magazine*, June 1905, p. 369, online at unz.org, accessed 10/05/2016.
20. Nicol to Cabell, 21 August 1951, R.P. For details of the birth of Amaryllis Nicol Cabell, Certificate of Death, 14 November 1983, R.P.
21. Edna Eldred, 'People Are More Important Than Happenings', Typed MS, no date, p. 6, Leslie Gelb and R.P.
22. Robert Nicol to Amaryllis Nicol Cabell, 27 July 1851, R.P.
23. See *Out West*, January 1900, p. 1, online at archive.org/stream/outwestland, accessed 15/08/2011.
24. Gertrude Dix, 'The Passing of the Forty-Niner', *Out West*, May 1906, pp. 299–301, R.P.
25. Dix, 'The Passing of the Forty-Niner', p. 300.
26. Dix, 'The Passing of the Forty-Niner', p. 203.
27. 'Dix, Gertrude (Mrs Nicol)', *The Literary Year Book*, London: George Routledge & Sons; New York: E.P. Dutton, 1906, p. 108.
28. *The People's Magazine*, plugged by *The Salt Lake Herald*, 7 December 1906, p. 9.

29. *The People's Magazine* cover December 1906, described in *The Salt Lake Herald*, 7 December 1906, p. 9.

30. Gertrude Dix, 'The Wandering Angels', *The People's Magazine*, December 1906. Reprinted in *The Star*, 29 May 1908, and *Burnley Express and Advertiser*, 14 April 1909.

31. Dix, 'The Wandering Angels'.

32. Gertrude Dix, 'The Last Flicker of the Candle', *Out West*, January to June 1907, no date, p. 524, R.P.

33. Dix, 'The Last Flicker of the Candle', p. 535.

34. UK Incoming Passenger Lists, Clement Dix, 4 May 1907; UK Incoming Passenger Lists, Gertrude Dix, 28 October 1907. Details of the birth of Robert Dix Nicol, California Birth Index, 1905–1995, R.P.

35. Gertrude Dix, 'The Apples of Hesperides', *Out West*, January 1908, p. 153, online at archive.org/stream/outwestland, accessed 15/08/2011.

36. Dix, 'The Apples of Hesperides', p. 155.

37. Dix, 'The Apples of Hesperides', p. 154.

38. Dix, 'The Apples of Hesperides', pp. 157–8.

39. Gertrude Dix, 'The Mystery of Miranda', *Out West*, July to December 1908, no date, p. 228, R.P.

40. Dix, 'The Mystery of Miranda', p. 229.

41. Dix, 'The Mystery of Miranda', p. 229.

42. Dix, 'The Mystery of Miranda', p. 229.

43. Dix, 'The Mystery of Miranda', pp. 230–1.

44. Dix, 'The Mystery of Miranda', p. 233.

45. Dix, 'The Mystery of Miranda, p. 233.

46. Margot de Silva, 'Her Father's Daughter', Typed MS, no date, pp. 20, 28, R.P.

47. Eldred, 'People Are More Important Than Happenings', Typed MS, no date, p. 6, Leslie Gelb and R.P.

48. De Silva, 'Her Father's Daughter', p. 60.

49. De Silva, 'Her Father's Daughter', p. 60.

50. Lardner and Brock, *History of Placer and Nevada Counties*, pp. 243–4.

19. Bundles of Contradictions: 1903–1907

1. Helen Tufts to Horace Traubel, 2 January 1903, L. of C., c. 104.

2. William Bailie, 'The Rule of the Monopolists', *Liberty*, February 1903, p. 4; on Tucker's critique of the Trusts, see Martin, *Men Against the State*, pp. 271–3.

3. Bailie 'The Rule of the Monopolists', p. 5. Ghent was a journalist sympathetic to Fabian socialism. He and William are addressing a debate in the newly formed Socialist Party on the monopolies and public ownership; see Ira Kipnis, *The American Socialist Movement, 1897–1912*, Chicago: Haymarket Books, 2004 (1st edition 1952), pp. 63–8.

4. Bailie, 'The Rule of the Monopolists', p. 5.

5. William Bailie, 'Twentieth-Century Benevolence', *Liberty*, March 1903, pp. 3–4.

6. William Bailie, 'The Steel Trust's Balance Sheet', *Liberty*, May 1903, p. 3.

7. Bailie, 'The Steel Trust's Balance Sheet', p. 3; William Bailie, 'The Senile State', *Liberty*, September 1903, p. 3.

8. William Bailie, 'Loria and Economic Interpretations', *Liberty*, December 1903, p. 5.

9. Bailie, 'Loria and Economic Interpretation', p. 4.
10. Bailie, 'Loria and Economic Interpretations', p. 4.
11. H.T.J., 29 February 1904, p. 115.
12. H.T.J., 7 March 1904, p. 115.
13. H.T.J., 28 March 1904, p. 115.
14. H.T.J., 28 March 1904, p. 115; 18 June 1904, pp. 115–16.
15. H.T.J., 18 May 1904, p. 115.
16. H.T.J., 19 June 1904, pp. 116–17.
17. H.T.J., 19 June 1904, p. 117.
18. H.T.J., 19 June 1904, p. 118.
19. H.T.J., 2 July 1904, p. 118.
20. H.T.J., Note added to 1901–1904 in July 1951, p. 113.
21. H.T.J., 21 October 1904, p. 119.
22. H.T.J., 31 December 1904, p. 122.
23. H.T.J., 27 December 1904, p. 120.
24. H.T.J., 27 December 1904, p. 120.
25. H.T.J., 29 January 1905, p. 123.
26. H.T.J., 30 January 1905, p. 123; 19 February 1905, pp. 123–4.
27. H.T.J., 4 April 1905, p. 124.
28. H.T.J., Note added, p. 114; see Richard R. Adelstein '"Islands of Conscious Power": Louis D. Brandeis and the Modern Corporation', *Business History Review*, Vol. 63, No. 3, Autumn 1989; on McClennan, see Melvin Urovsky and David W. Levy, *Letters of Louis D. Brandeis, Vol. 2*, New York: State University of New York Press, 1972, p. 18, note 1.
29. H.T.J., 4 April 1905, p. 124.
30. H.T.J., 1 May 1905, p. 125.
31. Notice enclosed in Helen Tufts to Horace Traubel, 23 March 1904, L. of C., c. 104; H.T.J.,1 May 1905, p. 125.
32. H.T.J., 1 May 1905, p. 125.
33. H.T.J., 4 April 1905, p. 125.
34. H.T.J., 23 January 1905, pp. 122–3; 30 January 1905, p. 123.
35. H.T.J., 27 June 1905, p. 126.
36. H.T.J., 15 August 905, p. 126.
37. William Bailie, *Josiah Warren: The First American Anarchist: A Sociological Study*, Boston: Small, Maynard and Co., 1906, p. 25.
38. Bailie, *Josiah Warren*, Appendix, p. 128.
39. Bailie, 'The Anarchist Spirit', *Josiah Warren*, p. xii.
40. Bailie, 'The Anarchist Spirit', *Josiah Warren*, pp. xvi–xviii.
41. Bailie, 'The Anarchist Spirit', *Josiah Warren*, p. xiv.
42. Bailie, 'The Anarchist Spirit', *Josiah Warren*, pp. xxi–xxii.
43. Bailie, 'The Anarchist Spirit', *Josiah Warren*, pp. xxiv–xxv.
44. Bailie, 'The Anarchist Spirit', *Josiah Warren*, p. xxv.
45. Bailie, *Josiah Warren*, p. 82; on their inception see Mass Moments, 3 June 1893: 'Massachusetts Creates Nation's First Regional Park System'; online at http://www.massmoments.org, accessed 12/02/2013.
46. William Bailie to Benjamin Tucker, 18 March 1906, Tucker Papers, New York Public Library.
47. 'Mr Bailie's Life of Josiah Warren', *Liberty*, February 1906, p. 14.

48. Bailie to Tucker, 18 March 1906, Tucker Papers; on Rabbi Fleischer, see Mann, *Yankee Reformers*, p. 71.
49. Bailie to Tucker, 18 March 1906, Tucker Papers.
50. H.T.J., 18 March 1906, p. 128.
51. H.T.J., 2 May 1906, p. 129.
52. H.T.J., 23 October 1907, p. 134.
53. C.L.S., 'The First American Anarchist', *Liberty*, April 1906, p. 52.
54. C.L.S., 'The First American Anarchist', pp. 54–5.
55. C.L.S., 'The First American Anarchist', p. 56.
56. Helen Tufts to Agnes Inglis, 24 April 1947, L.C.
57. William Bailie, 'Murder Entirely Satisfactory', *Liberty*, April 1906, p. 46.
58. William Bailie to Benjamin Tucker, 18 September 1906, Tucker Papers, New York Public Library.
59. H.T.J., 30 November 1906, p. 131.
60. Helen Tufts, 'What is a Mob?', *Liberty*, June 1906, pp. 28–30; on early theorists of the crowd, see Ewen, *P.R.*, pp. 64–81.
61. H.T.J., 19 March 1906, pp. 128–9.
62. H.T.J., 16 May 1906, p. 129.
63. H.T.J., 19 March 1906, p. 129.
64. H.T.J., 8 May [*sic*] 1906, p. 130. This entry, which follows May 16, could be May 18.
65. H.T.J., 19 March 1906, p. 128.
66. H.T.J., 10 October 1906, p. 130.
67. H.T.J., 16 October 1907, p. 133.
68. H.T.J., 30 November 1906, p. 131.
69. Freeman et al., *Who Built America?* Volume 2, pp. 167–78; Kipnis, *The American Socialist Movement*, pp. 106–63.
70. Joyce L. Kornbluh, ed., *Rebel Voices: An IWW Anthology*, Chicago: Charles H. Kerr Publishing Company, 1988, pp. 1–4; Bedford, *Socialism and the Workers in Massachusetts*, p. 231.
71. H.T.J., 27 January 1907, p. 131.
72. Trade Catalogs from Bailie Basket Co., Smithsonian Institution, record ID: SILNMAHTL_8560.
73. Walter Hough, 'Otis Tufton Mason', *American Anthropologist*, Vol. 10, April–June 1908, p. 189.
74. William Bailie to Otis Tufton Mason, 5 December 1907, Smithsonian Institution, National Museum of Natural History.
75. Bailie to Mason, 5 December 1907, Smithsonian.
76. Bailie to Mason, 9 February 1908, Smithsonian.
77. Hough, 'Otis Tufton Mason', p. 187.
78. On Ely's visit, William Bailie to John B. Andrews, 4 December 1907, Un-catalogued Manuscripts, L.C.; on Ely, Mann, *Yankee Reformers*, pp. 78–9, 92, 98; Arthur J. Vidich and Stanford M. Lyman, 'Secular Evangelism at the University of Wisconsin', *Social Research*, Vol. 49, No. 4, Winter 1982, pp. 1049–53
79. Richard T. Ely, 'Josiah Warren: The First American Anarchist', *The American Political Science Review*, Vol. 2, No. 1, November 1907, p. 125.
80. See John Calvin Colson, 'Academic Ambitions and Library Development: The American Bureau of Industrial Research and the State Historical Society of Wisconsin 1904–18', University of Illinois Graduate School of Library and Information Science,

Occasional Papers, No. 159, May 1983; Richard A. Gonce, 'John R Commons's "Five Big Years" 1899–1904', *American Journal of Economics and Sociology*, Vol. 61, No. 4, October 2002, pp. 756, 760, 772.

81. Bailie to Andrews, 4 December 1907, Un-catalogued Manuscripts, L.C.; for Emma Goldman's response, see Emma Goldman to John B. Andrews, New York, 2 December 1907, in Falk, Pateman, Moran, *Emma Goldman, Volume 2, 1902–1909*, p. 263, on Andrews, p. 508.

82. On the visit to Beatrice Taylor and the Ferrer material: H.T.J., 22 October 1940, p. 300; H.T.J., Note added after 'Jan. 27', 1907, p. 131; Helen Tufts Bailie to Agnes Inglis, 10 May 1945, L.C.

83. H.T.J., Note added after 'Jan. 27', 1907, p. 131; on Gilliard's book, Robert Gilliard to Edward Carpenter, 2 January 1905, MS 271-90, C.C.; 'The Late Mr Gilliard', Cutting, *Western Daily Mail*, 22 November 1921, Bristol Socialist Society Scrapbook B19561, Samuel Bale Collection, Bristol Central Library.

84. H.T.J., Note added after 'Jan. 27', 1907, pp. 131–2.

85. Kumari Jayawardena, *Doreen Wickremasinghe: A Western Radical in Sri Lanka*, pamphlet, Women's Education & Research Centre, Colombo, 1991, pp. 6–11; W. Young, *Robert Weare, An Appreciation, and Four of His Essays*, pamphlet [For Private Circulation], printed by the Cooperative Wholesale Society, Manchester, no date, Y9137516, Bristol Central Library.

86. H.T.J., Note added after 'Jan. 27', 1907, p. 132.

87. Helen Tufts to Horace Traubel and Anne Montgomerie, 30 September 1907, L. of C., c. 104; on 'The Eagle Street College', see Robertson, *Worshipping Walt*, pp. 198–231; Paul Salveson, 'Loving Comrades: Lancashire's Links to Walt Whitman', W.W.Q.R., Vol. 14, Nos. 2–3, Fall 1996/Winter 1997; Paul Salveson, *With Walt Whitman in Bolton: Spirituality, Sex and Socialism in a Northern Mill Town*, Huddersfield: Little Northern Books, 2008.

88. Tufts to the Traubels, 30 September 1907, L. of C., c. 104.

89. On Charles Sixsmith, see Rowbotham, *Edward Carpenter*, pp. 184–5, 450.

90. Tufts to the Traubels, 30 September 1907, L. of C., c. 104.

91. Robertson, *Worshipping Walt*, pp. 278–9.

92. Tufts to the Traubels, 30 September 1907, L. of C., c.104.

93. Helen Tufts to Charles Sixsmith, 5 November 1907 (letter inserted in copy of ed. Tufts, W.I.D., John Rylands Library, Manchester).

94. Tufts to the Traubels, 30 September 1907, L. of C., c. 104.

95. H.T.J., Note added after 'Jan. 27', 1907, p. 132.

20. *Political Reorientation and a New Arrival: 1907–1914*

1. William Bailie to John B. Andrews, 4 December 1907, Un-catalogued Manuscript, L.C.

2. See Sidney Fine, 'Richard T. Ely, Forerunners of Progressivism 1880–1901', *The Mississippi Valley Historical Review*, Vol. 37, No. 4, March 1951, pp. 604–5; Selig Perlman, 'John Rogers Commons', *American Economic Review*, Vol. 35, No. 4, September 1945, pp. 783–4; Richard A. Gonce, 'John R. Commons, "Five Big Years", 1899–1904', *American Journal of Economics and Sociology*, Vol. 61, No. 4, October 2002, pp. 760–4.

3. On Filene, see Gerald W. Johnson, *Liberal's Progress: Edward A. Filene, Shopkeeper to Social Statesman*, New York: Coward-McCann, 1948, pp. 48–59, 100; James A. Merino, 'Co-operative Schemes for Greater Boston, 1890–1920', *The New England Quarterly*, Vol. 45, No. 2, June 1972, p. 214; Kim McQuaid, 'An American Owenite: Edward A. Filene and the Parameters of Industrial Reform, 1890–1937', *American Journal of Economics and Sociology*, Vol. 35, No. 1, January 1976, p. 80; Kim McQuaid, *A Response to Industrialism: Liberal Businessmen and the Evolving Spectrum of Capitalist Reform, 1886–1960*, Washington, DC: Beard Books, 1986, pp. 50–97; on Boston Municipal Politics see, see Richard Heath, 'Woodbourne and the Boston 1915 Movement', Jamaica Plain Historical Society, online at jphs.org, accessed 09/05/2014; James J. Connolly, *The Triumph of Ethnic Progressivism: Urban Political Culture in Boston, 1900–1925*, Cambridge, MA: Harvard University Press, 1998, pp. 39–41.

4. George R. Nutter, 'The Boston City Charter', *National Municipal Review*, Vol. 2, Issue 4, October 1913, p. 588; Charles Phillips Huse, *The Financial History of Boston from May 1, 1822 to January 31, 1909*, Harvard Economic Studies, Vol. xv, Cambridge, MA: Harvard University Press, 1916, pp. 332–8; Connolly, *The Triumph of Ethnic Progressivism*, pp. 81–109; Frank Washburn Grinnell, 'George Read Nutter', *Proceedings of the Massachusetts Historical Society*, Vol. 68, October 1944–May 1947, p. 460.

5. Connolly, *The Triumph of Ethnic Progressivism*, pp. 80–99; Harvey N. Shepard, 'The Boston Finance Commission', *Proceedings of the American Political Science Association*, Vol. 5, Fifth Annual Meeting, 1908, pp. 122–30.

6. H.T.J., 30 November 1908, p. 143.

7. H.T.J., 21 January 1908, p. 135.

8. H.T.J., 10 February 1908, p. 135.

9. H.T.J., 22 December 1908, p. 143; on J.G. Phelps and Rose Pastor Stokes, see Rosalyn Fraad Baxandall, ed., *Words on Fire: The Life and Writing of Elizabeth Gurley Flynn*, New Brunswick: Rutgers University Press, 1987, pp. 173, 180.

10. H. Hamilton, 'The Evolution of a Subversive Tradition', in Coughlin et al., *Benjamin R. Tucker*, pp. 14–17.

11. H.T.J., 21 March 1908, p. 136.

12. H.T.J., 14 March 1908, p. 136.

13. H.T.J., 12 November 1908, p. 142.

14. See H.T.J., 14, 16, 29 February, 1, 22 March, 5 April 1908, p. 136; 24 May 1908, p. 137; on the fiddle, 25 June 1908, p. 139; on the safe, 26 May 1908, p. 137.

15. Copy of Helen Tufts to Sarah Holmes, in H.T.J., 17 June 1908, p. 137.

16. Tufts to Holmes in H.T.J., 17 June 1908, p. 138.

17. Tufts to Holmes in H.T.J., 17 June 1908, p. 138.

18. H.T.J., 22 January 1908, p. 135; 17 March 1908, p. 136; 24 April 1908, p. 136.

19. H.T.J., 3, 12 July 1908, p. 139.

20. H.T.J., 13 June 1908, p. 137.

21. H.T.J., 30, 31 October 1908, p. 141.

22. Copy of Helen Tufts to May Hurd, in H.T.J., 16 November 1908, p. 142.

23. H.T.J., 1 January 1909, p. 144.

24. H.T.J., 28 June, 3, 7 July 1908, p. 139.

25. H.T.J., 26 July 1908, p. 139.

26. H.T.J., 18, 30 August, 14 September 1908, p. 140.

27. William Bailie, *An Inquiry into Boston's Water Supply and Its Relation to the Public*

Health, with some startling Facts about the Pollution of Sources of Supply, pamphlet, Press of E. L. Grimes, Boston, 1909, H.B.P. (I am grateful to David Sachs for details of the contents.)

28. Bailie, *An Inquiry*, pp. 6–8, 16.
29. Bailie, *An Inquiry*, p. 19.
30. Bailie, *An Inquiry*, p. 24.
31. Bailie, *An Inquiry*, pp. 4–5, 12, 24. On the background, see 'Water Filter', Wikipedia; Sarah S. Elkind, *Bay Cities and Water Politics: The Battle for Resources in Boston and Oakland*, Lawrence: University Press of Kansas, 1998, pp. 79–95, 113.
32. H.T.J., 7 January 1909, p. 144; 21 January 1909, p. 145.
33. H.T.J., 12, 13, 14, 15, 21 January 1909, pp. 144–5.
34. Justin Kaplan, *Lincoln Steffens: A Biography*, New York: Simon and Schuster, 1974, pp. 116–72; Stanley K. Schultz, 'The Morality of Politics: The Muckrakers' Vision of Democracy', *The Journal of American History*, Vol. 52, No. 3, December 1965, pp. 531, 534–7, 540–2; Connolly, *The Triumph of Ethnic Progressivism*, pp. 77–104.
35. H.T.J., 20 January 1909, p. 145.
36. Kaplan, *Lincoln Steffens*, p. 132.
37. H.T.J., 20, 21 January 1909, p. 145.
38. H.T.J., 8 February 1909, p. 147.
39. H.T.J., 4, 7 May 1909, p. 154.
40. H.T.J., 26 July 1909, p. 159.
41. H.T.J., 4 August 1909, p. 159.
42. *Annual Report of the Metropolitan Water and Sewerage Board, Ninth Annual Report for the Year 1909*, Boston: Wright and Potter, 1910, p. 105; on Dug Pond see p. 107.
43. H.T.J., 2 March 1909, p. 149; 2, 3 June 1909, p. 155.
44. See Heath, 'Woodbourne and the Boston 1915 Movement', online at jphs.org; Johnson, *Filene*, pp. 89–115; Connolly, *The Triumph of Ethnic Progressivism*, pp. 39–41; Kaplan, *Lincoln Steffens*, pp. 167–72.
45. On the differing strands in Progressivism see John Whiteclay Chambers II, *The Tyranny of Change: America in the Progressive Era, 1890–1920*, New Brunswick: Rutgers University Press, 2001, pp. 132–57.
46. H.T.J., 24 January 1909, p. 145; on Robins, see Allen F. Davis, 'Raymond Robins, The Settlement Workers as Municipal Reformer', *Social Service Review*, Vol. 33, No. 2, June 1959, pp. 131–41; Angela John, *Elizabeth Robins: Shaping a Life, 1862–1952*, London: Routledge, 1995, pp. 121–38.
47. I am grateful to David Sachs for this information.
48. H.T.J., 29 September 1909, p. 165.
49. 'Boston 1915 Exhibition', *Art and Progress*, Vol. 1, No. 1, November 1909, p. 22.
50. On Storrow and Fitzgerald, see Connolly, *The Triumph of Ethnic Progressivism*, pp. 99–103; Peter K. Eisinger, 'Ethnic Political Transition in Boston, 1884–1933', *Political Science Quarterly*, Vol. 93, No. 2, Summer 1978, pp. 232–3.
51. H.T.J., 22 February 1909, p. 148; on N.A.W.S.A. and Shaw, see Gerda Lerner, *The Woman in American History*, Menlo Park, CA: Addison-Wesley Publishing Co., 1971, pp. 159–62.
52. H.T.J., 23 February 1909, p. 148; on socialist and militant currents in U.S. suffrage, see Temma Kaplan, 'On the Socialist Origins of International Women's Day', *Feminist Studies*, Vol. 11, No. 1, Spring 1985, pp. 164–6; Ellen Carol DuBois, *Harriot Stanton Blatch*, New Haven: Yale University Press, 1997, pp. 92–121; Sharon Hartman Strom,

'Leadership and Tactics in the American Woman Suffrage Movement', *The Journal of American History*, Vol. 62, No. 2, September 1975, pp. 306–13.

53. H.T.J., 22 March 1909, p. 150.

54. Charlotte Perkins Gilman, 'The Suffragists and Socialists Demand Votes for Women', *Call*, 1 March 1909, quoted in Kaplan, 'On the Socialist Origins of International Woman's Day', p. 166.

55. N.A.A.C.P. was originally the National Negro Committee. On O'Reilly, see Annelise Orleck, *Common Sense and a Little Fire: Women and Working-Class Politics in the United States, 1900–1965*, Chapel Hill: University of North Carolina Press, 1995, pp. 43–4, 59, 75, 91–102; 'Edward Russell', Wikipedia.

56. Sharon Hartman Strom, 'Florence Luscomb: For Suffrage, Labor and Peace', in Ellen Cantarow, ed., *Moving the Mountain: Women Working for Social Change*, Old Westbury, NY: The Feminist Press, 1980, pp. 15–17; Strom, 'Leadership and Tactics', pp. 304–11.

57. H.T.J., 26 July 1909, p. 159.

58. Strom, 'Leadership and Tactics', pp. 311–12. Back in Bristol, among those drawn to suffrage was a 'Mrs E.T. Daniel'. She was part of a W.S.P.U. contingent on the suffrage demonstration in London in June 1910, see 'Twenty-Five Years Ago', *Western Daily Press*, 13 June 1935.

59. H.T.J., 26 July 1909, p. 159.

60. H.T.J., Boston, Friday, 3 September 1909, p. 132a.

61. H.T.J., 21 September 1909, p. 164.

62. H.T.J., 30 June 1909, p. 159. The uprising was in the last week in July and the date of this entry, which is inserted between July 26 and August 4, is thus most probably July 30.

63. H.T.J., 10 October 1932, p. 336. This collection of material on Ferrer was later donated by Helen to the Labadie Collection. On the background, see Dolors Marin Silvestre, 'Barcelona July 1909: A City in Flames. Tragic week and the murder of Ferre', Kate Sharpley Library, online at katesharpleylibrary.net, accessed 7/09/2014; Falk, Pateman, Moran, *Emma Goldman, Volume 2*, pp. 520–1.

64. H.T.J., 5, 14, 24 February 1910, pp. 181–2.

65. H.T.J., 21 June 1910, p. 192.

66. H.T.J., 21 June 1910, p. 192. On Goldman and Ferrer, see Candace Falk, *Love, Anarchy and Emma Goldman*, New York: Holt, Rinehart and Winston, 1984, pp. 112–13; Avrich, *Anarchist Voices*, pp. 191–3.

67. H.T.J., 8 February 1911, p. 195; H.T.J., 10 October 1932, p. 336; Helen Tufts Bailie to Agnes Inglis, 15 May 1945, L.C.

68. See Leonard D. Abbott, ed., *Francisco Ferrer: His Life, Work and Martyrdom*, New York: Francisco Ferrer Association, 1910.

69. H.T.J., 14 June 1910, p. 191.

70. H.T.J., 18 February 1910, p. 184.

71. H.T.J., 9 October 1910, p. 194; on Fitzgerald's appeal to Boston's Irish Community, see Connolly, *The Triumph of Ethnic Progressivism*, pp. 98–104.

72. Kaplan, *Lincoln Steffens*, pp. 175–6; Johnson, *Liberal's Progress*, pp. 106–11.

73. On the 'City Beautiful', see Mel Scott, *American City Planning Since 1890*, Chicago: American Planning Association, 1995, pp. 47–109; William H. Wilson, *The City Beautiful Movement*, Baltimore: Johns Hopkins University Press, 1989, p. 79; Mary Ritter Beard, *Woman's Work in Municipalities*, New York: Arno Press, 1972 (1st edition

1915), pp. 300–7; Rowbotham, *Dreamers of a New Day*, pp. 125–47; John Nolen, 'City Planning and Civic Consciousness', *New Boston*, Vol. 2, No. 1, May 1911, p. 7; on Unwin, see Walter L. Creese, *The Legacy of Raymond Unwin: A Human Pattern for Planning*, Cambridge, MA: M.I.T. Press 1967, pp. 1–14; see also Mark Swenarton, *Artisans and Architects: The Ruskinian Tradition in Architectural Thought*, London: Macmillan, 1989.

74. H.T.J., 11 May 1911, p. 197.

75. William Bailie, 'Unwin, City Builder', *Boston Evening Transcript*, 6 May 1911.

76. H.T.J., 11 May 1911, p. 197.

77. William Bailie, 'Notes and Comment', *New Boston*, Vol. 2, No. 3, July 1911, pp. 87–8.

78. William Bailie, 'Comprehensive City Planning', *New Boston*, Vol. 2, No. 7, November 1911, pp. 229, 231, 232.

79. Bailie, 'Comprehensive City Planning', p. 232.

80. Bailie, 'Comprehensive City Planning', p. 230.

81. Bailie, 'Comprehensive City Planning', p. 232.

82. Bailie, 'Unwin, City Builder'.

83. H.T.J., 11 May 1911, p. 197.

84. H.T.J., 9 November 1911, p. 209; see John McCannon, 'Passageways to Wisdom: Nicolas Roerich, the Dramas of Maurice Maeterlinck and Symbols of Spiritual Enlightenment', *Russian Review*, Vol. 63, No. 3, July 2004, pp. 450–6, 460–3.

85. H.T.J., 5 September 1911, p. 206.

86. William Bailie to Miss MacGill, 26 January 1911, Typed copy, L.C.

87. Helen Tufts Bailie to Agnes Inglis, 22 June 1944, L.C.

88. H.T.J., 8 June 1911, p. 199; 23 June 1913, p. 243. Mrs James Storrow was Helen Osborne Storrow, and Boston Women's City Club, formed in 1912, aimed to promote solidarity among women and welfare in the city. Records of the Women's City Club of Boston 1913–1992, A Finding Aid, Schlesinger Library, Radcliffe Institute for Advanced Study, Harvard University, online at http://oasis.lib.harveard.edu, accessed 25/5/2014.

89. H.T.J., 21 November 1912, p. 227.

90. H.T.J., 7 September 1911, p. 207; H.T.J., 25 November 1911, p. 210; H.T.J., 14 December 1912, p. 228.

91. Helen Tufts Bailie to Leonard Abbott, copy in H.T.J., 1 January 1913, p. 230.

92. Tufts Bailie to Abbott, copy in H.T.J., 1 January 1913, p. 230; on Abbott and the Modern School, Maurice Hollod in Avrich, *Anarchist Voices*, pp. 204–8.

93. Tufts Bailie to Abbott, copy in H.T.J., 1 January 1913, p. 230.

94. H.T.J., 2 December 1913, p. 256.

95. H.T.J., 20 June 1912, p. 214.

96. H.T.J., 23 June 1912, p. 243.

97. H.T.J., 23 June 1913, p. 243.

98. H.T.J., 22 January 1913, p. 231.

99. H.T.J., 24 March 1913, p. 238.

100. H.T.J., 23 June 1913, p. 243.

101. H.T.J., 23 June 1913, p. 243.

102. H.T.J., 9 August 1913, p. 246.

103. H.T.J., 9 August 1913, p. 246.

104. H.T.J., 6 January 1914, p. 1.

21. Elusive Realities: 1908–1914

1. Lardner and Brock, *History of Placer and Nevada Counties*, pp. 213–16; 'Pages of the Past – Roseville Railroad History is Recalled', *Roseville Press-Tribune*, 21 March 1955; 'The Big Move', *Roseville Press-Tribune*, 6 May 2006; 'Railroad is Sound History of Roseville', *Sacramento Bee*, 23 August 1989; newspaper accounts submitted by Kathie Marynik, online at http://genealogytrails.com/cal/placer, accessed 23/01/2013. For a detailed history of Southern Pacific and its impact, see Richard J. Orsi, *Sunset Limited: Building the Southern Pacific Railroad and the Development of the American West 1850–1930*, Berkeley: University of California Press, 2005.

2. Deed, 24 June 1909; filed for record at the request of Wells Fargo Co., 29 June 1909; Placer County Archives and Research Center, Auburn.

3. UK Incoming Passenger Lists, 1878–1960.

4. Amaryllis Nicol Cabell, interviewed by Georges Rey, Nicol Tapes, R. P.

5. Margot de Silva, interviewed by Georges Rey, Nicol Tapes, R.P.

6. Eldred, 'People Are More Important Than Happenings', Typed MS, p. 6, Leslie Gelb and R.P.

7. Eldred, 'People Are More Important Than Happenings', Typed MS, p. 6, Leslie Gelb and R.P.

8. Amaryllis Nicol Cabell, interviewed by Georges Rey, Nicol Tapes, R.P.

9. Gertrude Dix, 'Manzanita', *Sunset*, Vol. 26, 1911, p. 324.

10. Gertrude Dix, 'Van Velsor's Apotheosis', *The Red Book Magazine*, June 1907, p. 199; Gertrude Dix, 'One Touch of Nature', *The Red Book Magazine*, June 1909, p. 258.

11. Robert A. Nicol, Letter to *The New Age*, Vol. VI, No. 19, 10 March 1910, p. 455.

12. Nicol, Letter to *The New Age*, p. 455. On the suffrage movement in 1910, see Joyce Marlow, *Votes for Women*, London: Virago, 2000, pp. 120–2; Martin Pugh, *The Pankhursts*, London: Allen Lane, 2001, pp. 205–33; Barbara Winslow, *Sylvia Pankhurst*, London: St. Martin's Press, London, 1996, pp. 9–25.

13. Emily Alice Haigh, *The New Age*, Vol. VI, No. 12, 20 January 1910, p. 273. See also Vol. VI, No. 14, 3 February 1910, p. 316. On Haigh/Hastings, see John Carswell, *Lives and Letters: A.R. Orage, Katherine Mansfield, Beatrice Hastings, John Middleton Murry, S.S. Koteliansky, 1906–1957*, New York: A New Directions Book, 1978, pp. 28–30, 59–60; on her time in Paris bohemian circles, Dan Franck, *The Bohemians*, London: Weidenfeld & Nicolson, 2001, pp. 220, 261.

14. 'D. Triformis', *The New Age*, Vol. VI, No. 18, 3 March 1910, p. 415. On Hastings and Feminism, see Lucy Delap, *The Feminist Avant-Garde: Transatlantic Encounters of the Early Twentieth Century*, Cambridge: Cambridge University Press, 2007, pp. 45, 56, 88, 158, 162, 318.

15. Carswell, *Lives and Letters*, pp. 64–5; Tom Steele, *Alfred Orage and the Leeds Arts Club, 1893–1923*, Aldershot: Scolar Press, 1990, pp. 45–61.

16. New York Passenger Lists 1820–1957, Record for Phyllis Snaith, 1 October 1910; 1911 England Census, Miriam Sunrise Nicol.

17. 'Bournemouth High School', *Hampshire and Isle of Wight Illustrated*, Bournemouth: W. Mate and Sons, 1905, p. 118, Bournemouth Reference Library.

18. 'Bournemouth High School', *Hampshire and Isle of Wight Illustrated*, p. 118.

19. *The Jubliee Book, Bournemouth High School, Talbot Heath, 1886–1946*, Bournemouth, 1946, pp. 19, 40–2, Bournemouth Reference Library.

20. *The Jubilee Book, Bournemouth High School*, p. 98.

21. F.M. Talconis, 'Russians at Tuckton', University of Southampton, Bournemouth Education Committee Workers Educational Association Leaflet, no. 77, March 1969, Bournemouth Reference Library; Nick Churchill, 'Viva lford: Bournemouth's radical Russian printers', *The Dorset Magazine*, September 2012, online at dorsetlife.co.uk, accessed 24/01/2013. On links to Carpenter, see Rowbotham, *Edward Carpenter*, p. 348.

22. New York Passenger Lists, 1820–1957, Record for Miriam Sunrise Nicol, 18 August 1911; Indenture and Deed of Trust between Robert A. Nicol and Gertrude Mary Dix Nicol and Mrs R.J. McChesney, witnessed by W. J. Prewett, 25 November 1912, Placer County Archives and Research Center, Auburn.

23. Eldred, 'People Are More Important Than Happenings', Typed MS, p. 6, Leslie Gelb and R.P.; Margot de Silva, interviewed by Georges Rey, Nicol Tapes, R.P.; Barbara Donnelly, telephone interview with Sheila Rowbotham, 20 July 2009; Georges Rey, email to Sheila Rowbotham, 21 September 2009.

24. Eldred, 'People Are More Important Than Happenings', Typed MS, p. 6, Leslie Gelb and R.P.

25. Robert Dix Nicol, Margot de Silva and Amaryllis Nicol Cabell, interviewed by Georges Rey, Nicol Tapes, R.P.

26. Amaryllis Nicol Cabell, interviewed by Georges Rey, Nicol Tapes, R.P. On Isadora Duncan, see also Gertrude Dix, 'To Isadora Duncan, Iphigenia in Aulis', *The New Age*, Vol. XXIII, No. 10, 4 July 1918, p. 160.

27. Robert Dix Nicol, Amaryllis Nicol Cabell, interviewed by Georges Rey, Nicol Tapes, R.P.

28. Amaryllis Nicol Cabell, interviewed by Georges Rey, Nicol Tapes, R.P.

29. De Silva, 'Her Father's Daughter' (H.F.D.), Typed MS, no date, pp. 24, 38–9, R.P.

30. De Silva, H.F.D., pp. 16, 38–9, 27.

31. Aunt Hilda quoted by Amaryllis Nicol Cabell, interviewed by Georges Rey, Nicol Tapes, R.P.

32. Amaryllis Nicol Cabell, interviewed by Georges Rey, Nicol Tapes, R.P.; on Robert Singleton Garnett, see Johnson, *Olive and Stepniak*, p. xii.

33. Amaryllis Nicol Cabell, interviewed by Georges Rey, Nicol Tapes, R.P.

34. Juliet Wartnaby Dix's death was 26 September 1913.

35. Incoming Passenger Lists New York, Gertrude Dix Nicol; Amaryllis Nicol Cabell, interviewed by Georges Rey, Nicol Tapes, R.P.

36. 'Dix, Gertrude (Mrs Nicol)', *The Literary Year Book*, 1912, p. 127.

37. Gertrude Dix, 'The Metamorphosis of a Toy Soldier', *Taunton Courier and Western Advertiser*, 12 August 1914.

38. Gertrude Dix, Letter to *The New Age*, Vol. XVI, No. 16, 18 February 1915, p. 439.

39. Amaryllis Nicol Cabell, interviewed by Georges Rey, Nicol Tapes, R.P.

40. Eldred, 'People Are More Important Than Happenings', Typed MS, p. 6, Leslie Gelb and R.P.

41. De Silva, H.F.D., pp. 89–90.

42. De Silva, H.F.D., pp. 46–47.

43. Robert Dix Nicol, Margot de Silva and Amaryllis Nicol Cabell, interviewed by Georges Rey, Nicol Tapes, R.P.

44. Margot de Silva, interviewed by Georges Rey, Nicol Tapes, R.P.

45. Amaryllis Nicol Cabell, interviewed by Georges Rey, Nicol Tapes, R.P.

46. De Silva, H.F.D., p. 4.

47. De Silva, H.F.D., p. 22.
48. De Silva, H.F.D., p. 41.
49. De Silva, H.F.D., p. 4.
50. De Silva, H.F.D., p. 65.
51. De Silva, H.F.D., p. 47.
52. De Silva, H.F.D., pp. 100–1.
53. De Silva, H.F.D., p. 78.
54. De Silva, H.F.D., p. 5.
55. De Silva, H.F.D., p. 90.
56. De Silva, H.F.D., pp. 68–9.
57. De Silva, H.F.D., p. 90.
58. De Silva, H.F.D., p. 51.
59. De Silva, H.F.D., p. 155.
60. De Silva, H.F.D., p. 156.
61. De Silva, H.F.D., pp. 7, 156.
62. De Silva, H.F.D., pp.155–7.
63. De Silva, H.F.D., pp. 205, 238.
64. De Silva, H.F.D., p. 213.
65. De Silva, H.F.D., p. 205.
66. De Silva, H.F.D., p. 40.
67. De Silva, H.F.D., p. 161.
68. De Silva, H.F.D., p. 205.
69. De Silva, H.F.D., p. 102.
70. De Silva, H.F.D., p. 102.
71. Margot de Silva, interviewed by Georges Rey, Nicol Tapes, R.P.; a notice of the marriage is in *Lincoln News Messenger*, 20 February 1914; 'Harley Lee', 1920 U.S. Census, Residents of Roseville, Placer County, California; Indenture between R.A. Nicol and Gertrude Mary Dix Nicol and Aubrey L. Wisker, 8 August 1914, Placer County Archives and Research Center, Auburn.

22. *Loose Endings*

1. U.S. Census, 1920; Harley Lee.
2. Margot de Silva, interviewed by Georges Rey, Nicol Tapes, R.P.
3. Cheyenne Wyoming City Directory, 1920; U.S. City Directories, 1921–1989.
4. Margot de Silva, interviewed by Georges Rey, Nicol Tapes, R.P.
5. U.S. Census, 1940; Harly Lee.
6. Margot de Silva, interviewed in the Poetry Column, *Soho News*, 22 May 1975, cutting in R.P.
7. De Silva, interviewed, *Soho News*, cutting in R.P.
8. Gertrude Dix's 'To Isadora Duncan' is marked 'S. Francisco', so she may have moved there the previous year or simply been visiting; *The New Age*, 4 July 1918, Vol. XXIII, No. 10, p. 160; Barbara Donnelly, interviewed by Sheila Rowbotham, 29 May 2011; U.S. Census, 1920; Doris Bassett; 'History of Mill Valley', Mill Valley Historical Society, cutting, no date, p. 15, R.P.; Indenture, 14 April 1921, between R.A. Nicol and Gertrude Dix Nicol and John Matrone and Maria Rangelo Matrone, Archives and Research Center, Auburn.

9. 'Dancer Makes Mill Valley Blush', *The San Francisco Examiner*, 6 May 1920, cutting in R.P.

10. *The San Francisco Examiner*, 8 May 1920, cutting in R.P.

11. Eldred, 'People Are More Important Than Happenings', Typed MS, p. 7, R.P.

12. Donnelly interviewed by Rowbotham, 29 May 2011; Cabell and De Silva interviewed by Rey, Nicol Tapes, R.P. Email from Georges Rey to Sheila Rowbotham, 28 June 2009; Eldred, 'People Are More Important Than Happenings', p. 7; Margot de Silva to Tamara Jean Nicol, 2 November 1980. (I am grateful to Leslie Gelb for this reference.)

13. On Margot: email from Georges Rey to Sheila Rowbotham, 28 June 2009; on San Francisco's Bohemia in the early 1920s, see Kenneth Rexroth, 'Bohemian San Francisco, Between the Wars', November–December 1975, Shaping San Francisco, online at shapingsf.org, accessed 05/07/2014; on women's position, see Linda Gordon, *Dorothea Lange: A Life Beyond Limits*, New York: W.W. Norton & Co., 2009, pp. 48–87; on embellishing one's past, Beth Gates Warren, *Artful Lives: Edward Weston, Margrethe Mather and the Bohemians of Los Angeles*, Los Angeles: The Getty Museum, 2011, pp. 17–19.

14. Eldred, 'People Are More Important Than Happenings', p. 6; Cabell interviewed by Rey, Nicol Tapes, R.P.

15. Bob Dix Nicol, interviewed by Rey, Nicol Tapes, R.P. Bob Nicol initially lived with a family in Laganitis and later with a farming family. Email from Barbara Donnelly to Sheila Rowbotham, 13 February 2016.

16. Cabell and De Silva, interviewed by Rey, Nicol Tapes, R.P.

17. Robert Nicol to Nora Keating, 1 March 1922, R.P.

18. I am grateful to Georges Rey and David Sachs for this information on Nora Keating.

19. Rey to Rowbotham, email, 28 June 2009.

20. Birth details for Tamara Jean Nicol, R.P.

21. Robert Nicol to Nora Keating, 24 January 1921, R.P.

22. Robert Nicol to Nora Keating, 27 November 1921, R.P.

23. Robert Nicol to Nora Keating, 1 March 1922, R.P.

24. Robert Nicol to Nora Keating, 24 April 1922, R.P.

25. Robert Nicol to Tamara Jean Nicol, no date, R.P.

26. Rey to Rowbotham, email, 28 June 2009.

27. Tamara Rey Patri, interviewed by Georges Rey, Nicol Tapes, R.P.

28. Rey to Rowbotham, email, 28 June 2009.

29. Gertrude's outburst is mentioned in Cabell and De Silva interviewed by Rey, Nicol Tapes, R.P.; Barbara Donnelly, email to Sheila Rowbotham, 7 May 2012.

30. Gertrude Dix, 'To An Idealist', *The New Age*, Vol. XXIV, No. 17, 27 February 1919, p. 271.

31. Gertrude Dix, 'To R.A.N.', Typed MS, no date, R.P.

32. Gertrude Dix to Amaryllis Nicol Cabell, 9 August 1943, R.P.

33. Gertrude Dix, 'Once More', Typed MS, no date, R.P.

34. Dix, 'Once More', R.P.

35. Dix, 'Once More', R.P.

36. Robert Nicol to Amaryllis Nicol Cabell, 26 July 1943, R.P.

37. Robert Nicol to Amaryllis Nicol Cabell, 31 December 1947, R.P.

38. Robert Allan Nicol, U.S. Naturalization Record Indexes, 1791–1992, 1440 Sutter St., San Francisco, Cal., 15 May 1950, R.P.

39. Robert Nicol to Amaryllis Nicol Cabell, 7 September 1949, R.P.

40. Gertrude Dix to Amaryllis Nicol Cabell, 7 September 1949, R.P.
41. Gertrude Dix, 'One World or None'; 'You Tell Us', Letter from 'Up-State N.Y.'; 'Our Birthday Message to Stalin', *Soviet Russia Today*, January 1950, pp. 22, 3, 5.
42. Information from David Sachs and R.P.
43. Gertrude Dix, 'Swings Wide the Gate', Typed MS, no date, R.P.
44. Certificate of Death, Gertrude Dix Nicol, October 1950, R.P.
45. Robert Nicol to Amaryllis Nicol Cabell, 7 November 1950 R.P.
46. Nicol to Cabell, 7 November 1950; Robert Nicol to Amaryllis Nicol Cabell, 8 August 1951, R.P.
47. Robert Nicol to Amaryllis Nicol Cabell, 25 March 1951, R.P.
48. Robert Nicol to Amaryllis Nicol Cabell, 22 April 1951, R.P.
49. Bob Dix Nicol to Margaret de Silva and Amaryllis Nicol Cabell, 8 July 1956, R.P.
50. I am grateful to Georges Rey's 'San Francisco's Cultural Ciopino', in email to Sheila Rowbotham, 28 June 2009, and for information from David Sachs.
51. De Silva, interviewed, *Soho News*, 22 May 1975, cutting in R.P.; I am grateful to Peggy Garrison for permission to quote her acute depiction of Margot and to Leslie Gelb for bringing it to my attention.
52. Information on Tamara Nicol Rey Patri from Georges Rey, David Sachs and material in R.P.
53. Georges Rey, 'A Memorial of Tamara Rey Patri', August 2001, in email to Sheila Rowbotham, 28 June 2009.
54. H.T.J., 26 May 1927, p. 156.
55. William Bailie, 'Ireland and Common Sense', *The Boston Sunday Globe*, 5 August 1917.
56. H.T.J., 17 December 1917, p. 194; 17 January 1919, p. 244; on the wartime context see Dawley, *Struggles for Justice*, pp. 184–228.
57. H.T.J., 2 February 1919, p. 251; on 'Marxian Socialism', 31 January 1919, p. 250.
58. Helena Bailie, in Avrich, *Anarchist Voices*, p. 15.
59. Bailie, in Avrich, *Anarchist Voices*, p. 14.
60. William Bailie, 'The Second Industrial Revolution', *The Christian Register*, Vol. 104, No. 1, 1 January 1925, p. 6.
61. Bailie, 'The Second Industrial Revolution', p. 5.
62. Bailie, 'The Second Industrial Revolution', p. 5.
63. H.T.J., 8 April 1925, p. 56.
64. H.T.J., 6 July 1925, p. 70.
65. H.T.J., 21 June 1927, p. 159.
66. H.T.J., 13 December 1927, p. 181.
67. H.T.J., 16 July 1927, p. 164.
68. H.T.J., 21 February 1957, p. 4; 19 November 1930, p. 255; 25 November 1931, p. 285.
69. Bailie, in Avrich, *Anarchist Voices*, p. 15.
70. H.T.J., 21 February 1926, p. 92.
71. H.T.J., 5 July 1926, p. 107.
72. Bailie, in Avrich, *Anarchist Voices*, p. 15. On the domestic conflict see also H.T.J., 19 September 1925, p. 75.
73. H.T.J., 16 July 1927, p. 164.
74. H.T.J., 22 March 1927, p. 142
75. H.T.J., 24 March 1927, p. 142.
76. H.T.J., 15 April 1927, p. 148; Helen Tufts 'Our Threatened Heritage: A Letter to the

Daughters of the American Revolution', 5 April 1928, Document 20, pp. 7, 9, in *Pacifism vs. Patriotism in Women's Organizations in the 1920s*, State University of New York at Binghamton, August 1998, online at http://womhist.alexanderstreet.com, accessed 14/05/2012.

77. Grace H. Brosseau, Opening Speech to the Third Women's Conference on National Defense, 1–3 February 1928, online at womhist.alexanderstreet.com, accessed 14/05/2012; Helena Huntington Smith, 'Mrs Brosseau and the D.A.R.', *Outlook and Independent*, 20 March 1929, pp. 460–3, 477–8; on the background, see Regin Schmidt, *Red Scare: FBI and the Origins of Anticommunism in the United States*, University of Copenhagen: Museum Tusculanum Press, 2000; Christine K. Erickson, '"So much for men"', Conservative Women and National Defense in the 1920s and 1930s', *American Studies*, Vol. 45, No. 1, Spring 2004; Delegard, *Battling Miss Bolsheviki*; Nielsen, *Un-American Womanhood*.

78. H.T.J., 24 March 1927, p. 142.

79. H.T.J., 7 October 1928, p. 236.

80. 'D.A.R. Drops Mrs Bailie', *New York Times*, 23 June 1928.

81. H.T.J., 17 April 1928, p. 206.

82. H.T.J., 11 July 1928, p. 217.

83. H.T.J., 7 October 1929, p. 236. 'Mr Menchell' is 'Minshall'. On Alf and Eleanor Barton, see Mathers, *Sheffield Municipal Politics, 1893–1926*, PhD, University of Sheffield, 1979, pp. 197, 205; Caminada, *Twenty-Five Years of Detective Work*, pp. 329–47; Sarah Irving, 'Alfred Barton: 19th century anarchism and the early 20th century Labour Party', 5 January 2010, online at https://radicalmanchester.wordpress.com, accessed 20/11 2014; Nick Heath, '1893: The Manchester Anarchists and the Fight for Free Speech', online at https://libcom.org/history, accessed 27/06/2015; 'Free Commune and Billy MacQueen', *Bulletin of the Kate Sharpley Library*, July 2012, pp. 1–2; George Cores, *Personal Recollections of the Anarchist Past*, pamphlet (1947), London: K.S.L. Publications, 1992, p. 9; Alderman Frank Thraves on Alfred Barton, 'Memorial Service to Edward Carpenter, July 7, 1946', pp. 9–10, Charles Frederick Sixsmith, Walt Whitman and Edward Carpenter Collection, John Rylands Library, Manchester. I am grateful to Herbert Stockton for reminding me of Frank Thraves' Appreciation. On Dan Irving, see Howell, 'Irving', *Oxford Dictionary of National Biography*, online, accessed 24/03/2010; Liddington, *The Life and Times of a Respectable Rebel*, pp. 62, 76, 113–18, 127, 131–2, 195. Crick, *The History of the Social Democratic Federation*, pp. 298, 308; on Robert Sharland, *Justice*, 10 April 1924, cutting in Bristol Socialist Society Album, Bristol Central Library, B19560, Samuel Bale Collection; see also Bryher, *Labour and Socialist Movement in Bristol* and *Minutes of the Bristol Socialist Society and Workers' Organising Committee*, B.R.O.

84. Will S. Monroe, 'Walt Whitman and other American Friends of Edward Carpenter', in Gilbert Beith, ed., *Edward Carpenter: In Appreciation*, London: George Allen & Unwin, 1931, p. 144.

85. H.T.J., 4 June 1930, p. 245c.

86. H.T.J., 17 January 1937, p. 110.

87. H.T.J., 4 February 1937, p. 115.

88. H.T.J., 16 June 1943, p. 87. See also her reflections on Simpson's politics after his death, H.T.J., 30 June 1945, p. 175. On Simpson in Britain see A.H. Simpson to George Schumm, 25 May 1935; A.H. Simpson to George Schumm, 23 August 1934, L.C.

89. A.H. Simpson to George Schumm, 13 September, no date, L.C.

90. Bertha Johnson to Agnes Inglis, 5 December 1941, L.C.

91. H.T.J., 25 January 1939, p. 222; Bailie, ed. Avrich, *Anarchist Voices*, p. 15.

92. H.T.J., 6 October 1932, p. 335.

93. H.T.J., 8 December 1938, pp. 217–18.

94. H.T.J., 12 December 1940, p. 311.

95. H.T.J., 16 June 1942, p. 29.

96. H.T.J., 21 June 1942, p. 311; Helen refers to the affair, H.T.J., 28 September 1939, p. 260.

97. H.T.J., 31 March 1943, p. 116.

98. On the ships' fenders and war money, H.T.J., 21 February 1957, p. 4; on Nantucket, H.T.J., 2 November 1945, p. 185; 15 March 1946, p. 197.

99. H.T.J., 12 May 1945, p. 172; 6 August 1945, pp. 177–8.

100. H.T.J., 24 March 1946, p. 198.

101. H.T.J., 15 July 1944, p. 125; Helen Tufts Bailie to Agnes Inglis, 21 April 1948; Helen Tufts Bailie to Agnes Inglis, 7 July 1948, L.C.

102. H.T.J., 16 July 1927, p. 164; 31 December 1941, p. 361.

103. H.T.J., 14 August 1953, p. 59; 12 September 1957, p. 1.

104. Helen Tufts Bailie, *My Darling Daughter*, New York: Greenwich Book Publishers, 1956.

105. H.T.J., 29 June 1957, p. 11.

106. H.T.J., 21 May 1958, no page nos.

107. H.T.J., 12 May 1958, no page nos.

108. H.T.J., 21 May 1958, no page nos.

109. H.T.J., 23 April 1959, no page nos.

110. Biographical Note, Helen Tufts Bailie Papers, Sophia Smith Collection, Smith College. I am grateful to Christine Ann Bailie Jolly for information on Helen's burial.

111. Christine Ann Bailie Jolly, interviewed on the telephone by Sheila Rowbotham, 2009.

Bibliography

Archives Consulted

Alexander Ellis (Ellis Family), Library of the Religious Society of Friends, Friends House.

American Woman Suffrage Association Records, Massachusetts Suffrage Associations, Library of Congress.

Angela Tuckett manuscript and papers on Enid Stacy, Working Class Movement Library.

Bailie family historical material from Christine Ann Bailie Jolly.

Basketry, Manuscript and Pamphlet File, National Anthropological Archives and Human Studies, United States National Museum, Smithsonian Institution.

Benjamin R. Tucker Papers, New York Public Library, Manuscripts and Archives Division, Astor, Lenox and Tilden Foundations.

Bolton Whitman Fellowship Collection, Bolton Library.

Boston Anarchist Club, Wisconsin Historical Society.

Bournemouth High School, Bournemouth Library.

Bristol and West of England Society for Women's Suffrage, Women's Library/London School of Economics.

Bristol Church Records, Bristol Record Office.

Bristol Socialist Society Album and Scrapbook, Bristol Reference Library.

Bristol Socialist Society and Workers' Organising Committee Minutes, Bristol Record Office.

Bristol Women's Liberal Association Reports, Bristol Reference Library.

Carpenter Collection, Sheffield Archives.

Cecil Reddie Letters, National Library of Scotland.

Charles Frederick Sixsmith, Walt Whitman and Edward Carpenter Collection, John Rylands Library, Deansgate, University of Manchester.

Charles Hodge Papers and Henry Van Dyke Family Papers, Princeton University Library Manuscripts Division, Department of Rare Books and Special Collections.

Charlotte Perkins Gilman Papers, Schlesinger Library, Radcliffe Institute.

Clifton College, Clifton College Archives.

Divorce Court Minutes, National Archives.

Elizabeth Porter Gould Papers, Boston Public Library.

Emma Goldman Papers, UC Berkeley.

Estlin Family Papers, Dr Williams's Library, London.

Fabian Papers, London School of Economics.

Fife Traders, Dunfermline Public Library.

Fowl House, Surrey History Centre.

Glasier Papers, Special Collections, Liverpool University Library.

Harry Lyman Koopman Papers, Special Collections, Brown University Library.

Havelock Ellis Papers, British Library.

Helen Priestman Bright Clark Papers, Clark Family Papers, Street.

Helen Tufts Bailie letters to Will S. Monroe, Department of Special Collections, Stanford University Libraries.

Helen Tufts Bailie Papers, Sophia Smith Collection, Smith College, Northampton, Mass.

Helena Born Papers, Tamiment Library and Robert F. Wagner Labor Archives, New York University.

Horace Traubel and Anne Montgomerie Traubel Papers and Gustave Percy Wiksell Collection, Library of Congress.

John Gregory Papers, Special Collections, University of Bristol.

Joseph A. Labadie Collection, Special Collections, University of Michigan.

Josephine Butler Letters, Women's History Library, London School of Economics.

Matriculation Records, University of Edinburgh.

Patrick Geddes Collection, Department of Special Collections, University of Strathclyde.

Placer County Museums and Archives, Deeds and Newspaper Cuttings.

Raymond Unwin Papers, Kantorowich Library, John Rylands Library, Manchester University.

Rey Papers, Georges Rey, Private Collection.

Robert Allan Nicol, Letters to Patrick Geddes, National Library of Scotland.

Socialist League Papers, International Institute for Social History, Amsterdam.

Sydney Olivier Papers, Rhodes House, University of Oxford.

Unitarian Church Records, Harris Manchester College, University of Oxford.

Unitarian Letterbooks, Grindall Reynolds Papers, Andover-Harvard Theological Library.

Walt Whitman Collection in the Charles E. Feinberg Collection, Library of Congress.

Women's Liberal Association Papers, Special Collections, University of Bristol.

Select Bibliography

Abbott, Leonard D. (ed.), *Francisco Ferrer: His Life, Work and Martrydom*, New York: Francisco Ferrer Association, 1910.

Abrams, Lynn, Gordon, Eleanor, Simonton, Deborah and Yeo, Eileen (eds), *Gender in Scottish History*, Edinburgh: Edinburgh University Press, 2006.

Alexander, Benjamin F., *Coxey's Army: Popular Protest in the Gilded Age*, Baltimore: Johns Hopkins University Press, 2015.

Armytage, W.H.G., *Heavens Below: Utopian Experiments in England 1560–1960*, London: Routledge and Kegan Paul, 1961.

Avrich, Paul (ed.), *Anarchist Voices*, Edinburgh: AK Press, 2005.

Avrich, Paul, *The Haymarket Tragedy*, Princeton: Princeton University Press, 1984.

Backwith, Dave, Ball, Roger, Hunt, Stephen E. and Richardson, Mike (eds), *Strikers, Hobblers, Conchies and Reds: A Radical History of Bristol, 1880–1939*, London: Breviary Stuff Publications, 2014.

Bailie, Helen Tufts, *My Darling Daughter*, New York: Greenwich Book Publishers, 1956.

Bailie, William, *Josiah Warren: The First American Anarchist: A Sociological Study*, Boston: Small, Maynard and Co. 1906.

Bailie, William, *Problems of Anarchism: Property, Labor and Competition* (1893), booklet prepared by Charles Johnson, Alliance of the Libertarian Left, 2011 and 2013, Las Vegas, Nevada.

Barrow, Logie and Bullock, Ian, *Democratic Ideas and the British Labour Movement, 1880–1914*, Cambridge: Cambridge University Press, 1996.

Beard, Mary Ritter, *Woman's Work in Municipalities*, New York: Arno Press, 1972.

Beaumont, Matthew, *Utopia Ltd: Ideologies of Social Dreaming in England, 1870–1900*, Chicago: Haymarket Books, 2009.

Bedford, Henry F., *Socialism and the Workers in Massachusetts, 1886–1912*, Amherst: University of Massachusetts Press, 1966.

Beith, Gilbert (ed.), *Edward Carpenter: In Appreciation*, London: George Allen & Unwin, 1931.

Bild, Ian, *Bristol's Other History*, Bristol: Bristol Broadsides Co-op, 1983.

Blatt, Martin Henry, *Free Love and Anarchism: The Biography of Ezra Heywood*, Urbana: University of Illinois Press, 1989.

Boardman, Philip, *The Worlds of Patrick Geddes*, London: Routledge & Kegan Paul, 1978.

Braude, Ann, *Radical Spirits: Spiritualism and Women's Rights in Nineteenth-Century America*, Bloomington: Indiana University Press, 2001.

Bristol Socialist Society, *Labour Songs*, London: The Twentieth Century Press, no date, c. 1889–90.

Brogan, Hugh, *The Penguin History of the United States*, London: Penguin Books, 1990.

Bryher, Samuel, *An Account of the Labour and Socialist Movement in Bristol*, Bristol: Bristol Labour Weekly, 1929.

Buhle, Mari Jo, *Women and American Socialism, 1870–1920*, Urbana: University of Illinois Press, 1983.

Buhle, Mari Jo, Buhle, Paul and Georgakas, Dan, *Encyclopedia of the American Left*, Chicago: University of Illinois Press, 1992.

Butler, H.E., *The Seven Creative Principles*, Boston: Esoteric Publishing Company, 1887.

Butterworth, Alex, *The World That Never Was: A True Story of Dreamers, Schemers, Anarchists and Secret Agents*, London: The Bodley Head, 2010.

Caminada, Jerome, *Twenty-Five Years of Detective Work*, Manchester: John Heywood, 1895.

Carpenter, Edward (ed.), *Chants of Labour*, London: George Allen & Unwin, London, 1888.

Carpenter Edward, *Civilisation: Its Cause and Cure*, London: Swan Sonnenschein, 1889.

Carpenter, Edward, *Ioläus: A History of Friendship*, London: Swan Sonnenschein, 1906.

Carpenter Edward, *Love's Coming of Age*, Manchester: Labour Press, 1896.

Carpenter, Edward, *Towards Democracy*, London: George Allen & Unwin, Complete Edition, 1903, Reprinted 1913.

Carswell, John, *Lives and Letters: A.R. Orage, Katherine Mansfield, Beatrice Hastings, John Middleton Murry, S.S. Koteliansky, 1906–1957*, New York: A New Directions Book, 1978.

Chesnutt, Charles W., *The Marrow of Tradition* (1901), ed. Werner Sollors, New York: W.W. Norton & Co., 2012.

Collins, Marcus, *Modern Love*, London: Atlantic Books, 2003.

Colman, Lucy, *Reminiscences*, Buffalo, NY: H.L. Green, 1891.

Connolly, James J., *The Triumph of Ethnic Progressivism: Urban Political Culture in Boston, 1900–1925*, Cambridge, MA: Harvard University Press, 1998.

Coughlin, Michael E., Hamilton, Charles H. and Sullivan, Mark A. (eds), *Benjamin R. Tucker and the Champions of Liberty: A Centenary Anthology*, St Paul: Michael E. Coughlin and Mark Sullivan Publishers, 1986.

Crawford, Elizabeth, *The Women's Suffrage Movement: A Reference Guide, 1866–1928*, London: UCL Press, 1999.

Crick, Martin, *The History of the Social Democratic Federation*, Keele: Ryburn Publishing, 1994.

Cross, Ira Brown, *A History of the Labor Movement in California*, Berkeley: University of California Publications in Economics, 1935.

Cullinane, Michael Patrick, *Liberty and Anti-Imperialism, 1898–1909*, New York: Palgrave Macmillan, 2012.

Daniell, Miriam, *Songs of Struggle & Sorrow*, ed. Charles Johnson, Alliance of the Libertarian Left, Auburn, Alabama, 2013 (pamphlet).

Daniell, Miriam and Nicol, Robert, *The New Trade Unionism: Its Relation to the Old and the Conditions of its Success*, Bristol, 1890 (pamphlet).

Daniel [sic], Miriam and Nicoll [sic], Robert, *The Truth about the Chocolate Factories or Modern White Slavery its Cause and Cure*, Facts for the Times, Vol. 1, Bristol, no date (pamphlet).

Davis, Mary (ed.), *Class and Gender in British Labour History*, London: Merlin, 2011.

Delap, Lucy, *The Feminist Avant-Garde*, Cambridge: Cambridge University Press, 2007.

Delegard, Kirsten Marie, *Battling Miss Bolsheviki: The Origins of Female*

Conservatism in the United States, Philadelphia: University of Pennsylvania Press, 2012.

Deutsch, Sarah, *Women and the City: Gender, Space and Power in Boston, 1870–1940*, New York. Oxford University Press, 2000.

Dix, Gertrude, *The Girl from the Farm*, London: John Lane; Boston: Roberts Bros., 1895, 2nd Edition 1896.

Dix Gertrude, *The Image Breakers*, New York: Frederick A. Stokes Co., 1900.

Dixon, Joy, *Divine Feminine: Theosophy and Feminism in England*, Baltimore: Johns Hopkins University Press, Baltimore, 2001.

Dixon, Thomas, *The Invention of Altruism*, Oxford: Oxford University Press, 2008.

Donoghue, Emma, *We Are Michael Field*, Bath: Absolute Press, 1998.

Dresser, Madge (ed.), *Women and the City: Bristol 1373–2000*, Bristol: Redcliffe Press and the Regional History Centre, University of the West of England, 2016.

Dresser, Madge and Ollerenshaw, Philip (eds), *The Making of Modern Bristol*, Bristol: Redcliffe Press, 1996.

Dubois, Ellen Carol, *Harriot Stanton Blatch and the Winning of Woman Suffrage*, New Haven: Yale University Press, 1997.

Edwards, Rebecca, *New Spirits: Americans in the Gilded Age*, Oxford: Oxford University Press, 2006.

Eichengreen, Barry, *The Gold Standard in Theory and History*, New York: Methuen, 1985.

Ellis, Havelock, *The New Spirit*, London: Bell, 1890.

Ellis, Havelock, *Women and Marriage; or Evolution in Sex*, London, 1889 (pamphlet).

Falk, Candace, *Love, Anarchy and Emma Goldman*, New York: Holt, Rinehart and Winston, 1984.

Falk, Candace, Pateman, Barry and Moran, Jessica (eds.), *Emma Goldman, A Documentary History of the American Years, Volume 1: Made for America, 1890–1901* and *Volume 2, Making Speech Free, 1902–1909*, The Emma Goldman Papers, Berkeley: University of California Press, 2003, 2005.

Freeman, Joshua et al., *Who Built America?* Volume Two, New York: Pantheon Books, 1992.

Fremantle, Anne, *This Little Band of Prophets: The Story of the Gentle Fabians*, London: George Allen & Unwin, 1960.

Frenchay Village Museum, *J.S. Fry and Sons*, Bristol, 2010 (booklet).

Glage, Liselotte, *Clementina Black: A Study in Social History and Literature*, Heidelberg: Carl Winter Universitätsverlag, 1981

Gordon, Linda, *Dorothea Lange: A Life Beyond Limits*, New York: W.W. Norton & Co., 2009.

Grönlund, Laurence, *The Cooperative Commonwealth*, Boston: Lee and Shepard, 1884.

Grosskurth, Phyllis, *Havelock Ellis: A Biography*, New York: New York University Press, 1985.

Haeckel, Ernst, *The Riddle of the Universe*, London: Watts & Co., 1929.

Hannam, June, *Isabella Ford*, Oxford: Basil Blackwell, 1989.

Harris, Thomas Lake, *God's Breath in Man and in Humane Society*, Published by the Author, Fountain Grove, Santa Rosa, California, 1891.

Henrick, George, *Henry Salt: Humanitarian Reformer and Man of Letters*, Urbana: University of Illinois Press, 1977.

Hine, Robert V., *California's Utopian Colonies*, New Haven: Yale University Press, 1966.

Hollis, Patricia, *Ladies Elect: Women in English Local Government, 1865–1914*, Oxford: Oxford University Press, 1987.

Holton, Sandra Stanley, *Quaker Women: Personal Life, Memory and Radicalism in the Lives of Women Friends, 1780–1930*, London: Routledge, 2007.

Holton, Sandra Stanley, *Suffrage Days: Stories from the Women's Suffrage Movement*, London: Routledge, 1996.

Houghton, Walter E., *The Victorian Frame of Mind*, New Haven: Yale University Press, 1957.

Huse, Charles Phillips, *The Financial History of Boston from May 1, 1822 to January 31, 1909*, Harvard Economic Studies, Vol. XV, Cambridge, MA: Harvard University Press, 1916

Ingram, Angela and Patai, Daphne (eds), *Rediscovering Forgotten Radicals: British Women Writers, 1889–1939*, Chapel Hill: University of North Carolina Press, 1993.

Jackson, Holbrook, *The Eighteen Nineties: A Review of Art and Ideas at the Close of the Nineteenth Century*, London: Penguin Books, 1950.

James, Edward T., *Notable American Women: A Biographical Dictionary, 1607–1950*, Cambridge, MA: Harvard University Press, 1971.

James, George F., 'University Extension', *The Official Organ of the American Society for the Extension of University Teaching*, Vol. 2, July 1892–June 1893, Philadelphia, 1893, Reprinted ICGtesting USA, no date.

Jayawardena, Kumari, *Doreen Wickremasinghe: A Western Radical in Sri Lanka*, Women's Education & Research Centre, Colombo, 1991 (pamphlet).

Jenkins, Philip, *A History of the United States*, London: Macmillan, 1997.

John, Angela V., *War, Journalism and the Shaping of the Twentieth Century: The Life and Times of Henry Nevinson*, London: I.B. Taurus, 2006.

Johnson, Barry C. (ed.), *Tea and Anarchy: The Bloomsbury Diary of Olive Garnett, 1890–1893*, London: Bartletts Press, 1989.

Johnson, Barry C. (ed.), *Olive & Stepniak: The Bloomsbury Diary of Olive Garnett, 1893–1895*, London: Bartletts Press, 1993.

Johnson, Gerald W., *Liberal's Progress: Edward A. Filene, Shopkeeper to Social Statesman*, New York: Coward McCann, 1948.

Jones, Pat, *The Colfax Connection: A History of Colfax*, Colfax Historical Society, 1997.

Jones, Peter d'A, *The Christian Socialist Revival, 1877–1914*, Princeton: Princeton University Press, 1968.

Kaplan, Justin, *Lincoln Steffens: A Biography*, New York: Simon and Schuster, 1974.

Kapp, Yvonne, *Eleanor Marx*, Volumes 1 and 2, London: Lawrence and Wishart, 1972 and 1976.

Katz, Jonathan Ned, *Gay/Lesbian Almanac*, New York: Harper Row, 1983.

Kenefick, William, *Red Scotland: The Rise and Fall of the Radical Left, c. 1872–1932*, Edinburgh: Edinburgh University Press, 2007.

Kerr, Howard and Crow, Charles L., *The Occult in America: New Historical Perspectives*, Urbana: University of Illinois Press, 1983.

Kortsch, Christine Bayles, *Dress Culture in Late Victorian Women's Fiction: Literacy, Textiles, and Activism*, Farnham: Ashgate, 2009.

Koven, Seth, *Slumming: Sexual and Social Politics in Victorian London*, Princeton: Princeton University Press, 2004.

Lardner, W.B. and Brock, M.J., *History of Placer and Nevada Counties, California*, Los Angeles: Historical Record Co., 1924.

Ledger, Sally, *The New Woman: Fiction and Feminism at the Fin de Siècle*, Manchester: Manchester University Press, 1997.

Ledger, Sally and McCracken, Scott, *Cultural Politics at the Fin de Siècle*, Cambridge: Cambridge University Press, 1995.

Leighton, Walter, *The Leighton Family*, Newton Center, Mass., Privately Printed, 1940.

Liddington, Jill, *The Life and Times of a Respectable Rebel, Selina Cooper (1864–1946)*, London: Virago, 1984.

Lloyd, William J., *The Red Heart in a White World: A Suggestive Manual of Free Society Containing a Method and a Hope*, New York: Holland Publishing Company, 1897, 2nd Edition, The Author, Westfield, New Jersey, 1898 (pamphlet).

Lockwood, George B., *The New Harmony Movement*, New York: D. Appleton and Co. 1902, 2nd Edition, 1905.

MacCarthy, Fiona, *The Simple Life: C.R. Ashbee in the Cotswolds*, London: Lund Humphries, 1981.

McElroy, Wendy, *Individualist Feminism of the Nineteenth Century*, Jefferson, NC: McFarland & Company, 2001.

McElroy, Wendy, *The Debates of Liberty: An Overview of Individualist Anarchism, 1881–1908*, Lanham: Lexington Books, 2003.

McMath, Robert C. Jr, *American Populism: A Social History, 1877–1898*, New York: Hill and Wang, The Noonday Press, 1993.

Mann, Arthur, *Yankee Reformers in the Urban Age: Social Reform in Boston, 1880–1900*, New York: Harper & Row, 1966.

Marlow, Joyce, *Votes for Women*, London: Virago, 2000.

Martin, James J., *Men Against the State: The Expositors of Individualist Anarchism in America, 1827–1908*, Colorado Springs: Ralph Myles, 1970.

Mavor, James, *My Windows on the Street of the World*, London: J.M. Dent, 1923.

Meller, Helen, *Patrick Geddes: Social Evolutionist and City Planner*, London: Routledge, 1957.

Meller, H.E., *Leisure and the Changing City, 1870–1914*, London: Routledge & Kegan Paul, 1976.

Nielsen, Kim E., *Un-American Womanhood: Anti-radicalism, Anti-feminism and the First Red Scare*, Columbus: Ohio State University Press, 2001.

Oliver, Hermia, *The International Anarchist Movement in Late Victorian London*, London: Croom Helm, 1983.

Olivier, Margaret (ed.), *Sydney Olivier: Letters and Selected Writings*, London: George Allen & Unwin, 1948.

Orleck, Annelise, *Common Sense and a Little Fire*, Chapel Hill: University of North Carolina Press, 1995.

Owen, Alex, *The Place of Enchantment: British Occultism and the Culture of the Modern*, Chicago: University of Chicago Press, 2004.

Pearson, Karl, *The Grammar of Science*, London: Adam & Charles Black, 1900.

Plazak, Dan, *A Hole in the Ground and a Liar at the Top: Fraud and Deceit in the Golden Age of American Mining*, Salt Lake City: University of Utah Press, 2010.

Puleo, Stephen, *A City So Grand: The Rise of the American Metropolis, Boston 1850–1900*, Boston: Beacon Press, 2010.

Quail, John, *The Slow Burning Fuse: The Lost History of British Anarchism*, London: Paladin, 1978.

Quint, Howard H., *The Forging of American Socialism: Origins of the Modern Movement*, Indianapolis: The Bobbs Merrill Co., 1953.

Raw, Louise, *Striking a Light: The Bryant and May Matchwomen and Their Place in History*, London: Continuum, 2011.

Reynolds, Siân, *Paris-Edinburgh: Cultural Connections in the Belle Epoque*, London: Routledge, 2007.

Richardson, Mike, *The Enigma of Hugh Holmes Gore: Bristol's Nineteenth-Century Christian Socialist Solicitor*, Bristol: Bristol Radical History Group, 2016.

Richardson, Mike, *The Maltreated and the Malcontents: Working in the Great Western Cotton Factory, 1838–1914*, Bristol: Bristol Radical History Group, 2016.

Robertson, Michael, *Worshipping Walt: The Whitman Disciples*, Princeton: Princeton University Press, 2008.

Robinson, David, *The Unitarians and the Universalists*, Westport, CT: Greenwood Press, 1986.

Rocca, Al M., *Old Shasta*, Charleston, SC: Arcadia, 2005.

Ross, Ellen, *Slum Travellers: Ladies and London Poverty, 1860–1920*, Berkeley: University of California Press, 2007.

Rowbotham, Sheila, *Dreamers of a New Day: Women Who Invented the Twentieth Century*, London: Verso, 2010.

Rowbotham, Sheila, *Edward Carpenter: A Life of Liberty and Love*, London: Verso, 2008.

Rowbotham, Sheila, *Hidden from History*, London: Pluto, 1973.

Rowbotham, Sheila and Weeks, Jeffrey, *Socialism and the New Life: The Personal and Sexual Politics of Edward Carpenter and Havelock Ellis*, London: Pluto, 1977.

Ruyter, Nancy Lee Chalfa, *The Cultivation of Body and Mind in Nineteenth-Century American Delsartism*, Westport, CT: Greenwood Press, 1999.

Salveson, Paul, *With Walt Whitman in Bolton: Spirituality, Sex and Socialism in a Northern Mill Town*, Huddersfield: Little Northern Books, 2008.

Satter, Beryl, *Each Mind a Kingdom: American Women, Sexual Purity and the New Thought Movement, 1875–1920*, Berkeley: University of California Press, 2001.

Schmidgall, Gary, *Conserving Walt Whitman's Fame*, Iowa: University of Iowa Press, 2006.

Schneider, Herbert W. and Lawton, George, *A Prophet and a Pilgrim: Being the Incredible History of Thomas Lake Harris and Laurence Oliphant*, New York: Columbia University Press, 1942.

Schultz, David E. and Joshi, S.T., *H.P. Lovecraft: Letters to James F. Morton*, New York: Hippocampus Press, 2011.

Schwartz, Laura, *Infidel Feminism: Secularism, Religion and Women's Emancipation, England 1830–1914*, Manchester: Manchester University Press, 2013.

Scott, Mel, *American City Planning Since 1890*, Chicago: American Planning Association, 1995.

Searle, G.R., *A New England? Peace and War 1886–1918*, Oxford: Clarendon Press, 2004.

Showalter, Elaine, *Daughters of Decadence: Women Writers of the Fin-de-Siècle*, London: Virago, London, 1993.

Sklar, Martin J., *The Corporate Reconstruction of American Capitalism, 1890–1916*, New York: Cambridge University Press, 1988.

Sommers, Arthur, *Auburn*, Charleston, SC: Arcadia, 2008.

Stetz, Margaret D. and Wilson, Cheryl A., *Michael Field and Their World*, High Wycombe: Rivendale Press, 2007.

Stirner, Max, *The Ego and His Own: The Case of the Individual Against Authority*, London: Verso, 2014.

Swenarton, Mark, *Artisans and Architects: The Ruskinian Tradition in Architectural Thought*, London: Macmillan, 1989.

Sypher, Eileen, *Wisps of Violence: Producing Public and Private Politics in the Turn-of-the-Century British Novel*, London: Verso, 1993.

Thompson, E.P., *William Morris: Romantic to Revolutionary*, London: Merlin Press, 1977.

Thompson, Lawrence, *The Enthusiasts: A Biography of John and Katharine Bruce Glasier*, London: Victor Gollancz, 1971.

Trevor, John, *My Quest for God*, London: Labour Prophet Office, 1897.

Tufts, Helen (ed.), *Whitman's Ideal Democracy and Other Writings by Helena Born*, Boston: The Everett Press, 1902.

Tufts, William Whittemore, *A Market for an Impulse* (1897), General Books, 2009.

Verbrugge, Martha H., *Able Bodied Womanhood: Personal Hygiene and Social Change in Nineteenth-Century Boston*, New York: Oxford University Press, 1988.

Verhuis, Arthur, *The Esoteric Origins of the American Renaissance*, New York: Oxford University Press, 2001.

Walker, Robert H., *The Poet and the Gilded Age: Social Themes in Late 19th Century American Verse*, Philadelphia: University of Pennsylvania Press, 1963.

Walter, Nicholas (ed.), *Charlotte Wilson: Anarchist Essays*, London: Freedom Press, 2000.

Warner, Sam Bass Jr, *Streetcar Suburbs: The Process of Growth in Boston, 1870–1900*, Cambridge, MA: Harvard University Press, 1978.

Wenley, Robert Mark, *The University Extension Movement in Scotland*, Glasgow: The University Press, Robert Maclehose and Co., 1895.

Wheeler, Sir Mortimer, *Still Digging*, London: Michael Joseph, 1955.

Whitman, Walt, *Leaves of Grass*, ed. Sculley Bradley and Harold W. Blodgett, New York: W.W. Norton, 1973.

Williams, Gwen Mary, *Mary Clifford*, Bristol: J.W. Arrowsmith, 1920.

Wilson, James M., *An Autobiography, 1836–1931*, London: Sidgwick & Jackson, 1932.

Winslow, Barbara, *Sylvia Pankhurst*, London: St Martin's Press, 1996.

Winsten, Stephen, *Salt and His Circle*, London: Hutchinson & Co., 1951.

Wittke, Carl, *Against the Current: The Life of Karl Heinzen*, Chicago: University of Chicago Press, 1945.

Yeo, Eileen Janes, *The Contest for Social Science*, London: Rivers Oram, 1996.

Young, W., *Robert Weare: An Appreciation and Four of His Essays*, Printed by the C.W.S., Manchester, For Private Circulation, no date (pamphlet).

Theses

Atkinson, Brian, *The Bristol Labour Movement, 1868–1906*, PhD, University of Oxford, 1969.

Cheadle, Tanya, *Realizing a 'More Than Earthly Paradise of Love': Scotland's Sexual Progressives, 1880–1914*, PhD, University of Glasgow, 2014.

Ferguson, Megan C., *Patrick Geddes and the Celtic Renascence of the 1890s*, PhD, University of Dundee, 2011.

Goldberg, Geoffrey C., *The Socialist and Political Labour Movement in Manchester and Salford*, MA, University of Manchester, 1975.

Mathers, Helen Eliza, *Sheffield Municipal Politics 1893–1926*, PhD, University of Sheffield, 1979.

Murdoch, Christina, 'A large and passionate humanity plays about her': *Women and Moral Agency in the Late Victorian Social Problem Novel*, PhD, University of Glasgow, 2012.

Rushton, John Ivor, *Charles Rowley and the Ancoats Recreation Movement*, PhD, University of Manchester, 1959.

Index

bold denotes photo

Abbott, Leonard D., 275, 276, 355, 356, 360
abolitionism, 101, 156, 185, 237, 241, 259
Adams, Anne, 153–4
Adler, Felix, 388
aesthetics, 2, 13, 15, 26, 32, 33, 34, 39, 51, 64, 111, 114, 147, 169, 183, 184, 185, 188, 216, 239, 281, 294, 296, 325, 357, 358, 373
Alexander, Kate, 91
Allen, Grant, 174, 201, 260
alternative belief systems, 211
alternative healers, 219, 316
alternative health, 198, 210, 211, 266, 396
alternative spiritual movements, 80, 136
altruism, 6, 20, 24, 48, 96, 129, 165, 174, 200, 209, 226, 247, 337, 344
altruistic reform, 58
American Bureau of Industrial Research, 340
American Federation of Labor (A.F.L.), 303, 345
American Socialist Party, 258, 275
Ames, Lucia, 391
anarchism, 4, 5, 7, 306–7, 313, 334. *See also* Boston Anarchist Club; communist anarchism; Individualist Anarchism/ individualist anarchism; Philosophical Anarchism/philosophical anarchism
anarchist communism, 102, 106, 112, 122, 123, 124, 128, 174, 192, 200, 227, 239, 254, 259, 262, 302, 305, 393
The Anarchist (Seymour), 215
anarchist economic theory, 130, 310

Anarchist Individualism, 261
Andrews, John B., 340–1, 344, 359
Andrews, Stephen Pearl, 333
animalism, 106, 144, 217
Animal Rights (Salt), 215
An Inquiry into Boston's Water Supply and Its Relation to the Public Health, with some startling Facts about the Pollution of Sources of Supply (Bailie), 349–50
Anthony, Susan B., 21, 73, 164, 205
Anti-Imperialist League, 245, 254, 263
antinomianism, 274
anti-slavery movement, 18, 19, 259. *See also* abolitionism
anti-vivisection movement, 13, 29, 114, 215, 356
Appeal to the Young (Kroptkin), 215
Applegate community (California), 100, 140, 145, 210, 211, 218, 382
The Arena, 208, 307
Art and Socialism (Morris), 118, 215
arts and crafts, 175, 282, 325
asceticism, 26, 81, 114, 169, 174
Association of University Women, 391
Association of Working Women, 84. *See also* Bristol Association of Working Women
Astor, William Waldorf, 283
Atkinson, Edward, 248, 388
attire
    fashionable attire, 29, 165, 172, 255, 284
    rational dress, 5, 16, 164
Austin, Kate, 311
avant-garde, 5, 109, 193, 201, 365
Avery, Martha Moore, 183, 259

Bailie, Annie, 119, 249, 250
Bailie, Ellen (née Donnan), 119, 125, 127, 229, 230, 243, 261, 338, 347–8, 359, 360
Bailie, Hannah (née Maxwell), 116
Bailie, Helena, 301, 388, 395
Bailie, Helen Tufts. *See also* Tufts, Helen
  as expelled from D.A.R., 3
  mention of on Google search, 2
  photos of, **167**, **226**, **231**, **242**
Bailie, James, 116
Bailie, Nellie, 359
Bailie, Terrill (Sonny), 390
Bailie, Viola, 347, 349, 356
Bailie, William
  assembling collection of Helena Born's writings with Helen Tufts, 272–4
  background of, 116–31
  basket making, 2, 5, 112, 127, 229, 230, 232, 264, 267, 329, 332–3, 339, 346, 361
  birth and death dates of, 2
  birth of daughter Helena, 362
  children of, 114, 338, 347, 348, 359–60. *See also* Bailie, Annie; Bailie, Helena; Bailie, Terrill (Sonny); Bailie, Viola; Bailie, William, Jr (Willie)
  death of, 395
  disharmony with Helen Tufts, 394
  divorce from Ellen, 338
  education of, 347
  emigration to US, 112, 125
  first encounter with Helena Born, 229–30
  founding of Pure Food Kitchen, 243–4
  friendship with Helen Tufts, 235–6, 240, 248
  furniture making, 332, 337
  health issues, 267, 268, 395
  hedonism of, 389
  interest in craft skills, 262
  involved with city planning, 359
  love of ideas of, 328
  marriage to Helen Tufts, 349
  Miriam Daniell as taking on, 113
  photo of, **131**
  poem by, 230, 231, 266
  political engagement of, 254, 313, 327–8
  political isolation of, 339
  pursuit of absolute truth by, 305
  as rejecting socialism, 263
  retirement of, 394
  romance with Helena Born, 232–4, 237, 238, 239, 240, 243, 261–2, 264, 269, 270
  romance with Helen Tufts, 301, 309, 329, 331, 338
  voracious appetite for knowledge of, 340

  water purification cause, 349–50, 351–2, 353
  work experience, 394. *See also* Nicol, Robert Allan, basket making; Nicol, Robert Allan, furniture making
  writings of, 303–5, 311, 313, 333–5, 336–7, 349–50, 358–9, 387, 388–9
Bailie, William, Jr (Willie), 119, 338, 347, 359–60
Bailie Basket Co., 332, 337, 339, 346, 347
Barlas, John, 293
Barnett, Francis Gilmore, 21, 33, 35, 60, 63, 85, 90
Barton, Alf, 121, 124, 392
Barton, Eleanor (née Stockton), 124
Baster, William, 15, 16, 35, 61, 87, 272
Baynes, Sophie Day, 29–30
Beardsley, Aubrey, 201
Beaumont, Donna Brooks, 221
'Beauty for Ashes' (Edinburgh University Socialist Society appeal), **47**
Beecher, Henry Ward, 155, 161
Beesly, Edward Spencer, 47, 68
Beith, Gilbert, 392
Bellamy, Edward, 163, 166
Bellamy Nationalists, 208, 263
Bennett, Arnold, 282, 293
Berlin, Fanny, 266, 267, 269
Besant, Annie, 54, 56, 70, 81, 119, 191, 200, 227, 353
Binns, Henry, 91
birth control, 47, 181, 212, 360, 389, 393. *See also* contraception
Black, Clementina, 69, 76
Blackie, John Stuart, 28
Blake, William, 26, 39, 51, 57, 241
Bodding, Carl, 385
bohemia, 4, 5, 19, 188, 379, 380
Boletin de la Escuela Moderna, 341
Bool, Henry, 250
Born, Elizabeth, 11, 16
Born, Helena
  as advocate of militant new unionism, 71
  arrival at Placer County, California, 144
  ashes of scattered, 300
  attention to detail of, 67
  as becoming minor celebrity after her death, 269–70
  birth and death dates of, 2
  Bristol Socialist Society meeting in memory of, 270–1
  Bristol Socialist Society member, 61, 83
  Cambridge, Massachusetts residency, 106, 133, 143, 149, 168–9
  as carrying great weight of contained anger, 135
  childhood, 12

collections of papers by, 3
companionships of with women, 17
compulsion of towards enquiry and
    duty, 16
death of, 269
diplomacy of, 67
dream of going to US, 92
effect of Patrick Geddes on, 49
emigration to US, 1, 92, 94–115, 137
first encounter with William Bailie,
    229–30
founding of Pure Food Kitchen, 243–4
friendship with Miriam Daniell, 1, 32,
    34, 38
friends of, 16
fund-raising subcommittee member, 63
health issues, 266–7
impact of Miriam Daniell's death on,
    168
inner rebellion of, 24
leaving Cambridge a second time, 143
meeting Helen Tufts, 4, 167, 172
meeting Miriam Daniell, 25–6
new found power of, 89
notebook, 96, 104, 106
obtaining job of her dreams, 142
as organiser, 2
origins of, 11
parting of path with Miriam Daniell,
    148
photos of, **22**, **167**, **226**, **242**
political radicalism of, 24
public speaking, 17, 19, 21–2, 24, 88,
    175–6, 255–7, 258–9
rejection of customary female behaviour
    by, 173
relief work, 37
religious upbringing, 13, 16, 17
return to Cambridge, 149, 168–9
return to US, 133
romance with William Bailie, 232–4,
    237, 238, 239, 240, 243, 261–2, 264,
    269, 270
scientific interests of, 13, 24
scrapbook, 13, 14, 16, 20, 23, 36, 104
sending money to Robert Allan Nicol,
    224, 225
as shy, 17, 65
as signing comradeship paper of C.F.S.,
    227
Strike Committee member, 61
visit to Britain, 103–6
Walt Whitman Fellowship committee
    member, 179
Walt Whitman Fellowship member, 170
work experience, 95–6, 264
as working behind the scenes, 65
writings of, 17, 24, 174–5, 177, 225,

227, 247–8, 272. *See also Whitman's
    Ideal Democracy and Other Writings by
    Helena Born* (Born)
    W.W.F. meeting in memory of, 270
Born, Maria Jane, 104
Born, Mary Helena, 11
Born, Richard, 11, 12, 16, 65, 71, 251,
    269, 272, 341, 361
Boston-1915 Movement, 352, 353, 357,
    358, 388
Boston Anarchist Club, 101, 126, 181, 229,
    263, 270, 327
Boston City Club, 344, 345, 346
Boston Social Science Club, 312
Boynton, Ray, 378
Bradlaugh, Charles, 14, 15, 16, 17, 28, 119
Bradley, Katharine, 114
Bradney, Emily, 124
Brand, Arthur, 378
Brandeis, Louis, 332, 345, 346, 351, 352,
    360
Bresci, Gaetano, 303, 306
Bright, Joseph, 18
Brinton, Daniel, 170, 173, 175
Bristol Association of Working Women,
    75, 90
Bristol May Day, 83–4, 191
Bristol Socialist Society, 2, 15, 24, 31, 32,
    34, 35, 53, 54, 55, 57, 59, 60, 61, 67, 70,
    74, 78, 79, 81, 83, 84, 88, 89, 92, 99,
    187, 188, 193, 196, 247, 271, 272, 275,
    289
Bristol Sunday Research and Recreation
    Society, 36
Bristol Sunday Society, 35, 120
Bristol Women's Liberal Association
    (B.W.L.A.), 4, 17–18, 19, 20, 21, 22, 23,
    25, 30, 32, 36, 38, 65, 89, 242
British Socialist League, 311
British Women's Liberal Association, 30
Brooks, John Graham, 347
Brosseau, Grace H. L., 390, 391, 395
Brown, Cora, 161, 361
Browning, Robert, 14, 114, 197, 232
Bryan, William Jennings, 178, 183, 254,
    263
Bucke, Richard Maurice, 173, 175, 177,
    183, 276
Bunyan, John, 92
Burns, John, 70
Butler, Hiram E., 100, 136, 140, 210, 211,
    382
Butler, Josephine, 45
Butler, Samuel, 115

Cambridge, Massachusetts, Miriam, Robert,
    and Helena's residencies in, 94–5, 106,
    133, 143, 168–9

Campaign for Nuclear Disarmament, 7
Campbell, Paul, 205
Campton, James S., 228, 254, 270, 274, 361
capitalism, 6, 7, 15, 31, 33, 57, 77, 126, 129, 138, 187, 199, 208, 220, 255, 256, 257, 258, 303, 304, 305, 327, 351, 353, 388, 389, 393
Career of a Nihilist (Stepnyak-Kravchinsky), 78
Carlyle, Thomas, 44, 166
Carnegie, Andrew, 41
Carpenter, Edward, 1, 4, 6, 15, 23, 26, 34, 39, 47, 64, 70, 77, 81, 91, 96–7, 98, 103, 106, 112, 123, 169, 176, 188, 191, 204, 207, 208, 212, 214, **219**, 220, 222–3, 229, 232, 257, 271, 272, 291, 292, 310, 358, 392
Carpenter, J. Estlin, 13
Carter, Leslie, 252
Catt, Carrie Chapman, 259
Chamberlain, J. E., 275
Champney, Adeline, 312
Charcot, Jean-Martin, 197
Chatterton, Thomas, 189
Chatterton, William, 189
Chernyshevsky, N. G., 102
Chesnutt, Charles W., 308
Chesterton, G. K., 294
Chicago martyrs, 124, 181, 263, 311, 312
chiliasm, 24, 57, 79, 122, 384
Christian altruism, 344
Christian belief, questioning of, 6
Christian Science, 219, 244, 285, 293, 323
Christian Socialist movement, 15, 23, 24, 30, 32, 33, 35, 57, 66, 67, 83, 88, 90, 98, 128, 187, 205, 208, 271, 289, 308, 340
Civilisation: Its Cause and Cure (Carpenter), 208
Claims of Decorative Art (Crane), 186
Clark, Helen Priestman Bright, 18, 21, 22, 260
Clarke, Helen Archibald, 170–1, 173, 175, 179–80, 183, 234, 245, 268, 270
class injustice, 129, 308
class struggle, 122, 123, 374
Claxton, John G. (pseudonym), 221
Clement, Edward Henry, 356
Clifford, Mary, 69, 70, 71, 75, 84, 203
Clifton (Bristol suburb), 12–13
Clothed with the Sun, 312
Clough, Arthur Hugh, 232
Coan, Marie Terry Jutie, 281
Coan, Raymond, 281
Coffin, George, 246
Colby, Maria, 20, 21, 65
collectivism, 5, 24, 123, 129, 166, 247, 305, 336

Collectivist Socialism, 123
Colman, Lucy, 241–2, **242**, 243
Colman, Mary, 21
The Coming Light, 234
Commons, John R., 340, 344, 345
Commonweal (journal), 34, 48, 55, 65, 66, 83, 102, 120, 121, 122, 123, 124, 125, 128, 311
The Commonwealth of Oceana (Harrington), 328
Communism/communism, 7, 123, 125, 129, 239, 248, 305, 385. *See also* anarchist communism
communist anarchism, 122. *See also* anarchist communism
communities
    Applegate community (California), 100, 140, 145, 210, 211, 218, 382
    Epsom, New Hampshire. *See* Epsom, New Hampshire
    Godspeace, 282, 283, 292
    Home anarchist community, 307, 312, 313
    imagined communities, 6
    Modern Times community, 101, 127, 313, 333
    New Harmony community (Indiana), 311, 313, 333
    Purleigh, Essex, Tolstoyan community, 292
    Starnthwaite community, 198, 199, 250, 289, 291
    White-nights ranch. *See* White-nights ranch
comrade-love, 310
Comradeship of Free Socialists (C.F.S.), 226, 228, 235, 236, 239, 261, 276
The Comrade (journal), 275, 307
Comte, Auguste, 24, 43
consciousness, 3, 69, 75, 77, 85, 123, 153, 192, 201, 217, 247, 256, 292, 304, 341. *See also* cosmic consciousness; inner consciousness; revolutionary consciousness; social consciousness
The Conservator (journal), 149, 170, 171, 173–4, 175, 227, 241, 247, 253, 271, 301, 308, 309
Contagious Diseases Acts, efforts to repeal, 13, 14, 18, 19, 20, 29, 45
contraception, 49, 136. *See also* birth control
Conway, Katharine St John, 66–7, 83, 93, 104, 187, 188, 191, 193, **194**, 195, 196, 197, 198, 199, 202, 282, 291
Conway, Moncure, 19, 333
Cooke, George Willis, 313
Cooper, Edith, 114
co-operative association, 5, 254, 255

The Cooperative Commonwealth (Grönlund), 57
co-operative voluntarism, 358
Cores, George, 124
cosmic consciousness, 173, 217
Cosmic Consciousness (Bucke), 276
cosmic enlightenment, 214
Cox, Harold, 191
Coxey, Jacob S., 166
Craig, Gordon, 297
Cramer, Malinda E., 219, 281
Crane, Walter, 35, 159, 186, 233
Creelman, Ellen, 218
Crooke, Kate, 105, 272
Crosby, Ernest, 308, 313
Cunningham, William, 328
Czolgosz, Leon, 305–6, 307, 308, 310–11, 312

Dalmas, Phillip, 204
Daniell, Edward Tuckett, 25–6, 29, 30, 32, 33, 37, 39, 50, 52, 54, 55, 58, 64, 87, 139, 361
Daniell, James Livett, 29, 56, 114
Daniell, Miriam (née Wheeler), 63
    accusation of maladministration, 77–8
    as acquiring celebrity, 112
    as advocate of militant new unionism, 71
    as arousing devotion, 65
    arrival at Placer County, California, 144
    art interest of, 30
    birth and death dates of, 2
    birth of daughter, 95
    Bristol Socialist Society member, 61, 83
    as B.W.L.A. member, 25
    Cambridge, Massachusetts residency, 106, 133, 143, 149, 168–9
    as catalyst in Helena Born's life, 4
    as challenging Benjamin Tucker, 114–15
    death of, 149
    disregard for gender codes of Victorian womanhood by, 59
    distribution of writings of by Helen Tuft, 149
    divorce, 31, 52–3, 54, 58, 139, 142, 149
    dream of California, 143–4
    dream of going to US, 92
    effect of Helena Born on, 51
    effect of Patrick Geddes on, 49
    effect of Robert Allan Nicol on, 51
    elected to Sunday Society Committee, 35
    emigration to US, 92, 94–115, 137
    entry into labour organising, 53
    force of personality of, 64
    friendship with Helena Born, 1, 32, 34, 38
    health issues, 31–2, 52, 134, 136, 139,
        142, 144, 146–9
    intimacy with Robert Allan Nicol, 52
    letter to *Western Daily Press*, 31
    marriage, 29
    meeting Helena Born, 25–6
    meeting Robert Allan Nicol, 39, 49–50
    meeting William Bailie, 112
    as new woman, 136
    as organiser, 2
    original name Elizabeth Miriam, 27
    origins of, 27
    parting of path with Helena Born, 148
    photo of, **36**
    poems by, 4, 98, 106, 107–10, 113, 132, 141, 146, 147, 148, 149–50, 169, 207, 308
    pregnancy, 87–8, 94
    preoccupation with achieving harmony through occult divination, 101
    as provoking antipathy, 65
    relief work, 37
    religious upbringing, 27, 28
    Strike Committee member, 61
    as strike organiser, 60
    summoning of Helena, 133
    Victorian upbringing of, 28
    as woman of extreme and complex contradictions, 133
    Workers' Organising Committee (W.O.C.) member, 73
    writings of, 223. *See also* Daniell, Miriam (née Wheeler), poems by; *The New Trade Unionism: Its Relation to the Old; and the Condition of Its Success* (Daniell and Nichol); *The Truth about the Chocolate Factories or Modern White Slavery its Cause and Cure* (Daniell and Nicol)
    writing stories and poems for *Liberty*, 106–12, 113, 132
Daniell, Sophie (née Baynes), 30, 32, 56
Darling Daughter: A Satire (Tufts), 395
Darrow, Clarence, 339
Darwin, Charles, 17
Daughters of the American Revolution (D.A.R.), 3, 390, 391, 392, 394, 395
Davenport, Mary D., 234
Davenport, William N., 351
Davis, Ella, 164, 165, 184, 185, 246
Dawson, Charles Edwin (C.E.), 282, 283
Debs, Eugene, 166, 258, 271, 339
The Decline and Fall of the Roman Empire (Gibbons), 331
De Leon, Daniel, 183, 220, 258, 259
Dell, Robert E., 82
Delsarte, François, 216, 378
De Mattos, William S., 191, 193, 194–5, 196, 197, 289

The Demonstrator (journal), 312, 313
Denis, Ruth Saint, 378
Denton, Carrie, 237
Denton, May, 362. *See also* Hurd, May
  Clifford
Denton, Sherman, 237
Denton, William, Jr, 237, 270, 348
Denton, William, Sr, 237
de Silva, Alvaro, 386
desire, 136
  emancipation of, 109
  ethical endorsement of, 49
  modern psychological approaches to,
    223
  personal desire, 6
  physical desire, 211, 240
  same-sex desire, 223
  sensuous desire, 81
  subordination of, 99
Desjardins, Paul, 177, 218
determinism, 304, 328
Dharmapala, Anagarika, 185
Dillon, John, 23
The Divine Basis of Society (Gilliard), 341
divine healing, 218, 219
Divine Science Church, 219, 281
divorce, 177, 282. *See also* Bailie, William,
  divorce from Ellen; Daniell, Miriam (née
  Wheeler), divorce
Dix, Clement, 206, 223, 322, 365
Dix, Frank, 206
Dix, Gertrude
  biographical details, 297
  birth and death dates of, 2
  birth of, 297
  Bristol Socialist Society member, 83
  children of. *See* Nicol, Amaryllis; Nicol,
    Margaret (younger) (Margot); Nicol,
    Robert Dix (Bob)
  creator of Godspeace, 282
  death of, 385
  disregard for convention of, 369
  family of, 189, 206
  friendship with Raymond Unwin, 83
  as having common quests with Robert
    Allan Nicol, 206
  interest in writing, 190–1
  joining Robert Allan Nicol in California,
    297
  marriage to Robert Allan Nicol, 317
  migration of, 5
  as new woman, 93, 187, 217
  novels by, 2, 5, 198, 201–4, 281, 283,
    284–96, 297
  photo of, **318**
  poems by, 364, 383–4, 385
  political roles of, 33
  pregnancy, 317, 322–3

public speaking, 187–8, 205
  as representative of Clifton and Bristol
    Christian Socialists, 90
  romance with Robert Allan Nicol, 297–
    8, 314, 315, 382–3, 384
  Strike Committee member, 67
  as studying nursing, 188, 189–90
  Western short stories of, 321–5, 326
  Workers' Organising Committee
    (W.O.C.) member, 73, 83
  work experience, 191–2
  writings of, 205, 206, 283–4, 317–19,
    320–5, 363–4, 369. *See also* Dix,
    Gertrude, novels by; Dix, Gertrude,
    poems by
Dix, Helen, 206
Dix, Hilda, 206, 283, **368**
Dix, John Ross, 189
Dix, Juliet (née Warnaby), 189, 203, 367,
  368, 369
Dix, Phyllis, 206
Dix, William Chatterton, 189, 282
Donnan, Ellen, 119
Donnelly, Barbara (née Nicol), 366, 377,
  378, 382
Drake, Arathena B., 234, 270, 276
Dreier, Margaret, 353
Dryhurst, Nannie, 192
Dunbar, Eliza, 19, 22, 38, 50
Duncan, Isadora, 367, 378
Dunfermline, 39, 40

Eastern mysticism, 210
Eastern religious thinking, 54, 91
Eastern spirituality, 184
The Economic Foundations of Society (Loria),
  328
The Economic Interpretation of History
  (Rogers), 331
Eddy, Mary Baker, 219
Edgerly, Albert Webster, 214
Edinburgh Socialist League, 48
Edinburgh Social Union, 43
Edinburgh University Socialist Society, 47
Edinburgh University Social Reform
  Society, 48
Edward Carpenter: A Life of Liberty and Love
  (Rowbotham), 2
Edward Carpenter. In Appreciation (Beith),
  392
egalitarian social collectivity, 250
*The Ego and His Own: The Case of the
  Individual Against Authority* (Stirner), 102
Egoism/egoism, 4, 6, 129, 174, 206, 225,
  247, 248, 337
Ehrenburg, Ilya, 384
Eldred, Edna, 320, 366, 367, 378
Eliot, Charles William, 179, 347

Eliot, George, 14
Ellis, Alexander, 91, 140, 209, 218, 223
Ellis, Havelock, 6, 81, 103, 188, 189, 214, 223, 289, 292
Ely, Richard T., 340, 344, 345
Emerson, Ralph Waldo, 96–7, 154, 176, 274
Engels, Friedrich, 71
England's Ideal (Carpenter), 67, 188
Environmental Society, 42, 43
Epicureanism, 188, 193, 195, 197, 202
Epicurus, 188
Epsom, New Hampshire, 228, 229, 230, 231, 232, 234, 239, 240, 241, 242, 245, 268, 312, 332
equal suffrage, 354, 355
erotic comrades, 216
Esoteric Christians, 100, 215
esoterics, 4, 210, 211
The Esoteric, 100, 218
Esther Waters (Moore), 203
Estlin, Mary, 19, 21
Ethical Culture Society, 170, 388
The Evolution of Sex (Geddes and Thomson), 48, 49
external transformation, 175

Fabian Society, 5, 32, 34, 80, 82, 187, 191, 192, 193, 198, 205, 206, 263, 282, 291, 292
Factory Times, 66
The Fall of Paris (Ehrenburg), 384
fashionable attire, 29, 165, 172, 255, 284
Fellowship of the New Life, 32, 34, 80, 191
feminism, 5, 7, 18, 81, 109, 170, 171, 179, 205, 228, 284, 354
Ferrer, Francisco, 341, 355, 356, 360
Fetz, Beatrice, 182
Field, Michael (pseudonym), 114, 203
Fields, Factories and Workshops (Kropotkin), 246
Filene, Edward, 345, 351, 352, 353, 357, 388, 389
Fitzgerald, John F. (Honey Fitz), 345–6, 353, 356–7, 395
Fleischer, Charles, 246, 336
Flower, Benjamin O., 208
Flower and Needlework Guild, 25
Foote, Elizabeth M., 237
Footpaths Preservation, 33, 56
Ford, Isabella, 205
Forecasts of the Coming Century (Carpenter), 291
For Liberty (Herbert), 19
Francisco Ferrer: His Life, Work and Martyrdom, 356
Frankland, George, 381
free association, 6, 276

The Free Comrade (Lloyd), 271, 275
Freedom, 192, 292
free love, 5, 49, 59, 102, 109, 136, 174, 177, 180, 181, 193, 196, 197, 211, 228, 232, 235, 236, 238, 252, 260, 261, 264, 286, 289, 312, 348, 374, 378
Free Society, 146, 149, 254, 260, 263, 271, 275, 302, 303, 305, 306, 307, 310, 311
free speech, 306
free thought, 28, 101, 138, 197, 237, 242
French, Daniel Chester, 183, 269
Froebel, Friedrich, 105
From Adam's Peak to Elephanta (Carpenter), 219, 220
Fry, Francis James, 33, 53, 56
Fry, Joseph Storrs, 56, 57, 59, 60
future society, 271

Garland, Hamlin, 175
Garnett, Constance, 69
Garnett, Olive, 199, 200
Garnett, Richard, 199, 200
Garnett, Robert Singleton, 369
Garrison, Peggy, 386
Gas Workers and General Labourers' Union (G.W. & G.L.U.), 4, 53, 54, 59, 60, 61, 70, 71, 74, 75, 82, 84, 85, 123
Geddes, Anna (née Morton), 45, 64, 105
Geddes, Patrick, 6, 42–5, **42**, 46, 48, 49, 50, 64, 104–5, 145, 174, 177, 272, 358
Gems from Walt Whitman (Whitman), 179
A Geography of the Erotic Body (Margot Nicol), 386
George, Henry, 15, 24, 118, 353
Ghent, W. J., 327
Gibbons, Edward, 331
Gilchrist, Anne, 179
Gilliard, Mary, 87
Gilliard, Robert, 15, 16, 35, 57, 58, 59, 64, 73, 74, 81, 82, 86–7, 88, 89, 92, 188, 270–1, 272, 292, 341
Gilliard, Sydney, 216
Gilman, Charlotte Perkins, 6, 254, 354
Ginn, Edwin, 180
The Girl From the Farm (Dix), 2, 201–4, 284
Glasier, John Bruce, 199
Glover, Revd R., 66
Godspeace, 282, 283, 292
Goldman, Emma, 6, 302, 306, 311, 340, 355, 360, 387, 393
Goldstein, David, 259
Gompers, Samuel, 345
Good Government Association (G.G.A.), 345, 346, 351, 353, 357
Goodspeed, Charles Eliot, 309
Gordak, William Walstein, 102, 262
Gore, Hugh Holmes (H.H.), 23, 30, 31,

33, 53, 61, 62, 73, 82, 83, 85, 187
Gorky, Maxim, 337
Gould, Elizabeth Porter, 179
Graeff, Virginia E., 105, 145, 173, 264, 272
Graham, Cunninghame, 84
Graham, Revd J.R., 66
The Grammar of Science (Pearson), 301
Great Western Cotton Factory, 60, 61, 62, 69, 85
Green, J. F., 205
Gregory, John, 14–15, 60, 61, 72, 74, 75
Grönlund, Laurence, 31, 47, 48, 57, 58, 80, 188
Guest, Emily, 33
Gwynn, H.T.M.C., 22

Haeckel, Ernst, 17, 45, 300
Haigh, Emily Alice, 364–5
Hansen, Mary, 275
Hardy, Thomas, 203
Hare, William, 292
Hargrave, Jane, 14, 17
Hargrave, Revd William, 13–14, 17
Harman, Moses, 102, 236
Harmony, 281
Harmony School, 281, 298
Harrington, James, 328
Harris, Thomas Lake, 58, 80, 81, 100, 136, 191, 207, 210, 220
Hartley, Eustace, 199
Hartley, Margaret, 199
Harvey, Revd Thomas William, 35, 37, 66
Hatherleigh (Devon), 11–12
Haworth, James, 228, 239
Hawthorne, Nathaniel, 160
Hawver, Dr, 213
Haywood, Big Bill, 339
Heald, Louise, 329–30, 360
health food, 5
Hegel, Georg Wilhelm Friedrich, 174, 201, 203, 320
Heinemann, William, 283, 293
Heinzen, Henriette Schiller, 262
Heinzen, Karl, 103, 138, 262
Herbert, Auberon, 19
Her Father's Daughter (Margot Nicol), 367–76
Herron, George D., 308
heterodox spirituality, 6
Heywood, Angela, 102
Heywood, Angela (née Tilton), 181
Heywood, Ezra, 102, 181
Hibbard, George A., 346
Hicks, Dana, 262
Hicks, Mary Dana, 173, 234
High Church Christians, 30, 33, 66, 67, 83, 187, 189, 284, 289, 296
Hill, Octavia, 45

Hinton, James, 81, 214
History of Our Own Time (McCarthy), 44
Hobson, Sam, 193, 197
Holmes, Lizzie, 311
Holmes, Oliver Wendell, 169, 182
Holmes, Sarah Elizabeth, 113, 181–2, **181**, 261, 262, 268, 347
Holmes, William T., 311
Home anarchist community, 307, 312, 313
Home Rule, 22, 28, 34, 36, 38, 47, 63, 117, 118, 254, 357, 387
Homogenic Love (Carpenter), 212, 213, 216, 222, 310
homosexuality, 204, 393–4
Hotchkiss, Douglas, 218, 219
Houghton Mifflin, 162, 166, 185, 186, 236, 244, 246, 275, 308, 329, 330, 332
Howard, Ebenezer, 358
Howe, Julia Ward, 184
Hudibras (Butler), 115
Hughes, Etti (or Hettie), 139
Hukin, George, 204
human agency, 328
humanitarianism, 6
Humanitarian League, 205, 215, 292
humorous fellowship, 74
Hunter, Edward H., 390
Hurd, May Clifford, 237, 260, 261, 270, 331, 348, 349, 362
Husband Brother (Conway), 282
Huxley, Thomas, 17, 35, 43
Hyde, Sim E., 214, 215, 218, 220
Hyndman, Henry, 24, 31, 47, 70, 78
hypnotism, 197

Ibsen, Henrik, 26, 188, 197
The Image Breakers (Dix), 2, 198, 199, 283, 284–96, 297, 325
imagined communities, 6
imperialism, 254, 263, 303, 305
Independent Labour Party (I.L.P.), 5, 83, 124, 191, 198, 199, 205, 233, 282, 291, 343, 392
individual development, 14, 101, 174, 272
individual expression, 4, 174, 175, 337. *See also* personal expression; self-expression
individual freedom, 14, 25, 26, 48, 101, 113, 205, 250, 305, 327, 333, 340, 347. *See also* personal freedom
individual fulfillment, 14
individualism, 5, 20, 23, 31, 129, 134, 163, 178, 238, 239, 247, 248, 255, 275, 375. *See also* Anarchist Individualism; Radical Individualism/radical individualism/ Individualist Anarchism/individualist anarchism, 4, 5, 19, 101, 125, 126, 180, 181, 182, 228, 254, 261, 271, 302, 305, 335, 339, 347, 388, 393, 397

individuality, 4, 23, 24, 25, 48, 127, 169, 203, 223, 247, 254, 271, 275, 276
individual reason, 387
individual rights, 6, 13, 20, 164, 336
The Individual (journal), 234
individual transformation, 366
Industrial Workers of the World (I.W.W.), 339
Ingersoll, Robert G., 17, 177
Inglis, Agnes, 393, 394
inner being, transformation of, 4
inner change, 80, 81, 303, 340
inner consciousness, 139, 257
inner development, 141
inner emotional bondage, 257
inner power, 185, 387
inner prefigurative change, 292
Instead of a Book (Tucker), 132
interconnecting radical networks, 354
International Council of Women, 21, 242
inward breath, 213
inward transformation, 175
Ioläus: An Anthology of Friendship (Carpenter), 309, 310
Irving, Clara, 194, 198
Irving, Dan, 23, 35, 60, 63, 73, 76, 77, 83, 87, 90–1, **90**, 194, 195, 196, 198, 199, 256, 257, 258, 269, 271, 291, 392
Isaak, Abe, 302
Isaak, Abe, Jr, 311
Isaak, Mary, 302

Jackson, Edward P., 169
James, C.L., 340
James, William, 165
Jex-Blake, Sophia, 28, 32
Johnson, Bertha F., 182, 393
Johnson, Pearl, 347
Jolly, Christine Ann Bailie, 395
Jolly, Walter, 395
Jones, Nahum, 157
Josiah Warren: The First American Anarchist (Bailie), 333, 334, 335, 336, 337, 340, 343, 351
'The Journals of Helen Matilda Tufts Bailie, from 1886' (Tufts), 153
Joynes, Bessie, 204
Justice, 119, 233, 343, 360

Karezza: Ethics of Marriage (Stockham), 232
Keating, Honora (Nora), 366, 381, 382
Keats, John, 14
Kennedy, Jim, 197, 198
Kennedy, William Sloane, 92, 170, 173, 175
Kenworthy, J.C., 292
Kingsford, Anna, 81, 215, 217
Konikow, Antoinette, 360

Koopman, Harry Lyman, 111, 115, 133, 134, 136, 137, 139, 140
Koopman, Helen, 134–5, 137, 139, 142–3, 147, 272
Kropotkin, Peter, 6, 45, 47, 102, 106, 112, 122, 174, 205, 215, 227, 246, 269, 335, 357, 393

Labadie, Joseph, 340
Labour Church, 125, 176, 205, 291
Labour Leader, 191, 282, 291
Labour League, 15, 23, 35, 47, 82
labour movement, 4, 53, 61, 70, 75, 85, 125, 126, 166, 220, 247, 345
Labour Party, 82, 289. *See also* Independent Labour Party (I.L.P.)
Labour Prophet, 128, 176
Labour Song Book, 78, **79**
Lamarck, J.B., 24
Lanchester, Elsa, 174
Lane, John, 201, 203
Law, Harriet, 184
Lease, Mary Elizabeth, 166, 167
Leaves of Grass (Whitman), 25, 102, 169, 176, 342
Le Devoir Présent (Desjardins), 177
Lee, Harley D., 375, 377
Lee, Marie, 377
Leffingwell, Albert, 215
Leighton, Dorothy, 200
Leighton, George, 235, 250
Leighton, Walter, Leatherbee, 235, 236, 237, 238, 239, 240, 244–5, 249, 250, 260, 300, 302, 304, 309
Le Play, Frederic, 43, 177
Lewis, Sinclair, 384
Liberal National Reform Union, 38
Liberal Party, 14, 18, 19, 22, 23
Libertas, 138
Liberty, 4, 5, 101, 102, 103, 106, 107, 112, 113, 125, 127, 128, 131, 182, 229, 271, 276, 302, 305, 327, 333, 336, 337
Littlehale, Cora, 160
Livett, James, 29
Living My Life (Goldman), 393
Lloyd, J. William, 182, 225, 226, 227, **227**, 228, 231, 261, 271, 275, 302
Lockwood, George, 311
Looking Backward (Bellamy), 163
Loria, Archille, 328
Love's Coming of Age (Carpenter), 176, 222, 223, 232, 288
Lucifer, 236
Lysaght, John, 53, 54, 77

MacDonald, Ramsay, 15, 205
MacDonald, Sarah, 171, 246
Mackay, John Henry, 103, 138, 141

MacLean, John, Jr, 155
MacMonnies, Frederick William, 185–6
Maeterlinck, Maurice, 359
magnetic powers/magnetism, 42, 133, 146,
    194, 211, 212, 214, 285
Maitland, Edward, 215, 217
Manchester Socialist League, 113, 120, 121,
    122, 392
Mandeville, John, 23
Mann, Tom, 60, 67, 70
The Man Versus the State (Spencer), 24
Markham, Edwin, 220–1, 308
Marlborough Workmen's Flower Show and
    Home Industry Society, 22
Marriage in Free Society (Carpenter), 174,
    208
The Marrow of Tradition (Chesnutt), 308
Marshall, James W. D., 35
Marshall, John, 41, 120, 123
Marx, Eleanor, 6, 47, 54, 55, 69, 70, 71,
    82, 84, 85, 86, 91, 233–4
Marx, Karl, 130, 262, 328
Mason, Otis Tufton, 339–40
Massachusetts Woman Suffrage Association
    (M.W.S.A.), 164, 259
Masson, David, 28, 50
materialism, 6, 14, 89, 99, 110, 140, 339
Mavor, James, 45, 50, 223
Maynard, Gertrude, 270
Maynard, Laurens, 170, 171, 179, 183,
    254, 270
McCarthy, Justin, 44
McClennen, Edward Francis, 332
McKinley, William, 178, 183, 245, 254,
    260, 263, 305, 306, 308, 310, 311, 312
Mead, Edwin D., 356
Melliet, Léo, 47
mental healing, 281
mental science, 218, 219
Merrill, George, 204
Michael, Arthur, 171
Michael, Helen Abbott, 171, 173, 179
Michel, Louise, 16, 192, 292
Mikol, David, 270, 302, 303, 356, 360
Mill, John Stuart, 121, 340
Miller, George Noyes, 103
Miller, Joseph Dana, 307
Mills, Revd B. Fay, 245
Mills, Revd Herbert V., 198, 199
Minshall, R. H., 392
Modern School, 341, 355, 360
Modern Times community, 101, 127, 313,
    333
Monroe, Will S., 392
Montgomerie, Anne, 269, 309
Monthly Record (journal), 75
Moore, George, 203
Morgan, Conway Lloyd, 33, 43, 50

Morgan, Lewis H., 328
Morley, John, 65
Morong, George F., 261
Morris, George Llewellyn, 282, 283
Morris, William, 15, 23, 24, 31, 32, 34, 47,
    112, 118, 120, 122, 159, 169, 215, 262,
    312, 338, 357, 358, 391
Morten, Honnor, 190, 205–6
Morton, Anna, 45
Morton, James F., Jr, 236, 238, 254, 263,
    302, 304, 307, 312
Most, Johann, 164
Mowbray, Charles, 124
Munro, J. E. C., 121
mutual banking, 128, 246
mycology, 5, 145
mystical revelation, 217
mysticism, 4, 5, 58, 81, 98, 99, 187, 210,
    248, 359. *See also* Neo-Platonic mysticism

National American Woman Suffrage
    Association (N.A.W.S.A.), 354
National Association for the Advancement
    of Colored People, 354
National Economic League, 346
National Woman's Day, 354
Neo-Platonic mysticism, 81, 91, 197, 359
Nethersole, Olga, 253
The New Age (journal), 233, 364, 365, 383
New Harmony community (Indiana), 311,
    313, 333
The New Harmony Communities
    (Lockwood), 311
new lifers, 34, 205, 213
new society, 6, 218
The New Spirit (Ellis), 188
New Thought, 219, 281
*The New Trade Unionism: Its Relation to
    the Old; and the Condition of Its Success*
    (Daniell and Nichol), 79, 80, 81, 82
new unionism, 53–4, 55, 60, 61, 70, 71,
    75, 76, 78, 79, 82, 84, 86, 89, 90, 91,
    112
new women, 1, 2, 3, 49, 93, 103, 136, 172,
    174, 178, 180, 184, 187, 188, 199, 200,
    201, 204, 205, 217, 255, 276, 282, 284,
    287, 293, 295, 324, 367, 384
New York City, Miriam, Robert, and
    Sunrise's move to, 106
New York Modern School, 355, 360
Nichols, Malcolm, 351
Nicol, Amaryllis, 297, 320, 322, **363**, 367,
    368, 369, 378, 380, **380**, 381
Nicol, Barbara, 385. *See also* Donnelly,
    Barbara (née Nicol)
Nicol, Davie, 214
Nicol, Jutie T. (née Coan), 297, 315, 317
Nicol, Margaret (younger) (Margot), 40,

42, 297, 317, 320, 322, **363**, 366, 367–75, 377–9, **379**, 380, 381, 386

Nicol, Miriam Sunrise (Sunrise), 95, 103, 106, 132, 134, 139, 141, 143, 144, 209, **209**, 210, 221, 224, 253, 297, 298, 317, 320, 362–3, **363**, 365–7, 369, 375, 377, 378

Nicol, Robert Allan
  arrival at Placer County, California, 144
  birth and death dates of, 2
  Cambridge, Massachusetts residency, 106, 133, 143, 149, 168–9
  children of. *See* Nicol, Amaryllis; Nicol, Margaret (younger) (Margot); Nicol, Robert Dix (Bob); Nicol, Tamara Jean
  as composer of song for *Labour Song Book*, 78
  death of, 386
  on death of Miriam, 207–8, 213
  as District Secretary of the G.W. & G.L.U., 74, 84, 92
  dream of California, 143–4
  early political influences, 48
  education of, 41–2, 44, 46
  effect of Patrick Geddes on, 49
  as elephant in the room within Helen Tufts' psyche, 277
  emigration to US, 92, 94–115, 137
  emotional oscillations of, 382
  entry into labour organising, 53
  establishment of Harmony School by, 281
  family home, 39–40
  fantasising of, 97
  fortune-seeking fanaticism of, 376
  friendship with Edward Carpenter, 216
  fund-raising subcommittee member, 63
  Gertrude Dix joining in California, 297
  grooming of for new job, 72
  as having buoyancy of character, 85
  as having common quests with Gertrude Dix, 206
  intimacy with Miriam Daniell, 52
  as landowner, 224
  as liking women as much as men, 217
  lofty muddles of, 223
  love affair with Honora (Nora) Keating, 381–2
  marriage to Gertrude Dix, 317
  marriage to Marie Terry Jutie Coan, 281
  meeting Miriam Daniell, 39, 50
  meeting Patrick Geddes, 43, 44
  meeting William Bailie, 112
  as mining engineer, 297
  mining work, 363
  Miriam Daniell's effect upon, 4
  photo of, **50**, 209, **316**
  post-Gertrude Dix's death, 385

  romance with Gertrude Dix, 297–8, 314, 315, 384
  sandal making, 208, 219–20
  search for mystical revelation by, 217
  shift away from science, 46
  Strike Committee member, 61
  as stuck without any particular place for self in US, 112
  as union organiser, 74
  Workers' Organising Committee (W.O.C.) member, 73, 74
  writings of, 364. *See also The New Trade Unionism: Its Relation to the Old; and the Condition of Its Success* (Daniell and Nichol); *The Truth about the Chocolate Factories or Modern White Slavery its Cause and Cure* (Daniell and Nicol)
  as yearning for personal immortality, 212

Nicol, Robert Dix (Bob), 323, 325, 366, 367, 369, 378, 380, 383, 386
Nicol, Robert, Jr, 40, 41, 44
Nicol, Robert, Sr, 39, 40, 41
Nicol, Tamara Jean, 381, 382, 386. *See also* Patri, Tamara Nicol Rey
Nicol, William, 42
Nicoll, David, 128
Nietzsche, Friedrich, 138, 335
Nightingale, Florence, 189
Nihilists, 73, 78, 99, 102, 107, 113, 200, 306, 375
Nolen, John, 357, 358
non-violent direct action, 7, 122
Nordgren, Anna, 200
Norton, Charles Eliot, 166
Nutter, George Read, 332, 345, 346, 351

Oliphant, James, 48
Olivier, Brynhild, 192
Olivier, Daphne, 192
Olivier, Margaret, 191, 192, 200
Olivier, Sydney, 191, 192, 200
On the Threshold (Ford), 205
Orage, Alfred, 365
O'Reilly, Leonora, 354
Osborn, Harris, 98, 141, 214, 216, 219, 220, 221
Our Benevolent Feudalism (Ghent), 327
Our Threatened Heritage: A Letter to the Daughters of the American Revolution (Tufts), 390
Owen, Robert, 246, 333
Owen, Robert Dale, 333

Paine, Tom, 17
Pankhurst, Emmeline, 124, 354, 364, 365
Parnell, Charles Stewart, 118
Parson, Albert, 238

Parsons, Lucy, 238
Pastor, Rose, 347
Pater, Walter, 26, 51
Patri, Giacomo, 386
Patri, Tamara Nicol Rey, 386–7
Pawling, Sidney S., 283
Pearson, Karl, 301
Pease, Edward, 34, 56, 192, 194
Pease, Susan, 34, 56
Pease, Thomas, 34, 56
Penhallow, Mattie D., 312
The People's Press (newspaper), 82, 90, 92
The Perfect Way (Kingsford and Maitland), 217
Perry, Bliss, 342
personal comradeship, 74, 272
personal energy, 223
personal expression, 25, 233. *See also* self-expression; *individual expression*
personal freedom, 6, 321. *See also* personal independence; *individual freedom*
personal growth, 141
personal independence, 187
personal moral agency, 34
personal relations, 249, 269, 292, 294, 313
personal transformation, 80, 285
Philosophical Anarchism/philosophical anarchism, 101, 271, 274
physical freedom, 255
picketing, 78
Pilgrim's Progress From This World to That Which is to Come: Delivered Under the Similitude of a Dream (Bunyan), 92
Pinkerton, Robert A., 306
The Pioneer (magazine), 256, 258, 259, 272
Pitman, Isaac, 330
Placer County, California, 100, 140, 142, 144, 145, 210, 315, 316, 325, 326, 363, 364, 377
Plato, 187, 189, 197, 200, 236, 293
Platt, Isaac, 173
Poet-Lore (journal), 170, 171, 183, 247
Poet-Lores, 179, 237, 246, 269, 270
political transformation, 80
Porter, Charlotte, 170–1, 173, 175, 179, 180, 183, 234, 245, 268, 270
pragmatism, 19, 357, 387
Prang, Louis, 262
Prang, Rosa, 262
Priestman, Anna Maria, 18, 20, 21, 22, 23, 65, 67
Priestman, Mary, 18
Progress and Poverty (George), 118
Proudhon, Pierre-Joseph, 101, 115, 128, 238, 246, 328, 335
psychological motivation, 387
Pure Food Kitchen, 243, 244, 251, 253, 264

Purleigh, Essex, Tolstoyan community, 292
Pyat, Félix, 103

Quakerism, 20, 57, 193, 205, 247

racism, 144, 185, 308, 336, 384
radical association, 255
Radical Individualism/radical individualism, 19, 23
radicalism, 2, 5, 13, 14, 24, 28, 101, 103, 176, 185, 237, 241, 272, 293, 333, 345
Radical Liberals, 14, 22, 23, 29, 271, 291
radical networks, 354
The Rag-picker of Paris (Pyat), 103
Ralstonism, 214, 215, 219
rational dress, 5, 16, 164
rationalism, 300, 366, 375
Rawle, Frank, 53, 54, 63, 65, 77
Reclus, Elie, 335
Reclus, Elisée, 45, 335
Reddie, Cecil, 34, 42, 50, 65, 209
The Red Heart in a White World: A Suggestive Manual of Free Society Containing a Method and a Hope (Lloyd), 225, 235
Redmond, John, 357
Reed, Mavorite, 158
Reflections from the Sun (Thacker), 211
relief work, 37
Religio-Philosophical Journal, 147, 208
revelatory enlightenment, 81
revolutionary consciousness, 122
revolutionary transformation, 344
Rey, Georges, 366, 367, 369, 378, 381, 382, 387
Rey, Noël, 386
The Riddle of the Universe (Haeckel), 300
The Rights of Women and the Sexual Relations: An Address to an Unknown Lady Reader (Heinzen), 103, 138
Ritson, John, 120
Robertson, John Mackinnon, 28, 105, 228
Robins, Raymond, 353
Rogers, John, 28
Rogers, Thorold, 328, 331
Romanticism/romanticism, 6, 14, 28, 197, 264, 271, 366
Roosevelt, Theodore, 245, 310, 337
Rosaline, Emily, 28
Rossetti, Dante Gabriel, 282
Rossetti, William Michael, 200, 292
Rowley, Charles, 120
Royce, Josiah, 165
Ruggli, Ida, 332
Ruskin, John, 6, 15, 23, 24, 33, 43, 335
Russell, Alan, 290, 291
Russell, Charles Edward, 354, 356
Russell, Edmund, 216, 218, 219, 221
Russell, Will, 210, 218

Sadler, Michael E., 121
Salt, Henry, 192, 215, 291, 292, 293
Salt, Kate, 192, 204, 292
same-sex desire, 1
same-sex love, 212, 223, 310
Sanborn, Franklin Benjamin, 183, 234–5
Sand, George, 188, 197, 203
Sapho (play), 253
Sartor Resartus (Carlyle), 44
scepticism, 67, 128, 185, 300, 303, 305, 339, 359
Schindler, Solomon, 163, 166, 336
Schopenhauer, Arthur, 165
Schreiner, Olive, 103
Schumm, Emma Heller, 137–8, 180, 182, 231, 254, 261, 262, 270, 276, 348
Schumm, George, 127, 137–8, 141, 180, 233, 246, 254, 262, 392
Scott, C.P., 198
Scott, J.W.A., 98
Scottish Land and Labour League, 47
secularism, 5, 6, 17, 112
Secular Positivists, 42, 43
secular rationalism, 300
self-determination, 6, 114, 154, 203, 248
self-development, 34, 261, 271, 276. *See also* individual development
self-expression, 6, 141, 187, 256, 272, 289. *See also* personal expression; individual expression
self-ownership, 6, 101, 106, 138, 177
self-realisation, 271
self-sovereignty, 242, 243
'The Sensible Skirt Vindicators,' 184
sensuousness, 26
sex hygiene, 359
Sex-Love in a Free Society (Carpenter), 208
sex pamphlets, 98, 208, 213
sex psychology, 5, 6, 81, 223
sexual autonomy, 136
sexual double standard, 6
sexual emancipation, 2, 48
sexual guilt, 212, 217
sexual prophets, 210–11
Seymour, Henry, 215
Sharland, Harold, 215
Sharland, John, 15, 16, 71
Sharland, Robert, 15, 16, 54, 60, 67, 74, 88, 176, 215, 271, 341, 343, 360, 392
Sharland, Will, 15, 16, 272
Shasta, California, 314
Shaw, Anna Howard, 354
Shaw, George Bernard, 102, 191, 192, 196, 199, 200, 204, 291, 297
Shelley, Percy Bysshe, 14, 15, 75, 175–6, 197, 272
She of the Holy Light (Beaumont), 221
Sherman, Charles D., 183

Shortland, Jim, 204
simplification/simple life, 1, 2, 34, 48, 64, 191, 192, 201, 225–6, 240, 241, 282, 294, 297, 325, 373
Simpson, Archibald H., 126, 127, **127**, 181, 229, 237, 238, 262, 268, 270, 306, 312, 388, 392–3
sister women, 106, 187, 198, 199, 289
Sixsmith, Charlie, 342, 343, 392
Sixsmith, Lucy, 342
Smart, George, 120
Smart, H. Russell, 197–8
Smith, Jessica, 385
Smith, Revd Samuel F., 236
Snaith, Phyllis, 365
Snellenberg, K. A., 270, 302
social amelioration, 344
social commitment, 155, 187, 205, 295
social consciousness, 7
Social Darwinism, 304
Social Democratic Federation (S.D.F.), 15, 24, 31, 32, 47, 70, 78, 112, 119, 120, 196, 205, 256, 262, 304
Social Democratic Party, 258, 259
social equality, 5, 167
social equity, 340
social housing, 357
social inequality, 284
social injustice, 14, 163
socialism, 1, 2, 5, 6, 7, 31, 32, 34–5, 48, 179, 257, 258–9, 272, 307, 334, 339, 341, 384. *See also* Collectivist Socialism
Socialist Labor Party (S.L.P.), 166, 181, 183, 220, 258, 259, 340
Socialist League, 31, 32, 34, 45, 47, 48, 54, 55, 65, 70, 78, 79, 84, 91, 102, 112, 120, 122, 129, 262, 357. *See also* *Commonweal*
Socialist League Club, 122, 123, 124, 125
socialist movement, 4, 84, 176, 191, 195, 250, 275, 284, 341, 372. *See also* Christian Socialist movement
Socialist Party, 339, 347, 354
The Socialist Spirit (journal), 275
Social Purity/social purity, 16, 21, 29, 56, 164
social reform, 6, 21, 33, 34, 35, 43, 45, 48, 68, 69, 70, 84, 147, 206, 332, 340, 344, 351, 356, 376, 391
Social Science Club, 312, 313
Social Statics (Spencer), 24
social transformation, 25, 33, 34, 48, 63–4, 80, 303, 366
Society of Christian Socialists, 340
sociology, 105, 313, 340, 344
Solar Biology, 210, 219
solidarity, 5, 7, 20, 54, 66, 71, 74, 75, 77, 83, 166, 255, 271, 276, 303

Southcombe, Elizabeth (Minnie), 11, 76, 96, 272
Southcombe, John, 11
Southcombe, Susannah, 11
Soviet Russia Today (journal), 385
Spafford, George, 61, 62, 63, 65
Spargo, John, 275
Spencer, Herbert, 24, 25, 334
spiritual enlightenment, 222, 281, 285
Spiritualism/Spiritualists, 57, 91, 100, 147, 181, 208, 211, 214, 236, 237
spirituality
    alternative kinds of, 4, 14
    Eastern spirituality, 184
    esoteric spirituality, 184
spiritual transformation, 80
Spurrell Printers, 264, 266
Stacy, Enid, 30, 31, 67, 83, 93, 98–9, **98**, 100, 101, 104, 187, 193, 194, 195, 196, 198, 199, 250, 251, 289, 290
Stacy, Henry, 30, 31, 32, 33, 84
Stacy, Paul, 30, 83, 88, 191, 193, 196
Stanley, H.M., 124
Stanton, Elizabeth Cady, 18, 164
Starnthwaite community, 198, 199, 250, 289, 291
Steffens, Lincoln, 351, 357
Stephen, Leslie, 17
Stepnyak-Kravchinsky, Sergey Mikhaylovich (Stepniak), 78, 102, 205
Stetson, Charlotte Perkins, 228, 241
Steunenberg, Frank, 339
Stevens, Mary, 171–2, 268, 269, 270
Stirner, Max, 4, 102, 138
Stockham, Alice B., 232
Stockton, Eleanor, 124
Stockton, Emily (née Bradney), 124
Stockton, Herbert, 121, 124
Stokes, Frederick A., 296
Stokes, J.G. Phelps, 347
Storrow, James J., 351, 352, 356, 357
The Story of an African Farm (Schreiner), 103
Street, Revd James Christopher, 118
Strike Committee, 61, 62, 63, 64, 65, 66, 67, 68, 69, 71, 72, 73, 82, 83
A Strike of a Sex (Miller), 103
Sturge, Emily, 18–19, 20, 21, 38, 65, 71
Sullivan, James, 174
Sullivan, John A., 313
Sunday Societies, 35
Swann, Louisa, 21, 23, 38, 65
Swartz, Clarence Lee, 237, 246, 254, 270, 336, 337
Swartz, Leslie, **242**
Swedenborg, Emmanuel, 57, 136
Swift, Morrison I., 166
Swinburne, Algernon, 14

symbolists, 5

tailoresses' union, 74–5, 76
Talbot, Mary, 75, 84, 90
Tanglewood Tales (Hawthorne), 160
Tanner, Margaret (Priestman), 18, 21, 22, 30, 65
Taylor, Beatrice, 16, 17, 19, 184, 265, 269, 341, 355, 392
Taylor, Clay, 297
Terrill, Daniel, 156
Terrill, Isabel, 156
Tess of the d'Urbervilles (Hardy), 203
Thacker, Sara, 211
Thackeray, William, 14
Theosophy/Theosophists, 54, 81, 100, 191, 200, 211, 216, 222, 227, 236, 353, 366
Thomas, C.P., 60
Thompson, C. Bertrand, 358
Thomson, Isabella, 46
Thomson, John Arthur, 42, 45–6, 48, 50, 174
Thoreau, Henry David, 1, 2, 34, 64, 94, 255, 256, 257, 272, 308, 335
Thorne, Will, 60
Thyrza Fleming (play), 200
Tillett, Ben, 53, 60, 61, 70, 75
Tilton, Angela, 181
Tilton, Flora, 181, 228, 229, 230, 242, **242**, 252, 268, 270, 392
Tilton, Josephine, 181, 228, 229, 241, **242**, 243, 267, 270
Tilton, Lucy, 181
Tina, Beatrice (pseudonym), 365
Tingley, Katherine, 222
Tolstoy, Leo, 103, 118, 169, 285, 290, 292, 308, 313, 334, 335, 367, 373, 374
The Torch, 200, 292
Tovey, Richard, 23
Tovey, Robert, 37, 53, 60, 73, 74, 75, 76, 84, 85, 290
Towards Democracy (Carpenter), 26, 34, 98, 104, 105, 176, 191, 213, 216, 218, 219, 220, 222, 247, 306, 315
trade unionism, 18, 20, 77, 79, 82, 98, 166, 345. *See also The New Trade Unionism: Its Relation to the Old; and the Condition of Its Success* (Daniell and Nichol)
Transcendentalism/Transcendentalists, 94, 101, 154, 157, 160, 178, 184, 235, 271, 309, 313
transformation
    external transformation, 175
    individual transformation, 366
    of inner being, 4
    inward transformation, 175
    personal transformation, 80, 285
    political transformation, 80

revolutionary transformation, 344
social transformation, 25, 33, 34, 48,
    63–4, 80, 303, 366
spiritual transformation, 80
theory of, 150
Traubel, Horace, 149, 170, 171, 173, 174,
    176, 177, 179, 180, 204, 228, 250, 254,
    258, 269, 272, 308, 309–10, 348, 388,
    394
Trevor, John, 125, 128, 176, 291
Triggs, Oscar Lovell, 175, 178
*The Truth about the Chocolate Factories or
    Modern White Slavery its Cause and Cure*
    (Daniell and Nicol), 55, 56, 57–8, 60, 63
Tubman, Harriet, 185
Tucker, Benjamin R., 4, 5, 6, 101–3, **102**,
    106, 112, 113, 114, 125, 128, 129, 130,
    132, 181, 182, 225, 249, 250, 337, 347
Tucker, Pearl, 393
Tuckett, Charles Helton, 65
Tuckett, Martha, 29
Tuckett, Richard Clapton, 33
Tufts, Anne Adams, 361
Tufts, Helen. *See also* Bailie, Helen Tufts
    abortions, 338
    aftermath of Helena Born's death,
        269–70
    assembling collection of Helena Born's
        writings with William Bailie, 272–4,
        308
    'Biographical Introduction' to *Whitman's
        Ideal Democracy*, 1, 12, 30, 37, 71,
        272, 273, 274, 276
    birth and death dates of, 2
    birth of, 153
    birth of daughter Helena, 362
    children of. *See* Bailie, Helena; Bailie,
        Terrill (Sonny)
    on children's innate inclinations for
        enlightenment, 356
    collections of papers by, 3
    death of, 395
    as desperate for independence, 248
    disharmony with William Bailie, 394
    education of, 159, 160, 161–2, 165,
        331, 347
    estrangement from parents, 359
    family of, 153–61
    friendship with William Bailie, 235–6,
        240, 248
    granddaughter of, 395
    journal, 153, 156, 185, 245, 300, 329,
        336, 349, 389, 394–5
    manuscript journal, 3
    marriage to William Bailie, 349
    meeting Helena Born, 4, 167, 172
    on nature and purposes of capitalist
        production as flawed, 33

pregnancy, 361–2
prejudices of, 4, 161, 336, 360, 393
as providing degree of respectability for
    Helena Born and William Bailie, 243
relationship with Walter Leighton,
    244–5, 249, 250, 260
romance with William Bailie, 301, 309,
    329, 331, 338, 390
as signing comradeship paper of C.F.S.,
    227
as taking charge of C.F.S., 239
vacation to England (1907), 341–3
work experience, 162, 164, 166, 244,
    330, 332
writings of, 253, 301, 302–3, 307, 308,
    309–10, 355, 356, 390, 395
Tufts, Helen Whittemore, 154
Tufts, Isabel (née Terrill), 158, 159, 160,
    164, 184, 241, 243, 249, 250, 251, 260,
    268, 309, 347, 348
Tufts, Joseph, 154, 161
Tufts, Peter, 153–4
Tufts, Russell, 157, 158, 160, 163, 164,
    172, 225, 239, 241, 249, 250, 253, 309,
    347, 348, 349
Tufts, William, 159, 178, 226, 239, **242**,
    243, 245, 248, 250–1, 252, 260, 308–9
Tufts, William Whittemore, 154–7
Twentieth Century Club, 177, 179, 356
Tyler, Wat (pseudonym), 303, 311
Tyndale, William, 28

Uncle Tom's Cabin (Stowe), 161
unconventional individuality, 4
Underwood, Benjamin Franklin, 147
Unitarian Church, 4, 5, 13, 16, 17, 154,
    157–8, 160, 163, 247, 301
Unitarian Women's Auxiliary Alliance, 160
Unwin, Ethel, 204, 210
Unwin, Raymond, 83, 112, 120, 122, 204,
    210, 214, 229, 291, 357, 358, 359
utopianism, 6, 47, 91, 95, 103, 107, 110,
    130, 140, 163, 176, 226, 228, 254, 259,
    264, 286, 292, 295, 297, 313, 333, 340,
    347, 357, 359, 373, 374

Van Dyke, Revd Henry J., 155
vegetarianism, 1, 16, 34, 111, 145, 178,
    184, 232, 243, 266, 282, 367, 381
Vest, Jacob, 239
Vickery, James, 54, 55, 60, 71, 85, 86
Vincent, Albert, 54, 59, 75, 84
Volkhovsky, Felix, 205
voluntary associations, 335, 346

Waisbrooker, Lois, 312
Walden (Thoreau), 34
Walden communal house, 341

Walker, Francis A., 130, 165
Wallace, Alfred Russel, 17
Wallace, Henry A., 385
Wallace, James William, 199, 341, 342
Wallas, Graham, 200
Walt Whitman Fellowship, 1
Walt Whitman Fellowship (W.W.F.), 1,
 169–70, 173, 177, 179, 180, 228, 234,
 235, 236, 245, 254, 255, 261, 262, 270,
 276, 313, 333, 337, 342, 348, 388
Walt Whitman: His Life and Works (Perry),
 342
Warnaby, Juliet, 189
Warren, Josiah, 127, 130, 238, 246, 249,
 311, 328, 333–5, 336, 340, 391
Watson, Edward J., 35, 73, 83, 88, 104,
 272
Watt, James, 188
Watts, J. Hunter, 120
*The Way Out: A Forecast of Coming Changes
 in American Business and Industry* (Filene),
 388
Weare, Robert, 15, 16, 34, 35, 36, 55, 60,
 61, 63, 67, 68, 70, 73, 74, 78, 188, 215,
 269, 271, 341, **342**
Webb, Sidney, 193, 291
Weimar, Placer County, California, 140,
 143, 144, 145, 149, 186, 218, 224, 315,
 316, 321, 363, 381, 385
Wellington, Amy, 254, 270
Weston, Edward, 380
Weston, Joseph, 62–3, 85
What's to be Done? (Chernyshevsky), 102
Wheeler, Catharine (née Freeman), 27–8
Wheeler, Catharine (younger), 29
Wheeler, Ellen, 29
Wheeler, Herbert, 28
Wheeler, Mary, 29, 64, 81, 93, 187
Wheeler, Mortimer, 27
Wheeler, Robert Mortimer, 28, 32, 45, 50,
 105
Wheeler, Robert Rogers, 27, 29, 31
The Wheelwoman, 283
Whitefield, William, 82, 85
White-nights ranch, 140, 145, 146, 207,
 209, 210, 212, 281, 315, 316, 319, 320,
 325, 363, 365, 373, 378
Whitman, Walt, 1, 2, 4, 15, 25, **25**, 34, 89,
 92, 102, 169, 170, 173, 176–7, 179, 188,
 212, 214, 221, 247, 255, 264, 271, 272,
 276, 310, 335, 342, 394
Whitman and His Contemporaries (Monroe),
 392
Whitmanite, Bolton, 199
*Whitman's Ideal Democracy and Other
 Writings by Helena Born* (Born), 1, 12, 30,
 71, 272, 274

Whittemore, Helen, 154
Wiksell, Gustave Percival, 175, 254, 270,
 310, 348
Wilcox, W. Dove, 90
Wilde, Oscar, 201, 222
Willway, Alice, 76
Wilmot, Isaac, 78
Wilson, Charlotte, 192
Wilson, Joseph Havelock, 85
Wilson, Revd James, 35, 37, 68
Wisker, Aubrey L., 376
Woman's Worst Enemy, Woman (Tina), 365
The Woman Who Did (Allen), 174, 201
Women and Economics (Stetson), 241
Women and Marriage: Evolution in Sex
 (Ellis), 188
Women in Soviet Russia (Smith), 385
Women's City Club, 359
women's equality, 260
Women's International League for Peace and
 Freedom, 391
Women's Liberal Association, 38, 50,
 88. *See also* Bristol Women's Liberal
 Association (B.W.L.A.); British Women's
 Liberal Association
women's liberation movement, 7
Women's Protective and Provident League,
 75
women's rights, 13, 14, 19, 49, 147, 182,
 211, 237, 241, 312, 355, 365
Women's Social and Political Union
 (W.S.P.U.), 365, 366
women's suffrage, 4, 18, 19, 20, 29, 65,
 114, 156, 164, 184, 272, 354, 388.
 See also Massachusetts Woman Suffrage
 Association (M.W.S.A.)
Women's Trades Association, 70
Women's Trades Union and Provident
 League, 66, 69, 75
Women's Union (Silvertown), 54
Women's Union Journal, 66
women's unions, 69, 71, 75
women writers, 114, 190, 204
Women Writers' Club, 206
Wood, Esther, 282, 283
The Word (journal), 101, 181
Workers' Organising Committee (W.O.C.),
 73, 74, 75, 76, 83, 84, 89, 98
Workman's Times (newspaper), 123
Wright, Frances, 333

Yarros, Victor, 182
The Yellow Book (journal), 201
Young, Will, 269, 392
The Youth's Companion (journal), 162

Zaza (play), 252